**ELEVENTH
EDITION**

# Conformity
# and Conflict

*Readings in Cultural Anthropology*

JAMES SPRADLEY

DAVID W. McCURDY
*Macalester College*

Boston   New York   San Francisco
Mexico City   Montreal   Toronto   London   Madrid   Munich   Paris
Hong Kong   Singapore   Tokyo   Cape Town   Sydney

*To Barbara Spradley and Carolyn McCurdy*

*Series Editor:* Jennifer Jacobson
*Editorial Assistant:* Tom Jefferies
*Marketing Manager:* Taryn Wahlquist
*Editorial-Production Service:* Omegatype Typography, Inc.
*Manufacturing Buyer:* JoAnne Sweeney
*Composition and Prepress Buyer:* Linda Cox
*Cover Administrator:* Linda Knowles
*Electronic Composition:* Omegatype Typography, Inc.

For related titles and support materials, visit our online catalog at www.ablongman.com.

**Library of Congress Cataloging-in-Publication Data**

Conformity and conflict : readings in cultural anthropology / [edited by] James Spradley, David W. McCurdy.—11th ed.
   p.   cm.
   Includes bibliographical references and index.
   ISBN 0-205-35479-3
   1. Ethnology.   2. Anthropology.   I. Spradley, James P.   II. McCurdy, David W.

   GN325 .C69 2003
   306—dc21

                                        2002016341

Printed in the United States of America
10  9  8  7  6  5  4  3  2  1   RRD-VA   07  06  05  04  03  02

**Photo Credits:** Part 1, Sean Sprague/Stock Boston; Part 2, Jim Cornfield/Corbis; Part 3, Charles & Josette Lenars/Corbis; Part 4, Gary Braasch/Corbis; Part 5, Sheila Nardulli/Liaison Agency; Part 6, Mike Elicson/AP Wide World; Part 7, Arne Hodalic/Corbis; Part 8, Pasquier/Liaison Agency; Part 9, Lionel Delevigne/Stock Boston.

# Contents

# TWO

# THREE

# FOUR

# FIVE

# SIX

# SEVEN

# Preface

Cultural anthropology has a twofold mission: to understand other cultures and to communicate that understanding. Thirty-two years ago, in preparing the first edition of this book, Jim Spradley and I sought to make communication easier and more enjoyable for teachers and students alike. We focused on the twin themes stated in the title—conformity, or order, and conflict, or change—while organizing selections into sections based on traditional topics. We balanced the coverage of cultures between non-Western and Western (including American) so students could make their own cultural comparisons and see the relation between anthropology and their lives. We chose articles that reflected interesting topics in anthropology, but we also looked for selections that illustrated important concepts and theories, because we believed that anthropology provides a unique and powerful way to look at experience. We searched extensively for scholarly articles written with insight and clarity. Students and instructors in hundreds of colleges and universities responded enthusiastically to our efforts, and a pattern was set that carried through ten editions.

This eleventh edition retains the features of earlier ones: the focus on stability and change, the coverage of a broad range of societies, the combination of professionalism and readability in selections, the view that anthropology provides a perspective on experience, and carefully integrated organization. As in previous editions, I have revamped topics and added or subtracted selections in response to the suggestions of instructors and students across the country. Anthropology and the world it seeks to understand have changed since the first edition of *Conformity and Conflict*. New articles have been chosen to reflect these changes. Most new selections have been written within the last seven years; thirteen articles were created especially for this volume and five are revised and updated versions of previous selections. There are revisions to the part introduction on economics and globalization. In all, out of thirty-nine articles, eleven are new, five are revised and updated, and one has been brought back from earlier editions. All sections have at least one new or revised selection.

I have also continued the expanded special features that have appeared in past editions. Part introductions include discussion of many basic anthropological definitions for instructors who do not want to use a standard textbook but find it useful to provide students with a terminological foundation. Article introductions seek to tie selections to anthropological concepts and explanations in a coherent and systematic way.

Several student aids are retained in the eleventh edition. Lists of key terms accompany each part introduction. Each article is followed by several review questions. Maps locating societies discussed in articles accompany each selection. There is also a glossary and subject index at the end of the book.

A complimentary instructor's manual and test bank is available from the publisher. The manual contains a summary of each article along with a large selection of true or false and multiple choice questions for articles and part introductions.

It has always been my aim to provide a book that meets the needs of students and instructors. To help with this goal, I encourage you to send your comments and ideas for improving *Conformity and Conflict* to me at dlorac@aol.com.

Many people have made suggestions that guided this revision of *Conformity and Conflict*. I am especially grateful to Abigail E. Adams, Central Connecticut State University; Margaret Brown, Washington University; Barbara E. Cook, California Polytechnic; and Barry J. Lyons, Wayne State University.

D. W. M.

## WORLD MAP AND GEOGRAPHICAL PLACEMENT OF READINGS

The numbers on this map correspond to the reading numbers and indicate the places on which the articles focus. Screened maps also accompany the readings themselves, and boxed areas on those maps highlight the subject locations. Readings labeled as world on this global map do not include boxed areas.

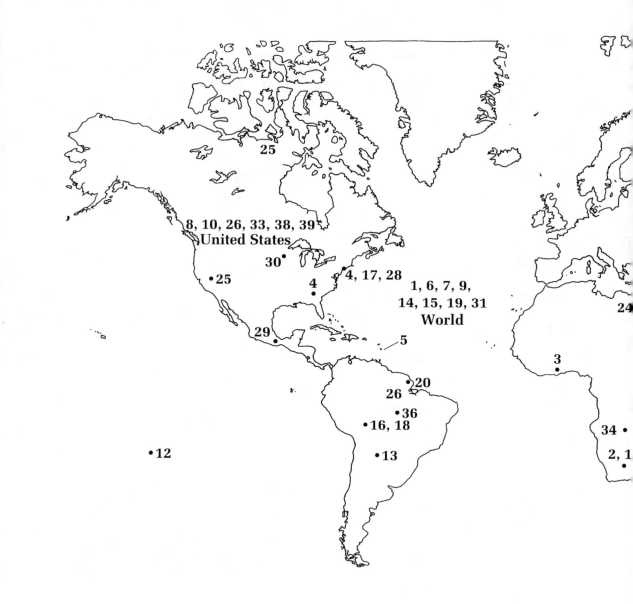

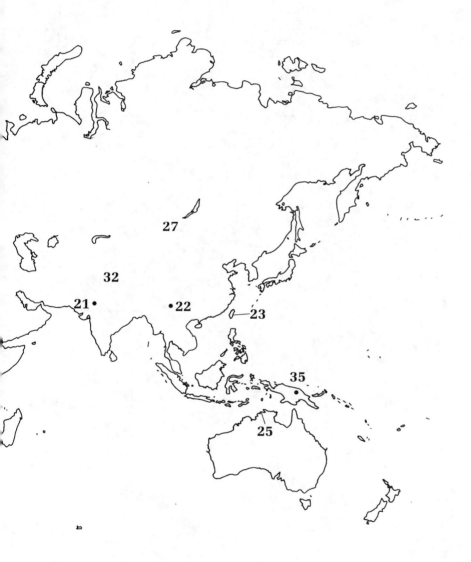

27

32

21 •

• 22

23

35

25

# ONE

# Culture and Ethnography

Culture, as its name suggests, lies at the heart of cultural anthropology. And the concept of **culture,** along with ethnography, sets anthropology apart from other social and behavioral sciences. Let us look more closely at these concepts.

To understand what anthropologists mean by culture, imagine yourself in a foreign setting, such as a market town in India, forgetting what you might already know about that country. You step off a bus onto a dusty street where you are immediately confronted by strange sights, sounds, and smells. Men dress in Western clothes, but of a different style. Women drape themselves in long shawls that entirely cover their bodies. They peer at you through a small gap in this garment as they walk by. Buildings are one- or two-story affairs, open at the front so you can see inside. Near you some people sit on wicker chairs eating strange foods. Most unusual is how people talk. They utter vocalizations unlike any you have ever heard, and you wonder how they can possibly understand each other. But obviously they do, since their behavior seems organized and purposeful.

Scenes such as this confronted early explorers, missionaries, and anthropologists, and from their observations an obvious point emerged. People living in various parts of the world looked and behaved in dramatically different ways. And these differences correlated with groups. The people of India had customs different from those of the Papuans; the British did not act and dress like the Iroquois.

Two possible explanations for group differences came to mind. Some argued that group behavior was inherited. Dahomeans of the African Gold Coast, for example, were characterized as particularly "clever and adaptive" by one British colonial official, while, according to the same authority, another African group was "happy-go-lucky and improvident." Usually implied in such statements was the idea that group members were born that way. Such thinking persists to the present and in its least discriminating guise takes the form of racism.

But a second explanation also emerged. Perhaps, rather than a product of inheritance, the behavior characteristic of a group was learned. The way people dressed, what they ate, how they talked—all these could more easily be explained as acquisitions. Thus a baby born on the African Gold Coast would, if immediately transported to China and raised like other children there, grow up to dress, eat, and talk like a Chinese. Cultural anthropologists focus on the explanation of learned behavior.

The idea of learning, and a need to label the lifestyles associated with particular groups, led to the definition of culture. In 1871, British anthropologist Sir Edward Burnet Tylor argued that "Culture . . . is that complex whole which includes knowledge, belief, art, law, morals, custom, and any other capabilities and habits acquired by man as a member of society."[1] The definition we present here places more emphasis on the importance of knowledge than does Tylor's. We will say that *culture is the learned and shared knowledge that people use to generate behavior and interpret experience.*

Important to this definition is the idea that culture is a kind of knowledge, not behavior. It is in people's heads. It reflects the mental categories they learn from others as they grow up. It helps them *generate* behavior and *interpret* what they experience. At the moment of birth, we lack a culture. We don't yet have a system of beliefs, knowledge, and patterns of customary behavior. But from that moment until we die, each of us participates in a kind of universal schooling that teaches us our native culture. Laughing and smiling are genetic responses, but as infants we soon learn when to smile, when to laugh, and even how to laugh. We also inherit the potential to cry, but we must learn our cultural rules for when crying is appropriate.

As we learn our culture, we acquire a way to interpret experience. For example, Americans learn that dogs are like little people in furry suits. Dogs live in our houses, eat our food, share our beds. They hold a place in our hearts; their loss causes us to grieve. Villagers in India, on the other hand, often view dogs as pests, that admittedly are useful for hunting in those few parts of the country where one still can hunt, and as watchdogs. Quiet days in Indian villages are often punctuated by the yelp of a dog that has been threatened or actually hurt by its master or a bystander.

Clearly, it is not the dogs that are different in these two societies. Rather, it is the meaning that dogs have for people that varies. And such meaning is cultural; it is learned as part of growing up in each group.

There are two basic kinds of culture, explicit and tacit. **Explicit culture** is cultural knowledge that people can talk about. As you grow up, for example, you learn that there are words for many things you encounter. There are items such as *clothes*, actions such as *playing*, emotional states such as *sadness*, ways to talk such as *yelling*, and people such as *mother*. Recognizing that culture may be explicit is important to the ethnographic process discussed below. If people

---

[1]Edward Burnet Tylor, *Primitive Culture* (New York: Harper Torchbooks, Harper & Row, 1958; originally published by John Murray, London, 1871), p. 1.

have words for cultural categories, anthropologists can use interviews or observations of people talking to uncover them. Because so much culture is explicit, words, both spoken and written, become essential to the discovery and understanding of a culture.

**Tacit culture** is cultural knowledge that people lack words for. For example, as we grow up we learn to recognize and use a limited number of sound categories such as /d/, /e/, and /f/. Although anthropological linguists have given sound categories a name *(phonemes)*, nonlinguists lack such a term. Instead, we learn our sound categories by hearing and replicating them and use them unconsciously. No parent said, "Now let's work on our phonemes tonight, dear," to us when we were little.

Anthropologist Edward Hall pioneered the study of tacit culture. He noted, for example, that middle-class North Americans observe four speaking distances—intimate, personal, social, and public—without naming them. (Hall, not his informants, invented the terms above.) Hall also noticed that people from other societies observed different tacit speaking distances, so that a Latin American's closer (than North American) personal speaking distance made North Americans uncomfortable because it seemed intimate. Because it is unspoken, tacit culture can only be discovered through behavioral observation.

**Ethnography** is the process of discovering and describing a particular culture. It involves anthropologists in an intimate and personal activity as they attempt to learn how the members of a particular group see their worlds.

But which groups qualify as culture-bearing units? How does the anthropologist identify the existence of a culture to study? This was not a difficult question when anthropology was a new science. As Tylor's definition notes, culture was the whole way of life of a people. To find it, one sought out distinctive ethnic units, such as Bhil tribals in India or Apaches in the American Southwest. Anything one learned from such people would be part of their culture.

But discrete cultures of this sort are becoming more difficult to find. The world is increasingly divided into large national societies, each subdivided into a myriad of subgroups. Anthropologists are finding it increasingly attractive to study such subgroups, because they form the arena for most of life in complex society. And this is where the concept of the microculture enters the scene.

**Microcultures** are systems of cultural knowledge characteristic of subgroups within larger societies. Members of a microculture will usually share much of what they know with everyone in the greater society but will possess a special cultural knowledge that is unique to the subgroup. For example, a college fraternity has a microculture within the context of a university and a nation. Its members have special daily routines, jokes, and meanings for events. It is this shared knowledge that makes up their microculture and that can serve as the basis for ethnographic study. More and more, anthropologists are turning to the study of microcultures, using the same ethnographic techniques they employ when they investigate the broader culture of an ethnic or national group.

More than anything else, it is ethnography that is anthropology's unique contribution to social science. Most scientists, including many who view people in social context, approach their research as **detached observers.** As social scientists, they observe the human subjects of their study, categorize what they see, and generate theory to account for their findings. They work from the outside, creating a system of knowledge to account for other people's behavior. Although this is a legitimate and often useful way to conduct research, it is not the main task of ethnography.

Ethnographers seek out the insider's viewpoint. Because culture is the knowledge people use to generate behavior and interpret experience, the ethnographer seeks to understand group members' behavior from the inside, or cultural, perspective. Instead of looking for a **subject** to observe, ethnographers look for an **informant** to teach them the culture. Just as a child learns its native culture from parents and other people in its social environment, the ethnographer learns another culture by inferring folk categories from the observation of behavior and by asking informants what things mean.

Anthropologists employ many strategies during field research to understand another culture better. But all strategies and all research ultimately rest on the cooperation of informants. An informant is neither a subject in a scientific experiment nor a **respondent** who answers the investigator's questions. An informant is a teacher who has a special kind of pupil: a professional anthropologist. In this unique relationship a transformation occurs in the anthropologist's understanding of an alien culture. It is the informant who transforms the anthropologist from a tourist into an ethnographer. The informant may be a child who explains how to play hopscotch, a cocktail waitress who teaches the anthropologist to serve drinks and to encourage customers to leave tips, an elderly man who teaches the anthropologist to build an igloo, or a grandmother who explains the intricacies of Zapotec kinship. Almost any individual who has acquired a repertoire of cultural behavior can become an informant.

Ethnography is not as easy to do as we might think. For one thing, Americans are not taught to be good listeners. We prefer to observe and draw our own conclusions. We like a sense of control in social contexts; passive listening is a sign of weakness in our culture. But listening and learning from others is at the heart of ethnography, and we must put aside our discomfort with the student role.

It is also not easy for informants to teach us about their cultures. Culture often lies below a conscious level. A major ethnographic task is to help informants remember their culture.

Naive realism may also impede ethnography. **Naive realism** is the belief that people everywhere see the world in the same way. It may, for example, lead the unwary ethnographer to assume that beauty is the same for all people everywhere or, to use our previous example, that dogs should mean the same thing in India as they do in the United States. If an ethnographer fails to control his or her own naive realism, inside cultural meanings will surely be overlooked.

Culture shock and ethnocentrism may also stand in the way of ethnographers. **Culture shock** is a state of anxiety that results from cross-cultural misunderstanding. Immersed alone in another society, the ethnographer understands few of the culturally defined rules for behavior and interpretation used by his or her hosts. The result is anxiety about proper action and an inability to interact appropriately in the new context.

Ethnocentrism can be just as much of a liability. **Ethnocentrism** is the belief and feeling that one's own culture is best. It reflects our tendency to judge other people's beliefs and behavior using values of our own native culture. Thus if we come from a society that abhors painful treatment of animals, we are likely to react with anger when an Indian villager hits a dog with a rock. Our feeling is ethnocentric.

It is impossible to rid ourselves entirely of the cultural values that make us ethnocentric when we do ethnography. But it is important to control our ethnocentric feeling in the field if we are to learn from informants. Informants resent negative judgment.

Finally, the role assigned to ethnographers by informants affects the quality of what can be learned. Ethnography is a personal enterprise, as all the articles in this section illustrate. Unlike survey research using questionnaires or short interviews, ethnography requires prolonged social contact. Informants will assign the ethnographer some kind of role and what that turns out to be will affect research.

The selections in Part One illustrate several points about culture and ethnography. The first piece, by the late James Spradley, takes a close look at the concept of culture and its role in ethnographic research. The second, by Richard Lee, illustrates how a simple act of giving can have a dramatically different cultural meaning in two societies, leading to cross-cultural misunderstanding. Laura Bohannan's article deals with the concept of naive realism and its role in cross-cultural misunderstanding. When she tells the classic story of *Hamlet* to African Tiv elders, the plot takes on an entirely different meaning as they use their own cultural knowledge in its interpretation. In the fourth selection, Claire Sterk describes how she conducted ethnographic field research under difficult circumstances. She sought to learn the culture of prostitutes working in New York City and Atlanta as part of a broader research interest in the spread and control of AIDS. Finally, the fifth article, by George Gmelch, explores how fieldwork in another culture can increase understanding of one's own.

# Key Terms

| | |
|---|---|
| culture  *p. 1* | informant  *p. 4* |
| culture shock  *p. 4* | microculture  *p. 3* |
| detached observer  *p. 4* | naive realism  *p. 4* |
| ethnocentrism  *p. 5* | respondent  *p. 4* |
| ethnography  *p. 3* | subject  *p. 4* |
| explicit culture  *p. 2* | tacit culture  *p. 3* |

# I

# Ethnography and Culture

*James P. Spradley*

*Most Americans associate science with detached observation; we learn to observe whatever we wish to understand, introduce our own classification of what is going on, and explain what we see in our own terms. In this selection, James Spradley argues that cultural anthropologists work differently. Ethnography is the work of discovering and describing a particular culture; culture is the learned, shared knowledge that people use to generate behavior and interpret experience. To get at culture, ethnographers must learn the meanings of action and experience from the insider's or informant's point of view. Many of the examples used by Spradley also show the relevance of anthropology to the study of culture in the United States.*

Ethnographic fieldwork is the hallmark of cultural anthropology. Whether in a jungle village in Peru or on the streets of New York, the anthropologist goes to where people live and "does fieldwork." This means participating in activities, asking questions, eating strange foods, learning a new language, watching ceremonies, taking fieldnotes, washing clothes, writing letters home, tracing out genealogies, observing play, interviewing informants, and hundreds of other things. This vast range of activities often obscures the nature of the most fundamental task of all fieldwork: doing ethnography.

Ethnography is the work of describing a culture. The central aim of ethnography is to understand another way of life from the native point of view. The goal of ethnography, as Malinowski put it, is "to grasp the native's point of view, his relation to life, to realize *his* vision of *his* world."[1] Fieldwork, then, involves the disciplined study of what the world is like to people who have learned to see, hear, speak, think, and act in ways that are different. Rather than *studying people*, ethnography means *learning from people*. Consider the following illustration.

George Hicks set out, in 1965, to learn about another way of life, that of the mountain people in an Appalachian valley.[2] His goal was to discover their culture, to learn to see the world from their perspective. With his family he moved into Little Laurel Valley, his daughter attended the local school, and his wife became one of the local Girl Scout leaders. Hicks soon discovered that stores and storekeepers were at the center of the valley's communication system, providing the most important social arena for the entire valley. He learned this by watching what other people did, by following their example, and slowly becoming part of the groups that congregated daily in the stores. He writes:

> At least once each day I would visit several stores in the valley, and sit in on the groups of gossiping men or, if the storekeeper happened to be alone, perhaps attempt to clear up puzzling points about kinship obligations. I found these hours, particularly those spent in the presence of the two or three excellent storytellers in the Little Laurel, thoroughly enjoyable. . . . At other times, I helped a number of local men gather corn or hay, build sheds, cut trees, pull and pack galax, and search for rich stands of huckleberries. When I needed aid in, for example, repairing frozen water pipes, it was readily and cheerfully provided.[3]

In order to discover the hidden principles of another way of life, the researcher must become a *student*. Storekeepers and storytellers and local farmers become *teachers*. Instead of studying the "climate," the "flora," and the "fauna" that made up the environment of this Appalachian valley, Hicks tried to discover how these mountain people defined and evaluated trees and galax and huckleberries. He did not attempt to describe social life in terms of what

---

[1] Bronislaw Malinowski, *Argonauts of the Western Pacific* (London: Routledge, 1922), p. 22.

[2] George Hicks, *Appalachian Valley* (New York: Holt, Rinehart, and Winston, 1976).

[3] Hicks, p. 3.

most Americans know about "marriage," "family," and "friendship"; instead he sought to discover how these mountain people identified relatives and friends. He tried to learn the obligations they felt toward kinsmen and discover how they felt about friends. Discovering the *insider's view* is a different species of knowledge from one that rests mainly on the outsider's view, even when the outsider is a trained social scientist.

Consider another example, this time from the perspective of a non-Western ethnographer. Imagine an Inuit woman setting out to learn the culture of Macalester College. What would she, so well schooled in the rich heritage of Inuit culture, have to do in order to understand the culture of Macalester College students, faculty, and staff? How would she discover the patterns that made up their lives? How would she avoid imposing Inuit ideas, categories, and values on everything she saw?

First, and perhaps most difficult, she would have to set aside her belief in *naive realism,* the almost universal belief that all people define the *real* world of objects, events, and living creatures in pretty much the same way. Human languages may differ from one society to the next, but behind the strange words and sentences, all people are talking about the same things. The naive realist assumes that love, snow, marriage, worship, animals, death, food, and hundreds of other things have essentially the same meaning to all human beings. Although few of us would admit to such ethnocentrism, the assumption may unconsciously influence our research. Ethnography starts with a conscious attitude of almost complete ignorance: "I don't know how the people at Macalester College understand their world. That remains to be discovered."

This Inuit woman would have to begin by learning the language spoken by students, faculty, and staff. She could stroll the campus paths, sit in classes, and attend special events, but only if she consciously tried to see things from the native point of view would she grasp their perspective. She would need to observe and listen to first-year students during their week-long orientation program. She would have to stand in line during registration, listen to students discuss the classes they hoped to get, and visit departments to watch faculty advising students on course selection. She would want to observe secretaries typing, janitors sweeping, and maintenance personnel plowing snow from walks. She would watch the more than 1,600 students crowd into the post office area to open their tiny mailboxes, and she would listen to their comments about junk mail and letters from home or no mail at all. She would attend faculty meetings to watch what went on, recording what professors and administrators said and how they behaved. She would sample various courses, attend "keggers" on weekends, read the *Mac Weekly,* and listen by the hour to students discussing things like their "relationships," the "football team," and "work study." She would want to learn the *meanings* of all these things. She would have to listen to the members of this college community, watch what they did, and participate in their activities to learn such meanings.

The essential core of ethnography is this concern with the meaning of actions and events to the people we seek to understand. Some of these meanings are directly expressed in language; many are taken for granted and communicated only indirectly through word and action. But in every society people make constant use of these complex meaning systems to organize their behavior, to understand themselves and others, and to make sense out of the world in which they live. These systems of meaning constitute their culture; ethnography always implies a theory of culture.

## Culture

When ethnographers study other cultures, they must deal with three fundamental aspects of human experience: what people do, what people know, and the things people make and use. When each of these is learned and shared by members of some group, we speak of them as *cultural behavior, cultural knowledge,* and *cultural artifacts.* Whenever you do ethnographic fieldwork, you will want to distinguish among these three, although in most situations they are usually mixed together. Let's try to unravel them.

Recently I took a commuter train from a western suburb to downtown Chicago. It was late in the day, and when I boarded the train, only a handful of people were scattered about the car. Each was engaged in a common form of *cultural behavior: reading.* Across the aisle a man held the *Chicago Tribune* out in front of him, looking intently at the small print and every now and then turning the pages noisily. In front of him a young woman held a paperback book about twelve inches from her face. I could see her head shift slightly as her eyes moved from the bottom of one page to the top of the next. Near the front of the car a student was reading a large textbook and using a pen to underline words and sentences. Directly in front of me I noticed a man looking at the ticket he had purchased and reading it. It took me an instant to survey this scene, and then I settled back, looked out the window, and read a billboard advertisement for a plumbing service proclaiming it would open any plugged drains. All of us were engaged in the same kind of cultural behavior: reading.

This common activity depended on a great many *cultural artifacts,* the things people shape or make from natural resources. I could see artifacts like books and tickets and newspapers and billboards, all of which contained tiny black marks arranged into intricate patterns called "letters." And these tiny artifacts were arranged into larger patterns of words, sentences, and paragraphs. Those of us on that commuter train could read, in part, because of still other artifacts: the bark of trees made into paper; steel made into printing presses; dyes of various colors made into ink; glue used to hold book pages together; large wooden frames to hold billboards. If an ethnographer wanted to understand the full cultural meaning in our society, it would involve a careful study of these and many other cultural artifacts.

Although we can easily see behavior and artifacts, they represent only the thin surface of a deep lake. Beneath the surface, hidden from view, lies a vast reservoir of *cultural knowledge.* Think for a moment what the people on that train needed to know in order to read. First, they had to know the grammatical rules for at least one language. Then they had to learn what the little marks on paper represented. They also had to know the meaning of space and lines and pages. They had learned cultural rules like "move your eyes from left to right, from the top of the page to the bottom." They had to know that a sentence at the bottom of a page continues on the top of the next page. The man reading a newspaper had to know a great deal about columns and the spaces between columns and what headlines mean. All of us needed to know what kinds of messages were intended by whoever wrote what we read. If a person cannot distinguish the importance of a message on a billboard from one that comes in a letter from a spouse or child, problems would develop. I knew how to recognize when other people were reading. We all knew it was impolite to read aloud on a train. We all knew how to feel when reading things like jokes or calamitous news in the paper. Our culture has a large body of shared knowledge that people learn and use to engage in this behavior called *reading* and make proper use of the artifacts connected with it.

Although cultural knowledge is hidden from view, it is of fundamental importance because we all use it constantly to generate behavior and interpret our experience. Cultural knowledge is so important that I will frequently use the broader term *culture* when speaking about it. Indeed, I will define culture as *the acquired knowledge people use to interpret experience and generate behavior*. Let's consider another example to see how people use their culture to interpret experience and do things.

One afternoon in 1973 I came across the following news item in the *Minneapolis Tribune:*

> ### Crowd Mistakes Rescue Attempt, Attacks Police
> *Nov. 23, 1973. Hartford, Connecticut.* Three policemen giving a heart massage and oxygen to a heart attack victim Friday were attacked by a crowd of 75 to 100 persons who apparently did not realize what the policemen were doing.
>
> Other policemen fended off the crowd of mostly Spanish-speaking residents until an ambulance arrived. Police said they tried to explain to the crowd what they were doing, but the crowd apparently thought they were beating the woman.
>
> Despite the policemen's efforts the victim, Evangelica Echevacria, 59, died.

Here we see people using their culture. Members of two different groups observed the same event, but their *interpretations* were drastically different. The crowd used their cultural knowledge (a) to interpret the behavior of the policemen as cruel and (b) to act on the woman's behalf to put a stop to what they perceived as brutality. They had acquired the cultural principles for acting and interpreting things in this way through a particular shared experience.

The policemen, on the other hand, used their cultural knowledge (a) to interpret the woman's condition as heart failure and their own behavior as a life-saving effort and (b) to give her cardiac massage and oxygen. They used artifacts like an oxygen mask and an ambulance. Furthermore, they interpreted the actions of the crowd in an entirely different manner from how the crowd saw their own behavior. The two groups of people each had elaborate cultural rules for interpreting their experience and for acting in emergency situations, and the conflict arose, at least in part, because these cultural rules were so different.

We can now diagram this definition of culture and see more clearly the relationships among knowledge, behavior, and artifacts (Figure 1). By identifying cultural knowledge as fundamental, we have merely shifted the emphasis from behavior and artifacts to their *meaning.* The ethnographer observes behavior but goes beyond it to inquire about the meaning of that behavior. The ethnographer sees artifacts and natural objects but goes beyond them to discover what meanings people assign to these objects. The ethnographer observes and records emotional states but goes beyond them to discover the meaning of fear, anxiety, anger, and other feelings.

As represented in Figure 1, cultural knowledge exists at two levels of consciousness. *Explicit culture* makes up part of what we know, a level of knowledge people can communicate about with relative ease. When George Hicks asked storekeepers and others in Little Laurel Valley about their relatives, he

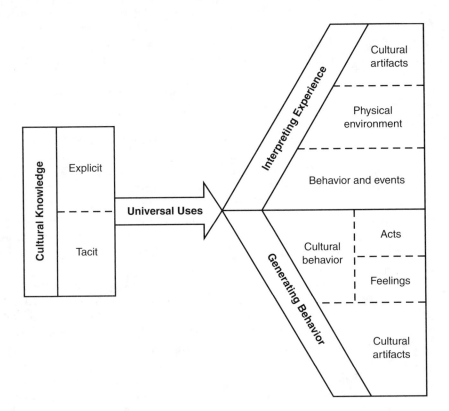

**FIGURE 1**

discovered that any adult over fifty could tell him the genealogical connections among large numbers of people. They knew how to trace kin relationships and the cultural rules for appropriate behavior among kins. All of us have acquired large areas of cultural knowledge such as this which we can talk about and make explicit.

At the same time, a large portion of our cultural knowledge remains *tacit*, outside our awareness. Edward Hall has done much to elucidate the nature of tacit cultural knowledge in his books *The Silent Language* and *The Hidden Dimension*.[4] The way each culture defines space often occurs at the level of tacit knowledge. Hall points out that all of us have acquired thousands of spatial cues about how close to stand to others, how to arrange furniture, when to touch others, and when to feel cramped inside a room. Without realizing that our tacit culture is operating, we begin to feel uneasy when someone from another culture stands too close, breathes on us when talking, touches us, or when we find furniture arranged in the center of the room rather than around the edges. Ethnography is the study of both explicit and tacit cultural knowledge. . . .

The concept of culture as acquired knowledge has much in common with symbolic interactionism, a theory that seeks to explain human behavior in terms of meanings. Symbolic interactionism has its roots in the work of sociologists like Cooley, Mead, and Thomas. Blumer has identified three premises on which this theory rests.

The first premise is that "human beings act toward things on the basis of the meanings that the things have for them."[5] The policemen and the crowd in our earlier example interacted on the basis of the meanings things had for them. The geographic location, the types of people, the police car, the policemen's movements, the sick woman's behavior, and the activities of the onlookers—all were *symbols* with special meanings. People did not act toward the things themselves, but to their meanings.

The second premise underlying symbolic interactionism is that the "meaning of such things is derived from, or arises out of, the social interaction that one has with one's fellows."[6] Culture, as a shared system of meanings, is learned, revised, maintained, and defined in the context of people interacting. The crowd came to share their definitions of police behavior through interacting with one another and through past associations with the police. The police officers acquired the cultural meanings they used through interacting with other officers and members of the community. The culture of each group was inextricably bound up with the social life of their particular communities.

The third premise of symbolic interactionism is that "meanings are handled in, and modified through, an interpretive process used by the person

---

[4] Edward T. Hall, *The Silent Language* (Garden City, NY: Doubleday, 1959); *The Hidden Dimension* (Garden City, NY: Doubleday, 1966).

[5] Herbert Blumer, *Symbolic Interactionism* (Englewood Cliffs, NJ: Prentice-Hall, 1969), p. 2.

[6] Blumer, p. 2.

dealing with the things he encounters."[7] Neither the crowd nor the policemen were automatons, driven by their culture to act in the way they did. Rather, they used their cultural knowledge to interpret and evaluate the situation. At any moment, a member of the crowd might have interpreted the behavior of the policemen in a slightly different way, leading to a different reaction.

We may see this interpretive aspect more clearly if we think of culture as a cognitive map. In the recurrent activities that make up everyday life, we refer to this map. It serves as a guide for acting and for interpreting our experience; it does not compel us to follow a particular course. Like this brief drama between the policemen, a dying woman, and the crowd, much of life is a series of unanticipated social occasions. Although our culture may not include a detailed map for such occasions, it does provide principles for interpreting and responding to them. Rather than a rigid map that people must follow, culture is best thought of as

> a set of principles for creating dramas, for writing script, and of course, for recruiting players and audiences. . . . Culture is not simply a cognitive map that people acquire, in whole or in part, more or less accurately, and then learn to read. People are not just map-readers; they are map-makers. People are cast out into imperfectly charted, continually revised sketch maps. Culture does not provide a cognitive map, but rather a set of principles for map making and navigation. Different cultures are like different schools of navigation to cope with different terrains and seas.[8]

If we take *meaning* seriously, as symbolic interactionists argue we must, it becomes necessary to study meaning carefully. We need a theory of meaning and a specific methodology designed for the investigation of it.

# Review Questions

1. What is the definition of *culture?* How is this definition related to the way anthropologists do ethnographic fieldwork?

2. What is the relationship among cultural behavior, cultural artifacts, and cultural knowledge?

3. What is the difference between tacit and explicit culture? How can anthropologists discover these two kinds of culture?

4. What are some examples of naive realism in the way Americans think about people in other societies?

[7] Blumer, p. 2.

[8] Charles O. Frake, "Plying Frames Can Be Dangerous: Some Reflections on Methodology in Cognitive Anthropology," *Quarterly Newsletter of the Institute for Comparative Human Development* 3 (1977): 6–7.

# 2

# Eating Christmas
# in the Kalahari

*Richard Borshay Lee*

*What happens when an anthropologist living among the !Kung of Africa de-
cides to be generous and to share a large animal with everyone at Christ-
mastime? This compelling account of the misunderstanding and confusion
that resulted takes the reader deeper into the nature of culture. Richard Lee
carefully traces how the !Kung perceived his generosity and taught the anthropologist something about his own culture.*

The !Kung Bushmen's knowledge of Christmas is thirdhand. The London Missionary Society brought the holiday to the southern Tswana tribes in the early
nineteenth century. Later, native catechists spread the idea far and wide among
the Bantu-speaking pastoralists, even in the remotest corners of the Kalahari
Desert. The Bushmen's idea of the Christmas story, stripped to its essentials, is
"praise the birth of white man's god-chief"; what keeps their interest in the

holiday high is the Tswana-Herero custom of slaughtering an ox for his Bushmen neighbors as an annual goodwill gesture. Since the 1930s, part of the Bushmen's annual round of activities has included a December congregation at the cattle posts for trading, marriage brokering, and several days of trance dance feasting at which the local Tswana headman is host.

As a social anthropologist working with !Kung Bushmen, I found that the Christmas ox custom suited my purposes. I had come to the Kalahari to study the hunting and gathering subsistence economy of the !Kung, and to accomplish this it was essential not to provide them with food, share my own food, or interfere in any way with their food-gathering activities. While liberal handouts of tobacco and medical supplies were appreciated, they were scarcely adequate to erase the glaring disparity in wealth between the anthropologist, who maintained a two-month inventory of canned goods, and the Bushmen, who rarely had a day's supply of food on hand. My approach, while paying off in terms of data, left me open to frequent accusations of stinginess and hardheartedness. By their lights, I was a miser.

The Christmas ox was to be my way of saying thank you for the cooperation of the past year; and since it was to be our last Christmas in the field, I was determined to slaughter the largest, meatiest ox that money could buy, insuring that the feast and trance dance would be a success.

Through December I kept my eyes open at the wells as the cattle were brought down for watering. Several animals were offered, but none had quite the grossness that I had in mind. Then, ten days before the holiday, a Herero friend led an ox of astonishing size and mass up to our camp. It was solid black, stood five feet high at the shoulder, had a five-foot span of horns, and must have weighed 1,200 pounds on the hoof. Food consumption calculations are my specialty, and I quickly figured that bones and viscera aside, there was enough meat—at least four pounds—for every man, woman, and child of the 150 Bushmen in the vicinity of /ai/ai who were expected at the feast.

Having found the right animal at last, I paid the Herero £20 ($56) and asked him to keep the beast with his herd until Christmas day. The next morning word spread among the people that the big solid black one was the ox chosen by /ontah (my Bushman name; it means, roughly, "whitey") for the Christmas feast. That afternoon I received the first delegation. Ben!a, an outspoken sixty-year-old mother of five, came to the point slowly.

"Where were you planning to eat Christmas?"

"Right here at /ai/ai," I replied.

"Alone or with others?"

"I expect to invite all the people to eat Christmas with me."

"Eat what?"

"I have purchased Yehave's black ox, and I am going to slaughter and cook it."

"That's what we were told at the well but refused to believe it until we heard it from yourself."

"Well, it's the black one," I replied expansively, although wondering what she was driving at.

"Oh, no!" Ben!a groaned, turning to her group. "They were right." Turning back to me she asked, "Do you expect us to eat that bag of bones?"

"Bag of bones! It's the biggest ox at /ai/ai."

"Big, yes, but old. And thin. Everybody knows there's no meat on that old ox. What did you expect us to eat off it, the horns?"

Everybody chuckled at Ben!a's one-liner as they walked away, but all I could manage was a weak grin.

That evening it was the turn of the young men. They came to sit at our evening fire. /gaugo, about my age, spoke to me man-to-man.

"/ontah, you have always been square with us," he lied. "What has happened to change your heart? That sack of guts and bones of Yehave's will hardly feed one camp, let alone all the Bushmen around /ai/ai." And he proceeded to enumerate the seven camps in the /ai/ai vicinity, family by family. "Perhaps you have forgotten that we are not few, but many. Or are you too blind to tell the difference between a proper cow and an old wreck? That ox is thin to the point of death."

"Look, you guys," I retorted, "that is a beautiful animal, and I'm sure you will eat it with pleasure at Christmas."

"Of course we will eat it; it's food. But it won't fill us up to the point where we will have enough strength to dance. We will eat and go home to bed with stomachs rumbling."

That night as we turned in, I asked my wife, Nancy, "What did you think of the black ox?"

"It looked enormous to me. Why?"

"Well, about eight different people have told me I got gypped; that the ox is nothing but bones."

"What's the angle?" Nancy asked. "Did they have a better one to sell?"

"No, they just said that it was going to be a grim Christmas because there won't be enough meat to go around. Maybe I'll get an independent judge to look at the beast in the morning."

Bright and early, Halingisi, a Tswana cattle owner, appeared at our camp. But before I could ask him to give me his opinion on Yehave's black ox, he gave me the eye signal that indicated a confidential chat. We left the camp and sat down.

"/ontah, I'm surprised at you; you've lived here for three years and still haven't learned anything about cattle."

"But what else can a person do but choose the biggest, strongest animal one can find?" I retorted.

"Look, just because an animal is big doesn't mean that it has plenty of meat on it. The black one was a beauty when it was younger, but now it is thin to the point of death."

"Well, I've already bought it. What can I do at this stage?"

"Bought it already? I thought you were just considering it. Well, you'll have to kill it and serve it, I suppose. But don't expect much of a dance to follow."

My spirits dropped rapidly. I could believe that Ben!a and /gaugo just might be putting me on about the black ox, but Halingisi seemed to be an impartial critic. I went around that day feeling as though I had bought a lemon of a used car.

In the afternoon it was Tomazo's turn. Tomazo is a fine hunter, a top trance performer . . . and one of my most reliable informants. He approached the subject of the Christmas cow as part of my continuing Bushman education.

"My friend, the way it is with us Bushmen," he began, "is that we love meat. And even more than that, we love fat. When we hunt we always search for the fat ones, the ones dripping with layers of white fat: fat that turns into a clear, thick oil in the cooking pot, fat that slides down your gullet, fills your stomach and gives you a roaring diarrhea," he rhapsodized.

"So, feeling as we do," he continued, "it gives us pain to be served such a scrawny thing as Yehave's black ox. It is big, yes, and no doubt its giant bones are good for soup, but fat is what we really crave, and so we will eat Christmas this year with a heavy heart."

The prospect of a gloomy Christmas now had me worried, so I asked Tomazo what I could do about it.

"Look for a fat one, a young one . . . smaller, but fat. Fat enough to make us //gom (evacuate the bowels), then we will be happy."

My suspicions were aroused when Tomazo said that he happened to know a young, fat, barren cow that the owner was willing to part with. Was Tomazo working on commission, I wondered? But I dispelled this unworthy thought when we approached the Herero owner of the cow in question and found that he had decided not to sell.

The scrawny wreck of a Christmas ox now became the talk of the /ai/ai water hole and was the first news told to the outlying groups as they began to come in from the bush for the feast. What finally convinced me that real trouble might be brewing was the visit from u!au, an old conservative with a reputation for fierceness. His nickname meant spear and referred to an incident thirty years ago in which he had speared a man to death. He had an intense manner; fixing me with his eyes, he said in clipped tones:

"I have only just heard about the black ox today, or else I would have come here earlier. /ontah, do you honestly think you can serve meat like that to people and avoid a fight?" He paused, letting the implications sink in. "I don't mean fight you, /ontah; you are a white man. I mean a fight between Bushmen. There are many fierce ones here, and with such a small quantity of meat to distribute, how can you give everybody a fair share? Someone is sure to accuse another of taking too much or hogging all the choice pieces. Then you will see what happens when some go hungry while others eat."

The possibility of at least a serious argument struck me as all too real. I had witnessed the tension that surrounds the distribution of meat from a kudu or gemsbok kill, and had documented many arguments that sprang up from a real or imagined slight in meat distribution. The owners of a kill may spend up to two hours arranging and rearranging the piles of meat under the gaze of a circle of recipients before handing them out. And I knew that the Christmas feast at /ai/ai would be bringing together groups that had feuded in the past.

Convinced now of the gravity of the situation, I went in earnest to search for a second cow; but all my inquiries failed to turn one up.

The Christmas feast was evidently going to be a disaster, and the incessant complaints about the meagerness of the ox had already taken the fun out of it for me. Moreover, I was getting bored with the wisecracks, and after losing my temper a few times, I resolved to serve the beast anyway. If the meat fell short, the hell with it. In the Bushmen idiom, I announced to all who would listen:

"I am a poor man and blind. If I have chosen one that is too old and too thin, we will eat it anyway and see if there is enough meat there to quiet the rumbling of our stomachs."

On hearing this speech, Ben!a offered me a rare word of comfort. "It's thin," she said philosophically, "but the bones will make a good soup."

At dawn Christmas morning, instinct told me to turn over the butchering and cooking to a friend and take off with Nancy to spend Christmas alone in the bush. But curiosity kept me from retreating. I wanted to see what such a scrawny ox looked like on butchering, and if there *was* going to be a fight, I wanted to catch every word of it. Anthropologists are incurable that way.

The great beast was driven up to our dancing ground, and a shot in the forehead dropped it in its tracks. Then, freshly cut branches were heaped around the fallen carcass to receive the meat. Ten men volunteered to help with the cutting. I asked /gaugo to make the breast bone cut. This cut, which begins the butchering process for most large game, offers easy access for removal of the viscera. But it also allows the hunter to spot-check the amount of fat on an animal. A fat game animal carries a white layer up to an inch thick on the chest, while in a thin one, the knife will quickly cut to bone. All eyes fixed on his hand as /gaugo, dwarfed by the great carcass, knelt to the breast. The first cut opened a pool of solid white in the black skin. The second and third cut widened and deepened the creamy white. Still no bone. It was pure fat; it must have been two inches thick.

"Hey /gau," I burst out, "that ox is loaded with fat. What's this about the ox being too thin to bother eating? Are you out of your mind?"

"Fat?" /gau shot back. "You call that fat? This wreck is thin, sick, dead!" And he broke out laughing. So did everyone else. They rolled on the ground, paralyzed with laughter. Everybody laughed except me; I was thinking.

I ran back to the tent and burst in just as Nancy was getting up. "Hey, the black ox. It's fat as hell! They were kidding about it being too thin to eat. It was a joke or something. A put-on. Everyone is really delighted with it."

"Some joke," my wife replied. "It was so funny that you were ready to pack up and leave /ai/ai."

If it had indeed been a joke, it had been an extraordinarily convincing one, and tinged, I thought, with more than a touch of malice, as many jokes are.

Nevertheless, that it was a joke lifted my spirits considerably, and I returned to the butchering site where the shape of the ox was rapidly disappearing under the axes and knives of the butchers. The atmosphere had become festive. Grinning broadly, their arms covered with blood well past the elbow, men packed chunks of meat into the big cast-iron cooking pots, fifty pounds to the load, and muttered and chuckled all the while about the thinness and worthlessness of the animal and /ontah's poor judgment.

We danced and ate that ox two days and two nights; we cooked and distributed fourteen potfuls of meat and no one went home hungry and no fights broke out.

But the "joke" stayed in my mind. I had a growing feeling that something important had happened in my relationship with the Bushmen and that the clue lay in the meaning of the joke. Several days later, when most of the people had dispersed back to the bush camps, I raised the question with Hakekgose, a Tswana man who had grown up among the !Kung, married a !Kung girl, and who probably knew their culture better than any other non-Bushman.

"With us whites," I began, "Christmas is supposed to be the day of friendship and brotherly love. What I can't figure out is why the Bushmen went to such lengths to criticize and belittle the ox I had bought for the feast. The animal was perfectly good and their jokes and wisecracks practically ruined the holiday for me."

"So it really did bother you," said Hakekgose. "Well, that's the way they always talk. When I take my rifle and go hunting with them, if I miss, they laugh at me for the rest of the day. But even if I hit and bring one down, it's no better. To them, the kill is always too small or too old or too thin; and as we sit down on the kill site to cook and eat the liver, they keep grumbling, even with their mouths full of meat. They say things like, 'Oh, this is awful! What a worthless animal! Whatever made me think that this Tswana rascal could hunt!' "

"Is this the way outsiders are treated?" I asked.

"No, it is their custom; they talk that way to each other, too. Go and ask them."

/gaugo had been one of the most enthusiastic in making me feel bad about the merit of the Christmas ox. I sought him out first.

"Why did you tell me the black ox was worthless, when you could see that it was loaded with fat and meat?"

"It is our way," he said, smiling. "We always like to fool people about that. Say there is a Bushman who has been hunting. He must not come home and announce like a braggart, 'I have killed a big one in the bush!' He must first sit down in silence until I or someone else comes up to his fire and asks, 'What did you see today?' He replies quietly, 'Ah, I'm no good for hunting. I saw nothing at all [pause] just a little tiny one.' Then I smile to myself," /gaugo continued, "because I know he has killed something big.

"In the morning we make up a party of four or five people to cut up and carry the meat back to the camp. When we arrive at the kill we examine it and cry out, 'You mean to say you have dragged us all the way out here in order to make us cart home your pile of bones? Oh, if I had known it was this thin I wouldn't have come.' Another one pipes up, 'People, to think I gave up a nice day in the shade for this. At home we may be hungry, but at least we have nice cool water to drink.' If the horns are big, someone says, 'Did you think that somehow you were going to boil down the horns for soup?'

"To all this you must respond in kind. 'I agree,' you say, 'this one is not worth the effort; let's just cook the liver for strength and leave the rest for the hyenas. It is not too late to hunt today and even a duiker or a steenbok would be better than this mess.'

"Then you set to work nevertheless; butcher the animal, carry the meat back to the camp and everyone eats," /gaugo concluded.

Things were beginning to make sense. Next, I went to Tomazo. He corroborated /gaugo's story of the obligatory insults over a kill and added a few details of his own.

"But," I asked, "why insult a man after he has gone to all that trouble to track and kill an animal and when he is going to share the meat with you so that your children will have something to eat?"

"Arrogance," was his cryptic answer.

"Arrogance?"

"Yes, when a young man kills much meat he comes to think of himself as a chief or a big man, and he thinks of the rest of us as his servants or inferiors. We can't accept this. We refuse one who boasts, for someday his pride will make him kill somebody. So we always speak of his meat as worthless. This way we cool his heart and make him gentle."

"But why didn't you tell me this before?" I asked Tomazo with some heat.

"Because you never asked me," said Tomazo, echoing the refrain that has come to haunt every field ethnographer.

The pieces now fell into place. I had known for a long time that in situations of social conflict with Bushmen I held all the cards. I was the only source of tobacco in a thousand square miles, and I was not incapable of cutting an individual off for noncooperation. Though my boycott never lasted longer than a few days, it was an indication of my strength. People resented my presence at the water hole, yet simultaneously dreaded my leaving. In short I was a perfect target for the charge of arrogance and for the Bushman tactic of enforcing humility.

I had been taught an object lesson by the Bushmen; it had come from an unexpected corner and had hurt me in a vulnerable area. For the big black ox was to be the one totally generous, unstinting act of my year at /ai/ai and I was quite unprepared for the reaction I received.

As I read it, their message was this: There are no totally generous acts. All "acts" have an element of calculation. One black ox slaughtered at Christmas does not wipe out a year of careful manipulation of gifts given to serve your own ends. After all, to kill an animal and share the meat with people is really no more than the Bushmen do for each other every day and with far less fanfare.

In the end, I had to admire how the Bushmen had played out the farce—collectively straight-faced to the end. Curiously, the episode reminded me of the

*Good Soldier Schweik* and his marvelous encounters with authority. Like Schweik, the Bushmen had retained a thoroughgoing skepticism of good intentions. Was it this independence of spirit, I wondered, that had kept them culturally viable in the face of generations of contact with more powerful societies, both black and white? The thought that the Bushmen were alive and well in the Kalahari was strangely comforting. Perhaps, armed with that independence and with their superb knowledge of their environment, they might yet survive the future.

# Review Questions

1. What was the basis of the misunderstanding experienced by Lee when he gave an ox for the Christmas feast held by the !Kung?

2. Construct a model of cross-cultural misunderstanding, using the information presented by Lee in this article.

3. Why do you think the !Kung ridicule and denigrate people who have been successful hunters or who have provided them with a Christmas ox? Why do Americans expect people to be grateful to receive gifts?

# 3

# Shakespeare in the Bush

*Laura Bohannan*

*All of us use the cultural knowledge we acquire as members of our own society to organize our perception and behavior. Most of us are also naive realists: we tend to believe our culture mirrors a reality shared by everyone. But cultures are different, and other people rarely behave or interpret experience according to our cultural plan. In this article, Laura Bohannan describes her attempt to tell the classic story of* Hamlet *to Tiv elders in West Africa. At each turn in the story, the Tiv interpret the events and motives in Hamlet using their own cultural knowledge. The result is a very different version of the classic play.*

Reprinted with permission by the author from *Natural History* Magazine, August/September 1966.

Just before I left Oxford for the Tiv in West Africa, conversation turned to the season at Stratford. "You Americans," said a friend, "often have difficulty with Shakespeare. He was, after all, a very English poet, and one can easily misinterpret the universal by misunderstanding the particular."

I protested that human nature is pretty much the same the whole world over; at least the general plot and motivation of the greater tragedies would always be clear—everywhere—although some details of custom might have to be explained and difficulties of translation might produce other slight changes. To end an argument we could not conclude, my friend gave me a copy of *Hamlet* to study in the African bush: it would, he hoped, lift my mind above its primitive surroundings, and possibly I might, by prolonged meditation, achieve the grace of correct interpretation.

It was my second field trip to that African tribe, and I thought myself ready to live in one of its remote sections—an area difficult to cross even on foot. I eventually settled on the hillock of a very knowledgeable old man, the head of a homestead of some hundred and forty people, all of whom were either his close relatives or their wives and children. Like the other elders of the vicinity, the old man spent most of his time performing ceremonies seldom seen these days in the more accessible parts of the tribe. I was delighted. Soon there would be three months of enforced isolation and leisure, between the harvest that takes place just before the rising of the swamps and the clearing of new farms when the water goes down. Then, I thought, they would have even more time to perform ceremonies and explain them to me.

I was quite mistaken. Most of the ceremonies demanded the presence of elders from several homesteads. As the swamps rose, the old men found it too difficult to walk from one homestead to the next, and the ceremonies gradually ceased. As the swamps rose even higher, all activities but one came to an end. The women brewed beer from maize and millet. Men, women, and children sat on their hillocks and drank it.

People began to drink at dawn. By midmorning the whole homestead was singing, dancing, and drumming. When it rained, people had to sit inside their huts: there they drank and sang or they drank and told stories. In any case, by noon or before, I either had to join the party or retire to my own hut and my books. "One does not discuss serious matters when there is beer. Come, drink with us." Since I lacked their capacity for the thick native beer, I spent more and more time with *Hamlet*. Before the end of the second month, grace descended on me. I was quite sure that *Hamlet* had only one possible interpretation, and that one universally obvious.

Early every morning, in the hope of having some serious talk before the beer party, I used to call on the old man at his reception hut—a circle of posts supporting a thatched roof above a low mud wall to keep out wind and rain. One day I crawled through the low doorway and found most of the men of the homestead sitting huddled in their ragged cloths on stools, low plank beds, and reclining chairs, warming themselves against the chill of the rain around a smoky fire. In the center were three pots of beer. The party had started.

The old man greeted me cordially. "Sit down and drink." I accepted a large calabash full of beer, poured some into a small drinking gourd, and tossed it down. Then I poured some more into the same gourd for the man second in seniority to my host before I handed my calabash over to a young man for further distribution. Important people shouldn't ladle beer themselves.

"It is better like this," the old man said, looking at me approvingly and plucking at the thatch that had caught in my hair. "You should sit and drink with us more often. Your servants tell me that when you are not with us, you sit inside your hut looking at a paper."

The old man was acquainted with four kinds of "papers": tax receipts, bride price receipts, court fee receipts, and letters. The messenger who brought him letters from the chief used them mainly as a badge of office, for he always knew what was in them and told the old man. Personal letters for the few who had relatives in the government or mission stations were kept until someone went to a large market where there was a letter writer and reader. Since my arrival, letters were brought to me to be read. A few men also brought me bride price receipts, privately, with requests to change the figures to a higher sum. I found moral arguments were of no avail, since in-laws are fair game, and the technical hazards of forgery difficult to explain to an illiterate people. I did not wish them to think me silly enough to look at any such papers for days on end, and I hastily explained that my "paper" was one of the "things of long ago" of my country.

"Ah," said the old men. "Tell us."

I protested that I was not a storyteller. Storytelling is a skilled art among them; their standards are high, and the audiences critical—and vocal in their criticism. I protested in vain. This morning they wanted to hear a story while they drank. They threatened to tell me no more stories until I told them one of mine. Finally, the old man promised that no one would criticize my style "for we know you are struggling with our language." "But," put in one of the elders, "you must explain what we do not understand, as we do when we tell you our stories." Realizing that here was my chance to prove *Hamlet* universally intelligible, I agreed.

The old man handed me some more beer to help me on with my storytelling. Men filled their long wooden pipes and knocked coals from the fire to place in the pipe bowls; then, puffing contentedly, they sat back to listen. I began in the proper style, "Not yesterday, not yesterday, but long ago, a thing occurred. One night three men were keeping watch outside the homestead of the great chief, when suddenly they saw the former chief approach them."

"Why was he no longer their chief?"

"He was dead," I explained. "That is why they were troubled and afraid when they saw him."

"Impossible," began one of the elders, handing his pipe on to his neighbor, who interrupted, "Of course it wasn't the dead chief. It was an omen sent by a witch. Go on."

Slightly shaken, I continued. "One of these three was a man who knew things"—the closest translation for scholar, but unfortunately it also meant witch. The second elder looked triumphantly at the first. "So he spoke to the dead chief, saying, 'Tell us what we must do so you may rest in your grave,' but the dead chief did not answer. He vanished, and they could see him no more. Then the man who knew things—his name was Horatio—said this event was the affair of the dead chief's son, Hamlet."

There was a general shaking of heads around the circle. "Had the dead chief no living brothers? Or was this son the chief?"

"No," I replied. "That is, he had one living brother who became the chief when the elder brother died."

The old men muttered: such omens were matters for chiefs and elders, not for youngsters; no good could come of being behind a chief's back; clearly Horatio was not a man who knew things.

"Yes, he was," I insisted, shooing a chicken away from my beer. "In our country the son is next to the father. The dead chief's younger brother had become the great chief. He had also married his elder brother's widow only about a month after the funeral."

"He did well," the old man beamed and announced to the others, "I told you that if we knew more about Europeans, we would find they really were very like us. In our country also," he added to me, "the younger brother marries the elder brother's widow and becomes the father of his children. Now, if your uncle, who married your widowed mother, is your father's full brother, then he will be a real father to you. Did Hamlet's father and uncle have one mother?"

His question barely penetrated my mind; I was too upset and thrown too far off balance by having one of the most important elements of *Hamlet* knocked straight out of the picture. Rather uncertainly I said that I thought they had the same mother, but I wasn't sure—the story didn't say. The old man told me severely that these genealogical details made all the difference and that when I got home I must ask the elders about it. He shouted out the door to one of his younger wives to bring his goatskin bag.

Determined to save what I could of the mother motif, I took a deep breath and began again. "The son Hamlet was very sad because his mother had married again so quickly. There was no need for her to do so, and it is our custom for a widow not to go to her next husband until she has mourned for two years."

"Two years is too long," objected the wife, who had appeared with the old man's battered goatskin bag. "Who will hoe your farms for you while you have no husband?"

"Hamlet," I retorted without thinking, "was old enough to hoe his mother's farms himself. There was no need for her to remarry." No one looked convinced. I gave up. "His mother and the great chief told Hamlet not to be sad, for the great chief himself would be a father to Hamlet. Furthermore, Hamlet would be the next chief: therefore he must stay to learn the things of a chief. Hamlet agreed to remain, and all the rest went off to drink beer."

While I paused, perplexed at how to render Hamlet's disgusted soliloquy to an audience convinced that Claudius and Gertrude had behaved in the best possible manner, one of the younger men asked me who had married the other wives of the dead chief.

"He had no other wives," I told him.

"But a chief must have many wives! How else can he brew beer and prepare food for all his guests?"

I said firmly that in our country even chiefs had only one wife, that they had servants to do their work, and that they paid them from tax money.

It was better, they returned, for a chief to have many wives and sons who would help him hoe his farms and feed his people; then everyone loved the chief who gave much and took nothing—taxes were a bad thing.

I agreed with the last comment, but for the rest fell back on their favorite way of fobbing off my questions: "That is the way it is done, so that is how we do it."

I decided to skip the soliloquy. Even if Claudius was here thought quite right to marry his brother's widow, there remained the poison motif, and I knew they would disapprove of fratricide. More hopefully I resumed, "That night Hamlet kept watch with the three who had seen his dead father. The dead chief again appeared, and although the others were afraid, Hamlet followed his dead father off to one side. When they were alone, Hamlet's dead father spoke."

"Omens can't talk!" The old man was emphatic.

"Hamlet's dead father wasn't an omen. Seeing him might have been an omen, but he was not." My audience looked as confused as I sounded. "It *was* Hamlet's dead father. It was a thing we call a 'ghost.' " I had to use the English word, for unlike many of the neighboring tribes, these people didn't believe in the survival after death of any individuating part of the personality.

"What is a 'ghost'? An omen?"

"No, a 'ghost' is someone who is dead but who walks around and can talk, and people can hear him and see him but not touch him."

They objected. "One can touch zombis."

"No, no! It was not a dead body the witches had animated to sacrifice and eat. No one else made Hamlet's dead father walk. He did it himself."

"Dead men can't walk," protested my audience as one man.

I was quite willing to compromise. "A 'ghost' is a dead man's shadow."

But again they objected. "Dead men cast no shadows."

"They do in my country," I snapped.

The old man quelled the babble of disbelief that rose immediately and told me with that insincere, but courteous, agreement one extends to the fancies of the young, ignorant, and superstitious, "No doubt in your country the dead can also walk without being zombis." From the depths of his bag he produced a withered fragment of kola nut, bit off one end to show it wasn't poisoned, and handed me the rest as a peace offering.

"Anyhow," I resumed, "Hamlet's dead father said that his own brother, the one who became chief, had poisoned him. He wanted Hamlet to avenge him. Hamlet believed this in his heart, for he did not like his father's brother." I took another swallow of beer. "In the country of the great chief, living in the same homestead, for it was a very large one, was an important elder who was often with the chief to advise and help him. His name was Polonius. Hamlet was courting his daughter, but her father and her brother . . . [I cast hastily about for some tribal analogy] warned her not to let Hamlet visit her when she was alone on her farm, for he would be a great chief and so could not marry her."

"Why not?" asked the wife, who had settled down on the edge of the old man's chair. He frowned at her for asking stupid questions and growled, "They lived in the same homestead."

"That was not the reason," I informed them. "Polonius was a stranger who lived in the homestead because he helped the chief, not because he was a relative."

"Then why couldn't Hamlet marry her?"

"He could have," I explained, "but Polonius didn't think he would. After all, Hamlet was a man of great importance who ought to marry a chief's daughter, for in his country a man could have only one wife. Polonius was afraid that if Hamlet made love to his daughter, then no one else would give a high price for her."

"That might be true," remarked one of the shrewder elders, "but a chief's son would give his mistress's father enough presents and patronage to more than make up the difference. Polonius sounds like a fool to me."

"Many people think he was," I agreed. "Meanwhile Polonius sent his son Laertes off to Paris to learn the things of that country, for it was the homestead of a very great chief indeed. Because he was afraid that Laertes might waste a lot of money on beer and women and gambling, or get into trouble by fighting, he sent one of his servants to Paris secretly, to spy out what Laertes was doing. One day Hamlet came upon Polonius's daughter Ophelia. He behaved so oddly he frightened her. Indeed"—I was fumbling for words to express the dubious quality of Hamlet's madness—"the chief and many others had also noticed that when Hamlet talked one could understand the words but not what they meant. Many people thought that he had become mad." My audience suddenly became much more attentive. "The great chief wanted to know what was wrong with Hamlet, so he sent for two of Hamlet's age mates [school friends would have taken long explanation] to talk to Hamlet and find out what troubled his heart. Hamlet, seeing that they had been bribed by the chief to betray him, told them nothing. Polonius, however, insisted that Hamlet was mad because he had been forbidden to see Ophelia, whom he loved."

"Why," inquired a bewildered voice, "should anyone bewitch Hamlet on that account?"

"Bewitch him?"

"Yes, only witchcraft can make anyone mad, unless, of course, one sees the beings that lurk in the forest."

I stopped being a storyteller, took out my notebook and demanded to be told more about these two causes of madness. Even while they spoke and I jotted notes, I tried to calculate the effect of this new factor on the plot. Hamlet had not been exposed to the beings that lurk in the forest. Only his relatives in the male line could bewitch him. Barring relatives not mentioned by Shakespeare, it had to be Claudius who was attempting to harm him. And, of course, it was.

For the moment I staved off questions by saying that the great chief also refused to believe that Hamlet was mad for the love of Ophelia and nothing else. "He was sure that something much more important was troubling Hamlet's heart."

"Now Hamlet's age mates," I continued, "had brought with them a famous storyteller. Hamlet decided to have this man tell the chief and all his homestead a story about the man who had poisoned his brother because he desired his brother's wife and wished to be chief himself. Hamlet was sure the great chief could not hear the story without making a sign if he was indeed guilty, and then he would discover whether his dead father had told him the truth."

The old man interrupted, with deep cunning. "Why should a father lie to his son?" he asked.

I hedged: "Hamlet wasn't sure that it really was his dead father." It was impossible to say anything, in that language, about devil-inspired visions.

"You mean," he said, "it actually was an omen, and he knew witches sometimes send false ones. Hamlet was a fool not to go to one skilled in reading omens and divining the truth in the first place. A man-who-sees-the-truth could have told him how his father died, if he really had been poisoned, and if there was witchcraft in it; then Hamlet could have called the elders to settle the matter."

The shrewd elder ventured to disagree. "Because his father's brother was a great chief, one-who-sees-the-truth might therefore have been afraid to tell it. I think it was for that reason that a friend of Hamlet's father—a witch and an elder—sent an omen so his friend's son would know. Was the omen true?"

"Yes," I said, abandoning ghosts and the devil; a witch-sent omen it would have to be. "It was true, for when the storyteller was telling his tale before all the homestead, the great chief rose in fear. Afraid that Hamlet knew his secret, he planned to have him killed."

The stage set of the next bit presented some difficulties of translation. I began cautiously. "The great chief told Hamlet's mother to find out from her son what he knew. But because a woman's children are always first in her heart, he had the important elder Polonius hide behind a cloth that hung against the wall of Hamlet's mother's sleeping hut. Hamlet started to scold his mother for what she had done."

There was a shocked murmur from everyone. A man should never scold his mother.

"She called out in fear, and Polonius moved behind the cloth. Shouting 'A rat!' Hamlet took his machete and slashed through the cloth." I paused for a dramatic effect. "He had killed Polonius!"

The old men looked at each other in supreme disgust. "That Polonius truly was a fool and a man who knew nothing! What child would not know enough to shout, 'It's me!'" With a pang, I remembered that these people are ardent hunters, always armed with bow, arrow, and machete; at the first rustle in the grass an arrow is aimed and ready, and the hunter shouts "Game!" If no human voice answers immediately, the arrow speeds on its way. Like a good hunter Hamlet had shouted, "A rat!"

I rushed in to save Polonius's reputation. "Polonius did speak. Hamlet heard him. But he thought it was the chief and wished to kill him to avenge his father. He had meant to kill him earlier that evening. . . ." I broke down, unable to describe to these pagans, who had no belief in individual afterlife, the difference between dying at one's prayers and dying "unhousell'd, disappointed, unaneled."

This time I had shocked my audience seriously. "For a man to raise his hands against his father's brother and the one who has become his father—that is a terrible thing. The elders ought to let such a man be bewitched."

I nibbled at my kola nut in some perplexity, then pointed out that after all the man had killed Hamlet's father.

"No," pronounced the old man, speaking less to me than to the young men sitting behind the elders. "If your father's brother has killed your father, you must appeal to your father's age mates; *they* may avenge him. No man may use violence against his senior relatives." Another thought struck him. "But if his father's brother had indeed been wicked enough to bewitch Hamlet and make him mad, that would be a good story indeed, for it would be his fault that Hamlet, being mad, no longer had any sense and thus was ready to kill his father's brother."

There was a murmur of applause. *Hamlet* was again a good story to them, but it no longer seemed quite the same story to me. As I thought over the coming complications of plot and motive, I lost courage and decided to skim over dangerous ground quickly.

"The great chief," I went on, "was not sorry that Hamlet had killed Polonius. It gave him a reason to send Hamlet away, with his two treacherous age mates, with letters to a chief of a far country, saying that Hamlet should be killed. But Hamlet changed the writing on their papers, so that the chief killed his age mates instead." I encountered a reproachful glare from one of the men whom I had told undetectable forgery was not merely immoral but beyond human skill. I looked the other way.

"Before Hamlet could return, Laertes came back for his father's funeral. The great chief told him Hamlet had killed Polonius. Laertes swore to kill Hamlet because of this, and because his sister Ophelia, hearing her father had been killed by the man she loved, went mad and drowned in the river."

"Have you already forgotten what we told you?" The old man was reproachful. "One cannot take vengeance on a madman; Hamlet killed Polonius in his madness. As for the girl, she not only went mad, she was drowned. Only witches can make people drown. Water itself can't hurt anything. It is merely something one drinks and bathes in."

I began to get cross. "If you don't like the story, I'll stop."

The old man made soothing noises and himself poured me some more beer. "You tell the story well, and we are listening. But it is clear that the elders of your country have never told you what the story really means. No, don't interrupt! We believe you when you say your marriage customs are different, or your clothes and weapons. But people are the same everywhere; therefore, there are always witches and it is we, the elders, who know how witches work. We told you it was the great chief who wished to kill Hamlet, and now your own words have proved us right. Who were Ophelia's male relatives?"

"There were only her father and her brother." Hamlet was clearly out of my hands.

"There must have been many more; this also you must ask of your elders when you get back to your country. From what you tell us, since Polonius was dead, it must have been Laertes who killed Ophelia, although I do not see the reason for it."

We had emptied one pot of beer, and the old men argued the point with slightly tipsy interest. Finally one of them demanded of me, "What did the servant of Polonius say on his return?"

With difficulty I recollected Reynaldo and his mission. "I don't think he did return before Polonius was killed."

"Listen," said the elder, "and I will tell you how it was and how your story will go, then you may tell me if I am right. Polonius knew his son would get into trouble, and so he did. He had many fines to pay for fighting, and debts from gambling. But he had only two ways of getting money quickly. One was to marry off his sister at once, but it is difficult to find a man who will marry a woman desired by the son of a chief. For if the chief's heir commits adultery with your wife, what can you do? Only a fool calls a case against a man who will someday be his judge. Therefore Laertes had to take the second way: he killed his sister by witchcraft, drowning her so he could secretly sell her body to the witches."

I raised an objection. "They found her body and buried it. Indeed Laertes jumped into the grave to see his sister once more—so, you see, the body was truly there. Hamlet, who had just come back, jumped in after him."

"What did I tell you?" The elder appealed to the others. "Laertes was up to no good with his sister's body. Hamlet prevented him, because the chief's heir, like a chief, does not wish any other man to grow rich and powerful. Laertes would be angry, because he would have killed his sister without benefit to himself. In our country he would try to kill Hamlet for that reason. Is this not what happened?"

"More or less," I admitted. "When the great chief found Hamlet was still alive, he encouraged Laertes to try to kill Hamlet and arranged a fight with machetes between them. In the fight both the young men were wounded to death. Hamlet's mother drank the poisoned beer that the chief meant for Hamlet in case he won the fight. When he saw his mother die of poison, Hamlet, dying, managed to kill his father's brother with his machete."

"You see, I was right!" exclaimed the elder.

"That was a very good story," added the old man, "and you told it with very few mistakes. There was just one more error, at the very end. The poison Hamlet's mother drank was obviously meant for the survivor of the fight, whichever it was. If Laertes had won, the great chief would have poisoned him, for no one would know that he arranged Hamlet's death. Then, too, he need not fear Laertes's witchcraft; it takes a strong heart to kill one's only sister by witchcraft.

"Sometime," concluded the old man, gathering his ragged toga about him, "you must tell us some more stories of your country. We, who are elders, will instruct you in their true meaning, so that when you return to your own land your elders will see that you have not been sitting in the bush, but among those who know things and who have taught you wisdom."

# Review Questions

1. In what ways does Bohannan's attempt to tell the story of Hamlet to the Tiv illustrate the concept of naive realism?

2. Using Bohannan's experience of telling the story of *Hamlet* to the Tiv and the response of the Tiv elders to her words, illustrate cross-cultural misunderstanding.

3. What are the most important parts of *Hamlet* that the Tiv found it necessary to reinterpret?

# 4

# Fieldwork on Prostitution in the Era of AIDS

*Claire E. Sterk*

*Many Americans associate social research with questionnaires, structured interviews, word association tests, and psychological experiments. They expect investigators to control the research setting and ask for specific information, such as age, income, place of residence, and opinions about work or national events. But ethnographic fieldwork is different. Cultural anthropologists may administer formal research instruments such as questionnaires, but largely their goal is to discover culture, to view the actions and knowledge of a group through the eyes of its members. In this sense, ethnographers are more like students; cultural informants are more like teachers. To implement ethnographic research, anthropologists must often become part of the worlds they seek to understand. They arrive as strangers, seek entrance into a group, meet and develop relationships of trust with informants,*

From *Tricking and Tripping* by Claire E. Sterk. (Putnam Valley, NY: Social Change Press, 2000), pp. 14–20. Reprinted by permission.

*and wrestle with the ethical dilemmas that naturally occur when someone wants to delve into the lives of others.*

*These are the challenges discussed in this selection by Claire Sterk. Working inside the United States, as many anthropologists do these days, she engaged in a long-term study of prostitutes in New York City and Atlanta. Her research required her to discover the places where her informants worked and hung out, introduce herself, develop rapport, and conduct open-ended interviews that permitted informants to teach her about their lives. During this process, she learned not to depend too much on contacts (gatekeepers) she met initially, that it was helpful to know something about respondents but to avoid an "expert" role, to refrain from expressing her own opinions about the culture and lives of her subjects, and to manage a variety of ethical questions. She ends by listing six themes that emerged from her ethnographic study.*

> Prostitution is a way of life. IT IS THE LIFE.
> We make money for pimps who promise us
>     love and more,
> but if we don't produce, they shove us out the door.
>
> We turn tricks who have sex-for-pay.
> They don't care how many times we serve
>     every day.
>
> The Life is rough. The Life is tough.
> We are put down, beaten up, and left for dead.
> It hurts body and soul and messes with
>     a person's head.
>
> Many of us get high. Don't you understand it is
>     a way of getting by?
>
> The Life is rough. The Life is tough.
> We are easy to blame because we are lame.
>                                         —Piper, 1987[1]

One night in March of 1987 business was slow. I was hanging out on a stroll with a group of street prostitutes. After a few hours in a nearby diner/coffee shop, we were kicked out. The waitress felt bad, but she needed our table for some new customers. Four of us decided to sit in my car until the rain stopped. While three of us chatted about life, Piper wrote this poem. As soon as she read it to us, the conversation shifted to more serious topics—pimps, customers, cops, the many hassles of being a prostitute, to name a few. We decided that if I ever finished a book about prostitution, the book would start with her poem.

This book is about the women who work in the lower echelons of the prostitution world. They worked in the streets and other public settings as well as

---

[1]The names of the women who were interviewed for this study, as well as those of their pimps and customers, have been replaced by pseudonyms to protect their privacy.

crack houses. Some of these women viewed themselves primarily as prostitutes, and a number of them used drugs to cope with the pressures of the life. Others identified themselves more as drug users, and their main reason for having sex for money or other goods was to support their own drug use and often the habit of their male partner. A small group of women interviewed for this book had left prostitution, and most of them were still struggling to integrate their past experiences as prostitutes in their current lives.

The stories told by the women who participated in this project revealed how pimps, customers, and others such as police officers and social and health service providers treated them as "fallen" women. However, their accounts also showed their strengths and the many strategies they developed to challenge these others. Circumstances, including their drug use, often forced them to sell sex, but they all resisted the notion that they might be selling themselves. Because they engaged in an illegal profession, these women had little status: their working conditions were poor, and their work was physically and mentally exhausting. Nevertheless, many women described the ways in which they gained a sense of control over their lives. For instance, they learned how to manipulate pimps, how to control the types of services and length of time bought by their customers, and how to select customers. While none of these schemes explicitly enhanced their working conditions, they did make the women feel stronger and better about themselves.

In this [article], I present prostitution from the point of view of the women themselves. To understand their current lives, it was necessary to learn how they got started in the life, the various processes involved in their continued prostitution careers, the link between prostitution and drug use, the women's interactions with their pimps and customers, and the impact of the AIDS epidemic and increasing violence on their experiences. I also examined the implications for women. Although my goal was to present the women's thoughts, feelings, and actions in their own words, the final text is a sociological monograph compiled by me as the researcher. . . .

## The Sample

. . . The research was conducted during the last ten years in the New York City and Atlanta metropolitan areas. One main data source was participant observation on streets, in hotels and other settings known for prostitution activity, and in drug-use settings, especially those that allowed sex-for-drug exchanges. Another data source was in-depth, life-history interviews with 180 women ranging in age from 18 to 59 years, with an average age of 34. One in two women was African-American and one in three white; the remaining women were Latina. Three in four had completed high school, and among them almost two-thirds had one or more years of additional educational training. Thirty women had graduated from college.

Forty women worked as street prostitutes and did not use drugs. On average, they had been prostitutes for 11 years. Forty women began using drugs an average of three years after they began working as prostitutes, and the average time they had worked as prostitutes was nine years. Forty women used drugs an average of five years before they became prostitutes, and on the average they had worked as prostitutes for eight years. Another forty women began smoking crack and exchanging sex for crack almost simultaneously, with an average of four years in the life. Twenty women who were interviewed were ex-prostitutes.

## Comments on Methodology

When I tell people about my research, the most frequent question I am asked is how I gained access to the women rather than what I learned from the research. For many, prostitution is an unusual topic of conversation, and many people have expressed surprise that I, as a woman, conducted the research. During my research some customers indeed thought I was a working woman, a fact that almost always amuses those who hear about my work. However, few people want to hear stories about the women's struggles and sadness. Sometimes they ask questions about the reasons why women become prostitutes. Most of the time, they are surprised when I tell them that the prostitutes as well as their customers represent all layers of society. Before presenting the findings, it seems important to discuss the research process, including gaining access to the women, developing relationships, interviewing, and then leaving the field.

## Locating Prostitutes and Gaining Entree

One of the first challenges I faced was to identify locations where street prostitution took place. Many of these women worked on strolls, streets where prostitution activity is concentrated, or in hotels known for prostitution activity. Others, such as the crack prostitutes, worked in less public settings such as a crack house that might be someone's apartment.

I often learned of well-known public places from professional experts, such as law enforcement officials and health care providers at emergency rooms and sexually transmitted disease clinics. I gained other insights from lay experts, including taxi drivers, bartenders, and community representatives such as members of neighborhood associations. The contacts universally mentioned some strolls as the places where many women worked, where the local police focused attention, or where residents had organized protests against prostitution in their neighborhoods.

As I began visiting various locales, I continued to learn about new settings. In one sense, I was developing ethnographic maps of street prostitution. After several visits to a specific area, I also was able to expand these maps by adding information about the general atmosphere on the stroll, general characteristics of the various people present, the ways in which the women and customers connected, and the overall flow of action. In addition, my visits allowed the regular actors to notice me.

I soon learned that being an unknown woman in an area known for prostitution may cause many people to notice you, even stare at you, but it fails to yield many verbal interactions. Most of the time when I tried to make eye contact with one of the women, she quickly averted her eyes. Pimps, on the other hand, would stare at me straight on and I ended up being the one to look away. Customers would stop, blow their horn, or wave me over, frequently yelling obscenities when I ignored them. I realized that gaining entree into the prostitution world was not going to be as easy as I imagined it. Although I lacked such training in any of my qualitative methods classes, I decided to move slowly and not force any interaction. The most I said during the initial weeks in a new area was limited to "How are you" or "Hi." This strategy paid off during my first visits to one of the strolls in Brooklyn, New York. After several appearances, one of the women walked up to me and sarcastically asked if I was looking for something. She caught me off guard, and all the answers I had practiced did not seem to make sense. I mumbled something about just wanting to walk around. She did not like my answer, but she did like my accent. We ended up talking about the latter and she was especially excited when I told her I came from Amsterdam. One of her friends had gone to Europe with her boyfriend, who was in the military. She understood from her that prostitution and drugs were legal in the Netherlands. While explaining to her that some of her friend's impressions were incorrect, I was able to show off some of my knowledge about prostitution. I mentioned that I was interested in prostitution and wanted to write a book about it.

Despite the fascination with my background and intentions, the prostitute immediately put me through a Streetwalker 101 test, and apparently I passed. She told me to make sure to come back. By the time I left, I not only had my first conversation but also my first connection to the scene. Variations of this entry process occurred on the other strolls. The main lesson I learned in these early efforts was the importance of having some knowledge of the lives of the people I wanted to study, while at the same time refraining from presenting myself as an expert.

Qualitative researchers often refer to their initial connections as gatekeepers and key respondents. Throughout my fieldwork I learned that some key respondents are important in providing initial access, but they become less central as the research evolves. For example, one of the women who introduced me to her lover, who was also her pimp, was arrested and disappeared for months. Another entered drug treatment soon after she facilitated my access. Other key respondents provided access to only a segment of the players on a scene. For example, if a woman worked for a pimp, [she] was unlikely . . . to introduce me to women working for another pimp. On one stroll my initial contact was with a pimp whom nobody liked. By associating with him, I almost lost the opportunity to meet other pimps. Some key respondents were less connected than promised—for example, some of the women who worked the street to support their drug habit. Often their connections were more frequently with drug users and less so with prostitutes.

Key respondents tend to be individuals central to the local scene, such as, in this case, pimps and the more senior prostitutes. Their function as gate-keepers often is to protect the scene and to screen outsiders. Many times I had to prove that I was not an undercover police officer or a woman with ambitions to become a streetwalker. While I thought I had gained entree, I quickly learned that many insiders subsequently wondered about my motives and approached me with suspicion and distrust.

Another lesson involved the need to proceed cautiously with self-nomi-nated key respondents. For example, one of the women presented herself as knowing everyone on the stroll. While she did know everyone, she was not a cen-tral figure. On the contrary, the other prostitutes viewed her as a failed street-walker whose drug use caused her to act unprofessionally. By associating with me, she hoped to regain some of her status. For me, however, it meant limited access to the other women because I affiliated myself with a woman who was marginal to the scene. On another occasion, my main key respondent was a man who claimed to own three crack houses in the neighborhood. However, he had a negative reputation, and people accused him of cheating on others. My initial alliance with him delayed, and almost blocked, my access to others in the neigh-borhood. He intentionally tried to keep me from others on the scene, not because he would gain something from that transaction but because it made him feel powerful. When I told him I was going to hang out with some of the other peo-ple, he threatened me until one of the other dealers stepped in and told him to stay away. The two of them argued back and forth, and finally I was free to go. Fortunately, the dealer who had spoken up for me was much more central and positively associated with the local scene. Finally, I am unsure if I would have had success in gaining entrance to the scene had I not been a woman.

## Developing Relationships and Trust

The processes involved in developing relationships in research situations am-plify those involved in developing relationships in general. Both parties need to get to know each other, become aware and accepting of each other's roles, and engage in a reciprocal relationship. Being supportive and providing practical assistance were the most visible and direct ways for me as the researcher to de-velop a relationship. Throughout the years, I have given countless rides, pro-vided child care on numerous occasions, bought groceries, and listened for hours to stories that were unrelated to my initial research questions. Gradually, my role allowed me to become part of these women's lives and to build rapport with many of them.

Over time, many women also realized that I was uninterested in being a prostitute and that I genuinely was interested in learning as much as possible about their lives. Many felt flattered that someone wanted to learn from them and that they had knowledge to offer. Allowing women to tell their stories and engaging in a dialogue with them probably were the single most important techniques that allowed me to develop relationships with them. Had I only wanted to focus on the questions I had in mind, developing such relationships might have been more difficult.

At times, I was able to get to know a woman only after her pimp endorsed our contact. One of my scariest experiences occurred before I knew to work through the pimps, and one such man had some of his friends follow me on my way home one night. I will never know what plans they had in mind for me because I fortunately was able to escape with only a few bruises. Over a year later, the woman acknowledged that her pimp had gotten upset and told her he was going to teach me a lesson.

On other occasions, I first needed to be screened by owners and managers of crack houses before the research could continue. Interestingly, screenings always were done by a man even if the person who vouched for me was a man himself. While the women also were cautious, the ways in which they checked me out tended to be much more subtle. For example, one of them would tell me a story, indicating that it was a secret about another person on the stroll. Although I failed to realize this at the time, my field notes revealed that frequently after such a conversation, others would ask me questions about related topics. One woman later acknowledged that putting out such stories was a test to see if I would keep information confidential.

Learning more about the women and gaining a better understanding of their lives also raised many ethical questions. No textbook told me how to handle situations in which a pimp abused a woman, a customer forced a woman to engage in unwanted sex acts, a customer requested unprotected sex from a woman who knew she was HIV infected, or a boyfriend had unrealistic expectations regarding a woman's earnings to support his drug habit. I failed to know the proper response when asked to engage in illegal activities such as holding drugs or money a woman had stolen from a customer. In general, my response was to explain that I was there as a researcher. During those occasions when pressures became too severe, I decided to leave a scene. For example, I never returned to certain crack houses because pimps there continued to ask me to consider working for them.

Over time, I was fortunate to develop relationships with people who "watched my back." One pimp in particular intervened if he perceived other pimps, customers, or passersby harassing me. He also was the one who gave me my street name: Whitie (indicating my racial background) or Ms. Whitie for those who disrespected me. While this was my first street name, I subsequently had others. Being given a street name was a symbolic gesture of acceptance. Gradually, I developed an identity that allowed me to be both an insider and an outsider. While hanging out on the strolls and other gathering places, including crack houses, I had to deal with some of the same uncomfortable conditions as the prostitutes, such as cold or warm weather, lack of access to a rest room, refusals from owners for me to patronize a restaurant, and of course, harassment by customers and the police.

I participated in many informal conversations. Unless pushed to do so, I seldom divulged my opinions. I was more open with my feelings about situations and showed empathy. I learned quickly that providing an opinion can backfire. I agreed that one of the women was struggling a lot and stated that I felt sorry for her. While I meant to indicate my genuine concern for her, she heard that I felt sorry for her because she was a failure. When she finally, after several weeks, talked with me again, I was able to explain to her that I was not judging her, but rather felt concerned for her. She remained cynical and many times asked me for favors to make up for my mistake. It took me months before I felt comfortable telling her that I felt I had done enough and that it was time to let go. However, if she was not ready, she needed to know that I would no longer go along. This was one of many occasions when I learned that although I wanted to facilitate my work as a researcher, that I wanted people to like and trust me, I also needed to set boundaries.

Rainy and slow nights often provided good opportunities for me to participate in conversations with groups of women. Popular topics included how to work safely, what to do about condom use, how to make more money. I often served as a health educator and a supplier of condoms, gels, vaginal douches, and other feminine products. Many women were very worried about the AIDS epidemic. However, they also were worried about how to use a condom when a customer refused to do so. They worried particularly about condom use when they needed money badly and, consequently, did not want to propose that the customer use one for fear of rejection. While some women became experts at "making" their customers use a condom—for example, by hiding it in their mouth prior to beginning oral sex—others would carry condoms to please me but never pull one out. If a woman was HIV positive and I knew she failed to use a condom, I faced the ethical dilemma of challenging her or staying out of it.

Developing trusting relationships with crack prostitutes was more difficult. Crack houses were not the right environment for informal conversations. Typically, the atmosphere was tense and everyone was suspicious of each other. The best times to talk with these women were when we bought groceries together, when I helped them clean their homes, or when we shared a meal. Often the women were very different when they were not high than they were when they were high or craving crack. In my conversations with them, I learned that while I might have observed their actions the night before, they themselves might not remember them. Once I realized this, I would be very careful to omit any detail unless I knew that the woman herself did remember the event.

## In-Depth Interviews

All interviews were conducted in a private setting, including women's residences, my car or my office, a restaurant of the women's choice, or any other setting the women selected. I did not begin conducting official interviews until I developed relationships with the women. Acquiring written informed consent prior to the interview was problematic. It made me feel awkward. Here I was asking the women to sign a form after they had begun to trust me. However, often I felt more upset about this technicality than the women themselves. As soon as they realized that the form was something the university required, they seemed to understand. Often they laughed about the official statements, and some asked if I was sure the form was to protect them and not the school. None of the women refused to sign the consent form, although some refused to sign it right away and asked to be interviewed later.

In some instances the consent procedures caused the women to expect a formal interview. Some of them were disappointed when they saw I only had a few structured questions about demographic characteristics, followed by a long list of open-ended questions. When this disappointment occurred, I reminded the women that I wanted to learn from them and that the best way to do so was by engaging in a dialogue rather than interrogating them. Only by letting the women identify their salient issues and the topics they wanted to address was I able to gain an insider's perspective. By being a careful listener and probing for additional information and explanation, I as the interviewer, together with the women, was able to uncover the complexities of their lives. In addition, the nature of the interview allowed me to ask questions about contradictions in a woman's story. For example, sometimes a woman would say that she always used a condom. However, later on in the conversation she would indicate that if she needed drugs she would never use one. By asking her to elaborate on this, I was able to begin developing insights into condom use by type of partner, type of sex acts, and social context.

The interviewer becomes much more a part of the interview when the conversations are in-depth than when a structured questionnaire is used. Because I was so integral to the process, the way the women viewed me may have biased their answers. On the one hand, this bias might be reduced because of the extent to which both parties already knew each other; on the other, a woman might fail to give her true opinion and reveal her actions if she knew that these went against the interviewer's opinion. I suspected that some women played down the ways in which their pimps manipulated them once they knew that I was not too fond of these men. However, some might have taken more time to explain the relationship with their pimp in order to "correct" my image.

My background, so different from that of these women, most likely affected the nature of the interviews. I occupied a higher socioeconomic status. I had a place to live and a job. In contrast to the nonwhite women, I came from a different racial background. While I don't know to what extent these differences played a role, I acknowledge that they must have had some effect on this research.

## Leaving the Field

Leaving the field was not something that occurred after completion of the field-work, but an event that took place daily. Although I sometimes stayed on the strolls all night or hung out for several days, I always had a home to return to. I had a house with electricity, a warm shower, a comfortable bed, and a kitchen.

My house sat on a street where I had no fear of being shot on my way there and where I did not find condoms or syringes on my doorstep.

During several stages of the study, I had access to a car, which I used to give the women rides or to run errands together. However, I will never forget the cold night when everyone on the street was freezing, and I left to go home. I turned up the heat in my car, and tears streamed down my cheeks. I appreciated the heat, but I felt more guilty about that luxury than ever before. I truly felt like an outsider, or maybe even more appropriate, a betrayer.

Throughout the years of fieldwork, there were a number of times when I left the scene temporarily. For example, when so many people were dying from AIDS, I was unable to ignore the devastating impact of this disease. I needed an emotional break.

Physically removing myself from the scene was common when I experienced difficulty remaining objective. Once I became too involved in a woman's life and almost adopted her and her family. Another time I felt a true hatred for a crack house owner and was unable to adhere to the rules of courteous interactions. Still another time, I got angry with a woman whose steady partner was HIV positive when she failed to ask him to use a condom when they had sex.

I also took temporary breaks from a particular scene by shifting settings and neighborhoods. For example, I would invest most of my time in women from a particular crack house for several weeks. Then I would shift to spending more time on one of the strolls, while making shorter and less frequent visits to the crack house. By shifting scenes, I was able to tell people why I was leaving and to remind all of us of my researcher role.

While I focused on leaving the field, I became interested in women who had left the life. It seemed important to have an understanding of their past and current circumstances. I knew some of them from the days when they were working, but identifying others was a challenge. There was no gathering place for ex-prostitutes. Informal networking, advertisements in local newspapers, and local clinics and community settings allowed me to reach twenty of these women. Conducting interviews with them later in the data collection process prepared me to ask specific questions. I realized that I had learned enough about the life to know what to ask. Interviewing ex-prostitutes also prepared me for moving from the fieldwork to writing.

It is hard to determine exactly when I left the field. It seems like a process that never ends. Although I was more physically removed from the scene, I continued to be involved while analyzing the data and writing this book. I also created opportunities to go back, for example, by asking women to give me feedback on parts of the manuscript or at times when I experienced writer's block and my car seemed to automatically steer itself to one of the strolls. I also have developed other research projects in some of the same communities. For example, both a project on intergenerational drug use and a gender-specific intervention project to help women remain HIV negative have brought me back to the same population. Some of the women have become key respondents in these new projects, while others now are members of a research team. For example, Beth, one of the women who has left prostitution, works as an outreach worker on another project.

## Six Themes in the Ethnography of Prostitution

The main intention of my work is to provide the reader with a perspective on street prostitution from the point of view of the women themselves. There are six fundamental aspects of the women's lives as prostitutes that must be considered. The first concerns the women's own explanations for their involvement in prostitution and their descriptions of the various circumstances that led them to become prostitutes. Their stories include justifications such as traumatic past experiences, especially sexual abuse, the lack of love they experienced as children, pressures by friends and pimps, the need for drugs, and most prominently, the economic forces that pushed them into the life. A number of women describe these justifications as excuses, as reflective explanations they have developed after becoming a prostitute.

The women describe the nature of their initial experiences, which often involved alienation from those outside the life. They also show the differences in the processes between women who work as prostitutes and use drugs and women who do not use drugs.

Although all these women work either on the street or in drug-use settings, their lives do differ. My second theme is a typology that captures these differences, looking at the women's prostitution versus drug-use identities. The typology distinguishes among (a) streetwalkers, women who work strolls and who do not use drugs; (b) hooked prostitutes, women who identify themselves mainly as prostitutes but who upon their entrance into the life also began using drugs; (c) prostituting addicts, women who view themselves mainly as drug users and who became prostitutes to support their drug habit; and (d) crack prostitutes, women who trade sex for crack.

This typology explains the differences in the women's strategies for soliciting customers, their screening of customers, pricing of sex acts, and bargaining for services. For example, the street-walkers have the most bargaining power, while such power appears to be lacking among the crack prostitutes.

Few prostitutes work in a vacuum. The third theme is the role of pimps, a label that most women dislike and for which they prefer to substitute "old man" or "boyfriend." Among the pimps, one finds entrepreneur lovers, men who mainly employ street-walkers and hooked prostitutes and sometimes prostituting addicts. Entrepreneur lovers engage in the life for business reasons. They treat the women as their employees or their property and view them primarily as an economic commodity. The more successful a woman is in earning them money, the more difficult it is for that woman to leave her entrepreneur pimp.

Most prostituting addicts and some hooked prostitutes work for a lover pimp, a man who is their steady partner but who also lives off their earnings. Typically, such pimps employ only one woman. The dynamics in the relationship between a prostitute and her lover pimp become more complex when both partners use drugs. Drugs often become the glue of the relationship.

For many crack prostitutes, their crack addiction serves as a pimp. Few plan to exchange sex for crack when they first begin using; often several weeks or months pass before a woman who barters sex for crack realizes that she is a prostitute.

Historically, society has blamed prostitutes for introducing sexually transmitted diseases into the general population. Similarly, it makes them scapegoats for the spread of HIV/AIDS. Yet their pimps and customers are not held accountable. The fourth theme in the anthropological study of prostitution is the impact of the AIDS epidemic on the women's lives. Although most are knowledgeable about HIV risk behaviors and the ways to reduce their risk, many misconceptions exist. The women describe the complexities of condom use, especially with steady partners but also with paying customers. Many women have mixed feelings about HIV testing, wondering how to cope with a positive test result while no cure is available. A few of the women already knew their HIV-infected status, and the discussion touches on their dilemmas as well.

The fifth theme is the violence and abuse that make common appearances in the women's lives. An ethnography of prostitution must allow the women to describe violence in their neighborhoods as well as violence in prostitution and drug-use settings. The most common violence they encounter is from customers. These men often assume that because they pay for sex they buy a woman. Apparently, casual customers pose more of a danger than those who are regulars. The types of abuse the women encounter are emotional, physical, and sexual. In addition to customers, pimps and boyfriends abuse the women. Finally, the women discuss harassment by law enforcement officers.

When I talked with the women, it often seemed that there were no opportunities to escape from the life. Yet the sixth and final theme must be the escape from prostitution. Women who have left prostitution can describe the process of their exit from prostitution. As ex-prostitutes they struggle with the stigma of their past, the challenges of developing a new identity, and the impact of their past on current intimate relationships. Those who were also drug users often view themselves as ex-prostitutes and recovering addicts, a perspective that seems to create a role conflict. Overall, most ex-prostitutes find that their past follows them like a bad hangover.

## Review Questions

1. Based on reading this selection, how is ethnographic research different from other social science approaches to research?

2. What can ethnographic research reveal that other forms of research cannot? What can the use of questionnaires and observational experiments reveal about people that ethnographic research might miss?

3. What were some of the techniques used by Sterk to enter the field, conduct her research, and leave the field? What problems did she face?

4. What advice does Sterk have for aspiring ethnographers?

5. What are some of the ethical issues faced by anthropologists when they conduct ethnographic research?

# 5

# Lessons from the Field

## George Gmelch

*Ethnographic fieldwork is a valued tradition in anthropology. Most anthropologists believe that the experience of living and working in another culture is essential to successful research. They also realize, however, that there is more to the experience than discovering and describing the culture of others. Like a rite of passage, fieldwork is an intense personal experience, one that yields deeper insight into one's own culture and personal life. It is this reflexive power of fieldwork that George Gmelch discusses. He bases his analysis on the experiences of undergraduate students he has sent to do fieldwork in Barbados since 1978. He argues that, after a stressful beginning, students gain valuable new insight into their own views on materialism, gender, race, social class, the United States, and the value of education as well as Barbadian culture.*

Sara, Eric, and Kristen heave their backpacks and suitcases—all the gear they'll need for the next ten weeks—into the back of the Institute's battered Toyota pick-up. Sara, a tense grin on her face, gets up front with me; the others climb in the back and make themselves comfortable on the soft luggage.

Leaving Bellairs Research Institute on the west coast of the island of Barbados, we drive north past the posh resort hotels. The scene changes abruptly as we move from tourism to agriculture, from the hustle and noise of the coast to the green and quiet of rolling sugar cane fields. There are no more white faces.

Graceful cabbage palms flank a large plantation house, one of the island's "great houses." On the edge of its cane fields is a tenantry, a cluster of small board houses whose inhabitants are the descendants of the slaves who once worked on the plantation.

Entering the village of Mile and a Quarter, so named because that is the distance from the village to nearby Speightstown, I point out the small orange and blue board house that one of my first students lived in. Sara and the others know of Ellen, as she became a documentary film maker and has made several films about the island which they have seen.

Two monkeys emerge from a cane field and scamper across the road. I mention that monkeys came to Barbados on early slave ships, 300 years ago. But Sara, absorbed in her own thoughts, doesn't seem to hear me. I've taken enough students to the "field" to have an idea of what's on her mind. She is wondering what her village will be like—the one we just passed through looked unusually poor. And will she like the family she is going to live with? Will they like her? Many people are walking along the road; clusters of men sit outside a rum shop shouting loudly while slamming dominoes on a wobbly plywood table. She is wondering how she will ever make friends with these people and gain their acceptance, which as a student anthropologist she must do.

Earlier in the day, Eric told me that many of the ten students on the field program thought they had made a mistake coming to Barbados. If they had chosen to go on the term abroad to Greece or England or even Japan, they mused, they would be together on a campus, among friends, and safe. They wouldn't have to live in a village, they wouldn't have to go out and make friends with all these strange people; and to do it all alone now seemed more of a challenge than many wanted.

We drive toward the northeastern corner of the island to the village of Pie Corner, where I had arranged for Sara to live with a family. This is the unsheltered side of the island. From several miles off we could see huge swells rolling in off the Atlantic and beating against the cliffs. The village only has a few hundred people but six small wooden churches, one of which—Bennett's Temple—has windows painted on the wall instead of real glass. Marcus Hinds and his family all come out to the truck to welcome Sara. Mrs. Hinds gives her a big hug, as though she were a returning relative, and daughter Yvette takes Sara into the backyard to show her the pigs and chickens. I explain to the Hinds, for a second time, the nature of the program, that Sara, like the other students, would be spending most of her time in the village talking to people and as much as possible participating in the life of the community, which meant everything from attending church to cutting sugar cane. Marcus is puzzled as my description doesn't fit his conception of what a university education is all about. The lives of Caribbean villagers are not something he thinks worthy of a university student's attention.

Back in the truck Eric and Kristen commented on the curiosity of the children and the stares from the houses we'd passed. But they also appeared relieved at seeing the warm welcome and friendliness of the family.

Things were different at Eric's village. Chalky Mount sits high on a narrow ridge, on land unsuitable for cultivation. The land drops away so abruptly that most residents have little flat ground so that many activities take place on the road. Most houses are simple wooden affairs with corrugated metal roofs. Eric's homestay "mother" shows him around. I see the disappointment in Eric's face when we are shown his bedroom. It is more cramped than he had ever imagined, barely larger than the bed. His new "mother," mostly out of her nervousness and uncertainty over what to do with a foreigner, much less a white man, seems aloof and uncaring. Later, Eric wrote about his arrival in his field notes:

> It was just awful. I expected my homestay mother to welcome me with open arms and be so excited. But she had nothing to say. The only solution was to go to my room and unpack.

Back in the truck, Kristen, who had seemed more relaxed after the first drop off, after meeting Sara's family, began to bite her nails.

For fifteen years I have been taking students to the field, and like most anthropologists I know a good deal about what they learn about the foreign culture in which they live. But it wasn't until serving on a committee that evaluated my college's international study programs that I ever thought much about what it is that they learn about their own culture by living in another. The notion that you have to live in another culture before you can truly understand your own has gained wide acceptance. But what is it that we learn?

I questioned other anthropologists who also took students to the field, and they too were unclear about its lessons. A search through the literature didn't help. All the research on the educational outcomes of foreign study has been on students who study at universities in foreign countries.

As a result, I decided to examine the experiences of my own students in Barbados. Using a variety of techniques—questionnaires, tape recorded interviews, and analysis of their daily field notes and journals—I looked at their adjustment to Bajan village life and what they learned about themselves and their own culture by living in Barbados. It is primarily the latter that I wish to address here.

Typically, my students go to Barbados expecting to learn a great deal about how people in this Caribbean society live and think. What they don't expect is that they will also learn much about themselves and their own culture. Nor do they imagine that they will discover attitudes and perspectives that they will take back home and incorporate into their own lives.

## Rural Life

Living in a Barbadian village brings many lessons in the difference between rural and urban. About 90 percent of my students come from suburbs or cities and have never lived in the countryside before. For them a significant part of their experience in Barbados is living among people who are close to the land. The host families, like most villagers, grow crops and raise animals. Each morning, before dawn, the students are awakened by the sounds of animals in the yard. They quickly begin to learn about the behavior of chickens, pigs, sheep, and cows. They witness animals giving birth and being slaughtered. They see the satisfaction families get from consuming food they have produced themselves. One student described the effect an everyday occurrence had on her:

> I was in Mrs. S.'s kitchen and she was making sugar cakes.
>     The recipe calls for a lime, and when she didn't have any in the kitchen she just walked into the yard and pulled a few off the nearest tree. It was nothing to her but I was amazed, and I thought how in that situation I would've had to drive to the supermarket.

In the villages most students live close to nature for a prolonged period of time. They may share their bedrooms with a green lizard or two, mice, cockroaches, and sometimes a whistling frog. They become aware of how different are the sounds of the countryside and are struck by the darkness of the sky and the brightness of the stars with no city lights to diminish their intensity. A student from Long Island described it as "like living in a planetarium."

The social world of the village is unlike anything most students know. In doing a household survey, for example, students discover that not only does everybody seem to know everybody else and that many families are related to one another, but that they know one another in more than one context—that people are tied to one another in multiple ways. Relationships are not single stranded as they often are in the urban America the students come from.

Students have never known a place of such intimacy, where relationships are so embedded with different meanings and a shared history. Some students reflect upon and compare the warmth, friendliness, and frequent sharing of food and other resources with the impersonality, individualism, and detachment of suburban life at home. But they also learn the drawbacks to living in small communities: there is no anonymity. People are nosy and unduly interested in the affairs of their neighbors. As the students become integrated into the community, they soon discover that they too may be the object of local gossip. Several female students learned from village friends that there were stories afoot that they were either mistresses to their host fathers or sleeping with their host brothers. The gossip hurt, for the students had worked hard to gain acceptance, greatly valued the friendships they had made, and naturally were concerned about the damage such rumors might do to their reputations (even though the students spend only ten weeks in their villages and most will never return, they still care greatly that villagers think well of them).

One of the biggest adjustments students must make to village life is to its slow pace, and the absence of the diversions and entertainment that they are accustomed to at home. Early in their stay there seems to be little to do apart from their research. At times they are desperate to escape the village but they are not allowed to leave except on designated days (all students initially hate this restriction, but by the end of the term they recommend that it be continued). The outcome of their forced isolation from other students is that they must satisfy their needs for companionship and recreation within their communities. They must learn to be resourceful in finding ways to entertain themselves. The outcome is that they spend a good deal of time hanging out—socializing—with people in the village, a practice which strengthens friendships and results in a good deal of informal education about culture. By the mid-point in the term most students have adapted so well to village life that they no longer report being bored or desperate to get away. And many no longer leave the village on their day off.

## Materialism

Many students arrive at a new awareness of wealth and materialism. One of the strongest initial perceptions the students have of their villages is that the people are poor—that most of their houses are tiny, that their diets are restricted, and that they have few of the amenities and comforts the students are accustomed to. Even little things may remind students of the difference in wealth, as anthropology major Betsy recounted after her first week in the field:

> At home [Vermont] when I go into a convenience store and buy a soda, I don't think twice about handing the clerk a 20 dollar bill. But here when you hand a man in the rum shop a 20 dollar bill [equals $10 U.S.] they often ask if you have something smaller. It makes me self-conscious of how wealthy I appear, and of how little money the rum shop man makes in a day.

The initial response of the students to such incidents and to the poverty they perceive around them is to feel embarrassed and even guilty that they, like many Americans, have so much wealth. However, such feelings are short-lived for as the students get to know the families better they no longer see poverty; even the houses no longer seem so small. They discover that most people not only manage quite well on what they have but that they are reasonably content. In fact, most students eventually come to believe that the villagers are, on the whole, actually more satisfied with their lives than are most Americans. Whether or not this is true, it's an important perception for students whose ideas about happiness have been shaped by an ethos which measures success and satisfaction by material gain. About his host family, Dan said:

> I ate off the same plate and drank from the same cup every night. We only had an old fridge, an old stove, and an old TV, and a few dishes and pots and pans. But that was plenty. Mrs. H. never felt like she needed any more. And after a while I never felt like I needed any more either.

Many students say that after Barbados they became less materialistic. Many said that when they returned home from Barbados they were surprised at how many possessions they owned; and that when they came back to campus they didn't bring nearly as many things with them as they usually do. A few had gone through their drawers and closets and given away to the Goodwill or Salvation Army the things they didn't really need. Most said they would no longer take for granted the luxuries, such as hot showers, that they are accustomed to at campus and home. Amy said:

> When I came back I saw how out of control the students here are. It's just crazy. They want so much, they talk about how much money they need to make, as if these things are necessities and you'll never be happy without them. Maybe I was like that too, but now I know I don't need those things; sure I'd like a great car, but I don't need it.

When alumni of the program were asked in a survey how they had been changed by their experience in Barbados, most believed they were less materialistic today.

## Gender

Female students quickly learn that gender relations are quite different in Barbados. Indeed, the most difficult adjustment for many women students is learning how to deal with the frequent and aggressive advances of Bajan men. At the end of her first week in the field, Jenny described a plight common to the students:

> When I walk through the village, the guys who hang out at the rum shop yell comments. I have never heard men say some of the things they tell me here. My friend Andrew tells me that most of the comments are actually compliments. Yet I still feel weird. . . . I am merely an object that they would like to conquer. I hate that feeling, so I am trying to get to know these guys. I figure that if they know me as a person and a friend, they will stop with the demeaning comments. Maybe it's a cultural thing they do to all women.

Indeed, many Bajan men feel it is their right—as males—to accost women in public with hissing, appreciative remarks, and offers of sexual services. This sexual bantering is tolerated by Bajan women who generally ignore the men's comments. Most women consider it harmless, if annoying; some consider it flattering. Students like Jenny, however, are not sure what to make of it. They do not know whether it is being directed at them because local men think white girls are "loose" or whether Bajan men behave in this fashion toward all women. Anxious to be accepted and not wanting to be rude or culturally insensitive, most female students tolerate the remarks the best they can, while searching for a strategy to politely discourage them. Most find that as people get to know them by name, the verbal harassment subsides.

But they still must get accustomed to other sexual behavior. For example, when invited to their first neighborhood parties most are shocked at the sexually explicit dancing, in which movements—*grinding*—imitate intercourse. One female student wrote, after having been to several *fetes,* or parties:

> I was watching everyone dance when I realized that even the way we dance says a lot about culture. We are so conservative at home. Inhibited. In the U.S. one's body is a personal, private thing, and when it is invaded we get angry. We might give a boyfriend some degree of control over our bodies, but no one else. Bajans aren't nearly as possessive about their bodies. Men and women can freely move from one dance partner to the next without asking, and then grind the other person—it's like having sex with your clothes on.

Students discover that, to an even greater degree than in the United States, women are regarded by men as both subordinates and sexual objects. Masculinity is largely based on men's sexual conquest of women and on their ability to give them pleasure. Being sexually active, a good sex partner, and becoming a father all enhance young men's status among male peers. As time passes, the students discover male dominance in other areas of Barbadian life as well—that women earn less than men, are more likely to be unemployed, and are less likely to attain political office. They conclude that while their own society is sexist, Barbados is far more so.

## Race

In Barbados my students become members of a racial minority for the first time in their lives. Everyone in the villages in which they live is black, while nearly all of my students have been white. Before going to Barbados, most of my students have had little contact with blacks and as a result they feel awkward and in some cases hold negative stereotypes. The students have never experienced racial prejudice themselves. During their first few weeks in the field, however, they become acutely aware of their own "race," of their being white while everyone around them is dark. Female students are often called "white girl" by people in the village until they get to know them personally. Village children ask if they can touch the students' skin, some want to feel the students' straight hair;

they marvel at the blue veins which show through the students' light skin, and sometimes ask those with freckles if they have a skin disease. Characteristically, during the second week one student wrote:

> I have never been in a situation before where I was a minority purely due to the color of my skin, and treated differently because of it. When I approach people I am very conscious of having white skin. Before I never thought of myself as having color.

A few students become hypersensitive to race during the early weeks of their stay. When students leave their villages, they travel by bus. The buses are often crowded, with the students usually being the only white person on board. Often they are stared at (sometimes because as the buses head into the countryside the passengers assume the student has missed her stop or taken the wrong bus). The students notice that as the bus fills up, the seat next to them is often the last to be taken. Here is the extreme reaction of one female student who has gone by bus to a remote area during her first week in Barbados. There she encounters a woman who stares at her:

> The woman glared at me as if she was seeing the evil white woman who has been responsible for the oppression of her people. I felt like I had chained, maimed, and enslaved every black person who had ever lived. The feelings were so strange . . . somehow I felt responsible for the entire history of the relationship between blacks and whites. I carried this woman's face with me for the rest of the day. When I got on the bus to go back to my village I felt very alone and very unwanted, like the mere presence of my color was making a lot of people very uneasy.

But concerns about race, even the very awareness of race, diminish rapidly as the students make friends and become integrated into their villages. In fact, by the end of the term most said they were "rarely" aware of being white. Several students described incidents in which they had become so unaware of skin color that they were shocked when someone made a remark or did something to remind them of their being different. Sara was startled when, after shaking the hand of someone in her village, the person remarked that she had never touched the hand of a white person before. Several students reported being surprised when they walked by a mirror and got a glimpse of their white skin. One student wrote that although she knew she wasn't black, she no longer felt white.

What is the outcome of all this? Do students now have an understanding of what it means to be a minority, and does this translate into their having more empathy at home? I think so. All the students from the previous Barbados programs whom I questioned about the impact of their experiences mentioned a heightened empathy for blacks, and some said other minorities as well. Several said that when they first returned home, they wanted to go up to any black person they saw and have a conversation. "But I kept having to remind myself," said one student, "that most blacks in America are not West Indians and they wouldn't understand where I am coming from." Another said her first, admittedly naive, reaction upon coming home and seeing black people was to want to hug every one of them.

# Social Class

American students, particularly compared to their European counterparts, have little understanding of social class. Even after several weeks in Barbados, most students are fairly oblivious to class and status distinctions in their villages. The American suburbs that my students grew up in are fairly homogenous in social composition and housing—most homes fall in the same general price range. In contrast, the Barbadian villages the students now live in exhibit a broad spectrum, ranging from the large two-story masonry homes of return migrants to tiny board houses of small farmers who eke out a living from a few acres. The students are slow to translate such differences in the material conditions of village households into status or class differences. Also, Barbadians' well-developed class consciousness, fostered by three centuries of British rule, is foreign to American students steeped in a culture that stresses, at least on an ideological level, egalitarianism. Hence, the students, who have never given much thought to social class, tend to view the population of the villages as all the same.

It is largely from the comments that their host families make about other people that students gradually become aware of status distinctions. But equally, they learn about class and status from making mistakes, from violating norms concerning relationships between different categories of people. Kristen learned that there are different standards of behavior for the more affluent families after she walked home through the village carrying a bundle on her head: "Mrs. C. told me never to do that again, that only poor people carry things on their heads, and that my doing it reflected badly on her family."

As in most field situations, the first villagers to offer the students friendship are sometimes marginal members of the community and this creates special problems in that the students are usually guests in the homes of "respectable" and often high-status village families. The host parents become upset when they discover their student has been seeing a disreputable man or woman. Most serious were, in the early years of the field program, female students who went out with lower-class local men. The women entered into these relationships oblivious to what the local reaction might be, and equally oblivious to how little privacy there is in a village where everyone knows everyone else's business. One student said she wrongly assumed that people would look favorably upon her going with a local man because it would show she wasn't prejudiced and that she found blacks just as desirable as whites. Another female student was befriended by some Rastafarians—orthodox Rastas who wore no clothes, lived off the land, and slept in caves in the hills above her village. When villagers discovered she had been seeing the Rastas, her homestay mother nearly evicted her and others gave her the cold shoulder. The student wrote:

> I have discovered the power of a societal norm: nice girls don't talk to Rastas. When girls who were formerly nice talk to Rastas, they cease to be known as nice. Exceptions none.

## New Perspectives on North America

In learning about Barbadian society, students inevitably make comparisons with their own culture. Especially in the early stages of fieldwork, students think about Barbadian customs in terms of how similar or different they are from customs at home. The students are often assisted in such comparisons by villagers who know a lot about North America from television, tourism, and for some, travel. Students quickly discover, however, that the villagers' perspectives are often at odds with their own. Based on a steady diet of American soap operas, many villagers, for example, believe that all students are wealthy, own late model cars, vacation in exotic places, etc.

Early in the term, many students find themselves defending the United States from criticism and from stereotypes. For example, one student described getting very annoyed when a guest at his host family's dinner table criticized the United States and talked about the chemical adulteration of American chicken. He knew this to be true, but later he said, "I couldn't take it anymore and fought back. I felt like an idiot afterward, defending American chicken."

Over time the students become less eager to defend their own society. Indeed, many become quite critical of the United States, or at least aspects of it. Why? What makes them question their own culture after a few months in Barbados? Part of the answer is found in their growing appreciation for Bajan life and their identification with local people. They come to see many things from the perspective of their village friends. Another factor is the students' exposure to North American tourists. When students go to the beach or town on their free day they encounter tourists and are sometimes embarrassed by what they see and hear—tourists entering shops and walking the street in skimpy beach attire, and their loud and intrusive voices. From a variety of sources, students learn about the social impacts of tourism—drug trafficking, materialism, crime, environmental damage, and American cultural penetration. Viewing tourism as part of a broader Americanization of the region, many students become critical not only of tourists but of America's presence abroad generally.

## Fieldwork and Education

Students learn more than about just cultural differences from their experience of living and doing anthropology alone in a Caribbean village. Most returned from Barbados with a more positive attitude toward education. This appears to stem both from their own experiences in doing research and from seeing the high value that villagers place on formal education, which is their chief means of upward mobility. They see that they are accorded respect and adult status largely because they are working toward a university degree. Also, as the weeks pass, most students become deeply involved in their own research. They are surprised at how much satisfaction they get from doing something that they previously regarded as "work." A number of the students from past terms have said they didn't see education as an end in itself, something to be enjoyed, until doing fieldwork in Barbados. One student wrote about her attitude after returning from the field:

> I feel isolated from many of my old friends on campus, and I no longer feel guilty missing social events. . . . I appreciate my education more and I do much more work for my own understanding and enjoyment rather than just for the exam or grades. I find myself on a daily basis growing agitated with those who don't appreciate what is being offered to them here. Several of my classmates blow off class and use other peoples' notes. A lot of what I feel is from seeing how important education was to my Bajan friends in Barbados compared to the lax attitude of my Union friends here.

Students spend much of their time in the field talking to people; a good part of each day is spent in conversations which they must direct onto the topics that they are investigating. To succeed at their studies, they must learn to be inquisitive, to probe sensitively into the villager's knowledge or memory of events and aspects of culture, and to concentrate, to listen to what they are being told, and later to be able to recall it so that they can record it in field notes. The students become proficient at maintaining lengthy conversations with adults and at asking pertinent questions. These are interpersonal skills they bring back with them and make use of in many aspects of their own lives.

While the students spend a semester discovering and making sense of the differences between their own culture and the Barbadians around them, most arrive at the notion that beneath differences in skin color and culture, Barbadians and Americans are basically alike, that beneath the veneer of custom there is something fundamental about "human nature" which is shared by everyone. In the words of one student, who is now an anthropologist:

> If I had to sum up my whole trip in one experience it would be this: It was late at night, a full moon, and I sat in a pasture with a local Rastafarian. After hours of talking, about everything from love to politics, the two of us came to an interesting conclusion. Although we lived a thousand miles away from each other, and that our skin color, hair style, and many personal practices were quite different, at heart we were the same people.

While this may seem like common sense it is surprisingly not a notion that many college students share today.

As the world's economies intertwine and its societies move closer to the "global village" Marshall McLuhan envisioned, it is more imperative than ever that we seek to understand other peoples and cultures. Without understanding there can be neither respect, nor prosperity, nor lasting peace. "The tragedy about Americans," noted Mexican novelist Carlos Fuentes, "is that they understand others so little." Students who study abroad, like those described in these pages, not only enrich themselves but in countless small ways help bridge the gulf between "us" and "them." Getting to know another culture is to look in the proverbial mirror and get glimpse of oneself and of what it means to be an "American."

# Review Questions

1. What are the main ways that fieldwork in Barbados has changed students' perceptions of their own culture and personal lives?

2. How has the behavior of U.S. tourists in Barbados changed students' perception of their own nation?

3. How has life in a Barbadian rural community affected students' views of U.S. materialism, gender, and social class?

4. How do you think fieldwork achieves the personal transformations described by Gmelch in the students he has sent to Barbados?

# TWO

# Language and Communication

$C$ulture is a system of symbols that allows us to represent and communicate our experience. We are surrounded by symbols: the flag, a new automobile, a diamond ring, billboard pictures, and, of course, spoken words.

A **symbol** is anything that we can perceive with our senses that stands for something else. Almost anything we experience can come to have symbolic meaning. Every symbol has a referent that it calls to our attention. The term *lawn*, for example, refers to a field of grass plants. When we communicate with symbols, we call attention not only to the referent but also to numerous connotations of the symbol. In U.S. culture we associate lawns with places such as homes and golf courses; actions such as mowing, fertilizing, and raking; and activities such as backyard games and barbeques. Human beings have the capacity to assign meaning to anything they experience in an arbitrary fashion, which allows limitless possibilities for communication.

Symbols greatly simplify the task of communication. Once we learn that a word such as *barn*, for example, stands for a certain type of building, we can communicate about a whole range of specific buildings that fit into the category. And we can communicate about barns in their absence; we can even invent flying barns and dream about barns. Symbols make it possible to communicate the immense variety of human experience, whether past or present, tangible or intangible, good or bad.

Many channels are available to human beings for symbolic communication: sound, sight, touch, and smell. Language, our most highly developed communication system, uses the channel of sound (or, for some deaf people, sight). **Language** is a system of cultural knowledge used to generate and interpret speech. It is a feature of every culture and a distinctive characteristic of the human animal. **Speech** refers to the behavior that produces vocal sounds. Our distinction between language and speech is like the one made between culture and behavior. Language is part of culture, the system of knowledge that generates behavior. Speech is the behavior generated and interpreted by language.

Every language is composed of three subsystems for dealing with vocal symbols: phonology, grammar, and semantics. Let's look briefly at each of these.

**Phonology** consists of the categories and rules for forming vocal symbols. It is concerned not directly with meaning but with the formation and recognition of the vocal sounds to which we assign meaning. For example, if you utter the word *bat,* you have followed a special set of rules for producing and ordering sound categories characteristic of the English language.

A basic element defined by phonological rules for every language is the phoneme. **Phonemes** are the minimal categories of speech sounds that serve to keep utterances apart. For example, speakers of English know that the words *bat, cat, mat, hat, rat,* and *fat* are different utterances because they hear the sounds /b/, /c/, /m/, /h/, /r/, and /f/ as different categories of sounds. In English, each of these is a phoneme. Our language contains a limited number of phonemes from which we construct all our vocal symbols.

Phonemes are arbitrarily constructed, however. Each phoneme actually classifies slightly different sounds as though they were the same. Different languages may divide up the same range of speech sounds into different sound categories. For example, speakers of English treat the sound /t/ as a single phoneme. Hindi speakers take the same general range and divide it into four phonemes: /t/, /t^h/, /T/, and /T^h/. (The lowercase *t*'s are made with the tongue against the front teeth, while the uppercase *T*'s are made by touching the tongue to the roof of the mouth further back than would be normal for an English speaker. The *h* indicates a puff of air, called *aspiration,* associated with the *t* sound.) Americans are likely to miss important distinctions among Hindi words because they hear these four different phonemes as a single one. Hindi speakers, on the other hand, tend to hear more than one sound category as they listen to English speakers pronounce *t*'s. The situation is reversed for /w/ and /v/. We treat these as two phonemes, whereas Hindi speakers hear them as one. For them, the English words *wine* and *vine* sound the same.

Phonology also includes rules for ordering different sounds. Even when we try to talk nonsense, we usually create words that follow English phonological rules. It would be unlikely, for example, for us ever to begin a word with the phoneme /ng/ usually written in English as "ing." It must come at the end or in the middle of words.

Grammar is the second subsystem of language. **Grammar** refers to the categories and rules for combining vocal symbols. No grammar contains rules for combining every word or element of meaning in the language. If this were the case, grammar would be so unwieldy that no one could learn all the rules in a lifetime. Every grammar deals with *categories* of symbols, such as the ones we call *nouns* and *verbs.* Once you know the rules covering a particular category, you can use it in appropriate combinations.

**Morphemes** are the categories in any language that carry meaning. They are minimal units of meaning that cannot be subdivided. Morphemes occur in more complex patterns than you may think. The term *bats*, for example, is actually two morphemes, /bat/ meaning a flying mammal and /s/ meaning plural. Even more confusing, two different morphemes may have the same sound shape. /Bat/ can refer to a wooden club used in baseball as well as a flying mammal.

The third subsystem of every language is semantics. **Semantics** refers to the categories and rules for relating vocal symbols to their referents. Like the rules of grammar, semantic rules are simple instructions for combining things; they instruct us to combine words with what they refer to. A symbol can be said to *refer* because it focuses our attention and makes us take account of something. For example, /bat/ refers to a family of flying mammals, as we have already noted.

Language regularly occurs in a social context, and to understand its use fully it is important to recognize its relation to sociolinguistic rules. **Sociolinguistic rules** combine meaningful utterances with social situations into appropriate messages.

Although language is the most important human vehicle for communication, almost anything we can sense may represent a **nonlinguistic symbol** that conveys meaning. The way we sit, how we use our eyes, how we dress, the car we own, the number of bathrooms in our house—all these things carry symbolic meaning. We learn what they mean as we acquire culture. Indeed, a major reason we feel so uncomfortable when we enter a group from a strange culture is our inability to decode our hosts' symbolic world.

The articles in this part illustrate several important aspects of language and communication. The first selection, by Martin Nowak, asserts that human language is grammatical, enabling people to use a limited number of sounds to produce an infinite number of messages. Grammatical language evolved in human ancestors because it enhanced their reproductive success. The second article, by Enid Schildkrout, looks at nonverbal symbols, notably those that humans send with body art. From tattoos to makeup, body art is used to convey life-changing events, group membership, and a variety of other messages. In the third article, David Thomson describes the hypothesis generated in the 1930s by a young linguist named Benjamin Lee Whorf. Whorf argued that, instead of merely labeling reality, the words and grammatical structure of a language can actually determine the way its speakers perceive the world. Thomson reviews and evaluates this hypothesis and shows that, although language may not create reality, it can affect our perceptions, as illustrated by the use of words in U.S. advertising and political doublespeak. The fourth article, by Sarah Boxer, illustrates the conscious attempts by people to create impressions with words. She traces the history of how military operations receive their names and points out that today, names such as "Just Cause" may actually create negative as well positive images in an audience. The final selection, by Deborah Tannen, looks at another aspect of language—conversation styles. Focusing on the different speaking styles of men and women in the workplace, she describes and analyzes how conversation styles themselves carry meaning and unwittingly lead to misunderstanding.

# Key Terms

grammar   *p. 60*                     phonology   *p. 60*
language   *p. 59*                    semantics   *p. 61*
morphemes   *p. 60*                   sociolinguistic rules   *p. 61*
nonlinguistic symbols   *p. 61*       speech   *p. 59*
phoneme   *p. 60*                     symbol   *p. 59*

# 6

# *Homo grammaticus*

*Martin A. Nowak*

*How did complex human language evolve? Other animals have effective communication systems, but these seem simple and limited by comparison to our own. What conditions have led to a human language system that permits us to produce an infinite number of unique utterances about virtually anything? Answers to this question are difficult to find. The evolution of language occurred in the past. Language, and the process that produced our ability to have it, does not fossilize, although there are some indications of growing speech ability found in fossil skulls. We see evidence, for example, of the development of an elongated pharynx to produce speech sounds and the growth of Broca's area in the brain, which is associated with complex speech. But how can we explain why the change to a complex language occurred? This is the question addressed by Martin Nowak in this article. Using observations of human and animal language systems and mathematical simulations, he argues that animal language has a simple, one-to-one relationship between signals and referents. A particular sound refers to a particular thing. By mathematically simulating this communication process, Nowak discovered that communication mistakes occur more frequently as the number of signals increases, until a point is reached where the signal system would reduce the reproductive fitness of the animals using it. In short, it starts to kill them, not help them survive. Human language, on the other hand, uses a limited number of vocal signals called* phonemes *(see page 60 for a definition) and combines them to make words. A limited number of these speech sounds can create an unlimited number of possible words, and thus an infinite number of meaningful units. In turn, words can be combined in different ways to produce even more complex utterances. This ability to combine small numbers of units into complex messages is called* grammar, *and a second mathematical computer simulation easily shows that grammatical ability means higher survivability for our species.*

Whenever I tell my four-year-old a dream, he also tells me a dream. His is often similar to mine. He doesn't distinguish between a story and a dream. Both my four- and my six-year-old have their own fantasy realms. Sometimes, when a fact proves contrary to their expectation, they hold comfortably to their version of reality in a different world. Their language is limited neither to actual experience nor to the context of this world. We can talk about everything.

Producing the sounds we use in an ordinary conversation is an anatomical feat. The motions of various parts of our vocal tract are coordinated within millimeters and timed within hundredths of a second. On the receptive end, a listener must process a stream of sounds instantaneously. When it comes to words, a six-year-old has a lexicon, or word store, of about 13,000. The rate of word learning in humans comes to about one word every ninety waking minutes from age one to age seventeen. This leaves a seventeen-year-old with about 50,000 words stored in her mental lexicon. When it comes to grammar, a four-year-old knows how to avoid 95 percent of the mistakes he could make. Children acquire the grammatical rules of their native language spontaneously and without formal education. All they need is the opportunity to talk to someone and to hear examples of sentences.

I could prove to you mathematically that what children do in acquiring language is not possible unless we add a further assumption: children must have a built-in sense of what grammar is. The linguist Noam Chomsky called this innate mechanism *universal grammar*. It is written in our genes and generated by neuronal circuitry in our brain.

Grammar is the computational system of human language. As used by linguists, the term *grammar* encompasses the patterns inherent in speech sounds, in word forms, and in sentence structures (syntax). All human languages use complex grammar. Grammar is what enables us to produce an infinite number of meaningful sentences, and it is what allows a child to speak sentences he has never heard before. The computations that are necessary for formulating or interpreting sentences cannot, so far, be performed by any computer, but they flow through our brain's language processor without conscious effort on our part. We can talk and listen without thinking about it.

The aim of my own work on language is to outline the fundamental principles that determine how natural selection shaped animal communication and led from there to human language. The main forces of evolution—mutation and natural selection—can be described by precise mathematical equations. As early as 1906, Oxford zoologist Walter Weldon remarked that "Darwinian evolution is intrinsically a mathematical theory and can only be tested by mathematical and statistical techniques." Hence, I and my colleagues at the Institute for Advanced Studies in Princeton are using mathematics to find out how language evolved.

Language was the most important evolutionary event in the history of the human species. Indeed, grammatical language defines humanity. The complex vocalizations of mammals such as dolphins and primates have been the subject of many studies, but so far, no natural animal communication appears to have a power of expression that is in any way close to human language. Animal communication can be based on a limited repertoire of calls (for example, warning or territorial calls) or consist of variations on a theme (such as birdsongs) or be a continuous, analog signal (the honeybee's dance, which transmits information on food sources). But the grammar inherent in human language enables us, in the words of Wilhelm von Humboldt, to "make infinite use of finite means." Language has changed us and the appearance of the planet and is responsible for the acceleration of cultural evolution during the last few millennia.

Human language originated after our human ancestors diverged from our closest relatives, the chimpanzees, about 5 to 7 million years ago. Since all currently living *Homo sapiens* have the same language ability, the most recent date for the origin of language would be the time of our last common ancestors, who lived in Africa perhaps 150,000 to 200,000 years ago. Evolution would not have had enough time to build our language ability from scratch but must instead have used existing structures that may originally have been employed for other purposes. Neuroanatomists describe certain areas in the brains of monkeys, for instance, that correspond to the human language areas but that are apparently not involved in producing calls or gestures. Monkeys use these brain regions to interpret sounds and control facial muscles. Evolution may have had an easy game here in adopting these structures to generate the neuronal circuits that control speech production and speech interpretation in humans.

Language evolved as a means of communicating information between individuals. In order to communicate on a basic level, a population of individual animals or hominids must discover that specific signals can be associated with specific referents—things being referred to—such as people, objects, actions, places, times, and events. A wolf, for example, may whine, growl, or howl, and this sound (along with extensive body language) can convey certain information to the members of its pack. We can imagine early hominids—perhaps Lucy and her fellow *Australopithecus afarensis,* who lived 4 million years ago—being capable of making a variety of sounds and transferring information about their world. If a wolf cub fails to learn the sounds and signals of its society, its life may be short. Similarly, hominids that were best able to transmit—and to hear and interpret—specific signals presumably benefited from this trait. They were fitter in the evolutionary sense, surviving longer and having offspring that knew how to communicate.

The computer simulation that I and my colleagues have been working on moves us from the realm of the presumed to the realm of mathematical analysis. The equations take into account mutation, forces of natural selection, and learning behavior. In the simulation, each individual in a group is characterized by what we call a lexical matrix, which links specific signals to specific referents. In the beginning of our simulation, all individuals are assigned very different, randomly chosen lexical matrices. Then individuals "talk" to each other. Whenever a simulated speaker uses a certain signal to denote a particular referent and the hearer interprets the signal as denoting that referent, they communicate correctly.

As the simulation continues, the individuals that are able to communicate well prosper and produce offspring who in turn inherit the genetically encoded mechanism for learning the language. The offspring will use this mechanism to learn the lexical matrix from their parents and others in the population or community. As a consequence of heterogeneity in the group and some errors occurring during language learning, children will not acquire the exact lexical matrix of their parents. Over time, the matrices will change and those individuals that communicate well will increase in abundance.

We have found that over a few generations, each signal tends to become associated with a single referent and that most individuals in the group will use the same signal for the same referent. But to be successful, this evolutionary process depends on conditions that we have quantified and that can also be expressed verbally: communication must contribute to biological fitness, and learners must have a sufficiently reliable lexicon-learning mechanism. Under these conditions, evolution can construct a communication system—but only a simple one.

Our model shows that while adding new signals or sounds to the repertoire may increase the number of things that can be described, such additions also carry a significant cost: a greater possibility of errors. What happens when a signal is misinterpreted, when a hearer misses the message? One monkey shouts "lion," but the other one understands "banana" and is attacked by the lion. We stretched our basic model by including the possibility of such perceptual errors into our equations. The mathematical analysis revealed an "error limit," a point at which having too many signals and referents creates confusion and becomes a liability rather than an evolutionary asset. In other words, the monkey might have been better off without a signal for banana that could be mistaken for the signal for lion.

Natural selection, then, prefers limited repertoires of signals. But how did human language overcome the error limit and come to be so vast? Our vocal apparatus can produce a large diversity of sounds. The roughly 6,000 languages on Earth have a total of about 1,000 phonemes—basic sound units, such as the

English pronunciation of the letters *g, d, p,* or *t.* Still, any one language uses only about 40 phonemes on average, with a range of about 10 to 100. So we use only a small fraction of all possible signals. We generally avoid mistakes among the phonemes that make up our native language but have a hard time with those of other languages.

How do we humans get such linguistic mileage from a small stock of sounds? In something of an evolutionary leap, we have combined them into words. Snippets of sound are spun out and blended into different configurations: the words "God" and "dog" or "top" and "pot" contain the same phonemes but have different referents. Word formation marks a transition from something like an analog (continuous) system to a digital (discrete and combinatorial) system of communication. Our equations show that for a simulated digital language, the error limit is much higher than for a simple analog signal system. Most animal communication, based on a simple system, must operate with a limited repertoire of signals, while human languages consist of more than 10,000 words (English has about 100,000 words).

Words still have to be memorized. Once we have them, however, words can be put into sentences governed by the rules of syntax. Mathematically put, the lexicon of a population cannot exceed the total number of chances an individual has to learn a new word. Syntax makes it possible to generate more sentences than the total number of sentences encountered by a learner. A child, for example, has to memorize the meaning of words but does not have to memorize the meaning of sentences. Syntax enables us to construct and understand an unlimited number of novel sentences.

What we know about animal communication suggests that it is largely nonsyntactic: signals refer to whole events. In contrast, human language is syntactic: signals consist of components that have independent meanings. To find out whether the latter situation confers more of an evolutionary advantage than the former, we built a mathematical model to analyze differences between the two kinds of communication in terms of natural selection. The equations resulting from our mathematical model indicated, fortunately, that syntactic communication is a bright idea, and for two main reasons. Unlike nonsyntactic communication (for example, the simple system obtained in the beginning of our simulation), syntactic communication not only allows the number of things that can be said to be larger than the number of things that have to be memorized but also enables us to generate messages that refer to novel and rare events—not just "dog bites man" but also "man bites dog."

Nevertheless, the equations reveal some limits: natural selection favors syntax only if there exist a large enough number of events that need to be communicated and only if these events can be broken down efficiently into components with meanings of their own, such as places, times, objects, and actions. We call this point the syntax threshold. Below it, nonsyntactic communication works well; above it, syntactic communication stands the users in better stead. We believe that many animal species have the capacity for a syntactic understanding of the world—monkeys and dogs, for example, perceive that the world consists of components, and they are able to relate the components to one another—but animals did not evolve syntactic communication because the syntax threshold was not reached.

We can envision the savannas and forests of Africa where, some 100,000 years ago, our young species lived among other mammals, all using their respective ways of transmitting information. For example, vervet monkeys (as shown by biologists Dorothy Cheney and Robert Seyfarth) have a handful of calls they use to denote the presence of potential predators. The call for "leopard" makes the monkeys jump up into a tree, where they can move faster than the cat. The call for "eagle" sends them running under a bush, where they can hide. However, a resident *Homo sapiens,* armed with syntax, can call out—give voice to objects and actions in a sequence—and indicate that a leopard is stalking ominously or that a leopard is sleeping benignly. A hearer may be warned of a danger approaching from a particular direction or be advised of a course of action. And the participants may one day recount to others the story of how they escaped from or killed a leopard.

The humans may also pass on information about new tools, faraway happenings, customs, and the history of the tribe. They may have names for one another, greatly facilitating social interactions, including planning and politicking, within the group. Syntax then gives rise to new and complex possibilities of cooperation and fairness, deception and manipulation.

Selected for and shaped by evolution, language has, most importantly, led to a new mode of evolution. Information drives evolution. For most of the 4 billion years of life on Earth, the only information that could be used for evolutionary purposes was encoded in gene sequences. Human language gave evolution a new playground. Relatively suddenly, vast amounts of information (at first in the form of orally transmitted ideas, stories, and legends, and later printed in books and journals and transmitted via Internet pages) could be exchanged between individuals and passed on to subsequent generations. Language lit the fuse that exploded the "big bang" of cultural evolution. In this sense, language, more than any other invention since the emergence of the nervous system some 500 million years ago, has affected and continues to affect the rules of evolution itself.

In the small red-brick building opposite my office window, where my four-year-old is at nursery, John von Neumann built the first programmable computer. The Hungarian-born mathematical genius realized that it was not a good idea to rewire a computer every time you wanted to calculate something different. The computer should be a general problem solver. Evolution had the same idea when it came up with a nervous system that allowed animals to learn. Not every task had to be solved by rewriting genetic code: a neuronal problem solver could be more efficient. Language was the next step. It provided an operating system, linked the neuronal problem solvers together, and enabled them to pass on solutions, to work on problems, and to exchange dreams. Language created *Homo sapiens.*

# Review Questions

1. What is the nature of nonhuman communication systems such as those employed by other primates?

2. What does Nowak mean by grammar? How is grammar reflected in the organization of human language?

3. How does Nowak demonstrate that human grammatical language confers a survivability advantage over more simply constructed animal languages?

4. If the ability to learn a grammatical language is inherited biologically, what evidence exists to believe that language is also a *cultural* system of communication?

# 7

# Body Art as Visual Language

### Enid Schildkrout

*Most people think language refers to speaking; talking stands out as a hall-mark of humanity. But virtually anything we can apprehend with our senses may act as a symbol that communicates meaning. Cars may suggest going places, traffic jams, social status, and personal identity. Smells can remind us of seasons, food, and people. In this article, Enid Schildkrout describes a special kind of nonverbal symbol, body art. Defined as any decorative addition to or alteration of the human body, body art may be temporary or permanent, dramatic or subdued, colorful or plain. It may appear in the form of tattoos, piercings, brands, painted designs, hairstyles, makeup, and many other varieties. However it is created and no matter where it is found, body art always transmits meanings, from ideals of beauty, important life transitions, and religious epics to social status and personal rebellion.*

"Body Art as Visual Language" and excerpt from "Teacher's Corner: Bodyart" by Enid Schildkrout as appeared in *AnthroNotes*, Vol. 22, No. 2, Winter 2001, pp. 1–3, 4–6.

Body art is not just the latest fashion. In fact, if the impulse to create art is one of the defining signs of humanity, the body may well have been the first canvas. Alongside paintings on cave walls created by early humans over 30,000 years ago, we find handprints and ochre deposits suggesting body painting. Some of the earliest mummies known—like the "Ice Man" from the Italian-Austrian Alps, known as Otzi, and others from central Asia, the Andes, Egypt, and Europe—date back to 5,000 years. People were buried with ornaments that would have been worn through body piercings, and remains of others show intentionally elongated or flattened skulls. Head shaping was practiced 5,000 years ago in Chile and until the 18th century in France. Stone and ceramic figurines found in ancient graves depict people with every kind of body art known today. People have always marked their bodies with signs of individuality, social status, and cultural identity.

## The Language of Body Art

There is no culture in which people do not, or did not, paint, pierce, tattoo, re-shape, or simply adorn their bodies. Fashions change and forms of body art come and go, but people everywhere do something or other to "package" their appearance. No sane or civilized person goes out in the raw; everyone grooms, dresses, or adorns some part of their body to present to the world. Body art communicates a person's status in society; displays accomplishments; and en-codes memories, desires, and life histories.

Body art is a visual language. To understand it one needs to know the vo-cabulary, including the shared symbols, myths, and social values that are written on the body. From tattoos to top hats, body art makes a statement about the per-son who wears it. But body art is often misunderstood and misinterpreted be-cause its messages do not necessarily translate across cultures. Elaborately pictorial Japanese tattooing started among men in certain occupational groups and depicts the exploits of a gangster hero drawn from a Chinese epic. The tat-toos have more meaning to those who know the stories underlying the images than they do to people unfamiliar with the tales. Traditional Polynesian tattooing is mainly geometric and denotes rank and political status but more recently has been used to define ethnic identity within Pacific island societies.

In an increasingly global world, designs, motifs, even techniques of body modification move across cultural boundaries, but in the process their original meanings are often lost. An animal crest worn as a tattoo, carved into a totem pole, or woven into a blanket may signify membership in a particular clan among Indians on the Northwest Coast of North America, but when worn by people outside these cultures, the designs may simply refer to the wearer's iden-tification with an alternative way of life. Polynesian or Indonesian tattoo de-signs worn by Westerners are admired for the beauty of their graphic qualities, but their original cultural meanings are rarely understood. A tattoo from Bor-neo was once worn to light the path of a person's soul after death, but in New York or Berlin it becomes a sign of rebellion from "coat and tie" culture.

Because body art is such an obvious way of signaling cultural differences, people often use it to identify, exoticize, and ostracize others. Tattoos, scarification, or head shaping may be a sign of high status in one culture and low status in another, but to a total outsider these practices may appear to be simply "mutilation." From the earliest voyages of discovery to contemporary tourism, travelers of all sorts—explorers and missionaries, soldiers and sailors, traders and tourists—have brought back images of the people they meet. These depictions sometimes reveal as much about the people looking at the body art as about the people making and wearing it. Some early images of Europeans and Americans by non-Westerners emphasized elaborate clothing and facial hair. Alternatively, Western images of Africans, Polynesians, and Native Americans focused on the absence of clothes and the presence of tattoos, body paint, and patterns of scars. Representations of body art in engravings, paintings, photographs, and film are powerful visual metaphors that have been used both to record cultural differences and to proclaim one group's supposed superiority over another.

## Body Art: Permanent and Ephemeral

Most people think that permanent modification of the skin, muscles, and bones is what body art is all about. But if one looks at body art as a form of communication, there is no logical reason to separate permanent forms of body art, like tattoos, scarification, piercing, or plastic surgery, from temporary forms, such as makeup, clothing, or hairstyles. Punks and sideshow artists may have what appears to be extreme body art, but everyone does it in one way or another. All of these modifications convey information about a person's identity.

Nonetheless, some forms of body art are undeniably more permanent than others. The decision to display a tattoo is obviously different from the decision to change the color of one's lipstick or dye one's hair. Tattooing, piercing, and scarification are more likely to be ways of signaling one's place in society, or an irreversible life passage like the change from childhood to adulthood. Temporary forms of body art, like clothing, ornaments, and painting, more often mark a moment or simply follow a fashion. But these dichotomies don't stand up to close scrutiny across cultures: tattoos and scarification marks are often done to celebrate an event and dying or cutting one's hair, while temporary, may signal a life-changing event, such as a wedding or a funeral.

## Cultural Ideals of Beauty

Ideas of beauty vary from one culture to another. Some anthropologists and psychologists believe that babies in all cultures respond positively to certain kinds of faces. The beautiful body is often associated with the healthy body and nonthreatening facial expressions and gestures. But this does not mean that beauty is defined the same way in all cultures. People's ideas about the way a healthy person should look are not the same in all cultures: some see fat as an indication of health and wealth while others feel quite the opposite. People in some cultures admire and respect signs of aging, while others do all they can to hide gray hair and wrinkles.

Notwithstanding the fact that parents often make decisions for their children, like whether or not to pierce the ears of infants, in general I would maintain that to be considered art and not just a marking, body art has to have some measure of freedom and intentionality in its creation. The brands put on enslaved people, or the numbers tattooed on concentration camp victims, or the scars left from an unwanted injury are body markings, not body art. . . .

## Body Art Techniques

### Body Painting

Body painting, the most ephemeral and flexible of all body art, has the greatest potential for transforming a person into something else—a spirit, a work of art, another gender, even a map to a sacred place including the afterlife. It can be simply a way of emphasizing a person's visual appeal, a serious statement of allegiance, or a protective and empowering coating.

Natural clays and pigments made from a great variety of plants and minerals are often mixed with vegetable oils and animal fat to make body paint. These include red and yellow ochre (iron rich clay), red cam wood, cinnabar, gold dust, many roots, fruits and flowers, cedar bark, white kaolin, chalk, and temporary skin dyes made from indigo and henna leaves. People all over the world adorn the living and also treat the dead with body paint.

The colors of body paint often have symbolic significance, varying from culture to culture. Some clays and body paints are felt to have protective and auspicious properties, making them ideal for use in initiation rituals, for weddings, and for funerals—all occasions of transition from one life stage to another.

Historically, body paints and dyes have been important trade items. Indians of North America exchanged many valuable items for vermilion, which is mercuric sulphide (an artificial equivalent of the natural dye made from cinnabar). Mixed with red lead by European traders, it could cause or sometimes caused mercury poisoning in the wearer.

### Makeup

Makeup consists of removable substances—paint, powders, and dyes—applied to enhance or transform appearance. Commonly part of regular grooming, makeup varies according to changing definitions of beauty. For vanity and social acceptance, or for medicinal or ritual purposes, people regularly transform every visible part of their body. They have tanned or whitened skin; changed the color of their lips, eyes, teeth, and hair; and added or removed "beauty" spots.

From the 10th to the 19th century, Japanese married women and courtesans blackened their teeth with a paste made from a mixture of tea and sake soaked in iron scraps; black teeth were considered beautiful and sexually appealing.

Makeup can accentuate the contrast between men and women, camouflage perceived imperfections, or signify a special occasion or ritual state.

Makeup, like clothing and hairstyles, allows people to reinvent themselves in everyday life.

Rituals and ceremonies often require people to wear certain kinds of makeup, clothing, or hairstyles to indicate that a person is taking on a new identity (representing an ancestor or a spirit in a masquerade, for example) or transforming his or her social identity as in an initiation ceremony, wedding, graduation, or naming ceremony. Male Japanese actors in Kabuki theater represent women by using strictly codified paints and motifs, and the designs and motifs of Chinese theatrical makeup indicate the identity of a character.

## Hair

Hair is one the easiest and most obvious parts of the body subject to change, and combing and washing hair is part of everyday grooming in most cultures. Styles of combing, braiding, parting, and wrapping hair can signify status and gender, age and ritual status, or membership in a certain group.

Hair often has powerful symbolic significance. Covering the head can be a sign of piety and respect, whether in a place of worship or all the time. Orthodox Jewish women shave their heads but also cover them with wigs or scarves. Muslim women in many parts of the world cover their heads, and sometimes cover their faces too, with scarves or veils. Sikh men in India never cut their hair and cover their heads with turbans. And the Queen of England is rarely seen without a hat.

Cutting hair is a ritual act in some cultures and heads are often shaved during rituals that signify the passage from one life stage to another. Hair itself, once cut, can be used as a symbolic substance. Being part, and yet not part, of a person, living or dead, hair can take on the symbolic power of the person. Some Native Americans formerly attached hair from enemies to war shirts, while warriors in Borneo formerly attached hair from captured enemies to war shields.

Reversing the normal treatment of hair, whatever that is in a particular culture, can be a sign of rebellion or of special status. Adopting the uncombed hair of the Rastafarians can be a sign of rebellion among some people, while for Rastafarians it is a sign of membership in a particular religious group. In many cultures people in mourning deliberately do not comb or wash their hair for a period of time, thereby showing that they are temporarily not part of normal everyday life.

What we do with our hair is a way of expressing our identity, and it is easy to look around and see how hair color, cut, style, and its very presence or absence, tells others much about how we want to be seen.

## Body Shaping

The shape of the human body changes throughout life, but in many cultures people have found ways to permanently or temporarily sculpt the body. To conform to culturally defined ideals of male and female beauty, people have bound the soft bones of babies' skulls or children's feet, stretched their necks with rings, removed ribs to achieve tiny waists, and most commonly today, sculpted the body through plastic surgery.

Becoming fat is a sign of health, wealth, and fertility in some societies, and fattening is sometimes part of a girl's coming of age ceremony. Tiny waists, small feet, and large or small breasts and buttocks have been prized or scorned as ideals of female beauty. Less common are ways of shaping men's bodies but developing muscles, shaping the head, or gaining weight are ways in which cultural ideals of male beauty and power have been expressed.

Head shaping is still done in parts of South America. For the Inca of South America and the Maya of Central America and Mexico, a specially shaped head once signified nobility. Because the skull bones of infants and children are not completely fused, the application of pressure with pads, boards, bindings, or massage results in a gently shaped head that can be a mark of high status or local identity.

While Western plastic surgery developed first as a way of correcting the injuries of war, particularly after WW II, today people use plastic surgery to smooth their skin, remove unwanted fat, and reshape parts of their bodies.

## Scarification

Permanent patterns of scars on the skin, inscribed onto the body through scarification, can be signs of beauty and indicators of status. In some cultures, a smooth, unmarked skin represents an ideal of beauty, but people in many other cultures see smooth skin as a naked, unattractive surface. Scarification, also called cicatrization, alters skin texture by cutting the skin and controlling the body's healing process. The cuts are treated to prevent infection and to enhance the scars' visibility. Deep cuts leave visible incisions after the skin heals, while inserting substances like clay or ash in the cuts results in permanently raised wheals or bumps, known as keloids. Substances inserted into the wounds may result in changes in skin color, creating marks similar to tattoos. Cutting elaborate and extensive decorative patterns into the skin usually indicates a permanent change in a person's status. Because scarification is painful, the richly scarred person is often honored for endurance and courage. Branding is a form of scarification that creates a scar after the surface of the skin has been burned. Branding was done in some societies as a part of a rite of passage, but in western Europe and elsewhere branding, as well as some forms of tattoo, were widely used to mark captives, enslaved peoples, and criminals. Recently, some individuals and members of fraternities on U.S. college campuses have adopted branding as a radical form of decoration and self-identification.

## Tattooing

Tattoo is the insertion of ink or some other pigment through the outer covering of the body, the epidermis, into the dermis, the second layer of skin. Tattooists use a sharp implement to puncture the skin and thus make an indelible mark, design, or picture on the body. The resulting patterns or figures vary according to the purpose of the tattoo and the materials available for its coloration.

Different groups and cultures have used a variety of techniques in this process. Traditional Polynesian tattooists punctured the skin by tapping a needle with a small hammer. The Japanese work by hand but with bundles of needles set in wooden handles. Since the late 19th century, the electric tattoo machine and related technological advances in equipment have revolutionized tattoo in the West, expanding the range of possible designs, the colors available, and the ease with which a tattoo can be applied to the body. Prisoners have used materials as disparate as guitar strings and reconstructed electric shavers to create tattoos. Tattoos are usually intended as permanent markings, and it is only recently through the use of expensive laser techniques that they can be removed.

While often decorative, tattoos send important cultural messages. The "text" on the skin can be read as a commitment to some group, an emblem of a rite of passage, or a personal or fashion statement. In fact, cosmetic tattooing of eyebrows and eyeliner is one of the fastest growing of all tattoo enterprises. Tattoos can also signify bravery and commitment to a long, painful process—as is the case with Japanese full body tattooing or Māori body and facial patterns. Though there have been numerous religious and social injunctions against tattooing, marking the body in this way has been one of the most persistent and universal forms of body art.

### Piercing

Body piercing, which allows ornaments to be worn in the body, has been a widespread practice since ancient times. Piercing involves long-term insertion of an object through the skin in a way that permits healing around the opening. Most commonly pierced are the soft tissues of the face, but many peoples, past and present, have also pierced the genitals and the chest. Ear, nose, and lip ornaments, as well as pierced figurines, have been found in ancient burials of the Inca and Moche of Peru, the Aztecs and Maya of ancient Mexico, and in graves of central Asian, European, and Mediterranean peoples.

The act of piercing is often part of a ritual change of status. Bleeding that occurs during piercing is sometimes thought of as an offering to gods, spirits, or ancestors. Particular ornaments may be restricted to certain groups—men or women, rulers or priests—or may be inserted as part of a ceremony marking a change in status. Because ornaments can be made of precious and rare materials, they may signal privilege and wealth. . . .

## Cultural Significance of Body Art

Body art takes on specific meanings in different cultures. It can serve as a link with ancestors, deities, or spirits. Besides being decorative, tattoos, paint, and scars can mediate the relationships between people and the supernatural world.

The decorated body can serve as a shield to repel evil or as a means of attracting good fortune. Tattoos in central Borneo had the same designs as objects of every-day use and shielded people from dangerous spirits. Selk'nam men in Tierra del Fuego painted their bodies to transform themselves into spirits for initiation cer-emonies. Australian Aborigines painted similar designs on cave walls and their bodies to indicate the location of sacred places revealed in dreams.

Transitions in status and identity, for example the transition between childhood and adulthood, are often seen as times of danger. Body art protects a vulnerable person, whether an initiate, a bride, or a deceased person, in this transitional phase. To ensure her good fortune, an Indian bride's hands and feet are covered in henna designs that also emphasize her beauty. For protection during initiation, a central African Chokwe girl's body is covered in white kaolin. In many societies, both the dead and those who mourn them are cov-ered with paints and powders for decoration and protection.

Worldwide travel, large-scale migrations, and increasing access to global networks of communication mean that body art today is a kaleidoscopic mix of traditional practices and new inventions. Materials, designs, and practices move from one cultural context to another. Traditional body art practices are given new meanings as they move across cultural and social boundaries.

Body art is always changing, and in some form or another always engag-ing: it allows people to reinvent themselves—to rebel, to follow fashion, or to play and experiment with new identities. Like performance artists and actors, people in everyday life use body art to cross boundaries of gender, national iden-tity, and cultural stereotypes.

Body art can be an expression of individuality, but it can also be an expres-sion of group identity. Body art is about conformity and rebellion, freedom and authority. Its messages and meanings only make sense in the context of culture, but because it is such a personal art form, it continually challenges cultural as-sumptions about the ideal, the desirable, and the appropriately presented body.

## Review Questions

1. What is the definition of body art? Are there marks on or alterations to the body that would not be classified as body art?

2. What is a symbol and why is body art classified as symbolic?

3. What forms can body art take?

4. What are some of the general meanings that examples of body art can have in different societies?

5. What effect has globalization had on the forms and meanings of body art?

# 8

# The Sapir-Whorf Hypothesis: Worlds Shaped by Words

*David S. Thomson*

*For many people, language mirrors reality. Words are labels for what we sense; they record what is already there. This view, which is another manifestation of what we have called* naive realism, *is clearly challenged by previous selections in this book. Members of different societies may not share cultural categories; words from one language often cannot be translated directly into another. In the 1930s, a young linguist named Benjamin Lee Whorf took the objection to the "words label reality" assertion one step further by arguing that words and grammatical structure actually shape reality. This piece by David Thomson describes Whorf's theory, shows how linguists have evaluated it, and applies it in modified form to the use of words, euphemisms, and doublespeak in the modern United States.*

The scene is the storage room at a chemical plant. The time is evening. A night watchman enters the room and notes that it is partially filled with gasoline drums. The drums are in a section of the room where a sign says "Empty Barrels." The watchman lights a cigarette and throws the still-hot match into one of the empty barrels.

The result: an explosion.

The immediate cause of the explosion, of course, was the gasoline fumes that remained in the barrels. But it could be argued that a second cause of the explosion was the English language. The barrels were empty of their original contents and so belonged under the empty sign. Yet they were not empty of everything—the fumes were still present. English has no word—no single term—that can convey such a situation. Containers in English are either empty or they are not; there is no word describing the ambiguous state of being empty and yet not empty. There is no term in the language for "empty but not quite" or "empty of original contents but with something left over." There being no word for such an in-between state, it did not occur to the watchman to think of the explosive fumes.

This incident is hypothetical, but the questions about language it raises are real. The example of the gasoline drums often was cited by Benjamin Lee Whorf to illustrate a revolutionary theory he had about language. Whorf was an unusual man who combined two careers, for he was both a successful insurance executive and a brilliant (and largely self-taught) linguistic scholar. Language, he claimed, may be shaped by the world, but it in turn shapes the world. He reasoned that people can think about only those things that their language can describe or express. Without the words or structures with which to articulate a concept, that concept will not occur. To turn the proposition around, if a language is rich in ways to express certain sorts of ideas, then the speakers of that language will habitually think along those linguistic paths. In short, the language that humans speak governs their view of reality; it determines their perception of the world. The picture of the universe shifts from tongue to tongue.

The originator of this startling notion came from an intellectually active New England family. Whorf's brother John became an artist of note and his brother Richard a consummately professional actor. Benjamin's early bent was not for drawing or acting but photography, especially the chemistry that was involved in developing pictures, and this interest may have influenced his choice of the Massachusetts Institute of Technology, where he majored in chemical engineering. After he was graduated from M.I.T. he became a specialist in fire prevention and in 1919 went to work for the Hartford Fire Insurance Company. His job was to inspect manufacturing plants, particularly chemical plants, that the Hartford insured to determine whether they were safe and thus good insurance risks. He quickly became highly skilled at his work. "In no time at all," wrote C. S. Kremer, then the Hartford's board chairman, "he became in my opinion as thorough and fast a fire prevention inspector as there ever has been."

Whorf was a particularly acute chemical engineer. On one occasion he was refused admittance to inspect a client's building because, a company official maintained, a secret process was in use here. "You are making such-and-such a product?" asked Whorf. "Yes," said the official. Whorf pulled out a pad and scribbled the formula of the supposedly secret process, adding coolly, "You couldn't do it any other way." Needless to say, he was allowed to inspect the building. Whorf rose in the Hartford hierarchy to the post of assistant secretary of the company in 1940. But then in 1941 his health, never strong, gave way, and he died at the early age of forty-four.

While Whorf was becoming a successful insurance executive, he was also doing his revolutionary work in linguistics. He started by studying Hebrew but then switched to Aztec and other related languages of Mexico. Later he deciphered Maya inscriptions, and tried to reconstruct the long-lost language of the ancient Maya people of Mexico and Central America. Finally he tackled the complexities of the still-living language of the Hopi Indians of Arizona. He published his findings in respected anthropological and linguistic journals, earning the praise and respect of scholars in the two fields—all without formal training in linguistic science. As his fame as a linguist spread, the Hartford obligingly afforded him vacations and leaves to travel to the Southwest in pursuit of the structure and lexicon of the Hopi. He also put in countless hours in the Watkinson Library in Connecticut, a rich repository of Mexican and Indian lore.

It was primarily his study of Hopi that impelled Whorf toward his revolutionary ideas. He was encouraged and aided by the great cultural anthropologist and linguist of Yale, Edward Sapir, and the idea that language influences a person's view of the world is generally known as the Sapir-Whorf hypothesis. Whorf formulated it a number of times, but perhaps his clearest statement comes from his 1940 essay "Science and Linguistics": "The background linguistic system (in other words, the grammar) of each language is not merely a reproducing instrument for voicing ideas but rather is itself the shaper of ideas. . . . We dissect nature along lines laid down by our native language. The categories and types that we isolate from the world of phenomena we do not find there because they stare every observer in the face; on the contrary, the world is presented in a kaleidoscopic flux of impressions which has to be organized by our minds—and this means largely by the linguistic systems in our minds."

These ideas developed from Whorf's study of the Hopi language. He discovered that it differs dramatically from languages of the Indo-European family such as English or French, particularly in its expression of the concept of time. English and its related languages have three major tenses—past, present, and future ("it was," "it is," "it will be")—plus the fancier compound tenses such as "it will have been." Having these tenses, Whorf argued, encourages Europeans and Americans to think of time as so many ducks in a row. Time past is made up of uniform units of time—days, weeks, months, years—and the future is similarly measured out. This division of time is essentially artificial, Whorf said, since people can only experience the present. Past and future are only abstractions, but Westerners think of them as real because their language virtually forces them to do so. This view of time has given rise to the fondness in

Western cultures for diaries, records, annals, histories, clocks, calendars, wages paid by the hour or day, and elaborate timetables for the use of future time. Time is continually quantified. If Westerners set out to build a house they establish a deadline; the work will be completed at a specified time in the future, such as May 5 or October 15.

Hopis do not behave this way; when they start to weave a mat they are not concerned about when it will be completed. They work on it desultorily, then quit, then begin again; the finished product may take weeks. This casual progress is not laziness but a result of the Hopi's view of time—one symptom of the fact that their language does not have the past, present, and future tenses. Instead it possesses two modes of thought: the objective, that is, things that exist now, and the subjective, things that can be thought about and therefore belong to a state of becoming. Things do not become in terms of a future measured off in days, weeks, months. Each thing that is becoming has its own individual life rhythms, growing or declining or changing in much the same manner as a plant grows, according to its inner nature. The essence of Hopi life, therefore, Whorf said, is preparing in the present so that those things that are capable of becoming can in fact come to pass. Thus weaving a mat is preparing a mat to become a mat; it will reach that state when its nature so ordains—whenever that will be.

This view of the future is understandable, Whorf noted, in an agricultural people whose welfare depends on the proper preparing of earth and seeds and plants for the hoped-for harvest. It also helps explain why the Hopi have such elaborate festivals, rituals, dances, and magic ceremonies: All are intended to aid in the mental preparation that is so necessary if the crops, which the Hopi believe to be influenced by human thought, are to grow properly. This preparing involves "much visible activity," Whorf said, "introductory formalities, preparing of special food . . . intensive sustained muscular activity like running, racing, dancing, which is thought to increase the intensity of development of events (such as growth of crops), mimetic and other magic preparations based on esoteric theory involving perhaps occult instruments like prayer sticks, prayer feathers, and prayer meal, and finally the great cyclic ceremonies and dances, which have the significance of preparing rain and crops." Whorf went on to note that the very noun for *crop* is derived from the verb that means "to prepare." *Crop* therefore is in the Hopi language literally "the prepared." Further, the Hopi prayer pipe, which is smoked as an aid in concentrating good thoughts on the growing fields of corn and wheat, is named *na'twanpi*, "instrument of preparing."

The past to the Hopi, Whorf believed, is also different from the chronological time sense of the speakers of Indo-European languages. The past is not a uniform row of days or weeks to the Hopi. It is rather an undifferentiated stream in which many deeds were done that have accumulated and prepared the present and will continue to prepare the becoming that is ahead. Everything is connected, everything accumulates. The past is not a series of events, separated and completed, but is present in the present.

To Whorf these striking differences in the Hopi language and sense of time implied that the Hopi live almost literally in another world from the speakers of Indo-European languages. The Hopi language grew out of its speakers' peculiar circumstances: As a geographically isolated agricultural people in a land where rainfall was scanty, they did the same things and prayed the same prayers year after year and thus did not need to have past and future tenses. But the language, once it had developed, perpetuated their particular and seemingly very different world view.

Many linguists and anthropologists who have worked with American Indians of the Southwest have been convinced that Whorf's theories are by and large correct. Other linguists are not convinced, however, and through the years since Whorf's death they have attacked his proposals. The controversy is unlikely to be settled soon, if ever. One of the problems is the difficulty of setting up an experiment that would either prove or disprove the existence of correlations between linguistic structure and nonlinguistic behavior. It would be fruitless to go about asking people of various cultures their opinions as to whether the language they spoke had determined the manner in which they thought, had dictated their view of the world. Nobody would be able to answer such a question, for a people's language is so completely embedded in their consciousness that they would be unable to conceive of any other way of interpreting the world.

Despite the near impossibility of proving or disproving Whorf's theory, it will not go away but keeps coming back, intriguing each succeeding generation of linguists. It is certainly one of the most fascinating theories created by the modern mind. It is comparable in some ways to Einstein's theory of relativity. Just as Einstein said that how people saw the phenomena of the universe was relative to their point of observation, so Whorf said that a people's world view was relative to the language they spoke.

And demonstrations of Whorf's ideas are not entirely lacking. They come mainly from studies of color—one of the very few aspects of reality that can be specified by objective scientific methods and also is rather precisely specified by people's naming of colors. In this instance it is possible to compare one person's language, expressing that person's view of the world, with another's language for exactly the same characteristic of the world. The comparison can thus reveal different views that are linked to different descriptions of the same reality. English-speakers view purple as a single relatively uniform color; only if pressed and then only with difficulty will they make any attempt to divide it into such shades as lavender and mauve. But no English-speaker would lump orange with purple; to the users of English, those colors are completely separate, for no single word includes both of them. If other languages made different distinctions in the naming of color—if lavender and mauve were always separate, never encompassed by a word for purple, or if orange and purple were not distinguished but were called by a name that covered both—then it would seem that the users of those languages interpreted those colors differently.

Such differences in color-naming, it turns out, are fairly widespread. Linguist H. A. Gleason compared the color spectrum as described by English-speaking persons to the way it was labeled by speakers of Bassa, a language spoken in Liberia, and by speakers of Shona, spoken in Rhodesia. English-speaking people, when seeing sunlight refracted through a prism, identify by name at least six colors—purple, blue, green, yellow, orange, and red. The speakers of Shona, however, have only three names for the colors of the spectrum. They group orange, red, and purple under one name. They also lump blue and green-blue under one of their other color terms and use their third word to identify yellow and the yellower hues of green. The speakers of Bassa are similarly restricted by a lack of handy terms for color, for they have only two words for the hues of the spectrum.

Gleason's observations prompted psychologists to perform an experiment that also showed the influence words can have on the way colors are handled intellectually and remembered. It was an ingenious and complex experiment with many checks and double checks of the results, but in essence it boiled down to something like this: English-speaking subjects were shown a series of color samples—rather like the little "chips" provided by a paint store to help customers decide what color to paint the living room. The subjects were then asked to pick out the colors they had seen from a far larger array of colors. It turned out that they could more accurately pick out the right colors from the larger selection when the color involved had a handy, ordinary name like "green." The subjects had difficulty with the ambiguous, in-between colors such as off-purples and misty blues. In other words, a person can remember a color better if that person's language offers a handy label for it, but has trouble when the language does not offer such a familiar term. Again the human ability to differentiate reality seemed to be affected by the resources offered by language.

Richness of linguistic resource undoubtedly helps people to cope with subtle gradations in the things they deal with every day. The Hanunóo people of the Philippine Islands have different names for ninety-two varieties of rice. They can easily distinguish differences in rice that would be all but invisible to English-speaking people, who lump all such grains under the single word *rice*. Of course, English-speakers can make distinctions by resorting to adjectives and perhaps differentiate long-grain, brown rice from small-grain, yellow rice, but surely no European or American would, lacking the terms, have a sufficiently practiced eye to distinguish ninety-two varieties of rice. Language is essentially a code that people use both to think and to communicate. As psychologist Roger Brown sums up the rice question: "Among the Hanunóo, who have names for ninety-two varieties of rice, any one of those varieties is highly codable in the array of ninety-one other varieties. The Hanunóo have a word for it and so can transmit it efficiently and presumably can recognize it easily. Among speakers of English one kind of rice among ninety-one other kinds would have very low codability."

Brown goes on to suppose that the Hanunóo set down in New York would be baffled by the reality around them partly because they would then be the ones lacking the needed words. "If the Hanunóo were to visit the annual Automobile Show in New York City, they would find it difficult to encode distinctively any particular automobile in that array. But an American having such lexical resources as *Chevrolet, Ford, Plymouth, Buick, Corvette, hard-top, convertible, four-door, station wagon,* and the like could easily encode ninety-two varieties."

The very existence of so many different languages, each linked to a distinctive culture, is itself support of a sort for Whorf's hypothesis. At least since the time of the Tower of Babel, no single tongue has been shared by all the people of the world. Many attempts have been made to invent an international language, one so simply structured and easy to learn it would be used by everyone around the globe as a handy adjunct to their native speech. Yet even the most successful of these world languages, Esperanto, has found but limited acceptance.

There are international languages, however, to serve international cultures. The intellectual disciplines of music, dance, and mathematics might be considered specialized cultures; each is shared by people around the world, and each has an international language, used as naturally in Peking as in Paris. English is a world language in certain activities that straddle national boundaries, such as international air travel; it serves for communications between international flights and the ground in every country—a Lufthansa pilot approaching Athens talks with the airport control tower neither in German nor in Greek but in English.

The trouble with most attempts to lend credence to the Sapir-Whorf hypothesis is that, while they indicate connections between culture and language, they do not really prove that a language shaped its users' view of the world. Just because the speakers of Shona have only three main distinctions of color does not mean that their "world view" is all that different from that of the English-speaker who has more convenient color terms. Shona speakers obviously see all the colors in the rainbow that English-speakers see. Their eyes are physiologically the same. Their comparative poverty of words for those colors merely means that it is harder for them to talk about color. Their "code" is not so handy; the colors' codability is lower.

Critics also point out that Whorf may have mistaken what are called dead metaphors for real differences in the Hopi language. All languages are loaded with dead metaphors—figures of speech that have lost all figurative value and are now just familiar words. The word "goodbye" is a dead metaphor. Once it meant "God be with you," but in its contracted form it conjures up no thought or picture of God. If a Whorfian linguist who was a native speaker of Hopi turned the tables and analyzed English he might conclude that English-speakers were perpetually thinking of religion since this everyday word incorporates a reference to God—a ridiculous misreading of a term that has lost all of its original religious significance. In like fashion, perhaps Whorf was reading too much into the Hopi lexicon and grammar, seeing significances where there were none.

The argument about how far Whorf's ideas can be stretched has gone on for several decades and promises to go on for several more. Most psychologists believe that all people see pretty much the same reality; their languages merely have different words and structures to approximate in various idiosyncratic ways a picture of that reality. And yet the experts accept what might be called modified Whorfism—a belief in the power of language to affect, if not to direct, the perception of reality. If a language is rich in terms for certain things or ideas—possesses extensive codability for them—then the people speaking that language can conceive of, and talk about, those things or ideas more conveniently. If different languages do not give their speakers entirely different world views, they certainly influence thinking to some degree.

Even within the Indo-European family of languages, some tongues have words for concepts that other tongues lack. German is especially rich in philosophical terms that have no exact counterparts in English, French, Italian—or any known language. One is *Weltschmerz,* which combines in itself meanings that it takes three English phrases to adequately convey—"weariness of life," "pessimistic outlook," and "romantic discontent." Another German word that has no direct translation is *Weltanschauung.* To approximate its meaning in English requires a number of different terms—"philosophy of life," "world outlook," "ideology"—for all of these elements are included in the German word. *Weltanschauung* is untranslatable into any single English term. It represents an idea for which only German has a word. Possessing the convenient term, German writers can develop this idea more easily than the users of other languages, and thus explore its ramifications further.

Even when a word from one language may seem to be easily translatable into another, it often is not really equivalent. The French term *distingué* would appear to translate easily enough into the English *distinguished.* But the French use their word in ways that no English-speaker would ever employ for *distinguished.* A Frenchman might reprimand his son by saying that his impolite behavior was not *distingué* or he might tell his wife that a scarf she has worn out to dinner is charmingly *distingué.* The word does not mean "distinguished" as English-speakers employ the term, but something more like "suitable," or "appropriate," or "in keeping with polite standards." It is simply not the same word in the two languages no matter how similar the spelling. It represents a different idea, connoting a subtle difference in mental style.

In some cases the existence of a word leads users of it down tortured logical paths toward dead ends. The common word *nothing* is one example. Since there is a word for the concept, points out philosopher George Pitcher, it tempts people to think that "nothing" is a real entity, that somehow it exists, a palpable realm of not-being. It has in fact led a number of philosophers, including the twentieth-century French thinker Jean-Paul Sartre, to spend a great deal of effort speculating about the nature of "nothing." The difficulty of this philosophic dilemma is indicated by a typical Sartre sentence on the subject: "The Being by which Nothingness arrives in the world must nihilate. Nothingness in its Being, and even so it still runs the risk of establishing Nothingness as a transcendent in the very heart of immanence unless it nihilates Nothingness in its being in connection with its own being." Sartre could hardly have gotten himself tangled up in such agonized prose had French lacked a noun for *le neant,* nothing, and the value to human welfare of his attempt to explain is open to question.

The power of language to influence the world can be seen not only in comparisons of one tongue to another, but also within a single language. The way in which people use their native tongue—choosing one term over another to express the same idea or action, varying structures or phrases for different situations—has a strong effect on their attitudes toward those situations. Distasteful ideas can be made to seem acceptable or even desirable by careful choices of words, and language can make actions or beliefs that might otherwise be considered correct appear to be obsolescent or naive. Value judgments of many kinds can be attached to seemingly simple statements. Shakespeare may have believed that "a rose by any other name would smell as sweet," but he was wrong, as other theatrical promoters have proved repeatedly. A young English vaudevillian known as Archibald Leach was a minor comedian until he was given the more romantic name of Cary Grant. The new name did not make him a star, but it did create an atmosphere in which he could demonstrate his talent, suggesting the type of character he came to exemplify.

If the power of a stage name to characterize personality seems of relatively minor consequence in human affairs, consider the effect of a different sort of appellation: "boy." It was—and sometimes still is—the form of address employed by whites in the American South in speaking to black males of any age. This word, many authorities believe, served as an instrument of subjugation. It implied that the black was not a man but a child, someone not mature enough to be entrusted with responsibility for himself, let alone authority over others. His inferior position was thus made to seem natural and justified, and it could be enforced without compunction.

Characterizing people by tagging them with a word label is a world-wide practice. Many peoples use a single word to designate both themselves and the human race. "The Carib Indians, for example, have stated with no equivocation, 'We alone are people,' " reported anthropologist Jack Conrad. "Similarly, the ancient Egyptians used the word *romet* (men) only among themselves and in no case for strangers. The Lapps of Scandinavia reserve the term 'human being' for those of their own kind, while the Cherokee Indians call themselves *Ani-Yunwiya,* which means 'principal people.' The Kiowa Indians of the Southwest are willing to accept other peoples as human, but the very name, *Kiowa,* meaning 'real people,' shows their true feeling." The effect of reserving a term indicating "human" to one group is far-reaching. It alters the perception of anyone from outside that group. He is not called "human," and need not be treated as human. Like an animal, he can be entrapped, beaten, or even killed with more or less impunity. This use of a word to demote whole groups from the human class is often a wartime tactic—the enemy is referred to by a pejorative name to justify killing him.

While language can be twisted to make ordinarily good things seem bad, it can also be twisted in the opposite direction to make bad things seem good or run-of-the-mill things better than they really are. The technique depends on the employment of euphemisms, a term derived from the Greek for "words of good omen." A euphemism is roundabout language that is intended to conceal something embarrassing or unpleasant. Some classes of euphemism—little evasions that people use every day—are inoffensive enough. It is when such cloudy doubletalk invades the vital areas of politics and foreign affairs that it becomes perilous.

A large and commonly used—and relatively harmless—class of euphemism has to do with bodily functions. Many people shy away from frank talk about excretion or sex; in fact, many of the old, vivid terms—the four-letter words—are socially taboo. So people for centuries have skirted the edge of such matters, inventing a rich vocabulary of substitute terms. Americans offered turkey on Thanksgiving commonly say "white meat" or "dark meat" to announce their preference. These terms date back to the nineteenth century when it was considered indelicate to say "breast" or "leg." *Toilet,* itself a euphemism coined from the French *toilette* ("making oneself presentable to the outside world"), long ago became tainted and too graphic for the prudish. The list of euphemistic substitutes is almost endless, ranging from the commonplace *washroom, bathroom,* and *restroom* (whoever rests in a restroom?) to *john, head,* and *Chic Sale* in the United States, and in England the *loo. Loo* may be derived from a mistaken English pronunciation of the French *l'eau,* water. Or it may be a euphemism derived from a euphemism. The French, with Gallic delicacy, once commonly put the number 100 on bathroom doors in hotels. It is easy to see how an English person might have mistaken the number for the word *loo.* Meanwhile, ladies in restaurants have adopted "I'm going to powder my nose" or, in England, where it once cost a penny to use public toilets, "I'm going to spend a penny."

Another generally harmless use of euphemistic language is the practice, especially notable in the United States, of giving prestigious names to more-or-less ordinary trades. As H. L. Mencken pointed out in *The American Language,* his masterly examination of English as spoken in the United States, ratcatchers are fond of calling themselves "exterminating engineers" and hairdressers have long since showed a preference for "beautician." The *-ician* ending, in fact, has proved very popular, doubtless because it echoes "physician" and thus sounds both professional and scientific. In the late nineteenth century undertakers had already begun to call themselves "funeral directors," but starting in 1916 ennobled themselves even further by battening on the newer euphemistic coinage, "mortician." Meanwhile a tree trimmer became a "tree surgeon" (that love of medicine again) and a press agent became a "publicist" or, even more grandly, a "public relations counsel."

Americans (and the English, too) not only chose high-sounding euphemisms for their professions but also gave new and gaudy names to their places of business. Thus pawn shops became "loan offices," saloons became "cocktail rooms," pool halls became "billiard parlors," and barber shops "hair-styling salons."

Purists might say that such shading or blunting of the stark truth leads to moral decay, but it is difficult to see why anybody should be the worse for allowing women to excuse themselves by pleading that they must powder their noses. There are euphemisms, however, that are clearly anything but harmless. These are evasive, beclouding phraseologies that hide truths people must clearly perceive if they are to govern themselves intelligently and keep a check on those in positions of power. Slick phrases, slippery evasions—words deliberately designed to hide unpleasant truth rather than reveal it—can so becloud political processes and so easily hide mistaken policies that the entire health of a nation is imperiled.

The classic treatise on the political misuse of language in modern times is the 1946 essay "Politics and the English Language" by the British writer George Orwell. "In our time, political speech and writing are largely the defence of the indefencible," Orwell said. "Thus political language has to consist largely of euphemism, question-begging and sheer cloudy vagueness." He concluded, "Such phraseology is needed if one wants to name things without calling up mental pictures of them. . . . When there is a gap between one's real and one's declared aims, one turns as it were instinctively to long words and exhausted idioms, like a cuttlefish squirting out ink."

Orwell supplied numerous examples to buttress his charges. "Defenceless villages are bombarded from the air, the inhabitants driven out into the countryside, the cattle machine-gunned, the huts set on fire with incendiary bullets: this is called *pacification*." He went on to observe that in Stalin's Russia people were "imprisoned for years without trial or shot in the back of the neck or sent to die of scurvy in Arctic lumber camps: this is called *elimination of unreliable elements*."

Orwell, who died at the age of forty-six in 1950, did not live to collect even more deplorable distortions of language. The French clothed their brutal war in Algeria with a veil of euphemism; the North Koreans accused the South Koreans of "aggression" when the North invaded the South. The United States invented a whole lexicon of gobbledygook to disguise the horror of the war in Vietnam: "protective reaction strike" (the bombing of a Vietnamese village); "surgical bombing" (the same as protective reaction strike); "free-fire zone" (an area in which troops could shoot anything that moved, including helpless villagers); "new life hamlet" (a refugee camp for survivors of a surgical bombing).

Perhaps the most appalling use of this type of euphemism was the word employed by the Nazis for their program to exterminate all of Europe's Jews. The word is *Endlösung*, which means final solution. Behind that verbal façade the Nazis gassed, burned, shot, or worked to death some six million Jews from Germany, France, Poland, and other conquered parts of Europe. Hitler and Gestapo chief Himmler often employed the euphemism among themselves, and it was always used in official records—but not necessarily to preserve secrecy for purposes of state security. Apparently the euphemism shielded the Nazis from themselves. Openly brutal and murderous as they were, they could not face up to the horrible reality of what they were doing, and they had to hide it in innocuous language.

Such distortion of language can do more than disguise truth. It can turn truth around, so that the idea conveyed is the opposite of actuality. After the USSR savagely crushed the Hungarian rebellion in 1956 the Soviet aggression was made to seem, in the twisted language used by other Communist dictatorships, an expression of friendship. The Peking radio commented after the rebellion was put down: "The Hungarian people can see that Soviet policy toward the people's democracies is truly one of equality, friendship, and mutual assistance, not of conquest, aggression, and plunder."

The possibility that such topsy-turvy language might ultimately make the world topsy-turvy—an ironic demonstration of the fundamental truth of Benjamin Lee Whorf's insights—was raised in a dramatic way by George Orwell. His novel *1984*, a chilling and convincing description of life in a totalitarian society, shows how language might destroy reality. In the imaginary nation of Oceania the official language is Newspeak, which is intended to facilitate "doublethink," the ability to accept simultaneously ideas contradicting each other. The Oceania state apparatus includes a Ministry of Truth, its headquarters building emblazoned with three slogans: "WAR IS PEACE"; "FREEDOM IS SLAVERY"; "IGNORANCE IS STRENGTH." There are also other ministries, Orwell explained: "The Ministry of Peace, which concerned itself with war; the Ministry of Love, which maintained law and order." Anyone who would use language this way, Orwell made clear, denies the meaning of his or her words. He or she has lost touch with reality and substituted for it an emptiness concealed in sounds that once had meaning.

There is another threat to language besides the intentional twisting of words by demagogues and others who would control people's thoughts. It is less obvious, but a danger nevertheless: simple imprecision, slovenliness, mindlessness in the use of the language. It seems a small matter that English-speakers increasingly confuse *uninterested* with *disinterested*, for example. But these words do not mean the same thing. *Disinterested* means impartial, not taking sides. *Uninterested* means lacking in interest, bored. A judge should be *disinterested* but never *uninterested*. Many such changes result from the inevitable evolution of language as it changes over the years, but the change can be a loss. The slow erosion of distinctions, visible in much writing, audible in many conversations, makes language imprecise and thus clumsy and ineffective as communication.

Among the symptoms of such erosion are stock phrases that people mindlessly repeat, substituting noise for thought. Everyone has heard speechmakers use such clichés as "having regard to," "play into the hands of," "in the interest of," "no axe to grind." Although this brief list is drawn from Orwell's essay of 1946 these exhausted clichés are still heard. Such verbal dead limbs do not distort thought but rather tend to obliterate it in a cloud of meaninglessness. "The slovenliness of our language makes it easier for us to have foolish thoughts," wrote Orwell. And ultimately, as has been pointed out by commentator Edwin Newman in his book *Strictly Speaking*, "Those for whom words have lost their value are likely to find that ideas have also lost their value."

# Review Questions

1. According to Thomson, what is the Sapir-Whorf hypothesis? Give some examples.

2. According to Whorf, how can grammar affect people's perceptions? Give examples.

3. The Sapir-Whorf hypothesis has been tested in several ways. What are some of the tests of the hypothesis described by Thomson, and how have these modified the theory?

4. What are some of the ways in which language affects or modifies perception in modern America? Can you add examples from your own experience to those presented by Thomson?

# 9

# The Military Name Game

## Sarah Boxer

*In the last article, we looked at Benjamin Whorf's assertion that words not only name things and ideas, but also affect our perception of them. Whether or not this is always true (doubters might argue that calling a crippled person "handicapped" does not really change perception of the disability), advertisers, politicians, and, indeed, all of us choose words to manipulate meaning. Thus a restaurant menu tells us its salad contains "crisp, garden-fresh greens." An automobile company sends the message that its SUVs are "like a rock." Especially articulate individuals can create word images on their feet, but corporations and government agencies often institutionalize the process. This selection, by Sarah Boxer, traces the history of one such bureaucratic process—the naming of military operations by members of the U.S. armed forces. Challenged by the need to generate public support for military actions, the naming process has taken on grand proportions. First used by the Germans in World War II, operations naming changed from a secret code to a positive statement designed to generate public support by 2001. At first, commanders chose the military operations' names. When these names were later revealed to the public, naming came to be seen as a form of public relations. By the Vietnam War, the U.S. military had created a computer program called "Code Word, Nickname, and Exercise Term System" or "NICKA" for short. Today each major military command has rights to certain letter combinations from which to create names for operations, but higher authorities may discard these names. Boxer concludes by noting that an unanticipated pitfall of the process is the potential for almost any word to offend some members of the national audience. For that reason, some of the best names may be those that have no meaning at all.*

For a few days in September [2001] it looked as if the United States would be fighting a war named Infinite Justice. By late September the name was gone. The Council on American-Islamic Relations had found the name offensive because it sounded too much like Eternal Retribution. In other words the United States seemed to be assuming God's role. On Sept. 25 Defense Secretary Donald H. Rumsfeld announced that the military operation would be called Enduring Freedom.

Never mind that Enduring Freedom presented its own troubling ambiguities: Is "enduring" supposed to be taken as an adjective, like long-lasting? Or as a present participle, as in "How long are we going to be enduring this freedom?"

This is not the first time that the name of a military operation has been floated then grounded. The history of naming such operations shows how an art that was once covert has slowly become bureaucratic propaganda.

As Lt. Col. Gregory C. Sieminski points out in his classic short history, "The Art of Naming Operations," published in 1995 in *Parameters*, the quarterly of the United States Army War College, the name of the 1989 United States invasion of Panama, Just Cause, was originally Blue Spoon, until the commander of the Special Operations Command, Gen. James Lindsay, asked an operations officer on the Joint Staff, Lt. Gen. Thomas Kelly, "Do you want your grandchildren to say you were in Blue Spoon?"

So who does create nicknames for military operations these days? There are 24 Defense Department entities, each of which is assigned "a series of two-letter alphabetic sequences," Colonel Sieminski explains. For example, AG-AL, ES-EZ, JG-JL, QA-QF, SM-SR, and UM-UR belong to the Atlantic Command. In order to name the invasion of Granada in 1983, the Atlantic Command started with the letters UR and came up with Urgent Fury. Once the name was generated, it was sent to the Joint Chiefs of Staff, who sent it to the Defense Secretary for the ultimate decision.

But all this can be overridden if the naming seems important enough. And that seems to be happening more and more. "Since 1989 U.S. military operations have been nicknamed with an eye toward shaping domestic and international perceptions," Colonel Sieminski notes.

A huge effort, for example, went into choosing the right name for the operation to defend Kuwait from Iraq. Gen. H. Norman Schwarzkopf wanted the name Peninsula Shield, even though the letters PE were not assigned to his command. Then Crescent Shield was proposed, with an eye to local sentiment. Finally it became Desert Shield. And then the word "desert" bloomed and multiplied: Desert Storm, Desert Saber, Desert Farewell, Desert Share.

The naming game began with the Germans. In World War II they seem to have been the first to give military operations code names, Colonel Sieminski writes. They ransacked mythology and religion for ideas: Archangel, St. Michael, St. George, Roland, Mars, Achilles, Castor, Pollux, and Valkyrie. Hitler himself named the invasion of the Soviet Union Barbarossa for the "12th-century Holy Roman Emperor Frederick I, who had extended German authority over the Slavs in the east," Colonel Sieminski writes.

Churchill, like Hitler, was partial to names that came from "heroes of antiquity, figures from Greek and Roman mythology, the constellations and stars, famous racehorses, names of British and American war heroes," Colonel Sieminski writes. And he set naming etiquette. Names should not "imply a boastful or overconfident sentiment," Churchill said; they should not have "an air of despondency"; they should not be frivolous or ordinary; and they should not be a target for fun. No widow or mother, Churchill said, should have "to say that her son was killed in an operation called 'Bunnyhug' or 'Ballyhoo.'"

For all of Churchill's pains with nomenclature, the names of British and American operations were originally designed to be secret, not meant for public ears until the war or operation was finished.

The United States named its first operations after colors. When the colors began to run out, the War Department drew up a list of "10,000 common nouns and adjectives," avoiding "proper nouns, geographical terms, and names of ships" that might give military clues away to the enemy, Colonel Sieminski writes. And each theater had its own blocks of code words; "the European Theater got such names as Market and Garden, while the Pacific Theater got names like Olympic and Flintlock."

Soon after World War II ended, the Pentagon began creating operation names that were especially designed for public ears. The first nickname was Operation Crossroads, for the 1946 atomic bomb tests conducted on Bikini Atoll. And then things opened up more. During the Korean War Gen. Douglas MacArthur "permitted code names to be declassified and disseminated to the press once operations had begun, rather than waiting until the end of the war," Colonel Sieminski writes.

What followed were some very "aggressive nicknames" for counteroffensives in China: Thunderbolt, Roundup, Killer, Ripper, Courageous, Audacious, and Dauntless.

The bloody names kept flowing in Vietnam, but public relations concerns soon stemmed the tide. The most controversial name, Colonel Sieminski notes, was Masher, the nickname for a "sweep operation through the Bong Son Plain." President Lyndon B. Johnson "angrily protested that it did not reflect 'pacification emphasis,'" In other words Masher somehow did not say "peace" to the world, Colonel Sieminski writes. Masher was reborn as White Wing. After 1966, operations tended to be named for towns and figures: Junction City, Bastogne, Nathan Hale. To rouse the troops at the Khe Sanh garrison, a "round-the-clock bombing attack" was called Operation Niagara, "to invoke an image of cascading shells and bombs," Colonel Sieminski notes.

By the end of the Vietnam War the process of naming had grown baroque. So in 1975 the Joint Chiefs of Staff created a computer system, the Code Word, Nickname, and Exercise Term System. "The NICKA system is not, as some assume, a random word generator for nicknames," Colonel Sieminski writes; "it is in fact merely an automated means for submitting, validating and storing them."

There is plenty of room for drama. But the fashion now, he writes, is "to make the names sound like mission statements by using a verb-noun sequence: Promote Liberty, Restore Hope, Uphold Democracy, Provide Promise." They are boring, unmemorable names.

Despite the monotonous trend, names are more important than they have ever been. With "the shrinking scale of military action," Colonel Sieminski writes, the nickname of an operation now may well become the name for the whole war and its rationale. Maybe that is the problem.

Robin Tolmach Lakoff, a professor of linguistics at the University of California, Berkeley, and the author of *The Language War,* a book about the unintentional overtones of language, said, "Whoever gives the name has control over it." Naming an operation is like naming a baby, she added. "Your creation is opaque, but the name suggests what you hope it will be." What then was the hope with Infinite Justice and then with Enduring Freedom?

The nouns in the name of the operation, she said, were no problem: freedom and justice. It was the adjectives that presented problems. The name had to please so many different kinds of people that every adjective seemed fraught with offensive overtones. "It is a virtue in times of peril," Ms. Lakoff said, "to find words without meaning."

# Review Questions

1. Why do military commanders and public officials take the naming of military actions so seriously?

2. How has the procedure for naming military actions changed since campaigns were first given names in World War II?

3. What pitfalls are there in choosing names for military actions in the United States today? Are there solutions to such problems?

4. What evidence supports or challenges the belief held by many in authority that the way something is portrayed in words does actually affect how people will understand it?

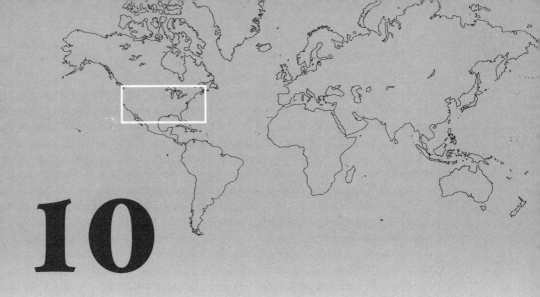

# 10

# Conversation Style: Talking on the Job

*Deborah Tannen*

*In Schildkrout's article, we looked at the important role played by nonverbal symbols in human communication. Speaking distances, gestures, smiles, and a host of other tacit signs make up this silent language. In this piece excerpted from her book about conversation in the workplace, Deborah Tannen discusses a second tacit dimension of communication, conversation style. Looking at the different ways men and women approach or avoid asking for help on the job, she argues that gender differences in conversation style are responsible for not only miscommunication but for misguided evaluations and moral judgments about the performance and character of coworkers.*

People have different conversational styles, influenced by the part of the country they grew up in, their ethnic backgrounds and those of their parents, their age, class, and gender. But conversational style is invisible. Unaware that these and other aspects of our backgrounds influence our ways of talking, we think we are simply saying what we mean. Because we don't realize that others' styles are different, we are often frustrated in conversations. Rather than seeing the culprit as differing styles, we attribute troubles to others' intentions (she doesn't like me), abilities (he's stupid), or character (she's rude, he's inconsiderate), our own failure (what's wrong with me?), or the failure of a relationship (we just can't communicate). . . .

Although I am aware of the many influences on conversational style and have spent most of my career studying and writing about them, [here] . . . style differences influenced by gender receive particular attention. This is not only because these are the differences people most want to hear about (although this is so and is a factor), but also because there is something fundamental about our categorization by gender. When you spot a person walking down the street toward you, you immediately and automatically identify that person as male or female. You will not necessarily try to determine which state they are from, what their class background is, or what country their grandparents came from. A secondary identification, in some places and times, may be about race. But, while we may envision a day when a director will be able to cast actors for a play without reference to race, can we imagine a time when actors can be cast without reference to their sex?

Few elements of our identities come as close to our sense of who we are as gender. If you mistake people's cultural background—you thought they were Greek, but they turn out to be Italian; you assumed they'd grown up in Texas, but it turns out they're from Kentucky; you say "Merry Christmas" and they say, "we don't celebrate Christmas; we're Muslim"—it catches you off guard and you rearrange the mental frame through which you view them. But if someone you thought was male turns out to be female—like the jazz musician Billy Tipton, whose own adopted sons never suspected that their father was a woman until the coroner broke the news to them after his (her) death—the required adjustment is staggering. Even infants discriminate between males and females and react differently depending on which they confront.

Perhaps it is because our sense of gender is so deeply rooted that people are inclined to hear descriptions of gender patterns as statements about gender *identity*—in other words, as absolute differences rather than a matter of degree and percentages, and as universal rather than culturally mediated. The patterns I describe are based on observations of particular speakers in a particular place and time: mostly (but not exclusively) middle-class Americans of European background working in offices at the present time. Other cultures evince very different patterns of talk associated with gender—and correspondingly different assumptions about the "natures" of women and men. I don't put a lot of store in talk about "natures" or what is "natural." People in every culture will tell you that the behaviors common in their own culture are "natural." I also don't put a lot of store in people's explanations that their way of talking is a natural response to their environment, as there is always an equally natural and opposite way of responding to the same environment. We all tend to regard the way things are as the way things have to be—as only natural.

The reason ways of talking, like other ways of conducting our daily lives, come to seem natural is that the behaviors that make up our lives are ritualized. Indeed, the "ritual" character of interaction is at the heart of this book. Having grown up in a particular culture, we learn to do things as the people we encounter do them, so the vast majority of our decisions about how to speak become automatic. You see someone you know, you ask "How are you?," chat, then take your leave, never pausing to ponder the many ways you could handle this interaction differently—and would, if you lived in a different culture. Just as an American automatically extends a hand for a handshake while a Japanese automatically bows, what the American and Japanese find it natural to say is a matter of convention learned over a lifetime.

No one understood the ritual nature of everyday life better than sociologist Erving Goffman, who also understood the fundamental role played by gender in organizing our daily rituals. In his article "The Arrangement Between the Sexes," Goffman pointed out that we tend to say "sex-linked" when what we mean is "sex-class-linked." When hearing that a behavior is "sex-linked," people often conclude that the behavior is to be found in every individual of that group, and that it is somehow inherent in their sex, as if it came hooked to a chromosome. Goffman suggests the term "genderism" (on the model, I assume, of "mannerism," not of "sexism") for "a sex-class linked individual behavioral practice." This is the spirit in which I intend references to gendered patterns of behavior: not to imply that there is anything inherently male or female about particular ways of talking, nor to claim that every individual man or woman adheres to the pattern, but rather to observe that a larger percentage of women or men *as a group* talk in a particular way, or individual women and men *are more likely* to talk one way or the other.

That individuals do not always fit the pattern associated with their gender does not mean that the pattern is not typical. Because more women or men speak in a particular way, that way of speaking becomes associated with women or men—or, rather, it is the other way around: More women or men learn to speak particular ways *because* those ways are associated with their own gender. And individual men or women who speak in ways associated with the other gender will pay a price for departing from cultural expectations.

If my concept of how gender displays itself in everyday life has been influenced by Goffman, the focus of my research—talk—and my method for studying it grow directly out of my own discipline, linguistics. My understanding of what goes on when people talk to each other is based on observing and listening as well as tape-recording, transcribing, and analyzing conversation. In response to my book *You Just Don't Understand,* I was contacted by people at many companies who asked whether I could help them apply the insights in that book to the problem of "the glass ceiling": Why weren't women advancing as quickly as the men who were hired at the same time? And more generally, they wanted to understand how to integrate women as well as others who were historically not "typical" employees into the increasingly diverse workforce. I realized that in order to offer insight, I needed to observe what was really going on in the workplace. . . .

## Women and Men Talking on the Job

Amy was a manager with a problem: She had just read a final report written by Donald, and she felt it was woefully inadequate. She faced the unsavory task of telling him to do it over. When she met with Donald, she made sure to soften the blow by beginning with praise, telling him everything about his report that was good. Then she went on to explain what was lacking and what needed to be done to make it acceptable. She was pleased with the diplomatic way she had managed to deliver the bad news. Thanks to her thoughtfulness in starting with praise, Donald was able to listen to the criticism and seemed to understand what was needed. But when the revised report appeared on her desk, Amy was shocked. Donald had made only minor, superficial changes, and none of the necessary ones. The next meeting with him did not go well. He was incensed that she was now telling him his report was not acceptable and accused her of having misled him. "You told me before it was fine," he protested.

Amy thought she had been diplomatic; Donald thought she had been dishonest. The praise she intended to soften the message "This is unacceptable" sounded to him like the message itself: "This is fine." So what she regarded as the main point—the needed changes—came across to him as optional suggestions, because he had already registered her praise as the main point. She felt he hadn't listened to her. He thought she had changed her mind and was making him pay the price.

Work days are filled with conversations about getting the job done. Most of these conversations succeed, but too many end in impasses like this. It could be that Amy is a capricious boss whose wishes are whims, and it could be that Donald is a temperamental employee who can't hear criticism no matter how it is phrased. But I don't think either was the case in this instance. I believe this was one of innumerable misunderstandings caused by differences in conversational style. Amy delivered the criticism in a way that seemed to her self-evidently considerate, a way she would have preferred to receive criticism herself: taking into account the other person's feelings, making sure he knew that her ultimate negative assessment of his report didn't mean she had no appreciation of his abilities. She offered the praise as a sweetener to help the nasty-tasting news go down. But Donald didn't expect criticism to be delivered in that way, so he mistook the praise as her overall assessment rather than a preamble to it.

This conversation could have taken place between two women or two men. But I do not think it is a coincidence that it occurred between a man and a woman. . . . Conversational rituals common among men often involve using opposition such as banter, joking, teasing, and playful put-downs, and expending effort to avoid the one-down position in the interaction. Conversational rituals common among women are often ways of maintaining an appearance of equality, taking into account the effect of the exchange on the other person, and expending effort to downplay the speakers' authority so they can get the job done without flexing their muscles in an obvious way.

When everyone present is familiar with these conventions, they work well. But when ways of speaking are not recognized as conventions, they are taken literally, with negative results on both sides. Men whose oppositional strategies are interpreted literally may be seen as hostile when they are not, and their efforts to ensure that they avoid appearing one-down may be taken as arrogance. When women use conversational strategies designed to avoid appearing boastful and to take the other person's feelings into account, they may be seen as less confident and competent than they really are. As a result, both women and men often feel they are not getting sufficient credit for what they have done, are not being listened to, are not getting ahead as fast as they should.

When I talk about women's and men's characteristic ways of speaking, I always emphasize that both styles make sense and are equally valid in themselves, though the difference in styles may cause trouble in interaction. In a sense, when two people form a private relationship of love or friendship, the bubble of their interaction is a world unto itself, even though they both come with the prior experience of their families, their community, and a lifetime of conversations. But someone who takes a job is entering a world that is already functioning, with its own characteristic style already in place. Although there are many influences such as regional background, the type of industry involved, whether it is a family business or a large corporation, in general, workplaces that have previously had men in positions of power have already established male-style interaction as the norm. In that sense, women, and others whose styles are different, are not starting out equal, but are at a disadvantage. Though talking at work is quite similar to talking in private, it is a very different enterprise in many ways.

## When Not Asking Directions
## Is Dangerous to Your Health

If conversational-style differences lead to troublesome outcomes in work as well as private settings, there are some work settings where the outcomes of style are a matter of life and death. Healthcare professionals are often in such situations. So are airline pilots.

Of all the examples of women's and men's characteristic styles that I discussed in *You Just Don't Understand*, the one that (to my surprise) attracted the most attention was the question "Why don't men like to stop and ask for directions?" Again and again, in the responses of audiences, talk-show hosts, letter writers, journalists, and conversationalists, this question seemed to crystallize the frustration many people had experienced in their own lives. And my explanation seems to have rung true: that men are more likely to be aware that asking for directions, or for any kind of help, puts them in a one-down position.

With regard to asking directions, women and men are keenly aware of the advantages of their own style. Women frequently observe how much time they would save if their husbands simply stopped and asked someone instead of driving around trying in vain to find a destination themselves. But I have also been told by men that it makes sense not to ask directions because you learn a lot about a neighborhood, as well as about navigation, by driving around and finding your own way.

But some situations are more risky than others. A Hollywood talk-show producer told me that she had been flying with her father in his private airplane when he was running out of gas and uncertain about the precise location of the local landing strip he was heading for. Beginning to panic, the woman said, "Daddy! Why don't you radio the control tower and ask them where to land?" He answered, "I don't want them to think I'm lost." This story had a happy ending, else the woman would not have been alive to tell it to me.

Some time later, I repeated this anecdote to a man at a cocktail party—a man who had just told me that the bit about directions was his favorite part of my book, and who, it turned out, was also an amateur pilot. He then went on to tell me that he had had a similar experience. When learning to fly, he got lost on his first solo flight. He did not want to humiliate himself by tuning his radio to the FAA emergency frequency and asking for help, so he flew around looking for a place to land. He spotted an open area that looked like a landing field, headed for it—and found himself deplaning in what seemed like a deliberately hidden landing strip that was mercifully deserted at the time. Fearing he had stumbled upon an enterprise he was not supposed to be aware of, let alone poking around in, he climbed back into the plane, relieved that he had not gotten into trouble. He managed to find his way back to his home airport as well, before he ran out of gas. He maintained, however, that he was certain that more than a few small-plane crashes have occurred because other amateur pilots who did not want to admit they were lost were less lucky. In light of this, the amusing question of why men prefer not to stop and ask for directions stops being funny.

The moral of the story is not that men should immediately change and train themselves to ask directions when they're in doubt, any more than women should immediately stop asking directions and start honing their navigational skills by finding their way on their own. The moral is flexibility: Sticking to habit in the face of all challenges is not so smart if it ends up getting you killed. If we all understood our own styles and knew their limits and their alternatives, we'd be better off—especially at work, where the results of what we do have repercussions for co-workers and the company, as well as for our own futures.

## To Ask or Not to Ask

An intern on duty at a hospital had a decision to make. A patient had been admitted with a condition he recognized, and he recalled the appropriate medication. But that medication was recommended for a number of conditions, in different dosages. He wasn't quite sure what dose was right for this condition. He had to make a quick decision: Would he interrupt the supervising resident during a meeting to check the dose, or would he make his best guess and go for it?

What was at stake? First and foremost, the welfare, and maybe even the life, of the patient. But something else was at stake too—the reputation, and eventually the career, of the intern. If he interrupted the resident to ask about the dosage, he was making a public statement about what he didn't know, as well as making himself something of a nuisance. In this case, he went with his guess, and there were no negative effects. But, as with small-plane crashes, one wonders how many medical errors have resulted from decisions to guess rather than ask.

It is clear that not asking questions can have disastrous consequences in medical settings, but asking questions can also have negative consequences. A physician wrote to me about a related experience that occurred during her medical training. She received a low grade from her supervising physician. It took her by surprise because she knew that she was one of the best interns in her group. She asked her supervisor for an explanation, and he replied that she didn't know as much as the others. She knew from her day-to-day dealings with her peers that she was one of the most knowledgeable, not the least. So she asked what evidence had led him to his conclusion. And he told her, "You ask more questions."

There is evidence that men are less likely to ask questions in a public situation, where asking will reveal their lack of knowledge. One such piece of evidence is a study done in a university classroom, where sociolinguist Kate Remlinger noticed that women students asked the professor more questions than men students did. As part of her study, Remlinger interviewed six students at length, three men and three women. All three men told her that they would not ask questions in class if there was something they did not understand. Instead, they said they would try to find the answer later by reading the textbook, asking a friend, or, as a last resort, asking the professor in private during office hours. As one young man put it, "If it's vague to me, I usually don't ask. I'd rather go home and look it up."

Of course, this does not mean that no men will ask questions when they are in doubt, nor that all women will; the differences, as always, are a matter of likelihood and degree. As always, cultural differences play a role too. It is not unusual for American professors to admit their own ignorance when they do not know the answer to a student's question, but there are many cultures in which professors would not, and students from those cultures may judge American professors by those standards. A student from the Middle East told a professor at a California university that she had just lost all respect for one of his colleagues. The reason: She had asked a question in class, and the offending professor had replied, "I don't know offhand, but I'll find out for you."

The physician who asked her supervisor why he gave her a negative evaluation may be unusual in having been told directly what behavior led to the misjudgment of her skill. But in talking to doctors and doctors-in-training around the country, I have learned that there is nothing exceptional about her

experience, that it is common for interns and residents to conceal their ignorance by not asking questions, since those who do ask are judged less capable.
Yet it seems that many women who are more likely than men to ask questions
(just as women are more likely to stop and ask for directions when they're lost)
are unaware that they may make a negative impression at the same time that
they get information. Their antennae have not been attuned to making sure they
don't appear one-down.

This pattern runs counter to two stereotypes about male and female styles:
that men are more focused on information and that women are more sensitive.
In regard to classroom behavior, it seems that the women who ask questions
are more focused on information, whereas the men who refrain from doing so
are more focused on interaction—the impression their asking will make on others. In this situation, it is the men who are more sensitive to the impression
made on others by their behavior, although their concern is, ultimately, the effect on themselves rather than on others. And this sensitivity is likely to make
them look better in the world of work. Realizing this puts the intern's decision
in a troubling perspective. He had to choose between putting his career at risk
and putting the patient's health at risk.

It is easy to see benefits of both styles: Someone willing to ask questions
has ready access to a great deal of information—all that is known by the people she can ask. But just as men have told me that asking directions is useless
since the person you ask may not know and may give you the wrong answer,
some people feel they are more certain to get the right information if they read
it in a book, and they are learning more by finding it themselves. On the other
hand, energy may be wasted looking up information someone else has at hand,
and I have heard complaints from people who feel they were sent on wild-goose
chases by colleagues who didn't want to admit they really were not sure of what
they pretended to know.

The reluctance to say "I don't know" can have serious consequences for an
entire company—and did: On Friday, June 17, 1994, a computer problem prevented Fidelity Investments from calculating the value of 166 mutual funds.
Rather than report that the values for these funds were not available, a manager decided to report to the National Association of Securities Dealers that the
values of these funds had not changed from the day before. Unfortunately, June
17 turned out to be a bad day in the financial markets, so the values of Fidelity's
funds that were published in newspapers around the country stood out as no-
ticeably higher than those of other funds. Besides the cost and inconvenience
to brokerage firms who had to re-compute their customers' accounts, and the
injustice to investors who made decisions to buy or sell based on inaccurate information, the company was mightily embarrassed and forced to apologize
publicly. Clearly this was an instance in which it would have been preferable to
say, "We don't know."

Flexibility, again, is key. There are many situations in which it serves one
well to be self-reliant and discreet about revealing doubt or ignorance, and others in which it is wise to admit what you don't know.

# Review Questions

1. What does Tannen mean by conversational style?

2. What is the important style difference in the way men and women ask for directions or help, according to Tannen?

3. What is Tannen's hypothesis about why males avoid asking other people for directions?

4. In Tannen's perspective, what conclusions do men and women draw about each other when they display typically different approaches to asking directions?

# THREE

# Ecology and Subsistence

**E**cology is the relationship of an organism to other elements within its environmental sphere. Every species, no matter how simple or complex, fits into a larger complex ecological system; each adapts to its ecological niche unless rapid environmental alterations outstrip the organism's ability and potential to adapt successfully. An important aim of ecological studies is to show how organisms fit within particular environments. Such studies also look at the effect environments have on the shape and behavior of life forms.

Every species has adapted biologically through genetically produced variation and natural selection. For example, the bipedal (two-footed) locomotion characteristic of humans is one possible adaptation to walking on the ground. It also permitted our ancestors to carry food, tools, weapons, and almost anything else they desired, enabling them to range out from a home base and bring things back for others to share.

Biological processes have led to another important human characteristic, the development of a large and complex brain. The human brain is capable of holding an enormous inventory of information. With it, we can classify the parts of our environment and retain instructions for complex ways to deal with the things in our world. Because we can communicate our knowledge symbolically through language, we are able to teach one another. Instead of a genetic code that directs behavior automatically, we operate with a learned cultural code. Culture gives us the ability to behave in a much wider variety of ways and to change rapidly in new situations. With culture, people have been able to live successfully in almost every part of the world.

**Cultural ecology** is the way people use their culture to adapt to particular environments. All people live in a **physical environment,** the world they can experience through their senses, but they will conceive of it in terms that seem most important to their adaptive needs and cultural perspective. We call this perspective the **cultural environment.**

All human societies must provide for the material needs of their members. People everywhere have to eat, clothe themselves, provide shelter against the elements, and take care of social requirements such as hospitality, gift giving, and proper dress.

Societies employ several different strategies to meet their material needs, strategies that affect their complexity and internal organization as well as relationships to the natural environment and to other human groups. Anthropologists often use these **subsistence strategies** to classify different groups into five types: hunter-gatherers, horticulturalists, pastoralists, agriculturalists, and industrialists. Let us look briefly at each of these.

People who rely on **hunting and gathering** depend on wild plants and animals for subsistence. Hunter-gatherers forage for food, moving to different parts of their territories as supplies of plants, animals, and water grow scarce. They live in small bands of from 10 to 50 people and are typically egalitarian, leading a life marked by sharing and cooperation. Because hunter-gatherer bands are so small, they tend to lack formal political, legal, and religious structure, although members have regular ways to make group decisions, settle disputes, and deal ritually with the questions of death, adversity, social value, and world identification.

Hunter-gatherers tend to see themselves as part of the environment, not masters of it. This view shapes a religious ritual aimed at the maintenance and restoration of environmental harmony. All people lived as hunter-gatherers until about 10,000 years ago, when the first human groups began to farm and dwell in more permanent settlements. Today few hunter-gatherers survive. Most have lost their habitats to more powerful groups bent on economic and political exploitation.

**Horticulture** represents the earliest farming strategy, one that continues on a diminishing basis among many groups today. Horticulturalists garden. They often use a technique called **slash-and-burn agriculture,** which requires them to clear and burn over wild land and, with the aid of a digging stick, sow seeds in the ashes. When fields lose their fertility after a few years, they are abandoned and new land is cleared. Although horticulturalists farm, they often continue to forage for wild foods and still feel closely related to the natural environment.

Horticulture requires a substantial amount of undeveloped land, so overall population densities must remain fairly low. But the strategy permits higher population densities than hunting and gathering, so horticulturalists tend to live in larger permanent settlements numbering from 50 to 250 individuals. (Some horticultural societies have produced chiefdomships with much larger administrative and religious town centers.) Although they are still small by our standards, horticultural communities are large enough to require more complex organizational strategies. They often display more elaborate kinship systems based on descent, political structures that include headmen or chiefs, political alliances, religions characterized by belief in a variety of supernatural beings, and the beginnings of social inequality. Many of today's so-called tribal peoples are horticulturalists.

**Pastoralism** is a subsistence strategy based on the herding of domesticated animals such as cattle, goats, sheep, and camels. Although herding strategies vary from one environment to another, pastoralists share some general attributes. They move on a regular basis during the year to take advantage of fresh sources of water and fodder for their animals. They usually congregate in large encampments for part of the year when food and water are plentiful, then divide into smaller groups when these resources become scarce. Pastoralists often display a strong sense of group identity and pride, a fierce independence, and skill at war and raiding. Despite attempts by modern governments to place them in permanent settlements, many pastoral groups in Africa and Asia continue their nomadic lifestyle.

**Agriculture** is still a common subsistence strategy in many parts of the world. Agriculture refers to a kind of farming based on the intensive cultivation of permanent land holdings. Agriculturalists usually use plows and organic fertilizers and may irrigate their fields in dry conditions.

Agrarian societies are marked by a high degree of social complexity. They are often organized as nation-states with armies and bureaucracies, social stratification, markets, extended families and kin groups, and some occupational specialization. Religion takes on a formal structure and is organized as a separate institution.

The term **industrialism** labels the final kind of subsistence strategy. Ours is an industrial society, as is much of the Western, and more recently, the Asian world. Industrial nations are highly complex; they display an extensive variety of subgroups and social statuses. Industrial societies tend to be dominated by market economies in which goods and services are exchanged on the basis of price, supply, and demand. There is a high degree of economic specialization, and mass marketing may lead to a depersonalization of human relations. Religious, legal, political, and economic systems find expression as separate institutions in a way that might look disjointed to hunter-gatherers or others from smaller, more integrated societies.

The study of cultural ecology involves more than an understanding of people's basic subsistence strategies. Each society exists in a distinctive environment. Although a group may share many subsistence methods with other societies, there are always special environmental needs that shape productive techniques. Andean farmers, for example, have developed approximately 3,000 varieties of potatoes to meet the demands of growing conditions at different elevations in their mountain habitat. Bhil farmers in India have learned to create fields by damming up small streams in their rugged Aravalli hill villages. Otherwise, they would find it difficult to cultivate there at all. American farmers learned to "contour-plow" parallel to slopes in response to water erosion and now increasingly use plowless (no-till) farming to prevent the wind from carrying away precious topsoil.

No matter how successful their microenvironmental adjustments are, most groups in the world now face more serious adaptive challenges. One difficulty is the exploitation of their lands by outsiders, who are often unconstrained by adaptive necessity. A second is the need to overexploit the environment to meet market demand (see Part Four for articles on market pressures). In either case, many local peoples find that their traditional subsistence techniques no longer work. They have lost control of their own environmental adjustment and must struggle to adapt to outsiders and what is left of their habitat.

Finally, just as humans adapt culturally to their environments, altering them in the process, environments may biologically adapt to humans. For example, intensive agriculture in the United States provides greater food sources for deer. In response, the number of deer has risen by as much as 400 percent. Animals domesticated by humans, such as cows, pigs, chickens, sheep, goats, dogs, and cats, have also experienced both genetic modification and increased numbers from their association with people. Less obviously, microbes have evolved to take advantage of the growing human presence. Some subsist on human wastes; others, including many that cause epidemic diseases, have evolved to subsist on people themselves.

The !Kung, described by Richard Lee in the first selection, provide an excellent example of a traditional foraging lifestyle. The update to this article by Richard Lee and Megan Biesele show that the same bands of people who once lived on wild foods in the Kalahari now find themselves confined to small government-mandated settlements. Cattle herders tend their animals on the desert lands once occupied by the !Kung. The second article, by Jared Diamond, describes the fate of Easter Islanders who overexploited their small island ecosystem. The example serves as a warning to people everywhere as populations grow and resources diminish. The third updated selection, by Richard Reed, is a sobering reminder of what can happen to a horticultural people who once subsisted in harmony with their tropical forest habitat, but who now find themselves being displaced by colonists. These outsiders have stripped the forest bare. Finally, the fourth article, by Jared Diamond, describes the evolution of crowd diseases among human beings. Evolving as new illnesses from microbe strains carried by herd animals, they decimated the Indians of the Americas and continue to trouble people today.

# Key Terms

agriculture   *p. 107*

cultural ecology   *p. 105*

cultural environment   *p. 106*

ecology   *p. 105*

horticulture   *p. 106*

hunting and gathering   *p. 106*

industrialism   *p. 107*

pastoralism   *p. 107*

physical environment   *p. 105*

slash-and-burn agriculture   *p. 106*

subsistence strategies   *p. 106*

# 11

# The Hunters: Scarce Resources in the Kalahari

*Richard Borshay Lee*

*Until about 10,000 years ago, everyone in the world survived by hunting and gathering wild foods. They lived in intimate association with their natural environments and employed a complex variety of strategies to forage for food and other necessities of life. Agriculture displaced foraging as the main subsistence technique over the next few thousand years, but some hunter-gatherers lived on in the more remote parts of the world. This study by Richard Lee was done in the early 1960s and describes the important features of one of the last foraging groups, the Ju/'hoansi-!Kung living in the Kalahari Desert. It argues against the idea, held by many anthropologists at that time, that hunter-gatherers live a precarious, hand-to-mouth existence. Instead,*

*Lee found that the !Kung, depending more on vegetable foods than meat, actually spent little time collecting food and managed to live long and fruitful lives in their difficult desert home. The update by Lee and Megan Biesele that appears at the end of the article details the events that have led the !Kung to settle down permanently to life as small-scale farmers and cattle raisers.*

The current anthropological view of hunter-gatherer subsistence rests on two questionable assumptions. First is the notion that these people are primarily dependent on the hunting of game animals, and second is the assumption that their way of life is generally a precarious and arduous struggle for existence.

Recent data on living hunter-gatherers show a radically different picture. We have learned that in many societies, plant and marine resources are far more important than are game animals in the diet. More important, it is becoming clear that, with few conspicuous exceptions, the hunter-gatherer subsistence base is at least routine and reliable and at best surprisingly abundant. Anthropologists have consistently tended to underestimate the viability of even those "marginal isolates" of hunting peoples that have been available to ethnographers.

The purpose of this paper is to analyze the food-getting activities of one such "marginal" people, the !Kung Bushmen of the Kalahari Desert. Three related questions are posed: How do the Bushmen make a living? How easy or difficult is it for them to do this? What kinds of evidence are necessary to measure and evaluate the precariousness or security of a way of life? And after the relevant data are presented, two further questions are asked: What makes this security of life possible? To what extent are the Bushmen typical of hunter-gatherers in general?

## Bushman Subsistence

The !Kung Bushmen of Botswana are an apt case for analysis. They inhabit the semi-arid northwest region of the Kalahari Desert. With only six to nine inches of rainfall per year, this is, by any account, a marginal environment for human habitation. In fact, it is precisely the unattractiveness of their homeland that has kept the !Kung isolated from extensive contact with their agricultural and pastoral neighbors.

Fieldwork was carried out in the Dobe area, a line of eight permanent waterholes near the South-West Africa border and 125 miles south of the Okavango River. The population of the Dobe area consists of 466 Bushmen, including 379 permanent residents living in independent camps or associated with Bantu cattle posts, as well as 87 seasonal visitors. The Bushmen share the area with some 340 Bantu pastoralists largely of the Herero and Tswana tribes. The ethnographic present refers to the period of fieldwork: October 1963 to January 1965.

The Bushmen living in independent camps lack firearms, livestock, and agriculture. Apart from occasional visits to the Herero for milk, these !Kung are entirely dependent upon hunting and gathering for their subsistence. Politically they are under the nominal authority of the Tswana headman, although they pay no taxes and receive very few government services. European presence amounts to one overnight government patrol every six to eight weeks. Although Dobe-area !Kung have had some contact with outsiders since the 1880s, the majority of them continue to hunt and gather because there is no viable alternative locally available to them.

Each of the fourteen independent camps is associated with one of the permanent waterholes. During the dry season (May–October) the entire population is clustered around these wells. Table 1 shows the numbers at each well at the end of the 1964 dry season. Two wells had no camp residents and one large well supported five camps. The number of camps at each well and the size of each camp changed frequently during the course of the year. The "camp" is an open aggregate of cooperating persons which changes in size and composition from day to day. Therefore, I have avoided the term "band" in describing the !Kung Bushman living groups.

Each waterhole has a hinterland lying within a six-mile radius that is regularly exploited for vegetable and animal foods. These areas are not territories in the zoological sense, since they are not defended against outsiders. Rather, they constitute the resources that lie within a convenient walking distance of a waterhole. The camp is a self-sufficient subsistence unit. The members move out each day to hunt and gather, and return in the evening to pool the collected foods in such a way that every person present receives an equitable share. Trade in foodstuffs between camps is minimal; personnel do move freely from camp to camp, however. The net effect is of a population constantly in motion. On the

**TABLE 1    Numbers and Distribution of Resident Bushmen and Bantu by Waterhole\***

| Name of Waterhole | No. of Camps | Population of Camps | Other Bushmen | Total Bushmen | Bantu |
|---|---|---|---|---|---|
| Dobe | 2 | 37 | — | 37 | — |
| !angwa | 1 | 16 | 23 | 39 | 84 |
| Bate | 2 | 30 | 12 | 42 | 21 |
| !ubi | 1 | 19 | — | 19 | 65 |
| !gose | 3 | 52 | 9 | 61 | 18 |
| /ai/ai | 5 | 94 | 13 | 107 | 67 |
| !xabe | — | — | 8 | 8 | 12 |
| Mahopa | — | — | 23 | 23 | 73 |
| Total | 14 | 248 | 88 | 336 | 340 |

\*Figures do not include 130 Bushmen outside area on the date of census.

average, an individual spends a third of his time living only with close relatives, a third visiting other camps, and a third entertaining visitors from other camps.

Because of the strong emphasis on sharing, and the frequency of movement, surplus accumulation of storable plant foods and dried meat is kept to a minimum. There is rarely more than two or three days' supply of food on hand in a camp at any time. The result of this lack of surplus is that a constant subsistence effort must be maintained throughout the year. Unlike agriculturalists, who work hard during the planting and harvesting seasons and undergo "seasonal unemployment" for several months, the Bushmen hunter-gatherers collect food every third or fourth day throughout the year.

Vegetable foods comprise from 60 to 80 percent of the total diet by weight, and collecting involves two or three days of work per woman per week. The men also collect plants and small animals, but their major contribution to the diet is the hunting of medium and large game. The men are conscientious but not particularly successful hunters; although men's and women's work input is roughly equivalent in terms of man-day of effort, the women provide two to three times as much food by weight as the men.

Table 2 summarizes the seasonal activity cycle observed among the Dobe-area !Kung in 1964. For the greater part of the year, food is locally abundant and easily collected. It is only during the end of the dry season in September and October, when desirable foods have been eaten out in the immediate vicinity of the waterholes, that the people have to plan longer hikes of 10 to 15 miles and carry their own water to those areas where the mongongo nut is still available. The important point is that food is a constant, but distance required to reach food is a variable; it is short in the summer, fall, and early winter, and reaches its maximum in the spring.

This analysis attempts to provide quantitative measures of subsistence status, including data on the following topics: abundance and variety of resources, diet selectivity, range size and population density, the composition of the work force, the ratio of work to leisure time, and the caloric and protein levels in the diet. The value of quantitative data is that they can be used comparatively and also may be useful in archeological reconstruction. In addition, one can avoid the pitfalls of subjective and qualitative impressions; for example, statements about food "anxiety" have proven to be difficult to generalize across cultures.

## Abundance and Variety of Resources

It is impossible to define "abundance" of resources absolutely. However, one index of *relative* abundance is whether or not a population exhausts all the food available from a given area. By this criterion, the habitat of the Dobe-area Bushmen is abundant in naturally occurring foods. By far the most important food is the mongongo (mangetti) nut (*Ricinodendron rautanenii* Schinz). Although tens of thousands of pounds of these nuts are harvested and eaten each year, thousands more rot on the ground each year for want of picking.

**TABLE 2  The Bushman Annual Round**

| | Jan. | Feb. | Mar. | April | May | June | July | Aug. | Sept | Oct. | Nov. | Dec. |
|---|---|---|---|---|---|---|---|---|---|---|---|---|
| *Season* | Summer Rains | | | Autumn Dry | | Winter Dry | | | Spring Dry | | | First Rains |
| Availability of water | Temporary summer pools everywhere | | | Large summer pools | | | Permanent waterholes only | | | | | Summer pools developing |
| Group moves | Widely dispersed at summer pools | | | At large summer pools | | | All population restricted to permanent waterholes | | | | | Moving out to summer pools |
| Men's subsistence activities | 1. Hunting with bow, arrows, and dogs (year-round) 2. Running down immatures 3. Some gathering (year-round) | | | | | Trapping small game in snares | | | | Running down newborn animals | | |
| Women's subsistence activities | 1. Gathering of mongongo nuts (year-round) 2. Fruits, berries, melons | | | | | Roots, bulbs, resins | | | | Roots, leafy greens | | |
| Ritual activities | Dancing, trance performances, and ritual curing (year-round) | | | | Boys' initiation* | | | | | | | † |
| Relative subsistence hardship | | | Water-food distance minimal | | | Increasing distance from water to food | | | | Water-food distance minimal | | |

*Held once every five years; none in 1963–64.

†New Year's: Bushmen join the celebrations of their missionized Bantu neighbors.

113

The mongongo nut, because of its abundance and reliability, alone accounts for 50 percent of the vegetable diet by weight. In this respect it resembles a cultivated staple crop such as maize or rice. Nutritionally it is even more remarkable, for it contains five times the calories and ten times the protein per cooked unit of the cereal crops. The average daily per capita consumption of 300 nuts yields about 1,260 calories and 56 grams of protein. This modest portion, weighing only about 7.5 ounces, contains the caloric equivalent of 2.5 pounds of cooked rice and the protein equivalent of 14 ounces of lean beef.

Furthermore, the mongongo nut is drought resistant, and it will still be abundant in the dry years when cultivated crops may fail. The extremely hard outer shell protects the inner kernel from rot and allows the nuts to be harvested for up to twelve months after they have fallen to the ground. A diet based on mongongo nuts is in fact more reliable than one based on cultivated foods, and it is not surprising, therefore, that when a Bushman was asked why he hadn't taken to agriculture, he replied: "Why should we plant, when there are so many mongongo nuts in the world?"

Apart from the mongongo, the Bushmen have available eighty-four other species of edible food plants, including twenty-nine species of fruits, berries, and melons and thirty species of roots and bulbs. The existence of this variety allows for a wide range of alternatives in subsistence strategy. During the summer months the Bushmen have no problem other than to choose among the tastiest and most easily collected foods. Many species, which are quite edible but less attractive, are bypassed, so that gathering never exhausts *all* the available plant foods of an area. During the dry season the diet becomes much more eclectic and the many species of roots, bulbs, and edible resins make an important contribution. It is this broad base that provides an essential margin of safety during the end of the dry season, when the mongongo nut forests are difficult to reach. In addition, it is likely that these rarely utilized species provide important nutritional and mineral trace elements that may be lacking in the more popular foods.

## Diet Selectivity

If the Bushmen were living close to the "starvation" level, then one would expect them to exploit every available source of nutrition. That their life is well above this level is indicated by the data in Table 3. Here all the edible plant species are arranged in classes according to the frequency with which they were observed to be eaten. It should be noted that although there are some eighty-five species available, about 90 percent of the vegetable diet by weight is drawn from only twenty-three species. In other words, 75 percent of the listed species provide only 10 percent of the food value.

In their meat-eating habits, the Bushmen show a similar selectivity. Of the 223 local species of animals known and named by the Bushmen, 54 species are classified as edible, and of these only 17 species were hunted on a regular basis. Only a handful of the dozens of edible species of small mammals, birds, reptiles,

**TABLE 3  !Kung Bushman Plant Foods**

| Food Class | Part Eaten | | | | | | | | Total Number of Species in Class | Totals (percentages) | |
|---|---|---|---|---|---|---|---|---|---|---|---|
| | Fruit and Nut | Bean and Root | Fruit and Stalk | Root, Bulb | Fruit, Berry, Melon | Resin | Leaves | Seed, Bean | | Estimated Contribution by Weight to Vegetable Diet | Estimated Contribution of Each Species |
| I. Primary<br>Eaten daily throughout year (mongongo nut) | 1 | — | — | — | — | — | — | — | 1 | c.50 | c.50* |
| II. Major<br>Eaten daily in season | 1 | 1 | 1 | 1 | 4 | — | — | — | 8 | c.25 | c.3† |
| III. Minor<br>Eaten several times per week in season | — | — | — | 7 | 3 | 2 | 2 | — | 14 | c.15 | c.1 |
| IV. Supplementary<br>Eaten when classes I–III locally unavailable | — | — | — | 9 | 12 | 10 | 1 | — | 32 | c.7 | c.0.2 |
| V. Rare<br>Eaten several times per year | — | — | — | 9 | 4 | — | — | — | 13 | c.3 | c.0.1‡ |
| VI. Problematic<br>Edible but not observed to be eaten | — | — | — | 4 | 6 | 4 | 1 | 2 | 17 | nil | nil |
| Total Species | 2 | 1 | 1 | 30 | 29 | 16 | 4 | 2 | 85 | 100 | — |

*1 species constitutes 50 percent of the vegetable diet by weight.
†23 species constitute 90 percent of the vegetable diet by weight.
‡62 species constitute the remaining 10 percent of the diet.

and insects that occur locally are regarded as food. Such animals as rodents, snakes, lizards, termites, and grasshoppers, which in the literature are included in the Bushman diet, are despised by the Bushmen of the Dobe area.

## Range Size and Population Density

The necessity to travel long distances, the high frequency of moves, and the maintenance of populations at low densities are also features commonly associated with the hunting and gathering way of life. Density estimates for hunters in western North America and Australia have ranged from 3 persons/square mile to as low as 1 person/100 square miles. In 1963–65, the resident and visiting Bushmen were observed to utilize an area of about 1,000 square miles during the course of the annual round for an effective population density of 41 persons/100 square miles. Within this area, however, the amount of ground covered by members of an individual camp was surprisingly small. A day's round-trip of twelve miles serves to define a "core" area six miles in radius surrounding each water point. By fanning out in all directions from their well, the members of a camp can gain access to the food resources of well over 100 square miles of territory within a two-hour hike. Except for a few weeks each year, areas lying beyond this six-mile radius are rarely utilized, even though they are no less rich in plants and game than are the core areas.

Although the Bushmen move their camps frequently (five or six times a year), they do not move them very far. A rainy season camp in the nut forests is rarely more than ten or twelve miles from the home waterhole, and often new campsites are occupied only a few hundred yards away from the previous one. By these criteria, the Bushmen do not lead a free-ranging nomadic way of life. For example, they do not undertake long marches of 30 to 100 miles to get food, since this task can be readily fulfilled within a day's walk of home base. When such long marches do occur they are invariably for visiting, trading, and marriage arrangements, and should not be confused with the normal routine of subsistence.

## Demographic Factors

Another indicator of the harshness of a way of life is the age at which people die. Ever since Hobbes characterized life in the state of nature as "nasty, brutish and short," the assumption has been that hunting and gathering is so rigorous that members of such societies are rapidly worn out and meet an early death. Silberbauer, for example, says of the Gwi Bushmen of the central Kalahari that "life expectancy . . . is difficult to calculate, but I do not believe that many live beyond 45." And Coon has said of hunters in general:

> The practice of abandoning the hopelessly ill and aged has been observed in many parts of the world. It is always done by people living in poor environments where it is necessary to move about frequently to obtain food, where food is scarce, and transportation difficult. . . . Among peoples who are forced to live in this way the

oldest generation, the generation of individuals who have passed their physical peak, is reduced in numbers and influence. There is no body of elders to hand on tradition and control the affairs of younger men and women, and no formal system of age grading.

The !Kung Bushmen of the Dobe area flatly contradict this view. In a total population of 466, no fewer than 46 individuals (17 men and 29 women) were determined to be over sixty years of age, a proportion that compares favorably to the percentage of elderly in industrialized populations.

The aged hold a respected position in Bushmen society and are the effective leaders of the camps. Senilicide is extremely rare. Long after their productive years have passed, the old people are fed and cared for by their children and grandchildren. The blind, the senile, and the crippled are respected for the special ritual and technical skills they possess. For instance, the four elders at !gose waterhole were totally or partially blind, but this handicap did not prevent their active participation in decision making and ritual curing.

Another significant feature of the composition of the work force is the late assumption of adult responsibility by the adolescents. Young people are not expected to provide food regularly until they are married. Girls typically marry between the ages of fifteen and twenty, and boys about five years later, so that it is not unusual to find healthy, active teenagers visiting from camp to camp while their older relatives provide food for them.

As a result, the people in the twenty to sixty age group support a surprisingly large percentage of nonproductive young and old people. About 40 percent of the population in camps contributes little to the food supplies. This allocation of work to young and middle-aged adults allows for a relatively carefree childhood and adolescence and a relatively unstrenuous old age.

## Leisure and Work

Another important index of ease or difficulty of subsistence is the amount of time devoted to the food quest. Hunting has usually been regarded by social scientists as a way of life in which merely keeping alive is so formidable a task that members of such societies lack the leisure time necessary to "build culture." The !Kung Bushmen would appear to conform to the rule, for as Lorna Marshall says:

> It is vividly apparent that among the !Kung Bushmen, ethos, or "the spirit which actuates manners and customs," is survival. Their time and energies are almost wholly given to this task, for life in their environment requires that they spend their days mainly in procuring food.

It is certainly true that getting food is the most important single activity in Bushman life. However, this statement would apply equally well to small-scale agricultural and pastoral societies too. How much time is *actually* devoted to the food quest is fortunately an empirical question. And an analysis of the work effort of the Dobe Bushmen shows some unexpected results. From July 6 to August 2, 1964, I recorded all the daily activities of the Bushmen living at the Dobe waterhole. Because of the coming and going of visitors, the camp population fluctuated in size day by day, from a low of 23 to a high of 40, with a mean of 31.8 persons. Each day some of the adult members of the camp went out to hunt and/or gather while others stayed home or went visiting. The daily recording of all personnel on hand made it possible to calculate the number of man-days of work as a percentage of total number of man-days of consumption.

Although the Bushmen do not organize their activities on the basis of a seven-day week, I have divided the data this way to make them more intelligible. The workweek was calculated to show how many days out of seven each adult spent in subsistence activities (Table 4, Column 7). Week II has been eliminated from the totals since the investigator contributed food. In week I, the people spent an average of 2.3 days in subsistence activities, in week II, 1.9 days, and in week IV, 3.2 days. In all, the adults of the Dobe camp worked about two and a half days a week. Since the average working day was about six hours long, the fact emerges that !Kung Bushmen of Dobe, despite their harsh environment, devote from twelve to nineteen hours a week to getting food. Even the hardest-working individual in the camp, a man named ≠oma who went out hunting on sixteen of the twenty-eight days, spent a maximum of thirty-two hours a week in the food quest.

Because the Bushmen do not amass a surplus of foods, there are no seasons of exceptionally intensive activities such as planting and harvesting, and no seasons of unemployment. The level of work observed is an accurate reflection of the effort required to meet the immediate caloric needs of the group.

**TABLE 4    Summary of Dobe Work Diary**

| Week | (1) Mean Group Size | (2) Adult- Days | (3) Child- Days | (4) Total Man- Days of Consumption | (5) Man- Days of Work | (6) Meat (lbs.) | (7) Average Workweek /Adult | (8) Index of Subsistence Effort |
|------|------|------|------|------|------|------|------|------|
| I (July 6–12) | 25.6 (23–29) | 114 | 65 | 179 | 37 | 104 | 2.3 | .21 |
| II (July 13–19) | 28.3 (23–27) | 125 | 73 | 198 | 22 | 80 | 1.2 | .11 |
| III (July 20–26) | 34.3 (29–40) | 156 | 84 | 240 | 42 | 177 | 1.9 | .18 |
| IV (July 27–Aug. 2) | 35.6 (32–40) | 167 | 82 | 249 | 77 | 129 | 3.2 | .31 |
| 4-wk. total | 30.9 | 562 | 304 | 866 | 178 | 490 | 2.2 | .21 |
| Adjusted total* | 31.8 | 437 | 231 | 668 | 156 | 410 | 2.5 | .23 |

*See text

Key: Column 1: Mean group size = $\dfrac{\text{total man-days of consumption}}{7}$.

Column 7: Workweek = the number of workdays per adult per week.

Column 8: Index of subsistence effort = $\dfrac{\text{man-days of work}}{\text{man-days of consumption}}$ (e.g., in Week I, the value of "S" = 21,

i.e., 21 days of work/100 days of consumption or 1 workday produces food for 5 consumption days).

This work diary covers the midwinter dry season, a period when food is neither at its most plentiful nor at its scarcest levels, and the diary documents the transition from better to worse conditions (see Table 2). During the fourth week the gatherers were making overnight trips to camps in the mongongo nut forests seven to ten miles distant from the waterhole. These longer trips account for the rise in the level of work, from twelve or thirteen to nineteen hours per week.

If food getting occupies such a small proportion of a Bushman's waking hours, then how *do* people allocate their time? A woman gathers on one day enough food to feed her family for three days, and spends the rest of her time resting in camp, doing embroidery, visiting other camps, or entertaining visitors from other camps. For each day at home, kitchen routines, such as cooking, nut cracking, collecting firewood, and fetching water, occupy one to three hours of her time. This rhythm of steady work and steady leisure is maintained throughout the year.

The hunters tend to work more frequently than the women, but their schedule is uneven. It is not unusual for a man to hunt avidly for a week and then do nothing at all for two or three weeks. Since hunting is an unpredictable business and subject to magical control, hunters sometimes experience a run of bad luck and stop hunting for a month or longer. During these periods, visiting, entertaining, and especially dancing are the primary activities of men. (Unlike the Hadza, gambling is only a minor leisure activity.)

The trance dance is the focus of Bushman ritual life; over 50 percent of the men have trained as trance-performers and regularly enter trance during the course of the all-night dances. At some camps, trance dances occur as frequently as two or three times a week, and those who have entered trances the night before rarely go out hunting the following day. . . . In a camp with five or more hunters, there are usually two or three who are actively hunting and several others who are inactive. The net effect is to phase the hunting and non-hunting so that a fairly steady supply of meat is brought into camp.

## Caloric Returns

Is the modest work effort of the Bushmen sufficient to provide the calories necessary to maintain the health of the population? Or have the !Kung, in common with some agricultural peoples, adjusted to a permanently substandard nutritional level?

During my fieldwork I did not encounter any cases of kwashiorkor, the most common nutritional disease in the children of African agricultural societies. However, without medical examinations, it is impossible to exclude the possibility that subclinical signs of malnutrition existed.

Another measure of nutritional adequacy is the average consumption of calories and proteins per person per day. The estimate for the Bushmen is based on observations of the weights of foods of known composition that were brought into Dobe camp on each day of the study period. The per-capita figure is obtained by dividing the total weight of foodstuffs by the total number of persons in the camp. These results are set out in detail elsewhere and can only be summarized

**TABLE 5    Caloric and Protein Levels in the !Kung Bushman Diet, July–August, 1964**

| | *Per-Capita Consumption* | | | | |
|---|---|---|---|---|---|
| *Class of Food* | *Percentage Contribution to Diet by Weight* | *Weight in Grams* | *Protein in Grams* | *Calories per Person per Day* | *Percentage Caloric Contribution of Meat and Vegetables* |
| Meat | 37 | 230 | 34.5 | 690 | 33 |
| Mongongo nuts | 33 | 210 | 56.7 | 1,260 | 67 |
| Other vegetable foods | 30 | 190 | 1.9 | 190 | |
| Total all sources | 100 | 630 | 93.1 | 2,140 | 100 |

here. During the study period 410 pounds of meat were brought in by the hunters of the Dobe camp, for a daily share of nine ounces of meat per person. About 700 pounds of vegetables were gathered and consumed during the same period. Table 5 sets out the calories and proteins available per capita in the !Kung Bushman diet from meat, mongongo nuts, and other vegetable sources.

This output of 2,140 calories and 93.1 grams of protein per person per day may be compared with the Recommended Daily Allowances (RDA) for persons of the small size and stature but vigorous activity regime of the !Kung Bushmen. The RDA for Bushmen can be estimated at 1,975 calories and 60 grams of protein per person per day. Thus it is apparent that food output exceeds energy requirements by 165 calories and 33 grams of protein. One can tentatively conclude that even a modest subsistence effort of two or three days' work per week is enough to provide an adequate diet for the !Kung Bushmen.

## The Security of Bushman Life

I have attempted to evaluate the subsistence base of one contemporary hunter-gatherer society living in a marginal environment. The !Kung Bushmen have available to them some relatively abundant high-quality foods, and they do not have to walk very far or work very hard to get them. Furthermore, this modest work effort provides sufficient calories to support not only active adults, but also a large number of middle-aged and elderly people. The Bushmen do not have to press their youngsters into the service of the food quest, nor do they have to dispose of the oldsters after they have ceased to be productive.

The evidence presented assumes an added significance because this security of life was observed during the third year of one of the most severe droughts in South Africa's history. Most of the 576,000 people of Botswana are pastoralists and agriculturalists. After the crops had failed three years in succession and over 100,000 head of cattle had died on the range for lack of water, the World Food Program of the United Nations instituted a famine relief program which has grown to include 180,000 people, over 30 percent of the population. This program did not touch the Dobe area in the isolated northwest corner of the country, and the Herero and Tswana women there were able to feed their families only by joining the Bushman women to forage for wild foods. Thus the natural plant resources of the Dobe area were carrying a higher proportion of population than would be the case in years when the Bantu harvested crops. Yet this added pressure on the land did not seem to adversely affect the Bushmen.

In one sense it was unfortunate that the period of my fieldwork happened to coincide with the drought, since I was unable to witness a "typical" annual subsistence cycle. However, in another sense, the coincidence was a lucky one, for the drought put the Bushmen and their subsistence system to the acid test and, in terms of adaptation to scarce resources, they passed with flying colors. One can postulate that their subsistence base would be even more substantial during years of higher rainfall.

What are the crucial factors that make this way of life possible? I suggest that the primary factor is the Bushmen's strong emphasis on vegetable food sources. Although hunting involves a great deal of effort and prestige, plant foods provide from 60 to 80 percent of the annual diet by weight. Meat has come to be regarded as a special treat; when available, it is welcomed as a break from the routine of vegetable foods, but it is never depended upon as a staple. No one ever goes hungry when hunting fails.

The reason for this emphasis is not hard to find. Vegetable foods are abundant, sedentary, and predictable. They grow in the same place year after year, and the gatherer is guaranteed a day's return of food for a day's expenditure of energy. Game animals, by contrast, are scarce, mobile, unpredictable, and difficult to catch. A hunter has no guarantee of success and may in fact go for days or weeks without killing a large mammal. During the study period, there were eleven men in the Dobe camp, of whom four did no hunting at all. The seven active men spent a total of 78 man-days hunting, and this work input yielded eighteen animals killed, or one kill for every four man-days of hunting. The probability of any one hunter making a kill on a given day was 0.23. By contrast, the probability of a woman finding plant food on a given day was 1.00. In other words, hunting and gathering are not equally felicitous subsistence alternatives.

Consider the productivity per man-hour of the two kinds of subsistence activities. One man-hour of hunting produces about 100 edible calories, and of gathering, 240 calories. Gathering is thus seen to be 2.4 times more productive than hunting. In short, hunting is a *high-risk, low-return* subsistence activity, while gathering is a *low-risk, high-return* subsistence activity.

It is not at all contradictory that the hunting complex holds a central place in the Bushmen ethos and that meat is valued more highly than vegetable foods. Analogously, steak is valued more highly than potatoes in the food preferences of our own society. In both situations the meat is more "costly" than the vegetable food. In the Bushman case, the cost of food can be measured in terms of time and energy expended. By this standard, 1,000 calories of meat "costs" ten man-hours, while the "cost" of 1,000 calories of vegetable foods is only four man-hours. Further, it is to be expected that the less predictable, more expensive food source would have a greater accretion of myth and ritual built up around it than would the routine staples of life, which rarely if ever fail.

## Conclusions

Three points ought to be stressed. First, life in the state of nature is not necessarily nasty, brutish, and short. The Dobe-area Bushmen live well today on wild plants and meat, in spite of the fact that they are confined to the least productive portion of the range in which Bushman peoples were formerly found. It is likely that an even more substantial subsistence would have been characteristic of these hunters and gatherers in the past, when they had the pick of African habitats to choose from.

Second, the basis of Bushman diet is derived from sources other than meat. This emphasis makes good ecological sense to the !Kung Bushmen and appears to be a common feature among hunters and gatherers in general. Since a 30 to 40 percent input of meat is such a consistent target for modern hunters in a variety of habitats, is it not reasonable to postulate a similar percentage for prehistoric hunters? Certainly the absence of plant remains on archeological sites is by itself not sufficient evidence for the absence of gathering. Recently abandoned Bushman campsites show a similar absence of vegetable remains, although this paper has clearly shown that plant foods comprise over 60 percent of the actual diet.

Finally, one gets the impression that hunting societies have been chosen by ethnologists to illustrate a dominant theme, such as the extreme importance of environment in the molding of certain cultures. Such a theme can best be exemplified by cases in which the technology is simple and/or the environment is harsh. This emphasis on the dramatic may have been pedagogically useful, but unfortunately it has led to the assumption that a precarious hunting subsistence base was characteristic of all cultures in the Pleistocene. This view of both modern and ancient hunters ought to be reconsidered. Specifically I am suggesting a shift in focus away from the dramatic and unusual cases, and toward a consideration of hunting and gathering as a persistent and well-adapted way of life.

## Epilogue: The Ju/'hoansi in 1994[1]

In 1963 perhaps three-quarters of the Dobe Ju/'hoansi were living in camps based primarily on hunting and gathering while the rest were attached to Black cattle posts. Back then there had been no trading stores, schools, or clinics, no government feeding programs, boreholes, or airstrips, and no resident civil servants (apart from the tribally-appointed headman, his clerk, and constable). By

[1] Excerpted from "A Local Culture in the Global System: The Ju/'hoansi-!Kung Today," Richard B. Lee and Megan Biesele, *General Anthropology*, 1:1, Fall 1994, pp. 1, 3–5.

1994 all these institutions and facilities were in place and the Dobe people were well into their third decade of rapid social change; they had been transformed in a generation from a society of foragers, some of whom herded and worked for others, to a society of small-holders who eked out a living by herding, farming, and craft production, along with some hunting and gathering.

Ju villages today look like others in Botswana. The beehive-shaped grass huts are gone, replaced by semi-permanent mud-walled houses behind makeshift stockades to keep out cattle. Villages ceased to be circular and tight-knit. Twenty-five people who lived in a space twenty by twenty meters now spread themselves out in a line village several hundred meters long. Instead of looking across the central open space at each other, the houses face the kraal where cattle and goats are kept, inscribing spatially a symbolic shift from reliance on each other to reliance on property in the form of herds.

Hunting and gathering, which provided Dobe Ju with over 85 percent of their subsistence as recently as 1964, now supplies perhaps 30 percent of their food. The rest is made up of milk and meat from domestic stock, store-bought mealie (corn) meal, and vast quantities of heavily-sugared tea whitened with powdered milk. Game meat and foraged foods and occasional produce from gardens makes up the rest of the diet. However, for most of the 1980s government and foreign drought relief provided the bulk of the diet. . . .

In the long run, Dobe-area Ju/'hoansi face serious difficulties. Since 1975, wealthy Tswana have formed borehole syndicates to stake out ranches in remote areas. With 99-year leases, which can be bought and sold, ownership is tantamount to private tenure. By the late 1980s borehole drilling was approaching the Dobe area. If the Dobe Ju do not form borehole syndicates soon, with overseas help, their traditional foraging areas may be permanently cut off from them by commercial ranching.

# Review Questions

1. How does Lee assess the day-to-day quality of !Kung life when they lived as foragers? How does this view compare with that held by many anthropologists in the early 1960s?

2. What evidence does Lee give to support his view about the !Kung?

3. According to Lee, !Kung children are not expected to work until after they are married; old people are supported and respected. How does this arrangement differ from behavior in our own society, and what might explain the difference?

4. What was a key to successful subsistence for the !Kung and other hunter-gatherers, according to Lee?

5. In what ways has life changed for the !Kung since 1964? What has caused these changes?

# 12

# Adaptive Failure: Easter's End

**Jared Diamond**

*Customs can often be explained as human responses to material necessity. But people may not always adapt successfully, as Jared Diamond shows in this discussion of the rise and fall of Easter Island civilization. Basing his conclusions on recent archaeological excavations, he notes that in A.D. 400, when the Polynesian ancestors of today's Easter Island population arrived on the island, they found a heavily forested and fertile land. Within a few hundred years the islanders numbered between 7,000 to 20,000 and lived in a politically complex, prosperous society. By the 1400s, however, the forest was destroyed, making it impossible for people to build ocean-going canoes or continue the manufacture of stone heads, for which the island later became famous. Bird and sea mammal populations, once a major source of food, had also been decimated. Political chaos ensued and islanders turned to cannibalism as a dietary supplement. Diamond concludes that Easter Island civilization declined because environmental destruction occurred slowly and because social concerns took precedence over conservation. In this sense, the island's fate serves as a warning about humanity's future in a highly stressed world environment.*

Among the most riveting mysteries of human history are those posed by vanished civilizations. Everyone who has seen the abandoned buildings of the Khmer, the Maya, or the Anasazi is immediately moved to ask the same question: Why did the societies that erected those structures disappear?

Their vanishing touches us as the disappearance of other animals, even the dinosaurs, never can. No matter how exotic those lost civilizations seem, their framers were humans like us. Who is to say we won't succumb to the same fate? Perhaps someday New York's skyscrapers will stand derelict and overgrown with vegetation, like the temples at Angkor Wat and Tikal.

Among all such vanished civilizations, that of the former Polynesian society on Easter Island remains unsurpassed in mystery and isolation. The mystery stems especially from the island's gigantic stone statues and its impoverished landscape, but it is enhanced by our associations with the specific people involved: Polynesians represent for us the ultimate in exotic romance, the background for many a child's, and an adult's, vision of paradise. My own interest in Easter was kindled over 30 years ago when I read Thor Heyerdahl's fabulous accounts of his *Kon-Tiki* voyage.

But my interest has been revived recently by a much more exciting account, one not of heroic voyages but of painstaking research and analysis. My friend David Steadman, a paleontologist, has been working with a number of other researchers who are carrying out the first systematic excavations on Easter intended to identify the animals and plants that once lived there. Their work is contributing to a new interpretation of the island's history that makes it a tale not only of wonder but of warning as well.

Easter Island, with an area of only 64 square miles, is the world's most isolated scrap of habitable land. It lies in the Pacific Ocean more than 2,000 miles west of the nearest continent (South America), 1,400 miles from even the nearest habitable island (Pitcairn). Its subtropical location and latitude—at 27 degrees south, it is approximately as far below the equator as Houston is north of it—help give it a rather mild climate, while its volcanic origins make its soil fertile. In theory, this combination of blessings should have made Easter a miniature paradise, remote from problems that beset the rest of the world.

The island derives its name from its "discovery" by the Dutch explorer Jacob Roggeveen, on Easter (April 5) in 1722. Roggeveen's first impression was not of a paradise but of a wasteland: "We originally, from a further distance, have considered the said Easter Island as sandy; the reason for that is this, that we counted as sand the withered grass, hay, or other scorched and burnt vegetation, because its wasted appearance could give no other impression than of a singular poverty and barrenness."

The island Roggeveen saw was a grassland without a single tree or bush over ten feet high. Modern botanists have identified only 47 species of higher plants native to Easter, most of them grasses, sedges, and ferns. The list includes just two species of small trees and two of woody shrubs. With such flora, the islanders Roggeveen encountered had no source of real firewood to warm themselves during Easter's cool, wet, windy winters. Their native animals included nothing larger than insects, not even a single species of native bat, land bird, land snail, or lizard. For domestic animals, they had only chickens.

European visitors throughout the eighteenth and early nineteenth centuries estimated Easter's human population at about 2,000, a modest number considering the island's fertility. As Captain James Cook recognized during his brief visit in 1774, the islanders were Polynesians (a Tahitian man accompanying Cook was able to converse with them). Yet despite the Polynesians' well-deserved fame as a great seafaring people, the Easter Islanders who came out to Roggeveen's and Cook's ships did so by swimming or paddling canoes that Roggeveen described as "bad and frail." Their craft, he wrote, were "put together with manifold small planks and light inner timbers, which they cleverly stitched together with very fine twisted threads. . . . But as they lack the knowledge and particularly the materials for caulking and making tight the great number of seams of the canoes, these are accordingly very leaky, for which reason they are compelled to spend half the time in bailing." The canoes, only ten feet long, held at most two people, and only three or four canoes were observed on the entire island.

With such flimsy craft, Polynesians could never have colonized Easter from even the nearest island, nor could they have traveled far offshore to fish. The islanders Roggeveen met were totally isolated, unaware that other people existed. Investigators in all the years since his visit have discovered no trace of the islanders' having any outside contacts: not a single Easter Island rock or product has turned up elsewhere, nor has anything been found on the island that could have been brought by anyone other than the original settlers or the Europeans. Yet the people living on Easter claimed memories of visiting the uninhabited Sala y Gomez reef 260 miles away, far beyond the range of the leaky canoes seen by Roggeveen. How did the islanders' ancestors reach that reef from Easter, or reach Easter from anywhere else?

Easter Island's most famous feature is its huge stone statues, more than 200 of which once stood on massive stone platforms lining the coast. At least 700 more, in all stages of completion, were abandoned in quarries or on ancient roads between the quarries and the coast, as if the carvers and moving crews had thrown down their tools and walked off the job. Most of the erected statues were carved in a single quarry and then somehow transported as far as six miles—despite heights as great as 33 feet and weights up to 82 tons. The abandoned statues, meanwhile, were as much as 65 feet tall and weighed up to 270 tons. The stone platforms were equally gigantic: up to 500 feet long and 10 feet high, with facing slabs weighing up to 10 tons.

Roggeveen himself quickly recognized the problem the statues posed: "The stone images at first caused us to be struck with astonishment," he wrote, "because we could not comprehend how it was possible that these people, who are devoid of heavy thick timber for making any machines, as well as strong ropes, nevertheless had been able to erect such images." Roggeveen might have added that the islanders had no wheels, no draft animals, and no source of power except their own muscles. How did they transport the giant statues for miles, even before erecting them? To deepen the mystery, the statues were still standing in

1770, but by 1864 all of them had been pulled down, by the islanders themselves. Why then did they carve them in the first place? And why did they stop?

The statues imply a society very different from the one Roggeveen saw in 1722. Their sheer number and size suggest a population much larger than 2,000 people. What became of everyone? Furthermore, that society must have been highly organized. Easter's resources were scattered across the island: the best stone for the statues was quarried at Rano Raraku near Easter's northeast end; red stone, used for large crowns adorning some of the statues, was quarried at Puna Pau, inland in the southwest; stone carving tools came mostly from Aroi in the northwest. Meanwhile, the best farmland lay in the south and east, and the best fishing grounds on the north and west coasts. Extracting and redistributing all those goods required complex political organization. What happened to that organization, and how could it ever have arisen in such a barren landscape?

Easter Island's mysteries have spawned volumes of speculation for more than two and a half centuries. Many Europeans were incredulous that Polynesians—commonly characterized as "mere savages"—could have created the statues or the beautifully constructed stone platforms. In the 1950s, Heyerdahl argued that Polynesia must have been settled by advanced societies of American Indians, who in turn must have received civilization across the Atlantic from more advanced societies of the Old World. Heyerdahl's raft voyages aimed to prove the feasibility of such prehistoric transoceanic contacts. In the 1960s the Swiss writer Erich von Däniken, an ardent believer in Earth visits by extraterrestrial astronauts, went further, claiming that Easter's statues were the work of intelligent beings who owned ultramodern tools, became stranded on Easter, and were finally rescued.

Heyerdahl and von Däniken both brushed aside overwhelming evidence that the Easter Islanders were typical Polynesians derived from Asia rather than from the Americas and that their culture (including their statues) grew out of Polynesian culture. Their language was Polynesian, as Cook had already concluded. Specifically, they spoke an eastern Polynesian dialect related to Hawaiian and Marquesan, a dialect isolated since about A.D. 400, as estimated from slight differences in vocabulary. Their fishhooks and stone adzes resembled early Marquesan models. Last year DNA extracted from 12 Easter Island skeletons was also shown to be Polynesian. The islanders grew bananas, taro, sweet potatoes, sugarcane, and paper mulberry—typical Polynesian crops, mostly of Southeast Asian origin. Their sole domestic animal, the chicken, was also typically Polynesian and ultimately Asian, as were the rats that arrived as stowaways in the canoes of the first settlers.

What happened to those settlers? The fanciful theories of the past must give way to evidence gathered by hardworking practitioners in three fields: archeology, pollen analysis, and paleontology.

Modern archeological excavations on Easter have continued since Heyerdahl's 1955 expedition. The earliest radiocarbon dates associated with human activities are around A.D. 400 to 700, in reasonable agreement with the approximate settlement date of 400 estimated by linguists. The period of statue construction peaked around 1200 to 1500, with few if any statues erected thereafter. Densities of archeological sites suggest a large population; an estimate of 7,000 people is widely quoted by archeologists, but other estimates range up to 20,000, which does not seem implausible for an island of Easter's area and fertility.

Archeologists have also enlisted surviving islanders in experiments aimed at figuring out how the statues might have been carved and erected. Twenty people, using only stone chisels, could have carved even the largest completed statue within a year. Given enough timber and fiber for making ropes, teams of at most a few hundred people could have loaded the statues onto wooden sleds, dragged them over lubricated wooden tracks or rollers, and used logs as levers to maneuver them into a standing position. Rope could have been made from the fiber of a small native tree, related to the linden, called the hauhau. However, that tree is now extremely scarce on Easter, and hauling one statue would have required hundreds of yards of rope. Did Easter's now barren landscape once support the necessary trees?

That question can be answered by the technique of pollen analysis, which involves boring out a column of sediment from a swamp or pond, with the most recent deposits at the top and relatively more ancient deposits at the bottom. The absolute age of each layer can be dated by radiocarbon methods. Then begins the hard work: examining tens of thousands of pollen grains under a microscope, counting them, and identifying the plant species that produced each one by comparing the grains with modern pollen from known plant species. For Easter Island, the bleary-eyed scientists who performed that task were John Flenley, now at Massey University in New Zealand, and Sarah King of the University of Hull in England.

Flenley and King's heroic efforts were rewarded by the striking new picture that emerged of Easter's prehistoric landscape. For at least 30,000 years before human arrival and during the early years of Polynesian settlement, Easter was not a wasteland at all. Instead, a subtropical forest of trees and woody bushes towered over a ground layer of shrubs, herbs, ferns, and grasses. In the forest grew tree daisies, the rope-yielding hauhau tree, and the toromiro tree, which furnishes a dense, mesquite-like firewood. The most common tree in the forest was a species of palm now absent on Easter but formerly so abundant that the bottom strata of the sediment column were packed with its pollen. The Easter Island palm was closely related to the still-surviving Chilean wine palm, which grows up to 82 feet tall and 6 feet in diameter. The tall, unbranched trunks of the Easter Island palm would have been ideal for transporting and erecting statues and constructing large canoes. The palm would also have been a valuable food source, since its Chilean relative yields edible nuts as well as sap from which Chileans make sugar, syrup, honey, and wine.

What did the first settlers of Easter Island eat when they were not glutting themselves on the local equivalent of maple syrup? Recent excavations by David Steadman, of the New York State Museum at Albany, have yielded a picture of Easter's original animal world as surprising as Flenley and King's picture of its plant world. Steadman's expectations for Easter were conditioned by his experiences elsewhere in Polynesia, where fish are overwhelmingly the main food at archeological sites, typically accounting for more than 90 percent of the bones in ancient Polynesian garbage heaps. Easter, though, is too cool for the coral reefs beloved by fish, and its cliffgirded coastline permits shallow-water fishing in only a few places. Less than a quarter of the bones in its early garbage heaps (from the period 900 to 1300) belonged to fish; instead, nearly one-third of all bones came from porpoises.

Nowhere else in Polynesia do porpoises account for even 1 percent of discarded food bones. But most other Polynesian islands offered animal food in the form of birds and mammals, such as New Zealand's now extinct giant moas and Hawaii's now extinct flightless geese. Most other islanders also had domestic pigs and dogs. On Easter, porpoises would have been the largest animal available—other than humans. The porpoise species identified at Easter, the common dolphin, weighs up to 165 pounds. It generally lives out at sea, so it could not have been hunted by line fishing or spearfishing from shore. Instead, it must have been harpooned far offshore, in big seaworthy canoes built from the extinct palm tree.

In addition to porpoise meat, Steadman found, the early Polynesian settlers were feasting on seabirds. For those birds, Easter's remoteness and lack of predators made it an ideal haven as a breeding site, at least until humans arrived. Among the prodigious numbers of seabirds that bred on Easter were albatross, boobies, frigate birds, fulmars, petrels, prions, shearwaters, storm petrels, terns, and tropic birds. With at least 25 nesting species, Easter was the richest seabird breeding site in Polynesia and probably in the whole Pacific.

Land birds as well went into early Easter Island cooking pots. Steadman identified bones of at least six species, including barn owls, herons, parrots, and rail. Bird stew would have been seasoned with meat from large numbers of rats, which the Polynesian colonists inadvertently brought with them; Easter Island is the sole known Polynesian island where rat bones outnumber fish bones at archeological sites. (In case you're squeamish and consider rats inedible, I still recall recipes for creamed laboratory rat that my British biologist friends used to supplement their diet during their years of wartime food rationing.)

Porpoises, seabirds, land birds, and rats did not complete the list of meat sources formerly available on Easter. A few bones hint at the possibility of breeding seal colonies as well. All these delicacies were cooked in ovens fired by wood from the island's forests.

Such evidence lets us imagine the island onto which Easter's first Polynesian colonists stepped ashore some 1,600 years ago, after a long canoe voyage from eastern Polynesia. They found themselves in a pristine paradise. What then happened to it? The pollen grains and the bones yield a grim answer.

Pollen records show that destruction of Easter's forests was well under way by the year 800, just a few centuries after the start of human settlement. Then charcoal from wood fires came to fill the sediment cores, while pollen of palms and other trees and woody shrubs decreased or disappeared, and pollen of the grasses that replaced the forest became more abundant. Not long after 1400 the palm finally became extinct, not only as a result of being chopped down but also because the now ubiquitous rats prevented its regeneration: of the dozens of preserved palm nuts discovered in caves on Easter, all had been chewed by rats and could no longer germinate. While the hauhau tree did not become extinct in Polynesian times, its numbers declined drastically until there weren't enough left to make ropes from. By the time Heyerdahl visited Easter, only a single, nearly dead toromiro tree remained on the island, and even that lone survivor has now disappeared. (Fortunately, the toromiro still grows in botanical gardens elsewhere.)

The fifteenth century marked the end not only for Easter's palm but for the forest itself. Its doom had been approaching as people cleared land to plant gardens; as they felled trees to build canoes, to transport and erect statues, and to burn; as rats devoured seeds; and probably as the native birds died out that had pollinated the trees' flowers and dispersed their fruit. The overall picture is among the most extreme examples of forest destruction anywhere in the world: the whole forest gone, and most of its tree species extinct.

The destruction of the island's animals was as extreme as that of the forest: without exception, every species of native land bird became extinct. Even shellfish were overexploited, until people had to settle for small sea snails instead of larger cowries. Porpoise bones disappeared abruptly from garbage heaps around 1500; no one could harpoon porpoises anymore, since the trees used for constructing the big seagoing canoes no longer existed. The colonies of more than half of the seabird species breeding on Easter or on its offshore islets were wiped out.

In place of these meat supplies, the Easter Islanders intensified their production of chickens, which had been only an occasional food item. They also turned to the largest remaining meat source available: humans, whose bones became common in late Easter Island garbage heaps. Oral traditions of the islanders are rife with cannibalism; the most inflammatory taunt that could be snarled at an enemy was "The flesh of your mother sticks between my teeth." With no wood available to cook these new goodies, the islanders resorted to sugarcane scraps, grass, and sedges to fuel their fires.

All these strands of evidence can be wound into a coherent narrative of a society's decline and fall. The first Polynesian colonists found themselves on an island with fertile soil, abundant food, bountiful building materials, ample lebensraum, and all the prerequisites for comfortable living. They prospered and multiplied.

After a few centuries, they began erecting stone statues on platforms, like the ones their Polynesian forebears had carved. With passing years, the statues and platforms became larger and larger, and the statues began sporting ten-ton red crowns—probably in an escalating spiral of one-upmanship, as rival clans tried to surpass each other with shows of wealth and power. (In the same way, successive Egyptian pharaohs built ever-larger pyramids. Today Hollywood movie moguls near my home in Los Angeles are displaying their wealth and power by building ever more ostentatious mansions. Tycoon Marvin Davis topped previous moguls with plans for a 50,000-square-foot house, so now Aaron Spelling has topped Davis with a 56,000-square-foot house. All that those buildings lack to make the message explicit are ten-ton red crowns.) On Easter, as in modern America, society was held together by a complex political system to redistribute locally available resources and to integrate the economies of different areas.

Eventually Easter's growing population was cutting the forest more rapidly than the forest was regenerating. The people used the land for gardens and the wood for fuel, canoes, and houses—and, of course, for lugging statues. As forest disappeared, the islanders ran out of timber and rope to transport and erect their statues. Life became more uncomfortable—springs and streams dried up, and wood was no longer available for fires.

People also found it harder to fill their stomachs, as land birds, large sea snails, and many seabirds disappeared. Because timber for building seagoing canoes vanished, fish catches declined and porpoises disappeared from the table. Crop yields also declined, since deforestation allowed the soil to be eroded by rain and wind, dried by the sun, and its nutrients to be leeched from it. Intensified chicken production and cannibalism replaced only part of all those lost foods. Preserved statuettes with sunken cheeks and visible ribs suggest that people were starving.

With the disappearance of food surpluses, Easter Island could no longer feed the chiefs, bureaucrats, and priests who had kept a complex society running. Surviving islanders described to early European visitors how local chaos replaced centralized government and a warrior class took over from the hereditary chiefs. The stone points of spears and daggers, made by the warriors during their heyday in the 1600s and 1700s, still litter the ground of Easter today. By around 1700, the population began to crash toward between one-quarter and one-tenth of its former number. People took to living in caves for protection against their enemies. Around 1770 rival clans started to topple each other's statues, breaking the heads off. By 1864 the last statue had been thrown down and desecrated.

As we try to imagine the decline of Easter's civilization, we ask ourselves, "Why didn't they look around, realize what they were doing, and stop before it was too late? What were they thinking when they cut down the last palm tree?"

I suspect, though, that the disaster happened not with a bang but with a whimper. After all, there are those hundreds of abandoned statues to consider. The forest the islanders depended on for rollers and rope didn't simply disappear one day—it vanished slowly, over decades. Perhaps war interrupted the moving teams; perhaps by the time the carvers had finished their work, the last rope snapped. In the meantime, any islander who tried to warn about the dangers of progressive deforestation would have been overridden by vested interests of carvers, bureaucrats, and chiefs, whose jobs depended on continued deforestation. Our Pacific Northwest loggers are only the latest in a long line of loggers to cry, "Jobs over trees!" The changes in forest cover from year to year would have been hard to detect: yes, this year we cleared those woods over there, but trees are starting to grow back again on this abandoned garden site here. Only older people, recollecting their childhoods decades earlier, could have recognized a difference. Their children could no more have comprehended their parents' tales than my eight-year-old sons today can comprehend my wife's and my tales of what Los Angeles was like 30 years ago.

Gradually trees became fewer, smaller, and less important. By the time the last fruit-bearing adult palm tree was cut, palms had long since ceased to be of economic significance. That left only smaller and smaller palm saplings to clear each year, along with other bushes and treelets. No one would have noticed the felling of the last small palm.

By now the meaning of Easter Island for us should be chillingly obvious. Easter Island is Earth writ small. Today, again, a rising population confronts shrinking resources. We too have no emigration valve, because all human societies are linked by international transport, and we can no more escape into space than the Easter Islanders could flee into the ocean. If we continue to follow our present course, we shall have exhausted the world's major fisheries, tropical rain forests, fossil fuels, and much of our soil by the time my sons reach my current age.

Every day newspapers report details of famished countries—Afghanistan, Liberia, Rwanda, Sierra Leone, Somalia, the former Yugoslavia, Zaire—where soldiers have appropriated the wealth or where central government is yielding to local gangs of thugs. With the risk of nuclear war receding, the threat of our ending with a bang no longer has a chance of galvanizing us to halt our course. Our risk now is of winding down, slowly, in a whimper. Corrective action is blocked by vested interests, by well-intentioned political and business leaders, and by their electorates, all of whom are perfectly correct in not noticing big changes from year to year. Instead, each year there are just somewhat more people, and somewhat fewer resources, on Earth.

It would be easy to close our eyes or to give up in despair. If mere thousands of Easter Islanders with only stone tools and their own muscle power sufficed to destroy their society, how can billions of people with metal tools and machine power fail to do worse? But there is one crucial difference. The Easter Islanders had no books and no histories of other doomed societies. Unlike the Easter Islanders, we have histories of the past—information that can save us. My main hope for my sons' generation is that we may now choose to learn from the fates of societies like Easter's.

# Review Questions

1. What was the ecology of Easter Island when Polynesians first arrived on the island about A.D. 400, according to Jared Diamond?

2. What were the main sources of food eaten by Easter Islanders in the early years of island habitation?

3. What changes occurred in the Easter Island environment due to human exploitation? How did these changes affect the life and social organization of the islanders?

4. How does Diamond explain the inability of Easter Islanders to see the effect they were having on their island's habitat?

5. How does the Easter Island case apply to what is happening in the world today?

# 13

# Cultivating the Tropical Forest

*Richard K. Reed*

*To most industrialized peoples, the practice of slash-and-burn agriculture seems wasteful. Horticulturalists use axes and machetes to fell forests, burn the debris, and then plant in the ashes. Within a few short years, the fields are abandoned and the farmer moves on. Because clearing is difficult and fields are left fallow for many years to recover, most land lies dormant. For people used to thinking of agriculture as intensively planted permanent fields, horticulture seems to epitomize "under-development." In this article, Richard Reed challenges this simplistic notion. Describing the subsistence practices of the Guaraní Indians living in the tropical forests of Paraguay, he shows that Indian slash-and-burn agriculture combined with foraging for wild game and plants represents the optimal use of the forest and a model for modern forest management programs. But modern times may change all that. The destruction of the forest has left many Guaraní villagers with little more than inhabited islands in a sea of destruction.*

The world's great tropical forests, which once seemed so forbidding and impenetrable, are now prime targets for economic exploitation. Developers and colonists, from Brazil to Indonesia, flock to the jungle frontiers armed with chain saws and bulldozers. They build roads, clear-cut timber, and denude the land of foliage, often burning the trees and brush as they go. The scope of this human invasion staggers the mind. Development destroys hundreds of square miles of virgin tropical forest each day. In the Amazon alone, an area half the size of Louisiana is cleared every year. At this rate, authorities predict that the forests will be gone by the year 2050.

Damage to the forest has not gone unnoticed. Publicized by newscasters, environmentalists, rock stars, and a host of others, the plight of rain forests is now familiar to many Americans. Concern has centered on the consequences of deforestation for the world ecosystem. Forests are the "lungs of the earth," producing crucial oxygen. Burning trees not only reduces world oxygen production, it releases large amounts of carbon dioxide, a greenhouse gas, into the atmosphere. A warmer world is the result.

Many authorities have also warned about the impact of deforestation on wildlife. Tropical forests contain the world's richest variety of animals and plants. As the trees disappear, so do countless irreplaceable species.

Curiously, there is less said about the plight of people who are native to the forests. In South America, for example, up to six million Indians once lived scattered across the vast lowland forests. Only a tenth of that population remains today, the rest having fallen victim to the colonial advance over the past 400 years. Each year, it is harder for these survivors to maintain their populations and communities.

The damage being done to these Indian societies is particularly distressing because they are the only humans who have managed to subsist in the forest without causing permanent harm. By employing a subsistence strategy that combines horticulture, gathering, and hunting, these indigenous peoples have managed to live in harmony with the forest environment for centuries.

We may ask what accounts for this successful adaptation. Is there a special genius to the social organization of indigenous peoples? What subsistence strategies permit them to live amicably with the forest? What happens to them when settlers and commercial development overtake them? Can such people provide a model for successful tropical forest management? If so, perhaps indigenous peoples will be as important to our future as the oxygen-giving forests they live in. Let's look at these questions in the context of one group living in the South American forest, the Guaraní of eastern Paraguay.

## The Guaraní

The Guaraní Indians provide an excellent example of a group well adapted to the forest environment. Like most horticulturalists, they live in small, widely scattered communities. Because their population densities are low, and because they practice a mixture of slash-and-burn agriculture and foraging, they place a light demand on forest resources. Small size also means a more personal social organization and an emphasis on cooperation and sharing. Although of greater size and complexity than hunter-gatherer bands, Guaraní villages contain many of the cultural values found in these nomadic societies.

I have conducted ethnographic fieldwork among the Guaraní for the past twenty years, mostly in the village of Itanaramí, located in eastern Paraguay. The residents of Itanaramí are among the last of the Guaraní Indians still living in the forests of southern South America. They are the remnants of an ethnic group that 400 years ago dominated southern Brazil and Paraguay from the Atlantic Ocean to the Andes. The Guaraní have suffered as disease, slavers, and colonists invaded their forests. Today, only 30,500 Guaraní remain in isolated settlements where the tropical forest survives—and even these are threatened.

The forests of Itanaramí have high canopies that shelter both animal and human populations. When I first arrived in the region, the expanse of trees was broken only by streams and rivers that drain westward to the broad, marshy valley of the Paraná River. Viewed from the ground, the density of the forest growth was matched only by the diversity of plant species.

Itanaramí itself is built along a small stream that gives the settlement its name. To my uninformed eye, it was difficult to recognize the existence of village at all. Homesteads, which consisted of a clearing, a thatched hut, and a field, were scattered in the forest, often out of sight of one another. A closer look revealed that pathways through the forest connected houses to each other and to a slightly larger homestead, that of the *tamoi*—(literally, *grandfather*), the group's religious leader. As in many small societies, households were tied together by kinship. People lived only a short distance from close relatives. Kinship wove a tapestry of relations that organized social affairs and linked Itanaramí to other Guaraní communities.

Guaraní culture emphasizes sharing and cooperation. Sisters often shared work and childcare. Brothers usually hunted together. Food was distributed among members of the extended family, including cousins, aunts, and uncles. People emphasized the general welfare, not personal wealth.

The *tamoi*, although in no sense a leader with formal authority, commanded considerable respect in the community. He settled disputes, chastised errant juniors, and led the entire community in evening religious ceremonies where all drank *kanguijy* (fermented corn), danced, and chanted to the gods.

The people of Itanaramí not only lived in the forest; they saw themselves as of it. The forest was basic to indigenous cosmology. The people referred to themselves as *ka'aguygua,* or "people of the forest." Villagers often named their children after the numerous forest songbirds, symbolizing their close personal ties to the environment.

## Subsistence

Guaraní have lived in their present locale for centuries and have dwelled throughout the tropical forests of lowland South America for thousands of years. During all this time, they have exploited flora, fauna, and soils of the forests without doing permanent harm. The secret of their success is in their production strategy. The Indians mix agriculture with gathering, hunting, and fishing in a way that permits the environment to recover. They even collect forest products for sale to outsiders, again without causing environmental damage.

Guaraní farming is well suited to forest maintenance. Using a form of shifting agriculture called slash-and-burn farming, the Indians permit the forest to recover from the damage of field clearing. The way Veraju, the *tamoi* of Itanaramí, and his wife, Kitu, farm provides a typical example. When the family needs to prepare a new field, it is Veraju who does the heavy work. He cuts the trees and undergrowth to make a half-acre clearing near his house. Then he, Kitu, and some of their five children burn the fallen trees and brush, creating an ash that provides a powerful fertilizer for the thin forest soils. When the field is prepared, Kitu uses a digging stick fashioned from a sapling to poke small holes in the ground, and plants the three staple Guaraní crops: corn, beans, and manioc root (from which tapioca is made). Interspersed with the basic staples, they add the slower-growing banana, sugar cane, and orange trees to round out their diet. When the crops mature, it is Kitu and her daughters who will harvest them

The secret to successful slash-and-burn agriculture is field "shifting" or rotation. Crops flourish the first year and are plentiful the next, but the sun and rain soon take their toll on the exposed soil. The thin loam layer, so typical of tropical forests, degenerates rapidly to sand and clay. Grasses, weeds, and insect pests, rare in the deep forest, eventually discover the vulnerable crops. By the third year, the poor soils are thick with weeds and grow only a sparse corn crop and few small manioc roots. Rather than replant a fourth time, Veraju and Kitu will clear a new field nearby where soils are naturally more fertile and the forest can be burned for additional ash fertilizer. Although fallow, their old field is not abandoned. They continue to return periodically for fruit and to root out the remaining manioc. The surrounding forest quickly reclaims the old field, roots penetrate the opening from the forest edge and animals wander through, dropping seeds in their path. As the forest returns, the decaying matter once again strengthens the depleted soil. After several years the plot will be distinguished only as one of the citrus groves that are scattered throughout the unbroken forest. In this way, the forest produces a sustained yield without degrading the natural ecosystem.

The forest recovers sufficiently fast for the same plot to be cleared and replanted within ten or fifteen years. This "swidden" system results in the cyclic use of a large area of forest, with a part under cultivation and a much larger portion lying fallow in various stages of recomposition.

If farming formed the only subsistence base, the Guaraní would have to clear much larger gardens. But they also turn to other forest resources—game, fish, and forest products—to meet their needs. Guaraní men often form small groups to hunt large animals, such as deer, tapir, and peccary, with guns purchased from outsiders or with the more traditional bows and arrows they make themselves. A successful hunt will provide enough meat to share liberally with friends. Men also trap smaller mammals, such as armadillo and paca (a large rodent). They fashion snares and deadfall traps from saplings, tree trunks, and cactus fiber twine. These are set near homesteads, along streams, and at the edges of gardens. Traps not only provide meat, but they also kill animals that would otherwise eat the crops.

Fish also supply protein for the Guaraní diet and reduce dependence on agricultural produce. Many rivers and streams flow near Itanaramí on flat bottomland. These watercourses meander in broad loops that may be cut off as the river or stream changes course during a flood. Meanders, called oxbows, make ideal fishing spots. In addition to hook and line, men capture the fish by using a poison extracted from the bark of the *timbo* vine. Floated over the surface of the water, the poison stuns the fish and allows people to catch them by hand.

The forest also supplies a variety of useful products for the Guaraní. They make houses from tree trunks and bamboo stalks; rhododendron vines secure thatched roofs. Villagers collect wild honey and fruit to add sweetness to their diets. If the manioc in the fields is insufficient, wild tubers provide a basic staple. Even several species of insect larva and ants are collected as tasty and nutritious supplements to the daily meal. Finally, the Indians know about a wide variety of medicinal plants. They process roots, leaves, flowers, and seeds to release powerful alkaloids, making teas and poultices for the sick and injured.

But the Guaraní have not been isolated from commercial goods. Almost five hundred years ago, White traders entered the forests of the Guaraní and gave Indians access to world markets. The Guaraní continue to produce for most of their needs, but items such as machetes, hooks, soap, and salt are more easily bought than manufactured or collected. As they do with farming and hunting, Guaraní turn to the forest to meet such economic needs. They regularly collect two forest products, *yerba mate* (a caffeinated tea) and oil extract from wild orange trees (used for flavorings and perfumes), to raise the necessary funds.

It is important to note the special Guaraní knowledge and values associated with subsistence activities. Because they have lived in the forest for such a long time, and because they would have nowhere to turn if their own resources disappeared, they rely on a special and complex knowledge of how the forest works and how it can be used.

For example, Guaraní, such as Veraju, distinguish among a variety of "ecozones," each with a unique combination of soil, flora, and fauna. They recognize obvious differences between the high forests on the hills, the deep swamps of river basins, and the grassy savannahs of the high plains. But they make more subtle distinctions within these larger regions. For example, they call the low scrub along rivers *ca'ati*. Flooded each year during the rainy season, *ca'ati* supports bamboo groves that harbor small animals for trapping and material for house construction. The forests immediately above the flood plain look like an extension of the *ca'ati*, but to the Guaraní they differ in important ways. This ecozone supports varieties of bamboo that are useless in house construction but that attract larger animals, such as peccary, that can be hunted. In all, the

Guaraní distinguish among nine resource zones, each with distinctive soils, flora, fauna, and uses. These subtle distinctions between ecozones enable the Guaraní to use the forest to its best benefit. By shifting their subsistence efforts from one zone to another, just as they shift their fields from one spot to the next, the Guaraní assure that the forest environment, with its rich variety of life, will always be able to renew itself.

## The Impact of Development

In the last few years, intensive commercial development has come to the region in which Itanaramí lies. Paraguay's deforestation rates are among the highest in the world, raising the specter of complete ecological destruction. White *colonos* (settlers), armed with chain saws and earthmovers, attack the trees. They vandalize the land without awareness of the carefully integrated ecozones. As the trees fall, the forest products, such as yerba mate, disappear. So do the mammals and fish, the bamboo and the rhododendron vines, the honey and the fruits, and the fallow fields. As these resources disappear, so does the economy of the once self-sufficient Guaraní. Without their traditional mode of subsistence, it becomes impossible to maintain their kin-organized society, the influence of the *tamoi*, and the willingness to share. Indian communities are destroyed by poverty and disease, and the members who remain join the legions of poor laborers who form the lowest class of the national society. In short, the Guaraní lose their ability to survive as an independent ethnic group.

Recent intensive development began near Itanaramí with a road that colonists cut through the jungle to within two hours' walk of the village. Through this gash in the forest moved logging trucks, bulldozers, farm equipment, and buses. Accompanying the machinery of development were farmers, ranchers, and speculators, hoping to make a quick profit from the verdant land. They descended from their vehicles onto the muddy streets of a newly built frontier town. They cleared land for general stores and bars, which were soon filled with merchandise and warm beer. By day, the air in the town was fouled by truck noise and exhaust fumes; by night it was infused with the glare of electric lights and the noise of blaring tape players.

Soon the settlers began to fell the forest, creating fields for cotton, soybeans, and pasture. Survey teams cleared boundaries and drew maps. Lumber gangs camped in the forests, clearcutting vast tracts of trees. Valuable timber was hauled off to newly established lumber mills; everything else was piled and burned. Massive bulldozers created expanses of sunlight in the previously unbroken forest. Within months, grass, cotton, and soybeans sprouted in the exposed soils. Where once the land had been home for game, it now provided for cattle. Herds often clogged the roads, competing with trucks hauling cotton to market and busses loaded with new colonists. Settlers fenced in the fields and cut lanes through the remaining forest to mark off portions that would be "private property," off limits to Indians.

The road and fields reached Itanaramí in 1994. A cement bridge was built over the stream and chain saws and logging trucks as well as bulldozers are now assaulting the forests the Guaraní once used for gardens, farming, and hunting. The footpath that once carried Guaraní to the *tamoi*'s house now carries their timber to market in Brazil. The families are left with barren house lots.

Moreover, by destroying the forest resources surrounding the Guaraní villages of the region, of which Itanaramí was only one, *colonos* set in motion a process that destroyed the native culture and society. Guaraní communities became islands surrounded by a sea of pastures and farm fields. Although the Indians held onto their gardens, they lost the forest resources needed to sustain their original mode of subsistence, which depended on hunting, fishing, and gathering in the forest as well as on farming. These economic changes forced alterations in Indian community.

First, without the forest to provide game, fish, and other products, the Guaraní became dependent on farming alone for their survival. Without wild foods, they had to plant more corn and beans. Without the forest production of yerba mate leaves to collect for sale, they were also forced to plant cash crops, such as cotton and tobacco. These changes forced them to clear gardens that were over twice the size of their previous plots.

While the loss of the forest for hunting and gathering increased their dependence on agriculture, the fences and land titles of the new settlers reduced the land available to the Indians for cultivation. Families soon cleared the last of the remaining high forests that they controlled. Even the once-forested stream banks were denuded.

After they cleared their communities' high forest, Indian farmers were forced to replant fields without allowing sufficient fallow time for soils to rejuvenate. Crops suffered from lack of nutrients and yields declined despite additional effort devoted to clearing and weeding. Commercial crops, poorly suited to the forest soils, did even worse. As production suffered, the Indians cleared and farmed even larger areas. The resulting spiral of poor harvests and enlarged farms outstripped the soil's capacity to produce and the Guaraní's ability to care for the crops. Food in the Indian communities grew scarce. The diet was increasingly restricted to non-nutritious manioc as a dietary staple because it was the only plant that could survive in the exhausted soils.

The Guaraní felt the ecological decline in other ways. The loss of game and poor crop yields exacerbated health problems. Settlers brought new diseases into the forest, such as colds and flu. The Guaraní have little inherited resistance to these illnesses and poor nutrition reduced their defenses even further. Disease not only sapped the adults' energy for farming and childcare, but it also increased death rates at all ages. Tuberculosis, which well-fed Guaraní rarely contract, became the major killer in the community.

The environmental destruction took a psychological toll as well. Guaraní began to fall into depression, get drunk on cheap cane liquor, and, all too often, commit suicide. A number of suicides were noted among the Guaraní in Brazil in 1996 and subsequent research in Paraguay showed that indigenous peoples were killing themselves at almost fifty times the national average. The epidemic hit 15- to 24-year-olds the hardest. These young people saw little future for themselves, their families, and their people.

Deforestation also disrupted social institutions. Without their subsistence base, many Guaraní needed additional cash to buy food and goods. Indian men were forced to seek work as farmhands, planting pasture and picking cotton on land where they once hunted. Women stayed at home to tend children and till the deteriorating soils of the family farms.

The search for wage labor eventually forced whole Guaraní families to move. Many jobs were available on the new farms that had replaced the forest. Entire families left home for hovels they constructed on the land of their employers. From independent farmers and gatherers, they became tenants of *patrones* (landowners). *Patrones* prohibited the Guaraní farmhands from planting gardens of their own, so the displaced Indians were forced to buy all their food, usually from the *patrones* themselves. Worse, *patrones* set their own inflated prices on the food and goods sold to Indians. Dependence on the *patrones* displaced the mutual interdependence of traditional Guaraní social organization.

As individuals and families left the Guaraní villages in search of work on surrounding farms and ranches, *tamoi* leaders lost influence. It became impossible to gather disparate relatives and friends for religious rituals. The distances were too great for the elders' nieces and nephews to seek out counsel and medicines. Moreover, the diseases and problems suffered by the Guaraní were increasingly caused by people and powers outside the forest. The *tamoi* could neither control nor explain the changing world.

Finally, as the forest disappeared, so did its power to symbolize Guaraní entity. No longer did young Indians see themselves as "people of the forest." Increasingly, they called themselves "*indios*," the pejorative slur used by their non-Indian neighbors.

Today, many of the Guaraní of eastern Paraguay remain in small but impoverished communities in the midst of a frontier society based on soybean farming and cattle ranching. The households that previously were isolated individual plots are now concentrated in one small area without forest for farming or privacy. The traditional *tamoi* continue to be the center of the social and religious life of the community, but no longer exert influence over village decisions, which are increasingly dominated by affairs external to the local community.

## Development and Ecology

Some people might argue that the plight of the Guaraní is inevitable and that in the long run, the Indians will be absorbed in a more modern, prosperous society. The forest, they claim, provides rich, nearly unlimited resources for development. Its exploitation, although painful for a few indigenous Indians, will provide an unequaled opportunity for the poor of Latin America.

Unfortunately, this argument makes forest development appear to be socially responsible. Yet, the long-run implications of forest clearing are disastrous, not simply for the Guaraní and other Indians, but for settlers and developers as well. The tropical forest ecosystem is extremely fragile. When the vegetable cover is destroyed, the soil quickly disappears. Erosion clogs rivers with silt, and the soils left behind are baked to a hardpan on which few plants can survive. Rainwater previously captured by foliage and soil is quickly lost to runoff, drying the winds that feed the regional rain systems. Although first harvests in frontier areas seem bountiful, long-term farming and ranching are unprofitable as the soils, deprived of moisture and the rejuvenating forces of the original forest, are reduced to a "red desert." Returning to Itanaramí today, one notices that many of the fields first cleared by ranchers in 1996 have already been abandoned. And even worse, leaving the cleared land fallow does not restore it. Once destroyed, the forest plants cannot reclaim the hardpan left by modern development.

Nor have developers been interested in husbanding the land. The *colonos* who clear the forests are concerned with short-term profit. Entrepreneurs and peasant farmers maximize immediate returns on their labor and investment, unaware of the environmental costs that subsidize their earnings. When the trees and soils of one area are exhausted, the farmers, ranchers, and loggers move farther into the virgin forest in search of new resources. The process creates a wave of development that leaves destruction in its wake. Unlike the Guaraní who remain on the land, developers do not stay and contend with the environmental destruction caused by their activities.

## Conservation

International agencies and national governments have begun to recognize the damage caused by uncontrolled rain forest development. Although deforestation continues unchecked in many regions of the Amazon Basin, forest conservation programs are being established in some areas. Several of these programs are attempting to use the experience of indigenous people to promote ecologically rational uses of the forest.

Such is the case in Paraguay where a program is being implemented to preserve the remaining tropical forests. Groups like the Guaraní of Itanaramí, so recently threatened by encroaching development, are providing a model for newcomers to earn a living from the natural resources while protecting the existing environment. The natural forests of the Guaraní are the last remaining undisturbed subtropical forest in eastern Paraguay. With the help of the Nature Conservancy, an area of 280 square miles has been set aside as a biosphere reserve. Although small, the program is attempting to protect a much larger buffer zone around the reserve by promoting rational land use by colonists. Aided by anthropologists who have made detailed studies of Indian subsistence techniques, planners are integrating the Indians' own models of agro-forestry into new production strategies for *colonos*. Guaraní techniques of commercial extraction have been of special interest, particularly the harvest of yerba mate, as it will economically outperform destructive farming in the long run. Teams of planners are teaching newcomers to tend and harvest their own tree crops. Far from being backward and inefficient, the mixed horticultural subsistence strategies of indigenous forest groups have turned out to be the most practical way to manage the fragile tropical forest environment.

# Review Questions

1. Anthropologists claim that subsistence strategies affect a society's social organization and ideology. Evaluate this assertion in light of reading about the way the Guaraní live in their rain forest environment.

2. Why is horticulture more environmentally sensible than intensive agricultural and pastoral exploitation of the Amazonian rain forest?

3. Guaraní Indians are largely subsistence farmers and foragers. How do they use their forest environment without destroying it?

4. How have *colonos* disrupted the lives of Guaraní villagers? What does this tell us about the relationship between subsistence and social structure?

5. How can the Guaraní use their rain forest habitat to make money, and what does their experience suggest as a way to integrate forest exploitation into a market economy without environmental destruction?

# 14

# Domestication and the Evolution of Disease

*Jared Diamond*

*All people exploit and often change their natural environments, as we have seen in the previous three articles. Not as obvious, but in some ways just as important, organisms living in the natural environment may biologically adapt to people. In this article, Jared Diamond shows that humans, once largely troubled by passive or slow-growing diseases such as parasites, provide a ready new ecological niche for animal-based microbes. With the advent of plant and animal domestication and rising populations, large sedentary human populations provide fertile ground for the evolution of diseases, such as smallpox, measles, and bubonic plague, all originally animal diseases that were once largely harmless to humans. Originating mostly in*

Originally published as "The Arrow of Disease" by Jared Diamond from *Discover,* October 1992. Copyright © 1992 by Jared Diamond. Reprinted with permission.

*the Old World, where agriculture, animal domestication, cities, and trade favored their development, crowd diseases brought by Europeans were responsible for killing 95 percent of the people living in the Americas.*

The three people talking in the hospital room were already stressed out from having to cope with a mysterious illness, and it didn't help at all that they were having trouble communicating. One of them was the patient, a small, timid man, sick with pneumonia caused by an unidentified microbe and with only a limited command of the English language. The second, acting as translator, was his wife, worried about her husband's condition and frightened by the hospital environment. The third person in the trio was an inexperienced young doctor, trying to figure out what might have brought on the strange illness. Under the stress, the doctor was forgetting everything he had been taught about patient confidentiality. He committed the awful blunder of requesting the woman to ask her husband whether he'd had any sexual experiences that might have caused the infection.

As the young doctor watched, the husband turned red, pulled himself together so that he seemed even smaller, tried to disappear under his bed sheets, and stammered in a barely audible voice. His wife suddenly screamed in rage and drew herself up to tower over him. Before the doctor could stop her, she grabbed a heavy metal bottle, slammed it onto her husband's head, and stormed out of the room. It took a while for the doctor to elicit, through the man's broken English, what he had said to so enrage his wife. The answer slowly emerged: he had admitted to repeated intercourse with sheep on a recent visit to the family farm; perhaps that was how he had contracted the mysterious microbe.

This episode, related to me by a physician friend involved in the case, sounds so bizarrely one of a kind as to be of no possible broader significance. But in fact it illustrates a subject of great importance: human diseases of animal origins. Very few of us may love sheep in the carnal sense. But most of us platonically love our pet animals, like our dogs and cats; and as a society, we certainly appear to have an inordinate fondness for sheep and other livestock, to judge from the vast numbers of them that we keep.

Some of us—most often our children—pick up infectious diseases from our pets. Usually these illnesses remain no more than a nuisance, but a few have evolved into far more. The major killers of humanity throughout our recent history—smallpox, flu, tuberculosis, malaria, plague, measles, and cholera—are all infectious diseases that arose from diseases of animals. Until World War II more victims of war died of microbes than of gunshot or sword wounds. All those military histories glorifying Alexander the Great and Napoleon ignore the ego-deflating truth: the winners of past wars were not necessarily those armies with the best generals and weapons, but those bearing the worst germs with which to smite their enemies.

The grimmest example of the role of germs in history is much on our minds this month, as we recall the European conquest of the Americas that began with Columbus's voyage of 1492. Numerous as the Indian victims of the murderous Spanish conquistadores were, they were dwarfed in number by the victims of murderous Spanish microbes. These formidable conquerors killed an estimated 95 percent of the New World's pre-Columbian Indian population.

Why was the exchange of nasty germs between the Americas and Europe so unequal? Why didn't the reverse happen instead, with Indian diseases decimating the Spanish invaders, spreading back across the Atlantic, and causing a 95 percent decline in *Europe*'s human population?

Similar questions arise regarding the decimation of many other native peoples by European germs, and regarding the decimation of would-be European conquistadores in the tropics of Africa and Asia.

Naturally, we're disposed to think about diseases from our own point of view: What can we do to save ourselves and to kill the microbes? Let's stamp out the scoundrels, and never mind what *their* motives are!

In life, though, one has to understand the enemy to beat him. So for a moment, let's consider disease from the microbes' point of view. Let's look beyond our anger at their making us sick in bizarre ways, like giving us genital sores or diarrhea, and ask why it is that they do such things. After all, microbes are as much a product of natural selection as we are, and so their actions must have come about because they confer some evolutionary benefit.

Basically, of course, evolution selects those individuals that are most effective at producing babies and at helping those babies find suitable places to live. Microbes are marvels at this latter requirement. They have evolved diverse ways of spreading from one person to another, and from animals to people. Many of our symptoms of disease actually represent ways in which some clever bug modifies our bodies or our behavior such that we become enlisted to spread bugs.

The most effortless way a bug can spread is by just waiting to be transmitted passively to the next victim. That's the strategy practiced by microbes that wait for one host to be eaten by the next—salmonella bacteria, for example, which we contract by eating already-infected eggs or meat; or the worm responsible for trichinosis, which waits for us to kill a pig and eat it without properly cooking it.

As a slight modification of this strategy; some microbes don't wait for the old host to die but instead hitchhike in the saliva of an insect that bites the old host and then flies to a new one. The free ride may be provided by mosquitoes, fleas, lice, or tsetse flies, which spread malaria, plague, typhus, and sleeping sickness, respectively. The dirtiest of all passive-carriage tricks is perpetrated by microbes that pass from a woman to her fetus—microbes such as the ones responsible for syphilis, rubella (German measles), and AIDS. By their cunning these microbes can already be infecting an infant before the moment of its birth.

Other bugs take matters into their own hands, figuratively speaking. They actively modify the anatomy or habits of their host to accelerate their transmission. From our perspective, the open genital sores caused by venereal diseases such as syphilis are a vile indignity. From the microbes' point of view, however, they're just a useful device to enlist a host's help in inoculating the body cavity of another host with microbes. The skin lesions caused by smallpox similarly spread microbes by direct or indirect body contact (occasionally very indirect, as when U.S. and Australian whites bent on wiping out "belligerent" native peoples sent them gifts of blankets previously used by smallpox patients).

More vigorous yet is the strategy practiced by the influenza, common cold, and pertussis (whooping cough) microbes, which induce the victim to cough or sneeze, thereby broadcasting the bugs toward prospective new hosts. Similarly the cholera bacterium induces a massive diarrhea that spreads bacteria into the water supplies of potential new victims. For modification of a host's behavior, though, nothing matches the rabies virus, which not only gets into the saliva of an infected dog but drives the dog into a frenzy of biting and thereby infects many new victims.

Thus, from our viewpoint, genital sores, diarrhea, and coughing are "symptoms" of disease. From a bug's viewpoint, they're clever evolutionary strategies to broadcast the bug. That's why it's in the bug's interests to make us "sick." But what does it gain by killing us? That seems self-defeating, since a microbe that kills its host kills itself.

Though you may well think it's of little consolation, our death is really just an unintended by-product of host symptoms that promote the efficient transmission of microbes. Yes, an untreated cholera patient may eventually die from producing diarrheal fluid at a rate of several gallons a day. While the patient lasts, though, the cholera bacterium profits from being massively disseminated into the water supplies of its next victims. As long as each victim thereby infects, on average, more than one new victim, the bacteria will spread, even though the first host happens to die.

So much for the dispassionate examination of the bug's interests. Now let's get back to considering our own selfish interests: to stay alive and healthy, best done by killing the damned bugs. One common response to infection is to develop a fever. Again, we consider fever a "symptom" of disease, as if it developed inevitably without serving any function. But regulation of body temperature is under our genetic control, and a fever doesn't just happen by accident. Because some microbes are more sensitive to heat than our own bodies are, by raising our body temperature we in effect try to bake the bugs to death before we get baked ourselves.

Another common response is to mobilize our immune system. White blood cells and other cells actively seek out and kill foreign microbes. The specific antibodies we gradually build up against a particular microbe make us less likely to get reinfected once we are cured. As we all know there are some illnesses, such as flu and the common cold, to which our resistance is only temporary; we can eventually contract the illness again. Against other illnesses, though—including measles, mumps, rubella, pertussis, and the now-defeated menace of smallpox—antibodies stimulated by one infection confer lifelong immunity. That's the principle behind vaccination—to stimulate our antibody production without our having to go through the actual experience of the disease.

Alas, some clever bugs don't just cave in to our immune defenses. Some have learned to trick us by changing their antigens, those molecular pieces of the microbe that our antibodies recognize. The constant evolution or recycling of new strains of flu, with differing antigens, explains why the flu you got two years ago didn't protect you against the different strain that arrived this year. Sleeping sickness is an even more slippery customer in its ability to change its antigens rapidly.

Among the slipperiest of all is the virus that causes AIDS, which evolves new antigens even as it sits within an individual patient, until it eventually overwhelms the immune system.

Our slowest defensive response is through natural selection, which changes the relative frequency with which a gene appears from generation to generation. For almost any disease some people prove to be genetically more resistant than others. In an epidemic, those people with genes for resistance to that particular microbe are more likely to survive than are people lacking such genes. As a result, over the course of history human populations repeatedly exposed to a particular pathogen tend to be made up of individuals with genes that resist the appropriate microbe just because unfortunate individuals without those genes were less likely to survive to pass their genes on to their children.

Fat consolation, you may be thinking. This evolutionary response is not one that does the genetically susceptible dying individual any good. It does mean, though, that a human population as a whole becomes better protected.

In short, many bugs have had to evolve tricks to let them spread among potential victims. We've evolved counter-tricks, to which the bugs have responded by evolving counter-counter-tricks. We and our pathogens are now locked in an escalating evolutionary contest, with the death of one contestant the price of defeat, and with natural selection playing the role of umpire.

The form that this deadly contest takes varies with the pathogens: for some it is like a guerrilla war, while for others it is a blitzkrieg. With certain diseases, like malaria or hookworm, there's a more or less steady trickle of new cases in an affected area, and they will appear in any month of any year. Epidemic diseases, though, are different: they produce no cases for a long time, then a whole wave of cases, then no more cases again for a while.

Among such epidemic diseases, influenza is the most familiar to Americans, this year having been a particularly bad one for us (but a great year for the influenza virus). Cholera epidemics come at longer intervals, the 1991 Peruvian epidemic being the first one to reach the New World during the twentieth century. Frightening as today's influenza and cholera epidemics are, though, they pale beside the far more terrifying epidemics of the past, before the rise of modern medicine. The greatest single epidemic in human history was the influenza wave that killed 21 million people at the end of the First World War. The black death, or bubonic plague, killed one-quarter of Europe's population between 1346 and 1352, with death tolls up to 70 percent in some cities.

The infectious diseases that visit us as epidemics share several characteristics. First, they spread quickly and efficiently from an infected person to nearby healthy people, with the result that the whole population gets exposed within a short time. Second, they're "acute" illnesses: within a short time, you either die or recover completely. Third, the fortunate ones of us who do recover develop antibodies that leave us immune against a recurrence of the disease for a long time, possibly our entire lives. Finally, these diseases tend to be restricted to humans; the bugs causing them tend not to live in the soil or in other animals. All four of these characteristics apply to what Americans think of as the once more-familiar acute epidemic diseases of childhood, including measles, rubella, mumps, pertussis, and smallpox.

It is easy to understand why the combination of those four characteristics tends to make a disease run in epidemics. The rapid spread of microbes and the rapid course of symptoms mean that everybody in a local human population is soon infected, and thereafter either dead or else recovered and immune. No one is left alive who could still be infected. But since the microbe can't survive except in the bodies of living people, the disease dies out until a new crop of babies reaches the susceptible age—and until an infectious person arrives from the outside to start a new epidemic.

A classic illustration of the process is given by the history of measles on the isolated Faeroe Islands in the North Atlantic. A severe epidemic of the disease reached the Faeroes in 1781, then died out, leaving the islands measles-free until an infected carpenter arrived on a ship from Denmark in 1846. Within three months almost the whole Faeroes population—7,782 people—had gotten measles and then either died or recovered, leaving the measles virus to disappear once again until the next epidemic. Studies show that measles is likely to die out in any human population numbering less than half a million people. Only in larger populations can measles shift from one local area to another, thereby persisting until enough babies have been born in the originally infected area to permit the disease's return.

Rubella in Australia provides a similar example, on a much larger scale. As of 1917 Australia's population was still only 5 million, with most people living in scattered rural areas. The sea voyage to Britain took two months, and land transport within Australia itself was slow. In effect, Australia didn't even consist of a population of 5 million, but of hundreds of much smaller populations. As a result, rubella hit Australia only as occasional epidemics, when an infected person happened to arrive from overseas and stayed in a densely populated area. By 1938, though, the city of Sydney alone had a population of over one million, and people moved frequently and quickly by air between London, Sydney, and other Australian cities. Around then, rubella for the first time was able to establish itself permanently in Australia.

What's true for rubella in Australia is true for most familiar acute infectious diseases throughout the world. To sustain themselves, they need a human population that is sufficiently numerous and densely packed that a new crop of susceptible children is available for infection by the time the disease would otherwise be waning. Hence the measles and other such diseases are also known as "crowd diseases."

Crowd diseases could not sustain themselves in small bands of hunter-gatherers and slash-and-burn farmers. As tragic recent experience with Amazonian Indians and Pacific Islanders confirms, almost an entire tribelet may be wiped out by an epidemic brought by an outside visitor, because no one in the tribelet has any antibodies against the microbe. In addition, measles and some other "childhood" diseases are more likely to kill infected adults than children, and all adults in the tribelet are susceptible. Having killed most of the tribelet, the epidemic then disappears. The small population size explains why tribelets can't sustain epidemics introduced from the outside; at the same time it explains why they could never evolve epidemic diseases of their own to give back to the visitors.

That's not to say that small human populations are free from all infectious diseases. Some of their infections are caused by microbes capable of maintaining themselves in animals or in soil, so the disease remains constantly available to infect people. For example, the yellow fever virus is carried by African wild monkeys and is constantly available to infect rural human populations of Africa. It was also available to be carried to New World monkeys and people by the transatlantic slave trade.

Other infections of small human populations are chronic diseases, such as leprosy and yaws, that may take a very long time to kill a victim. The victim thus remains alive as a reservoir of microbes to infect other members of the tribelet. Finally, small human populations are susceptible to nonfatal infections against which we don't develop immunity, with the result that the same person can become reinfected after recovering. That's the case with hookworm and many other parasites.

All these types of diseases, characteristic of small, isolated populations, must be the oldest diseases of humanity. They were the ones that we could evolve and sustain through the early millions of years of our evolutionary history, when the total human population was tiny and fragmented. They are also shared with, or are similar to the diseases of, our closest wild relatives, the African great apes. In contrast, the evolution of our crowd diseases could only have occurred with the buildup of large, dense human populations, first made possible by the rise of agriculture about 10,000 years ago, then by the rise of cities several thousand years ago. Indeed, the first attested dates for many familiar infectious diseases are surprisingly recent: around 1600 B.C. for smallpox (as deduced from pockmarks on an Egyptian mummy), 400 B.C. for mumps, 1840 for polio, and 1959 for AIDS.

Agriculture sustains much higher human population densities than does hunting and gathering—on average, 10 to 100 times higher. In addition, hunter-gatherers frequently shift camp, leaving behind their piles of feces with their accumulated microbes and worm larvae. But farmers are sedentary and live amid their own sewage, providing microbes with a quick path from one person's body into another person's drinking water. Farmers also become surrounded by disease-transmitting rodents attracted by stored food.

Some human populations make it even easier for their own bacteria and worms to infect new victims, by intentionally gathering their feces and urine and spreading it as fertilizer on the fields where people work. Irrigation agriculture and fish farming provide ideal living conditions for the snails carrying schistosomes, and for other flukes that burrow through our skin as we wade through the feces-laden water.

If the rise of farming was a boon for our microbes, the rise of cities was a veritable bonanza, as still more densely packed human populations festered under even worse sanitation conditions. (Not until the beginning of the twentieth century did urban populations finally become self-sustaining; until then, constant immigration of healthy peasants from the countryside was necessary to make good the constant deaths of city dwellers from crowd diseases.) Another bonanza was the development of world trade routes, which by late Roman times effectively joined the populations of Europe, Asia, and North Africa into one giant breeding ground for microbes. That's when smallpox finally reached Rome as the "plague of Antonius," which killed millions of Roman citizens between A.D. 165 and 180.

Similarly, bubonic plague first appeared in Europe as the plague of Justinian (A.D. 542–543). But plague didn't begin to hit Europe with full force, as the black death epidemics, until 1346, when new overland trading with China provided rapid transit for flea-infested furs from plague-ridden areas of Central Asia. Today our jet planes have made even the longest intercontinental flights briefer than the duration of any human infectious disease. That's how an Aerolíneas Argentinas airplane, stopping in Lima, Peru, earlier this year, managed to deliver dozens of cholera-infected people the same day to my city of Los Angles, over 3,000 miles away. The explosive increase in world travel by Americans, and in immigration to the United States, is turning us into another melting pot—this time of microbes that we previously dismissed as just causing exotic diseases in far-off countries.

When the human population became sufficiently large and concentrated, we reached the stage in our history when we could at last sustain crowd diseases confined to our species. But that presents a paradox: such diseases could never have existed before. Instead they had to evolve as new diseases. Where did those new diseases come from?

Evidence emerges from studies of the disease-causing microbes themselves. In many cases molecular biologists have identified the microbe's closest relative. Those relatives also prove to be agents of infectious crowd diseases—

but ones confined to various species of domestic animals and pets! Among animals too, epidemic diseases require dense populations, and they're mainly confined to social animals that provide the necessary large populations. Hence when we domesticated social animals such as cows and pigs, they were already afflicted by epidemic diseases just waiting to be transferred to us.

For example, the measles virus is most closely related to the virus causing rinderpest, a nasty epidemic disease of cattle and many wild cud-chewing mammals. Rinderpest doesn't affect humans. Measles, in turn, doesn't affect cattle. The close similarity of the measles and rinderpest viruses suggests that the rinderpest virus transferred from cattle to humans, then became the measles virus by changing its properties to adapt to us. That transfer isn't surprising, considering how closely many peasant farmers live and sleep next to cows and their accompanying feces, urine, breath, sores, and blood. Our intimacy with cattle has been going on for 8,000 years since we domesticated them—ample time for the rinderpest virus to discover us nearby. Other familiar infectious diseases can similarly be traced back to diseases of our animal friends.

Given our proximity to the animals we love, we must constantly be getting bombarded by animal microbes. Those invaders get winnowed by natural selection, and only a few succeed in establishing themselves as human diseases. A quick survey of current diseases lets us trace four stages in the evolution of a specialized human disease from an animal precursor.

In the first stage, we pick up animal-borne microbes that are still at an early stage in their evolution into specialized human pathogens. They don't get transmitted directly from one person to another, and even their transfer from animals to us remains uncommon. There are dozens of diseases like this that we get directly from pets and domestic animals. They include cat scratch fever from cats, leptospirosis from dogs, psittacosis from chickens and parrots, and brucellosis from cattle. We're similarly susceptible to picking up diseases from wild animals, such as the tularemia that hunters occasionally get from skinning wild rabbits.

In the second stage, a former animal pathogen evolves to the point where it does get transmitted directly between people and causes epidemics. However, the epidemic dies out for several reasons—being cured by modern medicine, stopping when everybody has been infected and died, or stopping when everybody has been infected and become immune. For example, a previously unknown disease termed *o'nyong-nyong* fever appeared in East Africa in 1959 and infected several million Africans. It probably arose from a virus of monkeys and was transmitted to humans by mosquitoes. The fact that patients recovered quickly and became immune to further attack helped cause the new disease to die out quickly.

The annals of medicine are full of diseases that sound like no known disease today but that once caused terrifying epidemics before disappearing as mysteriously as they had come. Who alive today remembers the "English sweating sickness" that swept and terrified Europe between 1485 and 1578, or the "Picardy sweats" of eighteenth- and nineteenth-century France?

A third stage in the evolution of our major diseases is represented by former animal pathogens that establish themselves in humans and that do not die out; until they do, the question of whether they will become major killers of humanity remains up for grabs. The future is still very uncertain for Lassa fever, first observed in 1969 in Nigeria and caused by a virus probably derived from rodents. Better established is Lyme disease, caused by a spirochete that we get from the bite of a tick. Although the first known human cases in the United States appeared only as recently as 1962, Lyme disease is already reaching epidemic proportions in the Northeast, on the West Coast, and in the upper Midwest. The future of AIDS, derived from monkey viruses, is even more secure, from the virus's perspective.

The final stage of this evolution is represented by the major, long-established epidemic diseases confined to humans. These diseases must have been the evolutionary survivors of far more pathogens that tried to make the jump to us from animals—and mostly failed.

Diseases represent evolution in progress, as microbes adapt by natural selection to new hosts. Compared with cows' bodies, though, our bodies offer different immune defenses and different chemistry. In that new environment, a microbe must evolve new ways to live and propagate itself.

The best-studied example of microbes evolving these new ways involves myxomatosis, which hit Australian rabbits in 1950. The myxoma virus, native to a wild species of Brazilian rabbit, was known to cause a lethal epidemic in European domestic rabbits, which are a different species. The virus was intentionally introduced to Australia in the hopes of ridding the continent of its plague of European rabbits, foolishly introduced in the nineteenth century. In the first year, myxoma produced a gratifying (to Australian farmers) 99.8 percent mortality in infected rabbits. Fortunately for the rabbits and unfortunately for the farmers, the death rate then dropped in the second year to 90 percent and eventually to 25 percent, frustrating hopes of eradicating rabbits completely from Australia. The problem was that the myxoma virus evolved to serve its own interest, which differed from the farmers' interests and those of the rabbits. The virus changed to kill fewer rabbits and to permit lethally infected ones to live longer before dying. The result was bad for Australian farmers but good for the virus: a less lethal myxoma virus spreads baby viruses to more rabbits than did the original, highly virulent myxoma.

For a similar example in humans, consider the surprising evolution of syphilis. Today we associate syphilis with genital sores and a very slowly developing disease, leading to the death of untreated victims only after many years. However, when syphilis was first definitely recorded in Europe in 1495, its pustules often covered the body from the head to the knees, caused flesh to fall off people's faces, and led to death within a few months. By 1546 syphilis had evolved into the disease with the symptoms known to us today. Apparently, just as with myxomatosis, those syphilis spirochetes evolved to keep their victims alive longer in order to transmit their spirochete offspring into more victims.

How, then, does all this explain the outcome of 1492—that Europeans conquered and depopulated the New World, instead of Native Americans conquering and depopulating Europe?

Part of the answer, of course, goes back to the invaders' technological advantages. European guns and steel swords were more effective weapons than Native American stone axes and wooden clubs. Only Europeans had ships capable of crossing the ocean and horses that could provide a decisive advantage in battle. But that's not the whole answer. Far more Native Americans died in bed than on the battlefield—the victims of germs, not of guns and swords. Those germs undermined Indian resistance by killing most Indians and their leaders and by demoralizing the survivors.

The role of disease in the Spanish conquests of the Aztec and Inca empires is especially well documented. In 1519 Cortés landed on the coast of Mexico with 600 Spaniards to conquer the fiercely militaristic Aztec Empire, which at the time had a population of many millions. That Cortés reached the Aztec capital of Tenochtitlán, escaped with the loss of "only" two-thirds of his force, and managed to fight his way back to the coast demonstrates both Spanish military advantages and the initial naïveté of the Aztecs. But when Cortés's next onslaught came, in 1521, the Aztecs were no longer naïve; they fought street by street with the utmost tenacity.

What gave the Spaniards a decisive advantage this time was smallpox, which reached Mexico in 1520 with the arrival of one infected slave from Spanish Cuba. The resulting epidemic proceeded to kill nearly half the Aztecs. The survivors were demoralized by the mysterious illness that killed Indians and spared Spaniards, as if advertising the Spaniards' invincibility. By 1618 Mexico's initial population of 20 million had plummeted to about 1.6 million.

Pizarro had similarly grim luck when he landed on the coast of Peru in 1531 with about 200 men to conquer the Inca Empire. Fortunately for Pizarro, and unfortunately for the Incas, smallpox had arrived overland around 1524, killing much of the Inca population, including both Emperor Huayna Capac and his son and designated successor, Ninan Cuyoche. Because of the vacant throne, two other sons of Huayna Capac, Atahuallpa and Huáscar, became embroiled in a civil war that Pizarro exploited to conquer the divided Incas.

When we in the United States think of the most populous New World societies existing in 1492, only the Aztecs and Incas come to mind. We forget that North America also supported populous Indian societies in the Mississippi Valley. Sadly, these societies too would disappear. But in this case conquistadores contributed nothing directly to the societies' destruction; the conquistadores' germs, spreading in advance, did everything. When De Soto marched through the Southeast in 1540, he came across Indian towns abandoned two years previously because nearly all the inhabitants had died in epidemics. However, he was still able to see some of the densely populated towns lining the lower Mississippi. By a century and a half later, though, when French settlers returned to the lower Mississippi, almost all those towns had vanished. Their relics are the great mound sites of the Mississippi Valley. Only recently have we come to realize that the mound-building societies were still largely intact when Columbus arrived, and that they collapsed between 1492 and the systematic European exploration of the Mississippi.

When I was a child in school, we were taught that North America had originally been occupied by about one million Indians. That low number helped justify the white conquest of what could then be viewed as an almost empty continent. However, archeological excavations and descriptions left by the first European explorers on our coasts now suggest an initial number of around 20 million. In the century or two following Columbus's arrival in the New World, the Indian population is estimated to have declined by about 95 percent.

The main killers were European germs, to which the Indians had never been exposed and against which they therefore had neither immunologic nor genetic resistance. Smallpox, measles, influenza, and typhus competed for top rank among the killers. As if those were not enough, pertussis, plague, tuberculosis, diphtheria, mumps, malaria, and yellow fever came close behind. In countless cases Europeans were actually there to witness the decimation that occurred when the germs arrived. For example, in 1837 the Mandan Indian tribe, with one of the most elaborate cultures in the Great Plains, contracted smallpox thanks to a steamboat traveling up the Missouri River from St. Louis. The population of one Mandan village crashed from 2,000 to less than 40 within a few weeks.

The one-sided exchange of lethal germs between the Old and New worlds is among the most striking and consequence-laden facts of recent history. Whereas over a dozen major infectious diseases of Old World origins became established in the New World, not a single major killer reached Europe from the Americas. The sole possible exception is syphilis, whose area of origin still remains controversial.

That one-sidedness is more striking with the knowledge that large, dense human populations are a prerequisite for the evolution of crowd diseases. If recent reappraisals of the pre-Columbian New World population are correct, that population was not far below the contemporaneous population of Eurasia. Some New World cities, like Tenochtitlán, were among the world's most populous cities at the time. Yet Tenochtitlán didn't have awful germs waiting in store for the Spaniards. Why not?

One possible factor is the rise of dense human populations began somewhat later in the New World than in the Old. Another is that the three most populous American centers—the Andes, Mexico, and the Mississippi Valley—were never connected by regular fast trade into one gigantic breeding ground for microbes, in the way that Europe, North Africa, India, and China became connected in late Roman times.

The main reason becomes clear, however, if we ask a simple question: From what microbes could any crowd diseases of the Americas have evolved? We've seen that Eurasian crowd diseases evolved from diseases of domesticated herd animals. Significantly, there were many such animals in Eurasia. But there were only five animals that became domesticated in the Americas: the turkey in Mexico and parts of North America, the guinea pig and llama/alpaca (probably derived from the same original wild species) in the Andes, the Muscovy duck in tropical South America, and the dog throughout the Americas.

That extreme paucity of New World domestic animals reflects the paucity of wild starting material. About 80 percent of the big wild mammals of the Americas became extinct at the end of the last ice age, around 11,000 years ago, at approximately the same time that the first well-attested wave of Indian hunters spread over the Americas. Among the species that disappeared were ones that would have yielded useful domesticates, such as American horses and camels. Debate still rages as to whether those extinctions were due to climate changes or to the impact of Indian hunters on prey that had never seen humans. Whatever the reason, the extinctions removed most of the basis for Native American animal domestication—and for crowd diseases.

The few domesticates that remained were not likely sources of such diseases. Muscovy ducks and turkeys don't live in enormous flocks, and they're not naturally endearing species (like young lambs) with which we have much physical contact. Guinea pigs may have contributed a trypanosome infection like Chagas' disease or leishmaniasis to our catalog of woes, but that's uncertain.

Initially the most surprising absence is of any human disease derived from llamas (or alpacas), which are tempting to consider as the Andean equivalent of Eurasian livestock. However, llamas had three strikes against them as a source of human pathogens: their wild relatives don't occur in big herds as do wild sheep, goats, and pigs; their total numbers were never remotely as large as the Eurasian populations of domestic livestock, since llamas never spread beyond the Andes; and llamas aren't as cuddly as piglets and lambs and aren't kept in such close association with people. (You may not think of piglets as cuddly, but human mothers in the New Guinea highlands often nurse them, and they frequently live right in the huts of peasant farmers.)

The importance of animal-derived diseases for human history extends far beyond the Americas. Eurasian germs played a key role in decimating native peoples in many other parts of the world as well, including the Pacific islands, Australia, and southern Africa. Racist Europeans used to attribute those conquests to their supposedly better brains. But no evidence for such better brains has been forthcoming. Instead, the conquests were made possible by Europeans' nastier germs, and by the technological advances and denser populations that Europeans ultimately acquired by means of their domesticated plants and animals.

So on this 500th anniversary of Columbus's discovery, let's try to regain our sense of perspective about his hotly debated achievements. There's no doubt that Columbus was a great visionary, seaman, and leader. There's also no doubt that he and his successors often behaved as bestial murderers. But those facts alone don't fully explain why it took so few European immigrants to initially conquer and ultimately supplant so much of the native population of the Americas. Without the germs Europeans brought with them—germs that were derived from their animals—such conquests might have been impossible.

# Review Questions

1. According to Diamond, why did Old World diseases kill 95 percent of the Indians of the Americas while so few illnesses traveled from the New World to Europe and Asia?

2. Diamond notes that animal diseases go through four stages as they evolve to infect humans. What are these stages?

3. What kinds of diseases did humans have before the advent of plant and animal domestication?

4. What accounts for the fact that so many "crowd diseases," such as small-pox and bubonic plague, occur only periodically in epidemics?

5. What conditions foster the development of crowd diseases among human beings? What are the most recent crowd diseases to develop?

# FOUR

# Economy and Globalization

P**eople** everywhere experience wants that can be satisfied only by the acquisition and use of material goods and the services of others. To meet such wants, humans rely on an aspect of their cultural inventory, the **economic system,** which we will define as the provision of goods and services to meet biological and social wants.

The meaning of the term *want* can be confusing. It can refer to what humans *need* for their survival. We must eat, drink, maintain a constant body temperature, defend ourselves, and deal with injury and illness. The economic system meets these needs by providing food, water, clothing, shelter, weapons, medicines, and the cooperative services of others.

But material goods serve more than just our survival needs: they meet our culturally defined *wants* as well. We need clothes to stay warm, but we want garments of a particular style, cut, and fabric to signal our status, rank, or anything else we wish to communicate socially. We need food to sustain life, but we want particular foods prepared in special ways to fill our aesthetic and social desires. Services and goods may also be exchanged to strengthen ties between people or groups. Birthday presents may not always meet physical needs, but they clearly function to strengthen the ties between the parties to the exchange.

Part of the economic system is concerned with **production,** which means rendering material items useful and available for human consumption. Production systems must designate ways to allocate resources. The **allocation of resources** refers to the cultural rules people use to assign rights to the ownership and use of resources. Production systems must also include technologies. Americans usually associate technology with the tools and machines used for manufacturing, rather than with the knowledge for doing it. But many anthropologists link the concept directly to culture. Here we will define

**technology** as the cultural knowledge for making and using tools and extracting and refining raw materials.

Production systems also include a **division of labor,** which refers to the rules that govern the assignment of jobs to people. In hunting and gathering societies, labor is most often divided along the lines of gender, and sometimes age. In these societies, almost everyone knows how to produce, use, and collect the necessary material goods. In industrial society, however, jobs are highly specialized, and labor is divided, at least ideally, on the basis of skill and experience. It is rarely that we know how to do someone else's job in our complex society.

The **unit of production,** meaning the persons or groups responsible for producing goods, follows a pattern similar to the way labor is divided in various societies. Among hunter-gatherers, there is little specialization; individuals, families, groups of friends, or sometimes bands form the units of production. But in our own complex society, we are surrounded by groups specially organized to manufacture, transport, and sell goods.

Another part of the economic system is **distribution.** There are three basic modes of distribution: market exchange, reciprocal exchange, and redistribution.

We are most conscious of market exchange because it lies at the heart of our capitalist system. **Market exchange** is the transfer of goods and services based on price, supply, and demand. Every time we enter a store and pay for something, we engage in market exchange. The price of an item may change with the supply. For example, a discount store may lower the price of a television set because it has too many of the appliances on hand. Prices may go up, however, if everyone wants the sets when there are few to sell. Money is often used in market systems; it enables people to exchange a large variety of items easily. Barter involves the trading of goods, not money, but it, too, is a form of market exchange because the number of items exchanged may also vary with supply and demand. Market exchange appears in human history when societies become larger and more complex. It is well suited for exchange between the strangers who make up these larger groups.

Although we are not so aware of it, we also engage in reciprocal exchange. **Reciprocal exchange** involves the transfer of goods and services between two people or groups based on role obligations. Birthday and holiday gift giving is a fine example of reciprocity. On these occasions we exchange goods not because we necessarily need or want them, but because we are expected to do so as part of our status and role. Parents should give gifts to their children, for example; children should reciprocate. If we fail in our reciprocal obligations, we signal an unwillingness to continue the relationship. Small, simply organized societies, such as the !Kung described earlier, base their exchange systems on reciprocity. Complex ones like ours, although largely organized around the market or redistribution, still manifest reciprocity between kin and close friends.

Finally, there is **redistribution,** the transfer of goods and services between a central collecting source and a group of individuals. Like reciprocity, redistribution is based on role obligation. Taxes typify this sort of exchange in the United States. We must pay our taxes because we are citizens, not because we are buying something. We receive goods and services back—education, transportation, roads, defense—but not necessarily in proportion to the amount we contribute. Redistribution may be the predominant mode of exchange in socialist societies.

Anthropologists also frequently talk about two kinds of economies. In the past, many of the world's societies had **subsistence economies** organized around the need to meet material necessities and social obligations. Subsistence economies are typically associated with smaller groups. They occur at a local level. Such economies depend most on the non-market-exchange mechanisms: reciprocity and redistribution. Their members are occupational generalists. Most people can do most jobs, although there may be distinctions on the basis of gender and age. The !Kung described by Richard Lee in Parts One and Three of this book had subsistence economies as do most horticulturalists.

**Market economies** differ from subsistence economies in their size and motive for production. Although reciprocity and redistribution exist in market economies, market exhange drives production and consumption. Market economies are larger (indeed, there is a growing world market economy that incudes almost everyone) and are characterized by high economic specialization, as well as impersonality. The American economy is market-driven as are most national system. If they have not been already, most subsistence economies will, in the near future, be absorbed into national market systems.

**Globalization** is a process that promotes economic, political, and other cultural connections among people living all over the world. Globalization is marked by an increase in the number and scope of multinational companies (a British company owns the publisher of this book, for example), almost instant communications via phone and Internet to any part of the world, rapid travel between countries, and the spread (anthropologists call the process *diffusion*) of other cultural characteristics from one part of the world to another. One result of globalization is that local people often find the invasion of people, goods, and ideas from other places threatening. It is common for outside forces and the internal cultural change they promote to increase social disorganization within a group and lead to conservative political and religious movements.

The selections in this part illustrate several of the concepts discussed. In the first article, Lee Cronk looks at gift giving, a classic example of reciprocity. He finds that gifts can cement relationships, confer prestige, and obligate subordinates. In the second selection, Jack Weatherford deals with the impact of the world market on the social organization and economy of the indigenous peoples of Peru, Bolivia, and Colombia who grow coca and prepare the drug for market. In the third article, Philippe Bourgois writes about why Latino African Americans work in the inner-city shadow economy of New York drug selling. Limited to service jobs in New York's formal economy, which they often find degrading, they prefer to perform the unpleasant work of selling drugs in the "informal" economy. The fourth article, by Nathan Williamson, describes the illegal logging activities of companies and small-scale timber smugglers in the eastern Bolivian lowlands. Attracted by the world market demand for tropical hardwoods, illegal logging, although an arduous process, yields enough money to help make ends meet on the frontier and thwart the conservation efforts of the Bolivian government and conservation groups. Finally, in the last article, Theodore Bestor illustrates the broad scope of globalization by showing the connection between American and European bluefin tuna fishermen and the Japanese love of sushi. The international interdependence between fishing and sushi grows as the Japanese culinary style spreads in popularity around the world.

# Key Terms

allocation of resources   *p. 159*
distribution   *p. 160*
division of labor   *p. 160*
economic system   *p. 159*
globalization   *p. 161*
market economies   *p. 161*
market exchange   *p. 160*

production   *p. 159*
reciprocal exchange   *p. 160*
redistribution   *p. 160*
subsistence economies   *p. 161*
technology   *p. 160*
unit of production   *p. 160*

# 15

# Reciprocity and the Power of Giving

*Lee Cronk*

*As we saw in the introduction to Part Four, reciprocity constitutes an important exchange system in every society. At the heart of reciprocal exchange is the idea of giving. In this article, Lee Cronk explores the functions of giving using a variety of examples from societies around the world. Giving may be benevolent. It may be used to strengthen existing relationships or to form new ones. Gifts may also be used aggressively to "fight" people, to "flatten" them with generosity. Givers often gain position and prestige in this way. Gifts may also be used to place others in debt so that one can control them and require their loyalty. Cronk shows that, in every society, from !Kung* hxaro *exchange to American foreign aid, there are "strings attached" to giving that affect how people and groups relate to each other.*

"Strings Attached" by Lee Cronk. This article is reprinted by permission of *The Sciences* and is from the May/June 1989 issue.

During a trek through the Rockies in the 1830s, Captain Benjamin Louis E. de Bonneville received a gift of a fine young horse from a Nez Percé chief. According to Washington Irving's account of the incident, the American explorer was aware that "a parting pledge was necessary on his own part, to prove that this friendship was reciprocated." Accordingly, he "placed a handsome rifle in the hands of the venerable chief; whose benevolent heart was evidently touched and gratified by this outward and visible sign of amity."

Even the earliest white settlers in New England understood that presents from natives required reciprocity, and by 1764, "Indian gift" was so common a phrase that the Massachusetts colonial historian Thomas Hutchinson identified it as "a proverbial expression, signifying a present for which an equivalent return is expected." Then, over time, the custom's meaning was lost. Indeed, the phrase now is used derisively, to refer to one who demands the return of a gift. How this cross-cultural misunderstanding occurred is unclear, but the poet Lewis Hyde, in his book *The Gift*, has imagined a scenario that probably approaches the truth.

Say that an Englishman newly arrived in America is welcomed to an Indian lodge with the present of a pipe. Thinking the pipe a wonderful artifact, he takes it home and sets it on his mantelpiece. When he later learns that the Indians expect to have the pipe back, as a gesture of goodwill, he is shocked by what he views as their short-lived generosity. The newcomer did not realize that, to the natives, the point of the gift was not to provide an interesting trinket but to inaugurate a friendly relationship that would be maintained through a series of mutual exchanges. Thus, his failure to reciprocate appeared not only rude and thoughtless but downright hostile. "White man keeping" was as offensive to native Americans as "Indian giving" was to settlers.

In fact, the Indians' tradition of gift giving is much more common than our own. Like our European ancestors, we think that presents ought to be offered freely, without strings attached. But through most of the world, the strings themselves are the main consideration. In some societies, gift giving is a tie between friends, a way of maintaining good relationships, whereas in others it has developed into an elaborate, expensive, and antagonistic ritual designed to humiliate rivals by showering them with wealth and obligating them to give more in return.

In truth, the dichotomy between the two traditions of gift giving is less behavioral than rhetorical: our generosity is not as unconditional as we would like to believe. Like European colonists, most modern Westerners are blind to the purpose of reciprocal gift giving, not only in non-Western societies but also, to some extent, in our own. Public declarations to the contrary, we, too, use gifts to nurture long-term relationships of mutual obligation, as well as to embarrass our rivals and to foster feelings of indebtedness. And this ethic touches all aspects of contemporary life, from the behavior of scientists in research networks to superpower diplomacy. Failing to acknowledge this fact, especially as we give money, machines, and technical advice to peoples around the world, we run the risk of being misinterpreted and, worse, of causing harm.

Much of what we know about the ethics of gift giving comes from the attempts of anthropologists to give things to the people they are studying. Richard Lee, of the University of Toronto, learned a difficult lesson from the !Kung hunter-gatherers, of the Kalahari desert, when, as a token of goodwill, he gave them an ox to slaughter at Christmas. Expecting gratitude, he was shocked when the !Kung complained about having to make do with such a scrawny "bag of bones." Only later did Lee learn, with relief, that the !Kung belittle all gifts. In their eyes, no act is completely generous, or free of calculation; ridiculing gifts is their way of diminishing the expected return and of enforcing humility on those who would use gifts to raise their own status within the group.

Rada Dyson-Hudson, of Cornell University, had a similar experience among the Turkana, a pastoral people of northwestern Kenya. To compensate her informants for their help, Dyson-Hudson gave away pots, maize meal, tobacco, and other items. The Turkana reaction was less than heartwarming. A typical response to a gift of a pot, for example, might be, "Where is the maize meal to go in this pot?" or, "Don't you have a bigger one to give me?" To the Turkana, these are legitimate and expected questions.

The Mukogodo, another group of Kenyan natives, responded in a similar way to gifts Beth Leech and I presented to them during our fieldwork in 1986. Clothing was never nice enough, containers never big enough, tobacco and candies never plentiful enough. Every gift horse was examined carefully, in the mouth and elsewhere. Like the !Kung, the Mukogodo believe that all gifts have an element of calculation, and they were right to think that ours were no exception. We needed their help, and their efforts to diminish our expectations and lessen their obligations to repay were as fair as our attempts to get on their good side.

The idea that gifts carry obligations is instilled early in life. When we gave Mukogodo children candies after visiting their villages, their mothers reminded them of the tie: "Remember these white people? They are the ones who gave you candy." They also reinforced the notion that gifts are meant to circulate, by asking their children to part with their precious candies, already in their mouths. Most of the youngsters reluctantly surrendered their sweets, only to have them immediately returned. A mother might take, at most, a symbolic nibble from her child's candy, just to drive home the lesson.

The way food, utensils, and other goods are received in many societies is only the first stage of the behavior surrounding gift giving. Although repayment is expected, it is crucial that it be deferred. To reciprocate at once indicates a desire to end the relationship, to cut the strings; delayed repayment makes the strings longer and stronger. This is especially clear on the Truk Islands, of Micronesia, where a special word—*niffag*—is used to designate objects moving through the island's exchange network. From the Trukese viewpoint, to return niffag on the same day it is received alters its nature from that of a gift to that of a sale, in which all that matters is material gain.

After deciding the proper time for response, a recipient must consider how to make repayment, and that is dictated largely by the motive behind the gift. Some exchange customs are designed solely to preserve a relationship. The !Kung have a system, called *hxaro*, in which little attention is paid to whether the items exchanged are equivalent. Richard Lee's informant !Xoma explained to him that "Hxaro is when I take a thing of value and give it to you. Later, much later, when you find some good thing, you give it back to me. When I find something good I will give it to you, and so will pass the years together." When Lee tried to determine the exact exchange values of various items (Is a spear worth three strings of beads, two strings, or one?), !Xoma explained that any return would be all right: "You see, we don't trade with things, we trade with people!"

One of the most elaborate systems of reciprocal gift giving, known as *kula*, exists in a ring of islands off New Guinea. Kula gifts are limited largely to shell necklaces, called *soulava*, and armbands, called *mwali*. A necklace given at one time is answered months or years later with an armband, the necklaces usually circulating clockwise, and the armbands counterclockwise, through the archipelago. Kula shells vary in quality and value, and men gain fame and prestige by having their names associated with noteworthy necklaces or armbands. The shells also gain value from their association with famous and successful kula partners.

Although the act of giving gifts seems intrinsically benevolent, a gift's power to embarrass the recipient and to force repayment has, in some societies, made it attractive as a weapon. Such antagonistic generosity reached its most elaborate expression, during the late nineteenth century, among the Kwakiutl, of British Columbia.

The Kwakiutl were acutely conscious of status, and every tribal division, clan, and individual had a specific rank. Disputes about status were resolved by means of enormous ceremonies (which outsiders usually refer to by the Chinook Indian term *potlatch*), at which rivals competed for the honor and prestige of giving away the greatest amount of property. Although nearly everything of value was fair game—blankets, canoes, food, pots, and, until the mid-nineteenth century, even slaves—the most highly prized items were decorated sheets of beaten copper, shaped like shields and etched with designs in the distinctive style of the Northwest Coast Indians.

As with the kula necklaces and armbands, the value of a copper sheet was determined by its history—by where it had been and who had owned it—and a single sheet could be worth thousands of blankets, a fact often reflected in its name. One was called "Drawing All Property from the House," and another, "About Whose Possession All Are Quarreling." After the Kwakiutl began to acquire trade goods from the Hudson's Bay Company's Fort Rupert post, in 1849, the potlatches underwent a period of extreme inflation, and by the 1920s, when items of exchange included sewing machines and pool tables, tens of thousands of Hudson's Bay blankets might be given away during a single ceremony.

In the 1880s, after the Canadian government began to suppress warfare between tribes, potlatching also became a substitute for battle. As a Kwakiutl man once said to the anthropologist Franz Boas, "The time of fighting is past. . . . We do not fight now with weapons: we fight with property." The usual Kwakiutl word for potlatch was *p!Esa*, meaning to flatten (as when one flattens a rival under a pile of blankets), and the prospect of being given a large gift engendered real fear. Still, the Kwakiutl seemed to prefer the new "war of wealth" to the old "war of blood."

Gift giving has served as a substitute for war in other societies, as well. Among the Siuai, of the Solomon Islands, guests at feasts are referred to as attackers, while hosts are defenders, and invitations to feasts are given on short notice in the manner of "surprise attacks." And like the Kwakiutl of British Columbia, the Mount Hagen tribes of New Guinea use a system of gift giving called *moka* as a way of gaining prestige and shaming rivals. The goal is to become a tribal leader, a "big-man." One moka gift in the 1970s consisted of several hundred pigs, thousands of dollars in cash, some cows and wild birds, a truck, and a motorbike. The donor, quite pleased with himself, said to the recipient, "I have won. I have knocked you down by giving so much."

Although we tend not to recognize it as such, the ethic of reciprocal gift giving manifests itself throughout our own society, as well. We, too, often expect something, even if only gratitude and a sense of indebtedness, in exchange for gifts, and we use gifts to establish friendships and to manipulate our positions in society. As in non-Western societies, gift giving in America sometimes takes a benevolent and helpful form; at other times, the power of gifts to create obligations is used in a hostile way.

The Duke University anthropologist Carol Stack found a robust tradition of benevolent exchange in an Illinois ghetto known as the Flats, where poor blacks engage in a practice called swapping. Among residents of the Flats, wealth comes in spurts; hard times are frequent and unpredictable. Swapping, of clothes, food, furniture, and the like, is a way of guaranteeing security, of making sure that someone will be there to help out when one is in need and that one will get a share of any windfalls that come along.

Such networks of exchange are not limited to the poor, nor do they always involve objects. Just as the exchange of clothes creates a gift community in the Flats, so the swapping of knowledge may create one among scientists. Warren Hagstrom, a sociologist at the University of Wisconsin, in Madison, has pointed out that papers submitted to scientific journals often are called contributions, and, because no payment is received for them, they truly are gifts. In contrast, articles written for profit—such as this one—often are held in low esteem: scientific status can be achieved only through *giving* gifts of knowledge.

Recognition also can be traded upon, with scientists building up their gift-giving networks by paying careful attention to citations and acknowledgments. Like participants in kula exchange, they try to associate themselves with renowned and prestigious articles, books, and institutions. A desire for recognition, however, cannot be openly acknowledged as a motivation for research, and it is a rare scientist who is able to discuss such desires candidly. Hagstrom was able to find just one mathematician (whom he described as "something of a social isolate") to confirm that "junior mathematicians want recognition from big shots and, consequently, work in areas prized by them."

Hagstrom also points out that the inability of scientists to acknowledge a desire for recognition does not mean that such recognition is not expected by those who offer gifts of knowledge, any more than a kula trader believes it is all right if his trading partner does not answer his gift of a necklace with an armband. While failure to reciprocate in New Guinean society might once have meant warfare, among scientists it may cause factionalism and the creation of rivalries.

Whether in the Flats of Illinois or in the halls of academia, swapping is, for the most part, benign. But manipulative gift giving exists in modern societies, too—particularly in paternalistic government practices. The technique is to offer a present that cannot be repaid, coupled with a claim of beneficence and omniscience. The Johns Hopkins University anthropologist Grace Goodell documented one example in Iran's Khūzestān Province, which, because it contains most of the country's oil fields and is next door to Iraq, is a strategically sensitive area. Goodell focused on the World Bank–funded Dez irrigation project, a showpiece of the shah's ambitious "white revolution" development plan. The scheme involved the irrigation of tens of thousands of acres and the forced relocation of people from their villages to new, model towns. According to Goodell, the purpose behind dismantling local institutions was to enhance central government control of the region. Before development, each Khūzestāni village had been a miniature city-state, managing its own internal affairs and determining its own relations with outsiders. In the new settlements, decisions were made by government bureaucrats, not townsmen, whose autonomy was crushed under the weight of a large and strategically placed gift.

On a global scale, both the benevolent and aggressive dimensions of gift giving are at work in superpower diplomacy. Just as the Kwakiutl were left only with blankets with which to fight after warfare was banned, the United States and the Soviet Union now find, with war out of the question, that they are left only with gifts—called concessions—with which to do battle. Offers of military cutbacks are easy ways to score points in the public arena of international opinion and to shame rivals, and failure either to accept such offers or to respond with even more extreme proposals may be seen as cowardice or as bellicosity. Mikhail Gorbachev is a virtuoso, a master potlatcher, in this new kind of competition, and, predictably, Americans often see his offers of disarmament and openness as gifts with long strings attached. One reason U.S. officials were buoyed last December [1988], when, for the first time since the Second World War, the Soviet Union accepted American assistance, in the aftermath of the Armenian earthquake, is that it seemed to signal a wish for reciprocity rather than dominance—an unspoken understanding of the power of gifts to bind people together.

Japan, faced with a similar desire to expand its influence, also has begun to exploit gift giving in its international relations. In 1989, it will spend more than ten billion dollars on foreign aid, putting it ahead of the United States for the second consecutive year as the world's greatest donor nation. Although this move was publicly welcomed in the United States as the sharing of a burden, fears, too, were expressed that the resultant blow to American prestige might cause a further slip in our international status. Third World leaders also have complained that too much Japanese aid is targeted at countries in which Japan has an economic stake and that too much is restricted to the purchase of Japanese goods—that Japan's generosity has less to do with addressing the problems of underdeveloped countries than with exploiting those problems to its own advantage.

The danger in all of this is that wealthy nations may be competing for the prestige that comes from giving gifts at the expense of Third World nations. With assistance sometimes being given with more regard to the donors' status than to the recipients' welfare, it is no surprise that, in recent years, development aid often has been more effective in creating relationships of dependency, as in the case of Iran's Khūzestān irrigation scheme, than in producing real development. Nor that, given the fine line between donation and domination, offers of help are sometimes met with resistance, apprehension and, in extreme cases, such as the Iranian revolution, even violence.

The Indians understood a gift's ambivalent power to unify, antagonize, or subjugate. We, too, would do well to remember that a present can be a surprisingly potent thing, as dangerous in the hands of the ignorant as it is useful in the hands of the wise.

# Review Questions

**1.** What does Cronk mean by *reciprocity*? What is the social outcome of reciprocal gift giving?

**2.** According to Cronk, what are some examples of benevolent gift giving?

**3.** How can giving be used to intimidate other people or groups? Give some examples cited by Cronk and think of some from your own experience.

**4.** How does Cronk classify gift-giving strategies such as government foreign aid? Can you think of other examples of the use of exchange as a political device?

# 16

# Cocaine and the Economic Deterioration of Bolivia

*Jack Weatherford*

*The demands of the world market have eroded local subsistence economies for centuries. Lands once farmed by individual families to meet their own needs now grow sugarcane, cotton, grain, or vegetables for market. Deprived of their access to land, householders must work as day laborers or migrate to cities to find jobs. Villages are denuded of the men, who have gone else-where for work, leaving women to farm and manage the family, The rhythm and structure of daily village life are altered dramatically. In this article, Jack Weatherford describes the impact of a new world market for cocaine on the structure and lives of rural Bolivians. Fed by an insatiable demand in Europe and the United States, the Bolivian cocaine trade has drawn males from the countryside, disrupted communications, destroyed families, unbalanced the local diet, and upset traditional social organization.*


"They say you Americans can do anything. So, why can't you make your own cocaine and let our children come home from the coca plantations in the Chapare?" The Indian woman asked the question with confused resignation. In the silence that followed, I could hear only the rats scurrying around in the thatched roof. We continued shelling corn in the dark. The large house around us had once been home to an extended clan but was now nearly empty.

There was no answer to give her. Yet it was becoming increasingly obvious that the traditional Andean system of production and distribution built over thousands of years was now crumbling. Accompanying the destruction of the economic system was a marked distortion of the social and cultural patterns of the Quechua Indians. Since early in Inca history, the village of Pocona where I was working had been a trading village connecting the highlands, which produced potatoes, with the lowlands, which produced coca, a mildly narcotic plant used by the Incas. Over the past decade, however, new market demands from Europe and the United States have warped this system. Now the commodity is cocaine rather than the coca leaves, and the trade route bypasses the village of Pocona.

Bolivian subsistence patterns range from hunting and gathering in the jungle to intensive farming in the highlands, and since Inca times many parts of the country have depended heavily on mining. In the 1980s all of these patterns have been disrupted by the Western fad for one particular drug. Adoption of cocaine as the "drug of choice" by the urban elite of Europe and America has opened up new jungle lands and brought new Indian groups into Western economic systems. At the same time, the cocaine trade has cut off many communities such as Pocona from their traditional role in the national economy. Denied participation in the legal economy, they have been driven back into a world of barter and renewed isolation.

The vagaries of Western consumerism produce extensive and profound effects on Third World countries. It makes little difference whether the demand is for legitimate products such as coffee, tungsten, rubber, and furs marketed through legal corporations, or for illegal commodities such as opium, marijuana, cocaine, and heroin handled through criminal corporations. The same economic principles that govern the open, legal market also govern the clandestine, illegal markets, and the effects of both are frequently brutal.

Before coming to this Bolivian village, I assumed that if Americans and Europeans wanted to waste their money on cocaine, it was probably good that some of the poor countries such as Bolivia profit from it. In Cochabamba, the city in the heart of the cocaine-producing area, I had seen the benefits of this trade among the *narco chic* who lived in a new suburb of houses styled to look like Swiss chalets, Spanish haciendas, and English country homes. All these homes were surrounded by large wrought-iron fences, walls with broken glass set in the tops, and with large dogs that barked loudly and frequently. Such homes cost up to a hundred thousand dollars, an astronomical sum for Bolivia. I had also seen the narco elite of Cochabamba wearing gold chains and the latest Miami fashions and driving Nissans, Audis, Ford Broncos, an occasional BMW, or even a Mercedes through the muddy streets of the city. Some of their children attended the expensive English-speaking school; much of Cochabamba's meager nightlife catered to the elite. But as affluent as they may be in Bolivia, this elite would probably not earn as much as working-class families in such cities as Detroit, Frankfurt, or Tokyo.

Traveling outside of Cochabamba for six hours on the back of a truck, fording the same river three times, and following a rugged path for the last twenty-five kilometers, I reached Pocona and saw a different face of the cocaine trade. Located in a valley a mile and a half above sea level, Pocona is much too high to grow the coca bush. Coca grows best below six thousand feet, in the lush area called the Chapare where the eastern Andes meet the western edge of the Amazon basin and rain forest.

Like the woman with whom I was shelling corn, most of the people of Pocona are older, and community life is dominated by women together with their children who are still too young to leave. This particular woman had already lost both of her sons to the Chapare. She did not know it at the time, but within a few months, she was to lose her husband to the same work as well. With so few men, the women are left alone to plant, work, and harvest the fields of potatoes, corn, and fava beans, but with most of the work force missing, the productivity of Pocona has declined substantially.

In what was once a moderately fertile valley, hunger is now a part of life. The daily diet consists almost exclusively of bread, potato soup, boiled potatoes, corn, and tea. The majority of their daily calories comes from the potatoes and from the sugar that they put in their tea. They have virtually no meat or dairy products and very few fresh vegetables. These products are now sent to the Chapare to feed the workers in the coca fields, and the people of Pocona cannot compete against them. The crops that the people of Pocona produce are now difficult to sell because truck drivers find it much more profitable to take goods in and out of the Chapare rather than face the long and unprofitable trip to reach such remote villages as Pocona.

Despite all the hardships caused by so many people being away from the village, one might assume that more cash should be flowing into Pocona from the Chapare, where young men easily earn three dollars a day—three times the average daily wage of porters or laborers in Cochabamba. But this assumption was contradicted by the evidence of Pocona. As one widowed Indian mother of four explained, the first time her sixteen-year-old son came home, he brought bags of food, presents, and money for her and the younger children. She was very glad that he was working in the Chapare. On the second visit home he brought only a plastic bag of white powder for himself, and instead of bringing food, he took away as much as he could carry on the two-day trip back into the Chapare.

The third time, he told his mother that he could not find enough work in the Chapare. As a way to earn more money he made his mother bake as much bread as she could, and he took Mariana, his ten-year-old sister, with him to sell the bread to the workers in the Chapare. According to the mother, he beat the little girl and abused her repeatedly. Moreover, the money she made disappeared. On one of Mariana's trips home to get more bread, the mother had no more wheat or corn flour to supply her son. So, she sent Mariana away to Cochabamba to work as a maid. The enraged son found where Mariana was working and went to the home to demand that she be returned to him. When the family refused, he tried but failed to have her wages paid to him rather than to his mother. Mariana was separated from her family and community, but at least she was not going to be one more of the prostitutes in the Chapare, and for her mother that was more important.

The standard of living in Pocona was never very high, but with the advent of the cocaine boom in Bolivia, the standard has declined. Ten years ago, Pocona's gasoline-powered generator furnished the homes with a few hours of electric light each night. The electricity also allowed a few families to purchase radios, and occasionally someone brought in a movie projector to show a film in a large adobe building on the main square. For the past two years, the people of Pocona have not been able to buy gasoline for their generator. This has left the village not only without electricity but without entertainment and radio or film contact with the outside world. A few boys have bought portable radios with their earnings from the Chapare, but their families were unable to replace the batteries. Nights in Pocona are now both dark and silent.

In recent years the national economy of Bolivia has been virtually destroyed, and peasants in communities such as Pocona are reverting to barter as the only means of exchange. The value of the peso may rise or fall by as much as 30 percent in a day; the peasants cannot take a chance on trading their crops for money that may be worth nothing in a week. Cocaine alone has not been responsible for the destruction of the Bolivian economy, but it has been a major contributor. It is not mere coincidence that the world's largest producer of coca is also the country with the world's worst inflation.

During part of 1986, inflation in Bolivia varied at a rate between 2,000 and 13,000 percent, if calculated on a yearly basis. Prices in the cities changed by the hour, and on some days the dollar would rise at the rate of more than 1 percent per hour. A piece of bread cost 150,000 pesos, and an American dollar bought between two and three million pesos on the black market. Large items such as airplane tickets were calculated in the billions of pesos, and on one occasion I helped a man carry a large box of money to pay for such a ticket. It took two professional counters half an hour to count the bills. Workers were paid in stacks of bills that were often half a meter high. Because Bolivia is too undeveloped to print its money, the importation of its own bills printed in West Germany and Brazil was one of the leading imports in the mid-1980s.

Ironically, by no longer being able to participate fully in the money economy, the villagers of Pocona who have chewed coca leaves for centuries now find it difficult to afford the leaves. The narcotics industry pays such a high price that the people of Pocona can afford only the rejected trash from the cocaine industry. Whether chewed or made into a tea, the coca produces a mild lift somewhat like a cup of coffee but without the jagged comedown that follows a coffee high. Coca also reduces hunger, thirst, headaches, stomach pains, and the type of altitude sickness known as *sorroche*.

Were this all, coca use might be viewed as merely a bad habit somewhat like drinking coffee, smoking cigarettes, or overindulging in chocolates, but unlike these practices coca actually has a number of marked health benefits. The coca leaf is very high in calcium. In a population with widespread lactose intolerance and in a country without a national system of milk distribution, this calcium source is very important. The calcium also severely reduces cavities in a population with virtually no dental services outside the city. Coca also contains large amounts of vitamins A, C, and D, which are often lacking in the starchy diets of the mountain peasants.

Without coca, and with an excess of corn that they cannot get to market, the people of Pocona now make more *chicha*, a form of home-fermented corn beer that tastes somewhat like the silage that American dairymen feed their cows. It is ironic that as an affluent generation of Americans are decreasing their consumption of alcohol in favor of drugs such as cocaine, the people of Pocona are drinking more alcohol to replace their traditional coca. *Chicha*, like most beers, is more nutritious than other kinds of distilled spirits but lacks the health benefits of the coca leaves. It also produces intoxication, something that no amount of coca leaves can do. Coca chewing is such a slow process and produces such a mild effect that a user would have to chew a bushel of leaves to equal the impact of one mixed drink or one snort of cocaine.

In many ways, the problems and complaints of Pocona echo those of any Third World country with a cash crop, particularly those caught in the boom-and-bust cycle characteristic of capitalist systems. Whether it is the sisal boom of the Yucatán, the banana boom of Central America, the rubber boom of Brazil, or the cocaine boom in Bolivia, the same pattern develops. Rural villages are depleted of their work forces. Family and traditional cultural patterns disintegrate. And the people are no longer able to afford certain local products that suddenly become valued in the West. This is what happened to Pocona.

Frequently, the part of a country that produces the boom crop benefits greatly, while other areas suffer greatly. If this were true in Bolivia, benefits accruing in the coca-producing area of the Chapare would outweigh the adjustment problems of such villages as Pocona. As it turns out, however, the Chapare has been even more adversely affected.

Most of the young men who go to the Chapare do not actually work in the coca fields. The coca bush originated in this area and does not require extensive care. One hectare can easily produce eight hundred kilograms of coca leaves in a year, but not much labor is needed to pick them. After harvesting, the leaves are dried in the sun for three to four days. Most of these tasks can easily be done by the farmer and his family. Wherever one goes in the Chapare one sees coca leaves spread out on large drying cloths. Old people or young children walk up and down these cloths, turning the drying leaves with their whisk brooms.

The need for labor, especially the labor of strong young men, comes in the first stage of cocaine production, in the reduction of large piles of leaves into a small quantity of *pasta*, or coca paste from which the active ingredient, cocaine, can then be refined. Three hundred to five hundred kilograms of leaves must be used to make one kilogram of pure cocaine. The leaves are made into *pasta* by soaking them in vats of kerosene and by applying salt, acetone, and sulfuric acid. To make the chemical reaction occur, someone must trample on the leaves for several days—a process very much like tromping on grapes to make wine, only longer. Because the corrosive mixture dissolves shoes or boots, the young men walk barefooted. These men are called *pisacocas* and usually work in the cool of the night, pounding the green slime with their feet. Each night the chemicals eat away more skin and very quickly open ulcers erupt. Some young men in the Chapare now have feet that are so diseased that they are incapable of standing, much less walking. So, instead, they use their hands to mix the *pasta*, but their hands are eaten away even faster than their feet. Thousands and possibly tens of thousands of young Bolivian men now look like lepers with permanently disfigured hands and feet. It is unlikely that any could return to Pocona and make a decent farmer.

Because this work is painful, the *pisacocas* smoke addictive cigarettes coated with *pasta*. This alleviates their pain and allows them to continue walking the coca throughout the night. The *pasta* is contaminated with chemical residues, and smoking it warps their minds as quickly as the acids eat their hands and feet. Like Mariana's brother, the users become irrational, easily angered, and frequently violent.

Once the boys are no longer able to mix coca because of their mental or their physical condition, they usually become unemployed. If their wounds heal, they may be able to work as loaders or haulers, carrying the cocaine or transporting the controlled chemicals used to process it. By and large, however, women and very small children, called *hormigas* (ants), are better at this work. Some of the young men then return home to their villages; others wander to Cochabamba, where they might live on the streets or try to earn money buying and selling dollars on the black market.

The cocaine manufacturers not only supply their workers with food and drugs, they keep them sexually supplied with young girls who serve as prostitutes as well. Bolivian health officials estimate that nearly half of the people living in the Chapare today have venereal disease. As the boys and girls working there return to their villages, they take these diseases with them. Increasing numbers of children born to infected mothers now have bodies covered in syphilitic sores. In 1985, a worse disease hit with the first case of AIDS. Soon after the victim died, a second victim was diagnosed.

In an effort to control its own drug problem, the United States is putting pressure on Bolivia to eradicate coca production in the Andean countries. The army invaded the Chapare during January of 1986, but after nearly three weeks of being surrounded by the workers in the narcotics industry and cut off from their supply bases, the army surrendered. In a nation the size of Texas and California combined, but with a population approximately the size of the city of Chicago, it is difficult for the government to control its own territory. Neither the Incas nor the Spanish conquistadores were ever able to conquer and administer the jungles of Bolivia, where there are still nomadic bands of Indians who have retreated deep into the jungle to escape Western encroachment. The army of the poorest government in South America is no better able to control this country than its predecessors. The government runs the cities, but the countryside and the jungles operate under their own laws.

One of the most significant effects of the coca trade and of the campaigns to eradicate it has come on the most remote Indians of the jungle area. As the campaign against drugs has pushed production into more inaccessible places and as the world demand has promoted greater cultivation of coca, the coca growers are moving into previously unexplored areas. A coca plantation has been opened along the Chimore river less than an hour's walk from one of the few surviving bands of Yuqui Indians. The Yuquis, famous for their eight-foot-long bows and their six-foot arrows, are now hovering on the brink of extinction. In the past year, the three bands of a few hundred Yuquis have lost eleven members in skirmishes with outsiders. In turn, they killed several outsiders this year and even shot the missionary who is their main champion against outside invaders.

According to the reports of missionaries, other Indian bands have been enlisted as workers in cocaine production and trafficking, making virtual slaves out of them. A Bolivian medical doctor explained to me that the Indians are fed the cocaine in their food as a way of keeping them working and preventing their escape. Through cocaine, the drug traffickers may be able to conquer and control these last remnants of the great Indian nations of the Americas. If so, they will accomplish what many have failed to do in the five-hundred-year campaign of Europeans to conquer the free Indians.

The fate of the Indians driven out of their homelands is shown in the case of Juan, a thirteen-year-old Indian boy from the Chimore river where the Yuquis live. I found him one night in a soup kitchen for street children operated in the corner of a potato warehouse by the Maryknoll priests. Juan wore a bright orange undershirt that proclaimed in bold letters Fairfax District Public Schools. I sat with him at the table coated in potato dust while he ate his soup with his fellow street children, some of whom were as young as four years old. He told me what he could remember of his life on the Chimore; he did not know to which tribe he was born or what language he had spoken with his mother. It was difficult for Juan to talk about his Indian past in a country where it is a grave insult to be called an Indian. Rather than talk about the Chimore or the Chapare, he wanted to ask me questions because I was the first American he had ever met. Was I stronger than everyone else, because he had heard that Americans were the strongest people in the world? Did we really have wolves and bears in North America, and was I afraid of them? Had I been to the Chapare? Did I use cocaine?

In between his questions, I found out that Juan had come to Cochabamba several years ago with his mother. The two had fled the Chapare, but he did not know why. Once in the city they lived on the streets for a few years until his mother died, and he had been living alone ever since. He had become a *polilla* (moth), as they call such street boys. To earn money he washed cars and sold cigarettes laced with *pasta*. When he tired of talking about himself and asking about the animals of North America, he and his two friends made plans to go out to one of the nearby *pasta* villages the next day.

Both the Chapare (which supplied the land for growing coca) and highland villages such as Pocona (which supplied the labor) were suffering from the cocaine boom. Where, then, is the profit? The only other sites in Bolivia are the newly developed manufacturing towns where cocaine is refined. Whereas in the past most of this refining took place in Colombia, both the manufacturers and the traffickers find it easier and cheaper to have the work done in Bolivia, closer to the source of coca leaves and closer to much cheaper sources of labor. The strength of the Colombian government and its closeness to the United States also make the drug trafficking more difficult there than in Bolivia, with its weak, unstable government in La Paz.

Toco is one of the villages that has turned into a processing point for cocaine. Located at about the same altitude as Pocona but only a half-day by truck from the Chapare, Toco cannot grow coca, but the village is close enough to the source to become a major producer of the *pasta*. Traffickers bring in the large shipments of coca leaves and work them in backyard "kitchens." Not only does Toco still have its young men at home and still have food and electricity, but it has work for a few hundred young men from other villages.

Unlike Pocona, for which there are only a few trucks each week, trucks flow in and out of Toco every day. Emblazoned with names such as Rambo, El Padrino (The Godfather), and Charles Bronson rather than the traditional truck names of San José, Virgen de Copacabana, or Flor de Urkupina, these are the newest and finest trucks found in Bolivia. Going in with a Bolivian physician and another anthropologist from the United States, I easily got a ride, along with a dozen Indians, on a truck which was hauling old car batteries splattered with what appeared to be vomit.

A few kilometers outside of Toco we were stopped by a large crowd of Indian peasants. Several dozen women sat around on the ground and in the road spinning yarn and knitting. Most of the women had babies tied to their shoulders in the brightly colored *awayu* cloth, which the women use to carry everything from potatoes to lambs. Men stood around with farm tools, which they now used to block the roads. The men brandished their machetes and rakes at us, accusing us all of being smugglers and *pisacocas*. Like the Indians on the truck with us, the three of us stood silent and expressionless in the melee.

The hostile peasants were staging an ad hoc strike against the coca trade. They had just had their own fields of potatoes washed away in a flash flood. Now without food and without money to replant, they were demanding that someone help them or they would disrupt all traffic to and from Toco. Shouting at us, several of them climbed on board the truck. Moving among the nervous passengers, they checked for a shipment of coca leaves, kerosene, acid, or anything else that might be a part of the coca trade. Having found nothing, they reluctantly let us pass with stern warnings not to return with cocaine or *pasta*. A few weeks after our encounter with the strikers, their strike ended and most of the men went off to look for work in the Chapare and in Toco; without a crop, the cocaine traffic was their only hope of food for the year.

On our arrival in Toco we found out that the batteries loaded with us in the back of the truck had been hollowed out and filled with acid to be used in making *pasta*. *Chicha* vomit had been smeared around to discourage anyone from checking them. After removal of the acid, the same batteries were then filled with plastic bags of cocaine to be smuggled out of Toco and into the town of Cliza and on to Cochabamba and the outside world.

Toco is an expanding village with new cement-block buildings going up on the edge of town and a variety of large plumbing pipes, tanks, and drains being installed. It also has a large number of motorcycles and cars. By Bolivian standards it is a rich village, but it is still poorer than the average village in Mexico or Brazil. Soon after our arrival in Toco, we were followed by a handful of men wanting to sell us *pasta,* and within a few minutes the few had grown to nearly fifty young men anxious to assist us. Most of them were on foot, but some of them circled us in motorcycles, and many of them were armed with guns and machetes. They became suspicious and then openly hostile when we convinced them that we did not want to buy *pasta*. To escape them we took refuge in the home of an Indian family and waited for the mob to disperse.

When we tried to leave the village a few hours later, we were trapped by a truckload of young men who did not release us until they had checked with everyone we had met with in the village. They wondered why we were there if not to buy *pasta*. We were rescued by the doctor who accompanied us; she happened to be the niece of a popular Quechua writer. Evoking the memory of her uncle who had done so much for the Quechua people, she convinced the villagers of Toco that we were Bolivian doctors who worked with her in Cochabamba, and that we were not foreigners coming to buy *pasta* or to spy on them. An old veteran who claimed that he had served in the Chaco War with her uncle vouched for us, but in return for having saved us he then wanted us to buy *pasta* from him.

The wealth generated by the coca trade from Bolivia is easy to see. It is in the European cars cruising the streets of Cochabamba and Santa Cruz, and in the nice houses in the suburbs. It is in the motorcycles and jeeps in Toco, Cliza, and Trinidad. The poverty is difficult to see because it is in the remote villages like Pocona, among the impoverished miners in the village of Porco, and intertwined in the lives of peasants throughout the highland districts of Potosí and Oruro. But it is in communities such as Pocona that 70 percent of the population of Bolivia lives. For every modern home built with cocaine money in Cochabamba, a tin mine lies abandoned in Potosí that lost many of its miners when the world price for tin fell and they had to go to the Chapare for food. For every new car in Santa Cruz or every new motorcycle in Toco, a whole village is going hungry in the mountains.

The money for coca does not go to the Bolivians. It goes to the criminal organizations that smuggle the drugs out of the country and into the United States and Europe. A gram of pure cocaine on the streets of Cochabamba costs five dollars; the same gram on the streets of New York, Paris, or Berlin costs over a hundred dollars. The price increase occurs outside Bolivia.

The financial differential is evident in the case of the American housewife and mother sentenced to the Cochabamba prison after being caught with six and a half kilograms of cocaine at the airport. Like all the other women in the prison, she now earns money washing laundry by hand at a cold-water tap in the middle of the prison yard. She receives the equivalent of twenty cents for each pair of pants she washes, dries, and irons. In Bolivian prisons, the prisoner has to furnish his or her own food, clothes, medical attention, and even furniture.

She was paid five thousand dollars to smuggle the cocaine out of Bolivia to the Caribbean. Presumably someone else was then to be paid even more to smuggle it into the United States or Europe. The money that the American housewife received to smuggle the cocaine out of the country would pay the salary of eighty *pisacocas* for a month. It would also pay the monthly wages of two hundred fifty Bolivian schoolteachers, who earn the equivalent of twenty U.S. dollars per month in pay. Even though her price seemed high by Bolivian standards, it is a small part of the final money generated by the drugs. When cut and sold on the streets of the United States, her shipment of cocaine would probably bring in five to seven million dollars. Of that amount, however, only about five hundred dollars goes to the Bolivian farmer.

The peasant in the Chapare growing the coca earns three times as much for a field of coca as he would for a field of papayas. But he is only the first in a long line of people and transactions that brings the final product of cocaine to the streets of the West. At the end of the line, cocaine sells for four to five times its weight in gold.

The United States government made all aid programs and loans to Bolivia dependent on the country's efforts to destroy coca. This produces programs in which Bolivian troops go into the most accessible areas and uproot a few fields of aging or diseased coca plants. Visiting drug-enforcement agents from the United States together with American congressmen applaud, make their reports on the escalating war against drugs, and then retire to a city hotel where they drink hot cups of coca tea and cocktails.

These programs hurt primarily the poor farmer who tries to make a slightly better living by growing coca rather than papayas. The raids on the fields and cocaine factories usually lead to the imprisonment of ulcerated *pisococas* and women and children *hormigas* from villages throughout Bolivia. Local authorities present the burned fields and full prisons to Washington visitors as proof that the Bolivian government has taken a hard stance against drug trafficking.

International crime figures with bank accounts in New York and Zurich get the money. Bolivia ends up with hunger in its villages, young men with their hands and feet permanently maimed, higher rates of venereal disease, chronic food shortages, less kerosene, higher school dropout rates, increased drug addiction, and a worthless peso.

# Review Questions

1. List and describe the major effects of the cocaine trade on rural Bolivian life.

2. Why have the production of coca and the manufacture of cocaine created a health hazard in Bolivia?

3. Why has the cocaine trade benefited the Bolivian economy so little?

4. How has the cocaine trade disrupted village social organization in Bolivia?

# 17

# Workaday World— Crack Economy

## Philippe Bourgois

*Market economies (usually linked to the global economy) seem to be a standard feature of most countries in today's world. Almost everywhere, there is a formal market economy identified by visible, legal, organized economic structures and activities, which economists attempt to measure and governments can tax and regulate. Banks, factories, corporations, retail outlets—these and other publicly organized economic units are usually part of the formal economy.*

    *But underneath the formal economy lies an informal market system often called the* shadow economy. *The shadow economy is usually small-scale, personal, and at times illegal. Governments find it difficult to measure and control the shadow economy. Yet it is the shadow economy that provides a living for hundreds of millions of largely poor men and women around the world today.*

    *In this article, Philippe Bourgois focuses on the shadow economy found in inner-city New York. There, Latino/a African Americans work for*

"Workaday World—Crack Economy" by Philippe Bourgois. Reprinted with permission from the December 4, 1995, issue of *The Nation*.

*little money under appalling conditions to sell drugs, even though they would
prefer to do legal work. Caught in a legal economy dominated by service jobs
in New York's finance, real estate, and insurance companies, these inner-city
men cannot do legal work and keep their dignity. Work selling drugs, no matter how unpleasant, is the only answer.*

I was forced into crack against my will. When I first moved to East Harlem—"El
Barrio"—as a newlywed in the spring of 1985, I was looking for an inexpensive
New York City apartment from which I could write about the experience of
poverty and ethnic segregation in the heart of one of the most expensive cities
in the world. I was interested in the political economy of inner-city street culture. I wanted to probe the Achilles' heel of the richest industrialized nation in
the world by documenting how it imposes racial segregation and economic marginalization on so many of its Latino/a and African-American citizens.

My original subject was the entire underground (untaxed) economy, from
curbside car repairing and baby-sitting to unlicensed off-track betting and drug
dealing. I had never even heard of crack when I first arrived in the neighborhood—no one knew about this particular substance yet, because this brittle
compound of cocaine and baking soda processed into efficiently smokable pellets was not yet available as a mass-marketed product. By the end of the year,
however, most of my friends, neighbors and acquaintances had been swept into
the multibillion-dollar crack cyclone: selling it, smoking it, fretting over it. I followed them, and I watched the murder rate in the projects opposite my crumbling tenement apartment spiral into one of the highest in Manhattan.

But this essay is not about crack, or drugs, per se. Substance abuse in
the inner city is merely a symptom—and a vivid symbol—of deeper dynamics
of social marginalization and alienation. Of course, on an immediately visible personal level, addiction and substance abuse are among the most immediate, brutal facts shaping daily life on the street. Most important, however,
the two dozen street dealers and their families that I befriended were not
interested in talking primarily about drugs. On the contrary, they wanted me
to learn all about their daily struggles for subsistence and dignity at the
poverty line.

Through the 1980s and 1990s, slightly more than one in three families in
El Barrio have received public assistance. Female heads of these impoverished
households have to supplement their meager checks in order to keep their children alive. Many are mothers who make extra money by baby-sitting their
neighbors' children, or by housekeeping for a paying boarder. Others may bar-
tend at one of the half-dozen social clubs and after-hours dancing spots scattered throughout the neighborhood. Some work "off the books" in their living
rooms as seamstresses for garment contractors. Finally, many also find themselves obliged to establish amorous relationships with men who are willing to
make cash contributions to their household expenses.

Male income-generating strategies in the underground economy are more publicly visible. Some men repair cars on the curb; others wait on stoops for unlicensed construction subcontractors to pick them up for fly-by-night demolition jobs or window renovation projects. Many sell "numbers"—the street's version of off-track betting. The most visible cohorts hawk "nickels and dimes" of one illegal drug or another. They are part of the most robust, multibillion-dollar sector of the booming underground economy. Cocaine and crack, in particular during the mid-1980s and through the early 1990s, followed by heroin in the mid-1990s, have become the fastest-growing—if not the only—equal-opportunity employers of men in Harlem. Retail drug sales easily outcompete other income-generating opportunities, whether legal or illegal.

Why should these young men and women take the subway to work minimum-wage jobs—or even double-minimum-wage jobs—in downtown offices when they can usually earn more, at least in the short run, by selling drugs on the street corner in front of their apartment or schoolyard? In fact, I am always surprised that so many inner-city men and women remain in the legal economy and work nine-to-five plus overtime, barely making ends meet. According to the 1990 Census of East Harlem, 48 percent of all males and 35 percent of females over 16 were employed in officially reported jobs, compared with a citywide average of 64 percent for men and 49 percent for women. In the census tracts surrounding my apartment, 53 percent of all men over 16 years of age (1,923 out of 3,647) and 28 percent of all women over 16 (1,307 out of 4,626) were working legally in officially censused jobs. An additional 17 percent of the civilian labor force was unemployed but actively looking for work, compared with 16 percent for El Barrio as a whole, and 9 percent for all of New York City.

## "If I Was Working Legal . . ."

Street dealers tend to brag to outsiders and to themselves about how much money they make each night. In fact, their income is almost never as consistently high as they report it to be. Most street sellers, like my friend Primo (who, along with other friends and co-workers, allowed me to tape hundreds of hours of conversation with him over five years), are paid on a piece-rate commission basis. When converted into an hourly wage, this is often a relatively paltry sum. According to my calculations, the workers in the Game Room crackhouse, for example, averaged slightly less than double the legal minimum wage—between 7 and 8 dollars an hour. There were plenty of exceptional nights, however, when they made up to ten times minimum wage—and these are the nights they remember when they reminisce. They forget about all the other shifts when they were unable to work because of police raids, and they certainly do not count as forfeited working hours the nights they spent in jail.

This was brought home to me symbolically one night as Primo and his co-worker Caesar were shutting down the Game Room. Caesar unscrewed the fuses in the electrical box to disconnect the video games. Primo had finished stashing the left-over bundles of crack vials inside a hollowed-out live electrical socket and was counting the night's thick wad of receipts. I was struck by how thin the handful of bills was that he separated out and folded neatly into his personal billfold. Primo and Caesar then eagerly lowered the iron riot gates over the Game Room's windows and snapped shut the heavy Yale padlocks. They were moving with the smooth, hurried gestures of workers preparing to go home after an honest day's hard labor. Marveling at the universality in the body language of workers rushing at closing time, I felt an urge to compare the wages paid by this alternative economy. I grabbed Primo's wallet out of his back pocket, carefully giving a wide berth to the fatter wad in his front pocket that represented Ray's share of the night's income—and that could cost Primo his life if it were waylaid. Unexpectedly, I pulled out fifteen dollars' worth of food stamps along with two $20 bills. After an embarrassed giggle, Primo stammered that his mother had added him to her food-stamp allotment.

> **Primo:**  I gave my girl, Maria, half of it. I said, "Here, take it, use it if you need it for whatever." And then the other half I still got it in my wallet for emergencies.
>
> Like that, we always got a couple of dollars here and there, to survive with. Because tonight, straight cash, I only got garbage. Forty dollars! Do you believe that?

At the same time that wages can be relatively low in the crack economy, working conditions are often inferior to those in the legal economy. Aside from the obvious dangers of being shot, or of going to prison, the physical work space of most crackhouses is usually unpleasant. The infrastructure of the Game Room, for example, was much worse than that of any legal retail outfit in East Harlem: There was no bathroom, no running water, no telephone, no heat in the winter and no air conditioning in the summer. Primo occasionally complained:

> Everything that you see here [sweeping his arm at the scratched and dented video games, the walls with peeling paint, the floor slippery with litter, the filthy windows pasted over with ripped movie posters] is fucked up. It sucks, man [pointing at the red 40-watt bare bulb hanging from an exposed fixture in the middle of the room and exuding a sickly twilight].

Indeed, the only furnishings besides the video games were a few grimy milk crates and bent aluminum stools. Worse yet, a smell of urine and vomit usually permeated the locale. For a few months Primo was able to maintain a rudimentary sound system, but it was eventually beaten to a pulp during one of Caesar's drunken rages. Of course, the deficient infrastructure was only one part of the depressing working conditions.

**Primo:** Plus I don't like to see people fucked up [handing over three vials to a nervously pacing customer]. This is fucked-up shit. I don't like this crack dealing. Word up.
[gunshots in the distance] Hear that?

In private, especially in the last few years of my residence, Primo admitted that he wanted to go back to the legal economy.

**Primo:** I just fuck up the money here. I rather be legal.

**Philippe:** But you wouldn't be the head man on the block with so many girlfriends.

**Primo:** I might have women on my dick right now, but I would be much cooler if I was working legal. I wouldn't be drinking and the coke wouldn't be there every night.
Plus if I was working legally I would have women on my dick too, because I would have money.

**Philippe:** But you make more money here than you could ever make working legit.

**Primo:** O.K. So you want the money but you really don't want to do the job.
I really hate it, man. Hate it! I hate the people! I hate the environment! I hate the whole shit, man! But it's like you get caught up with it. You do it, and you say, "Ay, fuck it today!" Another day, another dollar. [pointing at an emaciated customer who was just entering] But I don't really, really think that I would have hoped that I can say I'm gonna be richer one day. I can't say that. I think about it, but I'm just living day to day.
If I was working legal, I wouldn't be hanging out so much. I wouldn't be treating you [pointing to the 16-ounce can of Colt 45 in my hand]. In a job, you know, my environment would change . . . totally. 'Cause I'd have different friends. Right after work I'd go out with a co-worker, for lunch, for dinner. After work I may go home; I'm too tired for hanging out—I know I gotta work tomorrow.
After working a legal job, I'm pretty sure I'd be good.

## Burned in the FIRE Economy

The problem is that Primo's good intentions do not lead anywhere when the only legal jobs he can compete for fail to provide him with a livable wage. None of the crack dealers were explicitly conscious of the links between their limited options in the legal economy, their addiction to drugs and their dependence on the crack economy for economic survival and personal dignity. Nevertheless, all of Primo's colleagues and employees told stories of rejecting what they considered to be intolerable working conditions at entry-level jobs.

Most entered the legal labor market at exceptionally young ages. By the time they were 12, they were bagging and delivering groceries at the supermarket for tips, stocking beer off the books in local bodegas or running errands. Before reaching 21, however, virtually none had fulfilled their early childhood dreams of finding stable, well-paid legal work.

The problem is structural: From the 1950s through the 1980s second-generation inner-city Puerto Ricans were trapped in the most vulnerable niche of a factory-based economy that was rapidly being replaced by service industries. Between 1950 and 1990, the proportion of factory jobs in New York City decreased approximately threefold at the same time that service-sector jobs doubled. The Department of City Planning calculates that more than 800,000 industrial jobs were lost from the 1960s through the early 1990s, while the total number of jobs of all categories remained more or less constant at 3.5 million.

Few scholars have noted the cultural dislocations of the new service economy. These cultural clashes have been most pronounced in the office-work service jobs that have multiplied because of the dramatic expansion of the finance, real estate and insurance (FIRE) sector in New York City. Service work in professional offices is the most dynamic place for ambitious inner-city youths to find entry-level jobs if they aspire to upward mobility. Employment as mailroom clerks, photocopiers and messengers in the highrise office corridors of the financial district propels many into a wrenching cultural confrontation with the upper-middle-class white world. Obedience to the norms of highrise, office-corridor culture is in direct contradiction to street culture's definitions of personal dignity—especially for males who are socialized not to accept public subordination.

Most of the dealers have not completely withdrawn from the legal economy. On the contrary—they are precariously perched on its edge. Their poverty remains their only constant as they alternate between street-level crack dealing and just-above-minimum-wage legal employment. The working-class jobs they manage to find are objectively recognized to be among the least desirable in U.S. society; hence the following list of just a few of the jobs held by some of the Game Room regulars during the years I knew them: unlicensed asbestos remover, home attendant, street-corner flier distributor, deep-fat fry cook and night-shift security guard on the violent ward at the municipal hospital for the criminally insane.

The stable factory-worker incomes that might have allowed Caesar and Primo to support families have largely disappeared from the inner city. Perhaps if their social network had not been confined to the weakest sector of manufacturing in a period of rapid job loss, their teenage working-class dreams might have stabilized them for long enough to enable them to adapt to the restructuring of the local economy. Instead, they find themselves propelled headlong into an explosive confrontation between their sense of cultural dignity versus the humiliating interpersonal subordination of service work.

Workers like Caesar and Primo appear inarticulate to their professional supervisors when they try to imitate the language of power in the workplace; they stumble pathetically over the enunciation of unfamiliar words. They cannot decipher the hastily scribbled instructions—rife with mysterious abbreviations—that are left for them by harried office managers on diminutive Post-its. The "common sense" of white-collar work is foreign to them; they do not, for example, understand the logic in filing triplicate copies of memos or for postdating invoices. When they attempt to improvise or show initiative, they fail miserably and instead appear inefficient—or even hostile—for failing to follow "clearly specified" instructions.

In the highrise office buildings of midtown Manhattan or Wall Street, newly employed inner-city high school dropouts suddenly realize they look like idiotic buffoons to the men and women for whom they work. But people like Primo and Caesar have not passively accepted their structural victimization. On the contrary, by embroiling themselves in the underground economy and proudly embracing street culture, they are seeking an alternative to their social marginalization. In the process, on a daily level, they become the actual agents administering their own destruction and their community's suffering.

Both Primo and Caesar experienced deep humiliation and insecurity in their attempts to penetrate the foreign, hostile world of highrise office corridors. Primo had bitter memories of being the mailroom clerk and errand boy at a now-defunct professional trade magazine. The only time he explicitly admitted to having experienced racism was when he described how he was treated at that particular work setting.

> **Primo:** I had a prejudiced boss. . . . When she was talking to people she would say, "He's illiterate," as if I was really that stupid that I couldn't understand what she was talking about.
>
> So what I did one day—you see they had this big dictionary right there on the desk, a big heavy motherfucker—so what I just did was open up the dictionary, and I just looked up the word, "illiterate." And that's when I saw what she was calling me.
>
> So she's saying that I'm stupid or something. I'm stupid! [pointing to himself with both thumbs and making a hulking face] "He doesn't know shit."

In contrast, in the underground economy Primo never had to risk this kind of threat to his self-worth.

> **Primo:** Ray would never disrespect me that way; he wouldn't tell me that because he's illiterate too, plus I've got more education than him. I almost got a G.E.D.

The contemporary street sensitivity to being dissed immediately emerges in these memories of office humiliation. The machismo of street culture exacerbates the sense of insult experienced by men because the majority of office supervisors at the entry level are women. In the lowest recesses of New York City's FIRE sector, tens of thousands of messengers, photocopy machine operators and security guards serving the Fortune 500 companies are brusquely ordered about by young white executives—often female—who sometimes make bimonthly salaries superior to their underlings' yearly wages. The extraordinary wealth of Manhattan's financial district exacerbates the sense of sexist-racist insult associated with performing just-above-minimum-wage labor.

## "I Don't Even Got a Dress Shirt"

Several months earlier, I had watched Primo drop out of a "motivational training" employment program in the basement of his mother's housing project, run by former heroin addicts who had just received a multimillion-dollar private sector grant for their innovative approach to training the "unemployable." Primo felt profoundly disrespected by the program, and he focused his discontent on the humiliation he faced because of his inappropriate wardrobe. The fundamental philosophy of such motivational job-training programs is that "these people have an attitude problem." They take a boot-camp approach to their unemployed clients, ripping their self-esteem apart during the first week in order to build them back up with an epiphanic realization that they want to find jobs as security guards, messengers and data-input clerks in just-above-minimum-wage service-sector positions. The program's highest success rate had been with middle-aged African-American women who wanted to terminate their relationship to welfare once their children leave home.

I originally had a "bad attitude" toward the premise of psychologically motivating and manipulating people to accept boring, poorly paid jobs. At the same time, however, the violence and self-destruction I was witnessing at the Game Room was convincing me that it is better to be exploited at work than to be outside the legal labor market. In any case, I persuaded Primo and a half-dozen of his Game Room associates to sign up for the program. Even Caesar was tempted to join.

None of the crack dealers lasted for more than three sessions. Primo was the first to drop out, after the first day. For several weeks he avoided talking about the experience. I repeatedly pressed him to explain why he "just didn't show up" at the sessions. Only after repeated badgering on my part did he finally express the deep sense of shame and vulnerability he experienced whenever he attempted to venture into the legal labor market.

> **Philippe:**   Yo Primo, listen to me. I worry that there's something taking place that you're not aware of, in terms of yourself. Like the coke that you be sniffing all the time; it's like every night.

> **Primo:**   What do you mean?

**Philippe:**   Like not showing up at the job training. You say it's just pro-crastination, but I'm scared that it's something deeper that you're not dealing with. . . .

**Primo:**   The truth though—listen Felipe—my biggest worry was the dress code, 'cause my gear is limited. I don't even got a dress shirt, I only got one pair of shoes, and you can't wear sneakers at that program. They wear ties too—don't they? Well, I ain't even got ties—I only got the one you lent me.

I would've been there three weeks in the same gear: T-shirt and jeans. *Estoy jodido como un bón!* [I'm all fucked up like a bum!]

**Philippe:**   What the fuck kinda bullshit excuse are you talking about? Don't tell me you were thinking that shit. No one notices how people are dressed.

**Primo:**   Yo, Felipe, this is for real! Listen to me! I was thinking about that shit hard. Hell yeah!

Hell, yes, they would notice if somebody's wearing a fucked-up tie and shirt.

I don't want to be in a program all *abochornado* [bumlike]. I prob-ably won't even concentrate, getting dished, like . . . and being looked at like a sucker. Dirty jeans . . . or like old jeans, because I would have to wear jeans, 'cause I only got one slack. Word though! I only got two dress shirts and one of them is missing buttons.

I didn't want to tell you about that because it's like a poor excuse, but that was the only shit I was really thinking about. At the time I just said, "Well, I just don't show up."

And Felipe, I'm a stupid [very] skinny nigga'. So I have to be care-ful how I dress, otherwise people will think I be on the stem [a crack ad-dict who smokes out of a glass-stem pipe].

**Philippe:**   [nervously] Oh shit. I'm even skinnier than you. People must think I'm a total drug addict.

**Primo:**   Don't worry. You're white.

# Review Questions

1. What kinds of jobs, both legal and "shadow," can Latino African American men work at in East Harlem, New York City, according to Bourgois?

2. Why do so many poor Latino/a African American men and women hold legal jobs in New York?

3. What are the structural changes that have occurred in New York City's economy over the past forty years? How do these limit the work that is available to African American men and women?

4. How are Latino African Americans treated in the "FIRE" service economy?

5. Why did Bourgois's African American informants drop out of the motivational program some of them entered, and how did their response to this program resemble their reaction to work in the legal service economy?

# 18

# Illegal Logging and Frontier Conservation

## *Nathan Williamson*

*Conservation policy often seems to be based on a protective ideology and a faith in economic motivational theory. Too often, such policy ignores local reality, such as when the Indian government divided Aravalli Hill forests on the basis of a U.S. model. They designated ranges, lots, and sublots, hired forest guards, and began what was supposed to be a forty-two-year cutting cycle. The policy failed to conserve the forest because it ignored the fact that people lived in and used the forest every day. What is needed is a better understanding of what is actually going on, which, as this article by Nathan Williamson illustrates, is a possible role for anthropologists. Based on two years of fieldwork in and near the Chimanes forest in the eastern Bolivian lowlands, Williamson argues that forest conservation efforts by the Bolivian government and international organizations such as the International Tropical Timber Organization have largely failed to prevent illegal logging by commercial*

*companies, chain saw gangs, and Chimanes Indians. Major reasons for this
are the world demand for quality tropical hardwoods, the poverty of people
living on the Bolivian frontier, and the inability of a poor government to control illegal activities in such a remote area. The only solution, he concludes,
is for an international agreement to control demand for tropical hardwoods
or at least a plan that directs small-scale logging in a sustainable way.*

I hold up the microphone I am using during an impromptu interview and ask
Alfonso Campero if he is worried about hitting the tree that has emerged from
the darkness in front of us.[1] He and I are crouched in the bow of a balsa-wood
raft that carries his family, piles of green plantains, and bags of unshelled rice
down the Maniqui River. The Maniqui is an Amazonian tributary that cuts
through Bolivia's tropical lowlands. The river flows through parts of Beni Department (a department is roughly equivalent to a U.S. state), an area about the
size of Minnesota. Except for where lush hardwood forests butt up against the
Andes Mountains to the west, Beni is flat. This explains why the Maniqui meanders through endless curves and loops and why traveling on it by raft can be
painfully slow. Even so, the current is persistent and Alfonso doesn't have time
to answer me. The cumbersome raft hits the log and Alfonso and his father,
Jorge, swear and grunt as they push us away from the partly submerged hazard.

Navigation on the river is complicated by the fact that the Camperos are
also guiding a raft of timber, which they have cut illegally near their homestead
in the Chimanes Indian Reserve, down river to San Borja. San Borja is a frontier
town defined by unpaved streets, shacks, bars, prostitutes, and lumber mills. It
is also headquarters to several lumber companies, and it is to a small-scale lumber buyer that the Camperos will sell their timber. He, in turn, will mill the wood
in one of several small lumber mills found in San Borja and probably sell it to a
local lumber company. The company will ship it by truck up the perilous, single-
track dirt road to the Bolivian highlands, where it will likely be used to make furniture, flooring, or windows. Some of these products end up on the world market.

The Camperos are only a small part of the region's logging industry.
Largest are the several logging companies that, with government approval, are
supposed to conduct their logging at sustainable levels in forests set aside for
managed logging. The timber they cut there is considered to be legally harvested by the Bolivian government. But most of the logging companies are
closely tied to small illegal logging operations such as the Camperos' because
the companies can increase their profits by buying the valuable illegal timber
and claiming that it has come from their own forest ranges. They also buy timber from another small-scale source, the *cuartoneros* (chainsaw gang members), who scout for mahogany (and other hardwoods) found in the Chimanes
Reserve, cut it down, chainsaw it into timbers (*cuartones*), carry it piece by
piece to nearby streams, and float it down to San Borja. Working together and
motivated by the global demand for fine hardwoods, the logging company own-

---

[1]All names have been changed.

ers and workers, sawmill operators, truckers, Chimanes Indians, and *cuartoneros* form a single economic system.

But this system also works within another context, the international movement to conserve natural resources. The Bolivian government and world conservation groups, alarmed by the wholesale destruction of the world's prime forests and also motivated by the specter of lost revenue that accompanies it, have implemented plans designed to achieve sustainable logging in and around the Chimanes forest. On the face of it, their conservation policies appear sensible and workable. But in fact they are not. To be sure, the logging systems found in San Borja are not as destructive as the clear-cutting that goes on in many parts of the world, but they are slowly depleting the forest and will probably eventually lead to its destruction. Why have the carefully planned conservation efforts failed in this case? The answer lies in the geographic, economic, and political realities of frontier life in this part of Bolivia, and the actions of commercial timber companies driven by the high world demand for quality tropical hardwoods.

## Conservation Policy

The Bolivian government and several NGOs (nongovernmental organizations) have introduced plans to regulate logging in the Bolivian lowlands at a time when the forests still exist. The Chimanes forest has not yet suffered the effects of clear-cutting and the invasion of farmers and ranchers seen in other parts of the Amazon basin. Loggers are the major threat. With this in mind, Conservation International, a conservation organization based in Washington, D.C., arranged a debt-for-nature swap in the region in 1987. The organization bought (paid off) part of Bolivia's external national debt in exchange for the formation of a trust fund to pay for conservation projects in the region and permanent legal status for a biosphere reserve. Following the 1987 debt-for-nature swap, the International Tropical Timber Organization, an industry association, began funding its own sustainable forestry program inside the conservation and timber production areas. At the time, Conservation International, the International Tropical Timber Organization, and the Bolivian government hoped to demonstrate that economic development could be harmonious with forest conservation. The International Tropical Timber Organization's Chimanes program asked seven timber companies in the conservation area to change their harvesting practices in return for rights to cut in certain designated parts of the forest. They now would cut a variety of commercial species on a rotating schedule that would permit forest regeneration. The Chimanes program hoped to show that the forest could provide timber for the long term and that the forest's enhanced economic value in that role would discourage its destruction for use as pasture, colonization, and farming.

When I arrived in the Chimanes area for the first time in 1999, I quickly realized that what looked promising on paper was difficult to achieve on the ground. Despite an initial investment by the International Tropical Timber Organization of $1,200,000 and subsequent foreign assistance totaling $300,000 to $400,000 a year, the seven timber concessions in the conservation area did little to change their extraction techniques. It was more profitable for them to continue to cut only the most valuable species, primarily mahogany, than to search the forest for the less-valuable species that the sustainable forestry program required them to cut. It also did not work because the seven companies could buy timber from individuals—Chimanes Indians like the Camperos, and *cuartoneros*—who were willing and able to illegally harvest the most valuable trees in forests that were off limits to the big companies and logging altogether. In this way, some companies that were part of the legal economy "laundered" prime wood cut by people who were part of the "shadow," or illegal, economy. It is easy to understand why companies are motivated to do this. Timber extraction costs are high in this part of the world because it is so expensive to ship in equipment and send out the wood. Harvesting just the most valuable hardwoods is more economical; cutting cheaper wood is not. But what motivates the Chimanes Indians and *cuartoneros* to break the law, especially considering how much work it is for them to harvest timber by hand?

## Chimanes Economics

Economic necessity is the most obvious answer. About 8,000 Chimanes live in the Chimanes Reserve, which is about the size of Rhode Island. Only one or two logging roads carve up their vast tract of tropical forest and most of the people use the Maniqui River as their highway. The Chimanes seem to relish isolation, and remain hesitant to make strong connections with the rest of Bolivia. Few of them speak Spanish. Although some of them have married colonists, their contacts with outsiders are largely limited to trading, piloting rafts, and searching for the valuable trees that they or *cuartoneros* will cut. The Chimanes have often been mislabeled "nomads" because they move about the forest to hunt and fish. Nevertheless, virtually every Chimanes family has a small agricultural field and a more or less permanently located reed hut. Chimanes are expert fishermen, and, for this reason, most of their villages hug the banks of the Maniqui River.

Besides farming and hunting, many Chimanes produce some goods for sale. They grow and sell rice to river traders and weave two-foot-long shingles out of *jatata*, a small palm (*Genoma deversa*), which are used to roof houses in San Borja and other parts of the frontier.

The Chimanes are self-sufficient in many ways, but they still need to make money. They often buy (or trade for) tools, food, clothing, school supplies (for the children who go to school), and other goods they cannot produce themselves. Although the work is hard and the proceeds are meager, illegal logging is the easiest way to increase income.

The villagers living in Nápoles, a Chimanes settlement of about nineteen huts located up river from San Borja, harvest timber themselves or in partnership with timber buyers from San Borja. Jorge Campero, who, with his family, lives in Nápoles, figures that 50 percent of the villagers are employed in the illegal logging trade "right down to the schoolteacher," his son emphasized. Because the villagers don't have enough money to pay for a tractor to haul trees out of the woods, they use homemade oxcarts to bring the wood to the river.

This is how the Camperos harvested the timber we were rafting down the Maniqui. The Camperos cut four old-growth trees behind their house in late April of 2001 and used their cart to bring the wood to the river. Alfonso figured that he could sell the load for about $400 when they reached San Borja and clear about $220 after expenses. He would split the money with his father. This amount may appear small to many North Americans, especially if they knew how many dollars the wood would bring in the United States, but in Bolivia, where the average daily wage is about $2, the sum is significant. To the Camperos, who depend on illegal logging to earn a living, forest conservation means little.

## Cuartoneros

*Cuartoneros* log illegally for the same reasons that Chimanes do, but they work differently from the Indians. The Nápoles Chimanes community is unique in that many of its villagers are self-employed loggers, meaning they transport the wood themselves and sell it to small lumber mills or timber buyers in San Borja. Most of the other Chimanes villages sell their timber to traders who come up river to get it. In either case, most of their logging is done near the river. But in the more remote areas of the Chimanes Territory, it is the *cuartoneros,* or chainsaw crews, who mine the forest for its most valuable trees. And they do so without the help of mechanized equipment except for chainsaws and outboard motors. Mostly poor men from San Borja, they scout, often with the help of Chimanes Indians, for mahogany trees in the Chimanes Reserve, cut the trees down, saw them up with chainsaws, and carry the timbers to nearby streams. I joined a group of *cuartoneros* on a timber-cutting excursion in April 1999. Before we departed, team members loaded the outboard motor–powered dugout canoe with needed equipment, including a replacement chainsaw bar, a drum of gasoline, and food. The boat was a supply shuttle; its purpose was to drop me and the equipment off near a logging camp and return to town.

The Chimanes forest is well watered. It receives ninety-one inches of rain on average each year, which runs off to form small streams that flow into creeks and wide rivers. Once we were under way, it immediately became clear how important rivers and streams are to the *cuartoneros'* method of timber extraction. When the rivers run high, the timber can be floated to San Borja. When the rivers are low, crews must wait for rain to transport the wood.

Typically, the *cuartoneros* set up camp by a stream in an area where they believe uncut mahogany trees are located. They string up plastic tarpaulins to protect them and their equipment from the rain. They make a fire to cook the food they have brought with them or hunted in the forest. Next they contact local Chimanes Indians and ask them to scout the forest for suitable mahogany and other valuable hardwood trees. The search is more difficult than it might seem because broad-leafed mahogany trees grow at very low densities in Bolivia. Indeed, the loggers may only find one or two large-sized trees every twenty-five acres. If team members have already cut the trees closest to their camp, they may have to walk for several miles to reach the next tree they can fell.

Before they can cut the trees, however, the loggers must clear a trail from them to the nearest large stream or river. To do this, the men use machetes, cutting steps into inclines and chopping the brush back to form paths. Because of the large amount of labor involved in carrying the wood, trails must be as direct and level as possible. Bridges made from wood slabs are also placed over the brooks and streams that often block the way. Finally, the trail is carefully scouted for roots and other objects that might trip the loggers as they carry their heavy loads of wood to the river.

A chainsaw operator, who must work for hours each day with his heavy implement, does the actual cutting and processing of the trees. Mahogany grows up to six and one-half feet in diameter. To fell such a large tree, the chainsaw operator makes several cuts at its base. When the tree drops, the chainsawer's assistant, using wooden wedges and levers cut from smaller trees in the forest, must level it. Then the assistant measures the widths of the *cuartones* to be cut by marking the ends of the tree trunk. Finally, he uses an oil-soaked line to snap sawing guides along the length of the log.

The chainsaw operator, cutting along the snapped lines freehand, divides the tree into *planchones* (slabs) that are typically six and one-half inches thick and as wide as the log. The assistant flips the slabs over and snaps guidelines six or seven inches apart along their lengths. The chainsawer cuts along these lines to produce *cuartones*. Other loggers will carry these timbers, which weigh anywhere from 80 to 200 pounds, to the stream or river. While the carriers transport the wood, the chainsawer continues to saw *cuartones*.

To carry the *cuartones* to the river or stream, the men form a relay, with each worker responsible for his own section of the trail (*tramo*) that, depending on the difficulty of the terrain, is between 20 and 200 feet long. The first *lomero* (timber carrier) sets the pace. He upends a *cuarton*, balancing it horizontally on a shoulder pad. Trotting at a half jog, he plants the *cuarton* point down on the ground at the end of his *tramo*, and the next *lomero* picks it up on his shoulder and trots off toward the end of his section. The process is repeated over and over again until all the *cuartones* reach their final destination.

The work is exhausting. The loggers often have to carry the heavy timbers up steep hills, across narrow makeshift bridges, and down slippery descents. Even on the flat sections, the pace is hard because the *lomeros* run faster there. Despite the hard work, carrying is a slow way to move timber. It may take an entire day to move thirty timbers half a mile. As one logger recalled,

> Shit, my first day I almost fainted. Because they were heavy, those *cuartones*. I was saying it wasn't the kind of work for me because it seemed like they were going to kill me. "You will learn," they said. But all night my arms and legs were so sore. *They* [the other men] were relaxed! The other guys were playing. I said, shit, I am sick.

The work goes on for days until sufficient *cuartones* are cut and moved. Then the men drag the *cuartones* into the stream and wade, float, or push them to the nearest river. There, they lash them together to form rafts (*cayapos*), and float them to San Borja.

Why would anyone do this arduous and illegal work? The answer seems to be that there are few better alternatives for employment on the frontier. Jobs are hard to find in Bolivia, and the San Borja region is no exception. And by local standards (manual laborers, such as brush clearers and cowboys, receive about $33 to $35 a month), *cuartoneros* are paid well. In 1999, the foreman on a *cuartonero* crew made $5.26 a day. The chainsawer received four or five cents for each board foot he milled (I estimated that the crew produced about 2,200 board feet that month), while the timber carriers earned $5.30 a day. The chainsawer's assistant earned $4.38 and the camp cook, $3.50.

It is the lure of higher pay, combined with the fact that most men who work on chainsaw gangs are in debt to their *patrons,* the men who underwrite and organize the operation, which sends them back into the forest time and again. In this debt/peonage system, men are rarely able to earn enough to fully pay off what they owe. As a result, although the Chimanes forest is out of bounds to loggers, the attraction of higher pay and the need to pay off debts draws the men back into the illegal work time and again.

## Forest Conservation

Is it possible for industrial logging to be sustainable, to log in a way that permits forests to recover and produce timber for hundreds of years? Sustainable extraction for forests may actually work in some areas of North America. Unfortunately, the story in the tropics is more complex. Here large tracts of virgin rain forest remain, but logging them in a way that would let them recover is very expensive. For example, Bowles et al.[2] estimate that systems of logging that preserve tropical forests' biodiversity cost from 20 to 450 percent more than simply hacking the most valuable trees out of the forest and moving on to other untouched stands of trees.

But is illegal logging in the Chimanes forest and approved logging in other forests near San Borja that destructive? The answer is both yes and no. In the long run, the forest will be denuded of its most valuable trees. In the short run, illegal logging is less destructive than approved commercial logging. However, as markets for more tree species continue to open up for Bolivian logging companies, even approved companies will be tempted to log in more damaging ways.

Similar to slash-and-burn agriculture, which was once viewed as devastating to forests and wasteful but is now felt to permit forest sustainability if done in moderation, *cuartonero* and Chimanes logging have less impact on the forest than one might think. Unlike mechanized logging operations, these

[2]I. A. Bowles et al., "Policy, Logging and Tropical Forest Conservation," *Science* 280 (1998): 1900.

small-scale lumbermen do not clear wide skid roads that account for much of the ecological damage caused by logging in Bolivia. The forest quickly over-grows the five-foot-wide trails the *cuartoneros* clear to get timber out of the for-est. Chimanes logging is slightly more destructive because the Indians clear oxcart trails, which are much wider than footpaths, to transport the timber they cut and because they cut more trees in the forest near their houses.

Cuartoneros also spare almost all the less valuable rain forest tree species because it is only worth their time and hard labor to cut and carry the most valu-able trees. (Wood processed from a single large mahogany tree can bring $1,000 in San Borja and much more in the United States and Europe.) In addition, *cuar-tonero* timber harvests are limited to an area a few miles wide along large streams, because it does not make financial sense to carry the wood any farther.

Mechanized logging is more destructive. Industrial logging companies may have to cut and market less valuable rain forest species to justify the high cost of installing logging roads. And the roads, cut by bulldozers, are destruc-tive to the forest. Although commercial operations can theoretically rotate their cutting areas to allow for regrowth, these sustainable forest practices still re-quire extensive road networks to reach far into the forest.

But even the least destructive logging practices change the forest. Young ma-hogany trees do not usually produce seeds. It is the larger trees that regenerate the species and these are the ones that loggers cut down. In the end, the selective practice of cutting the most valuable trees will eliminate these species from the forest. The creation of logging roads, the migration of people into the frontier who are looking for work, and the likely improvement of the road up the mountains linking the region to La Paz in the highlands will all threaten the forest.

## Forest Management on the Frontier

In an attempt to stop the prolific illegal logging along the Maniqui River, both by large lumber companies and by the Chimanes and *cuartoneros,* the Bolivian Forestry Service recently approved two timber management plans for the Chi-manes Reserve. Both call for local people, the Chimanes and *cuartoneros,* to put down their chainsaws and cooperate with a group of timber companies that have been given exclusive rights to log in the management areas. Unfortunately, these plans provide good examples of what can go wrong with forestry projects in indigenous territories.

First, the Chimanes Indians possess no organized tribal government or agency that can deal effectively with the government or with logging compa-nies. Mindful of this, forestry projects in other areas of Bolivia (one is run by a Bolivian NGO working with the Nature Conservancy) try to establish a Western-style governing body among native groups. This was not necessary for the Chi-manes because the New Tribes evangelical missionaries had created something called the Chimanes Council, which is currently negotiating timber deals with outsiders on behalf of the tribe. Unfortunately, most Chimanes are unhappy with the results, and few believe the Council can fairly represent them.

A second problem is the Forest Service's choice of logging companies that have rights to do the work. One timber company that just received legal rights to log in the territory has long been involved in the illegal timber trade. Another is alleged to be a front for a U.S. timber company that is known for breaking Bolivian forestry laws.

A third problem concerns employment. At best, timber companies with new rights to log the Chimanes Territory will employ one or two men from each Chimanes village. The remaining men, who used to log illegally, are supposed to find other ways to earn a living. And although some *cuartoneros* may be hired by logging companies, their wages may be lower. If illegal logging ceases, many will lose their livelihoods.

In sum, it appears that the Bolivian Forest Department's new plan will not prevent current logging practices. Instead, the agreement will give local companies access to the Chimanes forest, which used to be out of bounds for cutting, and it probably won't stop small-scale cutting and smuggling.

## Conclusion

The Chimanes forest and other forests near San Borja are attractive natural resources ripe for exploitation by entrepreneurs. International environmental groups have sought ways to preserve the region's old-growth forests by suggesting various plans to promote sustainable logging. The Bolivian government has endorsed these plans or developed its own conservation programs, motivated partly by debt-for-nature agreements and partly by the economic argument that it is better to establish a longer-producing industry. But these programs have not worked well because poor Indians and colonists, driven by the need for work and money, ignore the agreements and because commercial logging companies in search of profits do as well.

On top of it all is the simple fact that logging law and policy cannot be enforced. San Borja and the Chimanes forest area are part of the Bolivian frontier. Just as frontier life in the United States bred lawlessness and opportunism, so does the Bolivian frontier. Located far from centers of government in La Paz in the highlands, the lowlands are barely connected to the rest of the country. The Bolivian nation is perpetually in debt. It does not have the resources, and perhaps, at times, the will, to control illegal frontier activity.

What possible solution is there to this difficult problem? The answer may ultimately lie with the world community. Just as demand drives the illegal international drug trade, the world market for quality old-growth forest hardwoods stimulates illegal logging. Controlling logging will require moderating demand by limiting imports of mahogany. One minor example of this approach is India's long-standing limit on the amount of pith it can produce for conversion into pith helmets. More dramatic are international agreements that limit whale hunting and define seasons on some varieties of fish.

Another approach might be to appeal to people's consciences. Wood produced in a sustainable manner can be labeled as environmentally friendly and priced higher to cover the costs of sustainable management. Conservation groups could run ad campaigns that are similar to those aimed at the fur coat industry. Building a home with unsustainably harvested mahogany paneling could be equated with the death of a priceless tropical forest ecosystem. Or perhaps it is possible to institute a program that permits Chimanes Indians and *cuartoneros* to log but also to replant the species they take. No matter what the approach, the dream of one day having sustainable logging in Bolivia and other parts of the world with tropical forests can only be realized if there is a worldwide determination to support it by using legal agreements, market mechanisms, and good forestry management.

In the meantime, the Camperos lose little sleep about whether their logging is sustainable. Their mission is simple: sell the wood to a small sawmill whose owner will sell the boards to someone with connections to get the shipments to a city where it can be re-sold and exported. Alfonso has his own and his family's life to worry about. Because it rained for several days, it has taken him over a month to harvest wood that will bring him $120. On that kind of money he has to feed, clothe, and school his eight children.

By nightfall the kids have fallen asleep in a big pile in the middle of the raft. They lie all tangled together under a sheet their father has hung over them to keep off the rain. As we near San Borja, he and Jorge become quiet. They are nervous about losing their wood because there have been rumors that local Forest Service agents are confiscating undocumented lumber. It has taken them 32 days to get their wood this far. They don't want to lose it now.

# Review Questions

1. According to Williamson, what plans and programs have been tried to promote sustainable logging in the Bolivian lowlands? How have they worked?

2. What are the three main types of logging employed by people in the Chimanes and nearby forests? How destructive to the forest is each?

3. What motivates the Chimanes Indians and *cuartoneros* to illegally cut timber in the Chimanes Forest Reserve? What role does the frontier nature of the area play in their ability to get away with these activities?

4. According to Williamson, why have the programs put forward by the Bolivian government and NGOs failed to work in the forests that surround San Borja? What does he suggest might be the way to promote sustainable logging there?

5. How are logging activities in the Bolivian lowlands connected to the world economy?

# 19

# How Sushi
# Went Global

## Theodore C. Bestor

*International trade, or at least intergroup trade, is nothing new. Tens of thousands of years ago, Upper Paleolithic peoples living in inland Europe made necklaces from shells traded to them from coastal peoples. Semiprecious stones from central India found their way to the Sumerian states by 4000 B.C. However, despite the increased world trade that accompanied more seaworthy oceangoing vessels and steam-powered ships and railroad trains in more recent times, most countries continued to depend largely on homebound manufacturing and commerce. But after World War II, world trade and global economic and cultural interdependence exploded. Today this globalization process means a world in which many companies are international conglomerates headquartered in countries other than one's own, communication with almost any place in the world is a keyboard away, and travel across national borders is free and easy. In this article, Theodore Bestor illustrates globalization with an unlikely example: the internationalization of a Japanese culinary custom, sushi, or the eating of raw fish. First, the Japanese love of bluefin tuna as a sushi centerpiece involved fishing industries in North America and Europe. The best bluefins were sent abroad to satisfy Japanese palates. A freak tuna glut depressed the Japanese market just as sushi became popular in the rest of the world, stimulating an increase in tuna fishing and the beginnings of tuna trapping and feeding in the Mediterranean. Despite its global reach, sushi is still a Japanese dish in the minds of most of its connoisseurs.*

A 40-minute drive from Bath, Maine, down a winding two-lane highway, the last mile on a dirt road, a ramshackle wooden fish pier stands beside an empty parking lot. At 6:00 P.M. nothing much is happening. Three bluefin tuna sit in a huge tub of ice on the loading dock.

Between 6:45 and 7:00, the parking lot fills up with cars and trucks with license plates from New Jersey, New York, Massachusetts, New Hampshire, and Maine. Twenty tuna buyers clamber out, half of them Japanese. The three bluefin, ranging from 270 to 610 pounds, are winched out of the tub, and buyers crowd around them, extracting tiny core samples to examine their color, fingering the flesh to assess the fat content, sizing up the curve of the body.

After about 20 minutes of eyeing the goods, many of the buyers return to their trucks to call Japan by cellphone and get the morning prices from Tokyo's Tsukiji market—the fishing industry's answer to Wall Street—where the daily tuna auctions have just concluded. The buyers look over the tuna one last time and give written bids to the dock manager, who passes the top bid for each fish to the crew that landed it.

The auction bids are secret. Each bid is examined anxiously by a cluster of young men, some with a father or uncle looking on to give advice, others with a young woman and a couple of toddlers trying to see Daddy's fish. Fragments of concerned conversation float above the parking lot: "That's all?" "Couldn't we do better if we shipped it ourselves?" "Yeah, but my pickup needs a new transmission now!" After a few minutes, deals are closed and the fish are quickly loaded onto the backs of trucks in crates of crushed ice, known in the trade as "tuna coffins." As rapidly as they arrived, the flotilla of buyers sails out of the parking lot—three bound for New York's John F. Kennedy Airport, where their tuna will be airfreighted to Tokyo for sale the day after next.

Bluefin tuna may seem at first an unlikely case study in globalization. But as the world rearranges itself—around silicon chips, Starbucks coffee, or sashimi-grade tuna—new channels for global flows of capital and commodities link far-flung individuals and communities in unexpected new relationships. The tuna trade is a prime example of the globalization of a regional industry, with intense international competition and thorny environmental regulations; centuries-old practices combined with high technology; realignments of labor and capital in response to international regulation; shifting markets; and the diffusion of culinary culture as tastes for sushi, and bluefin tuna, spread worldwide.

## Growing Appetites

Tuna doesn't require much promotion among Japanese consumers. It is consistently Japan's most popular seafood, and demand is high throughout the year. When the Federation of Japan Tuna Fisheries Cooperative (known as Nikkatsuren) runs ad campaigns for tuna, they tend to be low-key and whimsical, rather like the "Got Milk?" advertising in the United States. Recently, the federation launched "Tuna Day" (Maguro no hi), providing retailers with posters and recipe cards for recipes more complicated than "slice and serve chilled." Tuna Day's mascot is Goro-kun, a colorful cartoon tuna swimming the Australian crawl.

Despite the playful contemporary tone of the mascot, the date selected for Tuna Day carries much heavier freight. October 10, it turns out, commemorates the date that tuna first appeared in Japanese literature, in the eighth-century collection of imperial court poetry known as the *Man'yoshu*—one of the towering classics of Japanese literature. The neat twist is that October 10 today is a national holiday, Sports Day. Goro-kun, the sporty tuna, scores a promotional hat trick, suggesting intimate connections among national culture, healthy food for active lives, and the family holiday meal.

Outside Japan, tuna, especially raw tuna, hasn't always had it so good. Sushi isn't an easy concept to sell to the uninitiated. And besides, North Americans tend to think of cultural influence as flowing from West to East: James Dean, baseball, Coca-Cola, McDonald's, and Disneyland have all gone over big in Tokyo. Yet Japanese cultural motifs and material—from Kurosawa's *The Seven Samurai* to Yoda's Zen and Darth Vader's armor, from Issey Miyake's fashions to Nintendo, PlayStation, and Pokémon—have increasingly saturated North American and indeed the entire world's consumption and popular culture. Against all odds, so too has sushi.

In 1929, the *Ladies' Home Journal* introduced Japanese cooking to North American women, but discreetly skirted the subject of raw fish: "There have been purposely omitted . . . any recipes using the delicate and raw tuna fish which is sliced wafer thin and served iced with attractive garnishes. [These] . . . might not sound so entirely delicious as they are in reality." Little mention of any Japanese food appeared in U.S. media until well after World War II. By the 1960s, articles on sushi began to show up in lifestyle magazines like *Holiday* and *Sunset*. But the recipes they suggested were canapés like cooked shrimp on caraway rye bread, rather than raw fish on rice.

A decade later, however, sushi was growing in popularity throughout North America, turning into a sign of class and educational standing. In 1972, the *New York Times* covered the opening of a sushi bar in the elite sanctum of New York's Harvard Club. *Esquire* explained the fare in an article titled "Wake up Little

Sushi!" Restaurant reviewers guided readers to Manhattan's sushi scene, including innovators like Shalom Sushi, a kosher sushi bar in SoHo.

Japan's emergence on the global economic scene in the 1970s as the business destination du jour, coupled with a rejection of hearty, red-meat American fare in favor of healthy cuisine like rice, fish, and vegetables, and the appeal of the high-concept aesthetics of Japanese design all prepared the world for a sushi fad. And so, from an exotic, almost unpalatable ethnic specialty, then to haute cuisine of the most rarefied sort, sushi has become not just cool, but popular. The painted window of a Cambridge, Massachusetts, coffee shop advertises "espresso, cappuccino, carrot juice, lasagna, and sushi." Mashed potatoes with wasabi (horseradish), sushi-ginger relish, and seared sashimi-grade tuna steaks show Japan's growing cultural influence on upscale nouvelle cuisine throughout North America, Europe, and Latin America. Sushi has even become the stuff of fashion, from "sushi" lip gloss, colored the deep red of raw tuna, to "wasabi" nail polish, a soft avocado green.

## Angling for New Consumers

Japan remains the world's primary market for fresh tuna for sushi and sashimi; demand in other countries is a product of Japanese influence and the creation of new markets by domestic producers looking to expand their reach. Perhaps not surprisingly, sushi's global popularity as an emblem of a sophisticated, cosmopolitan consumer class more or less coincided with a profound transformation in the international role of the Japanese fishing industry. From the 1970s onward, the expansion of 200-mile fishing limits around the world excluded foreign fleets from the prime fishing grounds of many coastal nations. And international environmental campaigns forced many countries, Japan among them, to scale back their distant water fleets. With their fishing operations curtailed and their yen for sushi still growing, Japanese had to turn to foreign suppliers.

Jumbo jets brought New England's bluefin tuna into easy reach of Tokyo, just as Japan's consumer economy—a byproduct of the now disparaged "bubble" years—went into hyperdrive. The sushi business boomed. During the 1980s, total Japanese imports of fresh bluefin tuna worldwide increased from 957 metric tons (531 from the United States) in 1984 to 5,235 metric tons (857 from the United States) in 1993. The average wholesale price peaked in 1990 at 4,900 yen (U.S. $34) per kilogram, bones and all, which trimmed out to approximately U.S.$33 wholesale per edible pound.

Not surprisingly, Japanese demand for prime bluefin tuna—which yields a firm red meat, lightly marbled with veins of fat, highly prized (and priced) in Japanese cuisine—created a gold-rush mentality on fishing grounds across the globe wherever bluefin tuna could be found. But in the early 1990s, as the U.S. bluefin industry was taking off, the Japanese economy went into a stall, then a slump, then a dive. U.S. producers suffered as their high-end export market collapsed. Fortunately for them, the North American sushi craze took up the slack.

U.S. businesses may have written off Japan, but Americans' taste for sushi stuck. An industry founded exclusively on Japanese demand survived because of Americans' newly trained palates and a booming U.S. economy.

## A Transatlantic Tussle

Atlantic bluefin tuna ("ABT" in the trade) are a highly migratory species that ranges from the equator to Newfoundland, from Turkey to the Gulf of Mexico. Bluefin can be huge fish; the record is 1,496 pounds. In more normal ranges, 600-pound tuna, 10 feet in length, are not extraordinary, and 250- to 300-pound bluefin, six feet long, are commercial mainstays.

Before bluefin became a commercial species in New England, before Japanese buyers discovered the stock, before the 747, bluefin were primarily sports fish, caught with fighting tackle by trophy hunters out of harbors like Montauk, Hyannis, and Kennebunkport. Commercial fishers, if they caught bluefin at all, sold them for cat food when they could and trucked them to town dumps when they couldn't. Japanese buyers changed all of that. Since the 1970s, commercial Atlantic bluefin tuna fisheries have been almost exclusively focused on Japanese markets like Tsukiji.

In New England waters, most bluefin are taken one fish at a time, by rod and reel, by hand line, or by harpoon—techniques of a small-scale fisher, not of a factory fleet. On the European side of the Atlantic, the industry operates under entirely different conditions. Rather than rod and reel or harpooning, the typical gear is industrial—the purse seiner (a fishing vessel closing a large net around a school of fish) or the long line (which catches fish on baited hooks strung along lines played out for many miles behind a swift vessel). The techniques may differ from boat to boat and from country to country, but these fishers are all angling for a share of the same Tsukiji yen—and in many cases, some biologists argue, a share of the same tuna stock. Fishing communities often think of themselves as close-knit and proudly parochial; but the sudden globalization of this industry has brought fishers into contact—and often into conflict—with customers, governments, regulators, and environmentalists around the world (see Box 1).

Two miles off the beach in Barbate, Spain, a huge maze of nets snakes several miles out into Spanish waters near the Strait of Gibraltar. A high-speed, Japanese-made workboat heads out to the nets. On board are five Spanish hands, a Japanese supervisor, 2,500 kilograms of frozen herring and mackerel imported from Norway and Holland, and two American researchers. The boat is making one of its twice-daily trips to Spanish nets, which contain captured Mediterranean tuna being raised under Japanese supervision for harvest and export to Tsukiji.

Behind the guard boats that stand watch over the nets 24 hours a day, the headlands of Morocco are a hazy purple in the distance. Just off Barbate's white cliffs to the northwest, the light at the Cape of Trafalgar blinks on and off. For

20 minutes, the men toss herring and mackerel over the gunwales of the workboat while tuna the size (and speed) of Harley-Davidsons dash under the boat, barely visible until, with a flash of silver and blue, they wheel around to snatch a drifting morsel.

The nets, lines, and buoys are part of an *almadraba,* a huge fish trap used in Spain as well as Sicily, Tunisia, and Morocco. The *almadraba* consists of miles of nets anchored to the channel floor suspended from thousands of buoys, all laid out to cut across the migration routes of bluefin tuna leaving the strait. This *almadraba* remains in place for about six weeks in June and July to intercept tuna leaving the Mediterranean after their spawning season is over. Those tuna that lose themselves in the maze end up in a huge pen, roughly the size of a football field. By the end of the tuna run through the strait, about 200 bluefin are in the pen.

Two hundred fish may not sound like a lot, but if the fish survive the next six months, if the fish hit their target weights, if the fish hit the market at the target price, these 200 bluefin may be worth $1.6 million dollars. In November and December, after the bluefin season in New England and Canada is well over, the tuna are harvested and shipped by air to Tokyo in time for the end-of-the-year holiday spike in seafood consumption.

The pens, huge feed lots for tuna, are relatively new, but *almadraba* are not. A couple of miles down the coast from Barbate is the evocatively named settlement of Zahara de los Atunes (Zahara of the Tunas) where Cervantes lived briefly in the late 16th century. The centerpiece of the village is a huge stone compound that housed the men and nets of Zahara's *almadraba* in Cervantes's day, when the port was only a seasonally occupied tuna outpost (occupied by scoundrels, according to Cervantes). Along the Costa de la Luz, the three or four *almadraba* that remain still operate under the control of local fishing bosses who hold the customary fishing rights, the nets, the workers, the boats, and the locally embedded cultural capital to make the *almadraba* work—albeit for distant markets and in collaboration with small-scale Japanese fishing firms.

Inside the Strait of Gibraltar, off the coast of Cartagena, another series of tuna farms operates under entirely different auspices, utilizing neither local skills nor traditional technology. The Cartagena farms rely on French purse seiners to tow captured tuna to their pens, where joint ventures between Japanese trading firms and large-scale Spanish fishing companies have set up farms using the latest in Japanese fishing technology. The waters and the workers are Spanish, but almost everything else is part of a global flow of techniques and capital: financing from major Japanese trading companies; Japanese vessels to tend the nets; aquacultural techniques developed in Australia; vitamin supplements from European pharmaceutical giants packed into frozen herring from Holland to be heaved over the gunwales for the tuna; plus computer models of feeding schedules, weight gains, and target market prices developed by Japanese technicians and fishery scientists.

These "Spanish" farms compete with operations throughout the Mediterranean that rely on similar high-tech, high-capital approaches to the fish business. In the Adriatic Sea, for example, Croatia is emerging as a formidable tuna producer. In Croatia's case, the technology and the capital were transplanted by émigré Croatians who returned to the country from Australia after Croatia achieved independence from Yugoslavia in 1991. Australia, for its part, has developed a major aquacultural industry for southern bluefin tuna, a species closely related to the Atlantic bluefin of the North Atlantic and Mediterranean and almost equally desired in Japanese markets.

## Culture Splash

Just because sushi is available, in some form or another, in exclusive Fifth Avenue restaurants, in baseball stadiums in Los Angeles, at airport snack carts in

Amsterdam, at an apartment in Madrid (delivered by motorcycle), or in Buenos Aires, Tel Aviv, or Moscow, doesn't mean that sushi has lost its status as Japanese cultural property. Globalization doesn't necessarily homogenize cultural differences nor erase the salience of cultural labels. Quite the contrary, it grows the franchise. In the global economy of consumption, the brand equity of sushi as Japanese cultural property adds to the cachet of both the country and the cuisine. A Texan Chinese-American restauranteur told me, for example, that he had converted his chain of restaurants from Chinese to Japanese cuisine because the prestige factor of the latter meant he could charge a premium; his clients couldn't distinguish between Chinese and Japanese employees (and often failed to notice that some of the chefs behind his sushi bars were Latinos).

The brand equity is sustained by complicated flows of labor and ethnic biases. Outside of Japan, having Japanese hands (or a reasonable facsimile) is sufficient warrant for sushi competence. Guidebooks for the current generation of Japanese global *wandervogel* sometimes advise young Japanese looking for a job in a distant city to work as a sushi chef; U.S. consular offices in Japan grant more than 1,000 visas a year to sushi chefs, tuna buyers, and other workers in the global sushi business. A trade school in Tokyo, operating under the name Sushi Daigaku (Sushi University) offers short courses in sushi preparation so "students" can impress prospective employers with an imposing certificate. Even without papers, however, sushi remains firmly linked in the minds of Japanese and foreigners alike with Japanese cultural identity. Throughout the world, sushi restaurants operated by Koreans, Chinese, or Vietnamese maintain Japanese identities. In sushi bars from Boston to Valencia, a customer's simple greeting in Japanese can throw chefs into a panic (or drive them to the far end of the counter).

On the docks, too, Japanese cultural control of sushi remains unquestioned. Japanese buyers and "tuna techs" sent from Tsukiji to work seasonally on the docks of New England laboriously instruct foreign fishers on the proper techniques for catching, handling, and packing tuna for export. A bluefin tuna must approximate the appropriate *kata,* or "ideal form," of color, texture, fat content, body shape, and so forth, all prescribed by Japanese specifications. Processing requires proper attention as well. Special paper is sent from Japan for wrapping the fish before burying them in crushed ice. Despite high shipping costs and the fact that 50 percent of the gross weight of a tuna is unusable, tuna is sent to Japan whole, not sliced into salable portions. Spoilage is one reason for this, but form is another. Everyone in the trade agrees that Japanese workers are much more skilled in cutting and trimming tuna than Americans, and no one would want to risk sending botched cuts to Japan.

Not to impugn the quality of the fish sold in the United States, but on the New England docks, the first determination of tuna buyers is whether they are looking at a "domestic" fish or an "export" fish. On that judgment hangs several dollars a pound for the fisher, and the supply of sashimi-grade tuna for fishmongers, sushi bars, and seafood restaurants up and down the Eastern seaboard. Some of the best tuna from New England may make it to New York or Los Angeles, but by way of Tokyo—validated as top quality (and top price) by the decision to ship it to Japan by air for sale at Tsukiji, where it may be purchased by one of the handful of Tsukiji sushi exporters who supply premier expatriate sushi chefs in the world's leading cities.

## Playing the Market

The tuna auction at Yankee Co-op in Seabrook, New Hampshire, is about to begin on the second-to-last day of the 1999 season. The weather is stormy, few boats are out. Only three bluefin, none of them terribly good, are up for sale today, and the half-dozen buyers at the auction, three Americans and three Japanese, gloomily discuss the impending end of a lousy season.

In July, the bluefin market collapsed just as the U.S. fishing season was starting. In a stunning miscalculation, Japanese purse seiners operating out of Kesennuma in northern Japan managed to land their entire year's quota from that fishery in only three days. The oversupply sent tuna prices at Tsukiji through the floor, and they never really recovered.

Today, the news from Spain is not good. The day before, faxes and e-mails from Tokyo brought word that a Spanish fish farm had suffered a disaster. Odd tidal conditions near Cartagena led to a sudden and unexpected depletion of oxygen in the inlet where one of the great tuna nets was anchored. Overnight, 800 fish suffocated. Divers hauled out the tuna. The fish were quickly processed, several months before their expected prime, and shipped off to Tokyo. For the Japanese corporation and its Spanish partners, a harvest potentially worth $6.5 million would yield only a tiny fraction of that. The buyers at the morning's auctions in New Hampshire know they will suffer as well. Whatever fish turn up today and tomorrow, they will arrive at Tsukiji in the wake of an enormous glut of hastily exported Spanish tuna (see Box 2).

Fishing is rooted in local communities and local economies—even for fishers dipping their lines (or nets) in the same body of water, a couple hundred miles can be worlds away. Now, a Massachusetts fisher's livelihood can be transformed in a matter of hours by a spike in market prices halfway around the globe or by a disaster at a fish farm across the Atlantic. Giant fishing conglomerates in one part of the world sell their catch alongside family outfits from another. Environmental organizations on one continent rail against distant industry regulations implemented an ocean away. Such instances of convergence are common in a globalizing world. What is surprising, and perhaps more profound, in the case of today's tuna fishers, is the complex interplay between industry and culture, as an esoteric cuisine from an insular part of the world has become a global fad in the span of a generation, driving, and driven by, a new kind of fishing business.

Many New England fishers, whose traditional livelihood now depends on unfamiliar tastes and distant markets, turn to a kind of armchair anthropology to explain Japan's ability to transform tuna from trash into treasure around the

BOX 2

*Tokyo's Pantry*

Tsukiji, Tokyo's massive wholesale seafood market, is the center of the global trade in tuna. Here, 60,000 traders come each day to buy and sell seafood for Tokyo's 27 million mouths, moving more than 2.4 million kilograms of it in less than 12 hours. Boosters encourage the homey view that Tsukiji is *Tokyo no daidokoro*—Tokyo's pantry—but it is a pantry where almost $6 billion worth of fish change hands each year. New York City's Fulton Fish Market, the largest market in North America, handles only about $1 billion worth, and only about 13 percent of the tonnage of Tsukiji's catch.

Tuna are sold at a "moving auction." The auctioneer, flanked by assistants who record prices and fill out invoice slips at lightning speed, strides across the floor just above rows and rows of fish, moving quickly from one footstool to the next without missing a beat, or a bid. In little more than half an hour, teams of auctioneers from five auction houses sell several hundred (some days several thousand) tuna. Successful buyers whip out their cellphones, calling chefs to tell them what they've got. Meanwhile, faxes with critical information on prices and other market conditions alert fishers in distant ports to the results of Tsukiji's morning auctions. In return, Tsukiji is fed a constant supply of information on tuna conditions off Montauk, Cape Cod, Cartagena, Barbate, and scores of other fishing grounds around the world.

Tsukiji is the command post for a global seafood trade. In value, foreign seafood far exceeds domestic Japanese products on the auction block. (Tsukiji traders joke that Japan's leading fishing port is Tokyo's Narita International Airport.) On Tsukiji's slippery auction floor, tuna from Massachusetts may sell at auction for over $30,000 apiece, near octopus from Senegal, eel from Guangzhou, crab from Sakhalin, salmon from British Columbia and Hokkaido, snapper from Kyushu, and abalone from California.

Given the sheer volume of global trade, Tsukiji effectively sets the world's tuna prices. Last time I checked, the record price was over $200,000 for a particularly spectacular fish from Turkey—a sale noteworthy enough to make the front pages of Tokyo's daily papers. But spectacular prices are just the tip of Tsukiji's influence. The auction system and the commodity chains that flow in and out of the market integrate fishers, firms, and restaurants worldwide in a complex network of local and translocal economies.

As an undisputed hub of the fishing world, Tsukiji creates and deploys enormous amounts of Japanese cultural capital around the world. Its control of information, its enormous role in orchestrating and responding to Japanese culinary tastes, and its almost hegemonic definitions of supply and demand allow it the unassailable privilege of imposing its own standards of quality—standards that producers worldwide must heed.

world. For some, the quick answer is simply national symbolism. The deep red of tuna served as sashimi or sushi contrasts with the stark white rice, evoking the red and white of the Japanese national flag. Others know that red and white is an auspicious color combination in Japanese ritual life (lobster tails are popular at Japanese weddings for just this reason). Still others think the cultural prize is a fighting spirit, pure machismo, both their own and the tuna's. Taken by rod and reel, a tuna may battle the fisher for four or five hours. Some tuna literally fight to the death. For some fishers, the meaning of tuna—the equation of tuna with Japanese identity—is simple: Tuna is nothing less than the samurai fish!

Of course, such mystification of a distant market's motivations for desiring a local commodity is not unique. For decades, anthropologists have written of "cargo cults" and "commodity fetishism" from New Guinea to Bolivia. But the ability of fishers today to visualize Japanese culture and the place of tuna within its demanding culinary tradition is constantly shaped and reshaped by the flow of cultural images that now travel around the globe in all directions simultaneously, bumping into each other in airports, fishing ports, bistros, bodegas, and markets everywhere. In the newly rewired circuitry of global cultural and economic affairs, Japan is the core, and the Atlantic seaboard, the Adriatic, and the Australian coast are all distant peripheries. Topsy-turvy as Gilbert and Sullivan never imagined it.

Japan is plugged into the popular North American imagination as the sometimes inscrutable superpower, precise and delicate in its culinary tastes, feudal in its cultural symbolism, and insatiable in its appetites. Were Japan not a prominent player in so much of the daily life of North Americans, the fishers outside of Bath or in Seabrook would have less to think about in constructing their Japan. As it is, they struggle with unfamiliar exchange rates for cultural capital that compounds in a foreign currency.

And they get ready for next season.

# Review Questions

1. How did the Japanese love of bluefin tuna as a centerpiece of sushi dishes affect the U.S. fishing industry?

2. What part does the Tsukiji market play in the international tuna trade?

3. What example does Bestor cite that illustrates the dependence of U.S. fishermen on the Japanese market?

4. According to Bestor, does globalization necessarily mean cultural homogenization? What evidence does he cite to support his view?

# FIVE

## Kinship and Family

$S$ocial life is essential to human existence. We remain in the company of other people from the day we are born to the time of our death. People teach us to speak. They show us how to relate to our surroundings. They give us the help and the support we need to achieve personal security and mental well-being. Alone, we are relatively frail, defenseless primates; in groups we are astonishingly adaptive and powerful. Yet despite these advantages, well-organized human societies are difficult to achieve. Some species manage to produce social organization genetically. But people are not like bees or ants. We lack the genetically coded directions for behavior that make these insects successful social animals. Although we seem to inherit a general need for social approval, we also harbor individual interests and ambitions that can block or destroy close social ties. To overcome these divisive tendencies, human groups organize around several principles designed to foster cooperation and group loyalty. Kinship is among the strongest of these.

We may define **kinship** as the complex system of culturally defined social relationships based on marriage (the principle of **affinity**) and birth (the principle of **consanguinity**). The study of kinship involves consideration of such principles as descent, kinship status and roles, family and other kinship groups, marriage, and residence. In fact, kinship has been such an important organizing factor in many of the societies studied by anthropologists that it is one of the most elaborate areas of the discipline. What are some of the important concepts?

First is descent. **Descent** is based on the notion of a common heritage. It is a cultural rule tying together people on the basis of reputed common ancestry. Descent functions to guide inheritance, group loyalty, and, above all, the formation of families and extended kinship groups.

There are three main rules of descent. One is **patrilineal descent,** which links relatives through males only. In patrilineal systems, females are part of their father's line, but their children descend from the husbands.

**Matrilineal descent** links relatives through females only. Males belong to their mother's line; the children of males descend from the wives. **Bilateral descent** links a person to kin through both males and females simultaneously. Americans are said to have bilateral descent, whereas most of the people in India, Japan, and China are patrilineal. Such groups as the Apache and Trobriand Islanders are matrilineal.

Descent often defines groups called, not surprisingly, **descent groups.** One of these is the **lineage,** a localized group that is based on unilineal (patrilineal or matrilineal) descent and that usually has some corporate powers. In the Marshall Islands, for example, the matriline holds rights to land, which, in turn, it allots to its members. Lineages in India sometimes hold rights to land but are a more important arena for other kinds of decisions such as marriage. Lineage mates must be consulted about the advisability, timing, and arrangements for weddings. (See Article 21.)

**Clans** are composed of lineages. Clan members believe they are all descended from a common ancestor, but because clans are larger, members cannot trace their genealogical relationships to everyone in the group. In some societies, clans may be linked together in even larger groups called **phratries.** Because phratries are usually large, the feeling of common descent they offer is weaker.

**Ramages,** or cognatic kin groups, are based on bilateral descent. They often resemble lineages in size and function but provide more recruiting flexibility. An individual can choose membership from among several ramages where he or she has relatives.

Another important kinship group is the family. This unit is more difficult to define than we may think, because people have found so many different ways to organize "familylike" groups. Here we will follow anthropologist George P. Murdock's approach and define the **family** as a kin group consisting of at least one married couple sharing the same residence with their children and performing sexual, reproductive, economic, and educational functions. A **nuclear family** consists of a single married couple and their children. An **extended family** consists of two or more married couples and their children. Extended families have a quality all their own and are often found in societies where family performance and honor are paramount to the reputation of individual family members. Extended families are most commonly based on patrilineal descent. Women marry into such families and must establish themselves among the line members and other women who live there.

**Marriage,** the socially approved union of a man and a woman, is a second major principle of kinship. The regulation of marriage takes elaborate forms from one society to the next. Marriage may be **exogamous,** meaning marriage outside any particular named group, or **endogamous,** indicating the opposite. Bhil tribals of India, for example, are clan and village exogamous (they should marry outside these groups), but tribal endogamous (they should marry other Bhils).

Marriage may also be **monogamous,** where it is preferred that only one woman should be married to one man at a time, or **polygamous,** meaning that one person may be married to more than one person simultaneously. There are two kinds of polygamy, **polygyny,** the marriage of one man with more than one woman simultaneously, and **polyandry,** the marriage of one woman with more than one man.

Many anthropologists view marriage as a system of alliances between families and descent lines. Viewed in these terms, rules such as endogamy and exogamy can be explained as devices to link or internally strengthen various kinship groups. The **incest taboo,** a legal rule that prohibits sexual intercourse or marriage between particular classes of kin, is often explained as a way to extend alliances between kin groups.

Finally, the regulation of marriage falls to the parents and close relatives of eligible young people in many societies. These elders concern themselves with more than wedding preparations; they must also see to it that young people marry appropriately, which means they consider the reputation of prospective spouses and their families' economic strength and social rank.

The selections in Part Five illustrate several aspects of kinship systems. In the first article, Nancy Scheper-Hughes looks at the relationship that poor Brazilian mothers have with their infants. Because babies die so often, mothers must delay forming attachments to them until their children show that they can survive. The second article, by David McCurdy, looks at the way kinship organizes life for the inhabitants of a Rajasthani Bhil village. Arranging a marriage requires use and consideration of clans, lineages, families, and weddings. Despite its origin in peasant society, the Indian kinship system is proving useful as people try to cope with a modernizing society. The third article, by Lu Yuan and Sam Mitchell, describes the only society known in the world in which people do not marry. Despite this, the matrilineal Mosuo of China take lovers, have children, and build extended families consisting of women, their brothers, and their children. Finally, Margery Wolf looks at the structure of the Taiwanese extended family from the point of view of the women who constitute it. It is only by establishing her own uterine family that a woman can gain power within the patrilineal group.

# Key Terms

# 20

# Mother's Love: Death without Weeping

*Nancy Scheper-Hughes*

*Kinship systems are based on marriage and birth. Both, anthropologists as-sume, create ties that can link kin into close, cooperative, enduring struc-tures. What happens to such ties, however, in the face of severe hardship imposed by grinding poverty and urban migration? Can we continue to as-sume, for example, that there will be a close bond between mother and child? This is the question pursued by Nancy Scheper-Hughes in the following ar-ticle about the mother–infant relationship among poor women in a Brazil-ian shantytown. The author became interested in the question following a "baby die-off" in the town of Bom Jesus in 1965. She noticed that mothers seemed to take these events casually. After twenty-five years of research in the Alto do Cruzeiro shantytown there, she has come to see such indifference as a cultural response to high rates of infant death due to poverty and malnu-trition. Mothers, and surrounding social institutions such as the Catholic church, expect babies to die easily. Mothers concentrate their support on ba-bies who are "fighters" and let themselves grow attached to their children only*

From "Death Without Weeping," *Natural History*, October 1989. Copyright © 1989 by Nancy Scheper-Hughes. Reprinted by permission of the publisher.

*when they are reasonably sure that the offspring will survive. The article also
provides an excellent illustration of what happens to kinship systems in the
face of poverty and social dislocation. Such conditions may easily result in
the formation of woman-headed families, and in a lack of the extended kinship networks so often found in more stable, rural societies.*

> I have seen death without weeping
> The destiny of the Northeast is death
> Cattle they kill
> To the people they do something worse
> —Anonymous Brazilian singer (1965)

"Why do the church bells ring so often?" I asked Nailza de Arruda soon after I
moved into a corner of her tiny mud-walled hut near the top of the shantytown
called the Alto do Cruzeiro (Crucifix Hill). I was then a Peace Corps volunteer
and a community development/health worker. It was the dry and blazing hot
summer of 1965, the months following the military coup in Brazil, and save for
the rusty, clanging bells of N.S. das Dores Church, an eerie quiet had settled
over the market town that I call Bom Jesus da Mata. Beneath the quiet, however, there was chaos and panic. "It's nothing," replied Nailza, "just another little angel gone to heaven."

Nailza had sent more than her share of little angels to heaven, and sometimes at night I could hear her engaged in a muffled but passionate discourse
with one of them, two-year-old Joana. Joana's photograph, taken as she lay
propped up in her tiny cardboard coffin, her eyes open, hung on a wall next to
one of Nailza and Ze Antonio taken on the day they eloped.

Nailza could barely remember the other infants and babies who came and
went in close succession. Most had died unnamed and were hastily baptized in
their coffins. Few lived more than a month or two. Only Joana, properly baptized in church at the close of her first year and placed under the protection of
a powerful saint, Joan of Arc, had been expected to live. And Nailza had dan-
gerously allowed herself to love the little girl.

In addressing the dead child, Nailza's voice would range from tearful im-
ploring to angry recrimination: "Why did you leave me? Was your patron saint
so greedy that she could not allow me one child on this earth?" Ze Antonio advised me to ignore Nailza's odd behavior, which he understood as a kind of madness that, like the birth and death of children, came and went. Indeed, the
premature birth of a stillborn son some months later "cured" Nailza of her "inappropriate" grief, and the day came when she removed Joana's photo and carefully packed it away.

More than fifteen years elapsed before I returned to the Alto do Cruzeiro,
and it was anthropology that provided the vehicle of my return. Since 1982 I
have returned several times in order to pursue a problem that first attracted my

attention in the 1960s. My involvement with the people of the Alto do Cruzeiro now spans a quarter of a century and three generations of parenting in a community where mothers and daughters are often simultaneously pregnant.

The Alto do Cruzeiro is one of three shantytowns surrounding the large market town of Bom Jesus in the sugar plantation zone of Pernambuco in Northeast Brazil, one of the many zones of neglect that have emerged in the shadow of the now tarnished economic miracle of Brazil. For the women and children of the Alto do Cruzeiro the only miracle is that some of them have managed to stay alive at all.

The Northeast is a region of vast proportions (approximately twice the size of Texas) and of equally vast social and developmental problems. The nine states that make up the region are the poorest in the country and are representative of the Third World within a dynamic and rapidly industrializing nation. Despite waves of migrations from the interior to the teeming shantytowns of coastal cities, the majority still live in rural areas on farms and ranches, sugar plantations and mills.

Life expectancy in the Northeast is only forty years, largely because of the appallingly high rate of infant and child mortality. Approximately one million children in Brazil under the age of five die each year. The children of the Northeast, especially those born in shantytowns on the periphery of urban life, are at a very high risk of death. In these areas, children are born without the traditional protection of breast-feeding, subsistence gardens, stable marriages, and multiple adult caretakers that exists in the interior. In the hillside shantytowns that spring up around cities or, in this case, interior market towns, marriages are brittle, single parenting is the norm, and women are frequently forced into the shadow economy of domestic work in the homes of the rich or into unprotected and oftentimes "scab" wage labor on the surrounding sugar plantations, where they clear land for planting and weed for a pittance, sometimes less than a dollar a day. The women of the Alto may not bring their babies with them into the homes of the wealthy, where the often-sick infants are considered sources of contamination, and they cannot carry the little ones to the riverbanks where they wash clothes because the river is heavily infested with schistosomes and other deadly parasites. Nor can they carry their young children to the plantations, which are often several miles away. At wages of a dollar a day, the women of the Alto cannot hire baby sitters. Older children who are not in school will sometimes serve as somewhat indifferent caretakers. But any child not in school is also expected to find wage work. In most cases, babies are simply left at home alone, the door securely fastened. And so many also die alone and unattended.

Bom Jesus da Mata, centrally located in the plantation zone of Pernambuco, is within commuting distance of several sugar plantations and mills. Consequently, Bom Jesus has been a magnet for rural workers forced off their small subsistence plots by large landowners wanting to use every available piece of land for sugar cultivation. Initially, the rural migrants to Bom Jesus were squatters who were given tacit approval by the mayor to put up temporary straw huts on each of the three hills overlooking the town. The Alto do Cruzeiro is the oldest, the largest, and the poorest of the shantytowns. Over the past three decades many of the original migrants have become permanent residents, and the primitive and temporary straw huts have been replaced by small homes (usually of two rooms) made of wattle and daub, sometimes covered with plaster. The more affluent residents use bricks and tiles. In most Alto homes, dangerous kerosene lamps have been replaced by light bulbs. The once tattered rural garb, often fashioned from used sugar sacking, has likewise been replaced by store-bought clothes, often castoffs from a wealthy *patrão* (boss). The trappings are modern, but the hunger, sickness, and death that they conceal are traditional, deeply rooted in a history of feudalism, exploitation, and institutionalized dependency.

My research agenda never wavered. The questions I addressed first crystallized during a veritable "die-off" of Alto babies during a severe drought in 1965. The food and water shortages and the political and economic chaos occasioned by the military coup were reflected in the handwritten entries of births and deaths in the dusty, yellowed pages of the ledger books kept at the public registry office in Bom Jesus. More than 350 babies died in the Alto during 1965 alone—this from a shantytown population of little more than 5,000. But that wasn't what surprised me. There were reasons enough for the deaths in the miserable conditions of shantytown life. What puzzled me was the seeming indifference of Alto women to the death of their infants, and their willingness to attribute to their own tiny offspring an aversion to life that made their death seem wholly natural, indeed all but anticipated.

Although I found that it was possible, and hardly difficult, to rescue infants and toddlers from death by diarrhea and dehydration with a simple sugar, salt, and water solution (even bottled Coca-Cola worked fine), it was more difficult to enlist a mother herself in the rescue of a child she perceived as ill-fated for life or better off dead, or to convince her to take back into her threatened and besieged home a baby she had already come to think of as an angel rather than as a son or daughter.

I learned that the high expectancy of death, and the ability to face child death with stoicism and equanimity, produced patterns of nurturing that differentiated between those infants thought of as thrivers and survivors and those thought of as born already "wanting to die." The survivors were nurtured, while stigmatized, doomed infants were left to die, as mothers say, *a mingua*, "of neglect." Mothers stepped back and allowed nature to take its course. This pattern, which I call mortal selective neglect, is called passive infanticide by anthropologist Marvin Harris. The Alto situation, although culturally specific in the form that it takes, is not unique to Third World shantytown communities and may have its correlates in our own impoverished urban communities in some cases of "failure to thrive" infants.

I use as an example the story of Zezinho, the thirteen-month-old toddler of one of my neighbors, Lourdes. I became involved with Zezinho when I was called in to help Lourdes in the delivery of another child, this one a fair and robust little tyke with a lusty cry. I noted that while Lourdes showed great inter-

est in the newborn, she totally ignored Zezinho who, wasted and severely malnourished, was curled up in a fetal position on a piece of urine- and feces-
soaked cardboard placed under his mother's hammock. Eyes open and vacant,
mouth slack, the little boy seemed doomed.

When I carried Zezinho up to the community day-care center at the top of
the hill, the Alto women who took turns caring for one another's children (in
order to free themselves for part-time work in the cane fields or washing clothes)
laughed at my efforts to save Ze, agreeing with Lourdes that here was a baby
without a ghost of a chance. Leave him alone, they cautioned. It makes no sense
to fight with death. But I did do battle with Ze, and after several weeks of force-
feeding (malnourished babies lose their interest in food), Ze began to succumb
to my ministrations. He acquired some flesh across his taut chest bones, learned
to sit up, and even tried to smile. When he seemed well enough, I returned him
to Lourdes in her miserable scrap-material lean-to, but not without guilt about
what I had done. I wondered whether returning Ze was at all fair to Lourdes and
to his little brother. But I was busy and washed my hands of the matter. And
Lourdes did seem more interested in Ze now that he was looking more human.

When I returned in 1982, there was Lourdes among the women who
formed my sample of Alto mothers—still struggling to put together some sem-
blance of life for a now grown Ze and her five other surviving children. Much
was made of my reunion with Ze in 1982, and everyone enjoyed retelling the
story of Ze's rescue and of how his mother had given him up for dead. Ze would
laugh the loudest when told how I had had to force-feed him like a fiesta turkey.
There was no hint of guilt on the part of Lourdes and no resentment on the part
of Ze. In fact, when questioned in private as to who was the best friend he ever
had in life, Ze took a long drag on his cigarette and answered without a trace of
irony, "Why my mother, of course!" "But of course," I replied.

Part of learning how to mother in the Alto do Cruzeiro is learning when to
let go of a child who shows that it "wants" to die or that it has no "knack" or no
"taste" for life. Another part is learning when it is safe to let oneself love a child.
Frequent child death remains a powerful shaper of maternal thinking and practice. In the absence of firm expectation that a child will survive, mother love as
we conceptualize it (whether in popular terms or in the psychobiological notion of maternal bonding) is attenuated and delayed with consequences for infant survival. In an environment already precarious to young life, the emotional
detachment of mothers toward some of their babies contributes even further to
the spiral of high mortality–high fertility in a kind of macabre lock-step dance
of death.

The average woman of the Alto experiences 9.5 pregnancies, 3.5 child
deaths, and 1.5 stillbirths. Seventy percent of all child deaths in the Alto occur
in the first six months of life, and 82 percent by the end of the first year. Of all
deaths in the community each year, about 45 percent are of children under the
age of five.

Women of the Alto distinguish between child deaths understood as natural (caused by diarrhea and communicable diseases) and those resulting from

sorcery, the evil eye, or other magical or supernatural afflictions. They also recognize a large category of infant deaths seen as fated and inevitable. These hopeless cases are classified by mothers under the folk terminology "child sickness" or "child attack." Women say that there are at least fourteen different types of hopeless child sickness, but most can be subsumed under two categories—chronic and acute. The chronic cases refer to infants who are born small and wasted. They are deathly pale, mothers say, as well as weak and passive. They demonstrate no vital force, no liveliness. They do not suck vigorously; they hardly cry. Such babies can be this way at birth or they can be born sound but soon show no resistance, no "fight" against the common crises of infancy: diarrhea, respiratory infections, tropical fevers.

The acute cases are those doomed infants who die suddenly and violently. They are taken by stealth overnight, often following convulsions that bring on head banging, shaking, grimacing, and shrieking. Women say it is horrible to look at such a baby. If the infant begins to foam at the mouth or gnash its teeth or go rigid with its eyes turned back inside its head, there is absolutely no hope. The infant is "put aside"—left alone—often on the floor in a back room, and allowed to die. These symptoms (which accompany high fevers, dehydration, third-stage malnutrition, and encephalitis) are equated by Alto women with madness, epilepsy, and worst of all, rabies, which is greatly feared and highly stigmatized.

Most of the infants presented to me as suffering from chronic child sickness were tiny, wasted famine victims, while those labeled as victims of acute child attack seemed to be infants suffering from the deliriums of high fever or the convulsions that can accompany electrolyte imbalance in dehydrated babies.

Local midwives and traditional healers, praying women, as they are called, advise Alto women on when to allow a baby to die. One midwife explained: "If I can see that a baby was born unfortuitously, I tell the mother that she need not wash the infant or give it a cleansing tea. I tell her just to dust the infant with baby powder and wait for it to die." Allowing nature to take its course is not seen as sinful by these often very devout Catholic women. Rather, it is understood as cooperating with God's plan.

Often I have been asked how consciously women of the Alto behave in this regard. I would have to say that consciousness is always shifting between allowed and disallowed levels of awareness. For example, I was awakened early one morning in 1987 by two neighborhood children who had been sent to fetch me to a hastily organized wake for a two-month-old infant whose mother I had unsuccessfully urged to breast-feed. The infant was being sustained on sugar water, which the mother referred to as *soro* (serum), using a medical term for the infant's starvation regime in light of his chronic diarrhea. I had cautioned the mother that an infant could not live on *soro* forever.

The two girls urged me to console the young mother by telling her that it was "too bad" that her infant was so weak that Jesus had to take him. They were coaching me in proper Alto etiquette. I agreed, of course, but asked, "And what do *you* think?" Xoxa, the eleven-year-old, looked down at her dusty flip-flops and blurted out, "Oh, Dona Nanci, that baby never got enough to eat, but you must never say that!" And so the death of hungry babies remains one of the best kept secrets of life in Bom Jesus da Mata.

Most victims are waked quickly and with a minimum of ceremony. No tears are shed, and the neighborhood children form a tiny procession, carrying the baby to the town graveyard where it will join a multitude of others. Although a few fresh flowers may be scattered over the tiny grave, no stone or wooden cross will mark the place, and the same spot will be reused within a few months' time. The mother will never visit the grave, which soon becomes an anonymous one.

What, then, can be said of these women? What emotions, what sentiments motivate them? How are they able to do what, in fact, must be done? What does mother love mean in this inhospitable context? Are grief, mourning, and melancholia present, although deeply repressed? If so, where shall we look for them? And if not, how are we to understand the moral visions and moral sensibilities that guide their actions?

I have been criticized more than once for presenting an unflattering portrait of poor Brazilian women, women who are, after all, themselves the victims of severe social and institutional neglect. I have described these women as allowing some of their children to die, as if this were an unnatural and inhuman act rather than, as I would assert, the way any one of us might act, reasonably and rationally, under similarly desperate conditions. Perhaps I have not emphasized enough the real pathogens in this environment of high risk: poverty, deprivation, sexism, chronic hunger, and economic exploitation. If mother love is, as many psychologists and some feminists believe, a seemingly natural and universal maternal script, what does it mean to women for whom scarcity, loss, sickness, and deprivation have made that love frantic and robbed them of their grief, seeming to turn their hearts to stone?

Throughout much of human history—as in a great deal of the impoverished Third World today—women have had to give birth and to nurture children under ecological conditions and social arrangements hostile to child survival, as well as to their own well-being. Under circumstances of high childhood mortality, patterns of selective neglect and passive infanticide may be seen as active survival strategies.

They also seem to be fairly common practices historically and across cultures. In societies characterized by high childhood mortality and by a correspondingly high (replacement) fertility, cultural practices of infant and child care tend to be organized primarily around survival goals. But what this means is a pragmatic recognition that not all of one's children can be expected to live. The nervousness about child survival in areas of northeast Brazil, northern India, or Bangladesh, where a 30 percent or 40 percent mortality rate in the first years of life is common, can lead to forms of delayed attachment and a casual or benign neglect that serves to weed out the worst bets so as to enhance the life chances of healthier siblings, including those yet to be born. Practices similar to those that I am describing have been recorded for parts of Africa, India, and Central America.

Life in the Alto do Cruzeiro resembles nothing so much as a battlefield or an emergency room in an overcrowded inner-city public hospital. Consequently, morality is guided by a kind of "lifeboat ethics," the morality of triage. The seemingly studied indifference toward the suffering of some of their infants, conveyed in such sayings as "little critters have no feelings," is understandable in light of these women's obligation to carry on with their reproductive and nurturing lives.

In their slowness to anthropomorphize and personalize their infants, everything is mobilized so as to prevent maternal overattachment and, therefore, grief at death. The bereaved mother is told not to cry, that her tears will dampen the wings of her little angel so that she cannot fly up to her heavenly home. Grief at the death of an angel is not only inappropriate, it is a symptom of madness and of a profound lack of faith.

Infant death becomes routine in an environment in which death is anticipated and bets are hedged. While the routinization of death in the context of shantytown life is not hard to understand, and quite possible to empathize with, its routinization in the formal institutions of public life in Bom Jesus is not as easy to accept uncritically. Here the social production of indifference takes on a different, even a malevolent, cast.

In a society where triplicates of every form are required for the most banal events (registering a car, for example), the registration of infant and child death is informal, incomplete, and rapid. It requires no documentation, takes less than five minutes, and demands no witnesses other than office clerks. No questions are asked concerning the circumstances of the death, and the cause of death is left blank, unquestioned and unexamined. A neighbor, grandmother, older sibling, or common-law husband may register the death. Since most infants die at home, there is no question of a medical record.

From the registry office, the parent proceeds to the town hall, where the mayor will give him or her a voucher for a free baby coffin. The full-time municipal coffinmaker cannot tell you exactly how many baby coffins are dispatched each week. It varies, he says, with the seasons. There are more needed during the drought months and during the big festivals of Carnaval and Christmas and São Joao's Day because people are too busy, he supposes, to take their babies to the clinic. Record keeping is sloppy.

Similarly, there is a failure on the part of city-employed doctors working at two free clinics to recognize the malnutrition of babies who are weighed, measured, and immunized without comment and as if they were not, in fact, anemic, stunted, fussy, and irritated starvation babies. At best the mothers are told to pick up free vitamins or a health "tonic" at the municipal chambers. At worst, clinic personnel will give tranquilizers and sleeping pills to quiet the hungry cries of "sick-to-death" Alto babies.

The church, too, contributes to the routinization of, and indifference toward, child death. Traditionally, the local Catholic church taught patience and resignation to domestic tragedies that were said to reveal the imponderable workings of God's will. If an infant died suddenly, it was because a particular saint had claimed the child. The infant would be an angel in the service of his or her heavenly patron. It would be wrong, a sign of a lack of faith, to weep for a child with such good fortune. The infant funeral was, in the past, an event celebrated with joy. Today, however, under the new regime of "liberation theology," the bells of N. S. das Dores parish church no longer peal for the death of Alto babies, and no priest accompanies the procession of angels to the cemetery where their bodies are disposed of casually and without ceremony. Children bury children in Bom Jesus da Mata. In this most Catholic of communities, the coffin is handed to the disabled and irritable municipal gravedigger, who often chides the children for one reason or another. It may be that the coffin is larger than expected and the gravedigger can find no appropriate space. The children do not wait for the gravedigger to complete his task. No prayers are recited and no sign of the cross made as the tiny coffin goes into its shallow grave.

When I asked the local priest, Padre Marcos, about the lack of church ceremony surrounding infant and childhood death today in Bom Jesus, he replied: "In the old days, child death was richly celebrated. But those were the baroque customs of a conservative church that wallowed in death and misery. The new church is a church of hope and joy. We no longer celebrate the death of child angels. We try to tell mothers that Jesus doesn't want all the dead babies they send him." Similarly, the new church has changed its baptismal customs, now often refusing to baptize dying babies brought to the back door of a church or rectory. The mothers are scolded by the church attendants and told to go home and take care of their sick babies. Baptism, they are told, is for the living; it is not to be confused with the sacrament of extreme unction, which is the anointing of the dying. And so it appears to the women of the Alto that even the church has turned away from them, denying the traditional comfort of folk Catholicism.

The contemporary Catholic church is caught in the clutches of a double bind. The new theology of liberation imagines a kingdom of God on earth based on justice and equality, a world without hunger, sickness, or childhood mortality. At the same time, the church has not changed its official position on sexuality and reproduction, including its sanctions against birth control, abortion, and sterilization. The padre of Bom Jesus da Mata recognizes this contradiction intuitively, although he shies away from discussions on the topic, saying that he prefers to leave questions of family planning to the discretion and the "good consciences" of his impoverished parishioners. But this, of course, sidesteps the extent to which those good consciences have been shaped by traditional church teachings in Bom Jesus, especially by his recent predecessors. Hence, we can begin to see that the seeming indifference of Alto mothers toward the death of some of their infants is but a pale reflection of the official indifference of church and state to the plight of poor women and children.

Nonetheless, the women of Bom Jesus are survivors. One woman, Biu, told me her life history, returning again and again to the themes of child death, her first husband's suicide, abandonment by her father and later by her second husband, and all the other losses and disappointments she had suffered in her long forty-five years. She concluded with great force, reflecting on the days of Carnaval '88 that were fast approaching:

> No, Dona Nanci, I won't cry, and I won't waste my life thinking about it from morning to night. . . . Can I argue with God for the state that I'm in? No! And so I'll dance and I'll jump and I'll play Carnaval! And yes, I'll laugh and people will wonder at a *pobre* like me who can have such a good time.

And no one did blame Biu for dancing in the streets during the four days of Carnaval—not even on Ash Wednesday, the day following Carnaval '88 when we all assembled hurriedly to assist in the burial of Mercea, Biu's beloved *casula*, her last-born daughter who had died at home of pneumonia during the festivities. The rest of the family barely had time to change out of their costumes. Severino, the child's uncle and godfather, sprinkled holy water over the little angle while he prayed: "Mercea, I don't know whether you were called, taken, or thrown out of this world. But look down at us from your heavenly home with tenderness, with pity, and with mercy." So be it.

# Review Questions

1. What did Scheper-Hughes notice about mothers' reactions during the baby die-off of 1965 in Bom Jesus, Brazil?

2. How do poor Brazilian mothers react to their infants' illnesses and death? How do other institutions, such as the church, clinic, and civil authorities respond? Give examples.

3. How does Scheper-Hughes explain the apparent indifference of mothers to the death of their infants?

4. What does the indifference of mothers to the deaths of their children say about basic human nature, especially the mother–child bond?

# 21

# Family and Kinship in Village India

### David W. McCurdy

*Anyone who reads older ethnographic accounts of different cultures will inevitably run across terms such as* clan, lineage, avunculocal, levirate, extended family, polyandry, cross-cousin, *and* Crow *terminology. All these terms and many more were created by anthropologists to describe categories, groups, social arrangements, and roles associated with the complex kinship systems that characterized so many of the groups they studied. The importance of kinship for one of these societies, that found in an Indian village, is the topic of this article by David McCurdy. He argues that kinship forms the core social groups and associations in rural India in a system well adapted to family-centered land-holding and small-scale farming. He concludes by pointing out that Indians have used their close family ties to adapt to life in the emerging cash-labor-oriented modernizing world.*

On a hot afternoon in May, 1962, I sat talking with three Bhil men in the village of Ratakote, located in southern Rajasthan, India.[1] We spoke about the results of recent national elections, their worry over a cattle disease that was afflicting the village herds, and predictions about when the monsoon rains would start. But our longest discussion concerned kin—the terms used to refer to them, the responsibilities they had toward one another, and the importance of marrying them off properly. It was toward the end of this conversation that one of the men, Kanji, said, "Now sāb (Bhili for sāhīb), you are finally asking about a good thing. This is what we want you to tell people about us when you go back to America."

As I thought about it later, I was struck by how different this social outlook was from mine. I doubt that I or any of my friends in the United States would say something like this. Americans do have kin. We have parents, although our parents may not always live together, and we often know other relatives, some of whom are likely to play important parts in our lives. We grow up in families and we often create new ones if we have children. But we also live in a social network of other people whom we meet at work or encounter in various "outside" social settings, and these people can be of equal or even greater importance to us than kin. Our social worlds include such non-kin stuctures as companies and other work organizations, schools, neighborhoods, churches and other religious groups, and voluntary associations, including recreational groups and social clubs. We are not likely to worry much about our obligations to relatives with the notable exceptions of our children and grandchildren (middle-class American parents are notoriously child-centered), and more grudgingly, our aging parents. We are not supposed to "live off" relatives or lean too heavily on them.

Not so in Ratakote. Ratakote's society, like many agrarian villages around the world, is kinship-centered. Villagers anchor themselves in their families. They spend great energy on creating and maintaining their kinship system. This actually is not so surprising. Elaborate kinship systems work well in agrarian societies where families tend to be corporate units and where peoples' social horizons are often limited to the distance they can walk in a day. For the same reasons, families in the United States were also stronger in the past when more of them owned farms and neighborhood businesses.

What may come as a surprise, however, is how resilient and strong Indian kinship systems such as Ratakote's have been in the face of recent economic changes, especially the growth of wage labor. Let us look more closely at the Bhil kinship system, especially at arranged marriage, to illustrate these ideas.

## Arranging a Marriage

If there is anything that my American students have trouble understanding about India, it is arranged marriage. They can not imagine sitting passively by

---

[1] Ratakote is a Bhil tribal village located 21 miles southwest of Udaipur, Rajasthan, in the Aravalli hills. I did ethnographic research in the village from 1961 to 1963, and again in 1985, 1991, and 1994 for shorter periods of time.

while their parents advertise their charms and evaluate emerging nuptial candidates. The thought of living—to say nothing of having sex with—a total stranger seems out of the question to them. In our country, personal independence takes precedence over loyalty to family.

Not so in India. There, arranged marriage is the norm, and most young people, as well as their elders, accept and support the custom. (They often find it sexually exciting, too.) There are many reasons why this is so, but one stands out for discussion here. Marriage constructs alliances between families, lineages, and clans. The resulting kinship network is a pivotal structure in Indian society. It confers social strength and security. People's personal reputations depend on the quality and number of their allied kin. There is little question in their minds about who should arrange marriages. The decision is too important to leave up to inexperienced and impressionable young people.

As an aside I should note that young Indians play a greater part in the process than they used to. Middle class boys often visit the families of prospective brides, where they manage to briefly "interview" them. They also tap into their kinship network to find out personal information about prospects. Young women also seek out information about perspective grooms. Bhils are no exception. They often conspire to meet those to whom they have been betrothed, usually at a fair or other public event where their contact is likely to go unnoticed. If they don't like each other, they will begin to pressure their parents to back out of the arrangement.

The importance of arranging a marriage was brought home to me several times during fieldwork in Ratakote, but one instance stands out most clearly. When I arrived in the village for a short stay in 1985, Kanji had just concluded marriage arrangements for his daughter, Rupani.[2] What he told me about the process underscored the important role kinship plays in the life of the village.

Kanji started by saying that he and his wife first discussed Rupani's marriage the previous year when the girl first menstruated. She seemed too young for such a union then so they had waited nine months before committing to the marriage process. Even then, Rupani was still only 15 years old. Kanji explained that everyone preferred early marriage for their children because young people were likely to become sexually active as they grew older and might fall in love and elope, preempting the arrangement process altogether. Now they figured that the time had come, and they began a series of steps to find a suitable spouse that would eventually involve most of their kin.

The first step was to consult the members of Kanji's *lineage*. Lineage is an anthropological term, not one used by Bhils. But Bhils share membership in local groups of relatives that meet the anthropological definition. Lineages (in this case patrilineages) include closely related men who are all descended from a known ancestor. Kanji's lineage consists of his two married brothers, three married sons of his deceased father's brother (his father is also dead), and his own married son when the latter is home. All are the descendants of his grandfather who had migrated to Ratakote many years earlier. He had talked with all

2 Kanji and Rupani are not real people. Their experiences are a composite of several life histories.

of them informally about the possibility of his daughter's marriage before this. Now he called them together for formal approval.

The approval of lineage mates is necessary because they are essential to the marriage process. Each one of them will help spread the word to other villages that Rupani is available for marriage. They will loan money to Kanji for wedding expenses, and when it comes time for the wedding ceremony, they will provide much of the labor needed to prepare food and arrange required activities. Each family belonging to the lineage will host a special meal for the bride (the groom is similarly entertained in his village) during the wedding period, and one or two will help her make offerings to their lineal ancestors. The groom will also experience this ritual.

The lineage also has functions not directly related to marriage. It has the right to redistribute the land of deceased childless, male members, and it provides its members with political support. It sees to memorial feasts for deceased members. Its members may cooperatively plow and sow fields together and combine their animals for herding.

With lineage approval in hand, Kanji announced Rupani's eligibility in other villages. (Bhils are village exogamous, meaning they prefer to marry spouses from other communities.) Kanji and his lineage mates went about this by paying visits to feminal relatives in other villages. These are kin of the women, now living in Ratakote, who have married into his family. They also include the daughters of his family line who have married and gone to live in other villages, along with their husbands and husbands' kin.

Once the word has been spread, news of prospective candidates begins to filter in. It may arrive with feminal kin from other villages when they visit Ratakote. Or it may come from neighbors who are acting as go-betweens in Ratakote for kin who live in other villages and who seek partners for their children. Either way, a process of evaluation starts. Does the family of the suggested boy or girl have a good reputation? Are they hospitable to their in-laws? Do they meet their obligations to others? What is the reputation of the boy or girl they are offering in marriage? Is he or she tall or short, light or dark, robust or frail, cheerful or complaining, hardworking or lazy? What about their level of education? Does the family have sufficient land and animals? Have they treated other sons- and daughters-in-law well?

The most fundamental question to ask, however, is whether the prospective spouse is from the right clan. In anthropology, the term *clan* refers to an aggregate of people who all believe they are descended from a common ancestor. In Ratakote this group is called an *arak*. Araks are named and the names are used as surnames when Bhils identify themselves. Kanji comes from the pargi arak and is thus known as Kanji Pargi. There is Lalu Bodar, Naraji Katara, Dita Hiravat, Nathu Airi—all men named for one of the 36 araks found in Ratakote. Women also belong to their father's clan, but unlike many American women who adopt their husband's surname at marriage, they keep their arak name all their lives.

Araks are based on a rule of patrilineal descent. This means that their members trace ancestry through males, only. (Matrilineal descent traces the line through females only, and bilateral descent, which is found in U.S. society, includes both sexes.) Patrilineal descent not only defines arak membership, it governs inheritance. (Sons inherit equally from their fathers in Ratakote; daughters do not inherit despite a national law giving them that right.) It says that the children of divorced parents stay with the father's family. It bolsters the authority of men over their wives and children. It supports the rule of patrilocality. It even defines the village view of conception. Men plant the "seeds" that grow into children; women provide the fields in which the seeds germinate and grow.

The arak symbolizes patrilineal descent. It is not an organized group, although the members of an arak worship the same mother goddess no matter where they live. Instead it is an identity, an indicator that tells people who their lineal blood relatives are. There are pargis in hundreds of other Bhil villages. Most are strangers to Kanji but if he meets pargis elsewhere, he knows they share a common blood heritage with him.

It is this sense of common heritage that affects marriage. Bhils, like most Indians, believe that clan (arak) mates are close relatives even though they may be strangers. Marriage with them is forbidden. To make sure incest is impossible, it is also forbidden to marry anyone from your mother's arak or your father's mother's arak, to say nothing of anyone else you know you are related to.

This point was driven home to me on another occasion when a neighbor of Kanji's, Kamalaji Kharadi, who was sitting smoking with several other men, asked me which arak I belonged to. Instead of letting it go at "McCurdy," I said that I didn't have an arak. I explained that Americans didn't have a kinship group similar to this, and that was why I had to ask questions about kinship.

My listeners didn't believe me. After all, I must have a father and you get your arak automatically from him. It is a matter of birth and all people are born. They looked at each other as if to say, "We wonder why he won't tell us what his arak is?", then tried again to get me to answer. My second denial led them to ask, "OK, then what is your wife's arak?" (If you can't get at it one way, then try another.) I answered that she didn't have an arak either. This caused a mild sensation. "Then how do you know if you have not married your own relative?", they asked, secretly, I think, delighted by the scandalous prospect.

The third step that occurred during the arrangement of Rupani's marriage came after the family had settled on a prospective groom. This step is the betrothal, and it took place when the groom's father and some of his lineage mates and neighbors paid a formal visit to Kanji's house. When they arrive, Kanji must offer his guests a formal meal, usually slaughtering a goat and distilling some liquor for the occasion. The bride, her face covered by her sari, will be brought out for a brief viewing, as well. But most of the time will be spent making arrangements—when will the actual wedding take place?; who will check the couple's horoscopes for fit?; how much will the bride price (also called bride wealth by many anthropologists) be?

Bride price (*dapa*) deserves special comment. It is usually a standard sum of money (about 700 rupees in 1985), although it may also include silver ornaments or other valuables. The dapa is given by the groom's father and his line to the parents of the bride. Bhils view this exchange as a compensation for the loss of the bride's services to her family. It also pays for a shift in her loyalty.

The exchange points up an important strain on families in patrilineal societies, the transfer of a woman from her natal family and line to those of her husband. This transfer includes not only her person, but her loyalty, labor, and children. Although she always will belong to her father's arak, she is now part of her husband's family, not his.

This problem is especially troublesome in India because of the close ties formed there by a girl and her parents. Parents know their daughter will leave when she marries, and they know that in her husband's house and village, she will be at a disadvantage. She will be alone, and out of respect for his parents her husband may not favor her wishes, at least in public. Because of this, they tend to give her extra freedom and support. In addition, they recognize the strain she will be under when she first goes to live with her new husband and his family. To ease her transition, they permit her to visit her parents frequently for a year or two. They also may try to marry her into a village where other women from Ratakote have married, so that she has some kin or at least supporters.

After her marriage, a woman's parents and especially her brothers find it hard not to care about her welfare. Their potential interest presents a built-in structural conflict that could strain relations between the two families if nothing were done about it.

A solution to this problem is to make the marriage into an exchange, and bride price is one result. Bride price also helps to dramatize the change in loyalty and obligation accompanying the bride's entrance into her new family.

Bhils have also devised a number of wedding rituals to dramatize the bride's shift in family membership. The bride must cry to symbolize that she is leaving her home. The groom ritually storms the bride's house at the beginning of the final ceremony. He does so like a conquering hero, drawing his sword to strike a ceremonial arch placed over the entrance while simultaneously stepping on a small fire (he wears a slipper to protect his foot), ritually violating the household's sacred hearth. At the end of the wedding, the groom, with some friends, engages in a mock battle with the bride's brothers and other young men, and symbolically abducts her. The meaning of this ritual is a dramatic equivalent of a father "giving away the bride" at American weddings.

One additional way of managing possible tension between in-laws is the application of respect behavior. The parents of the bride must always treat those of the groom and their relatives with respect. They must not joke in their presence, and they must use respectful language and defer to the groom's parents in normal conversation. In keeping with the strong patrilineal system, a groom may not accept important gifts from his wife's family except on ritual occasions, such as weddings, when exchange is expected. A groom may help support his own father, but he should not do so with his in-laws. That is up to their sons.

Bride price exchange also sets in motion a life-long process of mutual hospitality between the two families. Once the marriage has taken place, the families will become part of each other's feminal kin. They will exchange gifts on some ritual occasions, open their houses to each other, and, of course, help one another make future marriages.

## The Future of Indian Kinship

On our last trip to India in 1994, my wife and I learned that Rupani had delivered three children since her wedding. Kanji had visited them a few months before we arrived, and he said that Rupani was happy and that he had wonderful grandchildren. But he also mentioned that her husband now spent most of his time in the nearby city of Udaipur working in construction there. He sent money home, but his absence left Rupani to run the house and raise the children by herself, although she did so with the assistance of his parents and lineage mates.

Rupani's case is not unusual. Every morning 70 or 80 men board one of the 20 or so busses that travel the road, now paved, that runs through Ratakote to the city. There they wait to be recruited by contractors for day labor at a low wage. If they are successful, gain special skills, or make good connections, they may get more permanent, better-paying jobs and live for weeks at a time in the city.

The reason they have to take this kind of work is simple. Ratakote has more than doubled in population since 1962. (The village had a population of 1,184 in 1963. By 1994 an estimate put the number at about 2,600.) There is not enough land for everyone to farm nor can the land produce enough to feed the growing population, even in abundant years. Work in the city is the answer, especially for householders whose land is not irrigated like Kanji's.

Cash labor has a potential to break down the kinship system that Bhils value so highly. It frees men and women from economic dependence on the family (since they make their own money working for someone else). It takes up time, too, making it difficult for them to attend the leisurely eleven-day weddings of relatives or meet other obligations to kin that require their presence. With cash labor, one's reputation is likely to hinge less on family than on work. For some, work means moving the family altogether. Devaji Katara, one of Kanji's neighbors, has a son who has moved with his wife and children to the Central Indian city of Indore. He has a good factory job there, and the move has kept them together. By doing so, however, he and they are largely removed from the kinship loop.

Despite these structural changes, kinship in Ratakote and for India as a whole remains exceptionally strong. Even though they may live farther away, Bhil sons and daughters still visit their families regularly. They send money home, and they try to attend weddings. They talk about their kin, too, and surprisingly, they continue the long process of arranging marriage for their children.

Perhaps one reason for kinship's vitality is the use to which kinship is put by many Indians. The people of Ratakote and other Indians have never given up teaching their children to respect their elders and subordinate their interests to those of the family. Family loyalty is still a paramount value. They use this loyalty to help each other economically. Family members hire each other in business. They take one another in during hard times. They offer hospitality to each other. Unlike Americans who feel guilty about accepting one-sided help from relatives, Indians look to the future. Giving aid now may pay off with a job or a favor later. Even if it doesn't, it is the proper thing to do.

Instead of breaking up the kinship network, work that takes men and families away from the village has simply stretched it out. An Indian student I know has found relatives in every American city he has visited. He knows of kin in Europe and southeast Asia too. Anywhere he goes he is likely to have relatives to stay with and to help him. When he settles down he will be expected to return the favor. Another Indian acquaintance, who went to graduate school in the United States and who continues to work here, has sent his father thousands of dollars to help with the building of a house. This act, which would surprise many Americans, seems perfectly normal to him.

Kanji is not disturbed by the economic changes that are overtaking the quiet agricultural pace of Ratakote. I last left him standing in front of his house with a grandson in his arms. His son, who had left the village in 1982 to be a "wiper" on a truck, returned to run the farm. He will be able to meet the family's obligation to lineage and feminal kin. For Kanji, traditional rules of inheritance have pulled a son and, for the moment at least, a grandson, back into the bosom of the family where they belong.

# Review Questions

1. What are the main ways that kinship organizes Bhil society in Ratakote, according to McCurdy?

2. What is meant by the terms *clan, lineage, family, patrilineal descent, patrilocal residence, alliance,* and *feminal kin group*? Give examples of each.

3. Why do Bhil parents feel that marriage is too important a matter to be left up to their children?

4. What attributes do Bhil parents look for in a prospective bride or groom? How do young people try to influence the marriage partner their parents choose for them?

5. Although the U.S. kinship system seems limited by comparison to India's, many argue that it is more important than most of us think. Can you think of ways this might be true?

# 22

# Matrilineal Kinship: Walking Marriage in China

*Lu Yuan and Sam Mitchell*

*As we noted in the introduction to Part Five, matrilineal descent links relatives through females only. A woman's children belong to her line, not their father's. Men belong to their mother's line but cannot pass such membership along to their offspring. Typically, women play a strong role in matrilineal systems. They often own property, manage families, and hold public office or at least influence group decisions. This does not mean that men have no place in matrilineal descent groups. They often hold leadership positions and feel responsibility for their sisters. They are close to their mothers and sisters, and it is often their sister's children who will look after them when they grow old.*

*Marriage is found in most matrilineal societies, although it may be a weak union because women can always fall back on their brothers and other matrilineal kin for support if things are not going well at home. Anthropologists usually define marriage as a socially recognized union between a man and a woman that confers legitimacy on their children. In the past most anthropologists felt marriage was universal, that it was found in all societies, although they also recognized that men and women could fashion less formal unions. But as Lu Yuan and Sam Mitchell show in this article about the Mosuo living in southwestern China, there is at least one society where marriage is absent. As a matrilineal group, women take lovers who often visit at night but return to their mother's houses in the morning. Women, their brothers, and their children live and work together in extended families. A man's responsibilities are to his sisters and their children.*

> There are so many skillful people,
> > but none can compare with my mother.
>
> There are so many knowledgeable people,
> > but none can equal my mother.
>
> There are so many people skilled at song and dance,
> > but none can compete with my mother.

We first heard this folk song around a blazing fire in southwestern China in the spring of 1995. It was sung enthusiastically by women of Luoshui village—members of the Nari, an ethnic group more commonly known to outsiders as the Mosuo. During the past few years, we have returned several times to visit these people, who celebrate women in more than song. Although the majority of China's ethnic groups follow a strong patrilineal tradition, the Mosuo emphasize matrilineal ties, with matrilineally related kin assisting one another to farm, fish, and raise children. Women also head most households and control most family property.

Marriage as other cultures know it is uncommon among the Mosuo; they prefer a visiting relationship between lovers—an arrangement they sometimes refer to in their language as *sisi* (walking back and forth). At about the age of twelve, a Mosuo girl is given a coming-of-age ceremony, and after puberty, she is free to receive male visitors. A lover may remain overnight in her room but will return in the morning to his own mother's home and his primary responsibilities. Children born from such a relationship live with their mother, and the male relatives responsible for helping to look after them are her brothers. Many children know who their fathers are, of course, but even if the relationship between father and child is quite close, it involves no social or economic obligation. And lovers can end their relationship at any time; a woman may signal her change of heart by simply no longer opening the door. When speaking Chinese, the Mosuo will call the *sisi* arrangement *zou hun* (walking marriage) or *azhu hunyin* (friend marriage, *azhu* being the Mosuo word for friend); nevertheless, the relationship is not a formal union.

Chuan-kang Shih, an anthropologist at the University of Illinois at Urbana-Champaign and an authority on the Mosuo, points out that many aspects of their family system have parallels elsewhere in the world. For example, although in most societies a husband and wife live together (usually near his relatives or hers), in others they continue to live in separate households, and one spouse must make overnight nuptial visits. Matrilineal kinship systems, in which a man looks after the interests of his sisters' children, are also well known. And although men commonly wield the power, even in matrilineal societies, women may play important political and economic roles. But the absence of a formal marital union may quite possibly be unique to the Mosuo. In this respect, only the precolonial practices of the matrilineal Nayar of southern India come close. As Shih explains, among some Nayar groups, a woman would take lovers (with due regard for social class), who would establish and maintain their relationships to her through a pattern of gift giving. Despite being expected to acknowledge paternity, the lovers incurred no obligations to their offspring. Still, the Nayar had a vestigial form of marriage: shortly before puberty, a girl would be wed to a young man; although this marriage lasted only three days and was often purely ceremonial in nature, the union marked the girl's transition to adult life and legitimized the birth of her children.

In Luoshui we stayed with thirty-year-old A Long, who runs a small guesthouse. His family consisted of his mother, grandmother, younger brother and the sister, and [the] sister's two-year-old son. Each evening A Long departed with his small overnight bag; each morning he returned to help his mother and sister. After several days of eating with the family and becoming friendly with them, we asked A Long what he thought about the *sisi* system. " 'Friend marriage' is very good," he replied. "First, we are all our mother's children, making money for her; therefore there is no conflict between the brothers and sisters. Second, the relationship is based on love, and no money or dowry is involved in it. If a couple feels contented, they stay together. If they feel unhappy, they can go their separate ways. As a result, there is little fighting." A Long told us that he used to have several lovers but started to have a stable relationship with one when she had her first child.

"Are you taking care of your children?" we asked.

"I sometimes buy candy for them. My responsibility is to help raise my sister's children. In the future, they will take care of me when I get old."

A Long's twenty-six-year-old sister, Qima, told us that the Mosuo system "is good because my friend and I help our own families during the daytime and only come together at night, and therefore there are few quarrels between us. When we are about fifty years old, we will not have 'friend marriage' anymore."

Ge Ze A Che is the leader of Luoshui, which has a population of more than 200 people, the majority of them Mosuo, with a few Han (China's majority ethnic group) and Pumi as well. He spoke proudly of this small settlement: "I have been the leader of the village for five years. There has been little theft, rape, or even argument here. 'Friend marriage' is better than the husband-wife system, because in large extended families everyone helps each other, so we are not afraid of anything. It is too hard to do so much work in the field and at home just as a couple, the way the Han do."

The Mosuo live in villages around Lugu Lake, which straddles the border between Yunnan and Sichuan provinces, and in the nearby town of Yongning. They are believed to be descendants of the ancient Qiang, an early people of the Tibetan plateau from whom many neighboring minority groups, including the Tibetans themselves, claim descent. As a result of Han expansion during the Qin dynasty (221–206 B.C.), some Qiang from an area near the Huang (Yellow) River migrated south and west into Yunnan. The two earliest mentions of the Mosuo appear during the Han dynasty (A.D. 206–222) and the Tang dynasty (618–907), in records concerning what is now southwestern China.

The Mosuo do not surface again in historical accounts until after Mongol soldiers under Kublai Khan subjugated the area in 1253. During the Yuan dynasty (1279–1368), a period of minority rule by the Mongols, the province of Yunnan was incorporated into the Chinese empire, and many Mongol soldiers settled in the Mosuo region. In fact, during the 1950s, when the government set out to classify the country's minority nationalities, several Mosuo villages surrounding Lugu Lake identified themselves as Mongol, and some continue to do so today. When we walked around the lake, as the Mosuo do each year in the seventh lunar month—a ritual believed to ensure good fortune during the coming year—we passed through villages that identified themselves variously as Mosuo, Mongol, Naxi, Pumi, and Han. The "Mongol" people we encountered dressed the same as the Mosuo and spoke the same language. Their dances and songs, too, were the same, and they sometimes even referred to themselves as Mosuo.

Tibetan Buddhism first entered the region in the late thirteenth century and has greatly influenced the lives and customs of the Mosuo. Before the area came under the control of the Communist government, at least one male from almost every family joined the monastic community. The local practice of Buddhism even incorporated aspects of the *sisi* system, although the women did the "commuting." On the eighth day of the fifth lunar month, monks traveling to Tibet for religious study would camp in front of Kaiji village. That night, each monk would be joined by his accustomed lover—a ceremonial practice believed to enable the monks to reach Lhasa safely and to succeed in completing their studies. And the local Mosuo monks, each of whom lived with his own mother's family, could also receive lovers. Such arrangements seem to defy the injunctions of many schools of Tibetan Buddhism, but by allowing the monks to live and work at home, outside the strict confines of monastic life, they helped the Mosuo maintain a stable population and ensure an adequate labor force to sustain local agriculture.

The area around Lugu Lake did not come under the full control of China's central government until 1956, seven years after the founding of the People's Republic. In 1958 and 1959, during the Great Leap Forward, the nearby monasteries, notably the one at Yongning, were badly damaged. Now, however, with a combination of government funds and donations from local people, they are slowly being rebuilt. One element of recent religious revival is the Bon tradition, which is accepted by the Dalai Lama as a school of Tibetan Buddhism but believed by many scholars to be derived from an earlier, animist tradition. During our walk around Lugu Lake, we witnessed a Bon cremation ceremony and visited the Bon temple on the eastern shore of the lake. The Mosuo also retain a shamanic and animist tradition of their own, known as Daba.

In the twentieth century, the West became acquainted with the Mosuo through the work of French ethnographers Edouard Chavannes and Jacques Bacot and through the contributions of Joseph Rock, a Vienna-born American who first journeyed to Yunnan in 1922 while on a botanical expedition. A flamboyant character, Rock traveled through remote Tibetan borderlands accompanied by trains of servants and bodyguards and equipped with such dubious necessities as a collapsible bathtub and a silver English tea set. He made the Naxi town of Lijiang his home for more than twenty years, until the victory of the Chinese Communist Party in 1949 spelled an end to foreign-funded research and missionary activity in the area.

Besides conducting botanical surveys and collecting plant and animal specimens, Rock took many photographs and became the West's foremost expert on the region's peoples and their shamanic practices. He identified the Mosuo as a subgroup of the Naxi, who, although their kinship system is patrilineal, speak a language closely related to that of the Mosuo. The Mosuo strongly contest this classification, but it has been retained by the present government, which has been reluctant to assign the Mosuo the status of a distinct minority. The Communists claim that the Mosuo do not fit the criteria for nationality status as defined for the Soviet Union by Joseph Stalin. According to Stalin, as he phrased it in a 1929 letter, "A nation is a historically constituted, stable community of people, formed on the basis of the common possession of four principal characteristics, namely: a common language, a common territory, a common economic life, and a common psychological make-up manifested in common specific features of national culture."

In keeping with Marxist interpretations of historical development, Chinese ethnologists have also regarded Mosuo society as a "living fossil," characterized by ancient marriage and family structures. This view draws on theories of social evolution formerly embraced by Western anthropologists, notably the American ethnologist Lewis Henry Morgan (1818–81). Morgan proposed that societies pass through successive natural stages of "savagery" and "barbarism" before attaining "civilization." He also proposed a sequence of marriage forms, from a hypothetical "group marriage" of brothers and sisters to monogamy. Chinese scholars have argued that a minority such as the Mosuo, with its unusual kinship system, fits into this scheme and thus validates Marxist views. Of course, the application of Morgan's theories to minority cultures in China has also enabled the Han majority to see itself as more advanced in the chain of human societal evolution. This kind of thinking, long discredited in the West, is only now beginning to be reexamined in China.

With the coming of the Cultural Revolution (1966–76), the Mosuo were pressured to change their way of life. According to Lama Luo Sang Yi Shi (a Mosuo who holds a county-government title but is primarily a spiritual leader), "during the Cultural Revolution, the governor of Yunnan came to Yongning. He went into Mosuo homes and cursed us, saying that we were like animals, born in a mess without fathers. At that time, all of the Mosuo were forced to marry and to adopt the Han practice of monogamy; otherwise, they would be punished by being deprived of food." During this period Mosuo couples lived with the woman's family, and divorce was not permitted. But even though they held marriage certificates and lived with their wives, the men kept returning to their maternal homes each morning to work.

Luo Sang Yi Shi criticized this attempt to change the Mosuo and explained that "at the end of the Cultural Revolution, the Mosuo soon returned to their former system of 'friend marriage.' A small family is not good for work. Also, mothers and their daughters-in-law cannot get along well."

Today the Mosuo maintain their matrilineal system and pursue *sisi* relationships. Yet how long will this remain the case? The government of Yunnan recently opened Lugu Lake to tourism, and vans full of visitors, both Chinese and foreign, are beginning to arrive. To some degree, this added exposure threatens to envelop the Mosuo in a society that is becoming increasingly homogeneous. Yet the tourists are drawn not only by the beauty of the lake but by the exotic qualities of the Mosuo people. Ironically, their unique qualities may well enable the Mosuo to endure and prosper.

We asked Ge Ze A Che, the Luoshui village leader, if tourism would change the lives of the Mosuo. "It has already changed their lives to some extent," he observed. "Our young people now like to wear Han clothes, speak Chinese, and sing Chinese songs. In the future they will lose our people's traditions and customs."

And what would happen to "friend marriage"? we wondered.

"It will also change—but very, very slowly!"

# Review Questions

1. What are the major organizational consequences of matrilineal descent?

2. What role do men play in a matrilineal-descent system?

3. The divorce rate is often higher in many matrilineal societies. Why is this the case?

4. The Mosuo lack marriage. How do they manage to produce children, organize families, and assign supportive kinship roles?

5. Why do the Han Chinese think that the Mosuo are "living fossils"?

# 23

# Uterine Families and the Women's Community

*Margery Wolf*

*The size and organization of extended families vary from one society to the next, but extended families often share some important attributes. They are most often based on a rule of patrilineal descent. For men, the patrilineal family extends in an unbroken line of ancestors and descendants. Membership is permanent; loyalty assured. For women, the patrilineal family is temporary. Born into one family and married into another, women discover that their happiness and interests depend on bearing children to create their own uterine family. This and the importance of a local women's group are the subjects of this article by Margery Wolf in her discussion of Taiwanese family life.*

Few women in China experience the continuity that is typical of the lives of the menfolk. A woman can and, if she is ever to have any economic security, must provide the links in the male chain of descent, but she will never appear in anyone's genealogy as that all-important name connecting the past to the future. If she dies before she is married, her tablet will not appear on her father's altar; although she was a temporary member of his household, she was not a member of his family. A man is born into his family and remains a member of it throughout his life and even after his death. He is identified with the family from birth, and every action concerning him, up to and including his death, is in the context of that group. Whatever other uncertainties may trouble his life, his place in the line of ancestors provides a permanent setting. There is no such secure setting for a woman. She will abruptly leave the household into which she is born, either as an infant or as an adult bride, and enter another whose members treat her with suspicion or even hostility.

A man defines his family as a large group that includes the dead, and not-yet-born, and the living members of his household. But how does a woman define her family? This is not a question that China specialists often consider, but from their treatment of the family in general, it would seem that a woman's family is identical with that of the senior male in the household in which she lives. Although I have never asked, I imagine a Taiwanese man would define a woman's family in very much those same terms. Women, I think, would give quite a different answer. They do not have an unchanging place, assigned at birth, in any group, and their view of the family reflects this.

When she is a child, a woman's family is defined for her by her mother and to some extent by her grandmother. No matter how fond of his daughter the father may be, she is only a temporary member of his household and useless to his family—he cannot even marry her to one of his sons as he could an adopted daughter. Her irrelevance to her father's family in turn affects the daughter's attitude toward it. It is of no particular interest to her, and the need to maintain its continuity has little meaning for her beyond the fact that this continuity matters a great deal to some of the people she loves. As a child she probably accepts to some degree her grandmother's orientation toward the family: the household, that is, those people who live together and eat together, including perhaps one or more of her father's married brothers and their children. But the group that has the most meaning for her and with which she will have the most lasting ties is the smaller, more cohesive unit centering on her mother, that is, the uterine family—her mother and her mother's children. Father is important to the group, just as grandmother is important to some of the children, but he is not quite a member of it, and for some uterine families he may even be "the enemy." As the girl grows up and her grandmother dies and a brother or two marries, she discovers that her mother's definition of the family is becoming less exclusive and may even include such outsiders as her brother's new wife. Without knowing precisely when it happened, she finds that her brother's interests and goals have shifted in a direction she cannot follow. Her mother does not push her aside, but when the mother speaks of the future, she speaks in terms of her son's future. Although the mother sees her uterine family as adding new members and another generation, her daughter sees it as dissolving, leaving her with strong particular relationships, but with no group to which she has permanent loyalties and obligations.

When a young woman marries, her formal ties with the household of her father are severed. In one of the rituals of the wedding ceremony the bride's father or brothers symbolically inform her by means of spilt water that she, like the water, may never return, and when her wedding sedan chair passes over the threshold of her father's house, the doors are slammed shut behind her. If she is ill-treated by her husband's family, her father's family may intervene, but unless her parents are willing to bring her home and support her for the rest of her life (and most parents are not), there is little they can do beyond shaming the other family. This is usually enough.

As long as her mother is alive, the daughter will continue her contacts with her father's household by as many visits as her new situation allows. If she lives nearby she may visit every few days, and no matter where she lives she must at least be allowed to return at New Year. After her mother dies her visits may become perfunctory, but her relations with at least one member of her uterine family, the group that centered on her mother, remain strong. Her brother plays an important ritual role throughout her life. She may gradually lose contact with her sisters as she and they become more involved with their own children, but her relations with her brother continue. When her sons marry, he is the guest of honor at the wedding feasts, and when her daughters marry he must give a small banquet in their honor. If her sons wish to divide their father's estate, it is their mother's brother who is called on to supervise. And when she dies, the coffin cannot be closed until her brother determines to his own satisfaction that she died a natural death and that her husband's family did everything possible to prevent it.

With the ritual slam of her father's door on her wedding day, a young woman finds herself quite literally without a family. She enters the household of her husband—a man who in an earlier time, say fifty years ago, she would never have met and who even today, in modern rural Taiwan, she is unlikely to know very well. She is an outsider, and for Chinese an outsider is always an object of deep suspicion. Her husband and her father-in-law do not see her as a member of their family. But they do see her as essential to it; they have gone to great expense to bring her into their household for the purpose of bearing a new generation for their family. Her mother-in-law, who was mainly responsible for negotiating the terms of her entry, may harbor some resentment over the hard bargaining, but she is nonetheless eager to see another generation added to *her* uterine family. A mother-in-law often has the same kind of ambivalence toward her daughter-in-law as she has toward her husband—the younger woman seems a member of her family at times and merely a member of the household at others. The new bride may find that her husband's sister is hostile or at best condescending, both attitudes reflecting the daughter's distress at an outsider who seems to be making her way right into the heart of the family.

Chinese children are taught by proverb, by example, and by experience that the family is the source of their security, and relatives the only people who can be depended on. Ostracism from the family is one of the harshest sanctions that can be imposed on erring youth. One of the reasons mainlanders as individuals are considered so untrustworthy on Taiwan is the fact that they are not subject to the controls of (and therefore have no fear of ostracism from) their families. If a timid new bride is considered an object of suspicion and potentially dangerous because she is a stranger, think how uneasy her own first few months must be surrounded by strangers. Her irrelevance to her father's family may result in her having little reverence for descent lines, but she has warm memories of the security of the family her mother created. If she is ever to return to this certainty and sense of belonging, a woman must create her own uterine family by bearing children, a goal that happily corresponds to the goals of the family into which she has married. She may gradually create a tolerable niche for herself in the household of her mother-in-law, but her family will not be formed until she herself forms it of her own children and grandchildren. In most cases, by the time she adds grandchildren, the uterine family and the household will almost completely overlap, and there will be another daughter-in-law struggling with loneliness and beginning a new uterine family.

The ambiguity of a man's position in relation to the uterine families accounts for much of the hostility between mother-in-law and daughter-in-law. There is no question in the mind of the older woman but that her son is her family. The daughter-in-law might be content with this situation once her sons are old enough to represent her interests in the household and in areas strictly under men's control, but until then, she is dependent on her husband. If she were to be completely absorbed into her mother-in-law's family—a rare occurrence unless she is a *simpua*—there would be little or no conflict; but under most circumstances she must rely on her husband, her mother-in-law's son, as her spokesman, and here is where the trouble begins. Since it is usually events within the household that she wishes to affect, and the household more or less overlaps with her mother-in-law's uterine family, even a minor foray by the younger woman suggests to the older one an all-out attack on everything she has worked so hard to build in the years of her own loneliness and insecurity. The birth of grandchildren further complicates their relations, for the one sees them as new members for her family and the other as desperately needed recruits to her own small circle of security.

In summary, my thesis contends . . . that because we have heretofore focused on men when examining the Chinese family—a reasonable approach to a patrilineal system—we have missed not only some of the system's subtleties but also its near-fatal weaknesses. With a male focus we see the Chinese family as a line of descent, bulging to encompass all the members of a man's household and spreading out through his descendants. With a female focus, however, we see the Chinese family not as a continuous line stretching between the vague horizons of past and future, but as a contemporary group that comes into existence out of one woman's need and is held together insofar as she has the strength to do so, or, for that matter, the need to do so. After her death the uterine family survives only in the mind of her son and is symbolized by the special attention he gives her earthly remains and her ancestral tablet. The rites themselves are demanded by the ideology of the patriliny, but the meaning they hold for most sons is formed in the uterine family. The uterine family has no ideology, no formal structure, and no public existence. It is built out of sentiments and loyalties that die with its members, but it is no less real for all that. The descent lines of men are born and nourished in the uterine families of women, and it is here that a male ideology that excludes women makes its accommodations with reality.

Women in rural Taiwan do not live their lives in the walled courtyards of their husband's households. If they did, they might be as powerless as their stereotype. It is in their relations in the outside world (and for women in rural Taiwan that world consists almost entirely of the village) that women develop sufficient backing to maintain some independence under their powerful mothers-in-law and even occasionally to bring the men's world to terms. A successful venture into the men's world is no small feat when one recalls that the men of a village were born there and are often related to one another, whereas the women are unlikely to have either the ties of childhood or the ties of kinship to unite them. All the same, the needs, shared interests, and common problems of women are reflected in every village in a loosely knit society that can when needed be called on to exercise considerable influence.

Women carry on as many of their activities as possible outside the house. They wash clothes on the riverbank, clean and pare vegetables at a communal pump, mend under a tree that is a known meetingplace, and stop to rest on a bench or group of stones with other women. There is a continual moving back and forth between kitchens, and conversations are carried on from open doorways through the long, hot afternoons of summer. The shy young girl who enters the village as a bride is examined as frankly and suspiciously by the women as an animal that is up for sale. If she is deferential to her elders, does not criticize or compare her new world unfavorably with the one she has left, the older residents will gradually accept her presence on the edge of their conversations and stop changing the topic to general subjects when she brings the family laundry to scrub on the rocks near them. As the young bride meets other girls in her position, she makes allies for the future, but she must also develop relationships with the older women. She learns to use considerable discretion in making and receiving confidences, for a girl who gossips freely about the affairs of her husband's household may find herself labeled a troublemaker. On the other hand, a girl who is too reticent may find herself always on the outside of the group, or worse yet, accused of snobbery. I described in *The House of Lim* the plight of Lim Chui-ieng, who had little village backing in her troubles with her husband and his family as the result of her arrogance toward the women's community. In Pei-hotien the young wife of the storekeeper's son suffered a similar lack of support. Warned by her husband's parents not to be too "easy" with the other villagers lest they try to buy things on credit, she obeyed to the point of being considered unfriendly by the women of the village. When she began to have serious troubles with her husband and eventually his family, there was no one in the village she could turn to for solace, advice, and, most important, peacemaking.

Once a young bride has established herself as a member of the women's community, she has also established for herself a certain amount of protection. If the members of her husband's family step beyond the limits of propriety in their treatment of her—such as refusing to allow her to return to her natal home for her brother's wedding or beating her without serious justification—she can complain to a woman friend, preferably older, while they are washing vegetables at the communal pump. The story will quickly spread to the other women, and one of them will take it on herself to check the facts with another member of the girl's household. For a few days the matter will be thoroughly discussed whenever a few women gather. In a young wife's first few years in the community, she can expect to have her mother-in-law's side of any disagreement given fuller weight than her own—her mother-in-law has, after all, been a part of the community a lot longer. However, the discussion itself will serve to curb many offenses. Even if the older woman knows that public opinion is falling to her side, she will still be somewhat more judicious about refusing her daughter-in-law's next request. Still, the daughter-in-law who hopes to make use of the village forum to depose her mother-in-law or at least gain herself special privilege will discover just how important the prerogatives of age and length of residence are. Although the women can serve as a powerful protective force for their defenseless younger members, they are also a very conservative force in the village.

Taiwanese women can and do make use of their collective power to lose face for their menfolk in order to influence decisions that are ostensibly not theirs to make. Although young women may have little or no influence over their husbands and would not dare express an unsolicited opinion (and perhaps not even a solicited one) to their fathers-in-law, older women who have raised their sons properly retain considerable influence over their sons' actions, even in activities exclusive to men. Further, older women who have displayed years of good judgment are regularly consulted by their husbands about major as well as minor economic and social projects. But even men who think themselves free to ignore the opinions of their women are never free of their own concept, face. It is much easier to lose face than to have face. We once asked a male friend in Peihotien just what "having face" amounted to. He replied, "When no one is talking about a family, you can say it has face." This is precisely where women wield their power. When a man behaves in a way that they consider wrong, they talk about him—not only among themselves, but to their sons and husbands. No one "tells him how to mind his own business," but it becomes abundantly clear that he is losing face and by continuing in this manner may bring shame to the family of his ancestors and descendants. Few men will risk that.

The rules that a Taiwanese man must learn and obey to be a successful member of his society are well developed, clear, and relatively easy to stay within. A Taiwanese woman must also learn the rules, but if she is to be a successful woman, she must learn not to stay within them, but to *appear* to stay within them; to manipulate them, but not to appear to be manipulating them; to teach them to her children, but not to depend on her children for her protection. A truly successful Taiwanese woman is a rugged individualist who has learned to depend largely on herself while appearing to lean on her father, her husband, and her son. The contrast between the terrified young bride and the loud, confident, often lewd old woman who has outlived her mother-in-law and her husband reflects the tests met and passed by not strictly following the rules and by making purposeful use of those who must. The Chinese male's conception of women as "narrow-hearted" and socially inept may well be his vague recognition of this facet of women's power and technique.

The women's subculture in rural Taiwan is, I believe, below the level of consciousness. Mothers do not tell their about-to-be-married daughters how to establish themselves in village society so that they may have some protection from an oppressive family situation, nor do they warn them to gather their children into an exclusive circle under their own control. But girls grow up in village society and see their mothers and sisters-in-law settling their differences to keep them from a public airing or presenting them for the women's community to judge. Their mothers have created around them the meaningful unit in their father's households, and when they are desperately lonely and unhappy in the households of their husbands, what they long for is what they have lost. . . . [Some] areas in the subculture of women . . . mesh perfectly into the main culture of the society. The two cultures are not symbiotic because they are not sufficiently independent of one another, but neither do they share identical goals or necessarily use the same means to reach the goals they do share. Outside the village the women's subculture seems not to exist. The uterine family also has no public existence, and appears almost as a response to the traditional family organized in terms of a male ideology.

# Review Questions

1. According to Wolf, what is a uterine family, and what relatives are likely to be members?

2. Why is the uterine family important to Chinese women who live in their husband's patrilineal extended families?

3. What is the relationship between a woman's uterine family and her power within her husband's family?

4. Why might the existence of the uterine family contribute to the division of extended families into smaller constituent parts?

5. How do you think a Chinese woman's desire to have a uterine family affects attempts to limit the Chinese population?

# SIX

## Identity, Roles, and Groups

For most of us, social interaction is unconscious and automatic. We associate with other people from the time we are born. Of course we experience moments when we feel socially awkward and out of place, but generally we learn to act toward others with confidence. Yet our unconscious ease masks an enormously complex process. When we enter a social situation, how do we know what to do? What should we say? How are we supposed to act? Are we dressed appropriately? Are we talking to the right person? Without knowing it, we have learned a complex set of cultural categories for social interaction that enables us to estimate the social situation, identify the people in it, act appropriately, and recognize larger groups of people.

Status and role are basic to social intercourse. **Status** refers to the categories of different kinds of people who interact. The old saying, "You can't tell the players without a program," goes for our daily associations as well. Instead of a program, however, we identify the actors by a range of signs, from the way they dress to the claims they make about themselves. Most statuses are named, so we may be heard to say things like, "That's President Gavin," or "She's a lawyer," when we explain social situations to others. This identification of actors is a prerequisite for appropriate social interaction.

**Roles** are the rules for action associated with particular statuses. We use them to interpret and generate social behavior. For example, a professor plays a role in the classroom. Although often not conscious of this role, the professor will stand, use the blackboard, look at notes, and speak with a slightly more formal air than usual. The professor does not wear blue jeans and a T-shirt, chew gum, sit cross-legged on the podium, or sing. These actions might be appropriate for this person when assuming the identity of "friend" at a party, but they are out of place in the classroom.

People also always relate to each other in **social situations,** the

## READINGS IN THIS SECTION

settings in which social interaction takes place. Social situations consist of a combination of times, places, objects, and events. For example, if we see a stranger carrying a television set across campus at four o'clock in the afternoon, we will probably ignore the activity. Most likely someone is simply moving. But if we see the same person carrying the set at four in the morning, we may suspect a theft. Only the time has changed, but it is a significant marker of the social situation. Similarly, we expect classrooms to be associated with lectures, and stethoscopes to be part of medical exams. Such places and objects mark the social situations of which they are part.

People also belong to groups. **Social groups** are organized collections of individuals. They are often named—the Republican Party, American Motorcyclist Association, General Motors—although some, such as friends who meet for drinks after work on Fridays, may be anonymous and less formal. Social groups have several attributes. The people who belong to them normally recognize their common membership and share the goals of the group. The group should share an "inside" culture and its members should interact with each other. Groups are also organized internally in some way. Tasks are often divided among members. Finally, groups usually link to one another. For example, when a couple marries, their union connects the families of the bride and groom. There are some collections of people that we might think of as groups that do not fit this definition. "Middle-class" people, for example, are an aggregate, not a social group, because they are not an interacting organized collective. No one says, "I am meeting tonight with my middle-class men's association."

As societies around the world grow larger, it becomes more difficult to identify groups. People may do most of their socializing in **social networks,** the individuals with whom they regularly interact. Networks are not groups; they are only defined in relation to a particular individual. Nonetheless they are important because they may involve a substantial part of an individual's social interaction. A "social messiness" also afflicts interaction worldwide. People freely travel and enter new social situations where culture is not fully shared. Individuals can interact in dozens of different social situations each day.

Groups form around several principles. Every society has kinship groups, the topic of the previous section of this book. Ethnic groups organize around a shared cultural background. Some groups, such as the American Association of Retired Persons, are based on age. Others, like the National Organization for Women, are based on gender. The Macalester/Groveland Community Association is a territorial group. Many groups, such as the Gold Wing Road Riders Association (a national motorcycle group), Ford Motor Company (an economic group), and Mothers Against Drunk Driving (an interest group) organize around common goals and interests. Many groups are built around several of these design principles at once.

Finally groups can also be organized around social hierarchy. Some degree of **inequality** is part of most human interaction. One spouse may dominate another; a child may receive more attention than his or her siblings; the boss's friends may be promoted faster than other employees. But inequality becomes most noticeable when it systematically affects whole classes of people. In its most obvious form, inequality emerges as **social stratification,** which is characterized by regularly experienced unequal access to valued economic resources and prestige.

Anthropologists recognize at least two kinds of social stratification: class and caste. **Class** stratification restricts individuals' access to valued resources and prestige within a partially flexible system. Although it is often a difficult process, individuals may change rank in a class system if they manage to acquire the necessary prerequisites.

Many sociologists and anthropologists believe that there is an American class system and use terms such as *lower class, working class, middle class,* and *upper class* to designate the unequal positions within it. Americans born into poverty lack access to goods and prestige in this system but can change class standing if they acquire wealth and symbols of higher standing on a continuing basis. Upward mobility is difficult to achieve, however, and few people at the bottom of the system manage to change rank significantly. Indeed, many social scientists feel there is now a permanent underclass in the United States.

**Caste** defines a second kind of social stratification, one based on permanent membership. People are born into castes and cannot change membership, no matter what they do. In India, for example, caste is a pervasive feature of social organization. South Asians are born into castes and remain members for life; intercaste marriage is forbidden. In the past, castes formed the building blocks of rural Indian society. They were governed by strict rules of deference and served to allocate access to jobs, land, wealth, and power. Cash labor and new industrial jobs have eroded the economic aspect of the system today, but caste persists as a form of rank throughout most of the Indian subcontinent.

Several anthropologists and sociologists have argued that American racial groups are the equivalent of Indian castes. Black and white Americans keep their racial identity for life; nothing can change one's race. Racial identity clearly affects chances for the acquisition of prestige and economic success.

Caste identity, whether Indian or American, tends to preserve and create cultural difference. There is noticeable cultural variation among members of castes in most Indian villages, just as cultural variation occurs among black and white people in the United States.

Using the idea of social stratification, anthropologists have constructed a rough classification of societies into three types: egalitarian, rank, and stratified. **Egalitarian societies** lack formal social stratification. They may display inequality in personal relations based on age, gender, or personal ability, but no category of persons within the same sex or age group has special privilege. Hunter-gatherer societies are most likely to be egalitarian.

**Rank societies** contain unequal access to prestige, but not to valued economic resources. In such societies there may be chiefs or other persons with authority and prestige, and they may gain access to rank by birth, but their positions give them no substantial economic advantage. Horticultural societies, including some chiefdomships, fit this category.

**Stratified societies** organize around formal modes of social stratification, as their name suggests. Members of stratified societies are likely to form classes or castes, and inequality affects access to both prestige and economic resources. Most complex societies, including agrarian and industrialized states, fit into this type.

Inequality may also be based on other human attributes, such as age and gender. In many societies, including our own, age and gender affect access to prestige, power, and resources. It is common for men to publicly outrank women along these dimensions, particularly in societies threatened by war or other adversity that requires male intervention.

The articles in this part explore the nature of status, role, and inequality. The first, by Elizabeth Fernea and Robert Fernea, describes the importance of the veil as a symbol defining the role and rank of women in the Middle East. The second selection, by Ernestine Friedl, explores the reasons behind difference in power experienced by women in hunting and gathering societies. Friedl concludes that women's power is governed by access to control over public resources. The third article, by Jeffrey Fish, looks at the way Americans define race. Seen by most Americans as a biologically determined subspecies of human beings, but actually a culturally defined taxonomy based on the classification of one's parents, race in the United States is entirely different from racial categories in Brazil. The fourth selection, by Jack Weatherford, looks at the topic of ethnic and religious identity. Focusing on central Asia, he shows that ethnic identities are shaped by circumstances such as economic conditions, politics, and religion. In the final selection, Dianna Shandy looks at the process by which Nuer refugees come to the United States and settle here. Fleeing the civil war that has wracked their home in southern Sudan, refugees must develop the skill and determination to pass through a series of bureaucratic hurdles to reach and adjust to life in the United States.

# Key Terms

caste   *p. 251*

class   *p. 251*

egalitarian societies   *p. 251*

inequality   *p. 250*

rank societies   *p. 251*

role   *p. 249*

social groups   *p. 250*

social networks   *p. 250*

social situation   *p. 249*

social stratification   *p. 251*

status   *p. 249*

stratified societies   *p. 252*

# 24

# Symbolizing Roles: Behind the Veil

*Elizabeth W. Fernea and Robert A. Fernea*

*Most societies have some things that serve as key symbols. The flag of the United States, for example, stands not only for the nation, but for a variety of important values that guide American behavior and perception. In this article, Elizabeth Fernea and Robert Fernea trace the meaning of another key symbol: the veil worn by women in the Middle East. Instead of reference to a national group, the veil codes many of the values surrounding the role of women. Often viewed by Westerners as a symbol of female restriction and inequality, for the women who wear it the veil signals honor, personal protection, the sanctity and privacy of the family, wealth and high status, and city life.*

Blue jeans have come to mean America all over the world; three-piece wool suits signal businessmen; and in the 1980s pink or green hair said "punk." What do we notice, however, in societies other than our own? Ishi, the last of a "lost" tribe of North American Indians who stumbled into twentieth-century California in 1911, is reported to have said that the truly interesting objects in the white culture were pockets and matches. Rifa'ah Tahtawi, one of the first young Egyptians to be sent to Europe to study in 1826, wrote an account of French society in which he noted that Parisians used many unusual objects of dress, among them something called a belt. Women wore belts, he said, apparently to keep their bosoms erect, and to show off the slimness of their waists and the fullness of their hips. Europeans are still fascinated by the Stetson hats worn by American cowboys; an elderly Dutch woman of our acquaintance recently carried six enormous Stetsons back to the Hague as presents for the male members of her family.

Like languages (Inca, French) or food (tacos, hamburgers), clothing has special meaning for people who wear it that strangers may not understand. But some objects become charged with meaning to other cultures. The veil is one article of clothing used in Middle Eastern societies that stirs strong emotions in the West. "The feminine veil has become a symbol: that of the slavery of one portion of humanity," wrote French ethnologist Germaine Tillion in 1966. A hundred years earlier, Sir Richard Burton, British traveler, explorer, and translator of the *Arabian Nights,* recorded a different view. "Europeans inveigh against this article [the face veil] . . . for its hideousness and jealous concealment of charms made to be admired," he wrote in 1855. "It is, on the contrary, the most coquettish article of women's attire . . . it conceals coarse skins, fleshy noses, wide mouths and vanishing chins, whilst it sets off to best advantage what in these lands is most lustrous and liquid—the eye. Who has not remarked this at a masquerade ball?"

In the present generation, the veil has become a focus of attention for Western writers, both popular and academic, who take a measure of Burton's irony and Tillion's anger to equate modernization of the Middle East with the discarding of the veil and to look at its return in Iran and in a number of Arab countries as a sure sign of retrogression. "Iran's 16 million women have come a long way since their floor-length cotton veil officially was abolished in 1935," an article noted in the 1970s, just before the Shah was toppled. Today [1986], with Ayatollah Khomeini in power, those 16 million Iranian women have put their veils back on again, as if to say that the long way they have come is not in the direction of the West.

The thousands of words written about the appearance and disappearance of the veil and of *purdah* (the seclusion of women) do little to help us understand the Middle East or the cultures that grew out of the same Judeo-Christian roots as our own. The veil and the all-enveloping garments that inevitably accompany it (the *milayah* in Egypt, the *abbayah* in Iraq, the *chadoor* in Iran, the *yashmak* in Turkey, the *burqa'* in Afghanistan, and the *djellabah* and the *haik* in North Africa) are only the outward manifestations of cultural practices and meanings that are rooted deep in the history of Mediterranean and Southwest Asian society and are now finding expression once again. Today, with the resurgence of Islam, the veil has become a statement of difference between the Middle East and the Western world, a boundary no easier to cross now than it was during the Crusades or during the nineteenth century, when Western colonial powers ruled the area.

In English, the word *veil* has many definitions, and some of them are religious, just as in the Middle East. In addition to a face cover, the term also means "a piece of material worn over the head and shoulders, a part of a nun's head dress." The Arabic word for veiling and secluding comes from the root word *hajaba,* meaning "barrier." A *hijab* is an amulet worn to keep away the evil eye; it also means a diaphragm used to prevent conception. The gatekeeper or doorkeeper who guards the entrance to a government minister's office is a *hijab,* and in a casual conversation a person might say, "I want to be more informal with my friend so-and-so, but she always puts a *hijab* [barrier] between us."

In Islam, the Koranic verse that sanctions a barrier between men and women is called the Sura of the *hijab* (curtain): "Prophet, enjoin your wives, your daughters and the wives of true believers to draw their garments close round them. That is more proper, so that they may be recognized and not molested. Allah is forgiving and merciful." Notice, however, that veils of the first true believers did not conceal but rather announced the religious status of the women who wore them, drawing attention to the fact that they were Muslims and therefore to be treated with respect. The special Islamic dress worn by increasing numbers of modern Muslim women has much the same effect; it also says, "Treat me with respect."

Certainly some form of seclusion and of veiling was practiced before the time of Muhammad, at least among the urban elites and ruling families, but it was his followers, the first converts to Islam, who used veiling to signal religious faith. According to historic traditions, the *hijab* was established after the wives of the Prophet Muhammad were insulted by people coming to the mosque in search of the Prophet. Muhammad's wives, they said, had been mistaken for slaves. The custom of the *hijab* was thus established, and in the words of historian Nabia Abbott, "Muhammad's women found themselves, on the one hand, deprived of personal liberty, and on the other hand, raised to a position of honor and dignity." It is true, nonetheless, that the forms and uses of veiling and seclusion have varied greatly in practice over the last thousand years since the time of the Prophet, and millions of Muslim women have never been veiled at all. It is a luxury poorer families cannot afford, since any form of arduous activity, such as working in the fields, makes its use impossible. Thus it is likely that the use of the veil was envied by those who could not afford it, for it signaled a style of life that was generally admired. Burton, commenting on the Muslims portrayed in the *Arabian Nights,* says, "The women, who delight in restrictions which tend to their honour, accepted it willingly and still affect it, they do not desire a liberty or rather a license which they have learned to regard as inconsistent with their time-honored notions of feminine decorum and delicacy. They would think very meanly of a husband who permitted them to be exposed, like hetairae, to the public gaze."

The veil bears many messages about its wearers and their society, and many men and women in Middle Eastern communities today would quickly denounce nineteenth-century Orientalists like Sir Richard Burton and deny its importance. Nouha al Hejelan, wife of the Saudi Arabian ambassador to London, told Sally Quinn of *The Washington Post,* "If I wanted to take it all off [the *abbayah* and veil], I would have long ago. It wouldn't mean as much to me as it does to you." Basima Bezirgan, a contemporary Iraqi feminist, says, "Compared to the real issues that are involved between men and women in the Middle East today, the veil itself is unimportant." A Moroccan linguist, who buys her clothes in Paris, laughs when asked about the veil. "My mother wears a *djellabah* and a veil. I have never worn them. But so what? I still cannot get divorced as easily as a man, and I am still a member of my family group and responsible to them for everything I do. What is the veil? A piece of cloth." However, early Middle Eastern feminists felt differently. Huda Sharawi, an early Egyptian activist who formed the first Women's Union, removed her veil in public in 1923, a dramatic gesture to demonstrate her dislike of society's attitude toward women and her defiance of the system.

"The seclusion of women has many purposes," states Egyptian anthropologist Nadia Abu Zahra. "It expresses men's status, power, wealth, and manliness. It also helps preserve men's image of virility and masculinity, but men do not admit this; on the contrary they claim that one of the purposes of the veil is to guard women's honor." The veil and *purdah* are symbols of restriction, in men's behavior as well as women's. A respectable woman wearing conservative Islamic dress today on a public street is signaling, "Hands off! Don't touch me or you'll be sorry." Cowboy Jim Sayre of Deadwood, South Dakota, says, "If you deform a cowboy's hat, he'll likely deform you." A man who approaches a veiled woman is asking for similar trouble; not only the woman but also her family is shamed, and serious problems may result. "It is clear," says Egyptian anthropologist Ahmed Abou Zeid, "that honor and shame which are usually attributed to a certain individual or a certain kinship group have in fact a bearing on the total social structure, since most acts involving honor or shame are likely to affect the existing social equilibrium."

Veiling and seclusion almost always can be related to the maintenance of social status. The extreme example of the way the rich could use this practice was found among the wealthy sultans of pre-revolutionary Turkey. Stories of their women, kept in harems and guarded by eunuchs, formed the basis for much of the Western folklore concerning the nature of male-female relationships in Middle Eastern society. The forbidden nature of seclusion inflamed the Western imagination, but the Westerners who created erotic fantasies in films and novels would not have been able to enter the sultans' palaces any more than they could have penetrated their harems! It was eroticism plus opulence and luxury, the signs of wealth, that captured the imagination of the Westerners— and still does, as witnessed by the popularity of "Dallas" and "Dynasty."

The meaning associated with veiling or a lack of veiling changes according to locality. Most village women in the Egyptian delta have not veiled, nor have the Berber women of North Africa, but no one criticizes them for this. "In the village, no one veils, because everyone is considered a member of the same large family," explained Aisha Bint Muhammad, a working-class wife of Marrakesh. "But in the city, veiling is *sunnah,* required by our religion." Veiling has generally been found in towns and cities, among all classes, where families feel that it is necessary to distinguish themselves from strangers. Some women who must work without the veil in factories and hotels may put such garments on when they go out on holidays or even walk on the streets after work.

Veiling and *purdah* not only indicate status and wealth; they also have some religious sanction and protect women from the world outside the home. *Purdah* delineates private space and distinguishes between the public and private sectors of society, as does the traditional architecture of the area. Older Middle Eastern houses do not have picture windows facing on the street, nor do they have walks leading invitingly to front doors. Family life is hidden away from strangers; behind blank walls may lie courtyards and gardens, refuges from the heat, cold, and bustle of the outside world, the world of nonkin that is not to be trusted. Outsiders are pointedly excluded.

Even within the household, among her close relatives, a traditional Muslim woman may veil before those kinsmen whom she could legally marry. If her maternal or paternal cousins, her brothers-in-law, or her sons-in-law come to call, she covers her head, or perhaps her whole face. To do otherwise, to neglect such acts of respect and modesty, would be considered shameless.

The veil does more than protect its wearers from known and unknown intruders; it can also conceal identity. Behind the anonymity of the veil, women can go about a city unrecognized and uncriticized. Nadia Abu Zahra reports anecdotes of men donning women's veils in order to visit their lovers undetected; women may do the same. The veil is such an effective disguise that Nouri Al-Sa'id, the late prime minister of Iraq, attempted to escape death from revolutionary forces in 1958 by wearing the *abbayah* and veil of a woman; only his shoes gave him away. When houses of prostitution were closed in Baghdad in the early 1950s, the prostitutes donned the same clothing to cruise the streets. Flashing open their outer garments was an advertisement to potential customers.

Political dissidents in many countries have used the veil for their own ends. The women who marched, veiled, through Cairo during the Nationalist demonstrations against the British after World War I were counting on the strength of Western respect for the veil to protect them against British gunfire. At first they were right. Algerian women also used the protection of the veil to carry bombs through French army checkpoints during the Algerian revolution. But when the French discovered the ruse, Algerian women discarded the veil and dressed like Europeans to move about freely.

The multiple meanings and uses of *purdah* and the veil do not fully explain how such practices came to be so deeply embedded in Mediterranean society. However, their origins lie in the asymmetrical relationship between men and women and the resulting attitudes about men's and women's roles. Women, according to Fatma Mernissi, a Moroccan sociologist, are seen by men in Islamic societies as in need of protection because they are unable to control their sexuality and hence are a danger to the social order. In other words, they need to be restrained and controlled so that men do not give way to the impassioned desire they inspire, and society can thus function in an orderly way.

The notion that women present a danger to the social order is scarcely limited to Muslim society. Anthropologist Julian Pitt-Rivers has pointed out that the supervision and seclusion of women was also found in Christian Europe, even though veiling was not usually practiced there. "The idea that women not subjected to male authority are a danger is a fundamental one in the writings of the moralists from the Archpriest of Talavera to Padre Haro, and it is echoed in the modern Andalusian *pueblo*. It is bound up with the fear of ungoverned female sexuality which had been an integral element of European folklore ever since prudent Odysseus lashed himself to the mast to escape the sirens."

Pitt-Rivers is writing about northern Mediterranean communities, which, like those of the Middle Eastern societies, have been greatly concerned with family honor and shame rather than with individual guilt. The honor of the Middle Eastern extended family, its ancestors and its descendants, is the highest social value. The misdeeds of the grandparents are indeed visited on their grandchildren, but so also grandparents may be disgraced by grandchildren. Men and women always remain members of their natal families. Marriage is a legal contract, but a fragile one that is often broken; the ties between brother and sister, mother and child, father and child are lifelong and enduring. The larger natal family is the group to which the individual man or woman belongs and to which the individual owes responsibility in exchange for the social and economic security that the family group provides. It is the group that is socially honored—or dishonored—by the behavior of the individual.

Both male honor and female honor are involved in the honor of the family, but each is expressed differently. The honor of a man, *sharaf*, is a public matter, involving bravery, hospitality, and piety. It may be lost, but it may also be regained. The honor of a woman, *'ard*, is a private matter involving only one thing, her sexual chastity. Once believed to be lost, it cannot be regained. If the loss of female honor remains only privately known, a rebuke may be all that takes place. But if the loss of female honor becomes public knowledge, the other members of the family may feel bound to cleanse the family name. In extreme cases, the cleansing may require the death of the offending female member. Although such killings are now criminal offenses in the Middle East, suspended sentences are often given, and the newspapers in Cairo and Baghdad frequently carry sad stories of runaway sisters "gone bad" in the city, and the revenge taken upon them in the name of family honor by their brothers or cousins.

This emphasis on female chastity, many say, originated in the patrilineal society's concern with the paternity of the child and the inheritance that follows the male line. How could the husband know that the child in his wife's womb was his son? He could not know unless his wife was a virgin at marriage. Marriages were arranged by parents, and keeping daughters secluded from men was the best way of seeing that a girl remained a virgin until her wedding night.

Middle Eastern women also look upon seclusion as practical protection. In the Iraqi village where we lived from 1956 to 1958, one of us (Elizabeth) wore the *abbayah* and found that it provided a great deal of protection from prying eyes, dust, heat, and flies. Parisian women visiting Istanbul in the sixteenth century were so impressed by the ability of the all-enveloping garment to keep dresses clean of mud and manure and to keep women from being attacked by importuning men that they tried to introduce it into French fashion. Many women have told us that they felt self-conscious, vulnerable, and even naked when they first walked on a public street without the veil and *abbayah*—as if they were making a display of themselves.

The veil, as it has returned in the last decade in a movement away from wearing Western dress, has been called a form of "portable seclusion," allowing women to maintain a modest appearance that indicates respectability and religious piety in the midst of modern Middle Eastern urban life. This new style of dress always includes long skirts, long sleeves, and a head covering (scarf or turban). Some outfits are belted, some are loose, and some include face veils and shapeless robes, as well as gloves so that no skin whatsoever is exposed to the public eye. However, these clothes are seldom black, like the older garments. The women wearing such clothes in Egypt may work in shops or offices or go to college; they are members of the growing middle class.

This new fashion has been described by some scholars as an attempt by men to reassert their Muslim identity and to reestablish their position as heads of families, even though both spouses often must work outside the home. According to this analysis, the presence of the veil is a sign that the males of the household are in control of their women and are more able to assume the responsibilities disturbed or usurped by foreign colonial powers, responsibilities which continue to be threatened by Western politics and materialism. Other scholars argue that it is not men who are choosing the garb today but women themselves, using modest dress as a way of communicating to the rest of the world that though they may work outside their homes, they are nonetheless pious Muslims and respectable women.

The veil is the outward sign of a complex reality. Observers are often deceived by the absence of that sign and fail to see that in Middle Eastern societies (and in many parts of Europe) where the garb no longer exists, basic attitudes are unchanged. Women who have taken off the veil continue to play the old roles within the family, and their chastity remains crucial. A woman's behavior is still the key to the honor and the reputation of her family, no matter what she wears.

In Middle Eastern societies, feminine and masculine continue to be strong poles of identification. This is in marked contrast to Western society, where for more than a generation greater equality between men and women has been reflected in the blurring of distinctions between male and female clothing. Western feminists continue to state that biology is not the basis of behavior and therefore should not be the basis for understanding men's and women's roles. But almost all Middle Eastern reformers, whether upper or middle class, intellectuals or clerics, argue from the assumption of a fundamental, God-given difference, social and psychological as well as physical, between men and women. There are important disagreements among these reformers today about what should be done, however.

Those Muslim reformers still strongly influenced by Western models call for equal access to divorce, child custody, and inheritance; equal opportunities for education and employment; abolition of female circumcision and "crimes of honor"; an end to polygamy; and a law regulating the age of marriage. But of growing importance are reformers of social practice who call for a return to the example set by the Prophet Muhammad and his early followers; they wish to begin by eliminating what they feel to be the licentious practices introduced by Western influence, such as sexual laxity and the consumption of alcohol. To them, change in the laws affecting women should be in strict accord with their view of Islamic law, and women should begin by expressing their modesty and piety by wearing the new forms of veiling in public life. Seclusion may be impossible in modern urban societies, but conservative dress, the new form of veiling, is an option for women that sets the faithful Muslim apart from the corrupt world of the nonbeliever as it was believed to do in the time of the Prophet.

A female English film director, after several months in Morocco, said in an interview, "This business about the veil is nonsense. We all have our veils, between ourselves and other people. The question is what the veils are used for, and by whom." Today the use of the veil continues to trigger Western reaction, for as Islamic dress, it is not only a statement about the honor of the family or the boundary between family and stranger. Just as the changes in the nun's dress in the United States tell us something about the woman who wears it and the society of which she is a part, the various forms of veiling today communicate attitudes and beliefs about politics and religious morality as well as the roles of men and women in the Middle East.

# Review Questions

1. What is the meaning to Westerners of the veil worn by Middle Eastern women? How does this view reflect Western values?

2. List the symbolic meanings of the veil to Middle Eastern women. How do these meanings relate to the Muslim concept of *purdah* and to other important Middle Eastern values?

3. There has been a resurgence of the veil in several Middle Eastern societies over the past few years. How can you explain this change?

4. Using this article as a model, analyze the meaning of some American articles of clothing. How do these relate to core values in the country?

# 25

# Society and Sex Roles

## Ernestine Friedl

*Many anthropologists claim that males hold formal authority over females in every society. Although the degree of masculine authority may vary from one group to the next, males always have more power. For some researchers, this unequal male–female relationship is the result of biological inheritance. As with other primates, they argue, male humans are naturally more aggressive, females more docile. Ernestine Friedl challenges this explanation in this selection. Comparing a variety of hunting and gathering groups, she concludes that relations between men and women are shaped by a culturally defined division of labor based on sex, not by inherited predisposition. Given access to resources that circulate publicly, women can attain equal or dominant status in any society, including our own.*

"Society and Sex Roles" by Ernestine Friedl as appeared in *Human Nature* Magazine, April 1978. Reprinted by permission of the author.

"Women must respond quickly to the demands of their husbands," says anthropologist Napoleon Chagnon, describing the horticultural Yanomamö Indians of Venezuela. When a man returns from a hunting trip, "the woman, no matter what she is doing, hurries home and quietly but rapidly prepares a meal for her husband. Should the wife be slow in doing this, the husband is within his rights to beat her. Most reprimands . . . take the form of blows with the hand or with a piece of firewood. . . . Some of them chop their wives with the sharp edge of a machete or axe, or shoot them with a barbed arrow in some nonvital area, such as the buttocks or leg."

Among the Semai agriculturalists of central Malaya, when one person refuses the request of another, the offended party suffers *punan*, a mixture of emotional pain and frustration. "Enduring *punan* is commonest when a girl has refused the victim her sexual favors," reports Robert Dentan. "The jilted man's 'heart becomes sad.' He loses his energy and his appetite. Much of the time he sleeps, dreaming of his lost love. In this state he is in fact very likely to injure himself 'accidentally.' " The Semai are afraid of violence; a man would never strike a woman.

The social relationship between men and women has emerged as one of the principal disputes occupying the attention of scholars and the public in recent years. Although the discord is sharpest in the United States, the controversy has spread throughout the world. Numerous national and international conferences, including one in Mexico sponsored by the United Nations, have drawn together delegates from all walks of life to discuss such questions as the social and political rights of each sex and even the basic nature of males and females.

Whatever their position, partisans often invoke examples from other cultures to support their ideas about the proper role of each sex. Because women are clearly subservient to men in many societies, like the Yanomamö, some experts conclude that the natural pattern is for men to dominate. But among the Semai no one has the right to command others, and in West Africa women are often chiefs. The place of women in these societies supports the argument of those who believe that sex roles are not fixed, that if there is a natural order, it allows for many different arrangements.

The argument will never be settled as long as the opposing sides toss examples from the world's cultures at each other like intellectual stones. But the effect of biological differences on male and female behavior can be clarified by looking at known examples of the earliest forms of human society and examining the relationship between technology, social organization, environment, and sex roles. The problem is to determine the conditions in which different degrees of male dominance are found, to try to discover the social and cultural arrangements that give rise to equality or inequality between the sexes, and to attempt to apply this knowledge to our understanding of the changes taking place in modern industrial society.

As Western history and the anthropological record have told us, equality between the sexes is rare; in most known societies females are subordinate. Male dominance is so widespread that it is virtually a human universal; societies in which women are consistently dominant do not exist and have never existed.

Evidence of a society in which women control all strategic resources like food and water, and in which women's activities are the most prestigious, has never been found. The Iroquois of North America and the Lovedu of Africa came closest. Among the Iroquois, women raised food, controlled its distribution, and helped to choose male political leaders. Lovedu women ruled as queens, exchanged valuable cattle, led ceremonies, and controlled their own sex lives. But among both the Iroquois and Lovedu, men owned the land and held other positions of power and prestige. Women were equal to men; they did not have ultimate authority over them. Neither culture was a true matriarchy.

Patriarchies are prevalent, and they appear to be strongest in societies in which men control significant goods that are exchanged with people outside the family. Regardless of who produces food, the person who gives it to others creates the obligations and alliances that are at the center of all political relations. The greater the male monopoly on the distribution of scarce items, the stronger their control of women seems to be. This is most obvious in relatively simple hunter-gatherer societies.

Hunter-gatherers, or foragers, subsist on wild plants, small land animals, and small river or sea creatures gathered by hand; large land animals and sea mammals hunted with spears, bows and arrows, and blow guns; and fish caught with hooks and nets. The three hundred thousand hunter-gatherers alive in the world today include the Eskimos, the Australian aborigines, and the Pygmies of Central Africa.

Foraging has endured for two million years and was replaced by farming and animal husbandry only ten thousand years ago; it covers more than 99 percent of human history. Our foraging ancestry is not far behind us and provides a clue to our understanding of the human condition.

Hunter-gatherers are people whose ways of life are technologically simple and socially and politically egalitarian. They live in small groups of 50 to 200 and have neither kings, nor priests, nor social classes. These conditions permit anthropologists to observe the essential bases for inequalities between the sexes without the distortions induced by the complexities of contemporary industrial society.

The source of male power among hunter-gatherers lies in their control of a scarce, hard to acquire, but necessary nutrient—animal protein. When men in a hunter-gatherer society return to camp with game, they divide the meat in some customary way. Among the !Kung San of Africa, certain parts of the animal are given to the owner of the arrow that killed the beast, to the first hunter to sight the game, to the one who threw the first spear, and to all men in the hunting party. After the meat has been divided, each hunter distributes his share to his blood relatives and his in-laws, who in turn share it with others. If an animal is large enough, every member of the band will receive some meat.

Vegetable foods, in contrast, are not distributed beyond the immediate household. Women give food to their children, to their husbands, to other members of the household, and rarely, to the occasional visitor. No one outside the family regularly eats any of the wild fruits and vegetables that are gathered by the women.

The meat distributed by the men is a public gift. Its source is widely known, and the donor expects a reciprocal gift when other men return from a successful hunt. He gains honor as a supplier of a scarce item and simultaneously obligates others to him.

These obligations constitute a form of power or control over others, both men and women. The opinions of hunters play an important part in decisions to move the village; good hunters attract the most desirable women; people in other groups join camps with good hunters; and hunters, because they already participate in an internal system of exchange, control exchange with other groups for flint, salt, and steel axes. The male monopoly on hunting unites men in a system of exchange and gives them power; gathering vegetable food does not give women equal power even among foragers who live in the tropics, where the food collected by women provides more than half the hunter-gatherer diet.

If dominance arises from a monopoly on big-game hunting, why has the male monopoly remained unchallenged? Some women are strong enough to participate in the hunt and their endurance is certainly equal to that of men. Dobe San women of the Kalahari Desert in Africa walk an average of 10 miles a day carrying from 15 to 33 pounds of food plus a baby.

Women do not hunt, I believe, because of four interrelated factors: variability in the supply of game; the different skills required for hunting and gathering; the incompatibility between carrying burdens and hunting; and the small size of seminomadic foraging populations.

Because the meat supply is unstable, foragers must make frequent expeditions to provide the band with gathered food. Environmental factors such as seasonal and annual variation in rainfall often affect the size of the wildlife population. Hunters cannot always find game, and when they do encounter animals, they are not always successful in killing their prey. In northern latitudes, where meat is the primary food, periods of starvation are known in every generation. The irregularity of the game supply leads hunter-gatherers in areas where plant foods are available to depend on these predictable foods a good part of the time. Someone must gather the fruits, nuts, and roots and carry them back to camp to feed unsuccessful hunters, children, the elderly, and anyone who might not have gone foraging that day.

Foraging falls to the women because hunting and gathering cannot be combined on the same expedition. Although gatherers sometimes notice signs of game as they work, the skills required to track game are not the same as those required to find edible roots or plants. Hunters scan the horizon and the land for traces of large game; gatherers keep their eyes to the ground, studying the distribution of plants and the texture of the soil for hidden roots and animal holes. Even if a woman who was collecting plants came across the track of an antelope, she could not follow it; it is impossible to carry a load and hunt at the same time. Running with a heavy load is difficult, and should the animal be sighted, the hunter would be off balance and could neither shoot an arrow nor throw a spear accurately.

Pregnancy and child care would also present difficulties for a hunter. An unborn child affects a woman's body balance, as does a child in her arms, on her back, or slung at her side. Until they are two years old, many hunter-gatherer children are carried at all times, and until they are four, they are carried some of the time.

An observer might wonder why young women do not hunt until they become pregnant, or why mature women and men do not hunt and gather on alternate days, with some women staying in camp to act as wet nurses for the young. Apart from the effects hunting might have on a mother's milk production, there are two reasons. First, young girls begin to bear children as soon as they are physically mature and strong enough to hunt, and second, hunter-gatherer bands are so small that there are unlikely to be enough lactating women to serve as wet nurses. No hunter-gatherer group could afford to maintain a specialized female hunting force.

Because game is not always available, because hunting and gathering are specialized skills, because women carrying heavy loads cannot hunt, and because women in hunter-gatherer societies are usually either pregnant or caring for young children, for most of the last two million years of human history men have hunted and women have gathered.

If male dominance depends on controlling the supply of meat, then the degree of male dominance in a society should vary with the amount of meat available and the amount supplied by the men. Some regions, like the East African grasslands and the North American woodlands, abounded with species of large mammals; other zones, like tropical forests and semideserts, are thinly populated with prey. Many elements affect the supply of game, but theoretically, the less meat provided exclusively by the men, the more egalitarian the society.

All known hunter-gatherer societies fit into four basic types: those in which men and women work together in communal hunts and as teams gathering edible plants, as did the Washo Indians of North America; those in which men and women each collect their own plant foods although the men supply some meat to the group, as do the Hadza of Tanzania; those in which male hunters and female gatherers work apart but return to camp each evening to share their acquisitions, as do the Tiwi of North Australia; and those in which the men provide all the food by hunting large game, as do the Eskimo. In each case the extent of male dominance increases directly with the proportion of meat supplied by individual men and small hunting parties.

Among the most egalitarian of hunter-gatherer societies are the Washo Indians, who inhabited the valleys of the Sierra Nevada in what is now southern California and Nevada. In the spring they moved north to Lake Tahoe for the large fish runs of sucker and native trout. Everyone—men, women, and children—participated in the fishing. Women spent the summer gathering edible berries and seeds while the men continued to fish. In the fall some men hunted deer, but the most important source of animal protein was the jackrabbit, which was captured in communal hunts. Men and women together drove the rabbits into nets tied end to end. To provide food for the winter, husbands and wives worked as teams in the late fall to collect pine nuts.

Since everyone participated in most food-gathering activities, there were no individual distributors of food and relatively little difference in male and female rights. Men and women were not segregated from each other in daily activities; both were free to take lovers after marriage; both had the right to separate whenever they chose; menstruating women were not isolated from the rest of the group; and one of the two major Washo rituals celebrated hunting while the other celebrated gathering. Men were accorded more prestige if they had killed a deer, and men directed decisions about the seasonal movement of the group. But if no male leader stepped forward, women were permitted to lead. The distinctive feature of groups such as the Washo is the relative equality of the sexes.

The sexes are also relatively equal among the Hadza of Tanzania, but this near-equality arises because men and women tend to work alone to feed themselves. They exchange little food. The Hadza lead a leisurely life in the seemingly barren environment of the East African Rift Gorge, which is, in fact, rich in edible berries, roots, and small game. As a result of this abundance, from the time they are ten years old, Hadza men and women gather much of their own food. Women take their young children with them into the bush, eating as they forage, and collect only enough food for a light family meal in the evening. The men eat berries and roots as they hunt for small game, and should they bring down a rabbit or a hyrax, they eat the meat on the spot. Meat is carried back to the camp and shared with the rest of the group only on those rare occasions when a poisoned arrow brings down a large animal—an impala, a zebra, an eland, or a giraffe.

Because Hadza men distribute little meat, their status is only slightly higher than that of the women. People flock to the camp of a good hunter and the camp might take on his name because of his popularity, but he is in no sense a leader of the group. A Hadza man and a woman have an equal right to divorce, and each can repudiate a marriage simply by living apart for a few weeks. Couples tend to live in the same camp as the wife's mother, but they sometimes make long visits to the camp of the husband's mother. Although a man may take more than one wife, most Hadza males cannot afford to indulge in this luxury. In order to maintain a marriage, a man must supply both his wife and his mother-in-law with some meat and trade goods, such as beads and cloth, and the Hadza economy gives few men the wealth to provide for more than one wife and mother-in-law. Washo equality is based on cooperation; Hadza equality is based on independence.

In contrast to both these groups, among the Tiwi of Melville and Bathurst Islands off the northern coast of Australia, male hunters dominate female gatherers. The Tiwi are representative of the most common form of foraging society, in which the men supply large quantities of meat, although less than half the food consumed by the group. Each morning Tiwi women, most with babies on their backs, scatter in different directions in search of vegetables, grubs, worms, and small game such as bandicoots, lizards, and opossums. To track the game, they use hunting dogs. On most days women return to camp with some meat and with baskets full of *korka,* the nut of a native palm, which is soaked and mashed to make a porridge-like dish. The Tiwi men do not hunt small game and do not hunt every day, but when they do they often return with kangaroo, large lizards, fish, and game birds.

The porridge is cooked separately by each household and rarely shared outside the family, but the meat is prepared by a volunteer cook, who can be male or female. After the cook takes one of the parts of the animal traditionally reserved for him or her, the animal's "boss," the one who caught it, distributes the rest to all near kin and then to all others residing with the band. Although the small game supplied by the women is distributed in the same way as the big game supplied by the men, Tiwi men are dominant because the game they kill provides most of the meat.

The power of Tiwi men is clearest in their betrothal practices. Among the Tiwi, a woman must always be married. To ensure this, female infants are betrothed at birth and widows are remarried at the gravesides of their late husbands. Men form alliances by exchanging daughters, sisters, and mothers in marriage, and some collect as many as twenty-five wives. Tiwi men value the quantity and quality of the food many wives can collect and the many children they can produce.

The dominance of the men is offset somewhat by the influence of adult women in selecting their next husbands. Many women are active strategists in the political careers of their male relatives, but to the exasperation of some sons attempting to promote their own futures, widowed mothers sometimes insist on selecting their own partners. Women also influence the marriages of their daughters and granddaughters, especially when the selected husband dies before the bestowed child moves to his camp.

Among the Eskimo, representative of the rarest type of forager society, inequality between the sexes is matched by inequality in supplying the group with food. Inland Eskimo men hunt caribou throughout the year to provision the entire society, and maritime Eskimo men depend on whaling, fishing, and some hunting to feed their extended families. The women process the carcasses, cut and sew skins to make clothing, cook, and care for the young; but they collect no food of their own and depend on the men to supply all the raw materials for their work. Since men provide all the meat, they also control the trade in hides, whale oil, seal oil, and other items that move between the maritime and inland Eskimos.

Eskimo women are treated almost exclusively as objects to be used, abused, and traded by men. After puberty all Eskimo girls are fair game for any interested male. A man shows his intentions by grabbing the belt of a woman, and if she protests, he cuts off her trousers and forces himself upon her. These encounters are considered unimportant by the rest of the group. Men offer their wives' sexual services to establish alliances with trading partners and members of hunting and whaling parties.

Despite the consistent pattern of some degree of male dominance among foragers, most of these societies are egalitarian compared with agricultural and industrial societies. No forager has any significant opportunity for political leadership. Foragers, as a rule, do not like to give or take orders, and assume leadership only with reluctance. Shamans (those who are thought to be possessed by spirits) may be either male or female. Public rituals conducted by women in order to celebrate the first menstruation of girls are common, and the symbolism in these rituals is similar to that in the ceremonies that follow a boy's first kill.

In any society, status goes to those who control the distribution of valued goods and services outside the family. Equality arises when both sexes work side by side in food production, as do the Washo, and the products are simply distributed among the workers. In such circumstances, no person or sex has greater access to valued items than do others. But when women make no contribution to the food supply, as in the case of the Eskimo, they are completely subordinate.

When we attempt to apply these generalizations to contemporary industrial society, we can predict that as long as women spend their discretionary income from jobs on domestic needs, they will gain little social recognition and power. To be an effective source of power, money must be exchanged in ways that require returns and create obligations. In other words, it must be invested.

Jobs that do not give women control over valued resources will do little to advance their general status. Only as managers, executives, and professionals are women in a position to trade goods and services, to do others favors, and therefore to obligate others to them. Only as controllers of valued resources can women achieve prestige, power, and equality.

Within the household, women who bring in income from jobs are able to function on a more nearly equal basis with their husbands. Women who contribute services to their husbands and children without pay, as do some middle-class Western housewives, are especially vulnerable to dominance. Like Eskimo women, as long as their services are limited to domestic distribution they have little power relative to their husbands and none with respect to the outside world.

As for the limits imposed on women by their procreative functions in hunter-gatherer societies, childbearing and child care are organized around work as much as work is organized around reproduction. Some foraging groups space their children three to four years apart and have an average of only four to six children, far fewer than many women in other cultures. Hunter-gatherers nurse their infants for extended periods, sometimes for as long as four years. This custom suppresses ovulation and limits the size of their families. Sometimes, although rarely, they practice infanticide. By limiting reproduction, a woman who is gathering food has only one child to carry.

Different societies can and do adjust the frequency of birth and the care of children to accommodate whatever productive activities women customarily engage in. In horticultural societies, where women work long hours in gardens that may be far from home, infants get food to supplement their mothers' milk, older children take care of younger children, and pregnancies are widely spaced. Throughout the world, if a society requires a woman's labor, it finds ways to care for her children.

In the United States, as in some other industrial societies, the accelerated entry of women with preschool children into the labor force has resulted in the development of a variety of child-care arrangements. Individual women have called on friends, relatives, and neighbors. Public and private child-care centers are growing. We should realize that the declining birth rate, the increasing acceptance of childless or single-child families, and de-emphasis on motherhood are adaptations to a sexual division of labor reminiscent of the system of production found in hunter-gatherer societies.

In many countries where women no longer devote most of their productive years to childbearing, they are beginning to demand a change in the social relationship of the sexes. As women gain access to positions that control the exchange of resources, male dominance may become archaic, and industrial societies may one day become as egalitarian as the Washo.

# Review Questions

1. According to Friedl, what factor accounts for the different degrees of dominance and power between males and females found in hunter-gatherer societies?

2. What are the four types of hunter-gatherer societies considered by Friedl in this article, and what is it about the structure of each that relates to the distribution of power and dominance between males and females?

3. Some anthropologists believe that male dominance is inherited. Comment on this assertion in light of Friedl's article.

4. Why does Friedl believe that women will gain equality with men in industrial society?

# 26

# Mixed Blood

*Jeffrey M. Fish*

*Many Americans believe that people can be divided into races. For them, races are biologically defined groups. Anthropologists, on the other hand, have long argued that U.S. racial groups are American cultural constructions; they represent the way Americans classify people rather than a genetically determined reality. In this article, Jeffrey Fish demonstrates the cultural basis of race by comparing how races are defined in the United States and Brazil. In America, a person's race is determined not by how he or she looks, but by his or her heritage. A person will be classified as black, for example, if one of his or her parents is classified that way no matter what the person looks like. In Brazil, on the other hand, people are classified into a series of* tipos *on the basis of how they look. The same couple may have children classified into three or four different* tipos *based on a number of physical markers such as skin color and nose shape. As a result, Fish's daughter, who has brown skin and whose mother is Brazilian, can change her race from black in the United States to* moreno *(brunette), a category just behind* branca *(blond) in Brazil, by simply taking a plane there.*

Last year my daughter, who had been living in Rio de Janeiro, and her Brazilian boyfriend paid a visit to my cross-cultural psychology class. They had agreed to be interviewed about Brazilian culture. At one point in the interview I asked her, "Are you black?" She said, "Yes." I then asked him the question, and he said "No."

"How can that be?" I asked. "He's darker than she is."

Psychologists have begun talking about race again. They think that it may be useful in explaining the biological bases of behavior. For example, following publication of *The Bell Curve*, there has been renewed debate about whether black–white group differences in scores on IQ tests reflect racial differences in intelligence. (Because this article is about race, it will mainly use racial terms, like black and white, rather than cultural terms, like African-American and European-American.)

The problem with debates like the one over race and IQ is that psychologists on both sides of the controversy make a totally unwarranted assumption: that there is a biological entity called "race." If there were such an entity, then it would at least be possible that differences in behavior between "races" might be biologically based.

Before considering the controversy, however, it is reasonable to step back and ask ourselves "What is race?" If, as happens to be the case, race is not a biologically meaningful concept, then looking for biologically based racial differences in behavior is simply a waste of time.

The question "What is race?" can be divided into two more limited ones. The answers to both questions have long been known by anthropologists, but seem not to have reached other social or behavioral scientists, let alone the public at large. And both answers differ strikingly from what we Americans think of as race.

The first question is "How can we understand the variation in physical appearance among human beings?" It is interesting to discover that Americans (including researchers, who should know better) view only a part of the variation as "racial," while other equally evident variability is not so viewed.

The second question is "How can we understand the kinds of racial classifications applied to differences in physical appearance among human beings?" Surprisingly, different cultures label these physical differences in different ways. Far from describing biological entities, American racial categories are merely one of numerous, very culture-specific schemes for reducing uncertainty about how people should respond to other people. The fact that Americans believe that Asians, blacks, Hispanics, and whites constitute biological entities called races is a matter of cultural interest rather than scientific substance. It tells us something about American culture—but nothing at all about the human species.

The short answer to the question "What is race?" is: There is no such thing. Race is a myth. And our racial classification scheme is loaded with pure fantasy.

Let's start with human physical variation. Human beings are a species, which means that people from anywhere on the planet can mate with others from anywhere else and produce fertile offspring. (Horses and donkeys are two different species because, even though they can mate with each other, their offspring—mules—are sterile.)

Our species evolved in Africa from earlier forms and eventually spread out around the planet. Over time, human populations that were geographically separated from one another came to differ in physical appearance. They came by these differences through three major pathways: mutation, natural selection, and genetic drift. Since genetic mutations occur randomly, different mutations occur and accumulate over time in geographically separated populations. Also, as we have known since Darwin, different geographical environments select for different physical traits that confer a survival advantage. But the largest proportion of variability among populations may well result from purely random factors; this random change in the frequencies of already existing genes is known as genetic drift.

If an earthquake or disease kills off a large segment of a population, those who survive to reproduce are likely to differ from the original population in many ways. Similarly, if a group divides and a subgroup moves away, the two groups will, by chance, differ in the frequency of various genes. Even the mere fact of physical separation will, over time, lead two equivalent populations to differ in the frequency of genes. These randomly acquired population differences will accumulate over successive generations along with any others due to mutation or natural selection.

A number of differences in physical appearance among populations around the globe appear to have adaptive value. For example, people in the tropics of Africa and South America came to have dark skins, presumably, through natural selection, as protection against the sun. In cold areas, like northern Europe or northern North America, which are dark for long periods of time, and where people covered their bodies for warmth, people came to have light skins—light skins make maximum use of sunlight to produce vitamin D.

The indigenous peoples of the New World arrived about 15,000 years ago, during the last ice age, following game across the Bering Strait. (The sea level was low enough to create a land bridge because so much water was in the form of ice.) Thus, the dark-skinned Indians of the South American tropics are descended from light-skinned ancestors, similar in appearance to the Eskimo. In other words, even though skin color is the most salient feature thought by Americans to be an indicator of race—and race is assumed to have great time depth—it is subject to relatively rapid evolutionary change.

Meanwhile, the extra ("epicanthic") fold of eyelid skin, which Americans also view as racial, and which evolved in Asian populations to protect the eye against the cold, continues to exist among South American native peoples because its presence (unlike a light skin) offers no reproductive disadvantage. Hence, skin color and eyelid form, which Americans think of as traits of different races, occur together or separately in different populations.

Like skin color, there are other physical differences that also appear to have evolved through natural selection—but which Americans do not think of as racial. Take, for example, body shape. Some populations in very cold climates, like the Eskimo, developed rounded bodies. This is because the more spherical an object is, the less surface area it has to radiate heat. In contrast, some populations in very hot climates, like the Masai, developed lanky bodies. Like the tubular pipes of an old-fashioned radiator, the high ratio of surface area to volume allows people to radiate a lot of heat.

In terms of American's way of thinking about race, lanky people and rounded people are simply two kinds of whites or blacks. But it is equally reasonable to view light-skinned people and dark-skinned people as two kinds of "lankys" or "roundeds." In other words, our categories for racial classification of people arbitrarily include certain dimensions (light versus dark skin) and exclude others (rounded versus elongated bodies).

There is no biological basis for classifying race according to skin color instead of body form—or according to any other variable, for that matter. All that exists is variability in what people look like—and the arbitrary and culturally specific ways different societies classify that variability. There is nothing left over that can be called race. This is why race is a myth.

Skin color and body form do not vary together: Not all dark-skinned people are lanky; similarly, light-skinned people may be lanky or rounded. The same can be said of the facial features Americans think of as racial—eye color, nose width (actually, the ratio of width to length), lip thickness ("evertedness"), hair form, and hair color. They do not vary together either. If they did, then a "totally white" person would have very light skin color, straight blond hair, blue eyes, a narrow nose, and thin lips; a "totally black" person would have very dark skin color, black tight curly hair, dark brown eyes, a broad nose, and thick lips; those in between would have—to a correlated degree—wavy light brown hair, light brown eyes, and intermediate nose and lip forms.

While people of mixed European and African ancestry who look like this do exist, they are the exception rather than the rule. Anyone who wants to can make up a chart of facial features (choose a location with a diverse population, say, the New York City subway) and verify that there are people with all possible admixtures of facial features. One might see someone with tight curly blond hair, light skin, blue eyes, broad nose, and thick lips—whose features are half "black" and half "white." That is, each of the person's facial features occupies one end or the other of a supposedly racial continuum, with no intermediary forms (like wavy light brown hair). Such people are living proof that supposedly racial features do not vary together.

Since the human species has spent most of its existence in Africa, different populations in Africa have been separated from each other longer than East Asians or Northern Europeans have been separated from each other or from Africans. As a result, there is remarkable physical variation among the peoples of Africa, which goes unrecognized by Americans who view them all as belonging to the same race.

In contrast to the very tall Masai, the diminutive stature of the very short Pygmies may have evolved as an advantage in moving rapidly through tangled forest vegetation. The Bushmen of the Kalahari desert have very large ("steat-opygous") buttocks, presumably to store body fat in one place for times of food scarcity, while leaving the rest of the body uninsulated to radiate heat. They also have "peppercorn" hair. Hair in separated tufts, like tight curly hair, leaves space to radiate the heat that rises through the body to the scalp; straight hair lies flat and holds in body heat, like a cap. By viewing Africans as constituting a single race, Americans ignore their greater physical variability, while assigning racial significance to lesser differences between them.

Although it is true that most inhabitants of northern Europe, east Asia, and central Africa look like Americans' conceptions of one or another of the three purported races, most inhabitants of south Asia, southwest Asia, north Africa, and the Pacific islands do not. Thus, the 19th century view of the human species as comprised of Caucasoid, Mongoloid, and Negroid races, still held by many Americans, is based on a partial and unrepresentative view of human variability. In other words, what is now known about human physical variation does not correspond to what Americans think of as race.

In contrast to the question of the actual physical variation among human beings, there is the question of how people classify that variation. Scientists classify things in scientific taxonomies—chemists' periodic table of the elements, biologists' classification of life forms into kingdoms, phyla, and so forth.

In every culture, people also classify things along culture-specific dimensions of meaning. For example, paper clips and staples are understood by Americans as paper fasteners, and nails are not, even though, in terms of their physical properties, all three consist of differently shaped pieces of metal wire. The physical variation in pieces of metal wire can be seen as analogous to human physical variation; and the categories of cultural meaning, like paper fasteners versus wood fasteners, can be seen as analogous to races. Anthropologists refer to these kinds of classifications as folk taxonomies.

Consider the avocado—is it a fruit or a vegetable? Americans insist it is a vegetable. We eat it in salads with oil and vinegar. Brazilians, on the other hand, would say it is a fruit. They eat it for dessert with lemon juice and sugar.

How can we explain this difference in classification?

The avocado is an edible plant, and the American and Brazilian folk taxonomies, while containing cognate terms, classify some edible plants differently. The avocado does not change. It is the same biological entity, but its folk classification changes, depending on who's doing the classifying.

Human beings are also biological entities. Just as we can ask if an avocado is a fruit or a vegetable, we can ask if a person is white or black. And when we ask race questions, the answers we get come from folk taxonomies, not scientific ones. Terms like "white" or "black" applied to people—or "vegetable" or "fruit" applied to avocados—do not give us biological information about people or avocados. Rather, they exemplify how cultural groups (Brazilians or Americans) classify people and avocados.

Americans believe in "blood," a folk term for the quality presumed to be carried by members of so-called races. And the way offspring—regardless of their physical appearance—always inherit the less prestigious racial category of mixed parentage is called "hypo-descent" by anthropologists. A sentence thoroughly intelligible to most Americans might be, "Since Mary's father is white and her mother is black, Mary is black because she has black 'blood.' " American researchers who think they are studying racial differences in behavior would, like other Americans, classify Mary as black—although she has just as much white "blood."

According to hypo-descent, the various purported racial categories are arranged in a hierarchy along a single dimension, from the most prestigious ("white"), through intermediary forms ("Asian"), to the least prestigious ("black"). And when a couple come from two different categories, all their children (the "descent" in "hypo-descent") are classified as belonging to the less prestigious category (thus, the "hypo"). Hence, all the offspring of one "white" parent and one "black" parent—regardless of the children's physical appearance—are called "black" in the United States.

The American folk concept of "blood" does not behave like genes. Genes are units which cannot be subdivided. When several genes jointly determine a trait, chance decides which ones come from each parent. For example, if eight genes determine a trait, a child gets four from each parent. If a mother and a father each have the hypothetical genes BBBBWWWW, then a child could be born with any combination of B and W genes, from BBBBBBBB to WWWWWWWW. In contrast, the folk concept "blood" behaves like a uniform and continuous entity. It can be divided in two indefinitely—for example, quadroons and octoroons are said to be people who have one-quarter and one-eighth black "blood," respectively. Oddly, because of hypo-descent, Americans consider people with one-eighth black "blood" to be black rather than white, despite their having seven-eighths white "blood."

Hypo-descent, or "blood," is not informative about the physical appearance of people. For example, when two parents called black in the United States have a number of children, the children are likely to vary in physical appearance. In the case of skin color, they might vary from lighter than the lighter parent to darker than the darker parent. However, they would all receive the same racial classification—black—regardless of their skin color.

All that hypo-descent tells you is that, when someone is classified as something other than white (e.g., Asian), at least one of his or her parents is classified in the same way, and that neither parent has a less prestigious classification (e.g., black). That is, hypo-descent is informative about ancestry—specifically, parental classification—rather than physical appearance.

There are many strange consequences of our folk taxonomy. For example, someone who inherited no genes that produce "African"-appearing physical features would still be considered black if he or she has a parent classified as black. The category "passing for white" includes many such people. Americans have the curious belief that people who look white but have a parent classified as black are "really" black in some biological sense, and are being deceptive if they present themselves as white. Such examples make it clear that race is a social rather than a physical classification.

From infancy, human beings learn to recognize very subtle differences in the faces of those around them. Black babies see a wider variety of black faces than white faces, and white babies see a wider variety of white faces than black faces. Because they are exposed only to a limited range of human variation, adult members of each "race" come to see their own group as containing much wider variation than others. Thus, because of this perceptual learning, blacks see greater physical variation among themselves than among whites, while whites see the opposite. In this case, however, there is a clear answer to the question of which group contains greater physical variability. Blacks are correct.

Why is this the case?

Take a moment. Think of yourself as an amateur anthropologist and try to step out of American culture, however briefly.

It is often difficult to get white people to accept what at first appears to contradict the evidence they can see clearly with their own eyes—but which is really the result of a history of perceptual learning. However, the reason that blacks view themselves as more varied is not that their vision is more accurate. Rather, it is that blacks too have a long—but different—history of perceptual learning from that of whites (and also that they have been observers of a larger range of human variation).

The fact of greater physical variation among blacks than whites in America goes back to the principle of hypo-descent, which classifies all people with one black parent and one white parent as black. If they were all considered white, then there would be more physical variation among whites. Someone with one-eighth white "blood" and seven-eighths black "blood" would be considered white; anyone with any white ancestry would be considered white. In other words, what appears to be a difference in biological variability is really a difference in cultural classification.

Perhaps the clearest way to understand that the American folk taxonomy of race is merely one of many—arbitrary and unscientific like all the others—is to contrast it with a very different one, that of Brazil. The Portuguese word that in the Brazilian folk taxonomy corresponds to the American "race" is "*tipo*." *Tipo*, a cognate of the English word "type," is a descriptive term that serves as a kind of shorthand for a series of physical features. Because people's physical features vary separately from one another, there are an awful lot of tipos in Brazil.

Since tipos are descriptive terms, they vary regionally in Brazil—in part reflecting regional differences in the development of colloquial Portuguese, but in part because the physical variation they describe is different in different regions. The Brazilian situation is so complex I will limit my delineation of tipos to some of the main ones used in the city of Salvador, Bahia, to describe people whose physical appearance is understood to be made up of African and European features. (I will use the female terms throughout; in nearly all cases the male term simply changes the last letter from *a* to *o*.)

Proceeding along a dimension from the "whitest" to the "blackest" tipos, a *loura* is whiter-than-white, with straight blond hair, blue or green eyes, light skin color, narrow nose, and thin lips. Brazilians who come to the United States think that a *loura* means a "blond" and are surprised to find that the American term refers to hair color only. A *branca* has light skin color, eyes of any color, hair of any color or form except tight curly, a nose that is not broad, and lips that are not thick. *Branca* translates as "white," though Brazilians of this tipo who come to the United States—especially those from elite families—are often dismayed to find that they are not considered white here, and, even worse, are viewed as Hispanic despite the fact that they speak Portuguese.

A *morena* has brown or black hair that is wavy or curly but not tight curly, tan skin, a nose that is not narrow, and lips that are not thin. Brazilians who come to the United States think that a *morena* is a "brunette," and are surprised to find that brunettes are considered white but *morenas* are not. Americans have difficulty classifying *morenas,* many of whom are of Latin American origin: Are they black or Hispanic? (One might also observe that *morenas* have trouble with Americans, for not just accepting their appearance as a given, but asking instead "Where do you come from?" "What language did you speak at home?" "What was your maiden name?" or even, more crudely, "What *are* you?")

A *mulata* looks like a *morena,* except with tight curly hair and a slightly darker range of hair colors and skin colors. A *preta* looks like a *mulata,* except with dark brown skin, broad nose, and thick lips. To Americans, *mulatas* and *pretas* are both black, and if forced to distinguish between them would refer to them as light-skinned blacks and dark-skinned blacks, respectively.

If Brazilians were forced to divide the range of tipos, from *loura* to *preta,* into "kinds of whites" and "kinds of blacks" (a distinction they do not ordinarily make), they would draw the line between *morenas* and *mulatas;* whereas Americans, if offered only visual information, would draw the line between *brancas* and *morenas.*

The proliferation of tipos, and the difference in the white–black dividing line, do not, however, exhaust the differences between Brazilian and American folk taxonomies. There are tipos in the Afro-European domain that are considered to be neither black nor white—an idea that is difficult for Americans visiting Brazil to comprehend. A person with tight curly blond (or red) hair, light skin, blue (or green) eyes, broad nose, and thick lips, is a *sarará.* The opposite features—straight black hair, dark skin, brown eyes, narrow nose, and thin lips—are those of a *cabo verde. Sarará* and *cabo verde* are both tipos that are considered by Brazilians in Salvador, Bahia, to be neither black nor white.

When I interviewed my American daughter and her Brazilian boyfriend, she said she was black because her mother is black (even though I am white). That is, from her American perspective, she has "black blood"—though she is a *morena* in Brazil. Her boyfriend said that he was not black because, viewing himself in terms of Brazilian tipos, he is a *mulato* (not a *preto*).

There are many differences between the Brazilian and American folk taxonomies of race. The American system tells you about how people's parents are classified but not what they look like. The Brazilian system tells you what they look like but not about their parents. When two parents of intermediate appearance have many children in the United States, the children are all of one race; in Brazil they are of many tipos.

Americans believe that race is an immutable biological given, but people (like my daughter and her boyfriend) can change their race by getting on a plane and going from the United States to Brazil—just as, if they take an avocado with them, it changes from a vegetable into a fruit. In both cases, what changes is not the physical appearance of the person or avocado, but the way they are classified.

I have focused on the Brazilian system to make clear how profoundly folk taxonomies of race vary from one place to another. But the Brazilian system is just one of many. Haiti's folk taxonomy, for example, includes elements of both ancestry and physical appearance, and even includes the amazing term (for foreigners of African appearance) *un blanc noir*—literally, "a black white." In the classic study *Patterns of Race in the Americas,* anthropologist Marvin Harris gives a good introduction to the ways in which the conquests by differing European powers of differing New World peoples and ecologies combined with differing patterns of slavery to produce a variety of folk taxonomies. Folk taxonomies of race can be found in many—though by no means all—cultures in other parts of the world as well.

The American concept of race does not correspond to the ways in which human physical appearance varies. Further, the American view of race ("hypo-descent") is just one among many folk taxonomies, not of which correspond to the facts of human physical variation. This is why race is a myth and why races as conceived by Americans (and others) do not exist. It is also why differences in behavior between "races" cannot be explained by biological differences between them.

When examining the origins of IQ scores (or other behavior), psychologists sometimes use the term "heritability"—a statistical concept that is not based on observations of genes or chromosomes. It is important to understand that questions about heritability of IQ have nothing to do with racial differences in IQ. "Heritability" refers only to the relative ranking of individuals *within* a population, under given environmental conditions, and not to differences *between* populations. Thus, among the population of American whites, it may be that those with high IQs tend to have higher-IQ children than do those with low IQs. Similarly, among American blacks, it may be that those with high IQs also tend to have higher-IQ children.

In both cases, it is possible that the link between the IQs of parents and children may exist for reasons that are not entirely environmental. This heritability of IQ *within* the two populations, even if it exists, would in no way contradict the average social advantages of American whites as a group compared to the average social disadvantages of American blacks as a group. Such differences in social environments can easily account for any differences in the average test scores *between* the two groups. Thus, the heritability of IQ *within* each group is irrelevant to understanding differences *between* the groups.

Beyond this, though, studies of differences in behavior between "populations" of whites and blacks, which seek to find biological causes rather than only social ones, make a serious logical error. They assume that blacks and whites are populations in some biological sense, as sub-units of the human species. (Most likely, the researchers make this assumption because they are American and approach race in terms of the American folk taxonomy.)

In fact, though, the groups are sorted by a purely social rule for statistical purposes. This can easily be demonstrated by asking researchers how they know that the white subjects are really white and the black subjects are really black. There is no biological answer to this question, because race as a biological category does not exist. All that researchers can say is, "The tester classified them based on their physical appearance," or "Their school records listed their race," or otherwise give a social rather than biological answer.

So when American researchers study racial differences in behavior, in search of biological rather than social causes for differences between socially defined groups, they are wasting their time. Computers are wonderful machines, but we have learned about "garbage in/garbage out." Applying complex computations to bad data yields worthless results. In the same way, the most elegant experimental designs and statistical analyses, applied flawlessly to biologically meaningless racial categories, can only produce a very expensive waste of time.

As immigrants of varied physical appearance come to the United States from countries with racial folk taxonomies different from our own, they are often perplexed and dismayed to find that the ways they classify themselves and others are irrelevant to the American reality. Brazilians, Haitians, and others may find themselves labeled by strange, apparently inappropriate, even pejorative terms, and grouped together with people who are different from and unreceptive to them. This can cause psychological complications (a Brazilian immigrant—who views himself as white—being treated by an American therapist who assumes that he is not).

Immigration has increased, especially from geographical regions whose people do not resemble American images of blacks, whites, or Asians. Intermarriage is also increasing, as the stigma associated with it diminishes. These two trends are augmenting the physical diversity among those who marry each other—and, as a result, among their children. The American folk taxonomy of race (purportedly comprised of stable biological entities) is beginning to change to accommodate this new reality. After all, what race is someone whose four grandparents are black, white, Asian, and Hispanic?

Currently, the most rapidly growing census category is "Other," as increasing numbers of people fail to fit available options. Changes in the census categories every 10 years reflect the government's attempts to grapple with the changing self-identifications of Americans—even as statisticians try to maintain the same categories over time in order to make demographic comparisons.

Perhaps they will invent one or more "multiracial" categories, to accommodate the wide range of people whose existence defies current classification. Perhaps they will drop the term "race" altogether. Already some institutions are including an option to "check as many as apply," when asking individuals to classify themselves on a list of racial and ethnic terms.

Thinking in terms of physical appearance and folk taxonomies helps to clarify the emotionally charged but confused topics of race. Understanding that different cultures have different folk taxonomies suggests that we respond to the question "What race is that person?" not by "Black" or "White," but by "Where?" and "When?"

# Review Questions

1. What is Jeffrey Fish's main point about the way Americans define race?

2. What is the difference between the way race is defined in the United States and in Brazil? List the Brazilian folk taxonomy of *tipos* and how to translate *tipos* into U.S. racial categories.

3. What evidence challenges the view that races are biologically defined types? What evidence would have to exist to prove that the human species is genetically divided into races?

4. Why does Fish feel it is important to understand that race as Americans use it does not represent a biological reality?

# 27

# Blood on the Steppes: Ethnicity, Power, and Conflict

## Jack Weatherford

*All of us assume a range of identities as we pursue our lives. We may be sons and daughters to our parents, students to our professors, drivers to pedestrians, and employees to our bosses. We also take on important group identities. We are Americans if we were born U.S. citizens and Texans if we were born or live in that state. We can be Gold Wing Road Riders if we hold membership in a certain motorcycle club, or docents at a zoo. Recently we, as well as many other people in the world, have often chosen to identify ourselves ethnically. We may be Latino or Asian, African American or Euro American, for example. How we form ethnic identities and the uses we put them to are the subject of this original article by Jack Weatherford. Focusing on the peoples of central Asia, Weatherford reveals the role of economics, politics, and religion in the formation of ethnic identities. He concludes that whereas the twentieth century was the age of groups united by ideology, the twenty-first may well be ruled by ethnicity.*

By the opening of the twenty-first century, Genghis Khan had won yet one more great political battle. Hundreds of years after his death, he had ousted Lenin's statues, portraits, and emblems and replaced them with his own symbols in Mongolia's capital city of Ulan Bator. The Mongolians tore down the giant stars, hammers, and sickles, and replaced them with the face of Genghis Khan, who now adorned office walls, postage stamps, paper money, web sites, and even the popular bottles of Genghis Khan Vodka.

After repeated bloody invasions and centuries of oppressive rule by Manchus, Chinese, and Russians, the Mongolians are today free of foreign domination. In the past, the Chinese had compelled them to accept a definition of themselves as barbarians, the Russians defined them as savages, and all their foreign rulers tried to force them to settle into permanent towns where they could be easily watched and controlled. For the first time in 600 years, the Mongolians are free to roam the steppes of their independent country and establish their own identity without fear of foreign intervention.

All people must deal with questions of self-identity as their culture changes over time. For some, questions of identity can be as simple as what kind of music they want their children to hear or whether foreign words should be allowed into their language. For Mongolians, it is more complicated. What kind of script should they use to write their language? What religion should they follow? What sort of political system can they build? They must reinvent themselves for a new era of globalized life.

Their solution has involved reaching back into their past, particularly that part of their past that the communists suppressed. As soon as communism collapsed, the Mongolians began to rebuild their shrines, bring their scriptures out of hiding, and rewrite their history. They enthusiastically returned to their native dress and to the rigors of nomadic life. They once again had the freedom to learn and use their ancient system of vertical writing in addition to the Cyrillic system imposed by Stalin. They composed songs about their horses rather than the beautiful tractors of the collective farm. They drank even more fermented mare's milk, and they celebrated their traditional sports of archery, wrestling, and horseback riding at their summer gathering of *Naadam* festivals around the country.

## Ethnicity and Subsistence

When examined outside of its social context, the resurgence of Mongolian culture may seem to represent some basic and primordial longing that people have to express a deep ethnic identity, one that may be suppressed for decades or centuries but can never be eradicated. The fuller meaning of the ethnic renaissance, however, can only be understood through a holistic analysis of ethnic identity as it relates to other social variables, such as politics, economics, religion, and kinship. For the Mongols, choosing to resurrect the past as a model for their identity was an economic adaptation.

The land-locked country of Mongolia stretches across an area of steppes and mountains that is roughly three times the size of France. Most of the nearly two and one-half million people in Mongolia are Mongols, with a small minority of Kazakh and other herders. A majority of the Mongols live spread out over the countryside in their traditional felt tents, or *gers*. What the vast steppes lack in people they compensate for in animals. Once again free to manage their own affairs, the nomads have increased their herds to nearly 50 million domesticated horses, camels, sheep, goats, cows, and yaks. In addition, Mongolia is still the home of millions of wild deer, marmots, wolves, horses, and vast flocks of migrating cranes, duck, and swans.

The return to a Mongol identity arose not merely from nostalgic sentiment; it also had a strong economic component. Without the Soviet subsidies that supported the Mongolian economy through the Cold War and the long series of border disputes with the Chinese, the Mongols had to learn to support themselves. Without Russian help there was no productive life in Ulan Bator and the smaller towns. The main option was to return to a life on the steppes where people could subsist by herding. Soon, Mongolia became the only country in the world where the majority of people live in tents.

As the need to pursue the traditional form of subsistence developed, the Mongols looked to the old culture for guidance, since that culture defined a proven way to survive. Without imported vehicles and expensive imported fuel to power them, people came back to the much cheaper, albeit slower, horses and camels, which fuel themselves from the ample supply of grass on the steppes. The traditional *del*, a thickly padded coat with long sleeves that hang down past the hands, proves to be better for horse riding than modern coats because the long sleeves cover the hands while allowing them freedom of motion for use with reins. The return to traditional clothing represented more than a mere nostalgic longing for the past; it proved more useful and appropriate than imported varieties.

Without money to heat the large, concrete apartment blocks of the city, people found the small felt *gers* to be ideal in the harsh Mongolian winter, when the rivers are frozen for six months each year and the temperature can easily drop to – 45 degrees Fahrenheit. Whereas fuel rises in cost, the large number of domesticated animals produce a large, virtually free, supply of dung that can be burned to keep the *gers* warm and to cook meals of boiled mutton.

The return to traditional culture appeared on many fronts, such as hunting with falcons as a replacement for the more expensive use of firearms. Instead of sugared tea, the people fell back on the traditional Mongol drink, salted milk tea, which was less expensive and proved better at keeping the body hydrated in the dry, cold winter. Being Mongol became a way of life again because it was economically adaptive.

But there are other strategies people may follow to establish a new identity. Ethnic identity and culture are not inherited at birth like eye color or a propensity for baldness. Ethnic identity is a culturally constructed concept that is constantly changing. It is shaped, as noted above, by politics, economics, religion, and the other aspects of social life, and in turn it can mold other institutions. Throughout history, groups and individuals have constantly reformulated ethnic identity in order to adapt it to myriad purposes.

The Mongol search for identity is just one of many in today's world. Across much of Central Asia the collapse of Soviet rule marked an end to a carefully maintained system of ethnic identities closely controlled by Soviet authorities. Stalin, who had served as the Minister of Nationality Affairs under Lenin, created a set of official ethnic groups. For each newly created nation, Soviet authorities developed a written language, created official songs and dances, and devised an official ethnic costume that often owed more to Hollywood films than to the ethnic history of the people themselves. Each group acquired a history, an ethnic identity, and all the cultural trappings to illustrate its place in the Soviet hierarchy.

Like the Mongol, the other groups that live across the vast expanse of Central Asia from Siberia and western China to the Caspian Sea faced a new ethnic challenge—the need (and opportunity) to formulate their own identities when Soviet rule ended. Different groups, however, faced quite different political, religious, and economic constraints on that identity.

## Ethnicity and Nationalism

Through the 1990s the newly independent republics of Central Asia faced the problem of how to establish their ethnicity in ways that were different from the hands-off approach of Mongolia. One solution was to create a new nationalism. Whereas the Mongols had very few economic opportunities and therefore chose the identity that would help them survive, the stronger economies in some of the other republics permitted greater freedom to create images of themselves. In Uzbekistan, for example, the government chose to create a national identity around a famous historical figure. They pulled down the statues of Marx and closed the Lenin museum, replacing them with statues and a museum dedicated to their national hero, Tamerlane. However, the Uzbekistan government went further. It organized a vigilant effort to force a pan-Uzbek identity on the population. The government changed street names to reflect Uzbek themes and changed the writing system from the Cyrillic alphabet to the Latin one. The president also sponsored an international academic conference of scholars to glorify Tamerlane and his contributions to world civilization.

Although there was no violence or organized government campaigns of ethnic cleansing, the equation of Uzbekistan's national identity with the dominant Uzbek ethnic group meant that Jews and Armenians, whose families had lived in the cities of Uzbekistan for more than a thousand years, felt compelled to flee. Minority groups of Russians, Ukrainians, Tartars, and Germans also began a steady migration out of the country. Only the Korean minority stayed on, seemingly unable to find a place of refuge outside the country.

## Ethnicity and Personal Power

In Turkmenistan, which occupies the arid steppe between Iran, Uzbekistan, and Afghanistan, the president of the country invented a new form of Stalinist tribalism to establish a national ethnic identity. Of the different avenues of power open to him, he chose to emphasize the tribal identity of Turkomen, as a symbol that clearly separated him and his followers from all neighbors. The president emphasized the tribal and kinship ties of the people. He seized on the great Turkomen horse and the wooly hats of the Turkomen soldiers as images of his newly independent country. He, like the Uzbek president, also organized an international academic conference, this one focused on the role of the Turkomen horse in world history.

Since the relatively small nation had no single individual such as Tamerlane or Genghis Khan to idealize in its new ethnic identity, the president decided to use himself as the symbol of the people. He changed his own name to Turkmenbashi, with the modest meaning "Father of the Turkomen." Turkmenbashi renamed the country's Caspian port after himself, and every city named a major street for him and erected a statue of him. His followers decorated the country with banners displaying his quotes, and they seemed to outdo one another in how many pictures of Turkmenbashi they could put up and how large they could make them. Giant portraits of the president graced the entrance to almost every government building in the country. Busts and smaller pictures adorned the insides of rooms and were displayed in airplanes, taxis, and buses. The president appeared on postage stamps and on all the money, and his profile even graced the upper corner of the television screen twenty-four hours a day no matter what program was being shown. Turkish investors, whom he attracted to build a textile factory in his country, felt obligated to name their blue jean production plant after him. Like a traditional tribal leader, he kept the focus on himself, but he did so with Stalinist efficiency as he attempted to make his country into a totalitarian, tribally based country somewhat like the strong tribal monarchies of the Persian Gulf and Arabian peninsula. He became the national symbol of the Turkomen ethnic image.

## Ethnicity and Religion

When people are forced to accept an alien national identity or are denied any direct expression of their own ethnic identity, they often search for an identity in a new realm, such as religion. In many areas of Central Asia, militant Islam has become the dominant form of identification and thereby the main route of resistance to central government authorities. This holds true particularly for people who feel the most cut off from the centers of power and government. Under the inspiration of the Afghan guerillas who defeated the Soviet army and the example of the Iranians who created a religious state, many groups in Central Asia turned to religion for their identity and as their form of resistance. For many, it is the only path open to them.

In the Osh valley of Uzbekistan during 1997, Muslim militants cut off the heads of five policemen and put them on public display. The militants dramatized their religious identity by displaying their triumph over government authority. The use of religion as a central focus of ethnic identification became even stronger across the mountains from Uzbekistan in the western province of China. There the Uighurs, a Turkic ethnic group related to the Uzbeks, struggled for autonomy in a tightly controlled, and still officially communist, state.

The Turkic-speaking Uighurs inhabit Xinjiang, the largest province in China. They were once Buddhists who gradually converted to Islam, but like most Turkic people, they have shown little historical interest in religious fundamentalism. They have a vibrant culture that draws heavily on Chinese and Persian influences as well as those of their fellow Turkic groups. As people with a long history of wine making, they show little of the dourness often associated with religious fanaticism.

Because Uighurs cannot express an ethnic identity in the face of Chinese control, they have adopted religion to symbolize their group. One strategy has been subtle. Uighurs make pilgrimages to the ancient oasis city of Kashgar to visit the mosque where there is a tomb of a heroine called Fragrant Concubine. According to tradition, she led a revolt against the Chinese in ancient times, but after the Chinese captured her and made her into an imperial concubine, she killed herself. Her tomb and the horse cart that supposedly brought her body home to the lands of the Uighurs have become sacred shrines. The Chinese authorities vehemently deny the authenticity of both the tomb and the cart, but such denials only increase the attraction the heroine has for young Uighurs.

Since the Uighurs cannot display religious symbols or any symbol of their ethnicity, they turned to portraits of this secular figure, Fragrant Concubine. She is shown with Western features and wearing medieval European armor. Her images look like Joan of Arc, who fought for the freedom of France from English rule. Both the display of portraits such as Fragrant Concubine and the idea of a woman as warrior are distinctly un-Muslim acts, yet Uighurs have managed to fit Sacred Concubine into their new, and awkwardly created, Muslim religious identity. By placing the remains and relics of this nearly mythical woman in the mosque, the Uighurs have made this very secular figure into a virtual saint. She represents a fusing of their religious identity as Muslims with their ethnic identity. They are also groping toward religious fundamentalism and fanaticism in other ways.

"The boys are preparing to die. They have given up alcohol and cigarettes. They run and exercise every morning to build their strength. They pray five times a day to build their faith. They are trying to learn Arabic, and they are ready to die for their people when the Chinese army attacks us." The words came from a young Uighur man, who under normal conditions would probably have been a college student. Under perceived pressure from the Chinese government, he feels that he has found his new identity in a militant version of Islam. He and others like him see that Islam allowed their Afghan neighbors across the mountains to defeat the Soviet Union, and increasingly the young Uighurs turn to it for their own salvation from Chinese rule.

Chinese threats seem real to Uighurs. The Chinese boast of the new roads they have built, the schools and hospitals they have opened, and the new prosperity they have brought. But the Uighurs point out that the Chinese have closed most of their mosques, deprived their children of the opportunity to study the Koran, forbade their muezzin from making the traditional call to prayer, and severely limited the number of pilgrims who can make the *haj* to Mecca. Government bureaucrats even control the number of children they can have. To demonstrate that they were serious about enforcing their rule, the Chinese authorities staged a public execution of seventeen Uighurs in 1998. The following year they poured more secret police and soldiers into the province. Undeterred, the Uighurs stepped up their movement toward Islamic fundamentalism.

## Ethnicity and Crime

Just as ethnicity serves as a potent tool for some people in their quest for political goals, it can also be used to create whole new identities for group of people. Take the Reebok Mafia, for example.

"I am Karakalpak," said the man proudly as blood splattered over his rubber boots from the gaffe hook he had embedded in a large fish he was struggling to haul out of his small boat. "But the Russians stole our identity. We don't even know who we are," he responded in a slightly puzzled manner. "The Russians took everything from us. They took our land and moved us away, and they took our language. We don't have clothes to wear or even know what religion we should be. Some people say that we are Muslims, but others said we were Christians even before the Russians themselves became Christians. I have seen rocks with pictures of Buddha and monsters from India; maybe they were our gods. We don't even know why we have this name. *Karakalpak,* they say it means 'black hat.' Why would we be called 'black hat people'? Maybe we should wear a black hat, but what kind? Who knows?

"Since I don't know how to be a Karakalpak I joined the Reebok Mafia," the fisherman explained with husky laugh. The man now lives and works on a clandestine mud island in the middle of the Ili estuary where it joins Lake Balkhash in the middle of Central Asia in Kazakhstan. As he repeated the name "Reebok Mafia," he pointed at his soiled shirt and brushed the flies away from the logo of the Reebok sports shoe and clothing company. Because of the almost identical pronunciation of the Russian word *rebak,* meaning *fisherman,* and the name of the company, the men who illegally fished the lake called themselves the

Reebok Mafia and wore shirts, hats, shoes, and anything else with the name *Reebok* on it as a way of proclaiming their occupation and identity. Although they fished in this natural park and environmental reserve illegally, the authorities rarely bothered to make the grueling day-long trek across dirt paths to reach this area unless they were coming to shake down the fishermen for money.

Under cover of darkness, trucks made the all-night trip from the nearest city of Almaty to Lake Balkhash. The independent drivers negotiate for a load of fish, which they then drive back to the city in their unrefrigerated trucks.

The Reebok Mafia included individuals from ethnic groups as varied as Kazakh, Mongol, Kirghiz, Ukrainians, and even some Germans dislocated during World War II. They used Russian as the only common language in the group, and to create solidarity and smooth social relationship among the various types of members, they invented their new identity and symbols around the international clothing manufacturer. The distinctive Reebok emblems and clothing allow the fisherman, truckers, and their customers to recognize one another in much the same way that the distinctive clothes of Los Angeles gang members or Amish farmers in Pennsylvania allow them to identify themselves and separate them from others.

## Sex and Ethnicity

Groups and individuals can use ethnicity as well as create it. The Kirghiz have reinvented their past traditional ethnic identity and this has legitimized what previously would have been illegal behavior, as became evident in a late-night discussion with a Kirghiz family. The elderly wife explained how in the old days her husband had kidnapped her in order to marry her. Bride capture had been practiced on the steppes for millennia, and it varied between true capture, as in raids and wars, and a culturally sanctioned way in which a man and woman might elope without bringing dishonor to her family.

"Even though I was totally surprised when he and his friends kidnapped me, he had written a beautiful song for me." At this point in her story, the now nearly toothless husband brought out his horsehead fiddle and began to sing in a high falsetto the song he had written for her. She grinned and lowered her eyes as her wrinkled cheeks turned red once again on hearing him sing of the irresistible beauty of her face.

In the intervening years since the kidnapping, the couple raised eight children, the first six of whom were married in the modern, bureaucratic format. With the fall of communism, young men in the area seized on the old custom of bride capture as an excuse to abduct young women. In two separate instances, each of the couple's two youngest daughters were abducted. One of the daughters fought so fiercely against her abductors that they finally killed her. The abductors claimed that they killed her by accident while merely trying to kidnap her in the traditional way. The men were more like criminal thugs than traditional Kirghiz, but they successfully used the ethnic revival as a form of camouflage for their acts of criminal rape and assault.

The ancient tradition also provided the local authorities with an excuse not to arrest or prosecute the men. Perhaps because the police feared the thugs or perhaps because they had succumbed to bribes, the authorities and the thugs used the convenient traditional cultural concept as an excuse for what they had done.

Ethnic identity, like most other cultural constructs, can be put to varied purposes, from subsistence and politics to crime and religion. It is a tool that can be used by individuals in pursuit of their personal goals such as power and wealth, or even sexual gratification. At the same time, ethnicity can be used by large groups of people as a way to pursue nationalist or religious goals.

## The Ethnic Future

The twentieth century often produced countries held together by ideologies. Nazis, communists, capitalists, fascists, and others used ideology to establish group identity while they suppressed identities based on ethnicity and religion. After two great world wars, a handful of smaller ones, and a protracted Cold War struggle of the "Free World" against the "Communist World," ideology seemed to lose its ability to unite or motivate people. Without central control and the threat of common enemies to unite them, people from around the world began to identify themselves in other ways.

As a result, masses of people turned to new forms of ethnic identity in an effort to give their lives meaning and structure. Without major external powers to threaten their way of life, countries from the United States and China to Albania and Rwanda began to feel the struggle of ethnic tensions within their borders.

Ethnicity certainly has not yet played itself out as a major factor on the world scene. Instead, it seems to be steadily increasing in power, scope, and importance for group relations both within countries as well as between them. In the twenty-first century, ethnicity may well become the compelling global force that ideology had been for people in the twentieth century.

## Review Questions

1. What ways have central Asian peoples used to create and spread ethnic identities?

2. Under what conditions will people adopt religious identities instead of ethnic ones?

3. Why have the Mongols elected to recreate their ancient identity as they seek to establish themselves in a global world?

4. Why have more and more people chosen to identify themselves ethnically in recent years?

# 28

# New Americans: The Road to Refugee Resettlement

*Dianna Shandy*

*In the early days of the discipline, anthropologists usually studied non-Western groups that they assumed were bounded and clearly definable. Such groups were named (often by outsiders) and were thought to have territories and a common language and culture. Although anthropologists recognized that many of the groups they studied had outside connections—that they freely borrowed culture, intermarried, and migrated—most still felt it was reasonable to talk about groups as if they were bounded units. However, the picture is changing, as this article by Dianna Shandy clearly shows. Today people are on the move. Some are migrants looking for economic opportunity; others are refugees. Here Shandy, using the case of the Nuer from southern Sudan, shows how refugees fleeing a perpetual civil war manage to gain relocation in the United States and how they have sought to adapt to the demands of life among Americans. A key to the process is the role played by the United Nations and social service agencies and the Nuer's own determination to better (in their terms) themselves.*

A Nuer youth, Thok Ding (*not his real name*) lies prone alongside two other boys on the dusty, clay ground on the outskirts of a village in southern Sudan. A man crouches over him with a razor blade. Beginning with the right side, the man makes six parallel cuts from each side of the youth's forehead to the center to create scars called *gaar*. This ritual scarification, which has been outlawed in Nuer areas since the 1980s, still marks entry into manhood for many Nuer young men.

A few years later in Minneapolis, Minnesota, Thok sits in pained concentration in front of a computer screen in a driver's license examination office. Still weak in English, he struggles to recall the multiple choice response sequence he memorized to pass the exam, in this stressful, but less painful, American rite of passage into adulthood.

When I began ethnographic work among Nuer refugees living in Minnesota, Iowa, and several other regions of the United States in 1997, I immediately was struck by the incongruity of their lives. The Nuer are a famous people in anthropology. They were the subject of three books by the well-known late British social anthropologist, Sir E. E. Evans-Pritchard, who described their pastoralist mode of subsistence, complex segmented kinship system, and religion. Evans-Pritchard conducted research among the Nuer in the 1930s. He described the Nuer as a tall, independent, confident people whose existence revolved around the needs of their cattle, especially the requirement to move the animals from high to low ground and back again each year. During the dry season from September to April, the cattle were herded to lower ground where there was still water and grass. During the rainy season, the lowlands became a swampy lagoon and the herds had to be moved to the highlands where rain had restored the range. This transhumant lifestyle and the need to guard cattle against raiders from nearby tribes had shaped Nuer society. (The Nuer were also the subject of a well-known ethnographic film, *The Nuer,* made by Robert Gardner and released in 1970, which showed them to be much as Evans-Pritchard had described them.)

So when I first met Nuer people in Minnesota in the mid 1990s, these Northeast African pastoralists seemed out of place. Tall (most men are well over six feet) and still displaying the scars received at their initiations (for men, not women), the Nuer had come to live in one of the coldest parts of the United States. Why had they left their ancestral home? What did their status as refugees mean and how did they get it? How had they managed to come to the United States? Why had they been located, as it turns out, in more than 30 different U.S. states? How would a people raised as cattle herders adapt to American urban settings? And finally, in a broader sense, what does all this tell us about the interconnectedness of a globalizing world and about anthropology's role in it?

## Becoming a Refugee

Until recently, most Americans called the people who settled here *immigrants*. No distinctions were made based on the reasons people had chosen to come here or the circumstances they had left behind. In general, their arrival was encouraged and welcome because the country was spacious and their skills and labor were needed.

Today, things are different. There are immigrants and *refugees*. In the past, refugees were a kind of immigrant. They were people who came here to escape from intolerable conditions in their homelands, such as pogroms, the threat of military conscription, civil wars, and famine. The fact that they were escaping from something, however, did not affect whether they could enter the United States. Most people, especially those from Europe, were welcome.

Over the last fifty years, however, refugees have come to occupy a formal status, both in the eyes of the United Nations and U.S. immigration officials. They are not just *internally displaced persons* (IDPs), those who have left their homes but who are still in their own country. Officially (meaning how the United Nations and national governments define them), a refugee group is one that shares a "well-founded fear of persecution" based on any number of factors such as race, religion, nationality, membership in a particular social group, or political opinion. How the U.N. or national governments apply this definition when they seek to certify individuals as refugees varies. But the number of people who claim to fit this description and who seek asylum skyrocketed at the end of the cold war in 1989 to an estimated 22 million by 2000.

Bureaucracies control who can be classified as a refugee. In 1950 the United Nations established a formal agency to help with the refugee "problem," headed by the United Nations High Commissioner for Refugees (UNHCR). The agency recognizes three options, or what it calls "durable solutions," to deal with refugees around the world: voluntary repatriation to the country of origin, integration into a country of asylum, or, rarely, third country resettlement, meaning a move from one country of asylum to one that offers possibilities for a more permanent home. Initially housed in refugee camps, displaced people can apply for official refugee status with the hope of resettlement in another country.

Many countries have agreed to take in a limited number of refugees as a way of settling them more permanently, and the United States is one of them. To do this, the United States sets a limit on the number of refugees it will accept each year and uses a bureaucratic process to screen prospective refugees it might be willing to take in. The process is complicated by the fact that the criteria for admission can change, different government officials interpret the criteria dissimilarly, and resettlement policy can shift from one year to the next. It is also complicated by cross-cultural misunderstanding. The U.S. bureaucracy works differently from the way governments operate in the refugee's country of origin. Languages are a major barrier. Categories of meaning are not shared. The screening process is intended to determine "real" refugees, or those who cannot be protected by their home governments, and "economic" migrants who leave their home voluntarily to seek a better life. In practice, the distinction is often difficult to establish.

The Nuer living in Minnesota and other regions of the United States have managed to come through this process successfully. They have made it to camps that process refugees, discovered how to enter the bureaucratic process designed to certify them as refugees, learned how to tell a sufficiently convincing refugee story to gain certification, and found a way to get on the list to be resettled in the United States.

Thok Ding's life illustrates this process. Thok was born in southern Sudan and lived in a small village. As in most Nuer households, Thok lived with his mother, father, siblings, and his father's extended family. Thok had family members who lived in town and attended school, but there was no school in his village. His first memory is of going to the forest to take care of his calves when he was seven or eight. He would leave home in the early morning with other boys his age, taking food with him to eat while he was grazing the cattle and protecting the calves from wild animals. Girls, on the other hand, would stay closer to home and were charged with milking the cows.

When he was in his early teens, he, along with other boys who were the same age, underwent the ritual scarification *gaar* ceremony ushering him into manhood. After undergoing this painful ritual, Thok said that now that he was a man, he could be "free": "You can do whatever you like. You can have a woman. You can have a home by yourself. You can live away from your parents."

Shortly after his initiation, the civil war that wracked the southern Sudan caught up with him. Civil war has engulfed the Sudan since just before it gained independence from joint English–Egyptian colonial rule until the present, with just a brief interlude of peace from the early 1970s until 1983. This ongoing strife in the Sudan frequently is attributed to social distinctions based on geography (north–south), ethnicity (Arab–African), and religion (Muslim–Christian). From a southern perspective, northern Muslim Arabs entered their land in the 1800s looking for ivory and slaves. Northerners were favored under colonial rule, which gave them more power and increased tension with people, such as the Nuer, living in the south. Today, it is the Khartoum government, located in the north, that is engaged in war with southerners who seek self-government.

Nuer society has suffered cataclysmic shifts in the decades since Evans-Pritchard conducted his fieldwork, a fact well documented by anthropologist Sharon Hutchinson in her book entitled *Nuer Dilemmas*, published in 1996. For example, instead of merely regulating Nuer seasonal cattle drives, the change of seasons in the southern Sudan also dictates the rhythm of the civil war. The dry season makes it possible to move heavy artillery across the clay plains; during the wet season the same plains are impassable. The war and the displacement of Nuer and other southern Sudanese it has caused are the major cause of migration.

In the late 1980s, government troops attacked Thok's village, killing many people, including his father. Although many of the survivors elected to stay and to keep herding cattle, with his father dead Thok felt it was wisest to leave Sudan after this tragedy. He traveled on foot for three days with his mother and siblings and their cattle to an Ethiopian refugee camp called Itang.

One feature of camp life was the presence of a Christian mission school, which provided Thok with his first taste of formal education, something that would prove useful later as he sought refugee status. He advanced quickly in school, skipping several grades. Seventh grade stands out for him as the real beginning of his education, however, because he passed a national exam. As a result, he was transferred to Gambela, another Ethiopian camp, to attend school, leaving his mother and siblings behind. Food scarcity made life in Gambela very difficult. Thok recalls that students were given only a small amount of corn each month. They would grind the grain into flour, cook the mixture with water, and eat it plain without a stew.

His education at Gambela progressed nicely, but was ended when war broke out in Ethiopia. Threatened by the dangers the war posed, Thok rejoined his mother and siblings. Together they returned to the Sudan, where the U. N. had established a temporary camp to care for the Sudanese refugees who were streaming back across the border from Ethiopia. Thok weighed his options and decided to return to Ethiopia on his own. He went to the capital of Ethiopia, Addis Ababa, where he encountered some friends from school who shared information on how to get to refugee camps in Kenya.

He traveled to Kenya by bus, negotiating his way past border and police checkpoints along the way. He was arrested once by Kenyan police and had to spend the night in jail before they turned him over to the U. N. authorities that ran the nearby refugee camp. Once in the camp, he filled out a form that documented his background, and requested that he be considered for resettlement in another country. Since Thok had no relatives who had been resettled in other countries, he applied for resettlement anywhere that would accept refugees from the Sudan. These included Australia, Canada, and Sweden as well as the United States, the country that finally admitted him.

Two years elapsed from the time Thok arrived in the camp until he was sent to the United States. Life in the Kenyan camp was much more difficult than the one he had stayed at in Ethiopia. There was nothing to do, no river, no place to keep cattle, and no garden plots. Thok did, however, meet some friends he had made earlier in school, and together they cooked food and found ways to pass the long days in the camp. He and his friends also listened to the stories other Nuer told of their encounters with the refugee officials who interviewed people requesting resettlement. In a tragic commentary on how devastation can seem "normal," they learned that the biggest mistake people made was to invent dramatic stories to make themselves eligible for resettlement. For example, one Nuer man said, "People feel they need a reason, so they tell the person interviewing them that they killed someone and if they return to Sudan they will be put in jail. But the story didn't work because the interviewer thought the refugee must be a violent man." The Nuer men who worked as interpreters in the camps believed there was a better approach. "We told the community, we need to tell them the reality. Don't say you killed someone, just say you were caught in the crossfire." They had learned that the refugee officials were looking for certain kinds of experiences to determine who fit the criteria for refugee resettlement.

In addition to recounting a plausible story that indicates why they would be persecuted if they returned home, refugees must also pass a medical screening, and to the surprise of many Americans, they must also sign a promissory note to repay the cost of their airfare to the United States once they have settled and found work. Thok passed through this process successfully, and with a ticket provided for him by the International Organization for Migration, flew to the United States. He was met at the airport by a representative from Lutheran Social Services, one of many U.S. voluntary agencies responsible for resettling refugees.

## Life and Adjustment in the United States

Some immigrants to the United States rely on family or friends to help them find a home, job, and place in America. But many refugees depend on voluntary agencies, or "volags," to help with settlement. These agencies are under contract to the U.S. government and receive a stipend for each refugee that they place. Volags help refugees with necessities such as finding a place to live, getting a job, learning to ride the bus, and buying food. They also help them complete paperwork documenting the existence of family members who were left behind, since there will be a chance to bring them over later. Volags emphasize how important it is for refugees to find a job and become self-sufficient. Volags provide refugees with a small initial cash stipend to help them get established. But the money doesn't last long and refugees are encouraged to start working as soon as possible, often within the first week or two after arrival. An agency helped place Thok in Minnesota and eventually Minneapolis, finding him an apartment and helping with a job search.

There were about thirty refugees from Sudan and Somalia on Thok's flight from Nairobi, Kenya, to New York's JFK International Airport. When Thok boarded the plane, he knew no one. By the time he arrived in New York many hours later, he felt like the eight Sudanese men he had traveled with were his new best friends. In a wrenching sort of dispersal, the eight men were all directed by airline staff to different gates at the airport to await the next leg of their journey to far-flung destinations, like San Diego, California; Nashville, Tennessee; Dallas, Texas; and Minneapolis, Minnesota.

A representative from Lutheran Social Services and a volunteer from a local church greeted Thok when he arrived on his own in Minneapolis. His few possessions fit in a small bag that he carried with him on the plane. The man from Lutheran Social Services gave him shampoo and a toothbrush and took him to Burger King. Thok found the food very strange and difficult to eat. Thok stayed the first night in the volunteer's home—a widower in his mid-sixties who regularly helped out Lutheran Social Services in this way. Thok spoke some English, but he relied mostly on gestures to communicate with his host. The next day the volunteer took Thok to Lutheran Social Services to complete paperwork.

When they finished with the paperwork, the case manager who had met Thok at the airport took him to what was to be his apartment. Thok found the place to be very dirty, particularly the carpeting that had not been cleaned after the last tenants departed. There was a strong smell of cigarette smoke, cockroaches in the kitchen, and a very leaky faucet in the bathroom. Despite these problems, Thok would have his own place that would be affordable when he got a job. Later, the man Thok had stayed with the previous night brought over some furniture that had been donated by church members.

Over the coming week, Thok met with his case manager to discuss getting a job. Where refugees work and the kinds of jobs that they can get depend somewhat on the level of education and training they received prior to arrival in the United States. Most Nuer, unfortunately, have little education and can only find jobs that most people born in the United States do not want, such as unskilled factory worker, security guard, parking lot attendant, fast food server, and nursing home assistant. Many of the Nuer who have settled in the upper Midwest have found work in meat packing plants. Thok first got a job filling beverage trays for airplanes at the airport after he arrived in the United States. His back and arms ached from the lifting he was required to do, and he did not like his boss.

Several weeks later, Thok spotted another Nuer man while he was shopping at Target. Thok did not know him personally, but after they started talking he discovered that he knew the village where the man was from in the Sudan. It was good to see someone from "home," and Thok invited him back to his apartment to cook a meal and eat together. This man had moved to Minnesota from Iowa and was able to tell Thok the names and even the phone numbers of some Nuer who were living in Des Moines. Thok knew some of these people from the refugee camps in Ethiopia, and the next day he bought a phone card to get in touch. Thok could hardly believe his ears when he heard his friend John Wal answer the phone. After a conversation that lasted until the phone card expired, Thok decided to board a bus and leave Minnesota to move to Iowa. John had talked about the sizable Nuer community living in Des Moines and the well-paying jobs offered by a meat packing company. Thok called his case manager and left a message saying that he was going. He packed his personal items, left the furniture in the apartment, and boarded a Greyhound bus.

In Des Moines, Thok moved in with John and another Nuer man. Thok worked in a packing plant for a while, but found it very difficult. At first his job was to kill pigs as they entered the processing line. He found it so hard to sleep at night after doing this over and over again all day that he asked to be transferred to some other part of the line. He still found the work exceedingly hard. One motivation to find a job quickly is to make it possible to bring over his family members to join him, but Thok has not managed to do this yet.

In addition to his mother and siblings, Thok would also like to bring over a wife. There are roughly three Nuer men for every Nuer woman in the United States, and most of the women are already married or engaged to be married. Thok and other Nuer men struggle with what they perceive as "the unreasonable levels of freedom" afforded to women in U.S. society. One way to marry a wife with more "traditional" Nuer values, or so men think, is to let their family facilitate a marriage in the Sudan or in Ethiopia and try to bring the wife over as a spouse or a refugee.

## Staying in Touch

Refugee groups are deliberately "scattered" geographically across the United States when they are resettled. Policy makers believe that dispersal increases individuals' ability to adapt successfully to their new environment and that it decreases any disruptive impact on the host community that receives the refugees. However, even though refugees are "placed" in particular locales in the United States, they seldom stay put. Hmong, originally from the highlands of South East Asia, and now residents of Saint Paul, Minnesota, are a case in point. They, like the Nuer, are well known for moving frequently after arrival in the United States. Nuer, who moved regularly as part of their lives in southern Sudan, continue a kind of nomadism in the United States. Nuer move frequently—from apartment to apartment, from city to city, and from state to state. As a result of having been resettled in more than thirty different states in America, Nuer have a tendency to move where they have relatives, friends, or jobs.

Staying in contact is very important to many Nuer refugees. They are amazingly adept at devising strategies for remaining in contact with other Nuer dispersed across the United States and those whom they left behind in Africa. The process of incorporation into the United States as a refugee is also about maintaining ties to Africa. One aspect of Nuer life that sets them apart from the experiences of previous waves of immigrants to the United States is the means by which they keep in contact with those who remain at home in the Sudan, in refugee camps in neighboring African states, and around the world.

Immigrants have always retained some ties with the homes they left. But, in a twenty-first century context, the possibilities for frequent, affordable, and rapid contact are greatly expanded. Anthropologists refer to these crosscutting social ties that span the borders of nation-states as *transnationalism*. For instance, Thok, who wants to marry, could phone his brother in Gambela, Ethiopia, to arrange the event. He can even use an informal banking system to send money to his brother to buy cows to give to the prospective bride's father. The Nuer groom gives U.S. dollars to a Somali man in Nashville who contacts his relative in Addis Ababa, Ethiopia, who gives Ethiopian money to the groom's brother who traveled there from Gambela. In Nuer eyes, the groom does not even need to be present for the marriage to be legitimate, but this is not true in the eyes of immigration authorities. Even though the groom can do his part to sponsor the marriage from the United States, he still must travel to Ethiopia for the marriage to be recognized officially for immigration purposes. The bride can apply as a refugee herself but increases her chances of resettlement by also applying as a spouse joining her husband.

The number of displaced Sudanese approaches three-quarters of a million people. Those in the diaspora maintain close ties with friends and family in the Sudan, in other African countries, and around the world. Therefore, a focus on the lives of Sudanese refugees in Africa is an important part of understanding Nuer refugees' lives in the United States. These transnational linkages influence Nuer peoples' decisions in the United States.

# Conclusion

Refugees are a special category of immigrant to the United States. Often seen as victims of tragic circumstances, refugees are also amazingly adept at finding ways to survive these same circumstances. Refugees' lives depend on an international and national bureaucracy, and those who pass through the process represent a very small percentage of people who are displaced. Starting a life in a vastly different cultural environment than the one they were raised in presents a number of hardships. Refugees cope with these challenges by trying to maintain their original ethnic group identity. Transnational communication is one way to do this. So is moving to find people they know from their homelands.

Anthropologists, such as Evans-Pritchard, used to journey to faraway places to study distant "others." Nowadays it is often the objects of study that make the journey to the land of the anthropologists. Refugees such as the Nuer are among the latest newcomers to urban and suburban areas in the United States, and anthropologists can play an important role in their lives. For example, some anthropologists work for voluntary agencies where what they learn about refugees through their ability to conduct ethnographic research helps to ease refugee adjustment to unfamiliar surroundings. Other anthropologists work at the federal and state levels to advise about the efficacy of the social programs designed to meet the needs of recently arrived populations and suggest changes if they are needed. Sometimes these roles take the form of advocacy.

But through it all, anthropologists still do fieldwork in much the same way. They learn the language of refugee populations, ask open-ended questions in interviews, conduct participant observation at such events as weddings, funerals, graduation ceremonies, and political meetings, and try to understand life from their informants' perspective.

Although he now knows an anthropologist, Thok Ding goes about his new life in America with the same independent determination that got him here in the first place. He will continue to move his residence if he thinks it will help him, increase his level of education, find better paying jobs, and eventually, if all works out, marry a woman from the Sudan, bring his whole family to the United States, and, in the end, become a new American.

# Review Questions

1. According to Shandy, what is the formal United Nations definition of a refugee?

2. What steps do displaced persons have to take to achieve resettlement as refugees?

3. How have Nuer refugees reorganized their lives to live successfully in the United States?

4. How have migrants to the United States changed the way anthropologists define groups they study and the focus of their research?

# SEVEN

## Law and Politics

$\mathbf{I}$deally, culture provides the blueprint for a smoothly oiled social machine whose parts work together under all circumstances. But human society is not like a rigidly constructed machine. It is made of individuals who have their own special needs and desires. Personal interest, competition for scarce resources, and simple accident can cause nonconformity and disputes, resulting in serious disorganization.

One way we manage social disruption is through the socialization of children. As we acquire our culture, we learn the appropriate ways to look at experience, to define our existence, and to feel about life. Each system of cultural knowledge contains implicit values of what is desirable, and we come to share these values with other people. Slowly, with the acquisition of culture, most people find they *want* to do what they *must* do; the requirements of an orderly social life become personal goals.

Enculturation, however, is rarely enough. Disputes among individuals regularly occur in all societies, and how such disagreements are handled defines what anthropologists mean by the legal system. Some disputes are **infralegal;** they never reach a point where they are settled by individuals with special authority. Neighbors, for example, would engage in an infralegal dispute if they argued over who should pay for the damage caused by water that runs off one's land into the other's basement. So long as they don't take the matter to court or resort to violence, the dispute will remain infralegal. This dispute may become **extralegal,** however, if it occurs outside the law and escalates into violence. Had the neighbors come to blows over the waterlogged basement, the dispute would have become extralegal. Feuds and wars are the best examples of this kind of dispute.

Legal disputes, on the other hand, involve socially approved mechanisms for their settlement. **Law** is the cultural knowledge that people use to settle disputes by means of agents who have the recognized authority to do so. Thus if the argument between neighbors cited previously ended up in court before a judge or referee, it would have become legal.

Although Americans often think of courts as synonymous with the legal system, societies have evolved a variety of structures for settling disputes. For example, some disputes may be settled by **self-redress,** meaning that wronged individuals are given the right to settle matters themselves. **Contests** requiring physical or mental combat between disputants may also be used to settle disputes. A trusted third party, or **go-between,** may be asked to negotiate with each side until a settlement is achieved. In some societies, supernatural power or beings may be used. In parts of India, for example, disputants are asked to take an oath in the name of a powerful deity or (at least in the past) to submit to a supernaturally controlled, painful, or physically dangerous test called an **ordeal.** Disputes may also be taken to a **moot,** an informal community meeting where conflict may be aired. At the moot, talk continues until a settlement is reached. Finally, disputes are often taken to **courts,** which are formally organized and include officials with authority to make and enforce decisions.

Political systems are closely related to legal ones and often involve some of the same offices and actors. The **political system** contains the process for making and carrying out public policy according to cultural categories and rules; **policy** refers to guidelines for action. The **public** are the people affected by the policy. Every society must make decisions that affect all or most of its members. The Mbuti Pygmies of the Ituri Forest described by anthropologist Colin Turnbull, for example, occasionally decide to conduct a communal hunt. Hunters set their nets together and wait for the appearance of forest game. Men, women, and children must work together as beaters to drive the animals toward the nets. When the Mbuti decide to hold a hunt, they make a political decision.

The political process requires that people make and abide by a particular policy, often in the face of competing plans. To do so a policy must have **support,** which is anything that contributes to its adoption and enforcement. Anthropologists recognize two main kinds of support: legitimacy and coercion. **Legitimacy** refers to people's positive evaluation of public officials and public policy. A college faculty, for example, may decide to institute the quarter system because a majority feel that quarters rather than semesters represent the "right length" for courses. Theirs is a positive evaluation of the policy. Some faculty members will oppose the change but will abide by the decision because they value the authority of faculty governance. For them the decision, although unfortunate, is legitimate.

**Coercion,** on the other hand, is support derived from the threat or use of force or the promise of short-term gain. Had the faculty members adopted the quarter system because they had been threatened with termination by the administration, they would have acted under coercion.

There are also other important aspects of the political process. Some members of a society may be given **authority,** the right to make and enforce public policy. In our country, elected officials are given authority to make certain decisions and exercise particular powers. However, formal political offices with authority do not occur in every society. Most hunting and gathering societies lack such positions, as do many horticulturalists. **Leadership,** which is the ability to influence others to act, must be exercised informally in these societies.

The first article, by James Spradley and David McCurdy, uses Zapotec cases collected by anthropologist Laura Nader to illustrate basic anthropological legal concepts such as substantive and procedural law, legal levels, and legal principles. They show that, for the Zapotec, social harmony is more important than punishment. In the second article, Anne Sutherland describes what happens when the substantive laws of two culturally different groups collide in court. A young Gypsy man is convicted of using another family member's social security number although he has no intention to defraud anyone. The third selection, by Marvin Harris, traces the development of political leadership. He argues that small groups characterized by reciprocal exchange have no recognizable political officers and that many horticultural societies with redistributive economic exchange may develop "big men" who lead by example but still have no formal authority.

# Key Terms

authority  *p. 302*
coercion  *p. 302*
contest  *p. 302*
court  *p. 302*
extralegal  *p. 301*
go-between  *p. 302*
infralegal  *p. 301*
law  *p. 301*
leadership  *p. 302*

legitimacy  *p. 302*
moot  *p. 302*
ordeal  *p. 302*
policy  *p. 302*
political system  *p. 302*
public  *p. 302*
self-redress  *p. 302*
support  *p. 302*

# 29

# Law and Order

## James P. Spradley and David W. McCurdy

*When we consider U.S. law, we are likely to think of formal written statutes, police, courts, lawyers, strict rules of evidence, the determination of guilt, and punishment. In our large society the system seems technical and impersonal. In this selection, Spradley and McCurdy discuss the structure of law in the context of fieldwork conducted by anthropologist Laura Nader, who did research in the Zapotec community of Ralu'a. They discuss several legal cases to illustrate such concepts as substantive and procedural law, legal levels, and legal principles. They conclude with Nader's argument that Zapotec law seeks "to make the balance," to attempt a settlement between disputants that will promote social harmony.*

The Land Rover disappeared in a cloud of dust on its way back to Oaxaca City. The anthropologist adjusted the shoulder straps on the backpack, turned away from the end of the road, and began to follow the two Zapotec Indian guides. The trail led north, climbing along the edge of steep valleys, crossing over mountain ridges, and winding back and forth to make a steady gain in altitude. Accustomed to living at 5,000 feet above sea level, the two guides walked rapidly, oblivious to the hard breathing of their American companion. In every direction, scattered over much of the 36,000 square miles of Oaxaca State in

"Law and Order" was written by James P. Spradley and David W. McCurdy.

southern Mexico, the anthropologist knew there were small Zapotec villages. The three of them headed toward the Rincon district, which means "the corner," calling attention to the fact that the area is partially encircled by three high mountain peaks. As they walked, the anthropologist could see the distant and formidable Zempoateptl Mountain reaching to more than 10,000 feet; Maceta and El Machin, the two other peaks, would come into view before they reached their destination, the pueblo of Ralu'a. One of the Zapotec men spoke Spanish and had told the anthropologist as they started, "We are called the people of the corner, *Rinconeros,* because we live between the peaks." The sun was high on this day in early May 1957 and the sky clear; it was several weeks before the rainy season would begin. Wild orchids were in bloom everywhere. The mountains had a kind of awesome beauty for the anthropologist, particularly since she had anticipated the sight for many months. As she walked behind the guides, she wondered why no other social scientist had ever come before to this place, to live and study among these people.

The Zapotec guides pushed on, stopping only for water now and then at the edge of fast-flowing mountain streams. During the first hour they had passed scattered fields of coffee plants in bloom and sugarcane, evidence that a pueblo or homestead was nearby, enfolded in some mountain niche. The anthropologist would like to have stopped to inquire about these settlements and to rest, but the two guides never hesitated, pressing on toward their destination. The sun had already disappeared behind the highest peak when, after a 3½-hour walk, they came to Ralu'a, a pueblo of 2,000 people. Unexpectedly, as they came over a rise, houses appeared everywhere; children played on the paths, and women could be seen carrying firewood. The anthropologist felt a sense of excitement as she looked down on the town that would be her home for many months to come. Here she would live and work and make friends; from here she would travel to other villages and nearby settlements in her efforts to discover the cultural ways of the Zapotec; and here she would try to understand Zapotec law, to describe the cultural rules these people used when settling disputes.

As they entered the edge of the pueblo, she wondered how these people would receive her. Would they understand why she had come? In Oaxaca City she had met an engineer, a government employee who had friends in Ralu'a. He had made tentative arrangements for her to stay with a family while she conducted her field study. All was excitement at the home of her hosts, for a fiesta was in progress to celebrate the return of religious pilgrims from the Sanctuario in Veracruz. Her hosts seemed polite but not enthusiastic as they invited her to join them in the fiesta meal of special foods. After they had eaten, the head of the household came to her and asked, "Are you a Catholic? If you are not a Catholic, you cannot stay here. We do not want Protestants in our town." Surprised by this question, she explained her role and assured him that she belonged to the original Catholic church (Eastern Orthodox).

It would be many weeks before she would fully appreciate what lay behind this simple question about her religion. She was to discover that it concerned authority, conflict, and the process of law and dispute settlement, the very areas she had come to investigate. Before two weeks had elapsed a message came from the priest: she was to come to his house immediately. She entered and, after a brief exchange in Spanish, he said, "You are a Protestant missionary! Why have you come to our pueblo?" Nothing would convince him that it was not so; even the letter of recommendation that she brought from a priest in Oaxaca was dismissed as a fake, and a wire of confirmation from that priest that she was an anthropologist and a good Christian did not convince him. Although others would eventually accept her, the priest in Ralu'a would remain unconvinced, spreading the word from the pulpit and in the streets that she was really a Protestant missionary. Several years earlier some missionaries had come to Ralu'a and, as a result of winning converts, conflicts erupted that led to burning of Protestant homes. The dispute reached enormous proportions for this small pueblo and was only settled through the process of law when the state government forced the town to pay heavy fines for damage inflicted.

When the anthropologist was called to the home of the priest in the Zapotec pueblo of Ralu'a, she became a party to a dispute. He accused her of being a Protestant missionary; she denied it. Although she appealed to another priest to confirm her identity, he did not have the authority to settle the dispute. Like many troubles that beset human interaction, this dispute was never settled, and the anthropologist had to work around the difficulties it created with other individuals in the village. The dispute remained below the level of the law, but it is conceivable that the priest or the anthropologist could have appealed to some agent whose authority was recognized and who could settle the case. It would then have become a legal matter.

One of the earliest disputes that came to the anthropologist's attention occurred at a Ralu'a well several months after she arrived among the Zapotec. She awoke as usual one morning to the sound of the women in the household getting ready to go to the mill. It was 5:00 A.M., and each morning at this time the women in Ralu'a arose to take their corn to nearby mills. The men were still asleep as the anthropologist dressed and prepared to go with the women. It was not yet light at this hour of the morning, but the daily walk to the mill was exhilarating. Other women greeted them and, at the mill, while they waited to have their corn ground, they visited with each other. Soon each would return home to prepare tortillas, fix breakfast for the family, and make lunches for the men who must walk many miles to their fields for a day of work. But now they caught up on the local news and enjoyed visiting.

This morning two women were earnestly discussing an argument that had occurred on the previous day at Los Remedios, one of the town wells. Carmen had gone to the well to wash the family clothes, and instead of using the flat slab of stone that belonged to her, she selected one near a friend so they could visit as they worked. Like other women she looked forward to this task because it enabled her to visit and gossip with others in the neighborhood, a pleasant change from working alone inside her house. But hardly 20 minutes had passed when the owner of the washing stone appeared, and instead of taking another place she angrily asked Carmen to move. As Carmen began to gather her wet clothes together, she loudly commented on the other woman's generosity. Insults began to fly, and the situation became especially tense when Carmen "accidentally" splashed water on the newcomer's dress as she went off to finish washing on her own slab. Some said Carmen should have moved to her own stone without comment; others declared that the second woman was wrong and should have gone quietly to another place to wash. Someone recalled a similar conflict several years earlier when a woman had taken the matter to the *municipio,* or town hall, where the *presidente* had settled the dispute. Some of the women wondered whether the trouble of yesterday would go that far.

It was the end of the summer before the dispute over washing stones reached the boiling point and became a case of law, but it did not happen in the way the anthropologist had expected, for no one took the dispute to the *municipio.* The incident at the well did not die down; the two women continued to make insulting remarks in public, and others began to take sides. Then a similar conflict arose between several other women who were not using the stones that belonged to them. At night in the *cantina* as the men drank *mescal,* an alcoholic drink made from the fermented juice of agave plants, they talked of the disputes they had learned about from their wives. Some men reported that at the wells where their wives washed clothes no such fights had occurred; everyone agreed that the problem was primarily at Los Remedios.

The bickering and fighting continued until one day people noticed that the water at Los Remedios had begun to dry up. Some said this was caused by the fighting. The men who belonged to the Well Association, a group that worked to maintain the wells, called a special meeting and decided that they must take action to save the water. They formed a work party and improved the well to ensure more water, but they also removed all the slabs of stone used for washing. In place of these privately owned washing places they constructed 24 shallow tubs from cement and announced that no one could own or reserve one of these spaces. They belonged to the well and were to be used on a first-come, first-serve basis. The priest blessed the new well, and the disputes were settled. Although some women complained that they liked the old way better, everyone recognized the authority of the men's Well Association, and the change was accepted. . . .

The ethnographer who investigates the process of law in a non-Western society must collect data on all kinds of disputes. Since any conflict can be transformed overnight into a legal dispute involving some agent with recognized authority, it is important to examine the range of ways that people handle such troubles. By means of various ethnographic discovery procedures, one begins to focus more and more on legal cases, those that are settled by people or groups with authority.

## The Structure of Legal Culture

By examining dispute cases, observing their outcome, and questioning the parties involved, one can describe a goodly portion of the law ways of a community. Such legal knowledge can be analyzed into three different aspects. First, the most explicit aspect of legal knowledge includes *substantive law* and *procedural law*, which are interrelated. At a more implicit level, underlying these rules, are the fundamental *legal principles* that determine the shape of the law in a particular society. Finally, there is a common core of *cultural values* that influence the legal principles and link the law of any culture to other domains of that culture. . . . .

## Substantive Law

The term "law" is most often used in our own society to refer to substantive law, the legal statutes that define right and wrong. Phrases such as "He broke the law" or "It is illegal to bring liquor across the state line" refer to substantive law. It is easy for us to assume that substantive rules can be equated with written statutes, but this is not always the case in our own society, and most of the world's cultures do not have written laws at all. But all people have agreed on substantive rules. Let us look at an example of an unwritten law from our own society.

Until recently every city in the United States had passed legislation that made it a crime to appear drunk in public. For many years in the city of Seattle this substantive rule was used to make more than 10,000 arrests each year. Although the law against public drunkenness seems clear and simple, ethnographic investigation of individual cases in Seattle shows that many other substantive rules of a complex nature were actually being used. In practice, the police used their own discretion to arrest some drunks but not others. The unwritten rule was, "If you see a poor man on skid row who is drunk, arrest him; those of the middle and upper class who are drunk in other parts of town need not be arrested." A tramp from skid row who had been arrested many times reported the following experience. Standing outside the University Club located several blocks from skid row, he observed men coming out of the club in states of obvious intoxication. A policeman not only saw the same men, but assisted them into cabs for transportation home.

The substantive law of Ralu'a contains many specific rules. Some are part of a written legal code, others must be inferred from what people say and do in dispute cases. Many cases end up in the town hall, the *municipio*, a two-room, adobe building in the center of town. Here certain officials hold a kind of court to settle disputes. Thirteen respected men make up an advisory group for the pueblo, the *principales*. Each year this group nominates three men for the position of village chairman, or *presidente*, one of whom is elected by the village to serve for 1 year. The *presidente*, in turn, appoints these same *principales* for another 1-year term. Working closely with the *presidente is* a man elected to the office of *sindico*, who runs the communal work program of the pueblo and is also head of the town police. There are 12 *policia* who serve under two lieutenants and a chief of police. Each year the outgoing men of this police force nominate other men, generally those who have been the biggest troublemakers during the year, to take over as replacements. They are then elected by the village as a whole, and the roughest man of all becomes the chief of police for the year. The *presidente* and the *sindico*, working together, handle minor disputes such as drunkenness, fighting, flirting, slander, boundary trespass, and theft. There is a third elected official, the *alcalde,* a kind of justice of the peace, who presides over more serious disputes. The *presidente* will often pass more serious cases as well as any cases that he cannot resolve directly to the *alcalde.* More serious cases or those that the *alcalde* cannot resolve are passed on to the district court. While the *presidente* and the *sindico* have various duties, the *alcalde* deals only with legal matters. We can see substantive law in action among the Zapotec if we examine two specific cases.

**The Case of the Flirting Husband.**    The first dispute involves a violation of rules that prohibit flirting. An unmarried woman, Señorita Zoalage, came to the *presidente* early on a Tuesday morning. She complained that a married man, Señor Huachic, had flirted with her. He appeared outside her house and made the equivalent of American wolf-calls shortly after dark on Monday night on his way home from the market. The *presidente* talked over the matter with the *sindico,* and someone was sent to notify Señor Huachic to appear in court that afternoon. It was now 2:00 P.M. and the *presidente* sat behind a long table at the front of the *presidencia,* one of the rooms in the town hall. Both Señor Huachic and Señorita Zoalage sat before him. After presenting the complaint to Señor Huachic, the *presidente* waited for his response. "Yes," he admitted, "I did what she said, but only because this woman here, Señorita Zoalage, flirted with me last week! She even invited me to come with her to collect firewood!" After some discussion about the particulars of the case the *presidente* said, "Señorita Zoalage, I am going to fine you 30 pesos for flirting with Señor Huachic. And Señor Huachic, you are fined 60 pesos for flirting with Señorita Zoalage. You are a married man and should have been at home with your wife." After warning them to refrain from further exhibitions of such behavior he dismissed them, they paid their fines, and returned to their homes. Each had violated a substantive rule that holds flirting to be illegal. In some cases individuals refuse to pay fines and, as a result, may be detained in jail or compelled to work on a community project.

**The Case of the Disobedient Son.**    The second case sheds light on substantive rules involving the relationships between parents and children. It was relatively easy to elicit cultural rules for this relationship. For example, one evening after the anthropologist had been in Ralu'a for 8 months, she was having dinner with a Zapotec family. The father had just told the others about a son who had been sent to jail in the district capital because when his father had beat him he had struck back, hitting his father. The anthropologist asked quizzically, "And for this they sent him to jail?"

"Of course," he said, looking rather surprised that she would ask such a stupid question.

"But," she said, seeking to enlarge on the discussion, "many men beat their wives, and they never go to jail for that!"

"Yes," the father responded, "but wives are one thing, fathers another."

It seemed a good place to introduce a hypothetical question and so she asked, "But what if the father beats his son harshly, and the father is in the wrong? Is it still wrong for the son to strike his father?"

The son in the family spoke up, entering the discussion with a serious tone. "Fathers are never in the wrong for beating their sons. They always do it for their own good."

Still not satisfied, the anthropologist asked one last question, "All right, but sons grow up and become men. Under your law could a father ever be proved guilty for doing wrong to a son, even if he is a grown man?"

The father's answer brought looks of agreement from the others, "A father cannot do wrong with his children." There the discussion ended, but several days later she observed a case in the *presidencia* that underscored this substantive rule of Zapotec law.[1]

Señor Benjamin Mendoza Cruz had complained to the court about his son, Clemente Mendoza, who was 25 years of age. Because the complaint had been made several days earlier, both men were sitting before the *presidente*. Señor Cruz repeated his charge. "I have coffee planted on my land near one of the neighboring *ranchos*. Someone harvested some of my ripe coffee beans, and I thought the thief was from the neighboring pueblo, but a woman who has the land next to mine said she saw my son harvesting the coffee. I demand that he repay me for the coffee he has stolen."

The *presidente* turned to the son, Clemente Mendoza, waiting for him to speak. His eyes were on the floor; he did not look at the *presidente* or his father as he spoke. "Yes," he said, "I admit that I went to his field and cut some coffee. A year ago he allowed me to cut some coffee on his property, and I was confident he would give the coffee to me, but I am at fault, and now he can decide how to punish me. I have committed a crime against him and now I wish he would forgive me." There was a long pause when the son finished speaking. The *presidente* sat silently as the secretary continued writing. Then the father spoke slowly. "I am, as his father, very sad that my son Clemente should have done this wickedness to me. I did not believe that it was he until the woman told me. Now I will leave it to his *Municipio Presidente* to decide what is suitable. As his father I have to help him and look after him, but he should not act this way, disposing of the fruit of my harvest without my consent."

Another period of silence followed; flies buzzed noisily around the room. It was warm and the *presidente* thought about the man and his son, how he would settle the case. He recalled that fathers should provide for their sons when they came asking for a bride price, but Señor Cruz had already given more than once to his son for this purpose; Clemente had spent it on other things. Yes, it was the son who was at fault. He turned to him now. "Now you heard what your father said, and I will tell you that your father does not have

---

[1]This case is presented in the excellent ethnographic film *To Make the Balance*, Berkeley: University of California Extension Media Center, and also in "Styles of Court Procedure: To Make the Balance," in *Law in Culture and Society*, Laura Nader (editor), Chicago: Aldine, 1969.

an obligation to give you, his son, *anything.*" He raised his voice on the last word as if to emphasize the great distance between fathers and sons. He continued, "Nor is a father obliged to give you what is his. If a father loves his son very much, he may give him something, but nobody can force him to do so. Now, you have abused him and, as you have admitted, there is no reason why your father should help you because you committed this wrong." Clemente Mendoza had been afraid of his father all of his life. After his mother died, his father remarried, and he found it even more difficult to get along with the old man. Now he sat in silence, his eyes shifting nervously, focused on the floor most of the time as he listened to the *presidente* ask, "Are you now both ready to come to an agreement?" They would accept his settlement.

"Clemente Mendoza," the *presidente* addressed the guilty son, "you shall repay your father for the coffee that you took without permission. Without delay you have to deliver the 25 pounds of dried coffee to your father, and the deadline is Friday, the 21st of this month, and for the wrong you have committed I impose on you a 200-peso fine, which you have to pay today." The secretary prepared an agreement that finalized the ending of the dispute, and it was soon ready for signing. More than an hour had passed since they first appeared before the *presidente*. The agreement showed the amount Clemente would repay his father as well as the fine payable to the *municipio*. The agreement was shown to both parties, and the *presidente* addressed them one more time.

"Clemente Mendoza, you should realize that both you and your father are bound by this agreement; you should not inflict reprisals on your father or stepmother, and you must realize that your father has the right, as a father, to correct any of your faults. You, as his son, must ask him for full permission to harvest some coffee or give you anything else, to avoid being offensive to your father. You should now go and behave as a good son should behave."

Turning to the father he said, "Señor Cruz, whenever you desire you can dispose of your property and give it to your son, you can help him in mutual agreement, but the father does not have any obligation to give his son anything; on the other hand, the son cannot demand his father to give him any of his property. It is entirely in the hands of the father whether he wants to give or not."

The two men, father and son, signed the agreement and turned to walk out of the *municipio*. It had been a rare occurrence for a father to bring his son to court. Most disputes of this sort are easily settled by the authority of the father. Although all sons feel the constraints of the father's authority, they know they will one day marry and have sons of their own and, like their father, require total obedience.

## Procedural Law

When a dispute moves into the settlement stage, numerous procedural rules come into play. Procedural law refers to the agreed-on ways to settle a dispute.

They guide not only the *presidente,* the *sindico,* the *alcalde,* or other authority agent, but also the parties to a dispute. Take, for example, the unwritten procedural rule about who should bring family disputes to the court. Although a large number of family cases are brought to the *presidente*'s court, only certain classes of persons would think of settling such disputes in the court. The *principales,* for example, are some of the most respected men in Ralu'a, and they take pride in their respectable families. Undoubtedly their authority in the pueblo enhances their authority within their families, giving them the power to arbitrate and settle any disputes that may arise. If any member complained about family problems in court, it would bring shame and dishonor to the entire family. There is, therefore, considerable social pressure to keep members abiding by the unwritten procedural rule that says that *principales and their families should not use the court to settle family disputes.* If the wife of a *principale* were to appear in court making a complaint against her husband, the *presidente* would be greatly surprised, and news of this event would quickly spread throughout the pueblo. Everyone would know that she had violated an implicit procedural rule of Zapotec law.

## Procedural Rules in U.S. Society

Procedural rules in our own legal system are not always clearly specified. The ethnographer seeks to make these rules explicit, thereby shedding light on substantive rules and the entire process of law. The ethnographic research among the tramps in Seattle, Washington, mentioned earlier, revealed an implicit procedural rule that held enormous significance for this population. It involves a procedural rule for sentencing that can be stated as follows.

> If a man is poor and has been arrested many times for being drunk in public, he shall be sentenced with greater severity than those with money or with no record of previous arrests for drunkenness.

On the basis of this rule, two men could be arrested at 10:00 P.M. on Monday on the same block in Seattle and plead guilty in court to public drunkenness. One would be given a 2-day suspended sentence and would walk out of the courtroom a free man. The other would be given 90 days in jail. Why this difference? The first man had not been arrested for this crime during the preceding 6 months, whereas the other had been arrested seven times.

The most significant part of this procedural rule, however, involves differences in wealth. Take two men, for example, who were arrested 10 to 15 times each year for public drunkenness. Each time they were picked up by the Seattle police they had to spend several hours in the jail "drying out." Then both men were allowed to post a $20 bail, *if they had the money.* Only one of the men had this amount, and he alone was immediately released from jail. He might be arrested again within a few days or weeks and repeat the process. Over the course of 15 or 20 years such a man might spend several thousand dollars for bail, each time walking away from jail after a few hours of sleep. Although a man who posted bail was expected to appear in court for his arraignment, no one did, choosing instead to forfeit this money than face a judge and possible jail sentence. The man who could not post bail, on the other hand, waited several days in the drunk tank, appeared in court, pleaded guilty, received his sentence, and then returned to the jail to serve his time. Thus violation of the same *substantive rule* can lead to enormously different consequences, depending on the nature of related *procedural rules*. . . .

## Legal Levels

In every culture the existence of different kinds of authority agents means that disputes can be settled at different levels. In our own society a dispute between a teacher and a student can be settled by the school principal. If the dispute continues, it could go to the town board of education. If still unsettled, it might go to the local court and even be appealed to a series of higher courts.

Among the Zapotec, several levels for settling disputes exist. Disputes can be settled by family elders, witches, local officials, the priest, supernatural beings, or officials in the *municipio*. If all else fails, the dispute can be taken to the district court in Villa Alta. Consider the following case.

Mariano's son Pedro married the only daughter of a family in the pueblo and went to live with her family. Mariano was pleased with the arrangement because he had helped decide the marriage. But soon trouble began to develop between his son and the new wife. It came to his attention directly when his daughter-in-law came to him and complained, "Your son Pedro is always drunk, he does not work now, and he argues with me all the time in the home of my parents." Mariano talked with her for some time and, on the following day, he warned Pedro that he should drink less and live at peace with his new wife. Like any son in Ralu'a, Pedro promised his father that he would change his behavior. However, within a month Mariano's daughter-in-law was back again with the same complaint. This time Mariano was angry. "She is back again so soon," he thought. "This son of mine does not learn from words." Mariano found his son and this time, amidst stern warnings, he whipped Pedro harshly.

The weeks passed and still Pedro did not change. His wife now turned to the *padrinos de pano,* the godparents of the marriage. But their warnings to Pedro were to no avail, and so she went to the priest. He talked to Pedro several times, and it seemed the penitent husband might change with his intervention. Then one night Pedro came home very drunk and began cursing at his wife and threatening her. Then he beat her, and she lay awake most of the night wondering what to do next. The fact that he had beat her was less important than that it was another stage in their deteriorating relationship and evidence that Pedro had not changed. Early in the morning while Pedro was still asleep she went to the *municipio* and made a complaint to the *presidente*. Pedro was cited and appeared in court later that same afternoon. He told the *presidente* that he had been drunk and did not know what he was doing, that he would change his ways, and that he would begin to work regularly in his fields. Pedro paid a fine of 50 pesos and signed an agreement that he would live at peace with his wife.

Disputes such as this can be resolved at various levels and through various remedy agents such as male family heads, church officials, village officials, and even by appeals directly to supernatural beings and individuals who are witches. For example, a man who is having trouble with his wife may go to a witch and say, "Somebody is gossiping about me and every time I come home my wife is after me because she is so upset. Can you do something about this person who is spreading bad tales about me?" The witch will reply, "Pay me 5 pesos and I'll find out who it is and do something about it." But whether a man goes to a witch or to the *presidente,* or whether a woman goes to her father-in-law is not left to happenstance. The procedural rules of a culture's law help define which authorities should be employed for various kinds of disputes.

## Legal Principles and Cultural Values

Underlying the settlement of disputes in every society we find legal principles based on the fundamental values of a culture. A legal principle is a broad conception of some desirable state of affairs that gives rise to many substantive and procedural rules. The witness is asked, "Do you promise to tell the truth, the whole truth, and nothing but the truth, so help you God?" We accept the value of telling the objective truth, getting at the facts, and we believe that humans are capable of telling the truth. In some societies, however, people hold different assumptions, asserting that it is not possible to tell objective truth. In other cultures the value placed on the facts is small when compared to the importance of restoring amicable relationships. In order to understand the decisions authorities make to settle disputes, we need to grasp the legal principles of a culture.

When the Zapotec talk about the characteristics of those wise men who have settled disputes in the proper way, they say, "He knows how to *make the balance."* This principle means that fault-finding in a particular trouble case is not as important as balancing the demands of all parties and restoring conditions of peaceful coexistence. The men's Well Association did not concern itself with seeking culprits who had violated rules about the use of private property. Instead, they sought to restore peace and prevent future conflicts at Los Remedios. Their goal—*hacer el balance*—to make the balance, was achieved.

The principle of balance does not mean people are never at fault, never violate substantive rules. Instead, it means that disputes are not settled merely by establishing the facts of the case, finding the guilty party, and administering punishment. When Clemente Mendoza harvested his father's coffee without permission, he was clearly in the wrong. But the *presidente,* acting as a kind of father to the citizens of Ralu'a, sought to restore the balance, to mend the relationship between father and son, eliciting a signed agreement from them that they would not hold grudges and continue the dispute.

## The Case of Fright

To the Zapotec, making the balance means settling disputes with an eye to the future of the relationships involved, not merely an examination of past events. Disputes create difficulties for people, financial losses, bitter feelings, and disrupted relationships. It would be possible to settle disputes without rectifying any of these conditions, but for the Zapotec this would not be sufficient, although the guilty person were given a life sentence for his or her crime. Take the case of Señora Juan. She complained to the *presidente* that she had been working, cutting coffee in the field of Señora Quiroz, when a young boy, Teodoro Garcia, had picked on her 6-year-old boy, hitting him. The experience had been so disconcerting to the smaller boy that he had come down with *susto*, or magical fright, an illness involving the loss of one's soul. "My little boy got frightened," she told the *presidente*, "and now he yells during the night and has diarrhea because of the fright. I am asking the *presidente* to help me make my little son well again." The *presidente* asked Teodoro Garcia about the dispute, and he answered that the son of Señora Juan was always calling him names and taunting him while he worked. Back and forth the discussion went, but the *presidente* did not seek to discover what really happened; *his goal was not to find out the facts.* He allowed people to express their feelings in the matter. It was difficult to tell who was at fault, but he could easily see that this upset had disturbed the equilibrium in social relationships of all those involved. A boy had *susto* as a result, and the *presidente* knew he could do something about that, restoring the balance required. The poor mother said she needed 30 pesos for the curer. After negotiation, Teodoro Garcia offered to settle for 20 pesos. The case was resolved, the boy taken to a curer, and the balance restored.

## Cultural Values

Underlying the legal principles of a society are the values that form the basis of social life. Making the balance in settling disputes is based on a widely held Zapotec cultural value of maintaining equilibrium. Direct confrontation between individuals in which one loses and another wins is unsettling to Zapotecans. As expressed by Laura Nader:

> This concern for equilibrium is evident through Ralu'a. Upon my making inquiries as to the motives for witchcraft in Ralu'a, an informant reported the following as causes: "because one works too much or not enough; because one is too pretty or too ugly or too rich; for being an only child; for being rich and refusing to lend money; for being antisocial—for example, for refusing to greet people." These are all situations that somehow upset the balance as Ralu'ans see it. It is no wonder that the zero-sum game (win or lose) as we know it in some American courts would

be a frightening prospect to a plaintiff, even though all "right" might be on his side. The plaintiff need not worry, however, for the *presidente* is equally reluctant to make such a clear-cut zero-sum game decision for a variety of reasons—among them that witchcraft is an all too possible tool of retaliation for such behavior. If a plaintiff wanted to play the zero-sum game he would go to a witch and not to the courts, where behavior is far too public.[2]

No doubt on that first day when the anthropologist entered the pueblo she had somehow upset some unseen sense of equilibrium in this Zapotec pueblo. A strange woman, dressed in strange clothes, with a strange reason for being there, asking strange questions; she must be a Protestant missionary, a person with supernatural power, at least someone to arouse suspicion. However, after weeks of persistently defining her role and participating in the daily round of life, she had overcome most of the suspicion and fear. Then one warm day when the excitement of a fiesta filled the air of Ralu'a, she had purchased a large barrel of *mescal* and donated it to the pueblo celebrations. It was a simple token, but the citizens of Ralu'a responded with enthusiasm. Public officials lauded her generosity and declared that she was now a true member of the pueblo. Others apologized for their suspicions and unfriendliness as they drank and laughed together. Without calculation she had *hacer el balance. . . .*

# Review Questions

1. What are the definitions of *law, substantive law, procedural law, legal levels,* and *legal principles*? What Zapotec dispute cases illustrate these concepts? Can you think of examples from our own society?

2. Based on the examples cited in this selection, how does Zapotec law differ from U.S. law? Illustrate your answer with specific examples.

3. Some anthropologists believe that every society has some *informal* substantive and procedural legal rules. Comment on this assertion using the Zapotec and American cases presented in this article.

4. Why do you think Zapotec law emphasizes "making the balance" while U.S. law seems more concerned with determining guilt?

[2]Laura Nader, "Styles of Court Procedure: To Make the Balance," in *Law in Culture and Society*, Laura Nader, ed. (Chicago: Aldine, 1969), pp. 73–74.

# 30

# Cross-Cultural Law: The Case of the Gypsy Offender

*Anne Sutherland*

*Every society recognizes a list of legal statutes, which anthropologists call substantive law, that define right from wrong. In the United States, for example, it is against the law for an individual to marry more than one person at a time. But what is proper in one country may be a crime in another. Unlike the United States, for example, in Iran it is legal for a person to be married simultaneously to more than one person. So what happens when members of one society live within and under the legal jurisdiction of another? This is the question explored by Anne Sutherland in this article on the legal plight of a young Gypsy man who is arrested for using the social security number of a relative on a car loan application. Despite the claim that using different identities of family members is a common Gypsy practice designed to hide their identities, and that he had no intention to defraud anyone by doing so, the young man receives a six-month jail term.*

It is often the case that a law made for one set of purposes has another, unintended impact on a particular group. A recent law making the use of a false social security number a federal felony is intended to help prosecution of major drug crime syndicates, but it has a special impact on Gypsies in the United States. Gypsies, traditionally a nomadic people, frequently borrow each others' "American" names and social security numbers, viewing them as a kind of corporate property of their kin group or *vitsa*. They also often lack birth certificates and must obtain midwife or baptismal certificates to use for identification purposes when they try to obtain credit, enter school, or apply for welfare.

In this article, I shall examine the case of a nineteen-year-old Gypsy man who was convicted under the new social security law and served six months in jail. Arguments for the defense in the case followed three lines of reasoning: 1) that this law unfairly singled out Gypsies for punishment; 2) that there was no intent to commit a crime; and 3) that in using the social security numbers of relatives, Gypsies were following a time-honored tradition to remain anonymous and separate from non-Gypsy society.

## Facts of the Case

In the fall of 1991 in St. Paul, Minnesota, a nineteen-year-old Gypsy man was convicted of the crime of using his five-year-old nephew's social security number to obtain credit to purchase a car. When the purchase was questioned by the car dealership, he returned the car and was arrested on a felony charge of using a false social security number. After he was arrested, police searched the apartment where he was staying. They found lists of names, addresses and social security numbers, leading them to suspect an organized crime ring.

In *The United States of America v. S.N.*,[1] it was "alleged that the defendant, S.N., while in the process of obtaining a new Ford Mustang from a car dealership, used a social security number that was not his own with intent to deceive." Under the statute 42 U.S.C. 408 (g)(2), a person who, with intent to deceive, falsely represents his or her number to obtain something of value or for any other purpose, is a felon.

In Mr. S.N.'s case there is no specific allegation that he intended to deprive another person permanently of property because the focus of the charging statute is false representation of numbers. The underlying purpose which motivates a person to falsely represent his or her number may be an essentially innocent purpose, but the statute, at least as it has been interpreted, does not appear to impose a burden of proof as to wrongful purpose.

The statute punishes the means (false number) which a person may employ to achieve any number of ends and it punishes those means as a felony.

---

[1] *United States v. Sonny Nicholas*, U.S. District Court, State of Minnesota, CR 4-91-137 (1991). Quotes from Philip Leavenworth, memorandum in support of a motion to declare 42 U.S.C. 408 (g)(2) unconstitutional.

The lawyer for the defense argued that the statute's failure to address the nature of the purpose to which false credentials are used is a serious flaw in the law and may punish those who would use the number for petty misconduct as felons. He also argued that there is a potential for discriminatory impact on Gypsies who use false credentials to conceal themselves from mainstream society. A Gypsy household may obtain a telephone by providing a false social security number and even if they pay the telephone bill without fail for years, they are felons under this law. S.N. not only made the payments for his car, but he returned it when the number was questioned. He is still a felon under this law.

The defense lawyer argued that the law is objectionable for two reasons. First, the law's disproportionate impact on the Gypsies is objectionable under the equal protection guaranteed in the Fifth Amendment of the U.S. Constitution. He argued that the law denies Gypsies equal protection of the law by irrationally and disproportionately punishing at the felony level certain traditional Gypsy actions which cause no positive injury to anyone. As evidence he used material from my book, *Gypsies: The Hidden Americans,* for testimony that Gypsies routinely use false social security numbers to acquire credit but do pay their bills and are available for repossession in case of default of payment. They get phone service, buy houses and cars and other household items on credit and have a record of payment that is probably better than the general population (*United States v. S. N., 1991*). They do this primarily to remain unknown by mainstream society rather than to cause loss or injury to any person.

Second, as the defense lawyer pointed out, there is a Supreme Court decision that requires the government to prove felonious intent when it seeks to punish a person for wrongful acquisition of another's property. S.N. maintained that he used a false social security number because of a Gypsy tradition to remain anonymous and because his own number had been used by other Gypsies. The government argued that there was a "ring" of Gypsies in the area where S.N. was living. At S.N.'s residence a number of false credentials and social security numbers were found which had been used to obtain cars illegally. Some of these cars are still missing. In other words, there was evidence that false identity had been used recently in the area to steal. In this case, however, S.N. had not stolen anything and was not being accused of stealing, but only of using a false social security number.

Because of the evidence of a ring of car thieves in the area, the prosecution hoped to use the threat of prosecution against S.N., the only Gypsy they had been able to arrest, to plea bargain for information regarding the other people involved in the alleged ring. These other people had disappeared immediately as soon as S.N. was arrested.

One of the problems in the case was that both the prosecution and even the defense had difficulty obtaining complete and accurate information on S.N. For example, they had difficulty determining his "real" name, a moot point for the Gypsies since they have a practice of using many "American" names although they only have one "Gypsy" name (*nav romano*). The Gypsy name of *o*

*Spiro le Stevanosko* (or Spiro the son of Stevan) uses the noun declension characteristic of the Sanskrit-rooted Rom language and is not immediately translatable into English since it does not employ a surname. Spiro's identity can be pinned down by finding out what *vitsa* (a cognatic descent group) he belongs to so that he will not be confused with any other Spiro le Stevanoskos. The Spiro of our example is a *Kashtare* which is part of a larger "nation" of Gypsies or *natsia* called *Kalderasha* (coppersmith). For his "American" names he may take any of a number used by his relatives such as Spiro Costello, John Costello, John Marks, John Miller, Spiro John or Spiro Miller. His nickname is Rattlesnake Pete.

## The Anthropologist as Cultural Broker

S.N.'s defense attorney contacted me after finding that he was less confused about S.N. after reading my book about Gypsies. He sought my help in determining whether S.N. was a Gypsy, what his name was, and any other cultural information (such as the use of social security numbers by Gypsies) that would help him with his case.

Consequently, one cold autumn day I drove to the federal holding prison, one and a half hours from the city, and met S.N. He was a thin young man, perpetually fearful of pollution from contact with non-Gypsies and suffering from the effects of several months of what for him was solitary confinement since he had not seen any of his people since being incarcerated. The telephone was his only link with people to whom he could relate, people from his own culture who spoke his language. His main contact was with a non-Gypsy woman who lived with one of his relatives. She was his link with the world he had known and the only "American" household he had been in before prison. Since my primary task was to determine if he was a Gypsy, first I talked to him about his relatives in Los Angeles and his *vitsa* (Yowane) and tried to establish what section of the *vitsa* I personally knew. This exchange of information about *vitsa* and Gypsies of mutual acquaintance is a normal one between Gypsies. The purpose was to establish a link between us.

Then I asked him about why he was in Minnesota. He talked about a seasonal expedition he and his brothers and cousins make to Minnesota to buy and sell cars and fix fenders before winter sets in. He claimed not to know where his brothers and cousins had gone or how he got into his present predicament.

For S.N., the most immediately effective action I could take was to see that he got the food he needed to stay "clean" in jail. When I met him he had lost fifteen pounds and was suffering demonstrable distress and nervousness. He was upset at being cut off from his culture and people for the first time in his life. In addition, he was distressed at being incarcerated and fearful for his safety. More importantly, he was worried he would become defiled or *marime*. A major concern of his was that if he ate food prepared by non-Gypsies who did not follow rules of cleanliness considered essential in the Gypsy culture, he would become *marime,* a condition of ritual impurity that would result in his being shunned by his relatives and other Gypsies. To protect himself, he avoided eating prison food in the hopes that when he was released from prison he would be able to return to his family without a period of physical exile, also called *marime* (or "rejected" as the Gypsies translate it into English). I arranged for his lawyer to provide him with money to buy food from the concession because it is packaged and untouched by non-Gypsies and therefore considered clean by Gypsy standards. He bought milk in cartons, candy bars and soft drinks and other packaged foods that, though they may lack in nutrition, at least were not defiling and kept him from starvation.

A further complicating factor for S.N. was that he spoke English as a second language. He had only a rudimentary ability to read, thus straining his grasp of his defense. And his only contact with relatives was by telephone since neither he nor they could write with any ease. Even though his limited English made it difficult for him to follow his own trial, the court did not provide a translator.

## The Trial

The trial was held in Federal Court and centered around the constitutionality of a law that unfairly targets a particular ethnic group and the question of intent to commit a crime. My testimony was intended to establish that Gypsies may use false identification for a number of cultural reasons which may have no connection to any intent to commit a crime. For a traditionally nomadic group with pariah status in the wider society and a pattern of secretiveness and autonomy, concealing identity is a long-established pattern.

This pattern is widespread in all Gypsy groups in Eastern Europe, Western Europe, Russia, Latin America and the United States. It is a mechanism they have developed over centuries to protect themselves from a wider society that has persecuted them or driven them away. The recent case of the German government paying large sums to Romania to take back Gypsy refugees is only the latest in a historically established tradition of discrimination against Gypsies. The persecution of Gypsies in the Holocaust, in medieval Europe and in the early part of the 20th century in the United States has been well documented. Current events in Eastern Europe have shown a resurgence of extreme prejudice against Gypsies. Interviews in recent *New York Times* articles have pointed to a hatred of Gypsies so deep that there is talk of extermination.[2] Because of the history of violence against them, Gypsies have developed elaborate mechanisms of secrecy and have hidden their identity in order to survive. It will

[2] See *New York Times,* November 17 and 28, 1993, for recent accounts of extreme prejudice against Gypsies.

not be easy to get them to change this pattern that has stood them in good stead for so many centuries.

The purpose of my testimony was to establish that S.N. *was* a Gypsy and that Gypsies often use false identification without intent to defraud. They do so because as members of a *vitsa,* or cognatic descent group, identification is corporate in nature. Members of the group have corporate access to property owned by other members of the group. That property includes forms of identification.

An additional problem in the S.N. case was the question of identification from photographs. Here we encountered the age-old problem that members of one culture and race have trouble identifying individuals from another culture and race. In simple terms, to many non-Gypsies, all Gypsies look alike. Part of the case involved clearing up erroneous identification of S.N. in photos provided by the prosecution.

I was also asked to testify on my own personal experience with discrimination against Gypsies by the Minneapolis Police Department. One instance of discrimination I related to the court occurred during a talk I gave to some twenty police officers to help them understand Gypsy culture. When I had spoken about the strong sense of family and community among the Gypsies and how much they value their children, a police officer suggested that since the main problem law enforcement officers have is how to detain the Gypsies long enough to prosecute them, removing Gypsy children from their homes on any pretext would be an effective way to keep the parents in town.

Prejudice against Gypsies often goes unrecognized even by culturally and racially sensitive people. The assistant district attorney prosecuting S.N. offered me an article that he used to understand the Gypsies, entitled "Gypsies, the People and their Criminal Propensity,"[3] which quotes extensively from my work, including the fact that Gypsies have several names and that the same or similar non-Gypsy names are used over and over. The article concentrates on "criminal" behavior and never mentions the possibility that there are Gypsies who may not engage in criminal activities. In one section, quotations from my book on the ways Gypsies deal with the welfare bureaucracy were placed under the title, "Welfare Fraud," although by far most of the practices I described were legal. These concluding words in Part II are representative of the tone of the article:

> Officers should not be misled into thinking these people are not organized. They are indeed organized and operate under established rules of behavior, including those that govern marriage, living quarters, child rearing, the division of money and participation in criminal acts.

The implication of such statements is inflammatory. Gypsies have a culture, history, language and social structure, but that fact is distorted to imply that their

[3] Terry Getsay, *Kansas State FOP Journal,* Parts I, II, and III (1982): 18–30.

social organization is partly for the purpose of facilitating criminal behavior. Their culture is viewed as a criminal culture. Gypsies have been fighting this view for hundreds of years. It is the view that they still combat in their relations with law enforcement and the criminal justice system. It is the view that was promoted by the prosecution in this case.

In spite of the best efforts of S.N.'s attorney and my testimony that use of a false social security number did not necessarily indicate intent to commit a crime, he was convicted of illegally using a social security number and served about six months in jail.

## Conclusions: Anthropology and Cultural Differences in the Courtroom

Anthropologists are often called in as expert witnesses in cases involving cultural difference. Most Native American legal cases, such as the *Mashpee* case reported by James Clifford,[4] center around Indian status, treaties and land rights. In St. Paul, a number of Hmong legal cases highlighted the conflict between traditional marriage (specifically, the age at which children may marry) and the legal status of minors in American law. With the Gypsies, there is yet another set of cultural issues in their contact with American law.

First is the question of the cultural conflict between a historically nomadic group and the state bureaucracy of settled people. Identification—a serious legal issue in a bureaucratic society composed of people with fixed abodes and a written language—has virtually no meaning for the nomadic Gypsies who consider descent and extended family ties the defining factor for identification.

Second is the conflict between Gypsy religious rules regarding ritual pollution and prison regulations. The Gypsies avoid situations, such as a job or jail, that require them to be in prolonged contact with non-Gypsies. Jail presents special problems because the Gypsies can become *marime,* that is, defiled by unclean food and living conditions. The psychological trauma that results from isolation from their community is compounded if they then emerge from jail and have to undergo a further isolation from relatives because of becoming *marime* in jail.

Finally, this case illustrates a cultural clash between the Rom Gypsy value on corporate kinship and the American value on individual rights. The rights and status of an individual Rom Gypsy is directly linked to his or her membership in the *vitsa*. Furthermore, the status of all members of the *vitsa* is affected by the behavior of each individual *vitsa* member. Since they are so intricately linked, reciprocity between *vitsi* members is expected. Members of a *vitsa* and

---

[4] "Identity in Mashpee," in *The Predicament of Culture* (Cambridge: Harvard University Press, 1988), pp. 277–346.

family share economic resources, stay in each other's homes, help each other in work and preparation of rituals, loan each other cars, information, identification, and money. They also share the shame of immoral or incorrect behavior by one member and the stigma (*marime*) attached to going to jail. For the Gypsies, the American ideal of each individual having only one name, one social security number, or a reputation based entirely on their own behavior is contrary to their experience and culture.

The analysis of an event such as a trial, especially an event that brings to the fore cultural difference, can be instructive for both cultures. In this article I have tried to present fundamental differences in the practices of American culture and U.S. law and the practices of Roma law and Gypsy culture. Understanding difference does not necessarily resolve conflict, but it can lead to a more humanitarian application of the law to different cultures. The United States, a country based on immigration and diversity, is in no position to ignore the cultural foundations of different ethnic groups, nor are different cultures in the United States exempt from a law because it is contrary to custom. However, the more aware the legal system is of cultural histories and custom, the greater its capacity for justice.

S.N. chose to pursue his case through the U.S. legal system. He made this choice partly because of the influence and advice of a brother who was married to an American lawyer. The rest of his family strongly opposed this decision, preferring to do it the way they always have, by fleeing or lying to avoid contact with the legal system. While he was in jail, the Gypsies in his community held a *Kris* (formal meeting) to explain his decision to work through the American courts rather than the traditional Gypsy way and to raise money for his defense. The outcome of that trial was that on his release S.N., as well as his brother and brother's wife, who was his lawyer, were "rejected" (*marime*) and totally ostracized by his family. At the same time, the conditions of his probation stipulated that S.N. could not associate with his family, and he was released early into the custody of his brother and his brother's wife. Ironically, in the end, both U.S. and Roma law were in agreement on the consequences of his "crime" but for opposite reasons. The American legal system viewed S.N.'s family as "criminal associates"; his family, on the other hand, viewed S.N. and his brother as *marime* for rejecting Gypsy culture. Nevertheless, the strength of Gypsy culture has always been its ability to keep its closely knit ties, and today S.N. and his brother are back in the bosom of the family.

As the world changes into the next millennium, more people than ever before in human history are on the move as migrants, immigrants, guest workers, refugees and even as tourists. At this time in history, many people are living in places that do not share their cultural and legal traditions. Studies of society and legal systems must search for ways to deal with this cultural encounter. Gypsies have probably the longest recorded history of continuous movement and adaptation to other societies and cultures. Their treatment is a barometer of justice and civilization.

# Review Questions

1. What aspect of the "crime" committed by a young Gypsy man is due to cross-cultural difference, according to Sutherland?

2. How did the police interpret the lists of social security numbers and other evidence found in the young man's apartment? How did their interpretation of this evidence differ from the Gypsy's?

3. How does this case illustrate the role cultural anthropologists can play in everyday American life?

4. Can you think of other cases where immigrants or culturally different people run afoul of American substantive law?

# 31

# Life without Chiefs

## Marvin Harris

*It may come as a surprise to most Americans, but there were, and in a few cases still are, societies in the world that lack formal political structure. Instead of presidents, mayors, senators, and directors of homeland security, there are headmen, big men, and chiefs who lead by their ability to persuade and impress without the authority to* make *people act. In this article, Marvin Harris traces the evolution of political leadership, associating* headmen *with small hunting and gathering societies marked by reciprocal exchange, and* big men *with slightly larger horticultural societies that employ redistributive exchange. Chiefs also occupied the center of redistribution systems but their societies were larger and chiefs could inherit their positions. He concludes that human biological inheritance was shaped by a hunter-gatherer existence; there is nothing inherited about the political formalism and social inequality that characterize large state societies.*

Can humans exist without some people ruling and others being ruled? To look at the modern world, you wouldn't think so. Democratic states may have done away with emperors and kings, but they have hardly dispensed with gross inequalities in wealth, rank, and power.

However, humanity hasn't always lived this way. For about 98 percent of our existence as a species (and for four million years before then), our ancestors lived in small, largely nomadic hunting-and-gathering bands containing about 30 to 50 people apiece. It was in this social context that human nature evolved. It has been only about ten thousand years since people began to settle down into villages, some of which eventually grew into cities. And it has been only in the last two thousand years that the majority of people in the world have not lived in hunting-and-gathering societies. This brief period of time is not nearly sufficient for noticeable evolution to have taken place. Thus, the few remaining foraging societies are the closest analogues we have to the "natural" state of humanity.

To judge from surviving examples of hunting-and-gathering bands and villages, our kind got along quite well for the greater part of prehistory without so much as a paramount chief. In fact, for tens of thousands of years, life went on without kings, queens, prime ministers, presidents, parliaments, congresses, cabinets, governors, and mayors—not to mention the police officers, sheriffs, marshals, generals, lawyers, bailiffs, judges, district attorneys, court clerks, patrol cars, paddy wagons, jails, and penitentiaries that help keep them in power. How in the world did our ancestors ever manage to leave home without them?

Small populations provide part of the answer. With 50 people per band or 150 per village, everybody knew everybody else intimately. People gave with the expectation of taking and took with the expectation of giving. Because chance played a great role in the capture of animals, collection of wild foodstuffs, and success of rudimentary forms of agriculture, the individuals who had the luck of the catch on one day needed a handout on the next. So the best way for them to provide for their inevitable rainy day was to be generous. As expressed by anthropologist Richard Gould, "The greater the amount of risk, the greater the extent of sharing." Reciprocity is a small society's bank.

In reciprocal exchange, people do not specify how much or exactly what they expect to get back or when they expect to get it. That would besmirch the quality of that transaction and make it similar to mere barter or to buying and selling. The distinction lingers on in societies dominated by other forms of exchange, even capitalist ones. For we do carry out a give-and-take among close kin and friends that is informal, uncalculating, and imbued with a spirit of generosity. Teen-agers do not pay cash for their meals at home or for the use of the family car, wives do not bill their husbands for cooking a meal, and friends give each other birthday gifts and Christmas presents. But much of this is marred by the expectation that our generosity will be acknowledged with expression of thanks.

Where reciprocity really prevails in daily life, etiquette requires that generosity be taken for granted. As Robert Dentan discovered during his field-work among the Semai of Central Malaysia, no one ever says "thank you" for the meat

received from another hunter. Having struggled all day to lug the carcass of a
pig home through the jungle heat, the hunter allows his prize to be cut up into
exactly equal portions, which he then gives away to the entire group. Dentan
explains that to express gratitude for the portion received indicates that you are
the kind of ungenerous person who calculates how much you give and take: "In
this context, saying 'thank you' is very rude, for it suggests, first, that one has
calculated the amount of a gift and, second, that one did not expect the donor
to be so generous." To call attention to one's generosity is to indicate that others are in debt to you and that you expect them to repay you. It is repugnant to
egalitarian peoples even to suggest that they have been treated generously.

Canadian anthropologist Richard Lee tells how, through a revealing incident, he learned about this aspect of reciprocity. To please the !Kung, the "bushmen" of the Kalahari desert, he decided to buy a large ox and have it slaughtered
as a present. After days of searching Bantu agricultural villages for the largest
and fattest ox in the region, he acquired what appeared to be a perfect speci-
men. But his friends took him aside and assured him that he had been duped
into buying an absolutely worthless animal. "Of course, we will eat it," they said,
"but it won't fill us up—we will eat and go home to bed with stomachs rumbling." Yet, when Lee's ox was slaughtered, it turned out to be covered with a
thick layer of fat. Later, his friends explained why they had said his gift was val-
ueless, even though they knew better than he what lay under the animal's skin:

"Yes, when a young man kills much meat he comes to think of himself as
a chief or a big man, and he thinks of the rest of us as his servants or inferiors.
We can't accept this. We refuse one who boasts, for someday his pride will make
him kill somebody. So we always speak of his meat as worthless. This way we
cool his heart and make him gentle."

Lee watched small groups of men and women returning home every
evening with the animals and wild fruits and plants that they had killed or collected. They shared everything equally, even with campmates who had stayed
behind and spent the day sleeping or taking care of their tools and weapons.

"Not only do families pool that day's production, but the entire camp—
residents and visitors alike—shares equally in the total quantity of food available," Lee observed. "The evening meal of any one family is made up of portions
of food from each of the other families resident. There is a constant flow of nuts,
berries, roots, and melons from one family fire-place to another, until each person has received an equitable portion. The following morning a different combination of foragers moves out of camp, and when they return late in the day,
the distribution of foodstuffs is repeated."

In small, prestate societies, it was in everybody's best interest to maintain
each other's freedom of access to the natural habitat. Suppose a !Kung with a
lust for power were to get up and tell his campmates, "From now on, all this
land and everything on it belongs to me. I'll let you use it but only with my permission and on the condition that I get first choice of anything you capture, collect, or grow." His campmates, thinking that he had certainly gone crazy, would
pack up their few belongings, take a long walk, make a new camp, and resume

their usual life of egalitarian reciprocity. The man who would be king would be left by himself to exercise a useless sovereignty.

## The Headman: Leadership, Not Power

To the extent that political leadership exists at all among band-and-village societies, it is exercised by individuals called headmen. These headmen, however, lack the power to compel others to obey their orders. How can a leader be powerless and still lead?

The political power of genuine rulers depends on their ability to expel or exterminate disobedient individuals and groups. When a headman gives a command, however, he has no certain physical means of punishing those who disobey. So, if he wants to stay in "office," he gives few commands. Among the Eskimo, for instance, a group will follow an outstanding hunter and defer to his opinion with respect to choice of hunting spots. But in all other matters, the leader's opinion carries no more weight than any other man's. Similarly, among the !Kung, each band has its recognized leaders, most of whom are males. These men speak out more than others and are listened to with a bit more deference. But they have no formal authority and can only persuade, never command. When Lee asked the !Kung whether they had headmen—meaning powerful chiefs—they told him, "Of course we have headmen! In fact, we are all headmen. Each one of us is headman over himself."

Headmanship can be a frustrating and irksome job. Among Indian groups such as the Mehinacu of Brazil's Zingu National Park, headmen behave something like zealous scoutmasters on overnight cookouts. The first one up in the morning, the headman tries to rouse his companions by standing in the middle of the village plaza and shouting to them. If something needs to be done, it is the headman who starts doing it, and it is the headman who works harder than anyone else. He sets an example not only for hard work but also for generosity: After a fishing or hunting expedition, he gives away more of his catch than anyone else does. In trading with other groups, he must be careful not to keep the best items for himself.

In the evening, the headman stands in the center of the plaza and exhorts his people to be good. He calls upon them to control their sexual appetites, work hard in their gardens, and take frequent baths in the river. He tells them not to sleep during the day or bear grudges against each other.

## Coping with Freeloaders

During the reign of reciprocal exchange and egalitarian headmen, no individual, family, or group smaller than the band or village itself could control access to natural resources. Rivers, lakes, beaches, oceans, plants and animals, the soil and subsoil were all communal property.

Among the !Kung, a core of people born in a particular territory say that they "own" the water holes and hunting rights, but this has no effect on the people who happen to be visiting and living with them at any given time. Since !Kung from neighboring bands are related through marriage, they often visit each other for months at a time and have free use of whatever resources they need without having to ask permission. Though people from distant bands must make a request to use another band's territory, the "owners" seldom refuse them.

The absence of private possession in land and other vital resources means that a form of communism probably existed among prehistoric hunting and collecting bands and small villages. Perhaps I should emphasize that this did not rule out the existence of private property. People in simple band-and-village societies own personal effects such as weapons, clothing, containers, ornaments, and tools. But why should anyone want to steal such objects? People who have a bush camp and move about a lot have no use for extra possessions. And since the group is small enough that everybody knows everybody else, stolen items cannot be used anonymously. If you want something, better to ask for it openly, since by the rules of reciprocity such requests cannot be denied.

I don't want to create the impression that life within egalitarian band-and-village societies unfolded entirely without disputes over possessions. As in every social group, nonconformists and malcontents tried to use the system for their own advantage. Inevitably there were freeloaders, individuals who consistently took more than they gave and lay back in their hammocks while others did the work. Despite the absence of a criminal justice system, such behavior eventually was punished. A widespread belief among band-and-village peoples attributes death and misfortune to the malevolent conspiracy of sorcerers. The task of identifying these evildoers falls to a group's shamans, who remain responsive to public opinion during their divinatory trances. Well-liked individuals who enjoy strong support from their families need not fear the shaman. But quarrelsome, stingy people who do not give as well as take had better watch out.

## From Headman to Big Man

Reciprocity was not the only form of exchange practiced by egalitarian band-and-village peoples. Our kind long ago found other ways to give and take. Among them the form of exchange known as redistribution played a crucial role in creating distinctions of rank during the evolution of chiefdoms and states.

Redistribution occurs when people turn over food and other valuables to a prestigious figure such as a headman, to be pooled, divided into separate portions, and given out again. The primordial form of redistribution was probably keyed to seasonal hunts and harvests, when more food than usual became available.

True to their calling, headmen-redistributors not only work harder than their followers but also give more generously and reserve smaller and less desirable portions for themselves than for anyone else. Initially, therefore, re-distribution strictly reinforced the political and economic equality associated with reciprocal exchange. The redistributors were compensated purely with admiration and in proportion to their success in giving bigger feasts, in per-sonally contributing more than anybody else, and in asking little or nothing for their effort, all of which initially seemed an innocent extension of the basic principle of reciprocity.

But how little our ancestors understood what they were getting themselves into! For if it is a good thing to have a headman give feasts, why not have sev-eral headmen give feasts? Or, better yet, why not let success in organizing and giving feasts be the measure of one's legitimacy as a headman? Soon, where conditions permit, there are several would-be headmen vying with each other to hold the most lavish feasts and redistribute the most food and other valu-ables. In this fashion there evolved the nemesis that Richard Lee's !Kung infor-mants had warned about: the youth who wants to be a "big man."

A classic anthropological study of big men was carried out by Douglas Oliver among the Siuai, a village people who live on the South Pacific island of Bougainville, in the Solomon Islands. In the Siuai language, big men were known as *mumis*. Every Siuai boy's highest ambition was to become a *mumi*. He began by getting married, working hard, and restricting his own consump-tion of meats and coconuts. His wife and parents, impressed with the serious-ness of his intentions, vowed to help him prepare for his first feast. Soon his circle of supporters widened and he began to construct a clubhouse in which his male followers could lounge about and guests could be entertained and fed. He gave a feast at the consecration of the clubhouse; if this was a success, the circle of people willing to work for him grew larger still, and he began to hear himself spoken of as a mumi. Larger and larger feasts meant that the mumi's demands on his supporters became more irksome. Although they grumbled about how hard they had to work, they remained loyal as long as their mumi continued to maintain and increase his renown as a "great provider."

Finally the time came for the new mumi to challenge the older ones. He did this at a *muminai* feast, where both sides kept a tally of all the pigs, coconut pies, and sago-almond puddings given away by the host mumi and his follow-ers to the guest mumi and his followers. If the guests could not reciprocate with a feast as lavish as that of the challengers, their mumi suffered a great social humiliation, and his fall from mumihood was immediate.

At the end of a successful feast, the greatest of mumis still faced a lifetime of personal toil and dependence on the moods and inclinations of his follow-ers. Mumihood did not confer the power to coerce others into doing one's bid-ding, nor did it elevate one's standard of living above anyone else's. In fact, because giving things away was the essence of mumihood, great mumis con-sumed less meat and other delicacies than ordinary men. Among the Kaoka, an-other Solomon Islands group, there is the saying, "The giver of the feast takes the bones and the stale cakes; the meat and the fat go to the others." At one great feast attended by 1,100 people, the host mumi, whose name was Soni, gave away thirty-two pigs and a large quantity of sago-almond puddings. Soni himself and some of his closest followers went hungry. "We shall eat Soni's renown," they said.

## From Big Man to Chief

The slide (or ascent?) toward social stratification gained momentum wherever extra food produced by the inspired diligence of redistributors could be stored while awaiting muminai feasts, potlatches, and other occasions of redistribution. The more concentrated and abundant the harvest and the less perishable the crop, the greater its potential for endowing the big man with power. Though others would possess some stored-up foods of their own, the redistributor's stores would be the largest. In times of scarcity, people would come to him, expecting to be fed; in return, he could call upon those who had special skills to make cloth, pots, canoes, or a fine house for his own use. Eventually, the redistributor no longer needed to work in the fields to gain and surpass bigman status. Management of the harvest surpluses, a portion of which continued to be given to him for use in communal feasts and other communal projects (such as trading expeditions and warfare), was sufficient to validate his status. And, increasingly, people viewed this status as an office, a sacred trust, passed on from one generation to the next according to the rules of hereditary succession. His dominion was no longer a small, autonomous village but a large political community. The big man had become a chief.

Returning to the South Pacific and the Trobriand Islands, one can catch a glimpse of how these pieces of encroaching stratification fell into place. The Trobrianders had hereditary chiefs who held sway over more than a dozen villages containing several thousand people. Only chiefs could wear certain shell ornaments as the insignia of high rank, and it was forbidden for commoners to stand or sit in a position that put a chief's head at a lower elevation. British anthropologist Bronislaw Malinowski tells of seeing all the people present in the village of Bwoytalu drop from their verandas "as if blown down by a hurricane" at the sound of a drawn-out cry warning that an important chief was approaching.

Yams were the Trobrianders' staff of life; the chiefs validated their status by storing and redistributing copious quantities of them acquired through donations from their brothers-in-law at harvest time. Similar "gifts" were received by husbands who were commoners, but chiefs were polygymous and, having as many as a dozen wives, received many more yams than anyone else. Chiefs placed their yam supply on display racks specifically built for this purpose next to their houses. Commoners did the same, but a chief's yam racks towered over all the others.

This same pattern recurs, with minor variations, on several continents. Striking parallels were seen, for example, twelve thousand miles away from the Trobrianders, among chiefdoms that flourished throughout the southeastern region of the United States—specifically among the Cherokee, former inhabitants of Tennessee, as described by the eighteenth-century naturalist William Bartram.

At the center of the principal Cherokee settlements stood a large circular house where a council of chiefs discussed issues involving their villages and where redistributive feasts were held. The council of chiefs had a paramount who was the principal figure in the Cherokee redistributive network. At the harvest time a large crib, identified as the "chief's granary," was erected in each field. "To this," explained Bartram, "each family carries and deposits a certain quantity according to his ability or inclination, or none at all if he so chooses." The chief's granaries functioned as a public treasury in case of crop failure, a source of food for strangers or travelers, and as military store. Although every citizen enjoyed free access to the store, commoners had to acknowledge that it really belonged to the supreme chief, who had "an exclusive right and ability . . . to distribute comfort and blessings to the necessitous."

Supported by voluntary donations, chiefs could now enjoy lifestyles that set them increasingly apart from their followers. They could build bigger and finer houses for themselves, eat and dress more sumptuously, and enjoy the sexual favors and personal services of several wives. Despite these harbingers, people in chiefdoms voluntarily invested unprecedented amounts of labor on behalf of communal projects. They dug moats, threw up defensive earthen embankments, and erected great log palisades around their villages. They heaped up small mountains of rubble and soil to form platforms and mounds on top of which they built temples and big houses for their chief. Working in teams and using nothing but levers and rollers, they moved rocks weighing fifty tons or more and set them in precise lines and perfect circles, forming sacred precincts for communal rituals marking the change of seasons.

If this seems remarkable, remember that donated labor created the megalithic alignments of Stonehenge and Carnac, put up the great statues on Easter Island, shaped the huge stone heads of the Olmec in Vera Cruz, dotted Polynesia with ritual precincts set on great stone platforms, and filled the Ohio, Tennessee, and Mississippi valleys with hundreds of large mounds. Not until it was too late did people realize that their beautiful chiefs were about to keep the meat and fat for themselves while giving nothing but bones and stale cakes to their followers.

## In the End

As we know, chiefdoms would eventually evolve into states, states into empires. From peaceful origins, humans created and mounted a wild beast that ate continents. Now that beast has taken us to the brink of global annihilation.

Will nature's experiment with mind and culture end in nuclear war? No one knows the answer. But I believe it is essential that we understand our past before we can create the best possible future. Once we are clear about the roots of human nature, for example, we can refute, once and for all, the notion that it is a biological imperative for our kind to form hierarchical groups. An observer viewing human life shortly after cultural takeoff would easily have concluded that our species was destined to be irredeemably egalitarian except for distinctions of sex and age. That someday the world would be divided into aristocrats and commoners, masters and slaves, billionaires and homeless beggars would have seemed wholly contrary to human nature as evidenced in the affairs of every human society then on Earth.

Of course, we can no more reverse the course of thousands of years of cultural evolution than our egalitarian ancestors could have designed and built the space shuttle. Yet, in striving for the preservation of mind and culture on Earth, it is vital that we recognize the significance of cultural takeoff and the great difference between biological and cultural evolution. We must rid ourselves of the notion that we are an innately aggressive species for whom war is inevitable. We must reject as unscientific claims that there are superior and inferior races and that the hierarchical divisions within and between societies are the consequences of natural selection rather than of a long process of cultural evolution. We must struggle to gain control over cultural selection through objective studies of the human condition and the recurrent process of history. Not only a more just society, but our very survival as a species may depend on it.

# Review Questions

1. What is the difference among headmen, big men, and chiefs according to Harris?

2. What does Harris see as the connection between forms of leadership and modes of economic exchange? How does this connection work?

3. Harris makes a distinction between biological evolution and cultural evolution. What is the distinction and how does he apply it to types of leadership?

# EIGHT

# Religion, Magic,
# and Worldview

$P$eople seem most content when they are confident about themselves and the order of things around them. Uncertainty breeds debilitating anxiety; insecurity saps people's sense of purpose and their willingness to participate in social activity. Most of the time cultural institutions serve as a lens through which to view and interpret the world and respond realistically to its demands. But from time to time the unexpected or contradictory intervenes to shake people's assurance. A farmer may wonder about his skill when a properly planted and tended crop fails to grow. A wife may feel bewildered when the man she has treated with tenderness and justice for many years runs off with another woman. Death, natural disaster, and countless other forms of adversity strike without warning, eating away at the foundations of confidence. At these crucial points in life, many people use religion to help account for the vagaries of their experience.

**Religion** is the cultural knowledge of the supernatural that people use to cope with the ultimate problems of human existence.[1] In this definition, the term **supernatural** refers to a realm beyond normal experience. Belief in gods, spirits, ghosts, and magical power often defines the supernatural, but the matter is complicated by cultural variation and the lack of a clear distinction in many societies between the natural and the supernatural world. **Ultimate problems,** on the other hand, emerge from universal features of human life and include life's meaning, death, evil, and transcendent values. People everywhere wonder why they are alive, why they must die, and why evil strikes some individuals and not others. In every society, people's personal desires and goals may conflict with the values of the larger group. Religion often provides a set of **transcendent values** that override differences and unify the group.

[1] This definition draws on the work of Milton Yinger, *Religion, Society, and the Individual: An Introduction to the Sociology of Religion* (New York: Macmillan, 1957).

## READINGS IN THIS SECTION

An aspect of religion that is more difficult to comprehend is its link to emotion. Ultimate problems "are more appropriately seen as deep-seated emotional needs," not as conscious, rational constructs, according to sociologist Milton Yinger.[2] Anthropologists may describe and analyze religious ritual and belief but find it harder to get at religion's deeper meanings and personal feelings.

Anthropologists have identified two kinds of supernatural power: personified and impersonal. **Personified supernatural force** resides in supernatural beings, in the deities, ghosts, ancestors, and other beings found in the divine world. For the Bhils of India, a *bhut,* or ghost, has the power to cause skin lesions and wasting diseases. *Bhagwan,* the equivalent of the Christian deity, controls the universe. Both possess and use personified supernatural force.

Impersonal supernatural force is a more difficult concept to grasp. Often called **mana,** the term used in Polynesian and Melanesian belief, it represents a kind of free-floating force lodged in many things and places. The concept is akin to the Western term *luck* and works like an electrical charge that can be introduced into things or discharged from them. Melanesians, for example, might attribute the spectacular growth of yams to some rocks lying in the fields. The rocks possess mana, which is increasing fertility. If yams fail to grow in subsequent years, they may feel that the stones have lost their power.

Supernatural force, both personified and impersonal, may be used by people in many societies. **Magic** refers to the strategies people use to control supernatural power. Magicians have clear ends in mind when they perform magic, and use a set of well-defined procedures to control and manipulate supernatural forces. For example, a Trobriand Island religious specialist will ensure a sunny day for a political event by repeating powerful sayings thought to affect the weather.

**Sorcery** uses magic to cause harm. For example, some Bhil *bhopas,* who regularly use magic for positive purposes, may also be hired to work revenge. They will recite powerful *mantras* (ritual sayings) over effigies to cause harm to their victims.

**Witchcraft** is closely related to sorcery because both use supernatural force to cause evil. But many anthropologists use the term to designate envious individuals who are born with or acquire evil power and who knowingly or unknowingly project it to hurt others. The Azande of Africa believe that most unfortunate events are due to witchcraft, and most Azande witches claim they were unaware of their power and apologize for its use.

Most religions possess ways to influence supernatural power or, if spirits are nearby, to communicate with it directly. For example, people may say **prayers** to petition supernatural beings. They may also give gifts in the form of **sacrifices** and offerings. Direct communication takes different forms. **Spirit possession** occurs when a supernatural being enters and controls the behavior of a human being. With the spirit in possession, others may talk directly with someone from the divine world. **Divination** is a second way to communicate

---

[2] Yinger, p. 9.

with the supernatural. It usually requires material objects or animals to provide answers to human-directed questions. The Bhils of India, for example, predict the abundance of summer rainfall by watching where a small bird specially caught for the purpose lands when it is released. If it settles on something green, rainfall will be plentiful; if it rests on something brown, the year will be dry.

Almost all religions involve people with special knowledge who either control supernatural power outright or facilitate others in their attempt to influence it. **Shamans** are religious specialists who directly control supernatural power. They may have personal relationships with spiritual beings or know powerful secret medicines and sayings. They are usually associated with curing. **Priests** are religious specialists who mediate between people and supernatural beings. They don't control divine power; instead, they lead congregations in ceremonies and help others petition the gods.

**Worldview** refers to a system of concepts and often unstated assumptions about life. It usually contains a **cosmology** about the way things are and a **mythology** about how things have come to be. Worldview presents answers to the ultimate questions: life, death, evil, and conflicting values.

Finally, anthropologists also study and report on the formation of new religions, especially those that occur as a result of deprivation and stress. These **revitalization movements,** as Anthony F. C. Wallace called them in 1956, are "deliberate, organized, conscious efforts by members of a society to construct a more satisfying culture."[3] Revitalization movements are usually related to rapid change that renders a traditional way of life ineffective. For example, when one cultural group becomes dominated by another, rapid change and loss of authority may make its original meaning system seem thin, ineffective, and contradictory. The resulting state of deprivation often causes members to rebuild their culture along what they consider to be more satisfying lines.

Wallace argued that revitalization movements go through five stages:

1. *A Steady State.* This is a normal state of society in which people, through their culture, are able to manage the chronic stresses of daily life.

2. *Period of Increased Individual Stress.* Individuals in a society experience new stress caused by such events as culture contact, defeat in war, political domination, or climatic change.

3. *Period of Cultural Distortion.* Stress levels continue to rise as normal stress-reducing techniques fail to work. Social organization begins to break down, causing additional stress, and various cultural elements become distorted and disjointed.

4. *Period of Revitalization.* This period is marked by its own stages. First, a prophet or leader comes forward with a new vision of the culture that

[3]Anthony F. C. Wallace, "Revitalization Movements: Some Theoretical Considerations for Their Comparative Study," *American Anthropologist* 58, no. 2 (1956): 264–281.

requires change. Called a *mazeway reformulation,* this vision is intended to produce a more integrated, satisfying, and adaptive culture. This is followed by the *communication* of the revitalization plan and, if it proves attractive, the plan's *organization* for wider dissemination, its *adoption* by many people, its *cultural transformation* of the society, and its *routinization* in daily life.

5. *A New Steady State.* If no additional stresses occur, the society should attain a new steady state at the end of the process.

Although not all revitalization movements are religious—the Marxist doctrine and communist revolution in Russia exemplify a political revitalization movement—most of the world's major religions probably started as revitalization movements and many smaller sects and movements fit the revitalization pattern today.

The first article, by Stanley Freed and Ruth Freed, describes how Sita, a low-caste Indian woman, is chronically possessed by the ghost of a friend who committed suicide. Stressed by the prospect of sexual relations with a new and strange husband, lack of support in her conjugal household, and the deaths of many friends and family members, ghost possession, argue the Freeds, reduces Sita's anxiety and gives her needed family support. The second article, by George Gmelch, is the latest revision of his earlier classic piece on the use of magic by American baseball players. He looks in detail at the rituals, taboos, and fetishes employed by the athletes. In the third selection, Charlanne Burke shows how beliefs in witchcraft among the Batswana have survived through time to explain causes of misfortune in the present. Focusing especially on youth, she describes the nature of Tswana witchcraft and its causes and cures. The final article, by Stephen Leavitt, analyzes a revitalization movement, the cargo cults and beliefs of New Guinea peoples. Noting that cargo movements originated as a response to changes and loss of power engendered by colonial control, he shows that cargo beliefs also connect people to their recently dead ancestors.

# Key Terms

cosmology  *p. 339*
divination  *p. 338*
magic  *p. 338*
mana  *p. 338*
mythology  *p. 339*
personified supernatural
    force  *p. 338*
prayer  *p. 338*
priest  *p. 339*
religion  *p. 337*

revitalization movement  *p. 339*
sacrifice  *p. 338*
shaman  *p. 339*
sorcery  *p. 338*
spirit possession  *p. 338*
supernatural  *p. 337*
transcendent values  *p. 337*
ultimate problems  *p. 337*
witchcraft  *p. 338*
worldview  *p. 339*

# 32

# Taraka's Ghost

## Stanley A. Freed and Ruth S. Freed

*Most people meet life's challenges by using an array of normal, and often ef-*
*fective, cultural responses. U.S. traffic is dangerous, for example, but we use*
*driving skills we have learned to survive with confidence on the road. But*
*some circumstances fall beyond our everyday abilities. We exercise and eat*
*properly, but still may unexpectedly become ill. We work diligently and skill-*
*fully at our jobs, yet fail to be promoted. Many anthropologists see a rela-*
*tionship between religion and the anxieties that are caused by stressful and*
*seemingly unmanageable aspects of life. In this article, Stanley Freed and*
*Ruth Freed describe such an association. They report that a low-caste girl,*
*Sita, is possessed by Taraka, the ghost of a childhood friend who committed*
*suicide. Sita is stressed by the need to have sex with a new husband, the lack*
*of support that meets a bride in her husband's household, and the deaths of*
*three friends and several brothers and sisters. Ghost possession reduces her*
*anxiety and gains her the support of her natal and conjugal families.*

When we saw our first ghost possession in a North Indian village, on a hot September day in the late 1950s, we were struck by the villagers' matter-of-fact response to what seemed an extraordinary event. We were seated with a group of low-caste villagers who were softly chatting in front of a mud hut. Sita, a newly married fifteen-year-old girl, was sitting on the ground, and, conforming to the proper behavior of a bride, she was inconspicuous and silent. Still wearing her bridal finery, her face veiled below the eyes, she worked her sewing machine, of which she was proud.

A man of her caste, who had recently lost his job, commented that sewing on a machine was man's work (at that time, it was mainly the province of the village tailor). The remark implied that Sita was doing something inappropriate, an insinuation to which, as a new bride, she could not respond. Moreover, the criticism struck at Sita's pride and joy, her sewing machine, which was part of her dowry. To her it was a talisman, protecting her and providing her with higher status than other brides of her caste, for she was the first to possess one.

Sita's mother-in-law, who had witnessed earlier ghost possessions of the girl, realized that the criticism had distressed Sita, and anticipating that Sita would again be possessed, the older woman abruptly began to discuss the ghost attacks that plagued the teen-ager. We couldn't imagine why the conversation had taken such a turn until Sita began to shiver, a symptom preceding possession. Despite the heat, she complained of feeling cold, so some women covered her with quilts. She moaned, breathed with difficulty, and then collapsed in a semiconscious state.

The spectators accepted that a ghost had possessed her and tried a variety of standard curing techniques. These ranged from engaging the ghost in conversation, identifying it, and trying to satisfy its wishes or demands so that it would leave voluntarily, to attempting to drive it away with verbal abuse and, if necessary, physically painful or unpleasant measures (applied to the victim but aimed at the ghost). First, the women propped Sita up in a sitting position and wafted smoke from some smoldering cow dung under her nose. She jerked violently, so they had to restrain her. Then they shouted at the ghost: "Who are you? Are you going?" The ghost, speaking through Sita, promised to leave, and the women released the girl. But they were not deluded. They suspected that the ghost would not leave permanently and that a cure would be difficult. "Ghosts don't keep their promises," they confided to us.

Sita again fell unconscious, a sign that the ghost had returned. To revive her, the women dropped stinging hookah water in her eyes and pulled her braids. Sita returned to semiconsciousness and emitted a high-pitched wail, which announced the ghost's presence and readiness to talk. There followed a conversation between the ghost (speaking through Sita) and Sita's in-laws and a few other women, in the course of which the ghost identified herself as Sita's cousin Taraka, who had committed suicide by drowning in a well. Taraka's ghost declared that she would not leave Sita. The spectators again attempted to drive out the ghost, but Sita finally relapsed into unconsciousness.

For a fortnight thereafter, Sita experienced a series of possessions, so her father-in-law called various exorcists. They used generally similar techniques, calling on their familiars—supernatural beings who served them—to assist with the cure. Among these familiars were Hanuman, the monkey god; Kalkaji, goddess of the cremation grounds, with whom ghosts are closely linked; Jahar or Guga Pir, a Hindu-Muslim saint, who cut off his maternal cousins' heads in battle and later buried himself alive; and the ghost of a conjurer from Dacca. Each curer began a session by calling on his familiars, thus reassuring Sita and her relatives as to his curing powers.

When Sita's possessions persisted, her father was notified. He brought two exorcists to collaborate in an all-night session to drive off the ghost. They first induced possession in Sita by the power of suggestion and by the hypnotic effects of chanting mantras (hymns) believed to have supernatural power and using a fire to focus her concentration. Then they tried to exorcise Taraka's ghost by verbal abuse, hitting Sita, squeezing rock salt between her fingers (which was painful), pulling her braids, and throwing bits of her hair into the fire. During the session, Sita alternated between seeing a ghost, falling into a semiconscious state while a ghost spoke through her, unconsciousness, and intermittent returns to consciousness. Sita was not cured, however, and soon thereafter left for an extended visit with her parents, who lived in another village.

During the rest of our stay in India, we came to learn more about the villagers' beliefs in ghosts and the particular circumstances that led to Sita's afflictions. In rural North India, almost all Hindus believe that the soul goes through a cycle of rebirths. Following a person's death, it becomes a ghost, lingering for thirteen days in the village cremation grounds. Villagers who adhere to the doctrines of the Arya Samaj, a reform sect of Hinduism, believe in only one God, Bhagwan, and expect his judgment after cremation. The majority of villagers, who follow a more traditional version of Hinduism with multiple supernatural beings, believe that the soul travels to the Land of the Dead, ruled by Yama, Lord of the Dead. There Yama and his scribe review the soul's past actions before deciding on its future.

The important element in what happens to the soul at death is its karma, the sum of its good and bad actions from all its past lives. After being judged, the soul may be reborn or, if the sum of its actions is unusually good, released from the cycle of rebirths to join with many other souls and the Universal Absolute, a neuter deity known also as the Ultimate Reality, the joining of all souls in one.

Many Hindus believe in an additional possibility: a soul may become a ghost that lingers, possibly for decades, haunting the places where it lived and died. These are the souls of people who die tortured, from disease, accident, suicide, or murder; who violate village norms of behavior; who die before the years allotted to them by Yama; or who never attain the satisfactions of adult life. The ghosts of persons who are murdered or commit suicide are the most malevolent and tarry longest.

Ghosts are feared because they are believed to attack the living to seize their souls. Many villagers, but not all, believe that being seized by a ghost can cause illness or death. Ghost possession is the most vivid form of attack, in which a ghost enters and speaks through its victim, who has fallen into semi-consciousness. After recovering, the victim does not remember what took place. Because people in a state of possession may attempt to commit suicide by drowning in a well or by jumping in front of a train, they are usually watched by relatives and neighbors.

There is often a relationship between a ghost and its victim. For example, we learned that Taraka was not only a cousin but also a very close friend of Sita's. Sita had lived with Taraka's family for six months. Engaged to a man of another village, Taraka had an illicit affair with a boy of her own village. Because she became pregnant, the loss of her premarital chastity could not be long concealed.

The virtue of daughters is crucial to family honor in North India, and a daughter's sexual misbehavior, if it becomes generally known, may force a father to get rid of her by inducing suicide or even by murder. Taraka's parents learned of her pregnancy and quickly arranged her wedding to her fiancé. They handed over only a small dowry, in case Taraka's in-laws, realizing she was pregnant, returned her.

When Taraka went to her husband's family to begin her marital life, her husband's parents immediately discovered that she was pregnant. Renouncing all rights to her, they returned her to her father. Despite Taraka's pleas, her father was unforgiving and told her to commit suicide. Shortly thereafter, when Taraka, Sita, and some other girls were playing, Taraka decided to leave the group and asked Sita to accompany her. Sita refused. Taraka ran from the group, went to a nearby well, jumped in, and drowned. Sita blamed herself for the suicide.

Taraka was one of Sita's three close childhood friends, all of whom she lost during the three years before her own marriage. Prior to Taraka's indiscretions and suicide, a schoolmate had been murdered by her father. She was raped by a schoolteacher, and even though the girl was the victim and the identity of the assailant was known, her father was furious and blamed her. He flew into a rage, raped and murdered her, and threw her into a well (villagers regard such crimes as family business and rarely interfere). Another of Sita's schoolmates died of typhoid and malaria, shortly after beginning sexual relations with her husband.

The episode of the untrustworthy schoolteacher worried Sita's mother, who took her daughter out of school. The abrupt end of her education was a shock to Sita, who wanted to be a schoolteacher herself. Instead, Sita and her mother went to visit her mother's brother in her mother's natal village. This was when Sita's life became entwined with Taraka's, for Taraka was this man's daughter.

In Sita's mind, the deaths of her friends were linked with mating, marriage, childbirth, and disappointed dreams of further education. This link was reinforced by other painful memories. As her parents' first-born child, Sita had lived through the deaths of four infant brothers and five infant sisters, who had died because they could not digest their mother's milk. Mother, daughter, and other villagers believed that a ghost had taken these infants' souls. (Two brothers born subsequently had survived.) With the memory of the deaths of her friends and infant siblings, the fifteen-year-old Sita went to her husband to consummate her marriage, on her second visit to her in-laws.

On the first night, Sita told her sister-in-law that she was afraid to sleep with her husband and implored her to stay with her instead. The sister-in-law did so, but when Sita awoke in the night, she found her husband sleeping beside her. They did not have sexual relations that night. The following day, Sita went to the well for water and either jumped or accidentally slipped and fell in. Fortunately, two men who were nearby threw her a rope and pulled her out. As a result of this incident, the young couple did not have sexual relations that night either, and the next day Sita returned to her parents' home.

The marriage was finally consummated on Sita's next visit to her husband, some months later. During the fourth night of sexual relations, however, Sita was possessed by Taraka's ghost, who said that Sita's husband was her husband. The statement indicated that Taraka's ghost had been with Sita at the time of Sita's wedding, which meant that both women were married to Sita's husband.

At best, a North Indian rural woman must make an extraordinary social and psychological adjustment when she marries. At an early age, she moves from her natal family, where she is loved, cherished, and indulged, to her marital family, where she is chaperoned and required to restrict her movements. She leaves her natal village to settle in the unfamiliar surroundings of her husband's village. She must adjust to her husband and his often large family, especially his parents, sisters, and brothers' wives. And in this rural society, where marriages are arranged by parents, the bride may not have even seen her husband before the wedding day (although nowadays at least some families arrange for the young couple to meet at the time of the engagement).

A married woman and her kin are regarded as social inferiors to her husband's kin. A new bride is expected to shoulder harder and more onerous household chores and farm work than the daughters in her husband's family (they too, when they marry and go to live with their husbands, will go through a similar experience). A new bride also is generally uninformed about the relation between menarche and childbirth and is apprehensive about beginning sexual relations with her husband. The social and psychological vulnerability of a bride makes her a prime candidate for attacks by ghosts. In Sita's case, with three friends who had all died before their allotted time and without issue, the ghosts were waiting in the wings. All three possessed Sita at one time or another, but Taraka's ghost was her main tormentor.

The transition from beloved and only surviving daughter to daughter-in-law was particularly stressful for Sita. Moreover, having been raised in a one caste village, she had faced little caste discrimination, but her husband's village was multicaste, and her caste was near the bottom of the hierarchy. Her fear of mating and bearing infants whose souls might be seized by ghosts was a source of stress, as were various physical ailments. These cultural, psychological, and physical stresses were preconditions for her possessions. Research by neuroscientists during the past two decades may shed light on the underlying physiological mechanism of ghost possession. Under the stress of mental or physical pain, the body produces morphinelike substances called endorphins, which relieve the pain and may trigger mental states called alternate, altered, or dissociative. Ghost possession is one such dissociative mental state.

Stress is not confined to brides or women in North India nor is ghost possession. On a return visit to the village in 1978, we recorded the cases of three young men who were troubled by ghosts. Although some of the details of the cases were different, they all involved the stresses of modern life, especially school examinations and job hunting. Education and employment are signs of economic responsibility that a girl's parents often require before entrusting their daughter to a young husband. For example, one of the young men, a 22-year-old member of the Potter caste, was desperate for a job because his wife's parents would not let their daughter come to live with him unless he found one.

The young man was possessed, according to his mother and sister, by the ghost of his mother's first husband's first wife. The belief that the ghost of a first wife will haunt her husband's next wife and children was a strong motif in village culture. In this case, the husband had subsequently passed away too, and his next wife had remarried and the children were of this marriage; but the principle was similar. Known as the Lady, this ghost had possessed the young man's older brother twenty years before under similar circumstances and was now intermittently possessing the younger man.

The young man was treated by two village exorcists. One was a high-caste Brahman. The other was the man whose remark had disturbed Sita twenty years before: unemployed at the time and subsequently saddened by the deaths of many of his infants and by his wife's long illness, he believed that the great god Shiva visited his home. Following this experience, he became an exorcist.

During our 1978 stay, we also interviewed Sita, who recounted her medical history. Now a poised, intelligent, 35-year-old woman, she recalled her early possessions, which had lasted three years until the birth of her first child. Then the possessions had become fits, which she described as follows:

> They start from the head. I feel giddy and drowsy. Then I can't see anything and everything goes dark. My legs, hands, and veins stiffen, then a pain goes to my stomach. I don't know what happens, but I have a pain in my heart, my eyes shut, and my tongue comes out. I shriek so loud that the whole village, even the Brahmans, know that I am having a fit. I have a weak heart. Whenever there is a fight in the family or elsewhere, or if I see a dead body, I have fits.

In 1978 Sita's fits were still taking place. Well acquainted with modern medicine—she went to modern hospitals for what she recognized as biological problems—she nonetheless blamed her twenty years of possessions and fits on Taraka's ghost. According to Sita, Taraka's ghost had possessed Taraka's mother, and she herself had then been infected through contact with Taraka's mother. She continued to consult indigenous curers, mainly exorcists, who drove off the ghost or gave her amulets to control it.

In the intervening years, Sita told us, her mother had given birth to three more infants who had died. The older of Sita's surviving brothers had died at age fourteen, and her grieving mother had died soon after. Sita's remaining brother became a schoolteacher with Sita's assistance, and she accompanied him and his wife on their honeymoon.

Sita's father was still alive, retired from military service. As a small child, Sita had idolized him—a soldier who traveled to other countries but came home every year for two months. The relationship persisted through the years. When she visited him every summer, free from the stress and anxiety of life in her marital family, she never had fits.

Sita detailed her pregnancies, illnesses, and operations in the years since we first met her. Pregnant nine times, she had six children born alive (one of whom died at age three), two miscarriages, and one induced abortion, prior to being sterilized in 1972. Sita's family had a history of an inability to digest milk, and her first child, a daughter, did not take Sita's milk. Sita's father arranged for Sita and her daughter to be hospitalized while the infant was fed glucose. Because of her father's influence, Sita thereafter went to hospitals for physical problems that she considered serious. She had an operation for kidney stones. She suffered from menstrual complaints and side effects from being sterilized. A constant worrier, she was badly disturbed when one of her brothers-in-law was diagnosed as having tuberculosis, for she feared that she might have it.

Nevertheless, with regard to her appearance, the maintenance of her household, and care of her children, she managed very well and, except for her fits, was in control of her life. The treatment for ghost possession and fits by exorcists and the various amulets they gave her for protection from Taraka's ghost relieved her anxiety and helped to reduce stress. They also brought her other advantages, especially support from her natal and marital families, a reduction in her workload, and permission to visit her retired father every summer. When we last saw her, Sita was the leader of the women of her family, confidently planning the education and future of her children.

# Review Questions

1. What aspects of her life make Sita a prime candidate for ghost possession in Indian society?

2. What happens to the souls of dead people according to Hindu village belief? What accounts for the presence of ghosts?

3. How did ghost possession help Sita adjust to her life as a married woman?

# 33

# Baseball Magic

## *George Gmelch*

*Americans pride themselves on their scientific approach to life and problem solving. But as George Gmelch demonstrates in this article, U.S. baseball players, much like people in many parts of the world, also turn to supernatural forces to ensure success. Following the pioneering analysis of Trobriand magic by Bronislaw Malinowski, Gmelch shows that, like Trobriand Islanders, baseball players use magic, including ritual, taboos, and fetishes, to manage the anxiety generated by unpredictable events that challenge human control.*

On each pitching day for the first three months of a winning season, Dennis Grossini, a pitcher on a Detroit Tiger farm team, arose from bed at exactly 10:00 A.M. At 1:00 P.M. he went to the nearest restaurant for two glasses of iced tea and a tuna fish sandwich. Although the afternoon was free, he changed into the sweatshirt and supporter he wore during his last winning game, and one hour before the game he chewed a wad of Beech-Nut chewing tobacco. After each pitch during the game he touched the letters on his uniform and straightened his cap after each ball. Before the start of each inning he replaced the pitcher's rosin bag next to the spot where it was the inning before. And after every inning in which he gave up a run, he washed his hands.

When asked which part of the ritual was most important, he said, "You can't really tell what's most important so it all becomes important. I'd be afraid to change anything. As long as I'm winning, I do everything the same."

Trobriand Islanders, according to anthropologist Bronislaw Malinowski, felt the same way about their fishing magic. Among the Trobrianders, fishing took two forms: in the *inner lagoon* where fish were plentiful and there was little danger, and on the *open sea* where fishing was dangerous and yields varied widely. Malinowski found that magic was not used in lagoon fishing, where men could rely solely on their knowledge and skill. But when fishing on the open sea, Trobrianders used a great deal of magical ritual to ensure safety and increase their catch.

Baseball, America's national pastime, is an arena in which players behave remarkably like Malinowski's Trobriand fishermen. To professional ballplayers, baseball is more than just a game. It is an occupation. Since their livelihoods depend on how well they perform, many use magic to try to control the chance that is built into baseball. There are three essential activities of the game—pitching, hitting, and fielding. In the first two, chance can play a surprisingly important role. The pitcher is the player least able to control the outcome of his own efforts. He may feel great and have good stuff warming up in the bullpen and then get into the game and not have it. He may make a bad pitch and see the batter miss it for a strikeout or see it hit hard but right into the hands of a fielder for an out. His best pitch may be blooped for a base hit. He may limit the opposing team to just a few hits yet lose the game, or he may give up a dozen hits but still win. And the good and bad luck don't always average out over the course of a season. Some pitchers end the season with poor won-lost records but good earned run averages, and vice versa. In 1990 Dwight Gooden gave up more runs per game than his teammate Sid Fernandez but had a won-lost record nearly twice as good. Gooden won 19 games and lost only 7, while Fernandez won only 9 games while losing 14. Both pitched for the same team—the New York Mets—which meant they had the same fielders behind them. Regardless of how well a pitcher performs, on every outing he depends not only on his own skill, but also upon the proficiency of his teammates, the ineptitude of the opposition, and luck.

Hitting, which Hall of Famer Ted Williams called the single most difficult task in the world of sports, is also full of risk and uncertainty. Unless it's a home run, no matter how well the batter hits the ball, fate determines whether it will go into a waiting glove, whistle past a fielder's diving stab, or find a gap in the outfield. The uncertainty is compounded by the low success rate of hitting: the average hitter gets only one hit in every four trips to the plate, while the very best hitters average only one hit every three trips. Fielding, as we will return to later, is the one part of baseball where chance does not play much of a role.

How does the risk and uncertainty in pitching and hitting affect players? What do they do to introduce some control over the outcomes of their performance? These are questions that I first became interested in many years ago as both a ballplayer and an anthropology student. I'd devoted much of my youth to baseball, and played professionally as first baseman in the Detroit Tiger organization in the 1960s. It was shortly after the end of one baseball season that I took an anthropology course called "Magic, Religion, and Witchcraft." As my professor described the magic practiced by a tribe in Papua New Guinea, it occurred to me that what these so-called "primitive" people did wasn't all that different from what my teammates and I had done to give ourselves luck and confidence in baseball.

The most common way players attempt to reduce chance and their feelings of uncertainty is to develop and follow a daily routine. By routine I mean a course of action which is regularly followed. Florida Marlins coach Rich Donnelly talked about the routines of his ballplayers:

> They're like trained animals. They come out here [ballpark] and everything has to be the same, they don't like anything that knocks them off their routine. Just look at the dugout and you'll see every guy sitting in the same spot every night. It's amazing, everybody in the same spot. And don't you dare take someone's seat. If a guy comes up from the minors and sits here, they'll say, 'Hey, Jim sits here, find another seat.' You watch the pitcher warm up and he'll do the same thing every time. And when you go on the road it's the same way. You got a routine and you adhere to it and you don't want anybody knocking you off it.

Routines are comforting, they bring order into a world in which players have little control. And sometimes practical elements in routines produce tangible benefits, such as helping the player to concentrate. But a lot of what players do often goes beyond mere routine and is what anthropologists define as *ritual*— prescribed behaviors in which there is no empirical connection between the means (e.g., tapping home plate three times) and the desired end (e.g., getting a base hit). Because there is no real connection between the two, rituals are not rational. Similar to rituals are the nonrational beliefs that form the basis of taboos and fetishes, which players also use to reduce chance and bring luck to their side. But first let's look closer at the ballplayers' rituals.

## Rituals

Most rituals are personal, that is, they're performed as individuals rather than as a team or group. Most are done in an unemotional manner, in much the same way as players apply pine tar to their bats to improve the grip or dab eye black on their upper cheeks to reduce the sun's glare. Baseball rituals are infinitely varied. A ballplayer may ritualize any activity—eating, dressing, driving to the ballpark—that he considers important or somehow linked to good performance. For example, White Sox pitcher Jason Bere listens to the same song on his Walkman on the days he is to pitch. Tampa's Wade Boggs eats chicken before every game (that's 162 meals of chicken per year), and he has been doing that for twelve years. Jim Leyritz eats turkey, and Dennis Grossini tuna fish. Infielder Julie Gotay always played with a cheese sandwich in his back pocket (he had a big appetite, so there might also have been a measure of practicality here). San Francisco Giant pitcher Ron Bryant added a new stick of bubble gum to the collection in his bulging back pocket after each game he won. Jim Ohms put another penny in the pouch of his supporter after each win. Clanging against the hard plastic genital cup, the pennies made an audible sound as he ran the bases toward the end of a winning season.

Many hitters go through a series of preparatory rituals before stepping into the batter's box. These include tugging on their caps, touching their uniform letters or medallions, crossing themselves, tapping or bouncing the bat on the plate, or swinging the weighted warm-up bat a prescribed number of times. Red Sox shortstop Nomar Garciaparra tightens his batting gloves and pounds the toes of his shoes into the earth several times before each pitch. Mike Hargrove, former Cleveland Indian first baseman, had a dozen elements in his batting ritual, from grabbing his belt to pushing his helmet down tight. And after each pitch he would step out of the batter's box and repeat the entire sequence, believing that his batting ritual helped him regain his concentration. His ritual sequence was so time consuming that he was known as the "human rain delay." Latin Americans draw upon rituals from their Catholic religion. Some make the sign of the cross or bless themselves before every at bat, and a few like the Rangers' Pudge Rodriquez do so before every pitch. Some, like Juan Gonzales, also visibly wear religious medallions around their necks, while others wear them discretely inside their undershirts.

One ritual associated with hitting is tagging a base when leaving and returning to the dugout between innings. Some players don't "feel right" unless they tag a specific base on each trip between the dugout and the field. Dave Jaeger added some complexity to his ritual by tagging third base on his way to the dugout only after the third, sixth, and ninth innings. Baseball fans observe a lot of ritual behavior, such as tagging bases, pitchers tugging their caps or touching the rosin bag after each bad pitch, smoothing the dirt on the mound before each new batter or inning, never realizing the importance of these actions to the player. The one ritual many fans do recognize, and that is a favorite of TV cameramen, is the "rally cap"—players in the dugout folding their caps and wearing them bill up in hopes of sparking a rally.

Most rituals grow out of exceptionally good performances. When a player does well, he seldom attributes his success to skill alone. He knows that his skills were essentially the same the night before. What was different about today which explains his three hits? He decides to repeat what he did today in an attempt to bring more good luck. And so he attributes his success, in part, to a food he ate, not having shaved, or just about any behavior out of the ordinary. By repeating that behavior, he seeks to gain control over his performance. Outfielder John White explained how one of his rituals started:

> I was jogging out to centerfield after the national anthem when I picked up a scrap of paper. I got some good hits that night and I guess I decided that the paper had

something to do with it. The next night I picked up a gum wrapper and had another good night at the plate. . . . I've been picking up paper every night since.

One of Mike Saccocia's rituals concerned food, "I got three hits one night after eating at Long John Silver's. After that when we'd pull into town, my first question would be, 'Do you have a Long John Silver's?' " Like most players, White and Sacciocia abandoned their rituals and looked for new ones when they stopped hitting.

Because starting pitchers play once every four days, they perform their rituals less frequently than do hitters. But their rituals are just as important to them, perhaps more so. A starting pitcher cannot make up for a poor performance the following day like other players can. And having to wait three days to redeem oneself can be miserable. Moreover, the team's performance depends more on the pitcher than on any other player. Considering the pressures to do well, it is not surprising that pitchers' rituals are often more complex than those of hitters. Mike Griffin begins his ritual a full day before he pitches by washing his hair. The next day, although he does not consider himself superstitious, he eats bacon for lunch. When Griffin dresses for the game he puts on his clothes in the same order, making certain he puts the slightly longer of his two stirrup socks on his right leg. "I just wouldn't feel right mentally if I did it the other way around," he explains. He always wears the same shirt under his uniform on the day he pitches. During the game he takes off his cap after each pitch, and between innings he sits in the same place on the dugout bench. He, too, believes his rituals provide a sense of order that reduces his anxiety about pitching.

Some pitchers involve their wives or girlfriends in their rituals. One wife reported that her husband insisted that she wash her hair each day he was to pitch. In her memoirs, Danielle Torrez reported that one "rule" she learned as a baseball wife was "to support your husband's superstitions, whether you believe in them or not. I joined the player's wives who ate ice cream in the sixth inning or tacos in the fifth, or who attended games in a pink sweater, a tan scarf, or a floppy hat."[1]

When in a slump, most players make a deliberate effort to change their rituals and routines in an attempt to shake off their bad luck. One player tried taking different routes to the ballpark; several players reported trying different combinations of tagging and not tagging particular bases in an attempt to find a successful combination. I knew one manager who would rattle the bat bin when his players weren't hitting, as if the bats were in a stupor and could be aroused by a good shaking. Similarly, I have seen hitters rub their hands along the handles of the bats protruding from the bin in hopes of picking up some power or luck from bats that are getting hits for their owners. Some players switch from wearing their contact lenses to glasses. Brett Mandel described how his Pioneer League team, the Ogden Raptors, tried to break a losing streak by using a new formation for their pre-game stretching.[2]

[1] Danielle Torrez, *High Inside: Memoirs of a Baseball Wife* (New York: G. P. Putnam's Sons, 1983).

[2] Brett Mandel, *Minor Player, Major Dreams* (Lincoln, NE: University of Nebraska Press, 1997).

## Taboos

Taboos are the opposite of rituals. The word *taboo* comes from a Polynesian term meaning prohibition. Breaking a taboo, players believe, leads to undesirable consequences or bad luck. Most players observe at least a few taboos, such as never stepping on the foul lines. One teammate of mine would never watch a movie on a game day, despite the fact that we played nearly every day from April to September. Another teammate refused to read anything before a game because he believed it weakened his batting eye.

Many taboos take place off the field, out of public view. On the day a pitcher is scheduled to start, he is likely to avoid activities he believes will sap his strength and detract from his effectiveness. Some pitchers avoid eating certain foods; others will not shave on the day of a game, and won't shave as long as they are winning. Early one season Oakland's Dave Stewart had six consecutive victories and a beard by the time he lost. Ex-St. Louis Cardinal Al Hrabosky took this taboo to extremes. Samson-like, he refused to cut his hair or beard during the entire season, which was part of the basis for his nickname, the "Mad Hungarian."

Taboos usually grow out of exceptionally poor performances, which players, in search of a reason, attribute to a particular behavior. During my first season of pro ball I ate pancakes before a game in which I struck out four times. A few weeks later I had another terrible game, again after eating pancakes. The result was a pancake taboo: I never again ate pancakes during the season. White Sox pitcher Jason Bere has a taboo that makes more sense in dietary terms: after eating a meatball sandwich and not pitching well he swore off them for good.

While most taboos are idiosyncratic, there are a few that all ballplayers hold and that do not develop out of individual experience or misfortune. These form part of the culture of baseball; some are learned as early as Little League. Mentioning a no-hitter while one is in progress is a well-known example. It is believed that if a pitcher hears the words "no-hitter," the spell accounting for this hard-to-achieve feat will be broken and the no-hitter lost. This taboo is also observed by many sports broadcasters, who use various linguistic subterfuges to inform their listeners that the pitcher has not given up a hit, never saying "no-hitter."

## Fetishes

Fetishes are material objects believed to embody "supernatural" power (i.e., luck) that can aid or protect the owner. Such charms are standard equipment for some ballplayers. These include a wide assortment of objects, from coins, chains, and crucifixes to a favorite baseball hat. In the words of Jim Snyder, "When you are going good you take notice of what you are doing. I still use my glove from college. It's kind of beat up but it's got 40 wins in it, so I still use it. I use my professional glove in practice and my college glove in games." The fetishized object may be a new possession or something a player found that happens to coincide with the start of a streak and which he holds responsible for his good fortune. While playing in the Pacific Coast League, Alan Foster forgot his baseball shoes on a road trip and borrowed a pair from a teammate. That night he pitched a no-hitter, which he attributed to the shoes. Afterward he bought them from his teammate and they became a fetish. Expo farmhand Mark LaRosa's rock has a very different origin and use:

> I found it on the field in Elmira after I had gotten bombed [pitched poorly]. It's unusual, perfectly round, and it caught my attention. I keep it to remind me of how important it is to concentrate. When I am going well I look at the rock and remember to keep my focus. It reminds me of what can happen when I lose my concentration.

For one season Marge Schott, owner of the Cincinnati Reds, insisted that her field manager rub her St. Bernard "Schotzie" for good luck before each game. When the Reds were on the road, Schott would sometimes send a bag of the dog's hair to the field manager's hotel room.

During World War II American soldiers used fetishes in much the same way. Social psychologist Samuel Stouffer and his colleagues found that in the face of great danger and uncertainty, soldiers developed magical practices, particularly the use of protective amulets and good luck charms (crosses, Bibles, rabbits' feet, medals), and jealously guarded articles of clothing they associated with past experiences of escape from danger.[3] Stouffer also found that pre-battle preparations were carried out in fixed "ritual" order, much as ballplayers and certain other athletes prepare for a game.

Uniform numbers have special significance for some players who request their lucky number. Since the choice is usually limited, they try to at least get a uniform that contains their lucky number, such as 14, 24, 34, or 44 for the player whose lucky number is four. Oddly enough, there is no consensus about the effect of wearing number 13. Some players will not wear it, others will, and a few request it. Number preferences emerge in different ways. A young player may request the number of a former star, hoping that—through what anthropologists call *imitative* magic—it will bring him the same success. Or he may request a number he associates with good luck. Vida Blue changed his uniform number from 35 to 14, the number he wore as a high-school quarterback. When 14 did not produce better pitching performance, he switched back to 35. Larry Walker has a fixation with the number three. Besides wearing 33, he takes three practice swings before stepping into the batter's box, and sets his alarm for three minutes past the hour. Fans in ballparks all across America rise from their seats for the seventh inning stretch before the home club comes to bat because the number seven is "lucky."

Articles of clothing, both the choice and the order in which they are put on, combine elements of both ritual and fetish. Some players put on their uniform in a ritualized order. Expos farmhand Jim Austin always puts on his left sleeve, left pants leg, and left shoe before the right. Most players, however, single out

---

[3] Samuel Stouffer, *The American Soldier* (New York: J. Wiley, 1965).

one or two lucky articles or quirks of dress. After hitting two home runs in a game, for example, infielder Jim Davenport discovered that he had missed a buttonhole while dressing for the game. For the remainder of his career he left the same button undone. For Brian Hunter the focus is shoes, "I have a pair of high tops and a pair of low tops. Whichever shoes don't get a hit that game, I switch to the other pair." At the time of our interview, he was struggling at the plate and switching shoes almost every day. For Birmingham Baron pitcher Bo Kennedy the arrangement of the different pairs of baseball shoes in his locker is critical:

> I tell the clubies [clubhouse boys] when you hang stuff in my locker don't touch my shoes. If you bump them move them back. I want the Pony's in front, the turfs to the right, and I want them nice and neat with each pair touching each other. . . . Everyone on the team knows not to mess with my shoes.

During streaks—hitting or winning—players may wear the same clothes day after day. Once I changed sweatshirts midway through the game for seven consecutive nights to keep a hitting streak going. Clothing rituals, however, can become impractical. Catcher Matt Allen was wearing a long-sleeve turtleneck shirt on a cool evening in the New York–Penn League when he had a three-hit game. "I kept wearing the shirt and had a good week," he explained. "Then the weather got hot as hell, 85 degrees and muggy, but I would not take that shirt off. I wore it for another ten days—catching—and people thought I was crazy." Also taking a ritual to the extreme, Leo Durocher, managing the Brooklyn Dodgers to a pennant in 1941, is said to have spent three and a half weeks in the same gray slacks, blue coat, and knitted blue tie. During a 16-game winning streak, the 1954 New York Giants wore the same clothes in each game and refused to let them be cleaned for fear that their good fortune might be washed away with the dirt.

Losing often produces the opposite effect. Several Oakland A's players, for example, went out and bought new street clothes in an attempt to break a 14-game losing streak. When I recently joined the Birmingham Barons for a road trip, outfielder Scott Tedder was in a slump. He changed batting gloves daily, and had already gone through a dozen pairs trying to find one that would change his luck and get him some hits.

Baseball's superstitions, like most everything else, change over time. Many of the rituals and beliefs of early baseball are no longer observed. In the 1920s and 1930s sportswriters reported that a player who tripped en route to the field would often retrace his steps and carefully walk over the stumbling block for "insurance." A century ago players spent time on and off the field intently looking for items that would bring them luck. To find a hairpin on the street, for example, assured a batter of hitting safely in that day's game. Today few women wear hairpins—a good reason the belief has died out. To catch sight of a white horse or a wagonload of barrels were also good omens. In 1904 the manager of the New York Giants, John McGraw, hired a driver and a team of white horses to drive past the Polo Grounds around the time his players were arriving at the ballpark. He knew that if his players saw white horses, they'd have more confidence and that could only help them during the game. Belief in the power of white horses survived in a few backwaters until the 1960s. A gray-haired manager of a team I played for in Quebec would drive around the countryside before important games and during the playoffs looking for a white horse. When he was successful, he'd announce it to everyone in the clubhouse before the game.

One belief that appears to have died out recently is a taboo about crossed bats. Some of my Latino teammates in the 1960s took it seriously. I can still recall one Dominican player becoming agitated when another player tossed a bat from the batting cage and it landed on top of his bat. He believed that the top bat might steal hits from the lower one. In his view, bats contained a finite number of hits, a sort of baseball "image of limited good." It was once commonly believed that once the hits in a bat were used up, no amount of good hitting would produce any more. Hall of Famer Honus Wagner believed each bat contained only 100 hits. Regardless of the quality of the bat, he would discard it after its 100th hit. This belief would have little relevance today, in the era of light bats with thin handles—so thin that the typical modern bat is lucky to survive a dozen hits without being broken. Other superstitions about bats do survive, however. Hitters on the Class A Asheville Tourists would not let pitchers touch or swing their bats, not even to warm up. The poor-hitting pitchers were said to pollute or weaken the bats.

## Uncertainty and Magic

The best evidence that players turn to rituals, taboos, and fetishes to control chance and uncertainty is found in their uneven application. They are associated mainly with pitching and hitting—the activities with the highest degree of chance—and not fielding. I met only one player who had any ritual in connection with fielding, and he was an error-prone shortstop. Unlike hitting and pitching, a fielder has almost complete control over the outcome of his performance. Once a ball has been hit in his direction, no one can intervene and ruin his chances of catching it for an out (except in the unlikely event of two fielders colliding). Compared with the pitcher or the hitter, the fielder has little to worry about. He knows that in better than 9.7 times out of 10 he will execute his task flawlessly. With odds like that there is little need for ritual.

Clearly, the ritual behavior of American ballplayers is not unlike that of the Trobriand Islanders studied by Malinowski many years ago.[4] In professional baseball, fielding is the equivalent of the inner lagoon while hitting and pitching are like the open sea.

Although Malinowski helps us understand how ballplayers and other people respond to chance and uncertainty, behavioral psychologist B. F. Skinner sheds light on why personal rituals get established in the first place.[5] With a few

---

[4] Bronislaw Malinowski, *Magic, Science and Religion and Other Essays* (Glencoe, IL: Free Press, 1948).

[5] B. F. Skinner, *Science and Human Behavior* (New York: Macmillan, 1953).

grains of seed Skinner could get pigeons to do anything he wanted. He merely waited for the desired behavior (e.g., pecking) and then rewarded it with some food. Skinner then decided to see what would happen if pigeons were rewarded with food pellets regularly, every 15 seconds, regardless of what they did. He found that the birds associate the arrival of the food with a particular action, such as tucking their head under a wing, or walking in clockwise circles. About 10 seconds after the arrival of the last pellet, a bird would begin doing whatever it associated with getting the food and keep doing it until the next pellet arrived. In short, the pigeons behaved as if their actions made the food appear. They learned to associate particular behaviors with the reward of being given seed. Ballplayers also associate a reward—successful performance—with prior behavior. If a player touches his crucifix and then gets a hit, he may decide the gesture was responsible for his good fortune, and touch his crucifix the next time he comes to the plate. If he gets another hit, the chances are good that he will touch his crucifix each time he bats. Unlike pigeons, however, most ball players are quicker to change their rituals once they no longer appear to work. Skinner found that once a pigeon associated one of its actions with the arrival of food or water, only sporadic rewards were necessary to keep the ritual going. One pigeon, apparently believing that hopping from side to side brought pellets into its feeding cup, hopped 10,000 times without a pellet before finally giving up. But, then, hasn't Wade Boggs continued to eat chicken, through slumps and good times, before every game for the past dozen years? Obviously the rituals and superstitions of baseball do not make a pitch travel faster or a batted ball find the gaps between the fielders, nor do the Trobriand rituals calm the seas or bring fish. What both do, however, is give their practitioners a sense of control and, with that, confidence. And they do so at very little cost to the practitioner.

# Review Questions

1. According to Gmelch, what is magic, and why do people practice it?

2. What parts of baseball are most likely to lead to magical practice? Why?

3. What is meant by the terms *taboo* and *fetish*? Illustrate these concepts using examples from this article.

4. How are Malinowski's and Skinner's theories of magic alike and different? What is each designed to explain?

5. Can you think of other areas of U.S. life where magic is practiced? Do the same theories used in this article account for these examples, too?

# 34

# Witchcraft
# Tswana Style

## Charlanne Burke

*We noted in the introduction to Part Eight that religion functions to answer
ultimate questions of life, such as the causes of death and evil. Some religions blame adversity on the malevolent actions of supernatural beings. Villagers in North India, for example, think that a goddess, Sitala Mata, causes
smallpox. For some Christians, Satan is behind adversity. People in many
societies also believe that human beings possess supernatural power that
can cause bad luck, illness, and death. In this selection, Charlanne Burke
describes such a belief system among people living in the African nation of
Botswana. Carried over from earlier times when witchcraft was a common
explanation for misfortune, modern Tswana continue to blame bad luck,
illness, death, and failure on the actions of witches. A person might bewitch
a pen so that it writes the wrong answers on school exams or cause a newly
built house to catch fire during a kitchen accident. Although it is hard to
think of witchcraft as positive, belief in witches can give people a sense of
control when things go wrong. It enables them to diagnose the cause of*

*trouble and use the power of local ritual specialists or Christian church congregations to fend off the evil causing the adversity.*

### Case 1, 1933

He [the accused] spoke to me about hunting for something as his tin was nearly empty. This tin was a medicine tin. I understood him to mean that he wanted the fat of a human being for medicine. . . . [H]e invited me to assist him in this hunt. I agreed. He offered to doctor me. . . . He then beckoned to me and I went to him. . . . I asked him what it was that he had with him. . . . He had the body of Motosa, a very young child, wrapped up in an overcoat. . . . At that time the child was breathing very slightly and a little further on accused (sic) killed him completely by striking him at the back of the head with a piece of wood which he picked up. When I joined accused, I noticed that the neck of the child had been twisted. . . . He took the body of the child across the river where he cut the stomach open with a knife. The child was already dead when he cut it open. I assisted accused to do this. I held the body in position whilst he cut it. . . . Accused took out the liver which he cut into small pieces and placed in his tin. He also took the meat from both flanks. He also cut one hand off which he took. . . . [1]

### Case 2, 1997

For the ulcer I went to the hospital, but my stomach became big. My parents suspected *sejeso,* and took me to the traditional doctor. The traditional doctor said I got a problem with a friend, who I am sitting next to in class. He's creating the problems. I believed by that time that he had a problem because he started ignoring me, this proved he had a problem with me. Even that boy's parents had a problem. When we separated, he never even went back to church. I was more intelligent than him, I was helping him in class. But his parents had a problem with me and were sending him to do those things. Because of jealousy. The traditional doctor gave me some medicine which I drank for a month. Then I returned to the hospital and learned it was an ulcer, and I shouldn't eat some foods. It was the traditional doctor who helped me, at the hospital they couldn't manage to remove the thing in my stomach.[2]

[The same youth talking about this incident in a letter the following year]

About the guy who tried to bewitch me of course we are relatives though we are not that close. His parents know us very well and they don't stay far from my home. I grew up with this boy at the lands as we are neighbours. . . . It is like this boy was sent by his grandmother to bewitch me. However, my mother knew before that the grandmother of this guy was very dangerous as she kept on advising me to take care when I visit him. And then unfortunately it happened.

[1]Botswana National Archives, *Rex v. Dintwe Dithupe,* testimony by Tete, an adult male. Mosarwa, 1933: pp. 7–9, S.357/3.

[2]Male youth, interview 1997.

These two stories, separated by nearly 65 years, describe two different types of witchcraft-related activities in Botswana. The first example is from government records about the trial of a man accused of *dipheko,* or ritual murder. Formerly called medicine murders, this kind of activity involves the killing and mutilation of a victim whose body parts will provide the ingredients for strong medicine. In the past, this medicine was said to protect cattle or to strengthen a chief's power. Today, on the other hand, people believe that this medicine will ensure business prosperity and political success. The second example depicts the less dramatic and more common form of witchcraft, where witches use their supernatural power to disrupt the lives of others. Despite extensive efforts by the colonial British government to eliminate witchcraft in the first half of the 20th century, these beliefs continue to be an important part of contemporary Botswana.

How do the Batswana explain witchcraft in their lives? Is this just a simple case of "uncivilized" superstition? This paper will examine witchcraft in Botswana, with particular emphasis on youth, in an effort to answer these questions.

## Botswana

Botswana, a democratic nation in southern Africa, has as bordering neighbors Namibia, South Africa, and Zimbabwe. Roughly the size of Texas, it is largely arid scrub country. The people who live here refer to themselves as the Batswana (plural; Motswana is singular), and they speak Setswana. Unlike many countries in Africa such as Kenya, Angola, or the Democratic Republic of Congo (formerly Zaire), Botswana was not colonized by a European power. Near the end of the 19th century, it requested protectorate status from the British, which complied in order to retain access to the African interior. However, because Botswana's mineral wealth had not yet been discovered, colonial exploitation and development were relatively absent. Missionaries from various denominations had arrived before the British government, and had begun providing limited formal schooling in the hopes of producing good Christians. They especially wanted to eliminate such customs as the initiation schools, polygamy, traditional medicine, and witchcraft. The missionary efforts were met with resistance from the Batswana who had their own ideas about what should happen to their customs, and what kind of education should be established within their country. Today, the Batswana have embraced the notion that the key to advancing in life is education and many of them have adopted Christianity. At the same time, traditional healers remain important, both for providing treatment for health problems and for dealing with witchcraft.

In 1966, Botswana gained peaceful independence from Great Britain, and in the early 1970s diamonds and other mineral resources were discovered, changing Botswana from one of Africa's poorest nations to one of its richest. The Tswana government used these newfound resources to improve and expand both the medical and educational facilities.

Tswana villages are historically large. For example, the village I lived in (called Moreneng) had nearly 30,000 people living in it. Traditionally, a village contained a number of wards (a cluster of households, or now, more like a neighborhood). Within each ward, family units managed their own affairs, although they were under the general control of the ward headman. The ward headman was subordinate to the head of several linked wards who was in turn subject to the chief. With the advent of protectorate status, a colonial political system was imposed on the indigenous system, rendering the latter system subordinate to the former. There now coexists a system of civil courts and laws based on Dutch Roman law alongside the traditional court system, and Botswana has a constitution ensuring the rights of its citizens.

The Batswana are cattle keepers and farmers, and they also grow maize (corn) and sorghum for their own consumption. The land supports cattle and beef is exported to Europe, although water (vital for cattle raising) is often a scarce resource. Cattle are an important form of wealth and are critical in negotiation of marriages. Marriage in Botswana has been called a process because often negotiation between families begins and the couple commences to live together and have children before the final cattle are transferred. Formerly, most young women got married (or began the marriage process) in their early twenties. Now, however, female-headed households in which the woman has children yet never gets married are on the rise. Ofaletse, whose story we turn to later, was raised in a number of female-headed households, and she appears to be forming one of her own.

## Boloi ba Botswana, or Witchcraft the Tswana Way

Witchcraft was a popular topic of research for anthropologists several decades ago, when it was assumed that these beliefs were evidence of the non-logical thought of uncivilized people. Colonial governments and missionaries asserted that the introduction of European culture and religion would eradicate these irrational beliefs and activities. Despite a substantial missionary presence, this did not happen in Botswana or many other African countries. In the 1990s anthropologists once again began to study witchcraft and discovered that although the beliefs and actions had changed to accommodate and incorporate new elements of the changing world, witchcraft as a coping mechanism was alive and well. Just as Batswana in the past blamed witches for crop failure or sickness in the family, today people blame witches for school failure and tuberculosis.

Witchcraft is perceived as a bad thing in Botswana, and no one would willingly admit to practicing it. However, witches are believed to be present in sufficient numbers that the women I knew took care not to disclose their pregnancies in case someone's envy led to witchcraft against them. Witchcraft often involves traditional healers and medicine and it is associated not only with bodily ailments but also with strained relationships and bad luck as well. Religious people (meaning ones who have become Christians) often claim not to believe in witchcraft, but most of the independent churches, which have prospered in Botswana, preach that Jesus and Christianity represent good while witchcraft and witches are evil.

Following Evans-Pritchard's pioneering work among the Azande in Africa, in which witchcraft is generally understood as the supernatural ability of one person to harm another person, anthropologists distinguish between witchcraft (an internal, inherited, often unconscious state) and sorcery (the malevolent intent to manipulate special powers and materials to hurt others). According to this distinction, there are no witches in Botswana because the Tswana do not believe that people are born with the innate capacity to do unwitting evil to others. There are only sorcerers, or those who willfully hurt their enemies. Witchcraft beliefs are also commonly divided into two classes: "black" magic, which is used for evil purposes, and "white" magic, which is used for good. Among the Tswana no linguistic distinction is made between black and white magic, and all witchcraft is called *boloi* (a witch is a *moloi* and more than one witch are *baloi*).

The Tswana used to distinguish between *baloi ba bosigo* (night witches) and *baloi ba motshegare* (day witches). Although these categories are not expressly stated much anymore, the two kinds of witches still exist. Night witches are said to be mainly elderly women who gather in groups at night, and who must give evidence of their commitment to join the group by killing a close family member. If a family member dies in an unusual accident, for example, a kinswoman, especially if she is prospering, may come under suspicion of practicing witchcraft. These witches are thought to travel around at night by various supernatural means, and are able to bewitch sleeping residents so that they do not awaken when the witches enter their huts, allowing the witches free reign to do what they want. They take body matter like hair or nail clippings which they use in medicine to make the person ill, insert bad objects inside someone to cause *sejeso,* or borrow their victims' bodies for their witchly deeds. They also exhume dead bodies and take parts to make medicine. Associated with these witches are various animals, like owls (which act as spies) and hyenas (upon which they are said to ride). Many of my informants were also leery of bats and cats. Bats were believed to be witches, moving about, while cats are agents of bewitching because they wrap themselves between a person's legs, spreading evil medicine on the limbs of the unsuspecting.

Day witches, on the other hand, do not habitually practice this kind of proactive malevolent magic, although they may do so occasionally to injure a specific enemy. These kinds of witches are ordinary men and women. Their methods require special herbs and other materials, which generally necessitates seeking the help of a *ngaka ya setswana* (traditional healer) who has the required expertise. Some of the methods of bewitching include sprinkling doctored blood or herbal medicine in the compound or on the path of victims. When the victims step on the blood they either die, lose the use of their legs, or suffer some other misfortune. One woman I knew believed she had stepped in such medicine in the recent past, and the resulting witchcraft explained her inability to find a job. Placement of doctored bundles within the victim's hut or compound ensures that someone in the household will become ill. A witch can also blow medicine in the direction of the intended victim, or conceal it in food or drink. This latter, called *sejeso,* is a common method and is considered very dangerous. Sorcerers can also direct lightning to strike victims or their huts or cattle.

Special medicines are not only used to harm one's enemies, but are also deployed for protective and positive measures as well. A person's compound and family can be doctored in advance to protect against future witchcraft or to ensure desired outcomes such as a promotion at work, attracting someone's love, or success at school. Friends recounted episodes of opposing football teams doctoring the playing field and goal posts before matches. This kind of activity, though, was not called witchcraft.

Older villagers explained *boloi* in 1983 to an African researcher.[3]

> Bangwato believed that evil befalling individuals and families was intimately associated with *boloi* (witchcraft). Thus the Bangwato took preventive methods for safeguarding themselves. Family doctors treated a whole family in case some evil neighbor or relative had intentions of bewitching them. This was such a strong belief in Bangwato society that newborn children were immediately treated by the family doctor to protect them in case they were handled by the people with malicious intents. *Baloi* (witches) were members of society who possessed special evil powers, utilizing herbs to bewitch other people. They were associated with jealousy. Their activities, often clandestine and nefarious, took place in the dead of the night. They were supposed to walk around nude, possessed magical powers to open locked doors, and could turn the sleeping enemy into an animal for nighttime transportation. They selected their targets carefully, stalked them at night, lulled them into sleep, and then poisoned them.

Current descriptions of witchcraft are similar to those noted above, and remain clandestine. There were few public accusations while I lived in Botswana (and even these were read about in the newspapers, not actually witnessed firsthand); people discussed these issues privately. For example, after the death of a 30-year-old woman, an informant referred to the fact that "people are saying that witchcraft is involved," yet there was no public accusation against anyone. Many different people were able to point out alleged witches. Ofaletse believed she was surrounded by the compounds of three witches. Another claimed to identify several witches living in town. A student thought there was witchcraft activity in the dorms at the local secondary school.

Formerly, when a person became ill or died, a traditional *setswana* doctor was called to discover the causes of the misfortune. Illness or death would often

[3]*Mgadla,* 1986: 51.

be attributed to the ancestors or to witchcraft. Usually the healer did not directly name the responsible person, but would suggest certain characteristics (such as sex, totem, and skin complexion) from which the victim or victim's family could identify a suspect. Such suspicions were confirmed by an inquiry, and the guilty party was taken to the chief who alone (up to the colonial period) could prosecute and punish witches. By the 1920s, local courts were no longer allowed to try cases of witchcraft. Unfounded accusations of witchcraft also contravened customary law, and diviners were punished in the past for falsifying the results of the bones (bones would be tossed and read by the *ngaka*, revealing key information with which to identify both the problem and the culprits). Today, witchcraft seems to go unpunished, at least publicly. In the cases that I was aware of, the bewitched were more concerned with alleviating the effects of the magic than with punishing the witch. However, in cases of suspected *dipheko* (ritual murder), the public often attacks and tries to kill the alleged murderer.

If found guilty in the past, the witches were ordered to undo the magic so the patient could recover. If the accused refused, they were tortured until they agreed. If victims died, the witches would be killed and tossed over a cliff or clubbed to death. Today church-goers explained that the church's prophet ferrets out a witch and leads a party of church members to the suspect's compound in a surprise "attack" to locate the magic bundle hidden in the thatch or somewhere else in the compound. Some prophets claim to be able to detect the presence of witches in their congregation and then to perform exorcisms. In one case a prophet had detected such a presence, and water, kerosene, and a candle were brought together to drive out the evil. Tragedy ensued when the mixture caught fire, congregation members could not escape from the dwelling, and several people died.

Witches may use other evil forces to attack people. For example, villagers said that a *thokolosi* (a mysterious, animal-like creature of the night) was sent by a witch to molest teachers in a village. Three teachers claimed that the creature had "pulled [their] breasts and had sex with [them] without [their] consent." Male teachers claimed that the *thokolosi* "pulled them by their private parts until they were swollen." Trainees refused to go to this school until the matter was resolved; and the chief recalled that a *thokolosi* used to terrorize the people in the village but had previously disappeared.[4]

Zombies are another set of supernatural characters. In Botswana, zombies (*setlotlwane*) are created when someone causes another person's death through witchcraft and then uses the body of the deceased to become wealthy. Special magic using medicine and the tip of the tongue ensures that the person, although looking dead and subsequently buried, gets up at night and works for the witch. Zombies have long, unwashed, uncombed hair, and they eat cooked, unsalted animal meat. An informant explained, "If you give one salty meat it

---

[4]*Gazette*, 1999.

will become very angry, can beat you, and you might die." Zombies enrich their makers because they can work incessantly. While the zombie's owner sleeps, the zombie is busy in productive tasks. One never has to reinvest profits in maintaining the zombie, and such a worker never tires, demands higher pay, complains, or quits. A zombie works in the night during a time inhabited by witches, ghosts, *tokolosi*, and thieves, when normal people sleep. They occupy a zone somewhere between alive and dead.

Witchcraft is not confined to Botswana. For example, it has become a troubling force in Botswana's neighbor, South Africa, over the past several years. There are many accounts of the brutal killings of suspected witches—as many as 60 deaths, mainly of old women, reported between 1995 and 1997. Ritual murder is also believed to be on the rise, with the discovery in South Africa of headless bodies, severed heads found in different locations, and missing body parts. Prices for brains, breasts, eyes, or genitals were said to range from $167 to $1,000, depending on the part.[5]

## Witchcraft and Youth

During my fieldwork in Botswana, I was investigating youths' lives, so my data primarily speak to the perspective of contemporary youth. Witchcraft can take bodily and psychological forms. What I learned was their belief that witchcraft can cause dizziness, headaches, eye problems, back and abdominal pains, general body pains, blindness, inability to speak or hold things, inability to see print on the page or chalkboard, infertility, and insanity. What medical personnel would identify as AIDS or a sexually transmitted disease is often attributed to witchcraft. The effects of witchcraft can be slow acting. A social worker remembered a friend who had done well throughout school, gone to university, and finally found a good job, at which point he died of witchcraft committed in his infancy. One's difficulties in life, such as unemployment, romantic problems, sexual troubles, and poverty, can also be caused by witchcraft.

The "doing" of witchcraft is a process, or a series of events, involving knowing, doing, diagnosing, and treatment. Before witchcraft can be done, some basic things about it must be known. For example, it is critical to know the particular skills and the location of the variety of traditional healers. All my informants agreed that youth do not know how to do witchcraft. Despite displaying physical symptoms, most aspects of a witchcraft episode are mediated through adults. Adults, they believe, do witchcraft to other adults and to youth. Youth cannot bewitch anyone without parental help, and then they can only bewitch other youth. A youth can approach her parents and express a desire for some goal, for example to be the best in her class at school. The parents determine the next steps

[5]*Gazette,* 1998.

without discussing the issue with the child. The parents might then approach a *ngaka ya setswana* (Tswana healer) to obtain the appropriate medicine, which will be passed to their son or daughter to administer.

Examples of witchcraft abound. Several people believed that a witch can borrow a classmate's pen or book and have it doctored by a traditional healer. When the owner regains her possession, she is bewitched and the pen will not write the correct answers, or it shoots off the edge of the page instead of writing. A book may be lost, and then found with blood in it, which will prevent the student from preparing for an exam. Students may get severe back pain, which prevents them from going to class or taking exams. This, too, is probably caused by witchcraft. Some believe that a student can have medicine on her hand and pat her friend's or a competitor's back or hair, shake or hold her hand, or borrow another's treated lip balm to cause trouble. Because of this, young people were hesitant to accept food from adults, because ingesting poisoned food or drink can result in *sejeso*. (*Sejeso* manifests itself as a burning, up-and-down movement in the throat and chest area, or as heart pain, and can be very dangerous.) When I pointed out to students that they routinely ate and drank what I offered, they laughed and said *makgoa* (white people) cannot bewitch people.

Adults also worried about witchcraft. Mothers were nervous about having their babies weighed at health clinics, since earlier visitors could have left medicine on the scales. People suspected that foreigners, especially those from Zimbabwe who sold fruit, practiced powerful magic. In one instance, some foreigners were accused of practicing witchcraft that caused money they used to buy things in local shops to return to them at night.

Adults control the diagnosis of witchcraft. Thus, a youth who experiences symptoms reports her malaise to her parents. They diagnose the problem and discuss it with their senior kin. If they suspect witchcraft, the parents usually accompany their afflicted child to an appropriate Tswana healer or church prophet. They divine the identity of the witch—usually a female relative or neighbor; strangers don't bewitch people—but keep it secret from the young person because they don't want her to confront the perpetrator.

Who is likely to be identified as a witch is an interesting subject in itself. I have found that identification seems to depend largely on factors such as the young person's family situation, chances at progressing in school, final performance on exams, parents' and youths' beliefs about witchcraft, and their valuation of education and its role in improving life. Students whose siblings had not done well in school experienced pressure to do well and lift the entire family from poverty. These students often claimed to experience witchcraft, such as pens that won't write on paper or eyes that can't see the exam questions, leading to school failure.

Adults also control treatment by traditional healers. Young people must be accompanied when they go to a healer for treatment because they cannot pay for it themselves and because, if the treatment fails and they die, someone will hold the *ngaka* responsible. However, treating witchcraft is a complicated process and traditional healers are not the only avenues of relief. Some people will first go to the hospital for treatment. If this doesn't work, they may appeal to their church. Often they will visit several churches looking for a solution. The prophets of these churches employ different methods, including prayer, cleansing with water, rituals involving flames, and singing. One young man had experienced much witchcraft in his life. As a student, his parents managed the treatment of these episodes, one of which almost killed him. But when he found himself living away from his parents, he relied on his church for protection and help. Before traveling, he and the other church members would perform an elaborate ritual involving whirling dancing and chanting, immersion in cold water while dressed, prayer, and the donation of travel funds. And, of course, many people try all three options at once.

## Ofaletse's Story

Ofaletse is a young woman who assisted me during my fieldwork in her village. Like many other girls her age, her first pregnancy occurred when she was 19 and in her final year at secondary school. She is now an unmarried mother of three children from different fathers although she is hoping to finalize marriage negotiations soon with the family of her third child's father. Unlike many girls, she successfully completed her senior secondary schooling and term of national service to the government. She is most concerned about finding a job (or going back to school to get training that would result in a job)—a plan that would allow her to provide for her children and to alleviate the poverty that envelops her and her immediate family members.

Her work as my assistant during my stay in the village was the sole source of wage income for a household that included her aged, blind maternal grandmother, an older sister and her three children by three fathers, the child of an absent sister, her own two children (all of these children were under the age of 8), and sometimes her younger brother and sister. The sixth of nine children, she lived in a barren compound on a plot of hard-packed bare dirt in a part of the village without electricity and running water. The compound contained huts for sleeping and cooking. Ofaletse's father is dead, and her mother rarely came to town from the fields where she lived and worked as an agricultural laborer. Ofaletse's siblings, offspring of five different fathers, have all had disparate life trajectories. She moved around as a child between relatives, spending part of her primary years with her paternal grandmother in a nearby village. When this grandmother died, she lived with a paternal aunt who was cruel to her. Ofaletse's secondary school years passed in a northern town with another paternal aunt who was nice but very strict. It was during her last year at secondary school that she became pregnant by a fellow student (although he was from Zambia, to which he ultimately returned, making contact between the two nearly nonexistent). She left her aunt's house without telling her about the pregnancy, and returned to Moreneng to live with her maternal grandmother. After her son's birth she was able to complete her TSP service.[6] It was during this year that she became pregnant, again by a village youth. She refused to disclose her condition even when questioned by the TSP social workers, and did not seek prenatal care or medical attention until the birth of the baby.

Although she was the youngest permanent resident (apart from the children) in the Palapye compound, she was the only one who finished her secondary schooling and her TSP (and is thus the one most likely to get a job). Her oldest brother was a "thief," while the whereabouts of the second sibling, a sister, were unknown. The third was the sister who lived in the compound with Ofaletse, and did not have a formal sector job. However, she cared for Ofaletse's children during working hours, and also spent more time at the fields trying to produce crops for the family than did her sister. She also took the grandmother to the food depot to pick up her monthly allotment of food. Her five other siblings went their own way in life and none contributed to her family.

The government has played an important role in Ofaletse's family. The government elderly assistance program supplied bread, flour, and sugar because her grandmother was eligible for the program. The babies received enriched food from the health clinic in a government-sponsored mother and child program.

Ofaletse had many worries. She was concerned about her mother, who was in her 60s and still toiling at agricultural work. She sometimes blamed the family's poverty and problems on her mother's inattention to them, however. She worried about her own children, and whether she would be able to afford pre-school expenses for the eldest. Threats by her second daughter's father and his family to take the child from her weighed on her mind daily, and she has gone to the Tswana civil courts in search of maintenance from the father.

Ofaletse's living conditions also worry her. A fallen-down hut is all that remains of her attempts to build her own home. Twice she built the hut and twice events beyond her control (bad weather, lack of labor, witchcraft) intervened to destroy it.

Ofaletse has become increasingly depressed by other misfortunes in her life as well. She believes that one of her neighbors, Sophie, is bewitching her and causing a sleep-time problem called *sebeteled*. She is unable to wake up, although are "things moving inside your body. You can't scream either. If you wake up you hear running and pounding, like dancing, outside." Sophie's

---

[6]Initiated by the government of Botswana in 1980, *Tirelo Setshaba* (known as *Tirelo Setshaba* participants, or TSPs) was meant to complement the education system as a national study-service plan to form ideal citizens. Open only to Tswana citizens, form 5 finishers (seniors) spent a year in a remote area of Botswana to learn about other people, national development, and different career possibilities. In the process, they would learn a set of life and career skills, mature, and develop self-confidence. TSP service was voluntary, but the government linked possession of a TSP completion certificate to entry into many tertiary educational institutions. After much criticism, it was discontinued in 1999.

jealousy and potency as a witch manifested itself frequently at Ofaletse's compound. One time Ofaletse's baby became ill and required several trips to indigenous healers, the chemist (pharmacist), and the hospital. A traditional healer, who attributed the illness to witchcraft and doctored her for future protection against it, eventually treated the baby.

Because of these misfortunes, Ofaletse revealed that she had twice tried to kill herself by hanging because of her depression about her mother's neglect and her own failures. She cannot find a job or a place at school, despite repeated written inquiries to various institutions, her excellent English skills, and her knowledge of computers. Her younger sister had been burned to death in an exorcism accident. During the girl's funeral, visiting mourners robbed the family of the limited clothing and photos they possessed. Even her studies have been affected. And the troubles continue: after I left, a fire destroyed all the clothes and household items I had given her, and she reported having spent several months living in the fields with her mother due to the direness of her life. Ofaletse attributes almost all of this travail to the actions of witches.

To counteract the witchcraft and change her luck, Ofaletse joined the congregation of a small, local independent church. This church was close to her compound, and several good friends belonged to it. She began wearing a headscarf, as good Tswana women are supposed to do, and told me she would avoid alcohol (although she didn't drink alcohol anyway), nonmarital sex, and being disrespectful. She felt regular church attendance was a must if she was to alleviate her problems. Since Ofaletse sought to confirm that witches had caused her troubles, she participated in a special church ceremony. Church prophets visited her compound, and an all-night prayer vigil revealed that, indeed, the source of her misfortune stemmed from a group of witches who met regularly to dance at night in her compound. A ritual would be required, they said, to counter this witchcraft. They would need a goat of specific size, color, and horns to sacrifice. To date, this ritual has not been performed because Ofaletse's family lacks the ability to organize it. She has since moved from this bad-luck compound to an even more isolated, barren plot. At least, she feels, this plot is far away from the witches who plagued her, and she is confident that the new hut she is building will remain standing.

## Conclusion

Witchcraft is a set of culturally defined beliefs and activities that people use to make sense of problems in their lives. In Botswana, the data reveal that those believed to engage in witchcraft are usually women, often kin or neighbors, and that they do so out of jealousy. My work among youth suggests that victims of witchcraft are often people without power who experience regular misfortune. Blaming misfortune on witches is a way of explaining it. Once diagnosed, traditional healers or church rituals designed to treat witchcraft can restore the afflicted's self-confidence and optimism.

# Review Questions

1. According to Burke, what kinds of people do Tswana think are most likely to be witches and how do these people work their evil? Do they confront witches?

2. What are the main cures for witchcraft?

3. How do anthropologists explain the existence of belief systems like witchcraft?

4. How do we explain misfortune in the United States? Are there any similarities between U.S. explanations and those found in Botswana?

# 35

# Cargo Beliefs and Religious Experience

*Stephen C. Leavitt*

*Revitalization movements usually respond to a feeling of loss and power-lessness caused by rapid change and colonial domination, and several have given rise to great world religions. One of the most unusual examples of re-vitalization movements, however, has occurred in New Guinea. These are cargo cults (cargo is pidgin for Western goods) that attempt, through ritual, to generate cargo wealth thought to be under the control of ancestral spirits. In this article, Stephen Leavitt reviews the history and social functions of cargo cults. But he goes a step further by showing how cargo cults meet the needs of individuals, especially the need for support from one's immediate ancestors.*

In August 1984 I began two years' research among the Bumbita Arapesh in the East Sepik Province of Papua New Guinea. I had planned to study religious experience in a secret men's cult. Soon after I arrived, though, I was told that the men's cult was gone forever: only two months earlier several Bumbita acting in the name of Jesus had revealed the cult secrets to women and children, making it impossible for the men to return to cult activities. Nevertheless, I had come at an opportune time, some said, for Jesus himself was due to arrive and usher in a new age in November.

The Bumbita and their neighbors were in the midst of what was locally known as a "revival," a period of widespread Evangelical Christianity. Missionaries had been in the area since the 1950s when the South Sea Evangelical Mission had established a station in Bumbita territory. However, they had had only limited success in converting local people; many people had been baptized at some point, but most had also left the church again after their enthusiasm had died down. All agreed, though, that 1984 was different. The revelation of cult secrets meant that there was no turning back to the old religion.

As time passed, I learned that some of the Bumbita Christian ideas were quite different from our own. Most Bumbita did find in Christianity a promise of a transformed world of happiness, and they believed that when Jesus came, there would no longer be illness, hunger, or death. But many also hoped for the arrival of vast material wealth. In their view, Jesus would bring with him huge quantities of rice, tinned meat, clothing, housing materials, and other goods. These are the kinds of goods that Europeans had brought with them into the area. As many Bumbita see it, all of this material wealth must have a magical or spiritual origin—it must be their own ancestors who really own the wealth, and somehow the Europeans figured out how to acquire some of it. Through Jesus' return, the ancestors would now be passing all their wealth onto their living descendants and rightful heirs.

These ideas were familiar to me because they were similar to those found in "cargo cults," the well-known religious movements that had been going on for generations in Papua New Guinea. Cargo cults are religious movements that involve attempts, usually through ritual, to attain vast amounts of material wealth thought to be under the control of ancestral spirits. In the early days of European colonization of the Pacific, when supplies of cargo were routinely unloaded from ships, the display of wealth made a strong impression on the local peoples. Although their own societies had complex ritual and social systems, and although they had developed intricate seafaring technologies, the Pacific islanders were truly amazed at what the Europeans possessed. It was not long before religious movements appeared, seeking to explain this seemingly miraculous access to wealth. Cult leaders would tell people that the Europeans must be following special rituals, that if they too could follow them carefully, the ancestors would return with the cargo. The rituals often involved imitating strange behaviors observed in Europeans, such as forming rigid lines and marching in unison or singing hymns for hours on end in church services. Frequently, cargo movements incorporated Christian ideas learned from missionaries, even though the missions opposed this kind of reinterpretation of the Christian message.

In some instances, the rituals became very elaborate. People built imitation communication centers and airstrips with bamboo control towers in hopes that cargo-laden planes would then land. In one well-known cult, now called the "Johnson cult," leaders even collected money from their followers to send to the United States in hopes of buying President Lyndon Johnson.

The largest movement to touch the Bumbita area occurred in 1971, when the cult leader Yaliwan claimed that the removal of two cement geological survey markers from the top of a well-known mountain would release cargo from the mountain. Yaliwan's organization collected membership fees from people over a wide area. The idea was that if one was an official member, one would be sure to get a share of the cargo when it came. On the appointed day villagers in even distant areas stayed in their houses, in fear of a terrible cataclysm. The markers were unearthed and carried down the mountainside, but the ancestors' failure to arrive did not stop the movement. In fact, Yaliwan was subsequently elected to represent his district in the national parliament.

The recurring cargo movements posed serious problems for colonial administrators because, although the cults were most active, people would neglect their gardens and other work in hopes that a new world would soon be upon them. There was also a concern that people would be duped into giving hard-earned money to cult leaders. In fact, money-collecting for cargo cult activity was made illegal by the colonial government, and when Papua New Guinea gained independence in 1975, those laws remained on the books. Today, although the term "cargo cult" has a bad name in Papua New Guinea, people continue to have strong beliefs in the ancestral control of cargo, and these beliefs continue to find expression in Christian religious movements like the Bumbita revival in 1984.

The seemingly bizarre beliefs typical of cargo cults have intrigued anthropologists interested in religious movements and the impact of colonial rule. Researchers saw similarities between these cults and religious movements in other parts of the world. The emphasis on ritual, the reliance on visions of charismatic leaders, and the hopes for a complete world transformation are common features of cults organized in response to colonial domination, In the nineteenth century, for example, Native American religious movements such as the Ghost Dance sought to create a new world through the performance of key rituals. These movements had arisen in response to crises over the loss of cultural traditions and the disappearance of the buffalo. Anthropologists saw the cargo cult as another example of the way people try to regenerate meaning in a time of cultural crisis.

But the emphasis on ancestral control of cargo was distinctive, and to explain this feature anthropologists looked to the pre-existing cultural understandings of Pacific peoples. The traditional religions of Papua New Guinea emphasized the role of ancestral spirits in taking care of people. A family could produce a thriving crop of yams or sweet potatoes only with magical assistance from ancestral spirits. It therefore made sense to think that European food and other goods might also come from this supernatural source. In addition, traditional cultures in Papua New Guinea placed a great deal of emphasis on exchange and the giving of gifts as a basis for building relationships and achieving prestige. People cemented friendships, built alliances, and resolved disputes by mounting large-scale exchanges of food with others. They also competed with rivals by engaging in competitive exchanges.

The Europeans who arrived did not share the same view of how relationships are built. They had control over extremely attractive material goods, but they refused to enter into proper exchange relations with the local people. Instead, they instituted colonial control and acted as superiors. Some anthropologists have argued, then, that the Papua New Guinean preoccupation with cargo is a way of rebuilding a sense of independence and prestige in the face of colonial rule.

My own research suggests that these explanations make sense, but that they cannot be the whole answer. Contemporary Papua New Guineans know quite a bit about how commerce works and where material goods come from. Many earn money through jobs or cash-cropping, and they buy Western goods for themselves. European colonial control has been replaced by an independent government. Nevertheless, many people today—people who have gone through schools, worked in plantations or factories, and participated in failed cargo cults—continue to look for a way to get cargo from ancestors. Why do cargo ideas persist after so many years?

Cargo ideology has to be understood as part of a religious world view that gives meaning to the larger questions in life while it also addresses the most deeply personal concerns of individual believers. Colonial rule is gone and some money is now available, but Papua New Guineans must still deal with the fact that they are relatively insignificant players on the world stage, and they have relatively little wealth in comparison to people elsewhere. Cargo ideology takes these diffuse and irresolvable existential problems and translates them into an idiom that is deeply personal. Instead of having to think about their position in the world at large, people can focus on their relations with those close to them. The "ancestors" that people turn to for cargo are not distant and anonymous supernatural beings; they are in fact the spirits of fathers, mothers, and other close kin. This means that to really understand the central idea behind cargo—that ancestors will bring wealth and bestow it upon the living—one needs to think in terms of what it means personally for a given individual. Cargo ideas are about relations with deceased parents. Often, getting cargo means receiving a sign, a gift, from one's own parents or grandparents showing that they forgive, that they still care.

When Bumbita men and women try to understand cargo in terms of their relationships with their own parents, they are looking for a way to give real meaning to all the bewildering changes that have been going on around them. It is a way for them to recast their colonial experience in terms that they can understand and deal with. But there is a cost. The problem is that for most people, the bulk of the cargo has not—and never will—arrive. As the Bumbita see it, the ancestors are for some unknown reason still holding back. This means that their religious experience remains filled with feelings of longing and remorse. It can be a difficult emotional predicament.

To illustrate the personal side to religious experience, my work focuses on detailed narratives or stories collected from several individuals. The idea is to speak with a few people in depth, recording their narratives carefully, so that I can later follow their line of thinking in detail. This method has the virtue of showing the personal side to religious belief while at the same time allowing people's words to stand for themselves. A major drawback is that such individual stories cannot be viewed as "representative" of the society as a whole. Personal stories must necessarily remain personal. Nevertheless. I believe this approach offers a richer sense of themes that might well be a part of other people's experience as well.

To illustrate, let's look at the stories of two older men who, when they converted, adopted the Christian names "Matthew" and "John." Each was around sixty years old when I did my interviews (some 25 hours total). I visited them at their houses or asked them to visit me, and we usually talked, alone, for one to two hours in a sitting. I tried not to guide them too much, but I did make it known that I was interested in their religious beliefs.

Matthew, a widower, first converted to Christianity in 1967, and he remains one of the most vocal proponents of the Christian cause in the Bumbita area. Before converting he was trained as a sorcerer, and he admits that he practiced sorcery. Matthew is well known for his preoccupation with the local missionaries and with Europeans in general. Everywhere he goes he carries a large sack containing Christian literature, calendars of years past, photographs of his favorite missionaries, and even some letters from them sent from various countries. Every item in his bundle is tattered, stained, and frayed, showing signs of frequent handling. His house also has mementos of his relations with missionaries, including a child's plastic gramophone with a stack of 78 r.p.m. records of sermons translated by the mission into the Bumbita Arapesh language. Matthew has been active in every cargo movement that has touched the Bumbita area.

Interviews with Matthew showed that one attraction of cargo beliefs for him was to resolve feelings of guilt that he had toward his father who had died some years before. Throughout his adult life, Matthew had a troubled relationship with his father. He says that his father once tried to seduce his fiancée, when she was living in their hamlet. Matthew claims that when he found out, he even tried to kill his father with a spear. As punishment, the father was banished for life from the village. Matthew believes that his father later retaliated with sorcery by killing Matthew's wife (she died in childbirth). Although he and his father were reconciled later, Matthew still longs for some sign that his father had forgiven him—a sign that he had not received before his father died.

Matthew's story will show that he was searching for a sign of forgiveness from his dead father by cultivating relationships with European missionaries. Matthew's most startling belief was that among these missionaries was one who was really the ghost of his own father. It is, in fact, a common belief among the Bumbita that some Europeans are the spirits of dead relatives. But Matthew, more than most people, appeared to be longing to find his personal ghost and to get from him a gift of cargo that would signal his father's forgiveness. All of this came out in a story Matthew told me about his parting with a local missionary who was going home to Germany. Matthew had brought the missionary some yams and greens as a farewell gift. He describes the subsequent interaction:

> [I asked the missionary about his leaving, and] he said that he would stay. But then when I asked him [again], he didn't answer and I sat down. He went and got a funnel and filled it with salt for me, and then I asked him. I said, "I think you are my father. I think you have the face of my father, Turingi, and your wife is like my mother, Tinga'wen. I can see the resemblance." And there was no answer. He did not answer me because he was ashamed. He said, "Just take the salt and go. You shouldn't come and blabber too much." [laughs] And now you see here, I have written their names in my book.

Matthew is claiming here that his father has returned from the dead as a European missionary. He says he can tell by the quiet way the man reacted when he gave him food—he was ashamed, so he silently gives Matthew a gift of salt and tells him to be quiet about this.

In reality, the missionary most likely thought he was paying Matthew for the yams and greens, but Matthew has come to see it in another way, as a gesture of intimate communication. The missionary says nothing, and Matthew takes it as a tacit confession, as if to say, "Yes, I am your father, you have guessed it, but say nothing to anyone about it." The gift was for Matthew a silent symbolic statement about the goodwill in their relationship. Although the gift of salt was a trivial one, Matthew's reaction to it shows his longing for more extensive cargo: he wants to be given material wealth by Europeans because he believes this cargo is really a gift from his own dead kin signaling their love for him.

My interviews with a second man, John, also showed that dreams of cargo had a deep personal significance. Unlike Matthew, John was a highly respected leader in his day. He was now sixty years old and retired. John was a short man by Bumbita standards, and he retained a lively demeanor. John also felt that his father would be the ultimate source of the cargo. But although Matthew looked for father figures among the missionaries, John saw God himself as his father.

John looked for God to give his approval by giving him secret knowledge as a key to material wealth. In the Bumbita view, it is proper to expect a father-ancestor to offer secrets and magical help, and John is extending this idea to include the concept of cargo. As John saw it, with the cargo he could then become a great and powerful leader by distributing it to others, just as traditionally Bumbita leaders had built power by giving away pigs and yams. Like Matthew, John feels that receiving the cargo will be final proof of his father's good will and approval.

John said God communicated with him mostly through dreams. In Bumbita culture, dreams are regarded as real experiences, albeit in a spiritual realm. People use dreams as omens to guide them in their hunting or in their pursuit of love relationships. Here John related to me one dream he had had some two months before the interview in which I recorded it. The dream went as follows:

> I dreamt that I had gone inside a house. I went and I sat like this. Everything here, the books, the money, were heaped around. I was on the edge of it all. It was a big house. A huge house. A house of iron. It had rooms that went on and on and I was sitting at the fence in front. Now I don't know how to write things; reading, yes, I can read some, but [someone else] would have to write [for me]. . . . But my [dream] spirit, when I went into this house, I went and I myself wrote everything and I myself checked everything over. I wrote and straightened the books and put them aside. . . . Then I got up to come back and a voice said, "Now you have come."—it was like a sign, right? When you can see it all. [It said,] "Later, when you come back, you will sit at this spot. Yes, you will straighten up everything later. Now you have seen it and written everything down and straightened it up and you will go. Later when you come back, you will straighten it all up, later, not now." . . . I woke up and remembered this and then went to sleep again, and a voice said, "This man, . . . he will come and stay at this house and check everything and distribute it to the people here. . . . This man will become a king. The king for distributing everything, for checking everything."

In this dream, John identifies himself with the clerks in the warehouses, with those people he sees as controlling the material wealth. His view is that clerks are very powerful because they preside over the goods. He says that God made him a clerk to show him that he will in fact be like "a king" in the new age, doling out the fates of the people. His main activity in the dream is writing, a skill still associated with Europeans and a sore point for adults who see their children learning to write in school. In this dream John shows that he looks to God to make him a great leader by giving him the power to distribute cargo.

A second dream has some of the same messages, but here John's ideas about the dream show that, as with Matthew, the core emotional content has to do with his own father. The high position that John sees for himself in the new age must be given to him by God, and for John, that God is his actual father. In this account, I follow John's statements step by step to show how his thoughts lead him from a dream about cargo to his personal relationship with his own father. He begins,

> [One night] I took the Bible inside and made a fire and just lay down. I said, "God"—I prayed—"God, I want you to show me my present now, where is it? I want to see it. . . .
>
> I want you yourself to show me so I can see it . . . I want to see my present."
> All right, when I went to sleep, I went straight to it. Man, I went inside, they—a big house.

At this point, he stumbled over his words because he felt he had to hide part of the dream as he related it to me. He later revealed to me that it had not been "a big house" that he had seen in the dream, but actually a graveyard. The dead were presiding over the cargo in the graveyard. John said that he had originally hidden this fact from me because he had not wanted to be accused of being a "cargo cultist." He went on to say that he was not a cargo cultist but a "good man," that he had not sought out the details of the dream—God himself had given them to him. He wants me to take him seriously and not write him off as a cultist. What he is about to say is important to him. He continues:

> They had put up a cloth from Hong Kong. They had hung it up and it went down like this, at the door. When I went and lifted up this cloth and pulled it up—Sorry! Huge huge boxes, more and more of them, going up to the clouds. Many many boxes. . . . In just one box, there would be so much inside. With two or three there would be even more. I just gazed up at them like this. When I looked down, I saw mushrooms growing on the boxes, and I thought, "They were good here, but some of them, I think they have already rotted. Everything has rotted so there are mush-rooms growing there." . . . I checked the ones that were on top and they were still good. You know, they went up and up and then at the top—I looked up, and I thought, "Hey, I hope a box doesn't come off and fall and break my head." So I lifted my leg onto one of the boxes and climbed on up and up and then I started and I was there lying in my bed. Then what did I do? I cried and cried over the pre-sent that God had shown me.

This dream conveys well the awe inspired by visions of cargo. The cargo here was under the control of the ancestors since, as he later confessed, the set-ting of the dream was really a graveyard and not a "house." As often happens in Bumbita dreams about the dead, an image of rot and decay appears in the dream, along with some anxiety, evident here in his fear that a case might fall on top of him. But unlike with most dreams about the dead, John interprets these images in a way that avoids unpleasantness. He points out that the decay indicates that God was saying that there would be so much cargo that much of it would rot with no one to use it, and he also succeeds in waking up before any boxes fall. John's euphoria over having had this dream points to the emotional power of the cargo itself. The cargo is a "present" that has deep meaning.

As his narrative continues, John then goes on immediately to link these cargo images to childhood memories of the amassed food of men from his fa-ther's generation. In Bumbita society, the ability to grow and display huge quan-tities of yams is the highest expression of male achievement. John continues,

> [Our ancestors] used to fill up the yams, in a huge bin. . . . We would dance and then go and give it to [our exchange partners]. So now I saw this image [of cargo in the dream], and it was just like what they used to do before, what [our fathers] did. It would go way up and up. Heaps and heaps of food, and given away. Now God has shown this to me. The present is hidden.

Here he links the heaps of food for exchange with the image of cargo from his dream. He talks of the mounds of food going "up and up," in what suggests a vision of a child's awe at the sight of such amounts of food. He links it with the awe he felt in the dream upon discovering the true extent of the wealth (the "present") controlled by the dead. Thus, the emotions he felt in his dream at the sight of the cargo were not unfamiliar—he remembers similar feelings from a time when senior men used to assemble food for exchange. In this way, John reveals what is for him a symbolic link between the ancestors of his dream and the senior adult male figures from his youth.

John then returns immediately to the significance of his having been shown the "present." He says:

> The present that [God] has shown me, the present here, it will all happen. You will see it, I am happy with him too. All of the time that I walk around my thinking dwells on only this. I don't stray from it. I think only of this that God has shown me. I think of it like this. If a man is no good, if a man has sins, if he prays and asks God for something, then God won't answer his prayer. No way. Because this thing, the sin, is there. It closes off the path to God. . . . How is God going to tell you? . . . If you are a holy man, free, and you are with God, he will hear it and God will answer. You will see God.

By this point, John has gone from a dream's image of splendid cargo to a sense of awe at the power of older generations, and finally to the argument that seeing cargo proves he is right with God. All that remains is for him to make the transition to his own father. And indeed, immediately following the passage cited above, he continues:

> A good man will see [God] here. God, I know, the God of the Christians. My God is—if I am Christian, then my God is Christian. Now he has died, and now I have seen him. I know now. It is finished. [laughs] Sorry, if I talk on like this, then the happiness is going to well up now! He will come. My God . . . [overcome with emotion, he laughs to avoid crying. He pauses]
>
> SL: You said you have seen him, what does he look like, God?
>
> My God? A big man, a big man. Before he was short, but now that he has gone, he's a big man. Happiness. I am happy with him. True, if before, he weren't Christian, yes, he would have gone and been lost. . . . But he was already Christian when he died. So now he's there. He will look after me, he is with me. He was Christian already. Now he has shown me everything. Who is he? God the father.

As he becomes absorbed with what he is saying, his description of God's position on revealing secrets to sinners becomes almost a reverie in the memory of his own father, of a short man who now seems big to him, of someone who looks after him, and above all, of someone who has shown him an image of the mass of wealth that the ancestors control. John is overcome by the recognition that his father/God has decided to reserve a special place for him in the new age, that he, John, will be the new leader.

Thus John's Christianity, with its concern about cargo and its inspired hopes for reunion with the dead, also works its way back to a personal relationship with his own father. John's God is his father, and the cargo is his sign of reassurance. John has become convinced that by being a Christian he will acquire that cargo.

For the Bumbita, Christian doctrines preach that the ancestors have good will, that in the end, in the transformation that will come with the return of Christ, they will demonstrate that good will and they will deliver. In his final summation of his thoughts about his father, John expresses with some eloquence the personal significance of getting the cargo, of knowing about and seeing God. He says in a whisper, again fighting tears:

> Now [in my life] I am just the same as I was before. But in my dreams, yes, I get it all. Life will go on until Jesus comes. Then I will get it, I will know about him, I will see him. His thinking. His wishes. The eyes of my father. Me and him. The eyes of father God, I will know them.

Although each of these stories bears the stamp of two different personalities, they both reveal a perspective that is a well-known part of New Guinean ideas about cargo. At the heart of it is the hope that the world will be transformed by renewed relationships with spirits of the dead. What these narratives suggest is that when some Bumbita think about their futures, whether it be their own personal lives or their larger place on the world stage, they do so in terms of a familiar family scenario, with parental figures (spirits) sharing or withholding gifts. By thinking of the situation in this way, they can take the bewildering and difficult problems of coping with the colonial experience and translate them into a much more personal and familiar set of ideas about love and nurture. In the end, cargo is important because it is a visible sign that the spirits are there and that they do care.

The stories of Matthew and John show how beliefs about cargo in Papua New Guinea can take the shape they do from the role they play in giving meaning to individuals. Although it is dangerous to make broad generalizations from the accounts of two people, their stories do point to a personal side of cargo ideas that has not been emphasized in most anthropological explanations. To have a more complete understanding of religious experience, one has to pay close attention to what individual believers say about the significance of their beliefs for their own lives. In the case of cargo beliefs, we can see that there is more going on than one might at first think. It is not just that the Bumbita have come to some unusual conclusions about how to interpret the changes in their world—they are also making an active effort to integrate the changes into their deepest personal sense of who they are.

# Review Questions

1. What are the main attributes of most cargo cults, according to Leavitt? Give some examples of the form cargo cults can take.

2. How have anthropologists tried to explain cargo cults?

3. Under what conditions do cargo cults occur, and what is their goal?

4. In what ways do cargo cults embrace the teaching of Christian missionaries?

5. Why does Leavitt think cargo cults persist? What is their religious function for individuals?

# NINE

# Culture Change and Applied Anthropology

Nowhere in the world do human affairs remain precisely constant from year to year. New ways of doing things mark the history of even the most stable groups. Change occurs when an Australian aboriginal dreams about a new myth and teaches it to the members of his band; when a loader in a restaurant kitchen invents a way to stack plates more quickly in the dishwasher; or when a New Guinea Big Man cites the traditional beliefs about ghosts to justify the existence of a new political office devised by a colonial government. Wherever people interpret their natural and social worlds in a new way, cultural change has occurred. Broad or narrow, leisurely or rapid, such change is part of life in every society.

Culture change can originate from two sources: innovation and borrowing. **Innovation** is the invention of qualitatively new forms. It involves the recombination of what people already know into something different. For example, Canadian Joseph-Armand Bombardier became an innovator when he mated tracks, designed to propel earth-moving equipment, to a small bus that originally ran on tires, producing the first snowmobile in the 1950s. Later, the Skolt Lapps of Finland joined him as innovators when they adapted his now smaller, more refined snowmobile for herding reindeer in 1961. The Lapp innovation was not the vehicle itself. That was borrowed. What was new was the use of the vehicle in herding, something usually done by men on skis.

Innovations are more likely to occur and to be adopted during stressful times when traditional culture no longer works well. Bombardier, for example, began work on his snowmobile after he was unable to reach medical help in time to save the life of his critically ill son during a Canadian winter storm. Frustrated by the slowness of his horse and sleigh, he set out to create a faster vehicle.

The other basis of culture change is **borrowing.** Borrowing—or **diffusion,** as it is sometimes called—refers to the adoption of something new from another group. Tobacco, for example, was first domesticated and grown in the New World but quickly diffused to Europe and Asia after 1492. Such items as the umbrella, pajamas, Arabic numerals, and perhaps even the technology to make steel came to Europe from India. Ideologies and religions may diffuse from one society to another.

An extreme diffusionist view has been used to explain most human achievements. For example, author Erich von Däniken argues that features of ancient New World civilizations were brought by space invaders. Englishman G. Elliot Smith claimed that Mayan and Aztec culture diffused from Egypt. Thor Heyerdahl sailed a reed boat, the *Ra II*, from Africa to South America to prove that an Egyptian cultural origin was possible for New World civilization.

Whether something is an innovation or borrowed, it must pass through a process of **social acceptance** before it can become part of a culture. Indeed many, if not most, novel ideas and things remain unattractive and relegated to obscurity. To achieve social acceptance, an innovation must become known to the members of a society, must be accepted as valid, and must fit into a system of cultural knowledge revised to accept it.

Several principles facilitate social acceptance. If a change wins the support of a person in authority, it may gain the approval of others. Timing is also important. It would have made little sense for a Lapp to attempt the introduction of snowmobiles when there was no snow or when the men who do the reindeer herding were scattered over their vast grazing territory. Other factors also affect social acceptance. Changes have a greater chance of acceptance if they meet a felt need, if they appeal to people's prestige (in societies where prestige is important), and if they provide some continuity with traditional customs.

Change may take place under a variety of conditions, from the apparently dull day-to-day routine of a stable society to the frantic climate of a revolution. One situation that has occupied many anthropologists interested in change is **cultural contact,** particularly situations of contact where one society politically dominates another. World history is replete with examples of such domination, which vary in outcome from annihilation, in the case of the Tasmanians and hundreds of tribes in North and South America, Africa, Asia, and even ancient Europe, to the political rule that indentured countless millions of people to colonial powers.

The process of change caused by these conditions is called **acculturation.** Acculturation results from cultural contact. Acculturative change may affect dominant societies as well as subordinate ones. After their ascendance in India, for example, the British came to wear *khaki* clothes, live in *bungalows,* and trek through *jungles*—all Indian concepts.

But those who are subordinated experience the most far-reaching changes in their way of life. From politically independent, self-sufficient people, they usually become subordinate and dependent. Sweeping changes in social structure and values may occur, along with a resulting social disorganization.

Although the age of colonial empires is largely over, the destruction of tribal culture continues at a rapid pace today. As we saw in Reed's article in Part Three of this book, hundreds of thousands of Amazonian Indians have already perished in the last few years because of intrusive frontier and development programs. Following almost exactly the pattern of past colonial exploitation, modern governments bent on "progress" displace and often kill off indigenous tribal populations. The frequent failure of development, coupled with its damaging impact on native peoples, has caused many anthropologists to reassess their role. As a result, more and more anthropologists have become part of native resistance to outside intrusion.

A less dramatic, but in many ways no less important, agent of change is the world economy. No longer can most people live in self-sufficient isolation. Their future is inevitably tied in with an overall system of market exchange. Take the Marshall Islanders described by anthropologist Michael Rynkiewich, for example. Although they cultivate to meet their own subsistence needs, they also raise coconuts for sale on the world market. Receipts from the coconut crop go to pay for outboard motors and gasoline, cooking utensils, and a variety of other goods they don't manufacture themselves but have come to depend on. Recently several major American food companies have eliminated coconut oil from their products because of its high level of saturated fat. This loss has created lower demand for copra (dried coconut meat), from which the oil is pressed. Reduced demand, in turn, may cause substantial losses to the Marshall Islanders. A people who once could subsist independently have now become prisoners of the world economic system.

Anthropologists may themselves become agents of change, applying their work to practical problems. **Applied anthropology,** as opposed to academic anthropology, includes any use of anthropological knowledge to influence social interaction, to maintain or change social institutions, or to direct the course of cultural change. There are four basic uses of anthropology contained within the applied field: adjustment anthropology, administrative anthropology, action anthropology, and advocate anthropology.

**Adjustment anthropology** uses anthropological knowledge to make social interaction more predictable among people who operate with different cultural codes. For example, take the anthropologists who consult with companies and government agencies about intercultural communication. It is often their job to train Americans to interpret the cultural rules that govern interaction in another society. For a business person who will work in Latin America, the anthropologist may point out the appropriate culturally defined speaking distances, ways to sit, definitions of time, topics of conversation, times for business talk, and so on. All of these activities would be classified as adjustment anthropology.

**Administrative anthropology** uses anthropological knowledge for planned change by those who are external to the local cultural group. It is the use of anthropological knowledge by a person with the power to make decisions. If an anthropologist provides knowledge to a mayor about the culture of constituents, he or she is engaged in administrative anthropology. So would advisers to chief administrators of U.S. trust territories such as once existed in places like the Marshall Islands.

**Action anthropology** uses anthropological knowledge for planned change by the local cultural group. The anthropologist acts as a catalyst, providing information but avoiding decision making, which remains in the hands of the people affected by the decisions.

**Advocate anthropology** uses anthropological knowledge by the anthropologist to increase the power of self-determination of a particular cultural group. Instead of focusing on the process of innovation, the anthropologist centers attention on discovering the sources of power and how a group can gain access to them. James Spradley took such action when he studied tramps in 1968. He discovered that police and courts systematically deprived tramps of their power to control their lives and of the rights accorded normal citizens. By releasing his findings to the Seattle newspapers, he helped tramps gain additional power and weakened the control of Seattle authorities.

Whether they are doing administrative, advocate, adjustment, or action anthropology, anthropologists take, at least in part, a qualitative approach. They do ethnography, discover the cultural knowledge of their informants, and apply this information in the ways discussed previously. In contrast to the quantitative data so often prized by other social scientists, they use the insider's viewpoint to discover problems, to advise, and to generate policy.

The articles in this part illustrate several aspects of cultural change and applied anthropology. The first, by Terence Turner, relates the case of how one people, the Kayapo of the Brazilian Amazon, have successfully resisted external threats to their existence as a people. By uniting Indians, environmental groups, and legislators, and using the international media, they have managed to protect and expand their forest area and advance the international environmental cause. The second selection, by medical anthropologist Sonia Patten, describes her experience as an applied anthropologist. Working with USAID funding, she and a team of specialists designed a program using milk goats to improve children's nutrition in Malawi. The third article, by David McCurdy, discusses the modern uses of anthropology. From studies of General Motors workers, to program assessment for people with AIDS, to participation in government health projects, to international counseling, professional anthropologists put their discipline to work. In this article, McCurdy looks at one way in which the ethnographic perspective can be put to work in a business setting. Finally, in the last article, John Omohundro tackles a question often asked by students: "What do you do with an anthropology major?" Basing his answer on years of work with his institution's career development office, he argues that anthropology teaches a number of skills that are useful in the world of work. The trick, he notes, is for students to translate these skills into resume language that employers can understand.

# Key Terms

| | |
|---|---|
| acculturation   *p. 384* | borrowing   *p. 383* |
| action anthropology   *p. 385* | cultural contact   *p. 384* |
| adjustment anthropology   *p. 385* | diffusion   *p. 383* |
| administrative anthropology   *p. 385* | innovation   *p. 383* |
| advocate anthropology   *p. 386* | social acceptance   *p. 384* |
| applied anthropology   *p. 385* | |

# 36

# The Kayapo Resistance

*Terence Turner*

*Until about 200 years ago, vast areas of the world were inhabited by native, mostly hunter-gatherer or horticultural, peoples. Few native groups, however, have survived the ravages of colonial and economic expansion, and those who are left seem destined to become victims of "progress." In this article, however, Terence Turner argues that "Fourth World" peoples, in this case the Kayapo of the Brazilian Amazon, have acted to conserve their own political autonomy while simultaneously aiding the world conservation movement. Apparently doomed to extinction by the relentless encroachment of Brazilian settlers, loggers, miners, and dam builders, the Kayapo have managed to mobilize not only themselves, but other Indians, environmentalists, legislators, and the world press in a united effort to defend the forest and their right to live in it.*

"The Role of Indigenous Peoples in the Environmental Crisis: The Example of the Kayapo of the Brazilian Amazon" by Terence Turner. From *Perspectives in Biology and Medicine 36:3* (1993), 526–545. © The Johns Hopkins University Press. Reprinted by permission of the Johns Hopkins University Press.

As increasing numbers of people have become aware of the imminence of the destruction of the world's tropical forests and the probable consequences for the atmosphere and climate of the planet, voices have increasingly been heard drawing attention to the need for concern for human populations of forest dwellers, as well as the floral and faunal components of the ecosystem. This has been motivated in part by humanitarian concerns, in part by more specific concerns for indigenous political and legal rights, in part by an awareness that native forest peoples may possess valuable knowledge of their environments, and also, at times, by a realization that the traditional adaptive activities of such peoples may make important functional contributions to the ecosystems in which they live. Whatever their specific point of departure, however, advocates of native forest peoples have tended to assume that recognition of the rights and contributions of the native inhabitants of the forests, as well as their physical and cultural survival, would depend, like the salvation of the forests themselves, upon them. That native forest peoples themselves, many of whom number among the most primitive and remote human societies on earth, should come to play an important role as allies and even leaders in the world struggle to save the forests is a prospect so apparently remote as to seem only a little less improbable than Martians arriving to lend a hand. Yet this is precisely what has been happening in the last few years, nowhere with more impressive scope and success than in the case of the Kayapo Indians of the Brazilian Amazon.

## The Kayapo: Ethnographic and Historical Background

The Kayapo are a nation of Ge-speaking Indians who inhabit the middle and lower reaches of the valley of the Xingu River, one of the major southern tributaries of the Amazon. Their total population is currently around 2,500, divided among 14 mutually independent communities. The largest of these communities, Gorotire, has about 800 inhabitants, but several others are little more than hamlets. Kayapo country is a mixture of forest and savannah land, with rather more forest than open country around most of the villages. The total area covered by Kayapo communities and their associated land-use patterns is about the size of Scotland.

The massive destruction of the Amazonian environment represented by the cutting and burning of the forest, the cutting of roads, and the soil erosion and river pollution caused by mining and the building of giant hydroelectric dams, have had a shattering impact on the environment and way of life of many forest Indians of the Amazon. Even groups whose lands have not yet been reached by these activities, or are just beginning to be affected by them, now live in the permanent shadow of the threat. To understand the meaning of this threat for indigenous peoples like the Kayapo, one must stand in a Kayapo village under the dense clouds of smoke that now darken the sky over Kayapo country at the end of every dry season, as Brazilian squatters and ranchers burn off vast stretches of previously forested land to the east and south, rapidly approaching the traditional borders of Kayapo territory along a 700-mile front. It is to feel one's world burning, with the ring of fire drawing even tighter.

For members of modern industrial societies, one of the most difficult points to grasp about the relation of native tropical forest peoples to their environment, as articulated through their modes of subsistence production, is that the relationship is not felt or conceived to comprise a separate, "economic" sphere in our sense. Rather, it forms an integral part of the total social process of producing human beings and social life. The threatened annihilation of such a society's environmental base of subsistence is therefore not felt merely as an "economic" threat, nor one that can be located and confined in an external, "environmental" sphere. It is a threat to the continuity and meaning of social life. Understanding this point is essential, not only to appreciate the traumatic effects of wholesale ecological devastation on traditional societies of subsistence producers like the Kayapo, but also to understand the nature of their political response and resistance to such threats.

## The Relation of the Kayapo to the Environment through Subsistence Production

For the Kayapo, like most other contemporary Amazonian native peoples, traditional patterns of subsistence adaptation are still the basic way of life. The Kayapo produce their means of subsistence by a combination of slash-and-burn horticulture, hunting, fishing, and foraging. According to the division of labor by gender and generation, men engage in all productive pursuits incompatible with the care of young children, while women perform those which can be carried out while caring for children. This means that men hunt, fish, do the heavy and dangerous work of clearing gardens, and gather certain wild forest products that grow at great distances, requiring overnight journeys. Women do the planting, weeding, and harvesting of gardens; cut firewood; cook the food; build traditional shelters (now done almost exclusively in trekking camps); forage for such wild products as can be found within a day's round-trip walk from the village or camp; and care for children. Girls begin to help their mothers with household and garden chores while still children, but boys do little productive labor until they are inducted into the men's house, a bachelors' dormitory and men's club which stands apart from the family houses in the middle of the round village plaza.

Kayapo gardens must be cleared from fresh forestland and produce for about three years for most crops. The Kayapo raise an impressive variety of garden produce: manioc (both the bitter and sweet varieties), maize, bananas, yams, sweet potatoes, fava beans, squash, *cissus* (a leafy creeper that is a unique domesticate of their own), tobacco, *urucu* (used to make red body paint), and cotton (used to make string, but not woven). In recent years, many Kayapo have added Brazilian-introduced crops such as papaya, rice, various species of beans, pineapples, watermelon, avocado, and mango. Most families maintain about three gardens in production at any one time and clear a new one every year. After a garden is abandoned, it requires about 25 years for reforestation to render it ready for reuse. A sizable village therefore needs an extensive area of forestland for the rotation of its garden plots.

The Kayapo supplement their horticultural diet with large quantities of fish and game. Included among the latter are wild pig, tapir, deer, monkey, tortoise, armadillo, and various species of birds and rodents. Gathered wild produce is also seasonally important, and includes *babassu* coconuts (used for body and hair oil), *piki, tucum,* and brazil nuts, honey, palmito, *acai, bacaba,* and a variety of less important fruits. Hunting or fishing for the men, and gardening for the women, are more or less daily activities while the community is settled in its base village.

For considerable periods of the year, however, the Kayapo abandon their base villages and go off on collective seminomadic treks through the surrounding forest and savannah. These may last from one to three months, and may take one of several forms. Individual age-sets (most frequently, the male bachelors' set) may be sent out to gather seasonally ripening nuts or fruits; the whole village may go together; the individual senior men's societies may trek as separate groups, each with its associated women, children, and bachelor dependents; or only part of the village may go on trek to gather food for a ceremonial feast, while the rest remain behind in the village. A community may go on two or three such treks per year, so that at least some of the village may spend as much as half the year on trek. Large areas may thus be covered by all the treks undertaken by the members of a single village in a given year. In spite of the low population density of Kayapo country, therefore, most of the area is actually used by the mobile trekking groups which continually sally forth from the widely scattered base villages.

The regular alternation between trekking and base village occupation thus appears to be an integral aspect of Kayapo social organization. Why this should be so is not immediately apparent. Trekking by large collective groups is a relatively inefficient way to exploit the wild floral and faunal resources of an area. Only the adult men of the camp do any hunting. The bachelors and younger boys are typically occupied either with clearing the trail to the next day's campsite and the campsite itself, or bringing up horticultural produce from the village gardens, while the women occupy themselves with pitching or breaking camp, cutting firewood, preparing food, and tending children. The camp is moved every one or two days, but usually only for a distance of one or two kilometers, about a 15-minute walk. More game could doubtless be captured by small groups of men working alone, free to move more rapidly over greater distances. Hunting and fishing are routinely done in this way while the community is residing in the base village, and it is certainly no less productive than the hunting done on trek. Trekking by whole communities or large groups, in other words, cannot be accounted for as the most efficient available method of acquiring needed protein or other foodstuffs.

A similar question arises over the frequency with which Kayapo bands moved their village sites in the days before peaceful relations were established with the Brazilians. There is in fact no ecological reason why Kayapo villages as large as two thousand would ever need to move as a group from their permanent village sites to remain supplied with the foods they require. Notwithstanding this fact, Kayapo villages before pacification tended to move as often as every two, or more usually five to ten years. A given community would have as many as a dozen village sites, and occupy most of them over a twenty-year period. This frequency of movement, again, cannot be accounted for simply as a result of material necessity. In common with trekking, it seems part of a dynamic inherent in Kayapo social organization.

## The Social Meaning of Subsistence Production

The high mobility of Kayapo society, and the large amount of territory it requires in consequence, thus cannot be understood, as some have attempted to do, as the result of nutritional deficiencies in the soil or lack of protein or other nutrients in the faunal or floral environment. They are, rather, the corollaries and effects of the organization of Kayapo society, with its central tension between female-centered and male-centered forms of social grouping. These forms themselves, however, are articulated in terms of their complementary roles in production, although this is production understood in the Kayapo sense of the social production of human beings and social relations, which includes but is not reducible to, material subsistence. This notion of social production calls for a more extended exegesis as it is essential to an understanding of the Kayapo relationship to their natural environment and their society per se.

Kayapo patterns of environmental adaptation and subsistence production are intricately interwoven with their ways of producing human individuals. This process of human production includes what we call "socializing" children, but continues through the life cycle and the final rites of death. This individual process, in turn, is treated by the Kayapo as an integral part of the process of reproducing collective social units like extended-family households, age-sets, and ceremonial organizations, and thus of society as a whole. As I have already indicated, the division of labor in the production of material subsistence is defined in relation to the division of labor in the production of social persons and relations, with women specializing in the socialization of children. It must be clearly understood that this is not simply a natural result but a culturally imposed social pattern. Women who do not happen to be raising young children nevertheless do not go hunting and fishing. At a higher level of organization, the nuclear family forms the social unit of cooperation in the production and consumption of material subsistence, but as a social unit it owes its form primarily to its role in producing new social persons, not its functions in expediting subsistence activities. Subsistence production thus finds its place as an integral part of the global process of social production, which also includes the socialization of children, the recruitment and reconstitution of families and collective groups, and the celebration of the great communal ceremonies. In these two-to-four month long symbolic dramas, all of these levels of activity are performed in an orchestrated pattern that asserts their essential interdependence as parts of a single whole.

The Kayapo attitude toward the nonhuman natural environment must be understood as a part of this same global pattern. The Kayapo do not oppose "nature" to human society as mutually exclusive, externally related domains; nor can they be said to possess a single, uniform concept of "nature" in our sense. They recognize that the forest and savannah beyond their village clearings are products of forces that are independent of humans and not under social control. They further recognize that they depend upon these natural forces and products for their own social existence, and that social persons are in fact largely "natural" beings, whose physical bodies, senses, and libidinal energies are as extra-social in origin as any forest tree or wild animal. Disease, death, shamanic trance, insanity, and periods of transition in left-crisis ritual are seen as moments when the continuity between the internal natural core of human social actors and the external natural environment of the forest and animal world asserts itself, short-circuiting and blacking out the interposed, insulating social veneer. At such times, the social person reverts to a "natural" state, here conceived as one of entropic dissolution of social form. At other times, as in the rituals of initiation at puberty or the everyday bringing in of game, gathered nuts, or garden produce from the forest, displacing or penetrating the boundary between nature and society has the opposite result: an infusion of energy which, directed into social channels, enables society to exist and renew itself. Human beings and society itself, in sum, are seen as partly "natural" entities, dependent on continual infusions of energy from their natural surroundings. The reproduction of human society, the reproduction of socialized human beings, and the reproduction of the natural forest and savannah environment are thus interconnected parts of a single great process.

Society and its members, in sum, are essentially seen as appropriating and channeling natural energy, and are thus dependent on the ability of the natural world (meaning the forest, animals, birds, rivers, and fish) to reproduce itself and continue as a great reservoir and source of the energy society must continually draw upon to live. The destruction of the forest, the killing or driving away of its animals, or the pollution of the rivers and killing of their fish, therefore, are not seen by the Kayapo simply as an attack on "the natural environment" in our sense, but as a direct assault upon them as a society and as individuals.

This view, it should immediately be added, is fully compatible with the destruction of trees and animals on a considerable scale for appropriation by the Kayapo of the energy stored in their flesh, fruits, or the soil on which they stand. The Kayapo operate with a rough rule of thumb derived from millennia of experience, a sense of the ability of the local environment to accommodate a certain level of destruction, inflicted by their traditional modes and levels of subsistence activity, and still regenerate itself. They have no mystical sense of reverence or respect for individual trees or animals and feel no hesitation about chopping them down or taking them as game whenever their interests demand. What concerns the Kayapo is nature in the aggregate, or more specifically, the survival and reproduction of a sufficient slice of the natural environment to support their traditional way of life. It was only when they realized that this aggregate capacity for regeneration was threatened by the vast scale of the destruction now being inflicted on the area that the Kayapo became aroused over the fate of the forest environment as such. Similarly, ecological concerns for tropical rain forests became transformed into urgent political issues in the developed world only when peoples of the developed countries realized the probable consequences of this destruction from the rest of the world's climate and population. Kayapo and First World modes of "ecological" consciousness and concern converged, in short, when, starting from very different premises, the members of both societies realized that the survival of their societies was at stake. The dramatic results of this convergence are the subject of the rest of this paper.

## The Kayapo Resistance and the Environmentalist Movement

The Kayapo area of Southern Para state is a representative microcosm of the destructive processes at work in the Amazon as a whole. Beginning in the late 1960s, the Kayapo have been confronted with virtually every major form of environmental destruction and land depredation found elsewhere in the region.

### The Kayapo Face the End of Their World

Since the 1960s there has been constant pressure from small squatters and large ranchers attempting to infiltrate Kayapo areas and clear small farms by burning off patches of forest. Land speculators have attempted to build illegal airstrips and to survey and sell off large chunks of Kayapo land to which they did not even hold legal title. In 1971, the Brazilian government built a major road of the Trans-Amazonica highway system through Kayapo country, secretly altering the route so as to amputate the Kayapo area of the Xingu National Park, which it then attempted to sell off to private owners, mostly speculators, would-be ranchers, and farmers. The road brought heavy truck and bus traffic carrying settlers and supplies to the new settlements farther west, bringing with them the perils of infectious disease and the potential for conflict with the Indians. Timber companies interested in the large stands of virgin mahogany within the boundaries of the remaining officially delimited Kayapo reserve, the Kayapo Indigenous Area, sought and obtained logging concessions for large tracts from Kayapo leaders in exchange for sizable money payments and the construction of modern housing and other facilities in Kayapo villages. Most of the money went into communal accounts in banks in neighboring frontier towns. These accounts were either explicitly or tacitly controlled by chiefs or the few literate Kayapo able to keep the accounts. Some of these individuals began to draw heavily on these "communal" funds for personal use, giving rise to tension and resentment by the rest of their communities. Rivalries between competing companies and their respective Kayapo sponsors almost led to war between two Kayapo villages in 1986.

The discovery of gold at the huge mine of Serra Pelada near the eastern border of the Kayapo Indigenous Area led to intense prospecting and exploratory gold-mining activity within the eastern borders of the Kayapo Indigenous Area. This culminated in 1983 with the opening of two large illegal gold mines only ten kilometers from Gorotire village. Three thousand Brazilian miners swarmed onto Kayapo land, and neither the Brazilian Indian Service (FUNAI) nor any other arm of the Brazilian government seemed willing or able to do anything to stop it. Tons of mercury from the mining operations began to pollute the Rio Fresco, the main fishery of several Kayapo communities. Then, in 1986, an even more ominous form of pollution threatened, when radioactive waste from a cancer treatment facility in the city of Goiania caused two dozen fatalities, and the federal government attempted to dump the material on the western border of Kayapo country.

As if all this were not enough, the Kayapo began to hear rumors that the Brazilian government was planning to build a series of hydroelectric dams along the Xingu and its tributaries, which would result in the flooding of large areas of Kayapo land and end the value of most of the river system as a fishery. The scheme was to be funded by loans from the World Bank. Repeated attempts to learn the truth about the government's plans were met with stonewalling and denials that any such plan existed. The rumors persisted, however, and construction sites began to be cleared at certain points along the river. The Kayapo were outraged by the government's disregard for their political and legal rights to be consulted about a project which would so heavily affect their lands and livelihood. They were equally concerned about the ecological effects. While Kayapo leaders strove unsuccessfully to penetrate the government's cover-up about the dam project, however, they were confronted by an even more direct threat to their legal and political rights, as Indians, to challenge governmental or private Brazilian infringements of their land rights, resources, or communal interests. At the convention called to draw up the new Brazilian constitution, a measure was introduced calling for the redefinition of any Indian who demonstrated the capacity to bring a legal action in a Brazilian court as an "acculturated" person who could no longer be considered an Indian, and therefore could no longer represent or bring an action on behalf of an Indian community in court. This "catch-22" provision would have destroyed the possibility of any legal or political resistance by native peoples against abuses of their rights, persons, lands, or environments within the terms of the Brazilian legal and political process.

This daunting array of threats to the Kayapo environment, communal lands and resource base, political and civil rights is a representative sample of the human face of the environmental crisis in the Amazon. The Kayapo confronted this apparently overwhelming onslaught beginning in the early 1970s as a still largely monolingual people of Ge-speakers scattered over a vast area in 14 mutually autonomous and politically uncoordinated settlements. In most of the villages, some of the men (but almost no women) spoke Portuguese, and a handful had learned to read, write, and do simple arithmetic. A few leaders had obtained some experience of Brazilian administrative and political ways through working in the Indian Service or as members of Brazilian expeditions to contact other tribes. They had a few contacts with the outside world through anthropologists and indigenous advocacy groups, and the Brazilian Indian Service (FUNAI) offered some support, although it could not be counted upon to represent the Indians' interests against the more threatening forms of economic development mounted by government or powerful private interests. Aside from this slender array of assets, the Kayapo had no political resources with which to defend themselves and their forest beyond their own largely intact tribal institutions and culture. These, however, were to serve them well in the trials that lay ahead.

## The Kayapo Resistance

This is what they did. The two western communities whose land had been severed by the road began an unrelenting campaign of armed attacks on all Brazilian intruders who attempted to open ranches or settle in the separated area. After 15 years and perhaps 50 Brazilian dead, with no Kayapo casualties, no Brazilian settler remained in the entire area. The leaders of the two Kayapo groups meanwhile carried out a campaign of diplomacy, making repeated trips to Brasília to pressure the government to return the stolen land and thus end the violent standoff in the area. The government capitulated in 1985, returning the area to the Kayapo and ceding an additional area immediately to the north of the old area (this became the Capoto Indigenous Area). The two communities of the region joined again into a single large village and have resolutely banned all Brazilian mining, timber, and agricultural interests and settlers from their reclaimed areas.

Also in 1985, the two illegally opened gold mines were assaulted and captured by 200 Kayapo, armed with a mixture of firearms and traditional weapons. The larger mine was accessible only by air, so the Kayapo seized and blockaded the landing strip, confronting the Brazilian government with a choice: either cede title and administrative authority over the mines to the Kayapo, together with a significant percentage of the proceeds (10% was the amount initially demanded), and legally demarcate the boundaries of the Kayapo Indigenous Area (thus making the government unambiguously responsible for the defense of the area against any further such incursions), or the Kayapo would allow no more planes to land or take off, either to supply or evacuate the three thousand miners at the site. After a tense ten-day standoff, the government gave in to the Kayapo demands.

The leaders of Gorotire, the nearest and largest Kayapo village, used the first income from the mine to purchase a light plane and hire a Brazilian pilot. They put the plane to use to patrol their borders from the air to spot intruders and would-be squatters. If any were seen, patrols were dispatched to expel or eliminate the invaders. Within a year, invasions effectively ceased. They have

also used the plane to fly to other Kayapo villages and to Brazilian cities to purchase goods and bring people out for medical assistance. In the nearest town
of Redencao, and the state capital of Belem, they have bought houses for the
use of Kayapo travelers and shoppers, and in the former they have established
a tribal office to deal with their bank accounts and official relations with the
local office of FUNAI.

All timber concessions on Kayapo land were suspended by the Indian Service (FUNAI) at the end of 1987, at the urging of the most influential Kayapo
leaders, Payakan and Ropni. Some concessions, however, were surreptitiously
continued by a few other leaders who have lined their own pockets with the fees
paid by the companies. Still other communities and leaders not previously involved with lumbering companies are under great pressure from the companies
to grant new concessions. Meanwhile, resistance to any new concessions continues to be strong, and one community (A'Ukre) has declared its part of the
Kayapo Indigenous Area an "extractive reserve" closed to all ecologically destructive forms of timber and mineral exploitation. This remains a conflicted
issue, with the ultimate outcome in doubt. Meanwhile, a substantial area of the
Kayapo Indigenous Area has been clear-cut. The fate of the captured gold mines
has also proved a divisive issue. Not only have the Kayapo not closed them
down, as they originally said they would do within two years of taking them
over, but some Kayapo have opened a couple of small new mines on their own
land. Other Kayapo vigorously oppose this and have strictly prohibited all mining activity, whether by Brazilians or Kayapo, from their areas of the reserve.
Meanwhile, five Gorotire Kayapo have become wealthy enough from the gold
and timber revenues to buy private houses for themselves in Redencao, where
they live for much of the time, keeping Brazilian servants and, in two cases, acquiring large ranches outside the reserve. This phenomenon has been paralleled
by the chief of the village of Kikretum, who owns an airplane, houses, and a
hotel in the neighboring town of Tucuma. The rise of this embryonic "new
class" has already given rise to significant tensions within Kayapo society and
is a factor in the unresolved conflicts over the future form of accommodation
between Kayapo society and the Brazilian economy.

Most of the other threats posed by the enveloping national society proved
less divisive, and the Kayapo were able to mount concerted, well-organized responses to them without internal dissension or conflict. When the government's
plan to dump the radioactive waste on traditional Kayapo land was announced,
the Kayapo sent a hundred men to Brasília to demonstrate against the plan.
Suitably painted and feathered, they staged a sit-in in the president's palace.
Nothing like this had happened in Brazil in the twenty years since the coup
d'etat that established the military regime that was then in the process of relin-
quishing power. The initial incredulity and indignation of the authorities, however, gave way to acquiescence to the Kayapo's demands, and the dumping plan
was abandoned. Pressing their advantage, the Kayapo next sent a deputation of
some 50 chiefs and leading citizens to the Constitutional Convention to lobby for
the defeat of the "catch-22" acculturation clause and other provisions injurious

to Indian interests. Presenting themselves as always, in traditional paint and feathers and carrying traditional weapons, they patiently attended the weeks of debates on the sections bearing on indigenous peoples' rights, gave press conferences, and lobbied the deputies. When the acculturation clause was defeated, and surprisingly strong safeguards of indigenous rights, lands, and resources were adopted by the Convention, the Kayapo received much of the credit in the Brazilian press.

In 1988, two Kayapo leaders were invited to the United States to participate in a conference on tropical forest ecology. From there, they traveled to Washington, met with members of Congress, and spoke with World Bank officials about the effects of the proposed Xingu dam scheme on the peoples and environment of the area. They were able to obtain copies of the entire dam project, the very existence of which the Brazilian government had continued to deny, from the Bank. Shortly after the Kayapos' visit, the World Bank announced that it was deferring action on the Brazilian loan request. Enraged, elements of the Brazilian national security and political establishment had criminal charges brought against them and their American interpreter under a law prohibiting participation in political activity in Brazil by foreigners. The charges were ridiculous in strictly legal terms; since the actions in question had taken place in the United States, the American had been acting in his own country, and the Kayapo were not in any case foreigners. The transparent attempt at legal terrorism boomeranged, as nongovernment organizations (NGOs), anthropologists, and the congressmen whom the Kayapo had met on their tour organized an international outcry.

When one of the Kayapo leaders came to Belem, the capital of the state of Para, where the charges had been brought, to be arraigned, the Kayapo organized a massive protest demonstration. More than five hundred Kayapo men and women danced through the streets and massed in the square before the Palace of Justice to support their kinsman and denounce Brazilian political repression. The defiance turned to ridicule when the judge refused to allow the Kayapo leader to enter the courthouse for arraignment until he changed his paint and feathers for "civilized" (Brazilian) clothes. The Kayapo refused and told the judge he would have to come to the Kayapo village of Gorotire if he wanted another chance to arraign him on the charges. Meanwhile, Kayapo orators unrolled the map of the Xingu dam scheme obtained from the World Bank in Washington on an easel erected in the square and explained the entire secret project in Kayapo and Portuguese for the benefit of the many Brazilian onlookers, who included reporters and TV crews. The government never again dared to try to arraign the Kayapo leader, and eventually dropped all the charges.

With the World Bank still actively considering the Brazilian government's request for a loan to enable the building of the Xingu dams, the proposed multi-dam hydroelectric scheme in the Xingu River valley now appeared to the Kayapo as the greatest threat, not only to their environment, but to their political and legal control over their lands and resources. Since the government still refused to disclose its plans to build the dams, the Kayapo resolved to force it to reveal its intentions and to receive, before an audience of national and world news media, their criticisms of the human and environmental effects of the dams, as well as of its deceit in attempting to conceal and deny its plans. To accomplish this, they decided to convene in great congress of Amazonian peoples at the site of the first of the dams the government hoped to build: Altamira, near the mouth of the Xingu. To the meeting would be invited representatives of the Brazilian governments representatives of the World Bank; representatives of the national and world news media; nongovernmental organizations active in the environmentalist, human rights, and indigenous peoples' support fields; delegates from as many indigenous nations of Amazonia as possible; and as many Kayapo as could be transported and accommodated. At the meeting, the government representatives would be asked to present their plans, to give an account of their probable effects on the environment and the human inhabitants of the region (Brazilian as well as native), and to explain why they had tried for so long to keep their plans secret from those who would be most affected by them.

The Kayapo leaders who envisioned this project saw that its success would depend on international public opinion, press attention, and financial support. Only the attendance of a large number of media and NGO representatives, they felt, would compel the Brazilian government to send its representatives to face certain humiliation at such a meeting. The leader chiefly responsible for the plan, Payakan, therefore embarked on a tour of seven European and North American countries (sponsored and coordinated by Friends of the Earth, the World Wildlife Federation, and the Kayapo Support Group of Chicago) in November, 1988, to publicize the Altamira gathering and appeal for support. At a more general level, Payakan also sought to bring the crisis of the Amazon forest and its native peoples to wider public attention, and to lobby government and international development bank officials against supporting economic development projects (such as the Xingu dam scheme) that would irreversibly damage the environment and require the expropriation or destruction of native lands.

Payakan, at the same time, also sought to bring about greater mutual trust, cooperation, and unity of purpose among the various kinds of nongovernmental organizations and sectors of public opinion involved in supporting the Indians and the environmental struggle. These included human rights, indigenous peoples' advocacy, anthropological, and environmentalist organizations. Among the latter were some groups specifically devoted to defending tropical rain forests, others concerned with saving endangered animal species, and still others dedicated to conservation and environmental quality in a more general sense. Payakan, in his dealings with these groups or their representatives, had quickly realized that they tended to work in isolation from one another, often mistrusted one another's politics, or viewed one another's work as irrelevant to their own concerns. With other Kayapo leaders, Payakan saw this situation as not only damaging the effectiveness of the work of these organizations, but as out of touch with the real interconnections of the issues with which the groups were attempting to deal. For both reasons, they felt, the support of the NGOs was less effective than it might otherwise be. Payakan therefore devoted much effort on his tour to appealing to these groups to join forces and recognize that they were really all involved in a single great struggle. As he put it in a speech at the University of Chicago:

> The forest is one big thing; it has people, animals, and plants. There is no point saving the animals if the forest is burned down; there is no point saving the forest if the people and animals who live in it are killed or driven away. The groups trying to save the races of animals cannot win if the people trying to save the forest lose; the people trying to save the Indians cannot win if either of the others lose; the Indians cannot win without the support of these groups; but the groups cannot win either without the support of the Indians, who know the forest and the animals and can tell what is happening to them. No one of us is strong enough to win alone; together, we can be strong enough to win.

Payakan's message was widely heard. His tour became a concrete example of the intergroup cooperation he preached. For many indigenous advocacy organizations, environmentalist groups, human rights groups, Latin Americanist social scientists and anthropologists, helping to organize Payakan's tour and attending his speeches was their first practical experience of cooperating and coming together around a common set of interests and commitments. This experience has been continually repeated since then in a series of cooperative efforts to support the Altamira meeting, aid new organizational initiatives by the Kayapo and other forest peoples in Brazil, and help with subsequent tours by Payakan and other Kayapo leaders. It is generally recognized by activists of the various support organizations concerned that the Kayapo campaign has become an important catalyst of increased contact and cooperation among them at the national and international level, and that this cooperation has brought increased efficacy in lobbying, fund-raising, and public opinion outreach efforts.

Payakan's tour successfully achieved all its goals. Enough money was raised to defray all the costs of the Altamira gathering (which eventually approached $100,000) without drawing upon any of the funds derived from timber or gold concessions, which Payakan and most of his closest Kayapo supporters opposed. Much publicity and media attention was generated, guaranteeing a strong international media presence at the Altamira gathering itself. The support base of the Kayapo campaign among European and American nongovernmental organizations, public opinion, and politicians was greatly strengthened. The stage was now set for one of the most remarkable events in the history of Amazonia, the environmentalist movement, and modern popular protest politics.

From February 19–24, 1989, 600 Amazonian Indians and a roughly equal number of Brazilian and international journalists, photographers, TV crews, documentary filmmakers, Brazilian and foreign politicians, and representatives of various nongovernmental support organizations converged on the small river town of Altamira. Among the Indians were some 500 Kayapo and 100 members of 40 other indigenous nations, whom the Kayapo had invited to join them in confronting the Brazilian government, and to make their own views on the issues of dams and the destruction of the forest known to the government representatives, the news media, and one another. Five days of meetings, speeches, press conferences, and ritual performances by Kayapo and other indigenous groups were programmed and carried out without a major hitch. The event represented an impressive feat of organization and political coordination. It required the transportation, lodging, and feeding of hundreds of indigenous participants, which involved constructing a large encampment with traditional Kayapo shelters outside the town and daily busing of its inhabitants to the meeting hall in the center. Much of the credit for the event belongs to the Brazilian indigenous peoples' support organization, The Ecumenical Center for Documentation and Information (CEDI), which effectively cooperated with Payakan and the rest of the indigenous leadership in handling many of the logistical tasks essential to the success of the meeting.

Some elements of the regional Brazilian populace, especially those linked with landowning and commercial interests who stood to gain from the construction of the dams, were hostile to the Indians and (even more) their Brazilian and foreign environmentalist supporters. There were fears that violent incidents might occur and spread out of control. That this did not happen can be attributed in part to the foresight and discipline of the Kayapo, who carefully sited their encampment far outside of town and refrained from street demonstrations within the city limits, but also in large measure to the presence of so many foreign and domestic media personnel and observers.

The event took on the aspect of an international media circus. The Pope sent a telegram of support. The rock star Sting flew in for a day and gave a press conference at the Kayapo encampment, denouncing the destruction of the forest and promoting his own project for the creation of a new Kayapo reserve. No doubt because this project depended on the goodwill of the Brazilian government, Sting avoided directly committing himself in support of the Kayapo campaign against the dams. Since this was the whole purpose of the Altamira meeting, his Kayapo hosts roundly criticized him for using their platform for his own project and then skipping off. A British member of Parliament, a Belgian member of the European Parliament, and a half-dozen Brazilian deputies of the National Congress, however, mounted the platform and gave unreserved support. A final communique was issued, on behalf of all native peoples of Amazonia, condemning the dam project. By the time the conference closed with a dance from the Kayapo New Corn ceremony (joined in by assorted Indians of other tribes, European and Brazilian activists and media personnel, momentarily giving it the air of a 1960s hippie love-in), the Altamira gathering had become an international media success of such proportions as to generate serious political pressure against any international funding of the dam scheme, or indeed any attempt to go on with the plan by the Brazilian government. Within two weeks after the end of the meeting, the World Bank announced that it would not grant the Brazilian loan earmarked for the dam project, and the Brazilian National Congress had announced plans for a formal investigation and debate on the whole plan.

The Kayapo have not rested on their laurels since Altamira. One major line of effort was the drive to get a large area of the west bank of the Xingu demarcated as a third major Kayapo reserve, linking the two largest existing reserves (the Capoto and Kayapo Indigenous Areas) in a continuous area the size of Britain. In this effort, the Kayapo were supported by Sting and his recently founded Rainforest Foundation, which raised close to two million dollars to support the project. President Sarney of Brazil made several public statements vaguely in favor of the plan, but in January 1990, when Sting came to Brazil with the money from the Rainforest Foundation to present to the government to start the demarcation of the reserve, Sarney noncommitally passed the buck by merely extending the official period for administrative decision on the proposal into the new administration of President-elect Collor without taking action. Collor finally proclaimed the new reserve in 1991; the actual demarcation of the boundary was finished in September 1992. The demarcation of the new reserve bears witness to the political pressure the Kayapo, and the Rainforest Foundation with its international and Brazilian support, were able to bring to bear. Meanwhile, Payakan established a Kayapo Foundation (the "Fundacao Mebengokre") to administer and raise money for the support of a series of programs, including the establishment of an "extractive reserve" within the Kayapo Indigenous Area. This is an area off-limits to all lumbering and mining operations, devoted exclusively to environmentally sustainable forms of forest exploitation such as the gathering of Brazil nuts and other wild forest products.

The Kayapo also made some attempt to follow up on the links of solidarity with other indigenous Amazonian peoples forged at Altamira. In November 1989, several Kayapo leaders and a Kayapo video-cameraman flew (in a Kayapo plane) to Boa Vista in the northern frontier state of Rondonia to investigate an incident in which Yanomamo villagers had been attacked and driven from their land by Brazilian gold miners. The Kayapo denounced the government policies leading to the incident and declared their support for the survivors. The government had banned the area to all non-Indians after the occurrence, attempting to cover up the affair and keep it out of the press. The government was clearly thinking only of local Yanomamo Indians, but the Kayapo, seizing upon the loophole opened up by the wording of the ban and capitalizing on their undeniable identity as "Indians," were able to penetrate the official smokescreen with their fact-finding and support mission.

## Wider Implications: The Kayapo Achievement in World Perspective

### The Environmentalist Movement

At the level of international environmentalist politics, the Kayapo are now an established presence. In 1990 alone, Kayapo spokesmen have traveled to various European countries, Canada, the U.S.A., and Japan. They were accorded audiences by heads of state (Mitterand of France), cabinet ministers responsible for loans, aid and financial dealings with Brazil, and members of parliaments and national assemblies (Canada, France, Belgium, England, and the U.S.A.). They have also met with indigenous groups and leaders in North America, notably the Cree of Northern Quebec in 1991 and 1992. All of this notoriety and attention has generated for them a measure of immunity from the cruder forms of abuse and exploitation that have so often been the lot of indigenous peoples in Amazonia and elsewhere.

A mere ten years ago, however, they themselves were the targets of many such abuses, as recounted above. They have succeeded, against fantastic odds, in turning the tables on their would-be exploiters and seizing the political advantage, drawing upon the support of international and urban Brazilian public opinion. The strength of this support owes much to the worldwide wave of concern for the fate of the tropical forests, but the Kayapo would not have been able to capitalize so effectively on the general climate of environmental concern without their shrewd grasp of the possibilities of contemporary news and informational media and their effective presentation of themselves and their cause through them. Other factors in the Kayapo successes have been the effective support of numerous nongovernmental organizations and the impressive capacity of the Kayapo themselves for mass organization and militant but disciplined confrontational tactics, as exemplified by their bold but nonviolent demonstrations in Brasília, Belem, and Altamira.

The success of the Kayapo in furthering their own cause, at the same time, has had an important effect upon the politics of the developed world, and in particular, of the environmentalist movement. The support of environmentalist groups and public opinion has been essential to the Kayapo victories, but it is equally true that the Kayapo have won important victories for the environmentalist movement, and partly as a result have exercised an important influence upon its thinking, strategies, and organizational tactics. Perhaps most importantly, in a few short years they have revolutionized the consciousness of many activists and ordinary persons concerned with the fate of the world's tropical forests, teaching them that indigenous forest-dwelling peoples are not just a passive part of the problem, but an active part of the solution. By their own example, they have demonstrated that native forest peoples, no matter how apparently primitive, remote, or numerically insignificant, can become potent combatants and allies in the struggle to avert ecological disaster. In addition, they have helped bring about working relations of mutual trust and collaboration between members of a number of important organizations, scientific specialists, and politicians, who had previously never considered working together, and in many cases mistrusted one another's politics and policies.

Before the advent of the Kayapo on the international stage, many environmentalists had realized that there could be no solution to the problem of saving the forests that did not include the human inhabitants of the forests. Many who had arrived at this relatively enlightened opinion, however, continued to think of aboriginal forest peoples, and even forest-dwelling members of national societies like the Brazilian rubber-tappers, as historical basket cases, with all the capacity for political action in their own behalf of endangered animal species like the black cayman or the Amazonian giant otter. It has been a humbling, disconcerting, but delightful surprise to many of these same good people suddenly to discover that some of these supposedly hapless victims of progress have assumed a leading role in the struggle environmentalists had thought (perhaps a tad condescendingly) *they* were leading, and that these same native peoples have even succeeded in bringing to the effort a degree of unity and effectiveness that had previously eluded its familiar leadership.

## The Rise of Ecological Resistance in the Fourth World

The Kayapo are not a unique case. Their story, in fact, conforms in its essential features to an emerging pattern of ethnic self-assertiveness and ecological militancy on the part of native forest peoples in the Amazon and other parts of the world. It is not new for native peoples (to refer, by this term, to the tribal societies and ethnic minorities comprising the "Fourth World") to attempt to resist the wholesale appropriation of their lands and resources by the peoples and governments of modern states. What is new is the combination of political, economic, environmental, and ideological pressures with revolutionary new media technologies that has enabled native peoples to take their case directly to the peoples and governments of the world, and to find a receptive hearing because of the convergence of their cause with the new levels of popular concern over the environment.

One major manifestation of this worldwide pattern is the organization, over the past twenty years, of many federations of native peoples, for the most part consisting of groups speaking the same or related languages. Over 50 such groups now exist in the Amazon alone. They typically unite around a program of defense of native land and resources, respect for civil and political rights, and the assertion of traditional values and cultural identity. These groups are increasingly in touch with one another, and in some areas intergroup coordinating organizations, such as the recently organized Coordinating Group of the Amazon Basin, COICA, have begun to appear.

The rise of these organizations and the political consciousness they express has been catalyzed by many factors. Among them are the extension of modern transportation and communications networks to many previously inaccessible areas inhabited by tribal peoples; improved medical technology and assistance; greater availability of manufactured tools and goods; the extension of effective national government administrative control over the contiguous national populations; the increase in the strength and effectiveness of nonindigenous, nongovernmental advocacy and support organizations; the increased interest and ability of national and international media to publicize abuse of native lands, rights and peoples; the increase in international economic and political interdependence, which has made many governments more sensitive to the repercussions of bad publicity over indigenous issues; and last but not least, the influence of a steady trickle of anthropological researchers, who have helped both to catalyze native groups' awareness of the value of their traditional cultures in the eyes of the outside world and to inform them of the existence of potential sources of support in that world for their struggles to resist economic, political, and cultural oppression.

These factors have converged in recent years with growing concern in world public opinion for human rights and environmental issues, which have favored the causes of native groups struggling to defend their traditional lands and resource bases. None of these external factors, however, would have been sufficient by themselves to generate the cultural and social resources, or the political organization and will to act, that have been shown by so many native peoples. This is the part of the story that remains least well known to the world at large. It is important that it become known, as an antidote to the hopelessness induced by apocalyptic but often inaccurate news stories of "genocide" and widespread romantic clichés like the inevitable disappearance of primitive peoples in the path of progress. (The two often have more in common than meets the eye.) These myths have had the harmful effect of discouraging support for the struggles of many native peoples with a fighting chance to win. As the Kayapo case shows, such support can make an enormous difference.

That is the rosy side of a picture which is in the main far from rosy. For every indigenous people who have found the courage, leadership, and ability to respond constructively to the threat of despoliation of their ecological bases or the theft of their lands, others have been or are being decimated, dispossessed, or destroyed. In spite of some shining cases of successful resistance to threats to the ambient life-world, other battles have been, or are being, lost. The sheer volume of environmental destruction, and the variety of its forms and causes, make the struggle appear almost hopeless. Nowhere, however, has this been more true than in the Kayapo area of the Amazon. What the Kayapo have managed to do shows that even the most apparently hopeless odds can be faced and overcome.

# Review Questions

1. How do the Kayapo Indians of Brazil subsist in their Amazon forest environment?

2. What forces threaten the livelihood and social existence of the Kayapo as a cultural group?

3. How have the Kayapo reacted to defend their forest environment and their existence as a cultural group?

4. Turner argues that the Kayapo have tried to unite and enlist the aid of several kinds of local and world groups in their fight to preserve their forest and lands. What are these groups? Use the case of the encampment at Altamira to illustrate how they could work together.

5. How have the Kayapo affected the world environmentalist movement?

# 37

# Medical Anthropology: Improving Nutrition in Malawi

## Sonia Patten

*Applied anthropologists work in many settings. They may conduct govern-
ment program evaluations, work on forest conservation projects, market or
advertise products, staff rural development programs, establish foreign offices for nongovernmental organizations or corporations, or advise hospital
staff, among other things. In this article, Sonia Patten describes her role as
an applied medical anthropologist on a project aimed at the improvement of
infant and child nutrition in the African nation of Malawi. As a medical anthropologist, her job was to collect cultural baseline data that would help to
shape the program and make it appropriate to village conditions in Malawi.*

*The article illustrates one kind of research medical anthropologists might do, as well as the fact that applied anthropologists must often work in teams whose members are not usually trained as ethnographers or sensitive to cross-cultural differences.*

Malawi—Welcome to the Warm Heart of Africa. This is the sign that greets travelers when they arrive in this southeastern African republic. The warm, open response to visitors that I have enjoyed each time I have traveled to Malawi contrasts starkly to the poverty that plagues its citizens.

Malawi is a small landlocked nation in southeast Africa that lies south of Tanzania, east of Zambia, and west of Mozambique. The country is long and thin, with its axis running north and south along the Great African Rift Valley. Part of the valley holds Lake Malawi, the third largest lake in Africa, which accounts for more than 20 percent of the country's total area of 119,100 square kilometers. Malawi is one of the ten poorest countries in the world. Its economy is based predominately on agriculture, which accounts for half the gross domestic product and virtually all the exports. Cotton, tobacco, and sugar are most likely to be sold to other countries. However, despite exports, food security for both households and the nation is a chronic problem, with annual "hungry seasons" a fact of life and the specter of famine never far from people's minds. Maize, or white corn, is the staple food for the nation, and it is rare when the nation's rain-fed agriculture produces enough of it to adequately feed the population. The Malawian government faces the enormous challenges of strengthening the economy, improving educational and health facilities, and dealing with the serious environmental issues of deforestation and erosion. The country depends heavily on the International Monetary Fund, the World Bank, and bilateral and multilateral donor assistance. It was a small project funded by the U.S. Agency for International Development (USAID) that brought me as a medical anthropologist to Malawi several times during the 1990s.

Medical anthropology is difficult to define because it covers such a variety of research and practical programming. In the broadest sense, it can be defined as the study of human health in a variety of cultural and environmental contexts. Over the past three decades, medical anthropology has become a distinct and important area within anthropology. Presently it has three major areas of emphasis. One is the study of cultural differences in health beliefs and systems of healing such as alternative therapies, shamanism, and folk concepts of disease. A second consists of biomedical studies of human adaptations to disease, including nutrition, genetics, and demography. The third is applied medical anthropology, which focuses on the application of anthropology to health-related problems and possible solutions.

Medical anthropologists often carry out research as members of interdisciplinary teams, where their main contribution is to discover a people's cultural conceptions of health, illness, and the more general cultural context within which ideas about health are situated. It was as an applied medical anthropologist that I came to be a member of such an interdisciplinary team that would work in Malawi.

In the early 1990s, I was on the faculty at one of three universities that had joined together to apply for a USAID grant under a program called University Development Linkages Program (UDLP). Two of the universities were American and one was the agricultural college that formed part of the University of Malawi system in Africa. A major goal of the UDLP was to strengthen developing nation colleges and universities by giving them access to U.S. faculties and other university resources. The program also sought to increase the involvement of U.S. faculty members with faculty in developing nations so that students at U.S. institutions would benefit from an internationalizing of the curriculum.

In this case, U.S. faculty scientists were asked to devise and implement a project that would benefit all collaborating institutions of higher education. Many teams of UDLP scientists that applied for grants designed projects intended to strengthen curricula at developing nation institutes. Our team, however, opted to design and implement a project addressing a major problem, child undernourishment in Malawi. We recognized that three out of five children in the country were undernourished. Worse, the mortality rate for children under five was 24 percent, or nearly one in four. The problem was caused by the fact that children received insufficient protein and calories, which left them vulnerable to a host of infectious diseases, potential mental impairment, serious deficiency diseases (such as kwashiorkor and marasmus), and premature death. This is the story of the people from two central Malawi villages and three universities as we worked to craft a program to reduce child undernourishment and increase child survival on a sustainable basis.

Faculty members who were participating in this effort represented a number of disciplines: anthropology, human nutrition, cooperative extension, animal science, veterinary medicine, and crop science. Several of the participating faculty members from Malawi had grown up in small villages, still had extended family in those villages, and were familiar with economic and cultural factors contributing to child undernourishment there. We learned from these people, and from field research, that mothers breastfeed their babies for two or three years. This assured that the children received sufficient protein and calories during their early years. However, that changed when the children were weaned. The indigenous weaning food is a thin gruel of water and corn flour, and babies receive small amounts of it beginning at about four months of age. When mothers wean their toddlers, it is this gruel that the children eat day after day. It is a nutritionally inadequate weaning food and children soon begin to show its effects—swollen bellies, stunted growth, and increased susceptibility to malaria, measles, and other infectious diseases. The weaning food is made from maize, the same crop that constitutes the staple food for adults, a boiled corn flour dish called *nsima*. The problem of a nutritionally inadequate weaning food is not unique to Malawi—it plagues many developing nations. In these countries there is often a high-carbohydrate food such as corn or rice that makes up as much as 90 percent of children's daily intake. If people survive into adulthood, their bodies have made an adaptation to this low-protein diet. But children do not thrive.

As our project searched for ideas about how to create a plan for addressing child nutrition, we decided to focus on a simple approach that would use indigenous resources and be manageable at the local level. This was the introduction of a protein- and calorie-rich additive to the local weaning food, goat milk. Although goats are plentiful in Malawi villages, they are meat goats, not dairy goats. They are like walking bank accounts, to be sold when a family needs money to pay for school fees for the children, health care, and rites of passage such as weddings and funerals. It would be a bold step to secure approval from male village political leaders and elders for the introduction of milk-producing goats to provide milk for the young children. Dairy goats would be put directly into the hands of women, not sold for meat. Would it work? Would women be willing to learn new animal management and food handling techniques? Would they have time to carry out the additional labor that would be required? Would the goat milk be given to the children who needed it? Would husbands or brothers take the valuable animals away from the women? Would the goats and the children flourish? As time went on, we learned the answers to all these questions and more. And the village women contributed very valuable insights and suggestions that made the project a model that has been adopted elsewhere in Malawi.

## The Program

Our work began with a series of planning meetings. Our goal was to create a program that would enable women to raise and keep dairy goats on a sustainable and manageable basis, and use the milk that was produced to supplement their children's diets and increase food security for their families. The plan we generated would have three parts: (1) generation of a database on the milk production and biological characteristics of goats; (2) development and implementation of demonstrations and outreach programs for distributing milk goats to rural women and teaching them how to care for the animals; and (3) formation and implementation of outreach programs for rural women so they could learn how to safely handle goat milk and use it as a regular part of the diet, especially for their children who were under five years of age. At our planning meetings we had to figure out what we were actually going to do, and in what sequence.

The animal scientists on the team knew that milk goats introduced into local villages would have to be hardy or they would die. They wanted to try out some breeding experiments using local goats and imported breeds of dairy goats to see just what kind of crossbred doe would result in the best combination of high milk production and ability to adapt to life in the village. They worked out a breeding scheme using local Malawi goats, imported Saanen dairy goats from South Africa, Damascus goats from Cyprus, and Anglo-Nubian goats from the United States. The breeding experiments were carried out at the farm that the Malawi members of our team used for teaching and research.

This kind of research can't be done in a hurry. Arranging for the importation of animals is a complex process because one has to find a supplier, arrange for payment, arrange for shipment (very few airlines are willing to transport large animals internationally), plan the feeding and watering of the animals while they are in transit, secure permits from the Malawi Ministry of Agriculture, and quarantine the animals for a period of weeks when they arrive in country. Only then can the breeding research begin.

To our dismay, none of the imported Anglo-Nubian goats survived very long in Malawi. And several of the Damascus goats also died. The Saanens, however, proved to be the hardiest—not surprising, since they originated from relatively close-by South Africa, where environmental conditions were similar to those in Malawi. And when bred with local Malawi goats, the crossbreed turned out to provide substantial weekly milk yields that would be enough for the goats' kids as well as for the young children of rural families. So the team decided to import more Saanens and continue the crossbreeding program. Crossbred does would be distributed to village women and most of the crossbred bucks would be sold to support the project. As the program developed, team members discovered that some local does produced relatively high average milk yields; this finding became important as the project unfolded.

My work as the team anthropologist involved the human side of the project. With the help of team nutritionists and the extension expert, I designed a survey to collect baseline cultural information in the villages where the milk goats would be distributed. It was important to document such things as women's daily activities, the meaning and use of goats, relationships between men and women, and ways children were fed in the target villages before the milk goats were introduced. Later we would look for changes we hoped would occur after the new goats arrived and for unexpected problems.

To proceed with the social research, we selected three villages, all relatively close to the college campus, in a rural setting about 25 km from the capital city of Lilongwe. To proceed, however, it was necessary to obtain permission from the people in each community. To do so we held meetings with the village chiefs, men and women elders, mothers of young children who would be affected by our project, and anyone else from the village that was interested in learning about the program.

In the central region of Malawi (where we were working), most people belong to the Chewa ethnic group. The Chewa have a matrilineal descent system and practice matrilocal residence. Thus, Chewa men and women inherit clan and lineage membership from their mothers. It is this membership that gives people the right to farm plots of land surrounding their villages. When women marry, they continue to live in the village of their birth with a group of related females—mother, grandmother, maternal aunts, sisters, maternal female cousins, and eventually adult daughters and their young children. When young men marry, they move to the villages of their brides. The village chief is almost always a man. He cannot be the son of the prior chief because a son is not part of his father's matriline. Instead, he is likely to be the son of the prior chief's sister—a maternal nephew. This system creates a situation where almost all of the women and the powerful men in a village are maternal kin to one another.

To introduce the project, we had to recognize the matrilineal nature of village social organization and the need for people's approval. We met with groups of interested women and men and the chiefs in two villages. We explained what we were proposing to do. We said we wanted to find out how the young children in the village were doing in terms of growth and health. Then we intended to make milk goats available to women who had children under five years old because we felt they would benefit from goat milk in their diet. We noted that it would not cost the women any money. (Most rural women lack the means to purchase even local goats, because they cost from $30 to $50. Milk goats would be even more expensive at nearly $250 each.) We said that women who received milk goats would be asked to return the first healthy kid, whether male or female, to the college farm and that this would constitute payment for the animal. We told them that women who took the goats would be asked to attend demonstrations to help them learn how to care for the animals, handle the milk, and feed the milk to their children. We also said that someone from the project would come to the village each week to weigh and measure the participants' children to see if goat milk in their diet was having an effect on weight and height of their offspring.

Village women were uniformly positive about the project—they wanted to participate. But men, including the chiefs, were more skeptical. They worried about the impact on social relations of such valuable animals going to women— it didn't seem appropriate. Couldn't the goats be given to the men of the village? The goats were not to be sold or slaughtered, we said. They would be there for the benefit of the children, and their care would involve extra work for the women. Everyone knew that children were suffering because of malnourishment—sometimes a child would become so seriously malnourished that relatives had to take it to the district hospital for nutritional rehabilitation. This meant a three-week hospital stay with a family member right there to feed and care for the child. The cost to the family was considerable. And the death of a child was a great sorrow. So eventually the men agreed that the project should go forward. The chiefs agreed that the goats should belong to the women and said they would resolve any disputes over ownership in favor of the women.

When we were ready to talk with people in a third village about the project, we learned something that quickly dissuaded us from continuing there. It seemed that there was animal theft going on in the area, and the prime suspects were a family living in the third village! Until the local system of justice had solved these crimes and dealt with the perpetrators, we could not take the risk of working in that village. Animal theft became a problem in the other two villages as well. The rural economy in Malawi has weakened in recent years because of droughts, floods, soil depletion, deforestation, erosion, low prices for commodities, and high rates of inflation. The annual hungry season, the period of time between when people consume the last of the food they have stored to the time when the next crops are harvested, used to begin in December and end in March. Now the hungry season often begins in September. People must reduce the amount of food they eat at a time when they have to carry out the heaviest agricultural labor—preparing fields and planting them when the annual rains begin. Both men and women do this work and nearly all agricultural labor is done by hand. In the depth of the hungry season, people may turn to eating maize bran, the portion of the corn ear that they normally feed to their animals, in order to have something in their bellies to assuage the hunger pangs. Under conditions such as these, it is no surprise that animal theft is on the rise in the countryside.

Women in the two villages who received milk goats responded vigorously to the threat of theft once a few animals had been stolen. They began to take their milk goats with them as they went to work in the fields, tethering them nearby rather than letting them range free. They built pens against the sides of their mud or brick houses, to provide shade and security. At night they brought the animals into their houses so the whole family could guard them.

Our research team hired two young women who were both native speakers of the local language, Chichewa, and who had grown up in villages. We asked them to administer the baseline survey in the two villages and to continue working on the project. They would help distribute animals to village women and later pay weekly visits to the recipients to weigh and measure their young children. One of these young women has remained with the project throughout, and is dedicated to working with the villagers. She has been a key to the success of our work.

The baseline survey of households with children under five years old revealed some interesting and useful information. Women headed 30 percent of the households, meaning there was no adult male regularly living with them. Almost 75 percent of the women were illiterate. A total of 35.4 percent of the children were underweight for their age, and 57.7 percent were short for their age. These figures are close to the national averages for a preharvest season, that is, the hungry season. A surprising finding was that children in female-headed households were less likely to be undernourished or have stunted growth. We can only speculate about why this was the case.

We gave women who participated in the baseline survey the opportunity to volunteer to receive a milk goat, with the understanding that they would attend demonstrations that taught how to manage the animals and keep them healthy, how to milk goats, how to keep the milk from spoiling, and how to add it to their children's food. We also pointed out that they would have to return first-born kids to project personnel so the females could be distributed to other women. However, all kids born after that would be theirs to keep. The female goats would increase their flock of milk producers, and the males could be sold to give the women much-needed cash. All women who received milk goats would also be provided with a bucket for milking, a pan for cooking, and a measuring cup to help them track milk production.

The program proved popular. Very quickly the project had more participants than it could accommodate, and we had to create a waiting list. We gave priority to those women who had children under five that were most seriously undernourished. Other women on the waiting list agreed to this. We also provided animals to some grandmothers who were raising young grandchildren orphaned when their parents died of AIDS. Care for AIDS orphans has become a major problem in Malawi, and is reflected at the village level. It is common to see women who are already struggling to care for immediate family members supporting children left behind by maternal relatives who have died of the disease.

Team members designed and began to present demonstrations for village women on goat management, goat health, milking, safe milk handling, and incorporation of milk in their children's food. Recipes using local ingredients and goat milk were developed and tested in the home economics kitchens at the college, and taste-tested by the women participants and their children at the village-based demonstrations. The recipes that passed the taste test were routinely used by the women; those that didn't were rejected.

When the women received their animals, all of the does were either pregnant or already had young kids. This is when project field assistants began their weekly visits to the villages. During each visit, the participating women gathered in a central area of the village with their children. Each woman would have her child or children weighed in a sling scale that was suspended from a tree branch. Once a month, team members measured the upper arm circumference and height of the children. The high incidence of child mortality was brought home to me in a very graphic way during this process. Some women initially objected to having their children's height measured because they thought it was too much like measuring the children for coffins. A few women persisted in their objection. In these cases, our field assistants could only estimate observable changes in height. The field assistants also asked women about the general health of their children during the previous week, the milk production of their goats, and the health of their goats. If a goat was ill, the field assistant arranged for a veterinarian or a veterinary assistant to travel to the village and examine the animal. If there was a significant health problem with a child, the field assistant notified faculty team members who would then take the information to the nearest clinic where they could arrange transport of the woman and child to a hospital, if necessary. Almost all the women who received animals were committed to caring for them and using the milk for their children. Ninety-eight percent of the recipients returned the first kid to the project. This is an astonishingly high rate of return and it implies that rural women would be very good risks for other kinds of so-called "payback schemes" that make local efforts to improve economic security sustainable.

We were gratified to see that those children who began to receive even small amounts of goat milk as an ingredient in their daily diets showed steady weight and height gains even when they were sick. In time, however, we began to see children hit plateaus or even temporarily lose ground. We learned from the village women why this was happening. Women who made up village committees approached the project team with a proposed solution. They told us that their milk goats had to have at least two kids before they could get a second high-yield doe, and this meant that there were periods of time when no milk was available for their children. The women asked if we could teach them how to grow soybeans. They were all familiar with soybean flour as a food for un-dernourished children because this is what they received when they took their malnourished children to maternal and child health clinics for treatment. Their plan was to grow soybeans and grind them into flour to feed their children when no goat milk was available.

Our project team went back to the drawing board and figured out how to incorporate this new effort. The team purchased soybean seed and distributed five kilograms of it to each woman in two villages. The village chiefs approved of this effort and provided more land to those women who needed it. Malawi team members developed and presented demonstrations on how to grow and process soybeans. The women agreed to pay back the five kilograms of seed after their first harvest, again a way to perpetuate the program over time and make it self-sustainable, and all did so. Women have now completed three or four successful growing seasons with soybeans, and are growing and storing enough beans to see them through the periods of time when their does produce no milk. They also save enough seed for the next planting season.

It also became clear after a short period of time that we would have to change the goat crossbreeding program. The college farm could not breed enough hardy milk goats to keep up with the demand. The animal scientists on our team looked for local Malawi goats that were the highest milk producers and these, when pregnant or with a kid, were distributed to women on the wait-ing list. Simultaneously, plans were made to build buck stations in each of the villages and to provide each with a Saanen or crossbred buck to breed with local milk goats. Village chiefs oversaw the project and men and women helped to feed and water the buck. When a doe came into heat, the owner would bring it to them to be inseminated. In this way the Saanen genes for high milk produc-tion spread more rapidly into the village flocks.

The breeding strategy has been successful. A veterinary assistant regularly checks the health and management of the bucks, which prove to be so valued by villagers that they are well cared for and diligently protected against theft. Villagers also know that their buck must be exchanged about every three years for another in order to avoid inbreeding.

## Conclusion

Our project team designed and tested a locally sustainable approach to allevi-ate infant and child malnourishment in rural Malawi. Data on changes in the participating children's weights, heights, and upper-arm circumferences show that relatively small amounts of goat milk included in the regular diet make a substantial difference in promoting normal growth in children. Results from a rapid appraisal survey that I helped design indicate that the project is highly valued by rural women. This is confirmed by key village women and by the fact that more women sought to join the program than project resources allowed. Presently some Malawi nongovernmental organizations (NGOs) have introduced similar efforts in other parts of the country. Several district hospitals that provide rehabilitation for severely malnourished children have established flocks of milk goats on their grounds and use the milk as an important part of the rehabilitation treatment. The agricultural college now offers training to Malawians and people from other southern African nations who are interested in replicating the program. And the two project villages will be demonstration sites for trainees who want to see how the project works "on the ground."

It was important to have an anthropologist on the project team. As the team anthropologist, I participated in every phase of the project, including management duties at times when it was necessary to keep our efforts on schedule. I was responsible for providing an ethnographic account of local culture and using this information to help shape how we could present the program to villagers. I was not trained to manage goat breeding or conduct some of the health measurements, but I could point out how I thought villagers would respond to our plans and to suggest how best to make them full participants in project planning and implementation. It is easy for people from any society to believe that those who are from elsewhere still see the world in the same way they do. Since cultures differ (Americans, for example find it difficult to understand the ramifications of a matrilineal descent system), anthropologists can act not only to discover what another culture is like, but also to translate this information in ways that are useful to other members of the interdisciplinary teams. Thus, we can shape programs to fit local conditions and help with cross-cultural communication. That is what I think happened in Malawi.

# Review Questions

1. What are the social and environmental conditions that lead to child malnutrition in Malawi, according to Patten?

2. What programs did the project team come up with to improve child nutrition in Malawi and what steps did they take to implement it?

3. How is anthropology useful for programs such as the one described by Patten in this article?

4. In what ways did team members involve local people in the design and implementation of the program?

# 38

# Using Anthropology

*David W. McCurdy*

*Some disciplines, such as economics, have an obvious relationship to the nonacademic world. Economic theory, although generated as part of basic research, may often prove useful for understanding the "real" economy. Anthropology, on the other hand, does not seem so applicable. In this article, David McCurdy discusses some of the professional applications of anthropology and argues that there is a basic anthropological perspective that can help anyone cope with the everyday world. He uses the case of a company manager to illustrate this point, asserting that ethnographic "qualitative" research is an important tool for use in the nonacademic world.*

In 1990, a student, whom I had not seen for fifteen years, stopped by my office. He had returned for his college reunion and thought it would be interesting to catch up on news about his (and my) major department, anthropology. The conversation, however, soon shifted from college events to his own life. Following graduation and a stint in the Peace Corps, he noted, he had begun to study for his license as a ship's engineer. He had attended the Maritime Academy and worked for years on freighters. He was finally granted his license, he continued, and currently held the engineer's position on a container ship that made regular trips between Seattle and Alaska. He soon would be promoted to chief engineer and be at the top of his profession.

As he talked, he made an observation about anthropology that may seem surprising. His background in the discipline, he said, had helped him significantly in his work. He found it useful as he went about his daily tasks, maintaining his ship's complex engines and machinery, his relationships with the crew, and his contacts with land-based management.

And his is not an unusual case. Over the years, several anthropology graduates have made the same observation. One, for example, is a community organizer who feels that the cross-cultural perspective he learned in anthropology helps him mediate disputes and facilitate decision making in a multiethnic neighborhood. Another, who works as an advertising account executive, claims that anthropology helps her discover what products mean to customers. This, in turn, permits her to design more effective ad campaigns. A third says she finds anthropology an invaluable tool as she arranges interviews and writes copy. She is a producer for a metropolitan television news program. I have heard the same opinion expressed by many others, including the executive editor of a magazine for home weavers, the founder of a fencing school, a housewife, a physician, several lawyers, the kitchen manager for a catering firm, and a high school teacher.

The idea that anthropology can be useful is also supported by the experience of many new Ph.D.'s. A recent survey has shown, for the first time, that more new doctorates in anthropology find employment in professional settings than in college teaching or scholarly research, and the list of nonacademic work settings revealed by the survey is remarkably broad. There is a biological anthropologist, for example, who conducts research on nutrition for a company that manufactures infant formula. A cultural anthropologist works for a major car manufacturer, researching such questions as how employees adapt to working overseas, and how they relate to conditions on domestic production lines. Others formulate government policy, plan patient care in hospitals, design overseas development projects, run famine relief programs, consult on tropical forest management, and advise on product development, advertising campaigns, and marketing strategy for corporations.

This new-found application of cultural anthropology comes as a surprise to many Americans. Unlike political science, for example, which has a name that logically connects it with practical political and legal professions, there is nothing in the term *anthropology* that tells most Americans how it might be useful.

The research subject of anthropology also makes it more difficult to comprehend. Political scientists investigate political processes, structures, and motivations. Economists look at the production and exchange of goods and services. Psychologists study differences and similarities among individuals. The research of cultural anthropologists, on the other hand, is more difficult to characterize. Instead of a focus on particular human institutions, such as politics, law, and economics, anthropologists are interested in cross-cultural differences and similarities among the world's many groups.

This interest produces a broad view of human behavior that gives anthropology its special cross-cultural flavor. It also produces a unique research strategy, called *ethnography*, that tends to be qualitative rather than quantitative. Whereas other social sciences moved toward *quantitative methods* of research designed to test theory by using survey questionnaires and structured, repetitive observations, most anthropologists conduct *qualitative research* designed to elicit the cultural knowledge of the people they seek to understand. To do this, anthropologists often live and work with their subjects, called *informants* within the discipline. The result is a highly detailed ethnographic description of the categories and rules people consult when they behave, and the meanings that things and actions have for them.

It is this ethnographic approach, or cultural perspective, that I think makes anthropology useful in such a broad range of everyday settings. I particularly find important the special anthropological understanding of the culture concept, ethnographic field methods, and social analysis. To illustrate these assertions, let us take a single case in detail, that of a manager working for a large corporation who consciously used the ethnographic approach to solve a persistent company problem.

## The Problem

The manager, whom we will name Susan Stanton, works for a large multinational corporation called UTC (not the company's real name). UTC is divided into a number of parts, including divisions, subdivisions, departments, and other units designed to facilitate its highly varied business enterprises. The company is well diversified, engaging in research, manufacturing, and customer services. In addition to serving a wide cross-section of public and private customers, it also works on a variety of government contracts for both military and nonmilitary agencies.

One of its divisions is educational. UTC has established a large number of customer outlets in cities throughout the United States, forming what it calls its "customer outlet network." They are staffed by educational personnel who are trained to offer a variety of special courses and enrichment programs. These courses and programs are marketed mainly to other businesses or to individuals who desire special training or practical information. For example, a small company might have UTC provide its employees with computer training, including instruction on hardware, programming, computer languages, and computer program applications. Another company might ask for instruction on effective management or accounting procedures. The outlets' courses for individuals include such topics as how to get a job, writing a resume, or enlarging your own business.

To organize and manage its customer outlet network, UTC has created a special division. The division office is located at the corporate headquarters and is responsible for developing new courses, improving old ones, training customer outlet personnel, and marketing customer outlet courses, or "products" as they are called inside the company. The division also has departments that develop, produce, and distribute the special learning materials used in customer outlet courses. These include books, pamphlets, video and audio tapes and cassettes, slides, overlays, and films. These materials are stored in a warehouse and are shipped, as they are ordered, to customer outlets around the country.

It is with this division that Susan Stanton first worked as a manager. She had started her career with the company in a small section of the division that designed various program materials. She had worked her way into management, holding a series of increasingly important positions. She was then asked to take over the management of a part of the division that had the manufacture, storage, and shipment of learning materials as one of its responsibilities.

But there was a catch. She was given this new management position with instructions to solve a persistent, although vaguely defined, problem. "Improve the service," they had told her, and "get control of the warehouse inventory." In this case, "service" meant the process of filling orders sent in by customer outlets for various materials stored in the warehouse. The admonition to improve the service seemed to indicate that service was poor, but all she was told about the situation was that customer outlet personnel complained about the service; she did not know exactly why or what "poor" meant.

In addition, inventory was "out of control." Later she was to discover the extent of the difficulty.

> We had a problem with inventory. The computer would say we had two hundred of some kind of book in stock, yet it was back ordered because there was nothing on the shelf. We were supposed to have the book but physically there was nothing there. I'm going, "Uh, we have a small problem. The computer never lies, like your bank statement, so why don't we have the books?"

If inventory was difficult to manage, so were the warehouse employees. They were described by another manager as "a bunch of knuckle draggers. All they care about is getting their money. They are lazy and don't last long at the job." Strangely, the company did not view the actions of the warehouse workers as a major problem. Only later did Susan Stanton tie in poor morale in the warehouse with the other problems she had been given to solve.

## Management by Defense

Although Stanton would take the ethnographic approach to management problems, that was not what many other managers did. They took a defensive stance, a position opposite to the discovery procedures of ethnography. Their major concern—like that of many people in positions of leadership and responsibility—was to protect their authority and their ability to manage and to get things done. Indeed, Stanton also shared this need. But their solution to maintaining their position was different from hers. For them, claiming ignorance and asking questions—the hallmark of the ethnographic approach—is a sign of weakness. Instead of discovering what is going on when they take on a new management assignment, they often impose new work rules and procedures. Employees learn to fear the arrival of new managers because their appearance usually means a host of new, unrealistic demands. They respond by hiding what they actually do, withholding information that would be useful to the manager. Usually, everyone's performance suffers.

Poor performance leads to elaborate excuses as managers attempt to blame the troubles on others. Stanton described this tendency.

> When I came into the new job, this other manager said, "Guess what? You have got a warehouse. You are now the proud owner of a forklift and a bunch of knuckle draggers." And I thought, management's perception of those people is very low. They are treating them as dispensable, that you can't do anything with them. They say the workers don't have any career motives. They don't care if they do a good job. You have to force them to do anything. You can't motivate them. It's only a warehouse, other managers were saying. You can't really do that much about the problems there so why don't you just sort of try to keep it under control.

Other managers diminished the importance of the problem itself. It was not "poor service" that was the trouble. The warehouse was doing the best it could with what it had. It was just that the customers—the staff at the customer outlets—were complainers. As Susan Stanton noted:

> The people providing the service thought that outlet staff were complainers. They said, "Staff complain about everything. But it can't be that way. We have checked it all out and it isn't that bad."

Making excuses and blaming others lead to low morale and a depressed self-image. Problems essentially are pushed aside in favor of a "let's just get by" philosophy.

## Ethnographic Management

By contrast, managers take the offensive when they use ethnographic techniques. That is what Stanton did when she assumed her new managerial assignment over the learning materials manufacturing and distribution system. To understand what the ethnographic approach means, however, we must first look briefly at what anthropologists do when they conduct ethnographic field research. Our discussion necessarily involves a look at the concepts of culture and microculture as well as ethnography. For as we will shortly point out, companies have cultures of their own, a point that has recently received national attention; but more important for the problem we are describing here, companies are normally divided into subgroups, each with its own microculture. It is these cultures and microcultures that anthropologically trained managers can study ethnographically, just as fieldworkers might investigate the culture of a !Kung band living in the Kalahari Desert of West Africa or the Gypsies living in San Francisco.

*Ethnography* refers to the process of discovering and describing culture, so it is important to discuss this general and often elusive concept. There are numerous definitions of culture, each stressing particular sets of attributes. The definition we employ here is especially appropriate for ethnographic fieldwork. We may define culture as the acquired knowledge that people use to generate behavior and interpret experience. In growing up, one learns a system of cultural knowledge appropriate to the group. For example, an American child learns to chew with a closed mouth because that is the cultural rule. The child's parents interpret open-mouthed chewing as an infraction and tell the child to chew "properly." A person uses such cultural knowledge throughout life to guide actions and to give meaning to surroundings.

Because culture is learned, and because people can easily generate new cultural knowledge as they adapt to other people and things, human behavior and perceptions can vary dramatically from one group to another. In India, for example, children learn to chew "properly" with their mouths open. Their cultural worlds are quite different from the ones found in the United States.

Cultures are associated with groups of people. Traditionally, anthropologists associated culture with relatively distinctive ethnic groups. Culture referred to the whole life-way of a society and particular cultures could be named. Anthropologists talked of German culture, Ibo culture, and Bhil culture. Culture was everything that was distinctive about the group.

*Culture* is still applied in this manner today, but with the advent of complex societies and a growing interest among anthropologists in understanding them, the culture concept has also been used in a more limited way. Complex societies such as our own are composed of thousands of groups. Members of these groups usually share the national culture, including a language and a huge inventory of knowledge for doing things, but the groups themselves have specific cultures of their own. For example, if you were to walk into the regional office of a stock brokerage firm, you would hear the people there talking an apparently foreign language. You might stand in the "bull pen," listen to brokers make "cold calls," "sell short," "negotiate a waffle," or get ready to go to a "dog and pony show." The fact that events such as this feel strange when you first encounter them is strong evidence to support the notion that you don't yet know the culture that organizes them. We call such specialized groups *microcultures*.

We are surrounded by microcultures, participating in a few, encountering many others. Our family has a microculture. So may our neighborhood, our college, and even our dormitory floor. The waitress who serves us lunch at the corner restaurant shares a culture with her coworkers. So do bank tellers at our local savings and loan. Kin, occupational groups, and recreational associations each tend to display special microcultures. Such cultures can be, and now often are, studied by anthropologists interested in understanding life in complex American society.

The concept of microculture is essential to Susan Stanton as she begins to attack management problems at UTC because she assumes that conflict between different microcultural groups is most likely at the bottom of the difficulty. One microculture she could focus on is UTC company culture. She knows, for example, that there are a variety of rules and expectations—written and unwritten—for how things should be done at the company. She must dress in her "corporates," for example, consisting of a neutral-colored suit, stockings, and conservative shoes. UTC also espouses values about the way employees should be treated, how people are supposed to feel about company products, and a variety of other things that set that particular organization apart from other businesses.

But the specific problems that afflicted the departments under Stanton's jurisdiction had little to do with UTC's corporate culture. They seemed rather to be the result of misunderstanding and misconnection between two units, the warehouse and the customer outlets. Each had its own microculture. Each could be investigated to discover any information that might lead to a solution of the problems she had been given.

Such investigation would depend on the extent of Stanton's ethnographic training. As an undergraduate in college, she had learned how to conduct ethnographic interviews, observe behavior, and analyze and interpret data. She was not a professional anthropologist, but she felt she was a good enough ethnographer to discover some relevant aspects of microcultures at UTC.

Ethnography is the process of discovering and describing a culture. For example, an anthropologist who travels to India to conduct a study of village culture will use ethnographic techniques. The anthropologist will move into a community, occupy a house, watch people's daily routines, attend rituals, and spend hours interviewing informants. The goal is to discover a detailed picture of what is going on by seeing village culture through the eyes of informants. The anthropologist wants the insider's perspective. Villagers become teachers, patiently explaining different aspects of their culture, praising the anthropologist for acting correctly and appearing to understand, laughing when the anthropologist makes mistakes or seems confused. When the anthropologist knows what to do and can explain in local terms what is going on or what is likely to happen, real progress has been made. The clearest evidence of such progress is when informants say, "You are almost human now," or "You are beginning to talk just like us."

The greatest enemy of good ethnography is the preconceived notion. Anthropologists do not conduct ethnographic research by telling informants what they are like based on earlier views of them. They teach the anthropologist how to see their world: the anthropologist does not tell them what their world should really be like. All too often in business, a new manager will take over a department and begin to impose changes on its personnel to fit a preconceived perception of them. The fact that the manager's efforts are likely to fail makes sense in light of this ignorance. The manager doesn't know the microculture. Nor have they been asked about it.

But can a corporate manager really do ethnography? After all, managers have positions of authority to maintain, as we noted earlier. It is all right for professional anthropologists to enter the field and act ignorant; they don't have a position to maintain and they don't have to continue to live with their informants. The key to the problem appears to be the "grace period." Most managers are given one by their employees when they are new on the job. A new manager cannot be expected to know everything. It is permissible to ask basic questions. The grace period may last only a month or two, but it is usually long enough to find out valuable information.

This is the opportunity that Susan Stanton saw as she assumed direction of the warehouse distribution system. As she described it:

> I could use the first month, actually the first six weeks, to find out what was going on, to act dumb and find out what people actually did and why. I talked to end customers. I talked to salespeople, people who were trying to sell things to help customer outlets with their needs. I talked to coordinators at headquarters staff who were trying to help all these customer outlets do their jobs and listened to what kinds of complaints they had heard. I talked to the customer outlet people and the guys in the warehouse. I had this six-week grace period where I could go in and say, "I don't know anything about this. If you were in my position, what would you do, or what would make the biggest difference, and why would it make a difference?" You want to find out what the world they are operating in is like. What do they value? And people were excited because I was asking and listening and, by God, intending to do something about it instead of just disappearing again.

As we shall see shortly, Stanton's approach to the problem worked. But it also resulted in an unexpected bonus. Her ethnographic approach symbolized unexpected interest and concern to her employees. That, combined with realistic management, gave her a position of respect and authority. Their feelings for her were expressed by one warehouse worker when he said:

> When she [Susan] was going to be transferred to another job, we gave her a party. We took her to this country-and-western place and we all got to dance with the boss. We told her that she was the first manager who ever tried to understand what it was like to work in the warehouse. We thought she would come in like the other managers and make a lot of changes that didn't make sense. But she didn't. She made it work better for us.

## Problems and Causes

An immediate benefit of her ethnographic inquiry was a much clearer view of what poor service meant to customer outlet personnel. Stanton discovered that learning materials, such as books and cassettes, took too long to arrive after they were ordered. Worse, material did not arrive in the correct quantities. Sometimes there would be too many items, but more often there were too few, a particularly galling discrepancy since customer outlets were charged for what they ordered, not what they received. Books also arrived in poor condition, their covers ripped or scratched, edges frayed, and ends gouged and dented. This, too, bothered customer outlet staff because they were often visited by potential customers who were not impressed by the poor condition of their supplies. Shortages and scruffy books did nothing to retain regular customers either.

The causes of these problems and the difficulties with warehouse inventory also emerged from ethnographic inquiry. Stanton discovered, for example, that most customer outlets operated in large cities, where often they were housed in tall buildings. Materials shipped to their office address often ended up sitting in ground-level lobbies, because few of the buildings had receiving docks or facilities. Books and other items also arrived in large boxes, weighing up to a hundred pounds. Outlet staff, most of whom were women, had to go down to the lobby, open those boxes that were too heavy for them to carry, and haul armloads of supplies up the elevator to the office. Not only was this time-consuming, but customer outlet staff felt it was beneath their dignity to do such work. They were educated specialists, after all.

The poor condition of the books was also readily explained. By packing items loosely in such large boxes, warehouse workers ensured trouble in transit. Books rattled around with ease, smashing into each other and the side of the box. The result was torn covers and frayed edges. Clearly no one had designed the packing and shipping process with customer outlet staff in mind.

The process, of course, originated in the central warehouse, and here as well, ethnographic data yielded interesting information about the causes of the problem. Stanton learned, for example, how materials were stored in loose stacks on the warehouse shelves. When orders arrived at the warehouse, usually through the mail, they were placed in a pile and filled in turn (although there were times when special preference was given to some customer outlets). A warehouse employee filled an order by first checking it against the stock recorded by the computer, then going to the appropriate shelves and picking the items by hand. Items were packed in the large boxes and addressed to customer outlets. With the order complete, the employee was supposed to enter the number of items picked and shipped in the computer so that inventory would be up to date.

But, Stanton discovered, workers in the warehouse were under pressure to work quickly. They often fell behind because materials the computer said were in stock were not there, and because picking by hand took so long. Their solution to the problem of speed resulted in a procedure that even further confused company records.

Most of the people in the warehouse didn't try to count well. People were looking at the books on the shelves and were going, "Eh, that looks like the right number. You want ten? Gee, that looks like about ten." Most of the time the numbers they shipped were wrong.

The causes of inaccurate amounts in shipping were thus revealed. Later, Stanton discovered that books also disappeared in customer outlet building lobbies. While staff members carried some of the materials upstairs, people passing by the open boxes helped themselves.

Other problems with inventory also became clear. UTC employees, who sometimes walked through the warehouse, would often pick up interesting materials from the loosely stacked shelves. More important, rushed workers often neglected to update records in the computer.

## The Shrink-Wrap Solution

The detailed discovery of the nature and causes of service and inventory problems suggested a relatively painless solution to Stanton. If she had taken a defensive management position and failed to learn the insider's point of view, she might have resorted to more usual remedies that were impractical and unworkable. Worker retraining is a common answer to corporate difficulties, but it is difficult to accomplish and often fails. Pay incentives, punishments, and motivation enhancements such as prizes and quotas are also frequently tried. But they tend not to work because they don't address fundamental causes.

Shrink-wrapping books and other materials did. Shrink-wrapping is a packaging device that emerged a few years ago. Clear plastic sheeting is placed around items to be packaged, then through a rapid heating and cooling process, shrunk into a tight covering. The plastic molds itself like a tight skin around the things it contains, preventing any internal movement or external contamination. Stanton described her decision.

> I decided to have the books shrink-wrapped. For a few cents more, before the books ever arrived in the warehouse, I had them shrink-wrapped in quantities of five and ten. I made it part of the contract with the people who produced the books for us.

On the first day that shrink-wrapped books arrived at the warehouse, Stanton discovered that they were immediately unwrapped by workers who thought a new impediment had been placed in their way. But the positive effect of shrink-wrapping soon became apparent. For example, most customer outlets ordered books in units of fives and tens. Warehouse personnel could now easily count out orders in fives and tens, instead of having to count each book or estimate numbers in piles. Suddenly, orders filled at the warehouse contained the correct number of items.

Employees were also able to work more quickly, since they no longer had to count each book. Orders were filled faster, the customer outlet staff was pleased, and warehouse employees no longer felt the pressure of time so intensely. Shrink-wrapped materials also traveled more securely. Books, protected by their plastic covering, arrived in good condition, again delighting the personnel at customer outlets.

Stanton also changed the way materials were shipped, based on what she had learned from talking to employees. She limited the maximum size of shipments to twenty-five pounds by using smaller boxes. She also had packages marked "inside delivery" so that deliverymen would carry the materials directly to the customer outlet offices. If they failed to do so, boxes were light enough to carry upstairs. No longer would items be lost in skyscraper lobbies.

Inventory control became more effective. Because they could package and ship materials more quickly, the workers in the warehouse had enough time to enter the size and nature of shipments in the computer. Other UTC employees no longer walked off with books from the warehouse, because the shrink-wrapped bundles were larger and more conspicuous, and because taking five or ten books is more like stealing than "borrowing" one.

Finally, the improved service dramatically changed morale in the division. Customer outlet staff members, with their new and improved service, felt that finally someone had cared about them. They were more positive and they let people at corporate headquarters know about their feelings. "What's happening down there?" they asked. "The guys in the warehouse must be taking vitamins."

Morale soared in the warehouse. For the first time, other people liked the service workers there provided. Turnover decreased as pride in their work rose. They began to care more about the job, working faster with greater care. Managers who had previously given up on the "knuckle draggers" now asked openly about what had got into them.

Stanton believes the ethnographic approach is the key. She has managers who work for her read anthropology, especially books on ethnography, and she insists that they "find out what is going on."

## Conclusion

Anthropology is, before all, an academic discipline with a strong emphasis on scholarship and basic research. But, as we have also seen, anthropology is a discipline that contains several intellectual tools—the concept of culture, the ethnographic approach to fieldwork, a cross-cultural perspective, a holistic view of human behavior—that make it useful in a broad range of nonacademic settings. In particular, it is the ability to do qualitative research that makes anthropologists successful in the professional world.

A few years ago an anthropologist consultant was asked by a utility company to answer a puzzling question: Why were its suburban customers, whose questionnaire responses indicated an attempt at conservation, failing to reduce their consumption of natural gas? To answer the question, the anthropologist conducted ethnographic interviews with members of several families, listening as they told him about how warm they liked their houses and how they set the heat throughout the day. He also received permission to install several video cameras aimed at thermostats in private houses. When the results were in, the answer to the question was deceptively simple: Fathers fill out questionnaires and turn down thermostats; wives, children, and cleaning workers, all of whom, in this case, spent time in the houses when fathers were absent, turn them up. Conservation, the anthropologist concluded, would have to involve family decisions, not just admonitions to save gas.

Over the past two or three years, anthropology's usefulness in the world of work has been discovered by the United States press. For example, *U.S. News and World Report* carried a story in 1998 entitled "Into the Wild Unknown of Workplace Culture: Anthropologists Revitalize Their Discipline," which traced changing trends in academic anthropology and highlighted the growth of the discipline's penetration of the business world.[1] Included in the article were examples of useful ethnography, such as the discovery by one anthropologist consultant that rank-and-file union members were upset with shop stewards because the latter spent more time recruiting new members than responding to grievances. In another instance, the article reported on the work of anthropologist Ken Erickson. Hired to find out why immigrant meatpackers had launched a wildcat strike, he was able to show that the workers struck because they felt their supervisors treated them as unskilled laborers, not because there was a language problem, as proposed by management. The workers had developed elaborate strategies to work quickly, effectively, and safely that were ignored or unknown to their supervisors.

In 1999, *USA Today* carried a story that further emphasized anthropology's usefulness. Entitled "Hot Asset in Corporate: Anthropology Degrees," the article began with, "Don't throw away the MBA degree yet. But as companies go global and crave leaders for a diverse workforce, a new hot degree is emerging for aspiring executives: anthropology."[2] The piece carried numerous examples—the hiring of anthropologist Steve Barnett as a vice president at Citicorp following his discovery of the early warning signs that identify people who do not pay credit card bills; the case of Hallmark, which sent anthropologists into immigrant homes to discover how holidays and birthdays are celebrated so that the company could design appropriate cards for such occasions; the example of a marketing consultant firm that sent anthropologists into bathrooms to watch how women shave their legs, and in the process, to discover what women want in a razor.

---

[1] Brendan I. Koerner, "Into the Wild Unknown of Workplace Culture: Anthropologists Revitalize Their Discipline," *U.S. News & World Report*, August 10, 1998, p. 56.

[2] Del Jones, "Hot Asset in Corporate: Anthropology Degrees," *USA Today*, February 18, 1999, section B, p. 1.

The article also listed executives who stressed how important their anthropology degree has been for their business successes. Motorola corporate lawyer Robert Faulkner says that the anthropology degree he received before going to law school has become increasingly valuable in his management job. Warned by his father that most problems are people problems, Michael Koss, CEO of the Koss headphone company, is another example. He received his anthropology degree from Beloit College. Katherine Burr, CEO of The Hanseatic Group, has an MA in anthropology and was quoted as saying, "My competitive edge came completely out of anthropology. The world is so unknown, changes so rapidly. Preconceptions can kill you." The article concluded with the observations of Ken Erickson of the Center for Ethnographic Research. "It takes trained observation. Observation is what anthropologists are trained to do."

In short, cultural anthropology has entered the world of business over the past twenty years. I argue that the key to its special utility and value in the commercial world is the ethnographic approach. Anthropologists have this ethnographic field experience and a sense of how social systems work and how people use their cultural knowledge. They have the special background, originally developed to discover and describe the cultural knowledge and behavior of unknown societies, needed to, in the words of Susan Stanton, "find out what is going on."

# Review Questions

1. What kinds of jobs do professional anthropologists do?

2. What is special about anthropology that makes fundamental knowledge of it valuable to some jobs?

3. What is meant by *qualitative research*? Why is such research valuable to business and government?

4. What difficulties did the company manager described in this article face? What solutions did she invent to deal with them? How did her knowledge of anthropology help her with this problem?

5. Why is ethnography useful in everyday life? Can you think of situations in which you could use ethnographic research?

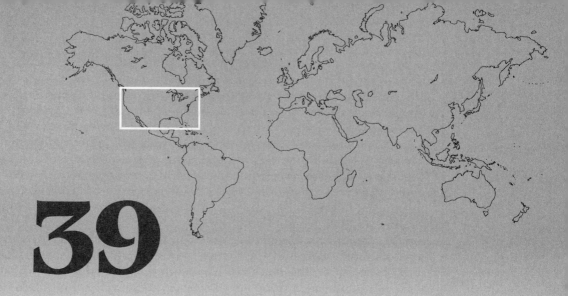

# 39

# Career Advice
# for Anthropology
# Undergraduates

*John T. Omohundro*

*In the previous article we learned that anthropologists regularly use their skills in the world of work and that employers are beginning to recognize the value of employees who are trained in anthropology. But the fact remains that many Americans do not fully understand what anthropology is and have little idea what students who major in anthropology can do for them. Worse, students themselves may not consciously recognize the work skills that anthropology has taught them or how to translate these skills into a language prospective employers can understand. John Omohundro tackles this problem of recognition and translation in this selection. Using a concept he calls "transcultural presentation," he lists some of the skills that anthropology teaches students and shows how these skills can be translated by graduating students into resume language for employers.*

The following scene happens at least once a semester. A distraught student pokes her (or his) head through my office door.

"Scuse me . . . Are you busy? I need to ask you something."

"No, Grebbleberry, come in, sit down. What's bothering you?"

"Well, I really like anthropology. In fact, I want to drop my major in [deleted] and declare anthropology. But I told my parents and they were freaked out. My mother cried and my father threatened to cut me off. And my friends think I've lost it completely. Now they have me scared. I'm afraid I won't be able to get a job. What am I going to do?"

This student has all the symptoms of anthro shock. I'm tempted to smile in recognition of the syndrome but to Grebbleberry there is nothing amusing here. I have two answers: the difficult answer and the easy answer. The difficult answer, which I would like to give, is a problem because students are not prepared to believe me. The difficult answer is:

"For most careers, it doesn't matter much what you major in, as long as you like the subject and are good at it. The point of a major in a liberal arts education is to give practice at studying something in depth. One's major is not the same thing as job training. The careers that follow from most undergraduate majors are not and cannot be specified, even if the world doesn't change— but it does, frequently. There is no direct, obvious, and inevitable connection between college disciplines and the occupational titles people carry."

Although many years of teaching and advising convince me that the difficult answer I've just described is true, I don't respond with that answer anymore. First, I have to treat the "anthro shock"—the fear gripping the student that, ". . . mocked and alone, I'm going to starve." So, instead I reply with the easy answer:

"Take courage. There are many things you can do for a living that use your anthropological knowledge and skills. I can help you discover them and prepare for them."

Only then does the student's color begin to return; the anthro shock is in remission. Later, perhaps, after we've begun a career development program, I might introduce the difficult answer. But Grebbleberry still won't believe me, because my answer goes against most of what pundits, peers, parents, and even some professors have told her. This article presents some of the evidence that I have gathered for the claims made in the "easy" answer, to assist advisors to respond quickly and effectively to anthro shock.

## Becoming a Career Advisor

Good advice is sorely needed and in short supply. Too many of the students I have supervised appeared flustered and ill-prepared when people ask them naive but usually sincere questions about what anthropology is, what it is good for, and what the student is going to "do with it." My advisees usually answered these questions apologetically or parried them with self-deprecating humor. Bill

Gates can get away with being apologetic and self-deprecating; my students need to present themselves more positively. Furthermore, many students and parents acquire their understanding of anthropology through students rather than professors, so it behooves us to raise the quality of the understanding that our major students impart. In turn, by improving their self-presentation our students will become more confident, more ambitious, and ultimately more successful in finding good work.

My career advising grew out of efforts to be a good teacher of the liberal arts, one who helps students move on to self-actualization in the world after college. The advising also grew out of my research in adaptive problem-solving by residents of small coastal communities in Newfoundland. Using the adaptive problem-solving approach, I ask, how do students find out about the world of work and how do they find their place in it? Twenty years ago, I began to develop career workshops within my department, then expanded them into workshops at anthropology conferences, and lately assembled those materials into a workbook, *Careers in Anthropology* (1998).[1] I use the book as a supplementary text in courses, as a workbook in careers workshops, and as an advising guide to students who declare anthropology as a major. This article is drawn from that book.

Because my experience with careers has been limited to academic ones, I collaborate with my college's career planning counselor. Lacking important parts of the whole picture, we are insufficient individually to advise anthropology majors. I have learned about résumés, interviews, and employer expectations, while my career planning colleagues have learned about the usefulness of anthropological perspectives and methods. Even if students consult both of us separately, they tend to perceive us as talking past one another, so they sometimes become frustrated and drop out of the process. But when the career planner and I work together, we see the value in each other's knowledge and how to blend it with concepts from our own fields. The career planners, for example, are delighted to learn that anthropology includes training in participant observation, object reconstruction and cataloguing, and cognitive mapping, among other activities. They in turn have taught me what employers call those activities and how to highlight them on student résumés to increase what linguistic anthropologists call "indexicality," or talking on the same wavelength.

While working with the career planners, and counseling and tracking my advisees, I discovered that undergaduate anthropology alumni not only find meaningful work in which they use their anthropology, but they can use their anthropology to get hired to do that work. To demonstrate this idea I drafted and field tested exercises in which anthropological research techniques, such as ethnosemantics, life history, demography, participant observation, social network analysis, key informant interviews, and survey data analysis, are applied to the tasks of selecting and pursuing interesting work. I also realized that when

---

[1] John T. Omohundro, *Careers in Anthropology* (Mountain View, CA: Mayfield Publishing Company, 1998).

they are advising for careers, professors can use anthropological perspectives and data-collection techniques to better understand what students and employers know and need. Let us look briefly at what that might be.

## Career Planning in Cross-Cultural Perspective

Except for a handful of publications distributed by the American Anthropological Association, few anthropologists have addressed the subject of career planning for undergraduate majors. One exception, James Spradley's "Career Education from a Cultural Perspective,"[2] shaped my conception of the problem. Spradley observes that in most cultures, such as the Amish in northern New York, the Inuit in central Canada, or the Masai in Kenya, children live close to the world of adult work. As they approach their own adulthood, youths understand clearly what adult work is and what they must do to take it up. There aren't many choices, but there isn't much anxiety either. The transition is smooth and supported by ritual, such as coming-of-age ceremonies.

The modern West, Spradley continues, is quite different. Career options are unclear to the beginner. A gulf yawns between their lives and what adults do. What kinds of careers are there over that gulf? What do people do in those positions? How do I decide which position is for me? How do I cross this gulf and get into the picture? The small-scale, nonindustrial cultures allowed twenty years of enculturation to adult careers. By comparison, Spradley observes, the postindustrial world expects youths to make a more complex transition from sixteen years of schooling to adult work in a matter of months or as little as a single weekend. And our culture has no ritual to ease the change.

It takes each student a while to assemble some kind of bridge across that gulf between college life and adult life. The average length of time in the U.S. between graduating with a B.A. and getting hired is six months to one year. That delay isn't usually because there aren't any jobs for liberal arts students. The delay is largely a cultural problem: new graduates simply don't know what to do next. A career counselor at Dartmouth College puts the problem like this: "Although liberal arts majors are qualified for dozens of jobs, they have no idea how to market themselves successfully."[3] They eventually figure it out and get back in the picture. Two years after graduation, two-thirds are employed full time (many of the others are in further study). Three-quarters of the employed are in positions related to their field of study.

My counseling efforts have aimed to enculturate students to the career life while they are still in college, thus abbreviating that limnal state after the

[2] James P. Spradley, "Career Education from a Cultural Perspective," in *Essays in Career Education*, Larry McClure and Carolyn Buan, eds. (Portland, OR: Northwest Regional Educational Laboratory, 1973), pp. 3–16.

[3] Burton Nadler, *Liberal Arts Power: What It Is and How to Sell It on Your Resume*, 2nd ed. (Princeton, NJ: Peterson's, 1989).

baccalaureate degree. Of course, that's a tactical calculation. Looking back on sixteen years of formal education and looking ahead to a worklife of forty or more years, many of my advisees want to enter a limnal state for awhile. Nevertheless, other students are eager to move on. Those who made the effort during their college years to select a starting career, identify some employers, and prepare themselves for that career were rewarded by finding interesting work more quickly than those who waited until after they graduated. Students will have to make some time for this work in a busy college life. As my career planning colleague says, "Looking for a job is itself a job."

If students take up this job of career planning, their anthropology teachers can be valuable motivators and informants. However, not all professors say much about careers to their advisees or their classes. I know this is so because for years I have advised students from other colleges who sought me out at conferences, or when they were home visiting their parents, because they were suffering from anthro shock untreated by their own professors.

Why are some professors avoiding giving career advice? Some feel that after years in the ivory tower they don't understand the work world that their students want to enter. Times have changed, they say, since they were looking for a position. It is widely repeated in the college community that after graduation many students will enter careers that don't exist yet. Also, it is widely repeated that most people change careers (not just employers, but lines of work) several times in their working life. My career planning colleagues have amassed evidence to support these popular conceptions. So, "how can we know what to advise students today?" some of my colleagues wonder. Other professors define career advice, just as they do elementary writing instruction, as a task someone else should do.

A third reason that some professors avoid counseling for careers is that they don't approve of the idea of college as a place to credential people for jobs. In their view, student "vocationalism," or seeing college as a route to a good career, shifts the professor's role from liberator of young minds to gatekeeper of yuppiedom. Professors who teach critical approaches to culture want to inculcate resistance and a desire to change, not a desire to join, the system.

Anthropologist Michael Moffatt, in an insightful ethnography of residence halls and student culture, caused me to re-think student concern about jobs.[4] Moffatt suggests that professors who disdain student "vocationalism" are being hypocritical. After all, professors got their job by going to college, so why shouldn't the students want the same? Students expect that what they call their "job" will place them in the American middle classes, where their occupation will be a key element in their identity. They expect that job to offer them challenge, growth, rewards, security, and a chance to make the world a better place—all of which are goals deserving support from anthropology professors.

---

[4] Michael Moffat, *Coming of Age in New Jersey* (Brunswick, NJ: Rutgers University Press, 1986).

## Translating the Skills

What does the student need to find that job and thus meet those goals? Career advice is partly a matter of teaching students to imagine themselves in a new way (the ethnographic "other's" way) and to construct a few basic models of what it's like in the working world.

Imagining themselves in a new way involves learning what employers (one of those ethnographic "others") really want (or think they want) and then reviewing one's education and experience for evidence of having acquired those desirable qualities. Seen in an anthropological light, this process may be called "trans-cultural self-presentation" and is similar to what the ethnographer initiates when entering the field and attempting to build rapport. Here are some data to assist that process.

Anthro shock contains the fear that one will acquire no marketable skills. "Marketable skills" implies there are other kinds as well. In fact, there are few skills that a liberal arts student acquires that aren't marketable. But there are temporary enthusiasms influencing which skills are considered desirable this year and what vocabulary is used to describe those skills. Anthropology students are well equipped to examine language, identify trends, and adapt to them by translating their own skills and knowledge into language appropriate for the setting.

Table 1 describes some skills that anthropology majors have an opportunity to develop at my college and, I am sure, at many other undergraduate institutions supporting a major. These are phrased in language immediately recognizable by the anthropology student and teacher.

Table 2 identifies twelve abilities often acquired through the undergraduate anthropology major. Fewer students and teachers will recognize their major as re-phrased in this table, but employers will take notice. I advise my students to select anthropology and other courses intentionally to increase their competence in the abilities listed in Table 1 and then, when presenting themselves to potential graduate schools or employers, to highlight those abilities in the terms used in Table 2. Summer jobs, internships, volunteer work, as well as college classes may provide practice in the desirable activities (read "marketable skills").

Advanced majors in our senior seminar practice this transcultural self-presentation with exercises in composing résumé language. I begin by examining a résumé as a cultural text, an element in the process of seeking and offering jobs. We consider when and how their intended readers approach résumés. I argue that the résumé, in little more than a page, is intended to provoke interest in the writer as a person who can do (or learn to do) what the reader wants. In one column students list in their own language the experiences, both in their major and in their lives, that they think might have value. In a second column they conduct the "first-order" extraction of what skills and abilities were expected or practiced in those activities. In the third column they rephrase these skills and abilities in résumé language. Usually an anxiety-generating activity, composing résumés this way seems to generate more self-confidence.

**TABLE 1\***   **Some Transferable Skills in the Anthropology Major**

—Interacting with people of diverse cultures, making allowance for difference in customs and beliefs
—Providing insight into social problems by supplying information about how problems, such as aging, conflict, or bereavement, are dealt with in other cultures
—Interviewing people to obtain information about their attitudes, knowledge, and behavior
—Using statistics and computers to analyze data
—Adapting approaches used in public relations, marketing, or politics to different population groups
—Appraising, classifying, and cataloging rare, old, or valuable objects
—Repairing, reconstructing, and preserving cultural artifacts by selecting chemical treatment, temperature, humidity, and storage methods
—Drawing maps and constructing scale models
—Photographing sites, objects, people, and events
—Interpreting or translating
—Using scientific equipment and measuring devices
—Analyzing craft techniques
—Cooperating in an ethnographic or archaeological research team
—Making policy based on social science research data, problem-solving methods, and professional ethical standards
—Designing research projects and applying for grants
—Producing a research paper in appropriate format and style
—Orally presenting research results
—Applying a variety of ethnographic data collection techniques: ethnosemantics, proxemics, life histories, ethnohistory, folklore, event analysis, genealogies, etc.
—Producing and editing a scholarly journal
—Leading a pre-professional organization such as a student anthropology society or honors society
—Developing public relations for a museum, field project, or conference
—Designing, building, installing, and acting as docent for museum exhibits
—Coaching, instructing, tutoring, and team-teaching with peers
—Studying a second language

\*Adapted from *Careers in Anthropology* (Omohundro, 1998)

## What Careers Do Anthropology B.A.'s Pursue?

Students can be brought out of anthro shock by infusions of empirical data. Surveys have been conducted to assess what work anthropology students are prepared for and what fields alumni actually entered. In *Anthropology and Jobs*, H. Russell Bernard and Willis Sibley identified thirteen fields that the anthropology B.A. could enter with no additional training.[5] These included journalism,

[5] H. Russell Bernard and Willis E. Sibley, *Anthropology and Jobs: A Guide for Undergraduates,* American Anthropological Association special publication (Washington, DC: American Anthropological Association, 1975).

**TABLE 2\*** **Résumé Language for Anthropological Abilities**

**Social agility**—In an unfamiliar social or career-related setting, you learn to size up quickly the "rules of the game." You can become accepted more quickly than you could without anthropology.

**Observation**—As you must often learn about a culture from within it, you learn how to interview and observe as a participant.

**Planning**—You learn how to find patterns in the behavior of a cultural group. This allows you to generalize about their behavior and predict what they might do in a given situation.

**Social sensitivity**—While other people's ways of doing things may be different from your own, you learn the importance of events and conditions that have contributed to this difference. You also recognize that other cultures view your ways as strange. You learn the value of behaving toward others with appropriate preparation, care, and understanding.

**Accuracy in interpreting behavior**—You become familiar with the range of behavior in different cultures. You learn how to look at cultural causes of behavior before assigning causes yourself.

**Challenging conclusions**—You learn that analyses of human behavior are open to challenge. You learn how to use new knowledge to test past conclusions.

**Interpreting information**—You learn how to use data collected by others, reorganizing or interpreting it to reach original conclusions.

**Simplifying information**—As anthropology is conducted among publics as well as about them, you learn how to simplify technical information for communication to non-technical people.

**Contextualizing**—Attention to details is a trait of anthropology. However, you learn that any detail might not be as important as its context, and can even be misleading when context is ignored.

**Problem-solving**—Often functioning within a cultural group, or acting upon culturally sensitive issues, you learn to approach problems with care. Before acting, you learn how to identify the problem, set your goals, decide upon the actions you will take, and calculate possible effects on other people.

**Persuasive writing**—Anthropology strives to represent the behavior of one group to another group, and is in continual need of interpretation. You learn the value of bringing someone else to your view through written argument.

**Social perspective**—You learn how to perceive the acts of individuals and local groups as cause and effect of larger sociocultural systems. This enables you to "act locally and think globally."

\*Source: Omohundro (1998)

police work, and the travel or tour industry. They also identified twenty-eight fields the anthropology B.A. could enter if additional training, up to the M.A. or M.S. level in the appropriate discipline, was acquired. These fields included dietetics, market research, city planning, museums, personnel, and community development, to name a few.

Ten years later, two of my students conducted a survey of anthropology alumni from 32 liberal arts colleges in the northeast U.S.[6] Of the 616

[6] Lawrence W. Kratts and Clarissa Hunter, "Undergraduate Alumni Survey Results," *Anthropology Newsletter*, November 1986.

respondents, 62% worked in the profit sector, 9% in the non-profit sector, and 6% in government. 16% were still in a graduate or professional school.

The respondents' occupations were sorted into seventeen categories. Academics accounted for 10%, some of whom were in disciplines other than anthropology, but managers ("director," "administrator," etc.) dominated at 19%. It appears that a large number of anthropology majors become actors in a bureaucracy, supervising others. Medicine, communications, and business together accounted for another 16% of respondents' current positions.

Does this range of work positions outside of anthropology, as usually conceived, signal a failure on our part to place our advisees in positions that will utilize their major? I don't think so, and neither do the alumni. 71% of the northeast alumni agreed with the statement, "my anthropology education helps me in my current work." An owner of a small business wrote, "All aspects of the [antique] business are satisfying: attending antique shows, unearthing an early item, researching its age and provenance, restoring or repairing it, and educating a potential customer about it. . . ."

Most (81%) of the alumni returning the survey claimed they were satisfied and challenged by their current work, and 74% felt their decision to major in anthropology was a good one. Some alumni waxed enthusiastic about anthropology as the foundation for a liberal arts education. A banker urged current majors, "Go for it: no one in business will ever hold a liberal arts education against you. . . . In the long run this will mark you as superior to a crowd of business students. . . ." Alumni highlighted the value in their current work of cultural relativism, examining human behavior holistically, and using qualitative research methods, all acquired in the major. A social services administrator reported, "I work as a management analyst in a county social services agency. While it is difficult to get an anthro degree recognized as relevant, the anthropological approach is, I feel, one of the best for this sort of job. I'm always translating. . . ."

More recent surveys of alumni, such as the six colleges in the North Carolina system in 1988[7] and a SUNY Plattsburgh survey in 1993,[8] produced similar results. The majority of anthropology majors are 1) glad they majored in anthropology, 2) using some or all of the skills and perspectives they acquired in the major, and 3) enjoying their work, even if few of them are hanging out shingles bearing the title "anthropologist."

Along with their satisfaction, the alumni have some complaints and some advice for current students and their teachers. Overall, alumni were disappointed with the quality and quantity of career advice they received while undergraduates. They also see now that they would have benefitted from more careful choices of electives and course work outside of anthropology.

The northeast alumni urged current students to take courses in math, statistics, communications, economics, science, and computing. This advice matches that offered by alumni from most majors, who recommend courses in

---

[7] Stanton Tefft, with Cathy Harris and Glen Godwin, "North Carolina Undergraduate Alumni Survey," *Anthropology Newsletter,* January 1988.

[8] James Armstrong, personal communication, 1993.

administration, writing, interpersonal relations, economics, accounting, and math. In our northeast survey, anthropology alumni also strongly urged students to gain as much practical experience as possible through field schools, lab and methods courses, senior theses, independent research projects, overseas study, and collaboration with professors' research.

## Conclusion

The purpose of this essay has been to help anthropology teachers deal with anthro shock among their students. I advocate swift first aid with the easy answer, but it is essential to have the evidence to back up that answer. I also advocate cooperation with careers planning professionals. Anthropology offers many marketable skills, or good training for a variety of fields of work, but students, working within the world view of college life and transcript semantics, often don't know how to translate their abilities into ones the rest of the world wants.

Surveys of alumni show that they pursue many lines of work, enjoy their work, are using their anthropological perspective and skills, and are glad they majored in anthropology. Their self-descriptions in surveys suggest that they majored in anthropology because its fundamental concepts and methods for understanding human behavior matched their long-established dispositions. After college, they found satisfying employment in positions where those same dispositions—now more developed through the major—were welcome and useful. This led me to a self-discovery theory of liberal arts education. That is, college is not a place where the student, as a blank slate ready to become a cog, learns "what I need to know to get a job." Instead, college is a place where the student discovers "what I like to do" and then refines his or her ability to do it. I've discovered that many career planning professionals knew this all along.

In sum, the evidence is that anthropology students not only find meaningful work, but they can use their anthropology to get that work, and we teachers can use our anthropology to improve our career advising. Not every anthropologist feels comfortable giving career advice, for several reasons, some of which I sympathize with and some I don't. Not every student needs to rush from college to a career, either, but I have discussed here some ways to help them if they want to move along.

Postscript: Grebbleberry recovered and is now doing fine as a technical illustrator in Oregon, coupling her artistic ability to her love of archaeology.

## Review Questions

1. According to Omohundro, what are the "hard" and "easy" answers to the question, "What can I do with an anthropology major?"

2. What is the difference between the way people in small-scale and complex societies make the transition into the world of work?

3. What does Omohundro mean by the term *transcultural presentation*?

4. List some of the skills acquired by undergraduate anthropology majors that are useful to employers. How can these be translated into résumé language that employers can understand?

5. According to available studies, in what job sectors do anthropology graduates most often find employment?

6. What advice do anthropology graduates have for anthropology programs and students?

# Glossary

**Acculturation**   The process that takes place when groups of individuals having different cultures come into first-hand contact, which results in change to the cultural patterns of both groups.

**Action anthropology**   Any use of anthropological knowledge for planned change by the members of a local cultural group.

**Adjustment anthropology**   Any use of anthropological knowledge that makes social interaction between persons who operate with different cultural codes more predictable.

**Administrative anthropology**   The use of anthropological knowledge for planned change by those who are external to a local cultural group.

**Advocate anthropology**   Any use of anthropological knowledge by the anthropologist to increase the power of self-determination for a particular cultural group.

**Affinity**   A fundamental principle of relationship linking kin through marriage.

**Agriculture**   A subsistence strategy involving intensive farming of permanent fields through the use of such means as the plow, irrigation, and fertilizer.

**Allocation of resources**   The knowledge people use to assign rights to the ownership and use of resources.

**Applied anthropology**   Any use of anthropological knowledge to influence social interaction, to maintain or change social institutions, or to direct the course of cultural change.

**Authority**   The right to make and enforce public policy.

**Bilateral (cognatic) descent**   A rule of descent relating someone to a group of consanguine kin through both males and females.

**Borrowing**   The adoption of something new from another group. Also see *diffusion*.

**Caste**   A form of stratification defined by unequal access to economic resources and prestige, which is acquired at birth and does not permit individuals to alter their rank.

**Clan**   A kinship group normally comprising several lineages; its members are related by a unilineal descent rule, but it is too large to enable members to trace actual biological links to all other members.

**Class**   A system of stratification defined by unequal access to economic resources and prestige, but permitting individuals to alter their rank.

**Coercion**   A kind of political support derived from threats, use of force, or the promise of short-term gain.

**Consanguinity**   The principle of relationship linking individuals by shared ancestry (blood).

**Contest**   A method of settling disputes requiring disputants to engage in some kind of mutual challenge such as singing (as among the Inuit).

**Cosmology**   A set of beliefs that defines the nature of the universe or cosmos.

**Court**   A formal legal institution in which at least one individual has authority to judge and is backed up by a coercive system to enforce decisions.

**Cultural contact**   The situation that occurs when two societies with different cultures somehow come in contact with each other.

**Cultural ecology**   The study of the way people use their culture to adapt to particular environments, the effects they have on their natural surrounding, and the impact of the environment

**439**

on the shape of culture, including its long-term evolution.

**Cultural environment**    The categories and rules people use to classify and explain their physical environment.

**Culture**    The knowledge that is learned, shared, and used by people to interpret experience and generate behavior.

**Culture shock**    A form of anxiety that results from an inability to predict the behavior of others or to act appropriately in cross-cultural situations.

**Descent**    A rule of relationship that ties people together on the basis of reputed common ancestry.

**Descent groups**    Groups based on a rule of descent.

**Detached observation**    An approach to scientific inquiry stressing emotional detachment and the construction of categories by the observer in order to classify what is observed.

**Diffusion**    The passage of a cultural category, culturally defined behavior, or culturally produced artifact from one society to another through borrowing.

**Distribution**    The strategies for apportioning goods and services among the members of a group.

**Divination**    The use of supernatural force to provide answers to questions.

**Division of labor**    The rules that govern the assignment of jobs to people.

**Ecology**    The study of the way organisms interact with each other within an environment.

**Economic system**    The provision of goods and services to meet biological and social wants.

**Egalitarian societies**    Societies that, with the exception of ranked differences between men and women and adults and children, provide all people an equal chance at economic resources and prestige. Most hunter-gatherer societies are egalitarian by this definition.

**Endogamy**    Marriage within a designated social unit.

**Ethnocentrism**    A mixture of belief and feeling that one's own way of life is desirable and actually superior to others'.

**Ethnography**    The task of discovering and describing a particular culture.

**Exogamy**    Marriage outside any designated group.

**Explicit culture**    The culture that people can talk about and of which they are aware. Opposite of *tacit culture*.

**Extended family**    A family that includes two or more married couples.

**Extralegal dispute**    A dispute that remains outside the process of law and develops into repeated acts of violence between groups, such as feuds and wars.

**Family**    A residential group composed of at least one married couple and their children.

**Globalization**    The process that promotes economic, political, and other cultural connections among people living all over the world.

**Go-between**    An individual who arranges agreements and mediates disputes.

**Grammar**    The categories and rules for combining vocal symbols.

**Horticulture**    A kind of subsistence strategy involving semi-intensive, usually shifting, agricultural practices. Slash-and-burn farming is a common example of horticulture.

**Hunting and gathering**    A subsistence strategy involving the foraging of wild, naturally occurring foods.

**Incest taboo**    The cultural rule that prohibits sexual intercourse and marriage between specified classes of relatives.

**Industrialism**    A subsistence strategy marked by intensive, mechanized food production and elaborate distribution networks.

**Inequality**    A human relationship marked by differences in power, authority, prestige, and access to valued goods and services, and by the payment of deference.

**Informant**    A person who teaches his or her culture to an anthropologist.

**Infralegal dispute** A dispute that occurs below or outside the legal process without involving regular violence.

**Innovation** A recombination of concepts from two or more mental configurations into a new pattern that is qualitatively different from existing forms.

**Kinship** The complex system of social relationships based on marriage (affinity) and birth (consanguinity).

**Language** The system of cultural knowledge used to generate and interpret speech.

**Law** The cultural knowledge that people use to settle disputes by means of agents who have recognized authority.

**Leadership** The ability to influence others to act.

**Legitimacy** A kind of political support based on people's positive evaluation of public policy or positive evaluation of the political structure and process that produces public policy.

**Lineage** A kinship group based on a unilineal descent rule that is localized, has some corporate powers, and whose members can trace their actual relationships to each other.

**Magic** Strategies people use to control supernatural power to achieve particular results.

**Mana** An impersonal supernatural force inherent in nature and in people. Mana is somewhat like the concept of "luck" in U.S. culture.

**Market economies** Economies in which production and exchange are motivated by market factors: price, supply, and demand. Market economies are associated with large societies where impersonal exchange is common.

**Market exchange** The transfer of goods and services based on price, supply, and demand.

**Marriage** The socially recognized union between a man and a woman that accords legitimate birth status rights to their children.

**Matrilineal descent** A rule of descent relating a person to a group of consanguine kin on the basis of descent through females only.

**Microculture** The system of knowledge shared by members of a group that is part of a larger national society or ethnic group.

**Monogamy** A marriage form in which a person is allowed only one spouse at a time.

**Moot** A community meeting held for the informal hearing of a dispute.

**Morpheme** The smallest meaningful category in any language.

**Mythology** Stories that reveal the religious knowledge of how things have come into being.

**Naive realism** The notion that reality is much the same for all people everywhere.

**Nonlinguistic symbols** Any symbols that exist outside the system of language and speech; for example, visual symbols.

**Nuclear family** A family composed of a married couple and their children.

**Ordeal** A supernaturally controlled, painful, or physically dangerous test, the outcome of which determines a person's guilt or innocence.

**Pastoralism** A subsistence strategy based on the maintenance and use of large herds of animals.

**Patrilineal descent** A rule of descent relating consanguine kin on the basis of descent through males only.

**Personified supernatural force** Supernatural force inherent in supernatural beings such as goddesses, gods, spirits, and ghosts.

**Phoneme** The minimal category of speech sounds that signals a difference in meaning.

**Phonology** The categories and rules for forming vocal symbols.

**Phratry** A group composed of two or more clans. Members acknowledge unilineal descent from a common ancestor but recognize that their relationship is distant.

**Physical environment** The world as people experience it with their senses.

**Policy** Any guideline that can lead directly to action.

**Political system**  The organization and process of making and carrying out public policy according to cultural categories and rules.

**Polyandry**  A form of polygamy in which a woman has two or more husbands at one time.

**Polygamy**  A marriage form in which a person has two or more spouses at one time. Polygyny and polyandry are both forms of polygamy.

**Polygyny**  A form of polygamy in which a man is married to two or more wives at one time.

**Prayer**  A petition directed at a supernatural being or power.

**Priest**  A full-time religious specialist who intervenes between people and the supernatural, and who often leads a congregation at regular cyclical rites.

**Production**  The process of making something.

**Public**  The group of people a policy will affect.

**Ramage**  A cognatic (bilateral) descent group that is localized and holds corporate responsibility.

**Rank societies**  Societies stratified on the basis of prestige only.

**Reciprocal exchange**  The transfer of goods and services between two people or groups based on their role obligations. A form of non-market exchange.

**Redistribution**  The transfer of goods and services between a group of people and a central collecting service based on role obligation. The U.S. income tax is a good example.

**Religion**  The cultural knowledge of the supernatural that people use to cope with the ultimate problems of human existence.

**Respondent**  An individual who responds to questions included on questionnaires; the subject of survey research.

**Revitalization movement**  A deliberate, conscious effort by members of a society to construct a more satisfying culture.

**Role**  The culturally generated behavior associated with particular statuses.

**Sacrifice**  The giving of something of value to supernatural beings or forces.

**Self-redress**  The actions taken by an individual who has been wronged to settle a dispute.

**Semantics**  The categories and rules for relating vocal symbols to their referents.

**Shaman**  A part-time religious specialist who controls supernatural power, often to cure people or affect the course of life's events.

**Slash-and-burn agriculture**  A form of horticulture in which wild land is cleared and burned over, farmed, then permitted to lie fallow and revert to its wild state.

**Social acceptance**  A process that involves learning about an innovation, accepting an innovation as valid, and revising one's cultural knowledge to include the innovation.

**Social groups**  The collections of people that are organized by culturally defined rules and categories.

**Social network**  An assortment of people with whom an individual regularly interacts but who themselves do not regularly form an organized group.

**Social situation**  The categories and rules for arranging and interpreting the settings in which social interaction occurs.

**Social stratification**  The ranking of people or groups based on their unequal access to valued economic resources and prestige.

**Sociolinguistic rules**  Rules specifying the nature of the speech community, the particular speech situations within a community, and the speech acts that members use to convey their messages.

**Sorcery**  The malevolent practice of magic.

**Speech**  The behavior that produces meaningful vocal sounds.

**Spirit possession**  The control of a person by a supernatural being in which the person becomes that being.

**Status**  A culturally defined position associated with a particular social structure.

**Stratified societies**  Societies that are at least partly organized on the principle of social stratification. Contrast with *egalitarian* and *rank societies*.

**Subject**   The person who is observed in a social or psychological experiment.

**Subsistence economies**   Economies that are local and that depend largely on the nonmarket mechanisms, reciprocity and redistribution, to motivate production and exchange.

**Subsistence strategies**   Strategies used by groups of people to exploit their environment for material necessities. Hunting and gathering, horticulture, pastoralism, agriculture, and industrialism are subsistence strategies.

**Supernatural**   Things that are beyond the natural. Anthropologists usually recognize a belief in such things as goddesses, gods, spirits, ghosts, and *mana* to be signs of supernatural belief.

**Support**   Anything that contributes to the adoption of public policy and its enforcement.

**Symbol**   Anything that humans can sense that is given an arbitrary relationship to its referent.

**Tacit culture**   The shared knowledge of which people usually are unaware and do not communicate verbally.

**Technology**   The part of a culture that involves the knowledge that people use to make and use tools and to extract and refine raw materials.

**Transcendent values**   Values that override differences in a society and unify the group.

**Ultimate problems**   Universal human problems, such as death, the explanation of evil and the meaning of life, and transcendent values that can be answered by religion.

**Unit of production**   The group of people responsible for producing something.

**Witchcraft**   The reputed activity of people who inherit supernatural force and use it for evil purposes.

**Worldview**   The way people characteristically look out on the universe.

# Index